CONTRI.

<small>FOR THE</small>

GENEALOGIES OF THE DESCENDANTS

<small>OF THE</small>

First Settlers

<small>OF THE</small>

PATENT AND CITY OF SCHENECTADY,

<small>FROM</small>

1662 TO 1800.

<small>BY</small>

JONATHAN PEARSON.

CLEARFIELD

Reprinted for
Clearfield Company, Inc. by
Genealogical Publishing Co., Inc.
Baltimore, Maryland
1998

Originally published: Albany, N.Y., 1873
Reprinted: Genealogical Publishing Co., Inc.
Baltimore, 1976, 1982
Library of Congress Catalogue Card Number 76-20240
International Standard Book Number 0-8063-0730-7
Made in the United States of America

PREFACE.

The First Settlers of Schenectady were citizens of Beverwyck. In 1661 Arent Van Curler extinguished the Indian title to lands at this place, and the following spring, with a little company of pioneers, commenced the first settlement. Two years later the lands were surveyed, allotted and patented to fifteen persons, a portion of whom being non-residents sold out their rights to permanent settlers.

For mutual safety they erected their cottages on the plat lying west of Ferry street, which was fortified with stockadoes. Their farming lands, embracing the islands, and rich flats lying on both sides of the Mohawk, produced bountiful crops of maize and wheat : a church was early formed under the occasional ministry of Dominie Schaets of the mother church at Albany : and in spite of its exposed position as the frontier settlement, the little hamlet prospered and grew in numbers and comforts until 1690, when in one night, the 8th of February, the entire village was destroyed and the inhabitants scattered or slain. Nothing better shows the hardihood and pluck of the survivors than the fact that few if any of them abandoned the settlement; they returned in the spring, rebuilt their cottages and the little church, cast the seed into the earth, and amid many alarms awaited the harvest. Though often threatened the place was never again attacked.

It is to this little band of hardy pioneers and their descendants that the following pages are mainly devoted. The sources of this compilation are chiefly the *Doop* and *Trouw Boeken* of the First Reformed church of this city. These registers of baptisms and marriages are nearly entire from the year 1691 to this date : those of the first 30 years after the settlement were probably burned in Dominie Thesschenmaecker's parsonage in 1690.

These *entire records* to 1800, and in a few cases later, have been copied and posted into families in this work. The records of the venerable mother church in Albany have also been carefully searched, and whenever entries have been found relating to Schenectady families, they have been inserted herein. Large additions have likewise been made to the above sources of information from the records of the secretary of state, of the clerks of the city and county of Albany, clerk of the court of appeals ; surrogate of the county of Albany ; from *Munsell's Annals and Collections of Albany ;* from family records and papers, and from gravestone inscriptions. Doubtless there is much additional information to be found by the patient and careful gleaner, especially such as relates to the later generations. In regard to the first two or three generations of descendants from the First Settlers, it is believed they will be found as completely set forth in these pages as they are likely ever to be from authentic sources.

The territory covered by this work is nearly that of the present county of Schenectady, extending about 22 miles along the Mohawk, and 4 miles on each side of that river. For the first hundred years after Schenectady was begun, the settlements were mainly confined to the river flats, gradually advancing westward, and consisted chiefly of descendants from the old Holland families of Albany and Schenectady, the Palatines being still farther west.

But after the French war and more especially after the Revolutionary war, New Englanders and Scotchmen immigrated largely to the high lands lying back from the river, which had hitherto been regarded as of little or no value.

All these new and foreign settlers, until they had churches of their own, brought their children either to Albany or Schenectady to be christened. Hence there will be found in this work many names of families then residing as far west as Caughnawaga and Canajoharie, south to the Helderberg and Schoharie, and north to Galway and Kayaderosseras patent.

The arrangement of these genealogies is simple and easily to be understood: — the tribal names are arranged alphabetically, and the families under each name are placed nearly in chronological order, and for divers reasons, are made to end with those which began to be entered in the church registers before 1800. Persons interested will find little difficulty in tracing back their pedigrees to the First Settlers, by keeping in mind the following facts. The names of all sons who subsequently became heads of families (so far as the complier could find), are printed in *italics :* the husbands of daughters and the parents of both husbands and wives are in all cases mentioned when discoverable. It should also be borne in mind that inasmuch as Schenectady was originally but an offshoot from Albany, the families of both places frequently intermarrying, in making up a pedigree of any old family of Albany county as anciently constituted, this work must be regarded as a complement of the *Genealogies of the First Settlers of Albany*, and that both works should be carefully consulted and compared.

The Vrooman arms facing page 276 was copied from an ancient painting long in possession of that family, and contributed by Doctor A. G. Brower of Utica.

J. P.

UNION COLLEGE,
Nov. 12, 1873.

GENEALOGIES

OF THE

FIRST SETTLERS OF SCHENECTADY.

ABBREVIATIONS used in the following pages: Ch : children ; b., born ; bp., baptized ; m., married ; a., aged ; d., died.

ABEEL.

CORNELIS (son of Jacobus of Albany) and Susanna Van Schoonhoven (dau. of Hendrik of Albany). Ch. b.: Elbertje Nov. 15, 1788; Hendrik Van Schoonhoven, Oct. 15, 1790; Alida, Mar. 14. 1793; Sarah, Sept. 15, 1796; Jacobus, Ap. 23, 1799; Nanning Visger, Feb. 9, 1802.

ADAIR.

PIETER, and Alida Van Slyck of Coxsackie; m. in Albany, Sept. 25, 1780. Ch : Hendrik, bp. Aug. 5, 1781.

JAMES, merchant. His widow m. James Bailey in 1801.

ADAMS,

EMANUEL, from Dublin, m. Maria, dau. of Jacob Truex, May 19, 1748. Ch : John, bp. Oct. 20, 1748; Jacob, bp. Ap. 15, 1750; Emanuel, bp. Aug. 9, 1752.

ROBERT, and Susanna Adams. Ch : Catharine, bp. Mar. 5, 1749.

CHARLES from Philadelphia and Annatie Erichzon, dau. of Gerard E., m. Nov. 6, 1762. Ch : Rachel, bp. Aug. 28, 1763; Gerrit, bp. Dec. 27, 1765.

Doct. WILLIAM, settled in Schenectady about the year 1757, as a physician. The following notice of him, taken from the Litchfield, Conn., *Post*, of June, 1827, is interesting, as showing his vigor and activity at an extreme old age: " Dr. William Adams, of Schenectady, N. Y., aged 97, arrived in this village, having borne without much apparent fatigue, the journey from Albany, a distance of more than 70 miles, in the stage, in one day. With the activity of middle age, he left his bed at one o'clock at night, and unattended, except by casual passengers, performed his long journey with the purpose of spending the summer with a beloved granddaughter, who resides in this village ; and the next day after his arrival, was seen moving, with ease and agility, around our streets and rejoicing in the pleasantness and beauty of spring. He has been more than 70 years a practicing physician in Schenectady, and was a surgeon under Sir Wm. Johnson, in the old French war." Dr. Adams had his residence on the lot now occupied by McCamus & Co., on State street. His wife, Margaret, d. Ap. 14, 1800, a. 66 yrs., leaving two sons, James, who d. Ap. 20, 1803, a. 35 yrs., and Archibald Hamilton.

JOHN and Engeltie Schermerhorn. Ch : Eva, born July 18, 1788.

Doct. ARCHIBALD HAMILTON, son of Dr. William Adams, was a physician; he m. Maria, dau. of Daniel McKinney; she d. July 6, 1810, a. 33 yrs. Dr. A. d. Ap. 5, 1811, a. 42 yrs. Ch. b.; Margariet, Sept. 8, 1795; Mary Anne, Sept. 21, 1797, d. June 5, 1810; Catharine Reed, Dec 25, 1800, d. Dec. 14, 1805; William, Jan. 27, 1802, d. Oct. 27, 1803; Matilda Beekman, Oct. 21, 1804 (?), d. June 17, 1810.

AIKLIN.

JOHN and Catlyntje Dodd. Ch : Peter Doremus, b. Aug. 4, 1794.

ALEXANDER.

ROBERT and Gaudy ..... Ch : Agnes, b. Oct. 20, 1785; Agnes b. Aug. 20, 1787.

ALEXANDER, merchant, a native of Scotland, made his will June 7, 1809, proved Sept. 15, 1809, in which he spoke of his bro. William and sister Anna, w. of William Henry. He d. Sept. 1, 1809, a. 44 yrs., 6 m., 12 d., leaving a son Stephen, now Professor in Princeton College, and a dau. Harriet.

JAMES, and Rachel Huges, m. Feb. 11, 1765.

ROBERT, Jr., and Jane Camp, m. Jan. 1, 1800.

ALLEN.

JOHN and Mary Misnet (Minatta, Minnet). Ch : John, 3 yrs. old, and Cornelius, bp. Feb. 13, 1785; James, b. June 13, 1787; Jenny, b. Sept. 8, 1789; David, b. Feb. 22, 1792; Mary, b. May 2, 1795.

Capt. ALLEN and Elisabeth Bratt, m. Aug. 29, 1735.

AMENT.

ELDERT, merchant, 1790, on south corner of Union and Ferry streets; m. Margarieta, dau. of Jan Viele. He d. shortly before March, 1798. Ch : Maria, bp. Oct. 3, 1779; Maria, bp. Feb. 25, 1781; John Viele, bp. May 22, 1783; William, b. Oct. 1, 1785; Hannah, b. Feb. 27, 1788; Maria, b. June 28, 1790; Edward Lewis, b. July 21, 1792; Rebecca, b. Nov. 3, 1797.

ANDERSON.

EZEKIEL, and Hannah Lawson. Ch : Isaac, b. Mar. 17, 1787.

ANDREW.

THOMAS, of *Halve Maan*, and Rachel Ostrander. Ch : Marytje, bp. Nov. 10, 1765; Sara, b. July, 1773.

ANDRUS.

JOSEPH, and Sarah Johnson. Ch : Joseph, b. Sept. 27, 1791.

ANTES.

JOHAN (Hans) and Aegie, dau. of Jacobus Cromwell, dwelling in the *Woestyne;* m. Jan. 16, 1726. Ch : Margariet, b. June 5, 1726 ; Johannes, bp. Dec. 22, 1745 ; *Frans.*

FRANS (son of Johannes) and Dorothea... Ch : Johannes, bp. Jan. 26, 1763.

ANTHONY.

GEORGE, of Schenectady, and Catharina Hazins, of Hellenbergh, m. in Cagnawago, in 1786.

APPEL.

ADRIAN Janse, alias Van Leyden, tavern keeper and schoolmaster at Albany, had two sons, Jan, who "was grievously wounded at the sacking of Schenectady, in 1690" and was on that account granted £6 by the Governor and Council ; and Willem who "was wounded in his limbs at the burning of Schenectady," and for that reason was exempted, in 1693, from the payment of 30s excise. They removed to New York about 1693. Willem had two ch. bp. in New York : Maria Magdalena, July 5, 1693 ; and Simon, bp. May 26, 1695. The dau. m. Johannes Vrooman of Schenectady. [See *Albany Families.*]

One Jacob Appel was member of the church in 1703.

APPLIE.

HENDERICK, and Eva Wagenaar, both of Rensselaerswyk ; m. October 6, 1767. Ch : Annatje, bp. Sept. 6, 1768 ; Pieter bp. Ap. 28, 1770.

ARNOLD.

THOMAS, and Elisabeth Dyer. Ch : Elisabeth, bp. Feb. 17, 1765 ; Thomas, bp. May 25, 1766.

ARROWSMITH.

CORNELIS, and Sarah Vedder. Ch : Elisabeth, bp. April 5, 1741 ; Cornelis, bp. Aug. 28, 1743 ; Hermanus, bp. Ap. 5, 1747.

ARENT, of Caughnawaga, and Catarina Feling, of Schenectady ; m. Oct. 2, 1762, (in the *Trouw-boek* he is called Smit). Ch : Benjamin, bp. Sept. 25, 1763.

ARWIN (ERWIN ?).

ANDREW, and Margariet Weeks. Ch : John, bp. Nov. 20, 1780.

ASTLE.

JAMES, and Elisabeth McLane ; m. Nov. 25, 1770.

ATERMAARCK.

BARTEL, and Anna Bastiaan. Ch : Engeltie, bp. May 5, 1782.

ATKINS.

WILLIAM, and Anna Freeman. Ch : Nehemiah, bp. Jan. 1, 1785.

AUGSBURGER.

DAVID, and Elisabeth Zell (Schelling, Scheltin). Ch : Christiaan, bp. May 18, 1764 ; Margarita, bp. Aug. 19, 1769 ; Elisabeth, bp. May 10, 1774.

AUKES.

DOUWE, alias De Freest, was born in 1639. He came over in Sept., 1663, in the ship *Stettin,* from Arnhem, and settled in Schenectady as an inn keeper on the lot on the south corner of Mill lane and State street, near the old church. Leisler made him justice of the peace in 1689. He married for his second wife, Maria, dau. of Aernout Cornelis Viele, and widow of Matthys Vrooman, in 1685, and had a dau., Margariet, bp. Mar. 21, 1686. In 1690, his wife, two children and negro woman, Francyn, were killed by the French and Indians in their attack upon the town. He escaped, and was living as late as 1718. In 1709 he conveyed all his real estate to Cornelis Viele, whom he calls his [adopted ?] son.

AUKST.

ADAM, and Barbara Reese. Ch : Elisabeth, bp. Jan. 21, 1741.

AVERY.

NICHOLAS and Ariaantje, dau. of Johannes (?) Heemstraten. Ch : Teunis, b. Oct. 3, 1785 ; Nehemiah, b. Jan. 5, 1789.

BAARD (BAAT).

FRANS, and Christina Kersenaar (Dorst). Ch : Helena, bp. Jan. 6, 1770 ; Maria Magdalena, bp. May 7, 1771 ; Maria Barbara, bp. Sept. 8, 1773 ; Sarah, bp. Jan. 24, 1776 ; Susanna, bp. Nov. 12, 1778 ; Johannes, bp. July 7, 1778.

BACHMAN.

ANDREAS Phillip, and Catarien Miller. Ch : Daniel Frederick, bp. Nov. 27, 1773 ; Christoffel, bp. Aug. 19, 1775.

BADLEY.

PETER, of Normanskil, and Annatje White. Ch : Willem, b. Ap. 8, 1786.

BAGGE,

BENT, was an inhabitant of the village from 1669 to 1681. He owned a house and land, which, in 1669, he leased to Jan Rinckhout for one year.

BAKHUYS (BACKUS).

JACOB, and Judith Murray. Ch : Jurry, b. Ap. 20, 1785 ; John, b. Mar. 8, 1787 ; Elisabeth, b. May 18, 1789.

BALDWIN.

ABRAM, and Catie McGalvie. Ch : Maria, b. Oct. 4, 1792.

BALL.

HENDERICK, and Maria Eliza Dietz. Ch : Willem, b. Dec., 1763.

JOHAN Jurry, and Elisabeth Dietz. Ch : Maria, bp. Aug. 30, 1765.

JOHANNES, and Geertruy Smitt. Ch : Magdalena, bp. Jan. 30, 1781 ; Simon, bp. Feb. 25, 1783.

BALLARD.

BENNONI, and Bata Quackenbosch. Ch : Johannes, b. Sept. 25, 1778.

BANCKER.

GERRIT, came from Amsterdam, where his brother Willem was a merchant as late as 1700. He was in New Amsterdam before 1655, and two years later in Beverwyck, where he continued to reside till his death, about 1691. His homelot, in Albany was on the south side of Yonker [now State] street, the third east from Pearl street, as it then was. When

Arent Van Curler began the settlement of Schenectady in 1662, he became one of the original fifteen proprietors. Farms number six on the Bouwland, were allotted to him, and his village lot comprised the northerly quarter of the block, bounded by Washington, Union, Church and State streets. His son Evert held this property till 1702, when he disposed of it to Isaac Swits. Gerrit Bancker married Elisabeth, daughter of Dirk Van Eps, and sister of Jan Van Eps, one of the first settlers of Schenectady. After the death of her husband, Mrs. Bancker removed to New York and engaged in trade. She died July 3, 1693, aged 70 years, leaving a large property for those times, to her only son Evert. Besides Evert, who was born in Albany, Jan. 24, 1665, Mr. Bancker had a daughter Anna, who married Johannes De Peyster of New York, Sept. 21, 1688, and perhaps a dau. Maria licenced to marry Cornelis De Peyster, also of New York, Sept. 19, 1694.

EVERT, son of Gerrit, was a merchant in Albany, but retired to his farm in Guilderland during the latter part of his life; he was buried on the 10th of July, 1734; 1692 he was justice of the peace; 1695–6 and 1707–9 mayor of Albany; he m. Elisabeth, dau. of Stoffel Janse Abeel, Sept. 24, 1686; she was born Mar. 23, 1671, and was buried Mar. 20, 1734. His home lot in Albany, was on the south side of Yonker [State] street, next east of his father's, and fourth east of Pearl street. He made his will Mar. 13, 1734, proved July 31, 1734, in which he gave to his son Johannes £50, "provided he continued to live with me till my decease, or till I dispose of my farm where I now live." He mentioned the following children, who are to share alike in his estate : Christoffel, Willem, Jannetie, Adriaan, Gerardus and Johannes. Ch : Gerardus, b. Feb. 11, 1688; Neeltie, b. Mar. 1, 1689; Gerardus, b. June 12, 1691; Elisabeth, b. July 29, 1693; *Christoffel*, b. Oct. 27, 1695; Anna, b. in New York, Oct. 3, 1697, and d. Oct. 2, 1706; *Willem*, b. Oct. 28, 1699; Jannetie, b. Aug. 28, 1701; *Adrianus*, b. Oct. 10, 1703; *Gerardus*, b. Ap. 1, 1706; Anna, b. June 12, 1708, and d. May 30, 1709; Johannes, b. Mar. 15, 1710, and d. Ap. 30,— *Johannes* (see his father's will).

CHRISTOPHER, of New York, son of Evert, m. Elisabeth Hooglant in New York, Oct. 16, 1719. Ch : Adriaan, bp. in New York, July 3, 1720.

ADRIAAN, of New York, son of Evert, m. Elisabeth Van Taerling in New York, Jan. 30, 1729.

GERRIT or Gerardus, son of Evert, m. Maria De Peyster, in New York, Oct. 31, 1731. Ch. bp. in Albany : Anna, Sept. 3, 1732; Evert, Aug. 10, 1734; Elisabeth, May 9, 1736; Johannes, Feb. 22, 1738.

WILLEM, son of Evert, settled in Schenectady, and m. Annatje, dau. of Gerrit Symonse Veeder, December 17, 1726. Ch : Evert, bp. Dec. 13, 1727; Elisabeth, bp. July 16, 1732, m. Hendericus Peek ;

Catharina, bp. Oct. 6, 1734, m. Jacobus Van Arnhem; Neeltie, bp. Dec. 21, (?) 1737, m. Albert A. Vedder; Annatie, bp. Aug. 16, 1740, m. Arent S. Vedder; Jannetje, bp. Mar. 25, 1744; Evert, bp. Sept. 21, 1746.

JOHANNES, son of Evert, settled on the Normanskil, and m. Magdalena, dau. of Gerrit Symonse Veeder, of Schenectady. Ch. bp. in Schenectady: Elisabeth, June 7, 1735, m. Simon H. Veeder; *Gerrit*, Feb. 27, 1737; *Thomas Brouwer* not registered.

GERRIT, son of Johannes, m. Hester, dau. of Jan Van Arnhem, of Albany, Sept. 1⁵̇, 1755. Ch: Magdalena, bp. May 11, 1756, m. Isaac A. Vrooman; Elisabeth, bp. Aug. 21, 1760; *Johannes*, bp. Dec. 25, 1764; Catarina, bp. Dec. 20, 1767.

THOMAS BROUWER, son of Johannes, built and lived in the house, No. 108 State street, now occupied by Mr. John Lake, his blacksmith shop being next east. He m. Anna, dau. of Jacob Mebie, Nov. 2, 1754, and d. May 25, 1807, in the 78th y. of his age. She d. July 2, 1776, a. 43 ys., 8 m., 28 d. Ch: Annatie, bp. Oct. 31, 1756; m. Daniel Toll Clute; Margarita, bp. Jan. 21, 1759; Elisabeth, bp. Nov. 1, 1761, d. June 28, 1836, a. 74 ys., 8 m. 6 d.; Catarina, bp. Feb. 17, 1765; m. Frederic Vedder, d. Mar. 28 (29), 1850, a. 85 ys.; Neeltie, bp. Feb. 1, 1767; m. Cornelis C. Clute; Magdalena, bp. May 7, 1769; m. Frans V. Vedder.

JOHN, m. Geertruy Jacobi in Albany, Ap. 19, 1778. Ch: Henry, b. Feb. 9, 1779, in Albany; Margarita, bp. in Albany, Oct. 27, 1780; Abram, b. Dec. 16, 1790.

JOHN, son of Gerrit and Annatje, dau. of Pieter Ouderkerk, both of Normanskil, m. Mar. 15, 1788. Ch: Gerrit, b. Mar. 26, 1789; Alida, b. June 30, 1791, Peter, b. Jan. 18, 1794; John, b. Aug. 17, 1796, d. 1864; Esther, b. Ap. 3, 1799; Isaac, b. Ap. —, 1802; Abraham, b. Nov. 2, 1805; Matilda, b. Dec; —, 1812.

BANTA.

ARIE, m. Elisabeth Le Sier. Ch: Pieter, bp. Feb. 20, 1774; *Hendrick, John, Dirk, Arie, Hellebrant.*

HENDRICK, of Clifton Park, son of Arie, m. Engeltie, dau. of Jacob Schermerhorn, June 7, 1787. Ch: Elisabeth, b. Sept. 16, 1788; Jacob, b. Jan. 22, 1791; Arie, b. Aug. 15, 1793; Christiaan, b. Sept. 19, 1795; John, b. June 30, 1798; Maria, b. Oct. 3, 1800.

JOHN, of Clifton Park, son of Arie, m. Engeltie, dau. of Albert Vedder, Feb. 23, 1790. Ch: Arie, b. Oct. 28, 1791; Esther, b. Aug. 16, 1795; Elisabeth, b. April 1, 1798; Albert, b. July 10, 1800.

DIRK, son of Arie, and Elisabeth Bensen. Ch: David, b. Dec. 27, 1793.

ARIE, son of Arie, and Catharina, dau. of Abraham Van Eps (?). Ch: Christina, b. Dec. 28, 1796.

HILLEBRANT, son of Arie, and Debora, daughter of Abraham Van Eps. Ch: Arie, b. Feb. 1, 1797.

BARBARO.

JOHN, of Montgomery county, m. Sara Van Petten, Jan. 30, 1791.

BARBER.

JOHN, and Jane McCrea. · Ch: William, b. Dec. 31, 1791.

BARHEIT or BARHEYT.

There were two early settlers of this name, Andries Hanse Barheit, "yeoman of ye Great Flatt neer Coxhacky" and Jeronimus Hanse Barheit, perhaps, of the same place. The latter m. for his second (?) wife Rebecca Evertse, Ap. 9, 1684, in Albany, where were baptised the following Ch: Margriet, Oct. 4, 1685, and *Wouter*, Aug. 4, 1691. He made his will Aug. 22, 1713, proved Feb. 23, 172⅔ in which he spoke of his wife Rebecca, son Wouter, and one daughter. He may have had a son *Johannes* by a former wife.

WOUTER, son of Jeronimus above, m. Rachel Winne of Albany, Mar. 28, 1715. He was buried Jan. 8, 1732. Ch. bp. in Albany: Hieronimus, Feb. 12, 1716; Teuntie, Sept. 1, 1717; Margarita, May 15, 1720; Margarita, May 5, 1723; Tytje, May 16, 1725.

JOHANNES, perhaps son of Jeronimus, m. first, Catharina dau. of John Gilbert, of Albany, July 6, 1701. Ch. bp. in Albany: *Johannes*, May 16, 1703, settled in Schenectady; Cornelia, Oct. 6, 1706; *Hieronimus*, Mar. 20, 1709; settled in Schenectady; Barentje, Oct. 14, 1711; Willem, July 10, 1715. He m. secondly, Catalyna, dau. of Adam Dingman, Mar. 23, 1718. Ch. bp. in Albany: Alida, Oct. 25, 1719; Adam, 6, 1723.

JOHANNES, "born in Albany, and dwelling in Schenectady," son of Johannes and Catharina, m. Cornelia, dau. of Arent Pootman, Aug. 1, 1734. Ch: *Johannes*, bp. June 7, 1735; *Cornelis*, bp. Dec. 21, 1737; Catharina, bp. June 14, 1740; m. Charles Denniston; *Teunis*, b. Oct. 3, 1742; Eva, bp. Nov. 25, 1744; m. John Coman; Jacomyntje, b.—, m. Wouter I. Vrooman; Anna, bp. June 10, 1750, m. Willem Hall; *Jacobus*, bp. Feb. 9, 1753; *Louis*, bp. Dec. 21, 1755.

HIERONIMUS, son of Johannes and Catharina, m. Maria, dau. of Jesse De Graaf, Ap. 9, 1737. Ch. bp: Johannes, Oct. 8, 1737; *Johannes*, Jan. 7, 1739; Alida, Aug. 16, 1740; Jesse,* Jan. 17, 1742; *Claas*, Nov. 3, 1745; Daniel, July 25, 1749, Alida, Jan. 26, 1752; Daniel, Nov. 26, 1758; Catarina, Sept. 12, 1762.

CORNELIS, son of Johannes and Cornelia, m. Rachel, dau. of Joseph Yates. She d. Aug. 3, 1809, in her 78th yr. Ch. bp: Cornelia, Dec. 13, 1761, m. John P. Truax; Eva, Nov. 20, 1763, m. Nicholas A. Van Petten; Lena, Oct. 27, 1765, m. Isaac Clute; *Johannes*, Aug. 30, 1767; Christoffel, Jan. 20, 1771.

* Jesse Barheit, of Princetown, made his will Aug. 24, 1805, proved July 11, 1812; spoke of dau. Katy, w. of George Kaley [Kelly] and of Lotty Van Buren, her dau.; also of Jesse, son of Jeroune Barheit.

JOHANNES, son of Hieronimus and Maria, m. Helena, dau. of Jacobus Peek. Ch. bp: Alida, Aug. 9, 1761; *Jacobus*, Oct. 2, 1763; *Hieronimus*, Nov. 2, 1765; Johannes, Jan. 15, 1768; *Johannes Sanders*, Mar. 10, 1771; Maria, Oct. 31, 1773; Maria, Dec. 10, 1775; *Hendrick*, Jan. 11, 1778.

JOHN, son of Johannes and Maria, m. Annatje, daughter of Pieter Van Slyck. Ch: Cornelia, bp. Nov. 3, 1765, m. Frederic Williams; *Petrus*, b. Mar. 17, 1768; Engelina, b. June 19, 1770, m. Petrus Williams; Maria ...... m. Gysbert C. Clau; Jacobus, bp. Dec. 14, 1777; Annatje, bp. Aug. 12, 1781; Catarina, bp. Oct. 11, 1783.

TEUNIS, son of Johannes and Maria, carpenter, of Remsen Bos, m. first, Jacomyntje, dau. of Johannes Van Vorst, Oct. 14, 1765; secondly, Cornelia Bovie, May 7, 1775, and thirdly, Catharina Vrooman of Normanskil, Jan. 14, 1786. Ch: Cornelia, bp. May 10, 1766, m. Thomas Mosher; Hannah, bp. May 8, 1768, m. Symon Van Sice; *Johannes*, bp. Oct. 28, 1770; Elisabeth, bp. Mar. 8, 1772; Matthias, bp. Aug. 4, 1776; Cornelis, bp. Nov. 1, 1778; Nicholas, bp. Mar. 4, 1781; Teunis, b. July 3, 1787; Maria, b. Mar. 20, 1790; Louis, b. June 15, 1792; Rachel, b. May 28, 1795.

NICOLAS, son of Hieronimus and Maria, m. Susanna, dau. of Abraham Van Antwerpe. Ch: Hieronimus, bp. May 14, 1779; Hieronimus, bp. Feb. 4, 1781; Abraham, b. Ap. 17, 1782, d. Oct. 31,

1843, a. 61ys., 6m., 14d.; Maria, bp. Mar. 20, 1785; Maria, b. Jan. 16, 1788; Johannes,* b. Sept. 15, 1790; Jeromimus, b. Jan. 20, 1793, d. Nov. 7, 1859; Peter, b. Sept. 4, 1795; Annatie, b. June 23, 1797; Annatje, b. June —, bp. July 7, 1799.

JACOBUS, son of Johannes and Cornelia, m. Maria Bovie. Ch: Cornelia, bp. May 20, 1781; Matthias, bp. Mar. 20, 1783; Marytje, b. June 22, 1785; Cornelia, b. Jan. 11, 1795.

LEWIS,* son of Johannes and Cornelia, m. Elsie Barheit. Ch: Johannes, bp. Oct. 26, 1783; Wouter, b. Apr. 1, 1785; Cornelia, b. Feb. 6, 1787; Cornelis, b. Jan. 22, 1789; Dirk, b. Sept. 6, 1791; Teunis, b. Aug. 16, 1793; Teunis, b. Jan. 8, 1798.

JEROONE, son of Johannes and Helena, m. Cornelia Becker, Jan. 4, 1789. He d. July 10, 1849, a. 85 ys., 8 m.; she d. Mar. 3, 1854, in her 86th yr. Ch. b: John, July 23, 1789; Gerrit Becker, Jan. 26, 1791; Jacobus, Oct. 15, 1792; Peter, Sept. 16, 1794; Maria, Ap. 20, 1797; Jesse, Jan. 9, 1799; Hendrick, Nov. 14, 1800; Lena, Sept. 18, 1802; Catrina, Sept. 7, 1804; Elly, Nov. 26, 1808; Jacob Becker, Oct. 20, 1810; Nicolas, June, 13, 1813.

JOHN C., son of Cornelis, m. Maria, dau. of Cornelis Van Slyck, Jan. 24, 1790; he d. Feb. 30, (*sic*) 1830, in his

---

* John N. B. d. June 30, 1849, a. 57 y., 9 m., 14d, Maria, w. of Jno. N. B., d. Dec. 30, 1836, in her 50th y.
* Lewis B. d. Mar. 7, 1829, in his 74th yr. Eleanor, w. of Lewis B., d. Nov. 26, 1801, a. 39 y., 2 m., 5 d.

63d yr., (see grave stone); she d. July 12, 1846, a. 76 ys., 9 m., 7 d. Ch. b: Cornelia, Oct. 3, 1790; Catharina, Dec. 29, 1792; Cornelius, Mar. 16, 1795, d. July 10, 1850; Rachel, June 9, 1797; Peter, June 15, 1800; Eva, Jan. 8, 1803; Peter, Oct. 12, 1805; Nicholas, June, 17, 1808; Adrian Van Slyck, June 1, 1811.

JACOBUS, son of Johannes and Helena, m. Christina Abel. Ch. b: Johannes, Oct. 9, 1791; Eva, June 23, 1795; David, Sept. 29, 1800; Lena, Nov. 17, 1802; John, Jan. 28, 1805; Dirk Van Schelluyne, Nov. 9, 1809.

JOHN, son of Teunis, and Catleyntie Pulver, both of Duanesburgh. The banns were proclaimed January 6, (?) 1791. Ch. b: Jacomyntje, Aug. 20, 1792; Maria, July 5, 1794; Teunis, July 21, 1796.

PETRUS, son of Johannes and Annatje, m. Susanna Bourns, b. Oct. 13, 1793. Ch. b: Annatje, May 31, 1794; Andries, Dec. 16, 1796.

JOHN SANDERS, of Glenville, son of Johannes and Helena, m. Catharina, dau. of Johannes Stevens, June 30, 1794; he d. July 27, 1852, a. 82 yrs., 5 m.; she d. July 20, 1805. Ch. b: Lena, Dec. 4, 1794; Lena, Oct. 10, 1796; Johannes, Oct. 26, 1798; Catlyntje, Feb. 2, 1801; Catlyntje, Mar. 28, 1803; Catharina, June 2, 1805.

HENDRICK, son of Johannes and Helena Peek, m. Catlyntje, dau. of Gerrit

Van Slyck. Ch. b: Johannes, Nov. 30, 1798; Elisabeth, Jan. 4, 1801; John, Aug. 25, 1802; Lena, Dec. 29, 1803; John, Oct. 29, 1805; John, Dec. 9, bp. Oct. 14, 1810. Sarah (?) Van Slyck made her will Sept. 11, 1802, proved Aug. 3, 1809; left her property to dau. Elisabeth, income to her father Gerrit; if her dau. died, then to her brother Harmanus. John H. Barheit, son of Henry Barheit, d. Sept. 13, 1802, a. 13 yrs., 9 m., 13 d.

BARKER.

ROBERT, a citizen of this city about 1800. In 1803, he bought of Maria (Bratt) Brouwer, the ancient house and lot No. 7 State street.

BARLOW.

RICHARD, "Sarjant," and Elisabeth .... Ch: Aaftje, bp. Aug. 10, 1756.

BARRET.

ROBERT, of Albany, and Wyntje Janse. She was buried Nov. 23, 1746, in Albany. Ch. bp. in Albany: Margriet, bp. Dec. 4, 1689; Tammus, bp. Mar. 5, 1692; Maria, bp. June 17, 1694; Sara, bp. Nov. 26, 1696; *Willem;* bp. Jan. 18, 1699; Magdalena, bp. Aug. 31, 1701.

WILLEM, carpenter, son of Robert, of Albany, m. Catalina, dau. of Dirk Bratt of Schenectady, Mar., 1725. His wife, Catalina, inherited from her father, the land on the south side of Union street, from No. 118 to, and including No. 154, extending south, beyond Liberty street. Willem Barret's dau. Anna, who m.

2

Jillis Van Vorst, inherited this property.
Ch: Robert, bp. in Albany, July 23,
1727; Wyntje, bp. Oct. 31, 1731; Maria, bp. Dec. 2, 1733, m. Thomas Bath;
Anna, bp. Jan. 18, 1736, m. Jillis Van
Vorst.

BARRON.

JOHN, m. Elisabeth Collon, July 24,
1758.

BARTELY.

DAMEN, and Maria Palmontier. Ch:
Rebecca, b. Nov. 6, 1770, bp. July 28,
1773; Abraham, bp. July 28, 1773; Elisabeth, bp. June 12, 1775; Maria, bp.
Aug. 29, 1777; Annatje, bp. Ap. 12,
1780; Catarien and Joseph, bp. Oct. 5,
1782.

ABRAHAM, and Margariet Ernst. Ch.
bp: Catarina, Oct. 30, 1774; Elisabeth,
Aug. 4, 1776; Neeltje, July 16, 1778.

BARTLEY.

JOCHIM, of Helderbergh, and Catharina Woester. Ch: A. Dorothea, b.
June 27, 1785.

EVERARD, of Helderbergh, and Regina Batter. Ch: Everard, bp. July 8,
1785.

BARTERAM.

CHRISTIAAN ERNST, and Dorothea
Maria Wilbreght. Ch: Henderick Andreas, bp. Aug. 3, 1755.

BARTON.

JOSIAH, m. Helena Phiney, Sept. 10,
1791.

BASELY.

THOMAS, m. Eve Rodgers, Aug. 20,
1798.

BASTIAANSE.

JOHANN JACOB, " Van Duytsland,"
and Catarina Reynhart. Ch: Elisabeth
and Hubertje, bp. Mar. 18, 1759; Elisabeth, bp. Nov. 30, 1760, m. Frederic
Weller; Maria, bp. Jan. 9, 1763; Maria,
bp. Jan. 13, 1764; Elisabeth, bp. Ap. 4,
1767.

JOHANNES, m. Eva, dau. of Sybrant
Van Schaick. Ch: Sybrant, bp. Nov.
22, 1778; Hendrick, bp. Mar. 20, 1783;
Evert Van de Bogart, b. June 19, 1785.

BAYLEY.

JOSEPH, and Debora Springer. Ch: Joseph, bp. Aug. 11, 1751.

BENJAMIN, and Eleanor McDougall.
Ch: Phebe, b. Dec. 13, 1792.

BAYARD.

STEPHEN N., was a merchant in Schenectady before 1800; treasurer of Union
College; removed to New York.

BEAVER (BEVER).

THOMAS, of Normanskil, and Margaret
Platto. Ch: Robert, bp. Oct. 27, 1779;
Maria, b. Dec. 22, 1785; Elisabeth, b.
Aug. 31, 1788.

EDWARD, and Rachel Adams. Ch:
Charles, b. Oct. 14, 1794.

BECK.

Capt. CALEB, settled in Schenectady
about 1703. He was an inn keeper, li-

cenced "to draw or sell liquor by retaile." His home lot was on the south corner of Church and Union streets, where after his death, in 1733, his widow continued the business, together with trade in groceries and dry goods, until her death. Caleb Beck made his will Mar. 8, 172⅜, proved Sept. 29, 1733, in which he spoke of his wife Anna, to whom he left the bulk of his property, which after her death was to pass to his son Caleb. He gave "to my son Caleb my waering cloaths from head to foot, and that he chues the best gun in the house and has it mended and prepared as he thinks fit for himself, and my Pocket Pistols and sword, with all my printed books and the Great New Chest." He married Anna (Harley) Mol, in New York, Nov. 2, 1705 (3 ?) Ch : Anna, bp. Oct. 7, 1704, m. Jacobus Van Vorst ; a dau. named ......, m. John Fairly ; Caleb, bp. June 21, 1712 ; *Caleb,* b. May 24, 1714 ; Engel, bp. Dec. 15, 1715, m. Isaac Ab. Truax, d. June 27, 1758, a. 42 ys., 6 m., 12 d. ; Margaret, m. John W. Brown.

CALEB, attorney at law, son of Caleb, m. Elisabeth, dau. of Abraham Truax, Nov. 1, 1747. She d. May 5, 1797, a. 71 ys., 11 m., 16 d He d. Dec. 9, 1787, a. 73 ys., 6 m., 16 d. Ch. bp: Anna, Oct. 6, 1748, m. Pieter Van Guysling ; Abraham, Dec. 15, 1751 ; Christina, Sept. 3, 1754 ; Caleb, Feb. 27, 1757 ; *Caleb,* Oct. 22, 1758 ; Engeltie, Ap. 5, 1761, m. Andrew Van Petten, d. July 13, 1817 ; Maria, Ap. 15, 1764 ; Elisabeth, Jan. 27, 1771.

CALEB, son of Caleb, studied law, but never practiced ; in 1788 was usher in Schenectady Academy ; d. in Oct., 1798. He m. Catharina Theresa, dau. of Rev. Dirk Romeyn, Aug. 26, 1790. She was b. June 5, 1768, d. August 28, 1853. Ch. b : *Theodric Romeyn,* August 11, 1791 ; Abraham, Oct. 21, 1792, d. 1821, in St. Louis ; John Brodhead, Sept. 18, 1794, d. 1851, in New York ; Nicholas Fairly, Nov. 7, 1796, d. June 30, 1830, in Albany ; Caleb Lewis [commonly written Lewis C.] Oct. 4, 1798, d. 1852.

THEODRIC ROMEYN, son of Caleb, m. Harriet, dau. of James Caldwell, in 1814. Ch : Catharine, who m. Pierre Van Cortland, and Helen, who m. William Parmalee.

BECKER (BACKER).

ABRAHAM, son of Johannes, of Albany, m. Elisabeth (Van der zee) Van Olinda, in Albany, July 17, 1742. Ch : Johannes, bp. Aug. 26, 1744. [*See Albany Families.*]

PIETER, of Schoharie, m. Gezina Vrooman, of Schenectady, Dec. 3, 1745.

(BEKKER).

FREDERIC, and Annatje Heger. Ch : Catarina, bp. Mar. 13, 1764.

JOHANNES, m. Sarah, dau. of Abraham Van Antwerpen, June 11, 1787. John G. Becker d. Jan. 4, 1794, in his 27th yr. After his death, Mrs. Becker m. Gilbert Van Sice ; she d. Feb. 10, 1826, in her 65th yr. Ch : Gerrit, b. Dec. 8, 1789 ; Abram, b. Nov. 14, 1792

ADAM, and Elisabeth Swart. Ch: Johannes, bp. May 13, 1772.

ZACHARIAS, and Rachel Young. Ch. b: Abram, June 23, 1786; Christina, July 14, 1793.

ALBERTUS, and Lena Becker. Ch. bp: Mar. 5, 1781.

ABRAHAM, and Elisabeth ...... Ch: Willem bp. Mar. 12, 1781.

NICHOLAS, and Jane Ferguson. Ch. b: Margariet, July 23, 1792; Nancy, Dec. 11, 1794; John, May 26, 1797.

GERRIT, and Maria Van Dyck. Ch. bp: Jacob, Ap. 14, 1782; Cornelius, Dec. 25, 1783.

BECON (BACON).

THOMAS, and Martha Withon (Whiton). Ch: Dinnis (Denis), bp. Dec 20, 1778.

BEDIE (BEDEUT)

STEPHEN, and Maria, dau. of Jan Pootman. Ch: Cornelia, bp. May 29, 1701.

BEEKMAN.

JOHANNES, son of Jacob, of Albany, m. Maria, dau. of Johannes Sanders, of Schenectady, Nov. 17, 1759. Ch: *Jacob*, bp. Aug. 9, 1761, d. Nov. 4, 1817.

JACOB, son of Johannes, m. Annatje, dau. of Daniel McKinney. He lived on lot No. 30 Washington street. Ch. b: John, Ap. 25, 1785, d. Aug. 13, 1791; Margarieta, Jan. 14, 1787, m. Rev. Stephen N. Rowan, D.D.; Hendrik, Nov.

29, 1788; he lived on south corner of Union and Canal streets.

BEERIGH.

CONRADT, Whitesmith, in 1788 owned lots Nos. 57 and 59 State street.

BEEROP (BARHOP).

THOMAS, trader, and Catarina Davis, Ch: *John*, bp. Oct. 23, 1763; *Andries*; Eafje, bp. Sept. 16, 1770; *Thomas*.

ANDRIES, son of Thomas, and Magdalena Creamer. Ch: Catrina, bp. May 4, 1783; Thomas, bp. Feb. 20, 1785; Margarietje, b. Dec. 28, 1787; Rachel, b. Sept. 22, 1793.

THOMAS, son of Thomas, and Gerritje Springsteen, both of Normanskil, m. Ap. 27, 1788. Ch. b: Andries, Dec. 11, 1788; Johannes, Mar. 22, 1794; Maria, Sept. 24, 1800.

JOHN, son of Thomas, m. Caty McGee, both of Normanskil, January 20, 1793. Ch. b: David, Nov. 12, 1793; John, Dec. 2, 1795; Catharina, Jan. 9, 1798; Andrew, Sept. 16, 1799; Thomas, Feb. 23, 1802; James, Jan. 29, 1804.

BELL.

JOHN, of Remsenbos, and Immetje Hendricksen. Ch: Rachel, bp. Aug. 2, 1775; Joseph, b. Oct. 18, 1778; Jannetje, b. June 29, 1780; Mary, b. Feb. —, 1785; Jannette, b. Aug. 29, 1786.

PETER, and ...... Van Slyck, both of the *Aalplaats*, m. July 23, 1797.

BELLINGER.

JOHANNES, and Ernestine Herder. Ch: Johannes, bp. Mar. 12, 1781. At the date of this baptism, the father was deceased.

BENJAMIN.

JONATHAN, of Remsenbush, and Fanny Staley of Duanesburgh, m. July 17, 1795. Ch: Ebenezer, b. May (?) 18, 1798.

BENSEN.

GERRIT, of Albany, and Dorothea Hoffman of Rensselaerswyk, m. Dec. 2, 1793. Ch. b. and bp. in Albany: Mary, Dec. 23, 1794; Gilbert, Nov. 9, 1796.

GERRIT, and Maria Van Vranken, dau. of Dirk. He d. Ap. 27, 1861, a. 91 ys. She d. Oct. 29, 1845, a. 70 ys. Ch. b: John, Feb. 9, 1798; Maria, Ap. 15, 1800; David, Nov. 1, 1802, d. in Albany, Nov. 17, 1853, a. 51; Sarah, May 19, 1805; Richard Van Vranken, Nov. 12, 1807; Nicholas, Jan. 17, 1811; Rebecca Ann, Ap. 29, 1813; Elisabeth, July 29, 1817.

ABRAHAM, of Albany, and Sarah Hagerdorn of *Aalplaats*, m. June 28, 1795. [*See Albany Families.*]

BERKLY (PIRKLY).

JOACHIM (Joseph), and Catarina Oosterman. Ch: Margarita, bp. June 19, 1779; Bartholomeus, b. Oct. 3, 1790.

(PERKLY).

MICHAEL, and Geertruy Say. Ch: Everhardt, Sept. 23, 1791.

BERRY (BERRIT ?).

WILLIAM, and Elisabeth Roseboom. Ch: William, bp. June 7, 1761.

BEST.

JACOB, and Jannetje Vredenburgh. Ch: Hendrik, b. Oct. 24, 1791.

BESTEDO (BEDSTEDO).

JACOB, and Clara Van Slyck. Ch. bp: David, Dec. 3, 1769; Elisabeth, Dec. 23, 1770; Ackus, Sept. 12, 1772; Louis and Gysbert, Oct. 3, 1775; Gysbert, Oct. 19, 1777; Joseph, Ap. 30, 1780.

BETH (BETT, BED, BATT, BATH).

THOMAS BATH, *Van Duytsland*, was perhaps the first settler of this name in Schenectady; his widow, Maria Berrit (dau. of Willem) joined the Church in 1758.

WILLEM, m. Elisabeth, dau. of Jillis Van Vorst, in Albany, Aug. 31, 1739. Ch. bp: Thomas, in Albany, June 1, 1740; Robert, Nov. 28, 1742; Gillis, Dec. 8, 1745; *Thomas*, Jan. 8, 1749; *Gillis*, Aug. 11, 1751.

WILLEM, (same as the last ?), m. Maria, dau. of Philip Bosie, May 3, 1755. Ch. bp: Elisabeth, Nov. 28, 1756, m. Jacob Bovie; Pieter Bovie, Nov. 5, 1758; Philip, Aug. 21, 1760; *Pieter Bosie*, May 8, 1762; Maria, Nov. 4, 1764; Margarita, Oct. 9, 1768; Philip, Aug. 19, 1771.

THOMAS, son of Willem, m. Maria, dau. of Willem Hall. Ch. bp: Willem,

Jan. 21, 1776; Elisabeth, July 19, 1778; Johannes, Jan. 16, 1780; *Robert*, Sept. 29, 1782; Annatje, Mar. 20, 1785; Jellis, Oct. 21, 1787; Elisabeth, Jan. 15, 1792.

ROBERT, son of Willem, m. Margarita, dau. of Daniel McKinney. Ch: Willem (?), bp. July 26, 1783; Margarietje, b. Jan. 6, 1788; Daniel, b. Aug. 1, 1792.

ROBERT, (same as last ?), m. Margarita, dau. of Cornelis P. Van Slyck. Ch. b: Marytje, Ap. 10, 1805; Catharine, July 26, 1807.

JELLIS, son of Willem, and Sarah Van Iveren. Ch. b: Elisabeth, Sept. 22, 1787; Maria, Aug. 22, 1789.

PIETER, son of Willem, m. Geertruy, dau. of Cornelis P. Van Slyck. Ch. b: William, Mar. 13, 1798; Catharina, June 10, 1801; William, Jan. 29, 1804; Caty, July 29, 1806; Maria Eliza, Feb. 19, 1809.

BETJER.

ANDRIES, of Normanskil, and Maria Fetherly. Ch: Maria, b. Ap. 3, 1786.

BETTIE.

WILLEM, member of the church 1761–85.

ROBERT, church member 1770–85.

BEVIER (BOVIER).

JOHN, (perhaps son of Matthias Bovier), m. Lena Schermerhorn. Ch: Mattheus, b. Sept. 21, 1799.

BIRGEN.

WILLIAM, of *de Willegen*, and Catrina Birns (Burns). Ch. bp: Catrina, Sept. 3, 1784; Martha, July 12, 1787.

BLANCHARD.

JAMES, and Elisabeth Bullock. Ch. b: Benjamin, July 1, 1782; Mary, Mar., 1784.

BLEEKER.

NICOLAS, son of Johannes, of Albany, and Margareta Roseboon, dau. of Johannes, of Albany. Ch: Nicolas, bp. May 16, 1745. [*See Albany Families.*]

RUTGER, son of Johannes Ruth of Albany, and Catrina Elmendorf. Ch: Elisabeth, bp. Oct. 5, 1777. She m. ...... Brinkerhoff, and d. in Albany, July 27, 1868, in her 91st yr. [*See Albany Families.*]

BLESSING.

MARTINUS, of Helderberg, and Margaret Syver. Ch: Frederic, b. June 16, 1785.

BLEY.

JOHANN, and Dorothea Herst. Ch: Johan Cornelius, bp. Oct. 8, 1780.

BLOEMENDAL.

JOHN, son of Pieter, of Albany, m. Jannetje, dau of Adam W. Vrooman, Feb. 13, 1780. Ch. b: Pieter, Aug. 13, 1786; Adam, Dec. 6, 1788.

BLOOD.

ROBERT, and Mary Simons. Ch: William Allen, b. June 2, 1799.

BOCHAAL.

JOSEPH, and Catarina Brosick. Ch: Joseph, bp. May 30, 1762.

ADAM, and Catarina Coks (Cox), Ch: Anna, bp. Dec. 19, 1781; Josina, b. June 13, 1784.

BODINE (BODYN).

JOHN, and Maria Van Hoesen. Ch. bp: Johannes, Mar. 18, 1770; Abraham, Jan. 9, 1785.

JACOB, and Susanna, dau. of Daniel Peek. She d. about January 1, 1798. Ch. b: Elisabeth, Nov. 31, 1796; Susanna, Jan. 1, 1798.

BOETS.

ANDREAS, and Elisabeth Rose. Ch: Barbara, bp. Mar. 30, 1760.

BOGAART.

PIETER PIETERSE, of Albany, m. Barbara, dau. of Ryckert Van Vranken of Schenectady, Mar. 11, 1758. [*See Albany Families.*]

BOGARDUS.

DAVID, and Maria Herrison. He resided in Amsterdam. Ch: Henderick, b. June 16, 1771; Johannes; Harmanus.

Rev. CORNELIUS, minister of the Dutch Church of Schenectady. He was ordained Nov. 27, 1808; Rev. John Bassett preached his installation sermon. He d. Dec. 15, 1812, a. 32 ys., 2 m., 19 d., and was buried in the burying ground belonging to the Church.

BOHAALT.

CASPER, and Margarita Conterman. Ch: Catharina, b. Mar. 21, 1786.

BOMPSTEAD.

JOHN, a citizen of Schenectady in 1715.

BOND.

RICHARD, and Engeltie, dau. of Johannes Van Antwerpen. Ch. b: Richard, July 9, 1787; Elisabeth, Dec. 8, 1792.

JOHN, and Annatje, dau. of Daniel Van Antwerpen. Ch. b: George, Feb. 24, 1786; Daniel, Aug. 14, 1788; Sarah, Aug. 5, 1791; Elisabeth, Oct. 29, 1794.

SAMUEL, of Normanskil, and Catharina Pulver of Duanesburgh, m. Nov., 1791. Ch. b: Richard, Aug. 28, 1792; Jacob, Oct. 12, 1794; Sarah, Mar. 3, 1797.

JOSEPH, and Gracy Williams (Williamson), both from the Normanskil in Corrysbos, m. July 12, 1791. Ch. b: Jenny, Aug. 21, 1793; Sarah, Dec. 27, 1795; James, Feb. 13, 1798.

BONNET.

PIETER, and Geesje Van Petten. Ch: Christiaan, b. Ap. 23, 1797.

BONNY.

JOHN, m. Annatje, dau. of Jacobus Teller, Mar. 16, 1788. He d. Aug. 6, 1835, a. 73 ys. Ch. b: Johannes Schoonmaker, Jan. 4, 1791, d. at Rahway, N. J., June 26, 1866; Joseph, Mar. 14, 1793, d. Sept. 8, 1827, a. 34 ys.; Jacobus Teller, Aug. 25, 1797.

JOHN, (same as last ?), and Polly Weller. Ch: Myndert Van Guysling, b. Sept. 1, 1805.

BONT (BENT, BINT, *alias* SASSIAN).

HENDRIK LAMBERTSE, before 1690 owned a bouwery above Schenectady, on the south bank of the Mohawk, called *Poversen's Landeryen,* which he sold to Douwe Aukes and removed to Claverak. This land, together with the island called Sassian's, afterwards came into the possession of the Viele family. He had a dau. Catalyntje, bp. in Albany, Ap. 28, 1686, and a son *Jan.*

JAN HENDRIKSE, m. Jannetje Scharp, in Albany, Jan. 20, 1704. He removed to Kinderhook. Ch. bp: Henderick, in Schenectady, June 18, 1704; Matthys in Albany, Jan. 13, 1706; Geesie, in Albany, Jan. 18, 1708.

BOOLMAN (BULMAN).

JOHN, and Lena Van Deusen, both from *de Willegen,* m. July 22, 1762. Ch: David, bp. Mar. 4, 1764.

BORDT.

JACOB, and Rachel Hegerman. Ch. b: Elisabeth, April 28, 1793; Andries, February 19, 1796; Catharine, Jan. 5, 1800.

BORN (BURN).

CAREL, and Bathseba, dau. of Andries Arentse Bratt. Ch. bp: Samuel, Aug. 5, 1716; Andries, Jan. 27, 1722; Jacomyna; Catelina, Mar. 26, 1714. Carel Born received conveyance from Arent Bratt, his wife's brother, of lot 100 ft.

square, on west corner of Union and Ferry streets; 1764, Francis Burn and wife, of Pounwell, N. H., conveyed said lot to Daniel Campbell, for £165 N. Y. currency.

BOWING (BOIN, BOON).

WILLEM, and Seyke Janse, both living at Albany, m. Jan. 22, 1690.

WILLEM, (same as last ?), m. Rachel, dau. of Jan Janse Yonkers of Schenectady, Sept. 13, 1702. Ch. bp: *Willem,* June 11, 1703; Maria, May 20, 1705; Sarah, Ap. 30, 1707; *Cornelis.*

CORNELIS, son of Willem, and Maria Pootman. Ch: Rachel, bp. Ap. 17, 1748.

WILLEM, son of Willem, of Maquaasland, m. Catarina, dau. of Daniel Van Antwerpen, Mar. 1, 1758. Ch. bp: Cornelia, Aug. 11, 1758; Pieter, Aug. 4, 1766.

BORNSEYD (BURNSIDE ?).

JAMES, and Debora Jansen. Ch. bp: Margaret, in Albany, July 22, 1759; Maria, Feb. 19, 1764.

JAMES, (same as last ?), and Debora Everse. Ch: Susannah, bp. Jan. 28, 1768.

BORRIN (BORN or BURN ?).

ANDREAS, and Sarah Gafe, m. Mar. 10, 1763.

BORSBOOM.

PIETER JACOBSE, *steen bakker* (brick maker), early settled in Beverwyck. In

1662, when the land was taken up at Schenectady, he became one of the fifteen first proprietors. His home lot in the village, was the north quarter of the block bounded by Front, Washington, Union and Church streets. He also had two farms allotted to him on the *bouwland.* In his will, which was recorded in New York, Oct. 18, 1686, he mentioned his son Cornelis, and four daughters. An inventory of his property was made May 30, 1689, by Barent Janse Van Ditmars, Isaac Cornelise Swits and Douwe Aukes; it amounted to 1630 guilders. His son Cornelis probably died young; his daughters who survived him were Anna, who m. Jan Pieterse Mebie; Maritie, wife of Hendrick Brouwer; Fytie, wife of Marte Van Benthuysen, and Tryntje, wife of John Oliver.

BORTEL.

JOHN, and Elisabeth Truax. Ch : Sarah, bp. Feb. 20, 1785.

BOSIE.

PHILIP, m. Grietje Bratt, Sept. 2, 1704. Ch. bp; Jannetje, Ap. 14, 1706, m. Dirk Van Vorst; Margarita, Oct. 10, 1708, m. Douwe Van Vorst; Gertrude, Jan. 21, 171⁹⁄₁, m. Johannes Marinus; Catalina. Oct. 28, 1715 ; Clara, Nov. 23, 1717, m. first, Cornelis Viele, secondly, Ephraim Bratt; Petrus, Mar. 19, 1720 ; *Petrus,* June 30, 1722 ; Catalina, b. Oct. 4, 1724 ; Maria, b. Sept. 25, 1726, m. Willem Beth.

PIETER, son of Philip, m. Margarieta, dau. of Nicolaas Fort, of Genistagione,

June 10, 1749. Ch. bp : Maria, Dec. 24, 1749 ; Maria, Mar. 24, 1751, m. Frans Veeder; Geertruy, Dec. 26, 1753, m. Jesse Peek.

BOVIE (BEAUFILS).

MATTHEUS, and Catrina Baroj (Barrois). He was a freeholder of Half Moon in 1720. Ch. bp : Anna, Jan. 18, 1702 ; Catrina, Jan. 7, 1705 ; *Francois,* in Albany, May 25, 1713. [*See also, Albany Families.*]

FRANS, son of Mattheus, of Rensselaerwyk, m. Machtelt, dau. of Claas Gerritse Van Vranken, of Connestigioune, Jan., 1735. Ch. bp : Elisabeth, June 13, 1736; *Mattheus,* in Albany, Oct. 22, 1738; Geertruy, in Albany, June 24, 1741.

RYCKERT, son of Claas, of Albany, m. Maria Huyk. Ch : Nicolaas, bp. Aug. 26, 1744. [*See Albany Families.*]

MATTHIAS, son of Frans and Maria Kool. Ch : Abraham, bp. Nov. 13, 1768.

MATTHIAS, and Baata, dau. of Joachim Van der Heyden, both of Nestongjoone, m. Oct. 11, 1760. Ch : *Johannes* (see John Bevier); Rachel, bp. Sept. 6, 1772; Elisabeth, bp. June 8, 1784. [*See Albany Families.*]

JACOB, and Elisabeth, dau. of Willem Beth. Ch : Antje, b. July 16, 1777 ; Willem, bp. Mar. 14, 1779 ; Maria, b. Oct. 23, 1780; Johannes, bp. Sept. 11, 1783; Pieter, b. Mar. 4, 1785; Jacob, b. Ap. 7, 1787; Maria, b. Jan. 15, 1789;

Isaac, b. Mar. 1, 1791; Philip, b. Sept. 18, 1792; Sarah, b. Sept. 26, 1794; Elisabeth, b. Mar. 6, 1797; Hendrikus, b. Feb. 20, 1801.

NICOLAAS J., and Sarah ...... Ch: Annatje, bp. Mar. 18, 1783.

NICOLAS, son of Ryckert, and Nancy Baptist, both living in the county of Montgomery, m. December 6, 1785. Ch. b: Maria, Sept. 22, 1786; John, Sept. 11, 1788; Jacob, July 5, 1790; Cornelia, Mar. 10, 1792; Jacob, Sept. 6, 1799.

JACOB M., son of Mattheus, and Jannetje Dodge. Ch. b; Polly, Oct. 25, 1789; Selia, May 21, 1791; Mattheus, July 24, 1793; Johannes, Sept. 26, 1795; Sarah, Oct. 19, 1797; Catlyntje, Feb. 22, 1800.

JACOB, son of Philip (?), and Jacomyntje, dau. of Johannes T. Marselis. Ch. b: Philip, Mar. 26, 1790; Annatje, Nov. 5, 1791; John, May 28, 1793.

ISAAC, m. Rebecca, dau of Albert H. Vedder, Ap. 19, 1789. Ch. b: Elisabeth, Ap. 16, 1793; Antje, Feb. 18, 1797; Albert, May 24, 1799; Jacob, Mar. 9, 1801.

ABRAM, m. Elisabeth, dau. of Albert H. Vedder, of Tjughtenoonda, Feb. 3, 1793. Ch. b: Antje, Feb. 11, 1794; Annatje, Jan. 28, 1795; Annatje, Jan. 29, 1796.

ABRAHAM, and Lydia Peek, both of Durloch, m. Feb. 19, 1797.

(BOVIER).

MATTHIAS, and Elisabeth Lansing. Ch: Maria, b. Aug. 4, 1796. [*See Albany Families.*]

MATTHIAS, son of Mattheus and Baata, m. Marytje Schermerhorn. Ch. b: Sarah, Nov. 22, 1799; Baata, Mar. 1, 1802; Isaac, Aug. 31, 1804.

HENDRICK and Alida (Aaltie) Sutphen. Ch. b: Mary, Mar. 31, 1798; John, Aug. 22, 1799.

ABRAHAM, son of Matthias and Maria, m. Annatje Warner. Ch: Maria, b. Nov. 22, 1798.

BOUWMAN (BOWMAN).

JACOB, m. Gerritje, dau. of Gerrit Luycase Wyngaard of Albany. Ch. bp: Gerrit Lucase, Mar. 17, 1738; Andries, July 4, 1742; Lucas, Sept. 23, 1744.

BOWMAN.

JOHN, of Corrysbush, m. Eva Barheyt, of Schenectady, Dec., 1767.

BOYD.

JAMES, m. Alida, dau. of Jesse Conde. Ch. b: Catharine, Nov. 17, 1785; John, Nov. 8, 1787.

BRADFORD.

JOHN, of Glenville, m. Rebecca, dau. of Symon Van Petten, Oct. 30, 1791; he d. Nov. 15, 1848, a. 79 ys. Ch. b: Jannetje, Jan. 15, 1792; Angelica, Aug. 17, 1798.

JAMES, and Nelly, dau. of Peter Hoogeboom. Ch: Ann, b. Oct. 25, 1805.

BRADSHAW.

JAMES, and Elisabeth Bullock. Ch: Joseph, b. Nov. 17, 1786.

BRAGHAM (BROCHAEL).

JOSEPH and Susannah, dau. of Simon Groot, Jr. Ch. bp: Simon,* June 14, 1718; Joseph, Mar. 19, 1720; Willem, Mar. 25, 1721; Joseph, Aug. 18, 1723; Johannes, b. Mar. 2, 1725; *Samuel*, b. Jan. 28, 1728; Elisabeth, bp. May 23, 1731; *Joseph*, May 5, 1734; Geertruy, Oct. 24, 1736; Sarah, July, 1739, m. Richard Bond; *Johannes*, Oct. 16, 1743.

JOSEPH, son of Joseph, m. Margaret Haggenbach of Rensselaerswyk, Dec. 15, 1765. Ch. bp: Susanna, Dec. 28, 1766; Elisabeth, Jan. 31, 1768, m. Alexander Shannon; Susanna, Mar. 6, 1769, m. Michael Shannon; Catarina, July 1, 1770; Joseph, Jan. 26, 1777; Johannes, Dec. 7, 1780.

SAMUEL, son of Joseph, and Debora, dau. of Albert Arentse Vedder. Ch. bp: *Samuel*, Oct. 30, 1776; Elisabeth, Mar. 13, 1780; Cornelius, May 5, 1782; Geertruy, Oct. 24, 1784; Albert, Mar. 12, 1786.

JOHN, son of Joseph, m. Margarita, dau. of Albert Arentse Vedder, Oct. 17, 1770. Ch. bp: Geertruy, Nov. 3, 1776; Arent, Oct. 19, 1778; Catarina, June 27, 1780; Johannes,. Nov. 30,

* In 1752 he owned one-third part of a lot 100 x 666 ft. beginning on north side of State street 55 ft. west of Jay street, which lot was inherited from his grandfather Groot. In 1786 his children conveyed this third part to the Dutch Church for £50; it afterwards passed to David Frank and George McQueen.

1783; Sarah, b. May 5, 1785; Willem, b. Mar. 26, 1787; Joseph, b. Sept. 26, 1788.

SAMUEL, Jr., son of Samuel, and Margaret Van Antwerpen, both of Normanskil, m. Nov. 25, 1798. Ch. b: Joseph, Ap. 12, 1799; Abram, Sept. 5, 1801; Debora, May 27, 1803; Caty, May 18, 1805.

BRAGHMAN (BRAGHAM?).

FREDERIC, and Susanna Brower, both of Normanskil, m. Mar. 8, 1791.

BRAKE.

WILLIAM, m. Alice Leonard, Aug. 22, 1742. Ch. bp: William, Dec. 18, 1743; Jannetje, Dec. 2, 1744.

BRATT (BRAT, BRADT).

Two brothers of this name, Albert Andriese and Arent Andriese, were among the early settlers of Albany. They often went by the name of *De Noorman.* The former remained in Albany, and is the ancestor of most of the name in that county; the latter became one of the first proprietors of Schenectady in 1662, about which time he died, leaving a widow and six children. His wife was Catalyntje, dau. of Andries De Vos, Deputy Director of Rensselaerswyk. After the death of her husband, the grants of land allotted to him, were 'confirmed to her. Her home lot in the village, was the west quarter of the block bounded by Washington, Union, Church and State streets, being about 200 ft. sq., Amsterdam measure. On this lot her grandson,

Arent A. Bratt, brewer, built the ancient Dutch house, now standing on the north side of State, near Washington street. On the 12th of Nov. 1664, being about to marry her second husband, Barent Janse Van Ditmars, she contracted with the guardians of her children, to set off for them from her estate, 1,000 guilders, and mortgaged her-bouwery, No. 1, on the *bouwland* to secure this sum to them. He was killed in the massacre of 1690. In 1691, she married Claas Janse Van Boekhoven, whom she also outlived. She died in 1712. In her marriage contract with Van Ditmars, (1664) the following children were mentioned, to wit: *Andries* Arentse, a. 11 ys.; Aeffie, a. 15 ys.; she m. Claas Van Petten; Ariaantje, a. 13 ys.; she m. Ryer Schermerhorn; *Samuel*, a. 5 ys.; *Dirk*, a. 3 ys.; Cornelia, a. 9 ys.; she m. Jan Pootman, and with her husband, was killed in the massacre of 1690.

ANDRIES, son of Arent, brewer, m. Margareta, dau. of Jacques Cornelise Van Slyck. He, with one of his children, was killed in the massacre cf 1690. His widow, about 1698, m. Manus Vedder. Ch: *Arent;* Bathseba, who m. Charles Burn.

SAMUEL, son of Arent, m. Susanna, dau. of Jacques Cornelise Van Slyck. Ch. bp: *Arent;* Margareta, Ap. 25, 1686, m. Capt. Daniel Toll; Anna, June 5, 1692; *Jacobus*, Jan. 3, 1695; Cornelia, Dec. 30, 1696; Johannes, Sept. 1, 1699; Catalyntje, Dec. 21, 1701, m. Jacobus Van Slyck; Susanna, Jan. 2, 1704, m. Bartholomeus Vrooman; *Andreas,*

Oct. 28, 1705; *Samuel*, Ap. 30, 1707; *Ephraim*, Feb. 12, 1712.

DIRK, son of Arent, m. Maritje, dau. of Jan Baptist Van Eps. He inherited his step-father Van Boekhoven's farm in Niskayuna, on the north side of the Mohawk, which farm by patent, dated Ap. 22, 1708, was extended one mile further north. Ch: Lysbet, b .Sept. 11, 1685, and bp. in Albany, Feb. 3, 1686; Jan, bp. in Albany, Aug. 27, 1693; Catalyntje, b. June 27, and bp. Oct. 9, 1695, m. Willem Berrit; Maria, b. Sept. 22, bp. Oct. 19, 1698, m. Ryckert Van Vranken; Anna, b. Sept. 27, bp. Sept. 29, 1700; *Johannes*, b. May 22, (old bible), bp. May 14, 1704; Andries, b. Jan. 15, 168⅜; *Dirk*, b. July 20, bp. Oct. 30, 1710. All the above ch. were living Jan. 16, 1727, save the second (Jan), when the father made his will.

Capt. ARENT, son of Andries, brewer, was heir of his grandfather, Arent Andriese, the first settler. He was member of the Provincial Assembly in 1745, and Trustee of Schenectady, from 1715 to 1767. He built and occupied till his death, the ancient brick house on the north side of State street, near Washington street. He m. Jannetje, dau. of Jan Hendrickse Vrooman, Oct. 14, 1704. Ch. bp: *Andreas*, Mar. 4, 1705; Catharina, Jan. 29, 1706, m. Henricus Wemple; Gezena, Ap. 30, 1707; *Johannes*, bp. in Albany, Jan. 5, 1709; Margrietje, Oct. 21, 1711, m. Cornelis Van Dyck; Magdalena, bp. in Albany, June 21, 1713; Magdalena, May 28, 1716, m.

Johannes Schermerhorn; Ariaantje, Jan. 11, 1718, m. Nicolaas Van Petten; *Harmanus*, Sept. 3, 1721; Simon Petrus, Jan. 6, 1723; Susanna, b. 1719; Jannetie (?).

ARENT, son of Samuel, built and resided in the ancient brick house, now standing southwest of the first lock above the city. He m. Catrina, dau. of Jan Pieterse Mebie. She d. in 1773, a. 82 ys., 2 m., 17 d. Ch: *Samuel*, bp. Oct. 16, 1715; *Johannes*, bp. Sept. 15, 1717; Susanna, bp. July (?) 9, 1719, m. Jacques Peek; Annatje, bp. Sept. 3, 1721, m. Johannes Helmerse Veeder; Margret, b. Sept. 15, 1723, m. Cornelis Vrooman; Eva, b. Mar. 10, 1726; *Abram*, b. Dec. 13, 1727; *Jacobus*, b. 1730; Engeltje, bp. Aug. 26, 1733, m. Daniel Campbell.

JACOBUS, son of Samuel, m. Margarita, dau. of Johannes Clute. Ch. bp: *Samuel*, Feb. 2, 1724; Johannes, b. Sept. 2, 1726; Elisabeth, Dec. 24, 1730; Bata, Jan. 30, 1732, m. Abraham Watson; Harmanus, Feb. 24, 1734; Jacobus, Feb. 27, 1737; Susanna, July, 1739; *Arent*.

Capt. ANDRIES, son of Arent, m. first, Ariaantje, dau. of Johannes Wemple, Nov. 28, 1728, and secondly, Elisabeth, dau. of Jan Barentse Wemple. Capt. Bratt was a brewer, and lived on north side of State street, between Church and Washington streets. He made his will Ap. 6, 1748, at which time all his children enumerated below, were living, except the first. Ch. bp: Catalina, b. Mar.

5, 1729; *Arent*, bp. Sept. 3, 1732; Cathalyntje, June 7, 1735, m. John Butler; the following are ch. of the second wife: *Johannes*, Mar. 22, 1741; Jannetje, Aug. 28, 1743, m. Christopher Yates; Helena, July 14, 1745, m. Andries Wemple; Adriaantje, December 26, 1747, m. Jellis Yates.

JOHANNES, son of Dirk Arentse, m. Margarita, dau. of Gerrit Ryckse Van Vranken, in Albany, February 10, 1732. Ch: Maria, bp. in Schenectady, Mar. 4, 1733; Barber, bp. in Albany, Jan. 29, 1835; Elisabeth, bp. in Albany, Oct. 3, 1736; Alida, bp. in Albany, Ap. 16, 1738; Cathalyna, bp. in Albany, May 4, 1740; Dirk, bp. in Albany, Sept. 20, 1741; Dirk, bp. in Albany, June 15, 1743; Anna, and Margarita, twins, bp. in Schenectady, June 2, 1745.

SAMUEL, son of Samuel, m. Catharina, dau. of Arent Van Petten, Oct. 1732. Ch. bp; Susanna, June 3, 1733; Jannetje, Mar. 23, 1735; *Samuel*, Ap. 10, 1737; Arent, Oct. 15, 1738; Maria, May 3, 1741; Jacobus, June 9, 1745; *Fredrik*, Nov. 20, 1748; *Ephraim*, Jan. 27, 1751; Susanna, June, 15, 1754.

DIRK, son of Dirk Arentse, of Connestagiouny, m. Annatje, dau. of Arent Danielse Van Antwerpen, Nov. 5, 1732. Ch. bp: Maria, Sept. 23, 1733, m. Jacob Volleweyser; *Dirk*, Nov. 24, 1734; Arent, Aug. 22, 1736; Andries, July 6, 1738.

JOHANNES, son of Arent Andriese, m. Maria, dau. of Abraham Truax, Nov. 19,

1732. He lived in the ancient brick house, still standing on the north side of State street, near Washington street; made his will in 1760, and d. June 23, 1760. His widow m. Evert Wendell of Albany, in 1761; he d. July 15, 1762. She d. April 15, 1782, aged 70 ys., 2 d. Ch : Arent, b. May 9, 1734, d. July 22, 1752.

ANDRIES, son of Samuel, m. Anna De Graaf, of Esopus, Jan. 29, 174¾. Ch : Samuel, bp. July 8, 1744.

SAMUEL, son of Arent Samuelse, m. Catharina, dau. of Myndert Van Guysling, Feb. 10, 174¾. He d. Aug. 3, 1799, a. 83 ys., 11 m., 11 d. She d. Dec. 29, 1803, aged 81 ys, 11 m. 21 d. Ch. bp : *Arent*, July 8, 1744 ; Zuster, Dec. 1, 1745, m. Johannes Peek ; Catharina, Dec. 30, 1747 ; Johannes, Jan. 1, 1749 ; Catharina, Ap. 8, 1750, d. May 3, 1801, a. 51 ys. 20 d.. Myndert, Aug. 30, 1752, d. June 7, 1806 ; Johannes, Nov. 17, 1754, d. Oct. 19, 1804 ; Elias, Sept. 14, 1756 ; Susanna, Nov. 2, 1758 ; Susanna, Nov. 18, 1759, m. Lucas W. Veeder ; *Cornelis*, b. Ap. 21, 1762, d. Aug. 16, 1814 ; Daniel Campbell, Nov. 9, 1766.

BERNARDUS, son of Daniel Barentse of Albany, m. Catharina, dau. of Johannes Van Vechten of Albany. Ch : Elisabeth, bp. Dec. 25, 1744. He m. secondly, Eva Toll, widow, Dec. 23, 1748. Ch : Maria, b. June 4, 1749, *obiit ante baptism :* Nicolaas, bp. July 8, 1750. [*See Albany Families.*]

ALBERT, of Albany, son of Andries Albertse, of Albany, m. Anna Karen (Carel) in Albany, November 24, 1743. Ch : Andries, bp. Oct. 7, 1744. [*See Albany Families.*]

HARMANUS, son of Arent Andriese, brewer and Indian trader, lived on lot No. 13 State street. Tradition says he was the wealthiest man in the village. He m. first, Elisabeth, dau. of Cornelis Van Dyck, Dec. 4, 1743 ; and secondly, Aefje, dau. of Hendrick Brouwer, Dec. 11, 1756. Ch. bp : Arent, Ap. 29, 1744 ; Arent, Jan. 19, 1746 ; Maria, June 18, 1749, m. Jillis Brouwer ; Andries, July 7, 1751 ; Jannetje, Feb. 19, 1758, m. Simon De Graaf ; Elisabeth, Sept. 2, 1759 ; Magdalena, Mar. 16, 1761 ; Andries ; Maria, Jan. 2, 1765, m. Lourens Vrooman ; *Arent*, Mar. 10, 1771.

JOHANNES, the fourth, son of Arent Samuelse, taylor, m. Anna Van Antwerpen. Ch : Arent, bp. Feb. 17, 1745.

JAN, of Albany, son of Pieter Bratt, of Albany, m. Susanna Zegers. Ch : *Gerrit*, bp. July 30, 1749. [*See Albany Families.*]

EPHRAIM, son of Samuel Arentse, carpenter, m. Claartje, dau. of Philip Bosie, and widow of Cornelis Viele, Jr., May, 1751. Ch. bp : Susanua, June 17, 1752, m. David Sege ; Cornelia, Jan. 14, 1759, m. Martin Van Benthuysen ; Margarita m. Nicolaas Van Petten.

SAMUEL, son of Jacobus, m. Annatje Mann. Ch. bp : *Jacobus*, Aug. 3, 1752 ;

Johannes, in Albany, Sept. 22, 1754; Annatje, Jan. 11, 1756; Margarita, Oct. 29, 1758; Susanna, Ap. 5, 1761; Elisabeth, Ap. 20, 1766; Elsje, Feb. 26, 1769; Samuel, Jan. 19, 1772; Lena, Jan. 8, 1775.

ARENT, son of Andries, cordwainer, m. Eva Van Antwerpen. Ch. bp: *Andries*, Aug. 27, 1755; Margarita, Ap. 16, 1758; Johannes, Jan. 18, 1761; Pieter, Ap. 10, 1763; Reyer, July 28, 1765; Pieter, Dec. 17, 1769. All these children, except Reyer, settled in the town of South, county of Lincoln, Upper Canada, where they were living in 1806. Margarita was the wife of Cornelis Ryckman. John made his will Oct. 17, 1826, proved Mar. 24, 1827, and left his property to his brother Andrew, only £1. 5s. to his dau. Nancy.

ABRAHAM, son of Arent Samuelse, of Rotterdam, m. Sarah, dau of Frederic Van Petten, Feb. 7, 1761. He made his will Aug. 4, 1806, proved Ap. 12, 1816, spoke of all his children as then living, except Arent and Rebecca; died Mar. 25, 1816, a. 88 ys., 3 m., 1 d. His wife d. Sept. 8, 1783, a. 45 ys., 11 m., 18 d. Ch. bp: Arent, Nov. 22, 1761; *Arent*, Jan. 9, 1762; Elisabeth, Ap. 7, 1765; *Frederick*, Aug. 16, 1767; *Johannes*, Ap. 1, 1770; *Nicolaas*, b. Aug. 24, 1772; Catarina, b. Feb. 23, 1775; Rebecca, bp. June 1, 1777; Eva, Ap. 14, 1780; Angelica; Sarah.

JOHANNES, son of Andries Arentse, inherited his uncle's house and brewery on the westerly end of State street. He m. Volkie, dau. of Reyer (?) Wemple, Mar. 4, 1761. Ch. bp: Andreas, Dec. 6, 1761; Andreas, July 3, 1763; Andreas, Oct. 14, 1768; Debora, Oct. 8, 1771, m. Jacobus Dellamont.

ANTHONY, of Albany, son of Daniel (?), of same place, m. Maria Veeder, Sept. 16, 1762. Ch. bp: Wyntje, July 31, 1763; *Cornelis*, Sept. 22, 1765; *Daniel*, May 22, 1768; *Nicolaas*, Dec. 23, 1770; Engeltie, July 11, 1773. [*See Albany Families.*]

SAMUEL, son of Samuel and Catharina Van Petten, m. Huybertje, daughter of Joseph Yates, December 10, 1763. Ch. bp: *Samuel*, Aug. 19, 1764; Joseph Yates, May 3, 1767; Annatie, Jan. 14, 1770, m. Walter Taylor; Joseph, Dec. 29, 1771.

SAMUEL, son of the last, m. Engeltie, dau. of Barent Veeder. He d. before July 1, 1804. Ch. b: Huybertje, May 7, 1785; Barent, Oct. 1, 1786; Jannetje, Dec. 12, 1788; Samuel, Nov. 6, 1790; Joseph, Dec. 14, 1792; Eve, July 1, 1804.

SAMUEL S., (perhaps same as the last), m. Clara, dau. of Jacob Heemstraat, of Nestigayune, Ap. 24, 1793. Ch. b: Annatje June 13, 1794; Jacob, Dec. 8, 1796; Samuel, July 27, 1799.

ARENT, son of Samuel, and Catharina Van Guysling, m. Maria Van Slyck. He d. Feb. 3, 1814, in his 71st year. Ch. bp: *Samuel*, Sept. 14, 1766; *Jo-

hannes, Dec. 10, 1769; *Frederic,* Nov. 17, 1771; Catarina, Aug. 1, 1774, m. John F. Quackenbos; Susanna, Sept. 22, 1776; Martinus and Margarita, Feb. 20, 1780; (Martinus d. June 16, 1845, a. 65 ys., 6 m., 11 d.); Arent, Oct. 13, 1782.

CORNELIS, son of Anthony, m. Annatje, dau. of Petrus Pieterse, Mar. 31, 1786. She d. Ap. 11, 1849, in her 80th year. Ch. b : Ariaantje, July 27, 1786; Daniel, Mar. 27, 1788; Rebecca, 1789; Maria, Feb. 8, 1793; Maria, Sept. 23, 1794; Peter, Sept. 7, 1796, d. May 8, 1850, a. 54 yrs.; Rachel, Oct. 8, 1798; Rachel, May 24, 1800; Ann Elisabeth, Ap. 21, 1802; Annatje, Sept. 1, and Sarah, Sept. 2, 1804, and both bp. Sept. 9, 1804; Annatje, Aug. 23, 1806; William Anderson, Dec. 25, 1809, and bp. Dec. 1, 1816.

JACOBUS, son of Arent and Catrina Mebie, m. Elisabeth, dau. of Jan Dellamont, Mar. 4, 1769. He d. Mar. 26, 1801, a. 71 ys.; she d. Dec. 25, 1819, a. 86ys., 11m., 22d. Ch. bp : Catarina, June 25, 1769, m. Johannes Jacobse Schermerhorn; Eva, Sept. 15, 1771, m. Takerus Vedder; Engeltje, March 26, 1775, m. Jacob Schermerhorn.

ARENT, son of Abraham, m. first, Engeltje Van Petten, May 7, 1786, and secondly, Jannetje, dau. of Gerrit Van Schaick. He was not living in 1809. Ch. b : Sarah, Oct. 2, 1791; Elisabeth, July 14, 1793; Abram, June 10, 1796; Engeltje, July 28, 1798; Lidia, Ap. 23,

1801; Gerrit Van Schaick, April 23, 1803.

DIRK, son of Dirk, and Aefje, dau. of Christiaan Christiaanse, both of Nistoungjoone, m. October 26, 1765. Widow Eve Bratt and son were buried in 1805. Ch : Evert, b. June 20, 1771; Annatje, bp. Sept. 26, 1779.

DANIEL, son of Anthony, m. Anna Olshaver, Feb. 24, 1793. She (widow,) d. Aug. 26, 1845, a. 74ys. Ch. b : Jannetje, Jan 27, and bp. Feb. 24, 1793, m. ...... McDowall, d. Dec. 31, 1850; Maria, Sept. 14, 1794; Margarieta, July 8, 1796; Sebastian Olshaver, August 24, 1798, d. at No. 3 Ferry street, Nov. 13, 1869; Anthony, Aug. 3, 1800, d. June 14, 1854; Peter, July 4, 1803; Angelica, Mar. 28, 1805; Nicholas, Nov. 30, 1808.

JACOBUS, son of Samuel and Annatje Mann, m. Susanna, dau. of Jacques Peek, Nov. 9, 1770. Ch : Catalyntje, bp. Sept. 1, 1771; Jakus, b. June 2, 1773; Samuel, bp. May 27, 1775; Eva, bp. Aug. 24, 1777; Jannetje, bp. Sept. 26, 1779; Dirk, bp. Feb. 11, 1787.

JACOBUS, (perhaps same as the last), m. Catharina Berrit. Ch. b : Annatje, Feb. 13, 1786; Walter Berrit, Oct. 19, 1788.

GERRIT, son of Jan Pieterse, m. Maria Van Antwerpe. Ch : *Arent Van Antwerpe,* bp. Nov. 4, 1773; Neeltie, bp. Aug. 13, 1775; Dirk, bp. Sept. 21, 1777; Harmanus, bp. Oct. 29, 1780; John, bp. August 29, 1784; Daniel, b

Sept. 26, 1787; Abraham, bp. Sept. 27, 1789; Elisabeth, b. Sept. 17, 1792; Andries, b. Aug. 20, 1795.

JOHN, and Maria Zeger, both of Rensselaerswyck, m. Mar. 5, 1774.

ARENT, and Geertruy Dalheymer. Ch: Dirk, bp. Aug. 30, 1775.

ANDRIES, son of Arent Andriese and Eva, m. Rachel, dau. of Johannes Rykman. Ch. b: Simon, Van Antwerp, Oct. 10, 1788; Eunice, Nov. 15, 1790.

FREDERICK, son of Samuel and Catharine Van Petten, m. Bata, dau. of Isaac Quackenbosch (?). Ch. bp: Catalyna, Oct. 29, 1775; Elisabeth, Dec. 14, 1777; Samuel, Nov. 28, 1779; Jacobus, Dec. 23, 1781, d. Ap. 24, 1854; Maria, Feb. 11, 1784; Rebecca, b. Feb. 26, 1786.

FREDERICK, son of Arent Samuelse and Maria Van Slyck, m. Catlyntje, dau. of Jacob Schermerhorn, July 7, 1792. Ch. b: Arent, Nov. 20, 1793; Maria, Feb. 6, 1797; Catharine, Ap. 7, 1801.

EPHRAIM, son of Samuel and Catharina Van Petten, m. Annatje, dau. of Hendrick Van Dyck. Ch. bp: Samuel, Feb. 23, 1777; Engeltje, Aug. 10, 1780; Henderick, Sept. 9, 1781; Arent, Dec. 7, 1783; Elisabeth, b. July 6, 1787.

S———,. and Annetje Hallenbeek. Ch: Treyntje, bp. Jan. 24, 1780.

SAMUEL, son of Arent Samuelse and Maria Van Slyck, m. Polly, (Maria) dau. of Benjamin Springer, of Normanskil, June 14, 1789. Ch. b: Arent, Sept.

24, 1789; Benjamin, Oct. 8, 1792; Maria, Dec. 24, 1794, d. Mar. 21, 1862, in her 68th year; Richard Oliver, April 21, 1797; Frederic, Dec. 10, 1799.

PIETER, of Albany (?), and Maria Bratt. Ch: Lydia, bp. Feb. 3, 1780.

NICOLAAS, son of Anthony Danielse, m. Elisabeth, dau. of Cornelis Van Deusen (?), of Albany. Ch. b: Maria, Ap. 29, 1792; Cornelius, Oct. 9, 1793; Anthony, Jan. 30, 1795; John, May 6, bp. May 1 (*sic*), 1796; Anthony, Feb. 8, 1798; Lea, Feb. 13, 1800; John, Nov. 28, 1801; Anthony, Sept. 25, 1803; Gerrit Simonse Veeder, Feb. 5, 1805; Lea, Sept. 7, 1806; Isaac Fonda, Sept. 3, 1808; Isaac Fonda, Nov. 11, 1809; Jacob Clute, Ap. 2, 1812.

HENDERICK, of Albany, and Maria Arnout. Ch: Wyntje, bp. Jan. 4, 1781. [*See Albany Families.*]

JOHANNES, son of Abraham, of the *Woestine*, m. Willempie, dau. of Cornelis Mebie, Jan. 19, 1793. He d. July 14, 1846, a. 76ys., 4m., 5d.; she d. Jan. 4, 1862, a. 87ys., 11m. Ch. b: Abram, June 9, 1793; Cornelius, July 2, 1796, m. Rebecca Van Patten; Abram, June 3, 1800; Esther, July 30, 1803; Arent, Aug. 13, 1806, d. Mar. 13, 1860; Sara, Ap. 18, 1809; Catharine, July 4, 1812, m. Cornelius Becker, and d. Jan. 5, 1850; Frederic, June 9, 1815.

WILLEM, and Elisabeth Arnhout. Ch: Frans, bp. Jan. 27, 1781. [*See Albany Families.*]

4

CORNELIUS, son of Samuel Arentse and Catharina Van Gyseling, m. Elisabeth Van Petten, June 13, 1790. Ch: Samuel, b. Mar. 7, 1794. Cornelius Bratt made his will May 2, 1814, proved Oct. 7, 1814, in which he spoke of wife Elisabeth and son Samuel, my sister Susanna, &c.; he d. Aug. 16, 1814. His son Samuel made his will Dec. 23, 1817, proved Aug. 1, 1818, and left all his estate to his mother Elisabeth.

JOSEPH, and Tanneke Van Buren, both of *Melatten Bos.*, m. Feb. 11, 1793.

JOHN, son of Arent and Maria Van Slyck, m. Lena, dau. of Barent Veeder, Mar. 16, 1789; she d. between Aug. 20, and Oct. 7, 1798. Ch. b: Maria, Oct. 1, 1789; Barent, Sept. 7, 1791; Jannetje, Dec. 16, 1793; Maria, Aug. 20, 1798.

JOHN A., (perhaps same as the last) m. Elsje Armstrong. Ch. b: Gilliam Armstrong, Dec. 8, 1800; Martinus, Sept. 2, 1803.

FREDERIC, son of Abraham and Sarah Van Petten, m. Annatje, dau. of Johannes Veeder, June 14, 1789; he d. May 7, 1822, a. 55ys. Ch. b: Abraham, Nov. 28, 1789, d. at Chittenango, May 13, 1845, in his 56th yr.; Magdalena, Dec. 21, 1791.

ARENT H., son of Harmanus and Elisabeth Van Dyck, m. Judith Van Ingen, Dec. 23, 1792. Ch. b: Harmanus, Aug. 20, 1793; Margarieta, Sept. 13, 1794; Eva, Dec. 15, 1796; Geertruy Van In-

gen, Jan. 8, 1799; Harmen John, Nov. 23, 1800, d. Mar. 28, 1852.

JAN, of Albany, (?) and Rachel Van Etten. Ch. b: Richard, Aug. 14, 1793; Albert, May 28, 1797; Rebecca, Sept. 2, 1799; John, Ap. 12, 1802.

NICOLAAS, son of Abraham and Sarah Van Petten, m. Margarita, dau. of Cornelis Mebie, Feb. 3, 1793, both of the *Woestine;* he d. July 9, 1850; she d. December 13, 1850, in her 75th year. Ch. b: Abram, Aug. 22, 1793, m. Maria Vedder, May 2, 1818, who d. May 12, 1833; Cornelius, Dec. 18, 1803, d. Nov. 2, 1842.

ARENT, son of Gerrit, m. Geertruy Henry, Sept. 28, 1794. Ch. b: Gerrit, Dec. 20, 1795; Elisabeth, Aug. 6, 1797; John, March 29, 1799; Marytje, June 19, 1801; Elisabeth, August 13, 1803; Henry Harmanus, July 26, 1807; Daniel, June 28, 1809.

JOHN, and Dorothea Ball. Ch: Nancy, b. July 29, 1798.

BREMLEY.

WILLIAM, of Normanskil, and Catarina, dau. of Johannes Kidney, of Albany. Ch. bp: Johannes Kidney, Dec. 28, 1777; Jacobus, Nov. 11, 1779; Geertruy, Oct. 25, 1783; Jannetje, b. Jan. 4, 1786.

BREWER.

GEORGE, and Catharine Larry. Ch: James, b. Sept. 29, 1796.

BREZIE.

PETER, and Rachel Lewis. Ch : Teunis, b. Feb. 28, 1786.

BRITTON.

ABRAM, and Lena Frederic. Ch : Fanny, b. Nov. 15, 1792.

BROAD.

JOHN, b. in New England, m. Debora, dau. of Albert Arentse Vedder, Aug. 27, 1765. Ch: Catarina, bp. Aug. 5, 1768.

BROKAW.

ABRAM, printer (?), and Femmetje Rappleje. Ch : Catharina, b. Oct. 10, 1795.

BRONK.

MATTHIAS, and Annatje Schram. Ch : Jacob, b. June 30, 1792.

ABRAHAM, and Catharina Radley. Ch: Matthew, b. Dec. 10, 1798.

BRONSTELE.

JONATHAN, and Maria Haverly, both of Normanskil, m. Mar. 1, 1791. [*See Albany Families.*]

BROOKS.

PHILIP, and Elisabeth Bay. Ch : Sarah, b. June 22, 1785.

BROUWER,

PHILIP HENDRICKSE, brewer. He was in Beaverwyck as early as 1655, where he owned a house, lot and brewery. He became one of the original proprietors of Schenectady in 1664; the following year he accidentally shot Claas Cornelise Swits there. He died in 1664. His wife's name was Elsje Tjerk. It is not known that he left any children. His village lot, 200 ft. square, on the north corner of Church and State streets, was sold to Cornelis Van Ness, after his death in 1664, by whom it was conveyed to his step-son Johannes Dirkse Van Eps.

WILLEM, (Hendrickse ?), perhaps brother of the last, in 1655 owned property in New Amsterdam ; was in Beverwyck in 1657, and was buried there Aug. 3, 1668, when the following entry was made in the deacon's book : *Tot die begravenisse van* Willem Brouwer 40 *guilders* 15 (*stuivers*). His two sons Hendrick and Willem settled early in Schenectady, and a dau. Maria m. Isaac Truex.

HENDRICK, son of the last, owned a house lot on the east side of Church street, commencing 108 feet north of the church, and extending probably to Front street. He made his will Dec. 12, 1706, proved Feb. 16, 170⅞. He was dead before the 10th of Mar., 1707. His widow Maritie, was an Indian trader in 1724. He m. Maria Pieterse, dau. of Pieter Jacobse Borsboom, and widow of Teunis Carstense, Mar. 26, 1692, in Albany. Benjamin Van Vleck in 1737, was called a son of Maritie Brouwer, probably by a former husband. Ch. of Hendrick Brouwer and Maria Borsboom, bp : Johannes, in Albany, Feb. 12, 1693 ; Elisabeth, Mar. 27, 1695, d. Aug. 1, 1783,

a. 88 ys., 6 m., 15 d.; *Pieter*, Nov. 10, 1697; Jacob, Jan. 9, 1700, an Indian trader, barbarously murdered at the falls, on the Oswego river, in the spring of 1730, by an Onondaga Indian; Eva, Mar. 29, 1702, m. Johannes Dellamont; Willem and *Cornelis*, twins, b. Jan. 23, 1704; *Henrik*, bp. in Albany, Dec. 25, 1706.

WILLEM, son of Willem, of Albany (?), m. Rebecca, dau. of Arent Vedder. Ch. bp: Johannes, June 21, 1712; Sara, Dec. 4, 1715; Arent, Mar. 29, 1718; Catharientje, Sept. 11, 1720, m. Harman Frederickse Visscher; *Harmanus*, Jan. 6, 1723; Wilhelmus, Sept. 26, 1725; Elisabeth, Jan. 3, 1731; Maria, May, 12, 1734, m. Machil Lantman.

CORNELIS, son of Hendrick, *geboren op dese plaats*, and Cornelia, dau. of Johannes Barheit, *geboren in Albanie*, m. June 27, 1730. He had a home lot on East side of Church street, the same as now owned by Henry Rosa. He made his will Aug. 13, 1765, proved Dec. 3, 1767, then spoke of his wife and children, Hendrick and Maritie; he d. Aug 13, 1765. Ch: *Hendrick*, b. Oct. 15, 1731; Catharina, b. Mar. 29, 1734, m. Gerrit Van Antwerpen; Marytje, b. Oct. 9, 1738, m. John Munro.

HENDRICK, son of Hendrick, cordwainer, m. Elisabeth, dau. of Evert Van Eps, June 3, 1732. Ch. bp: Aefje, Apr. 8, 1733, m. Harmanus Bratt; Maria, Feb. 29, 1736, m. Hendrik Brouwer, Jr.; Hendrik, March 13, 1743; Anna, Aug. 10, 1746.

PIETER, son of Hendrik, m. Lena, dau. of Gillis Fonda, March 6, 174½. *Myn vader* [*Pieter B.*] *in den Heer gerust*, June 3, 1758. Ch. b: Maria, April 20, 1743, d. Dec. 29, 1757; Gillis, Oct. 19, 1745; *Gillis*, Aug. 1, 1747

HARMANUS, son of Willem, m. Margariet, dau. of Jan Ekker, or Ekkerson, Feb. 8, 1755. Ch: Johannes, bp. Jan. 1, 1759.

HENDRICK, son of Cornelis, m. Maria, dau. of Hendrick Brouwer, Jan. 4, 1764; he d. Dec. 11, 1801. Ch. b: Cornelis, Sept. 6, 1765; Elisabeth, Dec. 19, 1768, m. Jacob Moon; Hendrick, Oct. 3, 1772.

GILLIS, son of Pieter, m. Maria, dau. of Harmanus Bratt, Dec. 7, 1770. He lived on the east corner of Washington and Front streets, and according to his grave stone, d. Oct. 14, 1800, a. 53ys. 2m. 14d. or according to record in the family Bible, Aug. 14, 1800, a. 53ys., 6m., 14d.; she d. Sept. 22, 1816, a. 67ys., 3m., 4d. Ch. b: Pieter, Sept. 3, 1771, d. Sept. 1, 1772; Elisabeth, May 29, 1773; Elisabeth, Aug. 15, 1775, d. Aug. 22, 1795; Helena, Mar. 27, 1778; *Pieter*, Mar. 3, 1780, d. Oct. 8, 1852; Harmanus, Aug. 15, 1782, d. April 1, 1857; Maria and Eva, bp. Jan. 6, 1785; the former d. aged 17d., the latter d. aged 9ds.; Maria, Sept. 30, 1786.

RICHARD, of Albany (?), and Mary Blann (Blean). Ch. bp: George Washington, Jan. 31, 1779; Petrus, Jan. 16, 1782.

PIETER, of Albany (?), and Catrina Chrisler. Ch: Abraham, bp. June 25, 1783; Johannes, b. March 13. 1787; Christina, b. Oct. 15, 1792 (?), bp. Aug. 31, 1793.

WILLIAM, of Albany, and Mary Marsshalk. Ch: Jeremia William, b. Sept. 11, 1790. [*See Albany Families.*]

MATTHEUS, of Albany, and Sarah West. Ch: Prudence, b. April 21, 1791 (?), bp. Feb. 5, 1792.

CORNELIUS, son of Hendrick, m. Jannetje Demorest, July 18, 1793. Ch. b: Hendrik, August 10, 1795; Fammetje (Febe), Dec. 4, 1798; Margarieta, Aug. 2, 1801.

Rev. THOMAS, the third minister of the church in Schenectady, 1715–1728. He probably ceased from the active duties of his office after 1723; died Jan. 15, 1728. He made his will Nov. 24, 1727, proved Mar. 20, 1728; spoke of neither wife, children or other relatives in this country; gave £25 to the Dutch Church, half of which was to be dispensed for the poor and needy; bequeathed many tokens of friendship, particularly to Gerrit Simonse Veeder's family, and to the Banckers; to his brothers, the Rev. Theodorus Brouwer and Gerardus Brouwer, the former preacher at Dalphin, Province of Overyssell in the Classis of Zwoll; the latter of Zwoll, in the same Province, he left the residue of his estate.

PIETER, son of Gillis, m. Ann Catharine Stevens, Aug. 25, 1808, in Elizabethtown, N. J. He d. Oct. 8, 1852; she was b. Aug. 18, 1790, and is still (1872) living. Ch. b: Maria Elisabeth, Aug. 8, 1809, m. Nathaniel McKenzie; George Washington, Feb. 22, 1811, m. first, Melinda Bettie; Sarah Elisabeth, Feb. 27, 1813, m. John Holliday, May 4, 1842, and d. April 23, 1851; *Giles*, Nov. 5, 1815, m. Ellen (Helen) Vrooman, Nov. 5, 1833, and d. April 23, 1861; Joseph Yates, Dec. 9, 1817, m. Isabella Beard, Feb. 3, 1842; Ann Catharine, May 17, 1820, d. unmarried May 16, 1851; Peter, Aug. 18, 1822, m. Antoinette Powell, Jan. 12, 1848; Sophia Willard, Jan. 18, 1824, m. Eugene Damon, June 17, 1861; Mary H., Dec. 11, 1826, m. Philip Seaver, Dec. 11, 1856; Archibald Craig, Oct. 9, 1828; in Chili, S. A.; Lawrence Stevens, Aug. 20, 1833 (?), d. in Cuba.

GILES, son of Peter, m. Ellen (Helen) Vrooman, Nov. 5, 1833. He d. April 23, 1861. She was b. May 27, 1817, and d. Aug. 15, 1867. Ch. b: *Abram Giles*, May 18, 1840; Maria Matilda, m. John Lodge.

ABRAM GILES, son of Giles, graduated at Union College 1859, studied medicine, and is now a physician in Utica. He m. Jennie Helen, dau. of Nicholas F. Vedder (b. Jan. 10, 1804), and his wife Cornelia Blandina Vedder (b. May 22, 1801, d. Sept. 12, 1867), Oct. 30, 1861. Ch. b: Jennie Cora, June 24, 1863, d. Nov. 11, 1871; Lena Vedder, Mar. 19, 1865 (?), d. Aug. 7, 1872.

BROWN.

JOHN W., of Albany in 1751, m. Margaret, dau. of Caleb Beck (?), May, 1751, and thereafter became a resident of Schenectady. He was a prominent member of the Episcopal Church in this city. Ch. bp: Dorothea, April 28, 1753; Elisabeth, Aug. 17, 1757; Dorothea, Nov. 11, 1762; *Abraham*. John W. Brown was born in 1727, and d. June 30, 1814.

ABRAM, son of John W., m. Jannetje, dau. of Daniel Kittel. Ch: John, bp. Aug. 9, 1783; David, b. Mar. 13, 1796; Myndert; Margaret.

ABRAM, (same as last ?), m. Margaret Van Vorst. Ch: Daniel, b. Nov., 1785.

JCHN, baker, had his shop at 96½ Ferry street; made will June 4, 1811, proved April 27, 1816; spoke of his wife Elisabeth, son Edward, and daughters.

BRUTEN.

BARTHOLOMEUS, and Catrina Poop. Ch. bp: Sarah, December 17, 1778; Johannes, Mar. 18, 1781.

BRYAN.

THOMAS C., and Elisabeth Bonney. Ch: John, b. April —, bp. April 10, 1785.

BUCHANAN (BOHANAN).

ROBERT, m. Margaret Steyber (Steyms, Ties, Meles!), April 12, 1764. Ch. bp: Annatje, Feb. 3, 1765; Maria, May 10, 1767; Margarita, Sept. 11, 1769; Hester, Dec. 22, 1771; Robert, Aug. 16, 1783.

FREDERIC, and Susanna Brouwer. Christoffel, b. Oct. 17, 1792.

THOMAS, m. Nancy, dau. of Major Snell, April 6, 1796. Ch. b: Robert, Mar. 23, 1798; William, June 30, 1805.

BULLOCK.

CHRISTINA, member of the church in 1738.

BULSEN (BULSING, BUNSING).

HENDRICK, and Cathalyna Goewey, both of Albany, had the following Ch. bp. in Albany: *Cornelis*, Mar. 18, 1732; Salomon, Jan. 6, 1734; Salomon, April 13, 1735; Benjamin, March 2, 1740; Alexander, Dec. 5, 1742; Alida, Sept. 8, 1745; Johannes, July 10, 1748; Gerardus, Aug. 30, 1752; Alida, Aug. 1, 1756. [*See Albany Families.*]

CORNELIS, son of Hendrick, m. Annatje (Hannah) Gonzalis (Consaul), Dec. 21, 1761. She d. May 23, 1815. Ch. b. in Albany: Catharine, Dec. 19, 1762, m. Jacob Joh: Vrooman; Sarah, Oct. 6, 1764; Henry, Sept. 20, 1766; *John*, Feb. 1 (28), 1769; Latte (Alida), June 31, 1771; Joseph, b. in Schenectady, Feb. 10, 1774, m. Alida Vedder, and d. Aug. 7, 1843; Francyntje, June 11, 1777.

JOHN, son of Cornelis, m. Angelitje, dau. of Johannes Vrooman, Mar. 31, 1798. Ch. b: Clara, April 28, 1799; Nancy, May 28, 1801; Cornelius, June 24, 1804; Catharine, April 5, 1809; John, April 8, 1812.

HENRY, and Annatie Lewis, both of Rensselaerswyck, m. Mar. 2, 1795.

BURCH.

WILLIAM, m. Marytje, dau. of Jan Christiaanse. Ch. bp: Neeltje, Feb. 14, 1742, m. Corset Vedder; John, Jan. 8, 1744; Sarah, m. Isaac Vedder.

JORIS (George), and Phebe Gordon. Ch: Catrina, bp. Dec. 15, 1780.

BURDETT (BOURDETT).

JOHN, and Antje Mayer. Ch: Margarietje, b. July, 1786.

BURGER.

LAMBERT, and Margarieta Ecker. Ch: Willemptje (Van) Santvoord, b. Jan 22, 1791.

DAVID, and Annatie Appel. Ch: Hendrik, b. Oct. 14, 1793. David Burger, and Elisabeth his wife, joined the church in 1758.

BURKE.

RICHARD, and Folkje Lanein *beide wonende in t' Maquaasland*, m. May 21, 1732. Ch: Elisabeth, bp. Sept. 30, 1733.

(BORKE).

JOHN, and Elisabeth Reimesnyder. Ch: Margarita, b. Nov. 4, 1780; Eldert, b. April 3, 1789. [*See Albany Families.*]

CHARLES, and Hester Bohanan. Ch: Robert, b. Sept. 28, 1790.

BURNET.

PETER, of Remsenbos, and Maria Strail. Ch. b: Gilbert, Sept. 21, 1789; Elisabeth, Mar. 5, 1796.

BURNHAM.

JOSHUA, and Susanna, dau. of William Teller. Ch: Joshua William, bp. July 10, 1797.

WILLIAM, a revolutionary soldier, d. Jan. 19, 1822, a. 62ys.

BURNS.

DAVID, of *de Willegen*, and Catharina, dau. of Jan Baptist Van Vorst. Ch. b: Samuel, Sept. 25, 1785; Jan Baptist, Dec. 15, 1788; Betsey; Lena.

DAVID, of Remsenbos, m. Maria Wiest of Duanesboro, January 26, 1786. Ch. b: Coenraadt, Feb. 20, 1787; Maria, Feb. 16, 1790.

BUTLER.

JOHN, and Catalyntje, dau. of Andries Bratt. Ch: Thomas, bp. Nov. 30, 1755; Andreas, May 13, 1759.

WILLIAM JOHNSON of Niagara, m. Eva, dau. of Christoffel Yates, Dec. 1, 1794. She d. between Nov. 28, 1800, and February 22, 1801. Ch: John, bp. January 1, 1797, Eve Eliza, b. Nov. 28, 1800.

BUYS.

JACOB, and Gouda Schoonhoven. Ch. bp: Willempje, Mar. 7, 1774; Samuel Witbeck, Jan. 11, 1782.

ABRAHAM, *geboren te Viskil*, m. Clara, dau. of Abraham Schermerhorn, Mar. 17, 1786. Ch. b : Hendrikus, Oct. 17, 1786; Abram, Feb. 15, 1788; Anna, Dec. 3, 1789; Jacobus, Dec. 27, 1791; Clara, Nov. 10, 1793; Maria, Nov. 30, 1795; Margareta and Rachel, Oct. 7, 1798; William, Jan. 11, 1800.

JOHN, and Engeltie Rutherford. Ch : Rachel, bp. Jan. 7, 1785.

JOHN, and Ann Rutherford (same as last ?). Ch : Lena Gyseling, b. Sept. 5, 1798.

(BIES).

GEORGE, and Anna Bullock. Ch : Johannes, b. Jan. 20, 1786.

(BORS).

FREDERICK, and Susanna Flagg. Ch : Margarieta, b. Mar. 17, 1793.

CADE (CADY ?).

DAVID, and Anna Schuyler. Ch : Schuyler, b. Sept. 9, 1785.

CAHALL.

JOHN, Revolutionary soldier, d. Mar. 1, 1822, a. 77ys.

CALY.

CHRISTIAAN, and Margarita .... Ch : Johan Jurry, bp. July, 1767.

CAMBEFORT (COMFORT).

GERARDUS, Mar. 8, 1694, contracted to sell to Carel Hansen Toll ten morgen of land, which he bought of the Indians *boven Kaquarrioone* (*now Towereune*) Isaac d' Treux Witness. The west bounds of Cambefort's land were also the west bounds of the township of Schenectady. He was in Schenectady as early as May 6, 1690, as late as 1697, and at Niska-yuna, May 18, 1707 to 1720. His first wife was Antje Raal. Ch : Gerardus, bp. in Albany, May 11, 1690, and probably settled in New York. His second wife was Ariaantje Uldrick, widow of Gerrit Claase Van Vranken, m. October 16, 1692. [*See Albany Families.*]

CAMERDINGER.

GOOTLIEB, and Magdalina Markwarden. Ch : Johannes, bp. Feb. 19, 1758.

CAMP.

JOHN, and Anna, dau. of Jacobus Van Vorst. Ch. bp : Joseph, July 20, 1761; Jacobus, Jan. 9, 1763; Rachel, Aug. 23, 1767.

CAMPBELL.

GEORGE LONDER, and Eleanor Cain. Ch : Gane, bp. Nov. 15, 1762.

KENNET, a Revolutionary soldier, a. 77 in 1820.

ALEXANDER, m. Magdalena, dau. of Johannes Van Seyse, May 23, 1768. Ch. bp : Catrina, July 27, 1769 ; Margarita, Mar. 31, 1771; Margarita, May 27, 1776; Catharine, wife of Alexander Campbell, d. July 12, 1767, a. 33ys.

DANIEL, a native of Ireland, "acquired great wealth at Schenectady as a merchant, a portion of which he left to a nephew, a Doctor Campbell of London, who resided in this country several years." *Documentary History N. Y.* iv., 263. He was in Schenectady as early as 1754, and was judge of the Court of Common Pleas for Albany County in 1771 By his will made July 16, 1801, the bulk of his large estate was left to his wife. He d. Aug. 16, 1802, a. 71ys., 10m., 28d. His wife was Engeltie, dau. of Arent Samuelse Bratt, by whom he had a son David, bp. Nov. 15, 1768. He made his will June 8, and d. June 29, 1801, leaving all his property to his father. Mrs. Campbell made her will May 27, 1811, proved Oct. 7, 1812, by which after leaving a large sum to her various relations, she made her nephew Daniel David Campbell Schermerhorn her residuary legatee. She d. Sept. 28, 1812.

HARMANUS, and Hester, dau of Cornelis Groot. Ch: Margarita, b. April 22, 1781; Joseph, bp. Feb. 13, 1785; Elisabeth, b. Oct. 25, 1789; Cornelius, b. Aug. 13, 1793.

CAIN (CANE).

ROBERT, and Rebecca Alin. Ch: William, bp. April 9, 1767.

CANE.

WILLIAM, perhaps son of the last, m. Peggy Bon (Bond) of Warrensburgh, Feb. 21, 1786. Ch: Jacob, b. July 19, 1787.

(CAIN).

BARNABAS, and Margariet Johnson. Ch. b: Hannah, Nov. 23, 1773; Johan, June 14, 1775.

PIETER WARREN, served in Capt. John Van Petten's company in the Revolutionary war, and was living, in 1832, in Glenville. His wife Engeltie Olin, then a widow, d. Jan. 3, 1843, reputed to be 102ys old. Ch: Pieter, bp. June 14, 1778; Pieter, bp. Nov. 18, 1780; Jannetje, b. Sept. 15, 1782; John, b. Oct. 4, 1788.

(CAIN, KAIN).

ERNEST, (Christiaan) and Catarina Millis (Wills, Mills). Ch: ...... Christina and Elisabeth, bp. Oct. 18, 1780; Catharina, b. Jan. 3, 1786; Lena, b. Nov. 9, 1791.

CANNADA.

JOHN and Mary (Kennedy in 1786), (Magdalena Veeder in 1785 according to the church records). Ch. b: James, Dec. 9, 1783; Hamilton, Mar. 26, 1786; Robert, Oct. 7, 1791; William, Feb. 22, 1796; John Ramsay, Dec. 29, 1800.

CANNET.

WILLIAM and Mary. Ch: Mary, b. May 7, 1763.

CARLEY.

JOSEPH, a soldier of the Revolutionary army, d. April 23, 1842 in his 80th year. He and Engeltie, dau. of Gerardus Quackenbos, both of Kayaderossera, were m. Feb. 1, 1789. Ch. b: Jacobus, Oct. 18, 1789, d. Oct. 13, 1854; Joseph Johnson, Oct. 13, 1791; Gerardus, Aug. 16, 1793; Gerardus Quackenbos, Feb. 5, 1796; Anna, Nov. 27, 1797.

5

CARLO.

STEPHEN *gebortigs' koningh's Brugge,* and Abigail Rider. Ch. bp : Sylvanus, Stephen, Uriel Independence, Lyman, Jane, Jan. 30, 1785; Jacob, Feb. 27, 1785; William Rider, b. Mar. 2, 1787.

CARMAN.

JOHN, and Elisabeth Teller. Ch : Abraham, bp. May 4, 1777; Jacomyntje, bp. Aug. 14, 1784; John Teller, b. Feb. 15, 1787.

CARNES.

WILLIAM, and Susanna Parleman. Ch. b : Jacob, Dec. 3, 1799; Elisabeth, July 29, 1803; Nancy, Dec. 15, 1808.

CAROL (CORL).

HENDRICK, and Maria Olin. Ch. bp : Johannnes, Jan. 12, 1755 ; *Johannes,* April 3, 1757 ; *Willem,* Nov. 16, 1760; *Hendrik,* Aug. 24, 1766 ; Eva, Aug. 20, 1769.

(CORLE).

WILLIAM, son of Hendrick, a private in Capt. John B. Vrooman's company in Col. Abraham Wemple's regiment in the Revolutionary war, died Mar. 19, 1848, a. 84ys. He m. Marytje, dau. of David Springer of Normanskil, July 8, 1787. She d. May 5, 1852, a. 91ys. Ch. b : David Springer, Aug. 9, 1788 ; Maria, May 18, 1790 ; Margarieta, Dec., 1791 ; Hendrik, Aug. 27, 1793 ; Eva, Dec. 20, 1795 ; Henry, Mar. 5, 1798 ; Susanna, Jan. 21, 1800 ; Desia (Desire), Mar. 31, 1803.

JOHN, son of Hendrick, private in Capt. Clute's company in the Revolutionary war, d. April 24, 1842. He m. Susanna, dau. of Jan Baptist Van Vorst. Ch. bp : Hendrick, Sept. 10, 1780; Jan Baptist, Nov. 10, 1782. Ch. b : Marytje, April 17, 1785 ; Willem, Aug. 10, 1786; Catharina, July 13, 1790; John Baptist, Oct. 21, 1792 ; Jellis, Oct. 31, 1794; Maria, Jan. 26, 1799.

(CORL).

HENRY, Jr., son of Hendrick, m. Nancy, dau. of Abraham Groot. He was a merchant in Schenectady as late as 1807. Ch : John ; Maria ; Cornelius.

CARSON (CARSTON, KARSON).

DAVID, and Ann Mackittrich (Catrak). Ch : Ann, bp. April 4, 1781 ; James, bp. July 7, 1783 ; Mary, b. Mar. 18, 1785.

CARSTENSEN.

TEUNIS, and Maritie Pieterse Borsboom. She took out letters of administration on the estate of her deceased husband, Oct. 8, 1691, at which time they had two Ch. living, viz. : Teunis, a. 19ys., and Elisabeth, a. 14ys. She m. Hendrick Willemse Brouwer, Mar. 26, 1692.

CARTER.

ROBERT, and Elisabeth, dau. of Jacobus Cromwell. Ch. bp : Maria ......, 1729 ; Anna, June 3, 1733 ; Elisabeth. Oct. 12, 1735 ; Jacobus, Oct. 9, 1743.

CAS (Cos).

COENRAT, and Gerritje De Vol (Voe). Ch. bp: Heyltje, Sept. 11, 1776; Johannes, March 3, 1780; Frederic, Jan. 16, 1782; Helena, Mar. 21, 1784; David, Feb. 23, 1790.

CASSIDY (CASSADA).

JAMES, m. Margarieta Nixon, April 26, 1760. Ch. bp: John, Oct. 25, 1761; Francis, Oct. 6, 1765.

CASSADA.

JOHN, and Margaret Van Antwerp, July 19, 1838, she deposed that she was married by Dominie Vrooman. At the time this deposition was made, she was 91ys. of age, and living in Naples, Ontario Co., N. Y. Ch : Elisabeth, bp. Aug. 31, 1777; Maria, b. Sept. 6, 1792.

CERSKEDDIN.

THOMAS, and Margaret Patterson. Ch : Catharine, bp. Jan. 9, 1785.

CHARLES.

JAN, and Maria Sebering. Ch. bp : Hendrik, May 30, 1731; Margarietje, May 6, 1733.

CHRISTIAANSE.

CHRISTIAAN. In 1671 he bought a morgen and a half of land at Schenectady of Paulus Janse, as bounded by patent of May 24, 1669. His village lot was on the north side of Union street, adjoining the church lot, and included the Riggs lot (now belonging to the church) and the lot of Mr. Aaron Baringer, and was 100ft. Amst. meas., wide in front. He sold this lot in 1694 to Neeltje Claase, widow of Hendrick Gardenier. His wife was Maritie Ysbrantse Elders. Ch. all bp. in Albany : Neeltje, Nov. 11, 1685 ; Elisabeth, July 11, 1693; Daniel, April 11, 1697; Christiaan; *Johannes; Cornelis.*

JOHANNES, son of Christiaan, of Half Moon, 1720, *geboren tot Schannechtede en wonende tot Conistagioene,* m. Neeltje Cornelise, June 30, 1709, in Albany. Ch. bp. in Albany : Marytje, July 3, 1709, m. William Birch; Elisabeth, Mar. 11, 1716; Sara, Nov. 15, 1718; Christiaan, in Schenectady, Dec. 3, 1720; Johannes, Feb. 26, 1724; *Christiaan,* Jan. 1, 1726; Neeltie, Jan. 5, 1729; Cornelis, Aug. 13, 1732. (Jan Christiaanse was buried Nov. 16, 1746).

CORNELIS, of Niskayuna, son of Christiaan, m. Annatje, dau. of Claas De Graaf. Ch. bp. in Schenectady : *Christiaan,* Feb. 3, 1716; Thomas, Nov. 30, 1717; Isaac, Jan. 31, 1719, d. Feb. 7, 1732; Immetje, Mar. 18, 1721, m. Reyer Vedder; *Thomas,* b. Dec. 1, bp. Feb. 1, 1725; *Jacob,* b. Feb. 12, bp. Mar. 12, 1727; Maria, —, 1729.

THOMAS, son of Cornelis, of Genistagione, m. Anneke, dau. of Ahasuerus Marselis, Sept. 1, 1744. Ch. bp : *Cornelis,* July 28, 1745 ; *Ahasuerus,* Feb. 26, 1749; Annatje, Sept. 8, 1751.

CHRISTIAAN, son of Cornelis, tanner, m. Anna, dau. of Evert Van Eps, Oct. 2, 1748. Ch. bp : Aefje, Nov. 12, 1749,

m. Dirk Bratt; *Cornelis*, May 26, 1760; Evert, Mar. 20, 1762.

CHRISTIAAN, son of Jan, m. Eunice Granger. Ch: Johannes, bp. July 24, 1767.

ABRAHAM, son of Cornelis, m. Marytje, dau. of Jan Dellamont. Ch. bp: Eva, Aug. 30, 1752; Annatje, June 20, 1756; Johannes, Mar. 26, 1758.

ABRAHAM, *geboren op Onestoungjoene*, (probably the same as the last), m. Jacomyntje Morry, *geboren in t' Maquaasland*, April 11, 1761. Ch. bp: John, Jan. 3, 1762; *Isaac*, Dec. 11, 1763; Judy, Jan. 14, 1766, m. Samuel Hagedorn; Annatje, April 3, 1769.

JOHAN JACOB, and Catalyntje Reynhart. Ch: Johannes, bp. Jan. 23, 1757.

JACOBUS, son of Cornelis, and Immetje Krankheit. Ch. bp: Cornelis, Jan. 25, 1761; Johannes, July 25, 1762; Martinus, Mar. 31, 1766.

CORNELIS, son of Thomas, m. Maria, dau. of Takel Marselis. Ch. bp: Thomas, June 13, 1779; Alexander, April 4, 1781; Annatje, Sept. 9, 1783. Ch. b: Johannes, Aug. 25, 1785; Douwe Van Vorst, June 5, 1787; Sara, Nov. 5, 1789; Emmetje, April 20, 1792.

AHASUERUS, son of Thomas, m. Maria Wagenaar, widow of Leendert Kryslaer, Aug. 21, 1785.

ISAAC, son of Abraham, and Maria McClelland Ch: Thomas, bp. June 3,

1781; Elisabeth, Feb. 2, 1783. Ch. b: Cornelis, April 6, 1785; Philippus, July 13, 1787, d. Nov. 3, 1857; Johannes, Mar. 13, 1790; Annatje, July 15, 1792.

ISAAC (probably the same as the last), and Catlyntje Barheit. Ch. b: Ahasuerus, April 20, 1801; Elsje, February 3, 1803; Jannetje, April 8, 1805; Ahasuerus and Cornelia, May 5, 1809.

CORNELIUS, son of Christiaan, and Elisabeth Bratt. Ch: Evert, bp. Aug. 15, 1784; Harmanus, b. March 17, 1786; Eva, Nov. 7, 1788; Andries Bratt, Dec. 2, 1790.

ISAAC, m. Marytje M. Youters, Nov. 11, 1787.

CHRISTOFFELSE.

DAVIDT, was perhaps son of Christoffel Davidtse, born in Bisscohopwyck, England, a. 42ys. in 1658. He owned a lot on the east side of Church street, 100ft. wide, and lying 100ft. south of Union street. He was slain with his wife and four children on Feb. 9, 1690, by the French and Indians when Schenectady was sacked and burnt.

CLARK.

WILLIAM, and Catharine McMasters. Ch. b: Esther, Nov. 25, 1785; Catharine, Feb. 27, 1788.

ROBERT, and Agnes Cophtry. Ch: Mary, b. Aug. 23, 1785.

JAMES, and Isabella McMasters. Ch: Rebecca, b. July 23, 1798.

(CLERK).

NATHAN, m. Sophia, dau. of Harmanus Peters, Oct. 31, 1787. Ch. b: Nathan Williams, July 5, 1788; Harmen, July 5, 1790; Elijah Goodale, May 7, 1792; James, May 4, 1794; Matthew, Feb. 13, 1799; John Dee, August 21, 1801.

CLAU.

GYSBERT, son of Lourens of Albany, of Normanskil, m. Maria, dau. of John C. Barheit, June 29, 1793. Ch. b: Annatie, Mar. 5, 1797; Lena, January 26, 1799; Lourens, June 28, 1800; Neeltje, Dec. 15, 1801; Maria, Nov. 15, 1803; Christina, Oct. 9, 1805; Catharine, April 4, 1808; John, Mar. 4, 1811. [*See Albany Families.*]

CLEMENT.

PIETER and Joseph Clement were stepsons of Benjamin Roberts, and inherited his property at Maalwyck, which they sold to Cornelis Viele and Carel Hanse. Joseph lived in Maquaasland In 1755.

PIETER, of the *Woestyne, jonge man geboren in* N. Utrecht *en wonende tot* Schannechtady, m, Anna Ruyting *geboren en wonende tot* Schannechtady, Nov. 26, 1707, in Albany. Ch. bp: Marytje, Oct. —, 1710, m. Ludovicus Davidts; Jannetie, in New York, Oct. 6, 1712; Alida, Dec. 18, 1714; ...... Pieter Clement *weduwenaar*, and Anna, dau. of Arent Vedder, both of the Woestyne, m. July 28, 1721. Ch. bp: Arent, April 8, 1722; Saartje, July 26, 1724, m. Nicolaas Van Petten; Susanna, b. Sept. 30,

1726, m. Nicolaas Sixberry; *Johannes,* bp. Sept. 24, 1732.

JOSEPH, brother of Pieter, m. Anna, dau. of Jacobus Peek. Ch. bp: Marigien, Dec. 25, 1715; *Jacobus,* Nov. 23, 1718; Elisabet, May 21, 1721; *Johannes,* July 7, 1723; *Ludovicus Cobes,* b. Nov. 30, 1725.

JACOBUS, son of Joseph; in 1755 the second interpreter to the Indians; m. Jannetie Van Woert, in Albany, Feb. 27, 1743. Ch. bp. in Albany: Marie, Feb. 6, 1747; Nicolaas, Oct. 23, 1748; *Nicolaas,* Dec. 2, 1750.

JOHANNES, son of Joseph, m. Rachel Redliff (Radcliffe) of Albany, Dec. 30, 1753. Ch. bp. in Albany: Annatie, Jan. 1, 1755.

JOHANNES, son of Pieter, m. Jannetie Bratt, July 14, 1760. Ch. bp: *Pieter,* Feb 22, 1761; Catalina, Mar. 13, 1763; Annatje, Sept. 8, 1765; *Samuel,* Sept. 13, 1767; Arent, May 15, 1774.

LOWIS COBES, son of Joseph, m. Catlyntje Pootman, June 21, 1748. Ch: Jacobus, bp. Aug. 4, 1764.

NICHOLAS, son of Jacobus, m. Rachel De Garmo of Albany. Ch: Jannetje, bp. July 3, 1774; Sara, b. in Albany, Dec. 12, 1777.

JOHANNES, and Margareta Flansburgh, m. Oct. 25, 1750.

PIETER, son of Johannes, m. Alida, dau. of Gerrit Veeder. Ch. b: Jannetie, July 18, 1785; Gerrit, May 14, 1787; Johannes, April 4, 1789; Annatje, July 10, 1791; Arent, June 21, 1793; Maria. July 6, 1795.

LAMBERT, *van Cagnawago*, m. Maria Vedder *van Rosendale*, Feb. 28, 1787.

SAMUEL, son of Johannes, m. Margareta, dau. of John Fairly. Ch. b : Johannes, June 25, 1793; John Fairly, Mar. 12, 1795.

JOHN, (of Niagara, Canada, 1802), m. Elisabeth Freeligh, Oct. 25, 1792. Ch. b : Margarieta, January 12, 1794 ; John Freeligh, January 17, 1796 ; Henry and James, April 25, 1798.

CLINCH.

ROBERT, kept an inn on the south side of State street, next east of Water street alley. At this house Washington stopped in his tour through the country in 1786. As early as 1774, he is said to have kept "a good house of entertainment." He died about 1786, when his widow, Hannah mortgaged the lot on the south corner of State street and Water street alley.

RALFE, perhaps son of Robert, died at Niagara, U. C., on the 19th Jan., 1828, of a paralytic affection, aged 68 yrs. He was a native of Schenectady, where he lived until the commencement of the Revolution, when he joined the Royal Standard as a cadet in the 42d regiment, and for his conduct in the action which terminated in the capture of Burgoyne, he obtained a commission in the 8th, or King's regiment, and shortly afterwards a lieutenancy in Butler's rangers, in which he served until the reduction of the corps in 1783. He was then appointed a clerk of the peace establishment under the government of Quebec, and after the division of the Province, he was continued in that situation in this district until his death. — *Niagara Herald.*

THOMAS B., was born Aug. 12, 1767 ; in 1813 kept an inn at No. 7 State street ; d. May 22, 1830. He m. Neeltje dau. of Bernard Freerman Schermerhorn, January 18, 1787. She d. May 8, 1849. Ch : Ariaantje, b. Dec. 24, 1787, m. Harmanus Peek, and d. April 18, 1812 ; Hannah Catharine, b. Jan. 28, 1791, m. G. V. S. Bleecker of Albany, and d. July 17, 1861 ; Freerman Schermerhorn, Dec. 29, 1795 ; Robert F. d. Sept. 15, 1805, in his 5th year ; Thomas D. d. Sept. 23, 1805, in his 2d year.

CLUTE.

Of this name there were three individuals who early became residents of Albany or its vicinity — Capt. Johannes, Johannes his nephew, and Frederick. Capt. Johannes Clute came to Beverwyck about 1656 from Neurenbergh, was a trader and considerable land holder, at Loonenburgh, Niskayuna, Albany &c. He was held in esteem by the Indians, from whom he obtained extensive tracts of land. It is not known that he had any family. On his death, his property passed to his nephew Johannes Clute, the *boslooper*.

JOHANNES, *alias de boslooper*, nephew of the last, settled in Niskayuna upon land received from his uncle. In 1707 he conveyed the Great Island in the Mohawk at Niskayuna and other lands to Robert Livingston for £706 to free himself from embarrassments. In 1692 he being a prisoner in Canada, his wife Baata managed his affairs at home. On the 28th of June she cited Sander Glen and Barent Wemp, administrators of Sweer Teunise Van Velsen's estate, before the court at Albany, demanding of them "nine pounds, six shillings and six pence for y⁰ remaining payᵗ of a negro named Jacob sold by old John Cloet to Sweer Teunise, and produces yᵉ book of sᵈ John Cloet Senʳ, kept by her husband, John Cloet Junʳ." The defendants asked time. Johannes Clute m. Baata, dau. of Gerrit Van Slichtenhorst. He was buried in Niskayuna November 26, 1725. All their children were baptised in Albany, except Gerardus and Baata. *Jacob;* Alida, Sept. 14, 1684, m. Pieter Ouderkerk; Elisabeth, Mar. 16, 1687, m. Abraham Ouderkerk; Gerardus, August 4, 1689; Margareta, July 11, 1693, m. Jacobus Bratt; *Gerardus*, in New York, Jan. 1, 1697; *Johannes*, May 12, 1700; Anna ......, m. Johannes Quackenbos; Baata, in Schenectady, May 7, 1704, m. Joachim Van der Heyden.

JACOB, of "Canistagioene," son of Johannes, m. Geertruy Van Vranken, April 12, 1707, in Albany, where the following Ch. were bp.: Gerrit, Jan. 4, 1708; *Gerrit*, July 10, 1709; Elisabeth, Feb.

10, 1712; Ariaantje, May 1, 1715; Baata, Aug. 18, 1717; *Johannes*, Nov. 15, 1719; *Petrus*, Aug. 12, 1722; *Nicolaas*, May 30, 1725.

JOHANNES, son of Johannes, m. Anna ...... Ch. bp. in Albany: *Johannes*, Sept. 15, 1728; Alida, July 2, 1731; Lysbeth, April 15th, 1733; Barber, b. April 27, 1735; Barber, Feb. 15, 1738; Baata, Nov. 18, 1739; Anna, Feb. 14, 1742; Gerrit, Mar. 11, 1744.

GERRIT (Gerardus), son of Johannes, m. Machtelt Heemstraat, May 28, 1725. His will was made May 15, 1746, proved June 1, 1767, in which he spoke of all the following children, except Jacobus and Maritie, also of his land at the *Boght* bought of Daniel Van Olinda. He was buried July 27, 1746. Ch: *Johannes*, b. July 10, bp. in Schenectady July 27, 1726; *Jacob*, bp. in Schenectady June 28, 1729 (?); Catie, bp. in Albany Dec. 31, 1732; Clara, bp. in Schenectady Jan. 14, 1733; *Gerardus*, bp. in Albany Oct. 19, 1735; Jacobus, Jan. 18, 1736, in Albany; Baata, Nov. 5, 1738; Elisabeth, Jan. 21, 1741; Maritie, May 1, 1743; Claartje, May 5, 1745; *Dirk.*

NICOLAAS, son of Jacob and Geertruy, m. Claartje, dau. of Johannes Heemstraat. She d. May 5, 1802, a. 65ys. He d. Nov. 30, 1812 (?). Ch. bp: Geertruy, Feb. 9. 1755; Baata, Aug. 21, 1757; Baata, in Albany Mar. 4, 1761; Catharina, b. Jan. 30, 1763; Jacob, bp. Nov. 10, 1765; *Johannes*, March 20, 1771; Maria, July 5, 1774; *Gerrit.*

JOHANNES, son of Johannes and Anna, m. Sarah, dau. of Abraham Van Arnhem, Sept. 27, 1752. Ch. bp. in Albany: Johannes, Sept. 9, 1753; Alida, in Schenectady, May 9, 1755; Alida, Feb. 6, 1757; Anna, April 1, 1759; Elisabeth, Jan. 24, 1762; Abraham, b. Jan. 11, 1764; Gerrit, b. Feb. 20, 1765; Abraham, b. May 16, 1767; Sara, bp. May 25, 1769; Abraham, April 16, 1773; Wouter, b. April 11, 1775.

JOHANNES, son of Jacob and Geertruy, m. Jannetie Ouderkerk, Oct. 6, 1753, in Albany. Ch. bp; Jacob in Albany, April 7, 1754; Wyntie, in Albany, Aug. 31, 1755; Geertruy. May 1, 1757; Johannes, in Albany, May 6, 1759; Baata, in Schenectady, Mar. 22, 1761; Frederick, July 10, 1763; Elisabeth, in Albany, Sept. 23, 1765; Nicolaas, in Schenectady, Nov. 29, 1767, d. June 8, 1827, in his 60th year.; Petrus, in Schenectady, Dec. 24, 1769; Abraham, in Albany, Nov. 12, 1771.

JOHANNES, son of Gerardus and Machtelt, m Catarina, dau. of Abraham Lansing of Albany, Jan. 17, 1754, in Schenectady. Ch: Gerardus, bp. in Albany, Sept. 21, 1755; Abraham, bp. in Albany, January 22, 1758; Dirk, bp. in Albany, April 19, 1760; Catarina, bp. in Schenectady, Mar. 21, 1762, m. Robert Sluyter.

JACOB, son of Gerardus and Machtelt, m. Maayke Lansing of Albany, June 12, 1761. Ch. bp. in Albany; Gerardus, b. Jan. 23, 1763; Hendrick, b. Oct. 27, 1765; Dirk, b. July 15, 1768.

DIRK, son of Gerardus and Machtelt, of Onestoungjoone, m. Annatie, dau. of Johannes Heemstraat of Albany, April 6, 1760. Ch. bp. in Schenectady: *Gerrit,* Mar. 18, 1761; Johannes, Jan. 8, 1764; Marritie, July 27, 1766; Dirk, Jan. 19, 1777.

GERARDUS, son of Gerardus and Machtelt, m. Alida, dau. of Nicolaas Visscher of Albany, and secondly, Sarah Abel, about 1775. Ch. bp. in Schenectady: Machtelt, Oct. 12, 1760; Annatje, June 19, 1762, m. Nicolaas Vandenbergh; Gerardus, May 27, 1765; Machtelt, Oct. 8, 1769; Maria, Feb. 16, 1772; Jacobus, b. Aug. 9, and bp. in Albany Sept. 22, 1776; Adam, Sept. 16, 1781.

GERRIT, son of Jacob and Geertruy, m. Maritie Heemstraat, Sept. 22, 1732. Ch. bp. in Albany: Dirk, Feb. 5, 1738; Geertruy, June 22, 1740; Gerrit, Nov. 7, 1742; *Gerardus,* June 17, 1750.

GERRIT, son of Dirk and Annatie, m. Bata Bovie. Ch. bp: Maria, bp. in Schenectady Jan. 25, 1783; Annatie, b. Jan. 15, 1788; Charles, b. Oct. 21, 1804.

GERRIT (Gerardus), son of Gerrit and Maritie, and Geertruy Clute, both of Nistoungjoone, m. June 17, 1775. Ch. bp, in Schenectady: Marritie, May 26, 1776; Gerrit, Dec. 11, 1780.

PETRUS, son of Jacob and Geertruy, of Onestoughjoone, m. Lea Hagedorn, May 7, 1761. Ch. bp. in Schenectady: *Jacob,* Dec. 12, 1761; Geertruy, Sept. 25, 1763.

JACOB, son of Petrus and Lea, of Normanskil, and Maria Ouderkerk. Ch. bp. in Schenectady: Johannes, Feb. 7, 1780; Peter, Nov. 30, 1783; Lea, July 23, 1784; Frederic, b. April 23, 1785; Isaac, b. Jan. 25, 1789; Harmanus Peek, b. Oct. 29, 1791; Magdalena, Jan. 23, 1803.

JACOB, son of Gerrit and Maritie (?), and Cornelia (Van) Valkenburgh. Ch. bp. in Schenectady: Gerrit, June 9, 1765; Maria, June 12, 1768.

GERRIT, of "Nestigaune," son of Nicolaas and Claartje, m. Ariaantje Clute of Rensselaerswyk, May 14, 1787. Ch: Nicholas, b. Dec. 13, 1787; Clara, bp. April 28, 1793; Catharina, b. Oct. 1, 1800.

JOHANNES, son of Nicolaas and Claartje of Normanskil, m. Catharine Teller, Aug. 9, 1789. She d. Oct. 11, 1815, a. 44ys., 10m., 15d. Ch: Nicolaas, b. Oct. 2, 1790.

GERARDUS (Gerrit) and Elisabeth, dau. of Simon Groot, both of "Canastagajoone," m. June 9, 1771. Ch. bp. in Schenectady: Bata, July 14, 1771; Bata, Nov. 4. 1773; Simon, July 19, 1778.

GERARDUS (Gerrit) and Elisabeth Bever. Ch: Elisabeth, b. Feb. 9, 1790.

JOHANNES, and Maria Hugery (Hugenen, Hugenot). Ch. bp: Pieter, May 28, 1778; Margarita, Mar. 14, 1780; Hendrick, May 15, 1782.

FREDERIC, from Montgomery, and Mercy Barnum Hinmain, from the Hellenbergh, m. Jan. 3, 1787.

JOHANNES J. Jr., and Lena Clute. Ch: Jannetje, bp. May 29, 1785.

FREDERIC, came from Kingston about 1703 and bought land of Johannes Clute in Niskayuna. What relationship, if any, existed between them is not known. He m. Francyntje Du Monds. Ch: Margarietje, who m. Andries De Graaf; *Johannes;* Anna Barber, who m. Abraham Fort; *Jacob;* Helena, who m. Johannes Quackenbos, Jr.; *Frederic; Walraven,* or Waldren; (perhaps these ch. were born before his removal to Niskayuna); Sarah, bp. in Albany Feb. 19, 1707; Magdalena, in Albany June 26, 1709; *Pieter,* in Albany April 20, 1712; Anna Catrina, in Schenectady, Dec. 8, 1716, m. Martin Van Olinda.

JOHANNES, son of Frederic, m. Tanneke, dau. of Gillis Fonda of Schenectay, Dec. 11, 1726. Ch. bp. in Schenectady: *Fredericus,* b. July 31, bp. Aug. 6, 1727; *Jacob,* April 25, 1731; Rachel, Jan. 18, 1733, m. Abraham De Graaf; Francyna, Feb. 16, 1735; Douwe, Feb. 27, 1737; Francyntje, June 27, 1742; *Gillis; Johannes.*

JACOB, son of Frederic, m. Maria Brouwer, Nov. 16, 1727, in Albany. Ch. bp. in Albany: Nelletie, Oct. 13, 1728; *Fredericus,* Feb. 22, 1730; *Pieter,* Oct. 31, 1731; Francyntie, Oct. 2, 1733; Johannes, June 14, 1735.

PIETER, son of Frederic, m. Ariaantje, dau. of Nicolaas Van Vranken. Ch. bp. in Albany: Geertruy, June 1, 1740; Francyntje, Feb. 20, 1743, in Schenec-

6

tady; Nicolaas, May 13, 1744, in Albany; Elisabeth, July 26, 1747; Pieter, Nov. 4, 1750; Rachel, April 12, 1752.

FREDERIC, son of Frederic, and Machtelt, dau. of Johannes Pieterse Quackenbos, both of "Genistagioene," m. May 22, 1742. Ch. bp. in Schenectady: Margareta, April 3, 1743; Annatje, Jan. 13, 1745; *Fredericus,* Nov. 10, 1751; Abraham, bp. in Albany Sept. 22, 1754; Willem, in Albany May 14, 1758.

WALDRON (Walraven) and Anna...... Ch. bp. in Albany: Antje, Oct. 21, 1722; Frederic, Mar. 8, 1724; Evert and Francyntje, Feb. 27, 1726; *Nicolaas,* July 7, 1728; Maria, Mar. 28, 1730; Willem, Oct. 10, 1731.

FREDERICUS, son of Johannes and Tanneke, made his will Aug. 16, 1803, proved Jan. 29, 1817, spoke of wife Elisabeth, sons Isaac, Johannes, Nicolaas and dau. Tanneke, and Frederic the eldest son of each of his 4 ch. He is said to have d. in 1808. He m. Elisabeth (Eva in the *trouw-boek*), dau. of Isaac De Graaf, April 4, 1752. Ch. bp. in Schenectady: *Johannes,* Mar. 5, 1754; *Isaac,* Mar. 15, 1756; Tanneke, Jan. 21, 1759; Tanneke, Jan. 18, 1761, m. Cornelius Williams; Rachel, July 5, 1766; *Nicolaas,* Aug. 21, 1768.

JACOB, son of Johannes and Tanneke, made his will August 17, 1797, proved May 17, 1821, spoke of wife Rachel, and daughters Eve and Tanneke; m. Rachel Swart, April 29, 1757. Ch. bp: Johannes, Aug. 20, 1758; Eva, Nov. 16, 1760;

m. Johannes Vedder; Tanneke, June 12, 1763, m. David Consaulus.

GILLIS, son of Johannes and Tanneke, made his will May 4, 1809, proved July 10, 1809, Joseph Mynderse executor: spoke of wife Maritie, "my eldest son Daniel, dau. Geertruy to have," "my house and lot bounded west by John Steers and north by Green street," Douwe and John to have "my house and lot lying east of my house and lot, and west of house and lot sold by me to Douwe." Elisabeth, wife of John Ouderkirk, to have land west of "Simon's kil," and land to child of deceased son Peter. He m. first, Geertruy, dau. of Capt. Daniel Toll, who d. Aug. 12, 1759, and secondly, Maria, dau. of Pieter Cornu, Feb. 11, 1758. Ch. bp: *Daniel Toll,* b. Nov. 29, and bp. Dec. 1, 1754; Tanneke, Feb. 15, 1756; Johannes, June 29, 1760; Geertruy Jan. 2, 1763; Pieter, April 14, 1765; Pieter, Aug. 30, 1767; Douwe, Mar. 10, 1771; *Douwe,* Feb. 28, 1773; Elisabeth, April 9, 1775, m. Benjamin Van Loon, and d. Dec. 10, 1851.

JOHANNES, son of Johannes and Tanneke, b. June 12, 1739, d. April 20, 1817 and Geesie, dau. of Bartholomew Vrooman, were licensed to m. April 20, 1762. She was b. January 23, 1740, d. April 12, 1812. Ch. bp: Johannes, Oct. 3, 1762, was licensed as a minister in the Reformed Dutch Church, but was drowned before entering on his work; *Bartholomew,* Jan. 6, 1765, is said to have been a Capt. of a company in the war of 1812; *Douwe,* Mar. 1, 1767;

Catarina, Aug. 27, 1769; *Cornelis*, Feb. 16, 1772; Jacob, Dec. 3, 1775; *Jacob*, b. Nov. 20, bp. Dec. 1, 1776, d. Dec. 25, 1852; Teunis, Oct. 27, 1782, d. April 8, 1855; his w. Nancy Crawford, d. Sept. 28, 1854, in her 66th year.—both buried in the *Woestyne.*

JACOB, son of Jacob and Maria Brouwer, both of Rensselaerswyck, m. July 4, 1765. Ch: Marytje, b. January 23, 1768.

PIETER, son of Jacob and Maria Brouwer, m. Catharina, dau. of Dirk Marselis. Ch. bp: Maria, April 13, 1755; Maria, Oct. 31, 1756; Dirk, Nov. 20, 1757; *Jacob*, Mar. 4, 1759; Maria, Oct. 4, 1760; *Jan Baptist*, May 24, 1762; Pieter, Jan. 15, 1764; *Pieter*, b. April 28, bp. April 28, 1765; Elisabeth, Nov. 22, 1767, m. Matthew McKinney; Dirk, Sept. 17, 1769; *Dirk*, b. Dec. 2, bp. Dec. 2, 1770, d. Sept. 2, 1849; Frederic, b. Aug. 1, bp. Aug. 2, 1772; *Frederick*, Dec. 25, 1773, d. Feb. 9, 1841; *Nicolaas*, Dec. 24, 1775; Sara, Nov. 2, 1777, m. Nicolaas Marselis; *Hendrick*, April 14, 1780. [This is the largest family recorded in the *Doop-boek.*]

FREDERICK, son of Jacob and Maria Brouwer, of Saratoga, m. Maria (De) Ridder, Nov. 2, 1754. Ch. bp. in Albany: Maria, Dec. 28, 1755; Maria, Jan. 28, 1759; Gerrit, Mar. 8, 1761; Annatie, Nov. 10, 1765; Annatie, Oct. 21, 1770.

FREDERIC son of Frederic and Machtelt. Ch: Machtelt, bp. Nov. 7, 1784.

DANIEL TOLL, son of Gillis, m. Annatie, dau. of Thomas Brouwer Bancker, June 25, 1775. He d. July 25, 1815; she d. April 28, 1807, in her 51st year. Ch: Annatje, bp. Dec. 29, 1776; Jillis, bp. Dec. 25, 1778; Jillis, bp. May 21, 1780; Geertruy, bp. Feb. 1783; Susanna, b. August 29, 1785; Thomas, b. July 26, 1788; Willem Bancker, b. Sept. 26, 1791; Tanneke, b. Mar. 26, 1794; Neeltje, b. Feb. 5, 1800.

DOUWE, son of Gillis, m. Maria, dau. of Richard Schermerhorn. Ch. b: John Mar. 10, 1798; Rykard Schermerhorn, Mar. 13, 1800; Jacob, Sept. 13, 1802; Annatje Schermerhorn, Mar. 29, 1805; Richard Schermerhorn, June 28, 1807; Anna Maria, Aug. 8, 1809; Ryer Schermerhorn, Aug. 16, 1812. [Douwe J. Clute d. Dec. 25, 1852, a. 76ys. (?).]

JOHANNES, son of Frederic and Elisabeth, m. Annatje, dau. of Wessel Wessels. Ch: Elisabeth, bp. Dec. 14, 1777; Wessel, bp. Aug. 6, 1780; Frederick, bp. Feb. 20, 1783; Wessel, b. May 14, 1785; Isaac, b. Feb. 26, 1788; Luykas, b. Dec. 20, 1790.

ISAAC, son of Frederic and Elisabeth, m. Lena, dau. of Cornelis Barheyt. Ch. bp: Elisabeth, Nov. 7, 1784; Rachel, Aug. 21, 1786. His widow Helen was living in 1838 in Syracuse.

NICOLAAS, son of Frederic and Elisabeth, m. Susanna dau. of Abraham Swits. Ch. b: Frederic, Mar. 12, 1797; Margarieta, Dec. 16, 1798, d. Feb. 4, 1810.

JACOB, son of Pieter and Catharina, served in the Revolutionary war under Capt. Nicolaas Veeder, and under Capt. Jacob Vrooman, d. Jan. 16, 1848. He m. Maria Huyk. Ch. b: Lenah, May 11, 1787; Catharina, March 13, 1789; Peter, Mar. 20, 1791; Elisabeth, May 26, 1793; Andrew; Henry; Sara, who m. ...... Marcelis.

JAN BAPTIST, son of Pieter, kept an inn in 1813, on east side of Washington street, a few doors south of Front street; made his will April 27, 1814, proved June 13, 1814, in which he spoke of his second wife Elisabeth, and of all the following children: One of his Ch., Catlina, if not more, was dau. of his second wife. His first wife was Catlyntje, dau. of Jillis Van Vorst; his second, Elisabeth Skiff, who d. Sept. 14, 1837, a. 73ys., 2m., 26d. Ch. b: Pieter, bp. Nov. 28, 1784, d. Feb. 8, 1870; Annatie, b. August 11, 1786; Wyntie, Aug. 5, 1788; Maria, Feb. 28, 1790; Jellis, Dec. 4, 1791; Abraham Oothout, May 14, 1801; John; Catharine; Sarah; Elisabeth; Catlina, Mar. 14, 1805.

PETRUS, son of Pieter and Catharina, m. Engelina, dau. of Cornelis Van Slyck, March 5, 1786. He d. July 7, 1835; she d. May 24, 1848, a. 84ys. Ch. b: Catharina, June 9, 1786; Cornelius, Nov. 14, 1788, d. August 30, 1870; Petrus, Nov. 17, 1790; John, Jan. 13, 1793; Jacob, Sept. 8, 1795; Maria, Jan. 31, 1798; Dirk, March 5, 1800; Adriaan Van Slyck, January 24, 1802; Nicholas, Aug. 7, 1804.

DIRK (Richard), son of Pieter and Catharina, m. Mary McMichael in Albany. He d. Sept. 2, 1849; she was b. Feb. 21, 1777, and d. Feb. 26, 1862.

FREDERIC, son of Pieter and Catharina, m. Elisabeth, dau. of Walter Swits, Dec. 12, 1795. He was b. Dec. 12, 1773, and d. Feb 9, 1841; she was b. Nov. 23, 1778, and d. Oct. 23, 1840. Ch. b: Petrus, Nov. 3, 1796, d. Sept. 9, 1834; Walter, Jan. 20, 1799, d. Aug. 17, 1847; Catharine, April 30, 1801; Sarah, May 2, 1804.

NICOLAAS, son of Pieter and Catharina, m. Lena, dau. of Richard Schermerhorn, Sept. 11, 1799. He d. Aug. 17, 1832; she d. Aug. 15, 1832, a. 50ys., 9m., 24d. Ch. b: Peter, June 1, 1800, d. Mar. 4, 1855; Rykard Schermerhorn, Aug. 30, 1802; Annatje, Jan. 26, 1805; Jacob, June 17, 1807; Hubartus Van Vechten, Oct. 2, 1809; John, Aug. 31, 1811; Ann Maria, May 18, 1813; Frederic, Oct. 22, 1815.

HENDRICK, son of Pieter, and Catharine, m. Margaret ...... He d. Mar. 2, 1855, a. 74ys., 9m., 27d.; she d. July 18, 1839, a. 58ys., 7m., 23d.

BARTHOLOMEUS, son of Johannes and Geesie, m. Margrietje, dau. of Hendrick Peek, Dec. —, 1787. Ch. b: Johannes, May 5, 1788; Elisabeth, Nov. 22, 1790; Hendrik, Sept. 28, 1793; Catharina, Dec. 27, 1794; Hendrick, Jan. 11, 1798, d. April 22, 1836; Cornelius, Feb. 16, 1801; James, Dec. 20, 1803; Margaret, Jan. 10, 1807; Margaret, Jan. 23, 1811.

DOUWE, son of Johannes and Geesie, m. first, Elisabeth Van Huysen, July 2, 1791; she d. Nov. 16, 1806, a. 35ys., 24d.; and secondly, Ann Shuter, who was b. Nov. 20, 1767, and d. July 6, 1835. He d. Dec. 2, 1827, a. 60ys., 9m., 26d. Ch. b: Catharina, Jan. 17, 1792, d. Sept. 14, 1793; John, Dec. 28, 1793; Harmanus, April 23, 1796, d. Aug. 13, 1815; David Campbell, April 7, 1798, d. Mar. 12, 1816; Jacob, May 19, 1800, removed to New York; Alexander Van Huysen, May 14, 1802; Catharine, Mar. 27, 1804; Elisabeth, Oct. 14, 1806.

CORNELIUS, son of Johannes and Geesie, m. Engeltie, dau. of Simon Groot, Sept. 2, 1792. He d. in Fredonia, April 11, 1855, a. 83ys.; she d. Oct. 27, 1830, a. 57ys. Ch. b: Gezina, Dec. 28, 1792; Annatie, May 7, 1798; Catharina, Dec. 7, 1801; Elisabeth, April 27, 1805.

JACOB, son of Johannes and Geesie, m. Elisabeth Marselis, who was b. Nov. 27, 1785, and d. Nov. 16, 1865. After the death of her first husband, on Dec. 25, 1852, she m. Roswell Perry. Ch. b: John, b. Mar. 19, 1807, editor living at Factoryville, S. I.; Catharina Gezina, b. Feb. 5, 1809, m. A. D. Clement, M.D., of New York, and d. Feb. 24, 1866; Nicholas Marselis, b. Dec. 17, 1814, d. in infancy; Helen Maria, b. Dec. 17, 1811, m. first, Rev. John Gile of Setauket, L. I., and secondly, Mr. David Lyon of Schenectady; Nicolas Marselis, b. Feb. 2, 1819, minister of Pres. church at Olean, N. Y.; Teunis; Frederic, m. Catharine McFarlane.

JACOB, b. at "Nestigune," dwelling at Normanskil, m. Sara Platto, dwelling at Normanskil, April 7, 1786.

JOHANNES J., m. Eva, dau. of Johannes Teller. She d. April 29, 1853, a. 80ys. Ch. b: Elisabeth, Oct. 17, 1797; Jannetje, Aug. 15, 1799; John, Nov. 1, 1801.

FREDERIC, of Saratoga, son of Walraven, m. Ariaantje (De) Ridder, Nov. 2, 1754. Ch. bp. in Albany: Evert, Aug. 31, 1755; Gerrit, Nov. 6, 1757; Annatie, June 19, 1760.

DIRK, and Rachel Lansing. Ch. bp. in Albany: Jacob, b. Oct. 13, 1785; Abraham, b. Oct. 31, 1787; Gerrit, b. Oct. 18, 1789.

GERRIT, m. Elisabeth Kane in Albany, Nov. 20, 1791. Ch. bp. in Albany; John, b. Aug. 28, 1792; Johanna, b. Jan. 1, 1794; William, b. Nov. 1, 1795; Ann, b. Mar. 3, 1798; Rebecca, b. April 5, 1800; Pieter Kane, b. June 3, 1806; Cornelia Ann, b. Mar. 19, 1810; [Elisabeth, widow of Gerrit Clute, d. Sept. 20, 1850, in her 85th year.]

COBES.

LODOVICUS, was b. in Herentals, in Brabant. He was Court Messenger in Beverwyck, as early as 1566; Notary Public and Secretary of Albany, 1668; Secretary of Schenectady in 1677. With Johannes Klein, his son-in-law, he purchased and settled upon the fourth flat, on the north side of the Mohawk above Schenectady. He also had a house lot in the village, on the north corner of Union and Church streets. After his death, his widow, Alida Pieterse, m. Dirk Ofmulder and resided upon her farm on the fourth flat until 1698, when she leased it to her son-in-law, Tomas Smit "of New England," during his life time, saving that at her death, her granddaughter, Clara Klein was to have two morgens of said land according to the will of her grandfather, Lodovicus Cobes. He had two children, Maria, who m. first, Gerrit Janse, and secondly, Thomas Smit, and a dau. who m. Johannes Klein. *'T Boekje van Lodovicus Cobes*, being the Register of his acts as Notary, Secretary and Schout of the village of Schenectady probably, was among the papers of the Dutch church as late as 1788.

COCHRANE.

GERRIT, and Hester Hemtom. Ch: Maria, bp. Mar. 24, 1784.

COCHRAN.

ANDREW, and Jemima Wilson. Ch: Andrew, b. Nov. 26, 1787.

COEN.

JACOB, and Maria Morey. Ch: Maria, bp. Feb. 16, 1784. He served 7ys. in the Revolutionary war.

COEYMAN.

JOHAN MELCHIOR, and Anna Maria Rees. Ch: Johannes, bp. Mar. 22, 1768.

COHOUN.

JOHN, and Rosanna Bagnall, m. Dec. 12, 1773.

COLBERSON.

WILLIAM and Sarah ...... Ch: William, bp. Oct. 16, 1764; Mary, b. —, 1766, bp. July 4, 1767; Margariet, bp. October 23, 1768; James, bp. Sept. 30, 1770; Henry Witfield, bp. Mar. 9, 1777.

COLE.

ABRAHAM, m. Engeltie, dau. of Jan Baptist Van Eps, Nov. 23, 1794. Ch. b: Alexander, Mar. 27, 1797; Jannetje, July 6, 1801; Jacob, Mar. 20, 1804.

(COOL).

JACOB, and Lena Bensen. Ch: Catharina, b. April 11, 1798.

COLLIER (CAILLER, COLJER).

JOHANNES, m. Machtelt Quackenbos, Dec. 31, 1727.

.... and Maria Palmontier. Ch: Neeltje, bp. Mar. 18, 1783.

(COLJER).

JOHANNES, and Susanna Mebie. Ch: Alida, b. Oct. 17, 1793.

COLLINS.

EDWARD, inn keeper, 1762, house on north corner of State and Jay streets.

COLSON (COLESON).

PETER, m. Elisabeth, dau. of Nicolaas Lighthall. Ch. b: Nancy, March 11, 1797; Peter, Oct. 17, 1798; Nicholas Lighthall, Dec. 6, 1800.

COMAN.

JOHN, m. Eva, dau. of Johannes Barheyt. Ch: Johannes, bp. Sept. 23, 1770.

COMBES (COMES).

PAUL, and Elsje Bed (Bett). Ch. bp: Sarah, Nov. 5, 1749; *John*, Sept. 8, 1751.

JOHN, son of Paul, m. Annatje, dau. of Henricus Veeder. Ch. bp: Elsje, Aug. 23, 1778; Elsje, Feb. 17, 1780; Hendricus, Jan. 14, 1782. Ch. b: Elsje, Feb. 22, 1785; Judith, Aug. 2, 1790; Maria, Mar. 25, 1792.

COMSTOCK.

WILLIAM, of Saratoga, m. Elisabeth Vining of Schenectady, Mar. 25, 1790.

CONDE (CONDESCHE).

ADAM, was high constable of Albany 1724, removed to Schenectady, and m. Catharine, dau. of Jesse De Graaf, Nov. 30, 1736. He was killed in the *Boeckendal* massacre in 1748. Ch. bp: Johannes, May 14, 1738; Susanna (?) July —, 1739; Alida, April 13, 1740; *Jesse*, March 13, 1743; Eva, July 21, 1745; *Adam*, Sept. 25, 1748, d. in Glenville, Sept. 22, 1824.

JESSE, son of Adam, settled in Charlton, m. Parthenia, dau. of Jonathan Ogden, July 8, 1762. Ch. bp: Alida, Jan. 16, 1763, m. James Boyd; Jonathan, Aug. 26, 1764; Jonathan, Dec. 14, 1766, d. in Charlton, Mar. 3, 1843; Adam, Feb. 12, 1769; *Albert*, June 9, 1771; Johannes, Oct. 17, 1773; Willmot, Feb. 11, 1776; Jesse, August 23, 1778; Susanna, August 16, 1780; De Graaf June 8, 1783; Isaac, August 21, 1785; Jesse, Sept. 4, 1791.

ADAM, son of Adam, m. Catelyntje, dau. of Pieter Truax, July (Jan. ?) 1, 1770. In 1770 he lived on the west corner of Church and Front streets; served in the Revolutionary war, under Captains Johannes Mynderse and Fonda; d. Sept. 22, 1824. His widow d. April 15, 1843, a. 92ys., 1m., 17d. Ch. bp: Johannes, Nov. 25, 1770; *Pieter*, July 25, 1773; Catharina, Oct. 3, 1775, m. Charles Taylor; Jacoba, Dec. 14, 1777; Eva, Mar. 26, 1780, m. Simon J. Van Petten; *Cornelius Santvoord*, Sept. 29, 1782. Ch. b: Jacobatje, Dec. 25, 1785; Alida, Nov. 8, 1788; Annatje, Feb. 28, 1791.

PETER, son of Adam, m. Clara, dau. of Philip Van Petten, Dec. 24, 1796. He d. in Charlton, May 17, 1843; she d. May 8, 1815, a. 45ys., 9m., 23d. Ch. b: Catlyntje, Feb. 10, 1797; Elisabeth, Feb. 11, 1799; Adam, April 30, 1801; Philip Van Petten, Sept. 8, 1803, d. Sept. 19, 1821; Alida, April 30, 1806; Sarah Ann, Sept. 8, 1808; Debora, Feb. 7, 1811.

CORNELIUS S., son of Adam, m. Sarah Truax, dau. of Abraham, July 13, 1805· He resided in Glenville, was for many years Justice of Sessions; d. May 13, 1869. Ch. b: John T., Jan. 17, 1807, resides in Milton; Adam C., March 7, 1809, d. April 30, 1871, in West Troy; Abram T., Dec. 20, 1810, resides in Glenville; Peter C., Dec. 2, 1812, of Schenectady; Cornelius B., Dec. 27, 1814, of Batavia, Ill.; Isaac H., Nov. 17, 1816, of Severns, Kas.; Simon V. P., Nov. 17,

1818, of Monroe, Wis., d. Dec. 30, 1863;
Platt S., August 20, 1820, of Ballston;
Andrew S., Aug. 19, 1822, d. July 5,
1837, in Glenville; Joseph S., July 31,
1824, d. at Burnt Hills. March 9, 1860;
George M., Nov. 6, 1826, of San Francisco; Benjamin L., Nov. 7, 1828, of
Schenectady; Alonzo B., Nov. 6, 1832,
of Trumansburgh. [This is the only instance which has come within the com-
piler's notice of a mother rearing 13 sons
to maturity. He is informed that she
also raised three other ch. whom she took
out of charity.]

ALBERT, son of Jesse, m. Esther, dau.
of Daniel Toll.   Ch. b : Parthenia, Aug.
5, 1798; Susan, April 8, 1803; Jesse,
Mar. 8, 1805; Daniel Toll, Feb. 2, 1807;
Henry Swits, May 30, 1809; Catharine,
Feb. 14, 1813.

CONNELL.

JOHN, and Lucretia Rught (Root ?).
Ch: Aaron, b. July, 1775.

CONNER.

OWEN, and Maria ...... Ch : Hester,
bp. Nov. 18, 1722.

GERRIT, m. Elisabeth, dau. of Ahasuerus Marselis.   Ch. b : Ariaantje, May
24, 1790; Gysbert, Sept. 3, 1791; Edward, Oct. 4, 1793; Nicholaas, Dec. 14,
1795; Gerrit, Nov. 24, 1797; Esther,
Jan. 17, 1800; John, June 20, 1802.

LANCASTER, m. Ariaantje, dau. of
Gerrit Van Antwerpen, Sept. 28, 1759.
Ch. bp : Lancaster, July 6, 1760; Maria,
Aug. 22, 1761; Annatje, Nov. 20, 1763;

Gerrit, July 5, 1766; Maria, Jan. 22,
1769; Ariaantje, July 19, 1772.

FRANS, and Marytje Kedney. Ch.
bp : Anna, Sept. 28, 1760; Franciscus,
Dec. 18, 1768.

CONNOLY.

JACOB, and Geertruy Minklaer.   Ch :
James, b. March 21, 1797.

CONSAUL (CONSAULUS, GONZALUS, ETC.).

EMANUEL CONSAUL was in Schenectady as early as 1684.   In 1767, two
families by this name lived neighbors, not
far from the intersection of the *Lisha's*
kil and the north manor line, probably on
what is now called the "Consaul road."

(CONSAULUS).

JOHANNES, of "Nistigioene," m. Machtelt, dau. of Johannes Hemstraat, in Albany, April 20, 1765.   Ch. bp. in Schenectady : *Johannes*, Nov. 5, 1767 ; Emmanuel, May 4, 1783; Machtelt, b. July
31, 1785; Annatje, b. Aug. 29, 1787.   Ch.
bp. in Albany : Sara, Nov. 3, 1765, m.
Hendrick J. Vrooman; Bastiaan, b. Nov.
16, 1769; Francyntje, b. Feb. 2, 1772,
m. William Lewis; Engeltie, b. Jan. 16,
1774; Bata, b. Jan. 31, 1776; Mattheus,
b. June 16, 1780.

PETER, and Sarah Van Vliet.   Ch.
bp. in Schenectady : Sarah, May 19,
1771 ; *Johannes*, Aug. 2, 1773 ; Teunis
and Emmanuel, May 14, 1775; Francina,
July 20, 1777 ; Neeltje, Jan. 3, 1779;
Catarina, Oct. 8, 1780; Pieter, Dec. 23,
1781; Catrina, Nov. 16, 1783.   Ch. b :

Annatje, Sept. 5, 1785; Elsje, June 11, 1787; Joseph, Jan. 8, 1789; Jenneke, April 13, 1791; Jacob, Mar. 1, 1793.

JOSEPH, of Rensselaerwyck, m. Hester, dau. of Nicolaas Groot, Nov. 28, 1773.

DAVID, m. Jannetje, dau. of Jacob Clute, Aug. 7, 1785. He made his will Sept. 6, 1817, proved May 7, 1818, spoke of wife Tanneke, dau. Margarieta, Rachel, Elisabeth, and sons Joseph, Jacob and John. Ch. b : Margarietje, June 1, 1786; Margarietje, August 4, 1787; Jacob, Dec. 3, 1789; Joseph, July 15, 1792; Rachel, May 12, 1795; Manuel, Nov. 16, 1797; Johannes, Sept. 1, 1800, d. Sept. 7, 1828; Elisabeth, Apr. 6, 1803.

JOHANNES, son of Johannes and Machtelt, m. Viney Manning. Ch. b : Johannes, Sept. 27, 1793; William, April 23, 1796; Magdalena, June 4, 1799; Lydia, Sept. 15, 1801.

JOHN, and Dirkje Hogen. Ch. b : Manuel, Nov. 13, 1794; Emmanuel, Oct. 12, 1796; Isaac Hogen, Nov. 23, 1792, and bp in Albany, Jan. 15, 1793.

JOSEPH, and Maria Manny. Ch. b : Gabriel, Sept. 7, 1795; Manuel, Nov. 19, 1797.

JOHN P., son of Pieter, and Jane Robbin, both of Rensselaerswyck, m. March 2, 1795. Ch. b : Sarah, Feb. 21, 1796; Christina, May 5, 1798.

MANUEL, and Lidia Manning, both of *Lysjes kil*, m. Aug. 7, 1794. Ch. b : Joseph, Feb. 10, 1797; William, Feb. 20, 1806.

BASTIAAN, m. Lena Lewis, May 19, 1793.

CONSTABLE.

JAMES, made his will Jan. 10, 1806, proved Sept. 2, 1809, remembers his nephews, William and John Constable, sister Harriet Pierce of Bristol, England, sister Euretta, wife of ...... Pinckard, and Mrs. (Anne ?) Constable, wife of my deceased brother William. Jane, widow of Doct. John Constable, "formerly of this city," d. Oct. 7, 1805, in her 73d year.

CONTERMAN.

NICHOLAS, and Anna Augsberger of Helderbergh. Ch : David, b. Feb. 4, 1786.

CONYN.

PIETER, son of Pieter of Albany, of Caughnawaga, m. Rebecca, dau. of Johannes Wemple. He made his will 1773, proved Sept. 5, 1774, when all his Ch. were living, also wife Rebecca. May 22, 1780, his house was burnt by Sir John Johnson's Indians. Ch : Petrus, eldest son; John; Abraham; Debora, bp. Sept. 30, 1750; Alida, m. Adam Ziele.

PIETER, son of the last (?), and Susanna Mebie. Ch : Alida, bp. Oct. 15, 1780.

COOK.

JOHN, of "Currybosch," and Mary Ledy of Rensselaerswyck, m. March 1, 1764. Ch. bp : Catrien, Feb. 2, 1765; Jane, Oct. 11, 1765.

NICHOLAS, and Margaret McDonald. Ch : Elisabeth, bp. Oct. 23, 1784.

JOHN LIDIUS of Duanesburgh, and Elisabeth Westly, m. Sept. 14, 1786. Ch. b: Alexander, Jan. 29, 1788; Margaret, March 1, 1790; Ann Hunt, May 25, 1792.

RICHARD, m. Sarah Shelly, Oct 16, 1794. He lived on south corner of Union and Ferry streets, d. June 17, 1833. Sarah, relict of R. C., d. at New York, at the house of her son-in-law, Rev. Dr. Hardenburgh, July 20 (19), 1848, in her 79th year. Ch: Richard; Margariet, b. Jan. 17, 1796.

COP.

JOHN, and Annatje Clopper. Ch: Harriet Van Dyck, bp. March 12, 1778.

COPPERNOL.

CLAAS WILLEMSE VAN, m. Lea, a Mohawk woman, who, after his death about 1692, m. Jonathan Stevens. In 1678, Coppernol and wife contracted to serve Jan Conell on his bouwery at Cattskil for one year for 42 beavers. In 1679 he hired a bouwery of Wm. Teller at Schenectady, and subsequently purchased and settled upon land at *de Willigen*, below Port Jackson. Ch: *Willem*, bp. May 22, 1691, in Albany.

WILLEM, son of the last, and Engeltie Lantgraaf. Ch: Claes, bp. Dec. 18, 1714; *Jurrian*, bp. April 14, 1716.

JURRIAN, son of the last, and Elisabeth Lucasse. Ch: Dirk, bp. Oct. 7, 1744.

CORLETT.

WILLIAM, trader, native of the Isle of Man, made his will Nov. 11, 1815, proved March 1, 1816, owned the lot on south corner of State and Washington streets, extending through to Water street, with store, brewery &c., besides other real estate, all of which was bequeathed to his partners in business, Daniel and Hugh R. Martin.

CORNU.

PIERRE, *geboren in Frankryk thans wonende in* Schenectady, m. Elisabeth, dau. of Carel Hanse Toll, Dec. 1, 1734. In 1738 he is said to have owned a house on the south side of State street, where the New York Central rail road now crosses; he also had land at *Toweraune*, inherited from his father-in-law, a portion, or all of which he conveyed to his brother-in-law, Johannes Van Eps. He was a carpenter, and built the *preeckstoel* in the church of 1734, for £20. Ch. bp: Maria, Aug. 3, 1735, m. Gillis Clute; Johannes, April 9, 1738; *Daniel*, Dec. 21, 1740; Carel Hansen, Sept. 25, 1743; Elisabet, April 27, 1746, m. John Knox; Carel Hansen, April 13, 1749.

DANIEL, son of Pierre, m. Sarah, dau. of Wessel Wessels, Sept. 26, 1761. His lot was on the north side of State street, extending from the Canal, easterly to the Given's Hotel lot, afterwards owned by Joseph and Thomas Kinsela. He was a resident of Montgomery county in 1785. Ch bp: Johannes, Nov. 8, 1761; Wessel, March 18, 1764; Pieter, July 5, 1766; Johannes, April 29, 1769; Elisabeth, Dec. 9, 1770; Johannes, Aug. 12, 1773; Lucas, March 3, 1776; Carel Hansen, Feb. 7, 1779; Maria, April 14, 1782.

COTTON.

NATHANIEL, and Mary Spoor. Ch.
b : Judith, Sept. 15, 1790; Willem, Oct.
12, 1792; Nicolaas, Jan. 2, 1795.

COULON.

JEAN, and Elisabet Warmoet. Ch.
bp : Catharina, July 8, 1744; Wilhelmus,
June 3, 1746; Willem, Jan. 17, 1748.

COWEN.

PETER, merchant in Church street in
1788.

ANDREW, with William Hannah, purchased the tannery on the east corner of
State and Jay streets in 1797.

COWENHOVEN.

SAMUEL, of Noormanskil, m. Sarah
Van Petten. Ch : Chrystyntje, b. March
31, 1786.

CRANNON.

MARTIN, and Catharine Bokkus. Ch :
Catharine, b. Dec. 12, 1796.

CRANSEY.

FREDERIC, and Barber Weber. Ch.
bp : Frederic, Jan. 30, 1770; Coenrat,
May 13, 1772.

CRAS (CRAST).

JOHANNES, and Annatje Rigter. Ch :
Johannes, bp. Sept. 15, 1765.

JOHANNES, and Lena Morry. Ch :
Catrien, bp. Aug. 25, 1781.

HENDRICK, and Lena Trommer. Ch :
Anna, bp. July 2, 1781.

CRAWFORD.

WILLIAM, and Rejoice Hudson. Ch :
William, bp. April 29, 1750.

JOHN, m. Mary Wildy, Aug. 16, 1765.
Ch. bp : William, June 7, 1766; Thomas,
March 1, 1769.

JOHN, m. Catalyntje dau. of Abraham
Schermerhorn. Ch. bp : Joseph, May 15,
1774; Rebecca, May 19, 1776; Arent,
April 26, 1778; Clara, July 17, 1784;
Mary, b. Sept. 13, 1792.

ALEXANDER, and Ann Staley. Ch :
Alexander, b. Sept. 1, 1781; Matthew,
b. April 11, 1785; Catharine, b. Oct. 5,
1787; Henry, May 5, 1790.

JOSEPH, and Margaret Shawkirk
(Shanklin). Ch : Andrew, bp. Sept. 28,
1783; Sarah, b. April 14, 1785.

JURRY, and Rosina Keeley. Ch : William, b. Sept. 14, 1790.

CREAMER (CREEMER).

JOOST, and Anna Kelly. Ch : Catharina, b. Aug. —, 1791.

CREY (GRAY ?).

ROBERT, and Susanna De La Grange.
Ch : Gerrit, bp. June 22, 1783. [*See
Albany Families.*]

CROM.

WILLIAM, and Wyntje Rosa. Ch :
Geertruy, bp. Feb. 21, 1705.

CROMWELL.

JACOBUS, m. Maria Philipse, Sept. 26,
1703. He was an inn keeper, and in 1711

bought a house in Front street, of Wouter Vrooman for £130. After his death, his widow married David Lewis, inn keeper, 1717. Ch. bp: Aegje, Jan. 29, 1706, m. Johan Antes; Lysbeth, Oct. 16, 1707, m. Robert Carter; *Stephanus*, March 6, 1709, in Albany; *Jan Philipse*, Jan. 21, 1711.

STEPHANUS, son of Jacobus, m. Cornelia Pootman, dau. of Arent. Ch. bp: Arent, Jan. 13, 1745; Jan Philipse, Jan. 11, 1747.

JAN PHILIPSE, son of Jacobus m. Agnietje, daughter of Harmen Philipse. Ch. bp: Aeghtje, June 3, 1746; Anna, Jan. 22, 1749; Harmanus, Dec. 18, 1751.

CROUL.

JOHN, of Remsenbos, and Mary Coss. Ch; Frederic, b. July 6, 1785.

CROWSHORN (CROUSEHORN).

JOHN, tanner, lived in Schenectady before the Revolutionary war, on the lot east corner of State and Jay streets. Perhaps *Coehorn* kil is a corruption for Crowshorn kil.

CRYSLER.

JOHN, and Maria Hagedorn. Ch: Baltus, b. July 3, 1790.

CULBERTSON.

WILLIAM, m. Mary Gordon, Dec. 31, 1787.

CUMMINS.

JOHN, m. Sarah, dau. of Johannes Gonzalis. He was buried Aug. 25, 1801;

she d. about Feb. 6, 1789. Ch: Sarah, b. Nov. 6, 1788.

CUNNINGHAM.

JAMES, and Peggy Van Vorst. Ch: Robert, b. Aug. 16, 1789.

CUSICK.

NICHOLAS, and Elisabeth Cusick. Ch: Johannes Krontewdnie, bp. Feb. 16, 1784.

CUYLER.

JOHANNES, merchant, son of Johannes A. of Albany, m. Susanna, dau. of Harmanus Vedder, and widow of ...... Van Petten, July 5, 1763. She d. March 23, 1784, a. 50ys., 11m., 21d. Ch. bp: Catarina, April 22, 1764; Harmanus Vedder, July 20, 1766; Annatje, Feb. 5, 1769; Elsje, April 28, 1771; Johannes, Jan. 8, 1775; Vedder, Aug. 9, 1777.

CORNELIUS, merchant, son of Johannes A. of Albany, m. Anna Wendell. She d. May —, 1775, and was buried in the church. Ch. bp: Jacob, June 9, 1765; Johannes, Dec. 7, 1766; Harmanus, Oct. 9, 1768; Jannetje, June 10, 1770.

CORNELIUS, perhaps same as the last, m. Jannetje Yates. Ch: Elsje, b. May 22, 1788. [*See Albany Families.*]

CYBEL.

JURRY ADAM, and Sophia Freeman. Ch: Jacob, bp. Sept. 28, 1760.

MICHAEL, and Engeltie Miller. Ch: Engeltje, bp. Aug. 24, 1778.

DAASEN (DAWSON).

WILLEM, cooper, m. Ariaantje, dau. of Volkert Veeder, Feb. 22, 1729. Ch: *Folkert*, bp. Sept. 26, 1731.

FOLKERT, son of Willem, m. Geertruy, dau. of Ryckert Hilton of Albany. Ch: Richard, bp. Dec. 11, 1763. [*See Albany Families.*]

DAWSON.

WILLIAM, and Gennet McArthur. Ch: Gennet, b. Nov. 2, 1789.

DALY.

NATHANIEL, and Sarah Teerpenning, both of Clifton Park, m. Oct. 31, 1793. Ch. b: Mary, March 28, 1794; Lourens, Jan. 10, 1797; Rachel, Dec. 31, 1799.

DANCE (DENS).

JOSEPH, m. Hillegonda Erichzon, June 30, 1729. Ch. b: Wilko, April 3, 1730; Wilko, Aug. 25, 1732; John, bp. Dec. 21, 1737; *Wouter.*

WOUTER, son of Joseph, and Clara Marinus. Ch. bp: *Joseph*, March 18, 1770; *Jacobus*, April 25, 1773; Jacob, Aug. 14, 1783.

JACOBUS, son of Wouter, m. Engeltie, dau. of Jacobus Bratt. Ch. b: Marytje, Oct. 22, 1794; Jacobus, Feb. 13, 1797; Barent Bratt, Nov. 7, 1798; William, Oct. 15, 1801.

JOSEPH, son of Wouter, m. Catharina Van Alen. Ch. b: Claartje, Nov. 8, 1795; Peter, June 21, 1801; Maria, Nov. 17, 1797; Nicholas Hall, Sept. 18, 1799.

ALEXANDER, m. Anna Crawford, June 27, 1786.

DANIELSON.

JOHN, and Jannetie Leane. Ch: Johannes, bp. Aug. 19, 1772.

DAVENPORT.

JOHN, cordwainer of Kingston, Ulster county, m. Henrikje Benneway (Benoit) of Kingston, Sept. 22, 1748. Ch: Petrus, bp. Sept. 23, 1750.

DAVIDS.

LUDOVICUS, b. in this place and living in the Maquaasland, and Maria, dau. of Peter Clement, born and living in the Woestyne, m. May 14, 1731. Ch: Catharina, bp. Dec. 19, 1731.

(DAVIDSE).

JAN, and Anna ...... Ch: David, bp. Aug. 16, 1780.

DAVIDSON.

ALEXANDER, and Christina Grant. Ch. bp: Jannet, Nov. 1, 1781; Alexander, March 26, 1785.

DAVIE (DAVIDS, DAVY, DAVIS).

THOMAS, m. Catarina, dau. of Johannes Klein, Dec. 14, 1701. Ch. bp: Margarita, Oct. 18, 1702; Johannes, April 29, 1705, Thomas, October 16, 1707; Lewis, May 4, 1710; Maria, October 9, 1715; Willem, Sept. 3, 1721; Pieter, May 31, 1724.

DAVIS.

JOHN, of Albany, m. Helena Post, Jan. 23, 1763. Ch. bp: Maria, May 20, 1764; Cornelius Post, Dec. 7, 1766

ABRAHAM, and Catarina Rogers. Ch:
Frans, bp. Nov. 2, 1780.

JOHN, and Mary Tint. Ch: David,
b. Jan. 15, 1772.

JOHN, and Cicely Connor, m. Aug. 6,
1761.

JACOB, and Catarina Reemsnyder.
Ch: Robert Bohannan and Hendrick,
bp. Oct. 13, 1781.

WILLEM, of Normanskil, and Jannetie
Relyea. Ch. b: Annatie, Oct. 13, 1784;
David, Sept. 20, 1788; John, May 22,
1790.

JOOST HENDRIK, and Catharina Bar-
tram. Ch: Christiaan, b. Feb. 25, 1787.

DE CLERK (now CLARK).

MATTHIAS, m. Immetje Page, Jan. 2,
1774, in Albany. He was born in Tap-
paan, d. Dec. 14, 1814, a. 72ys. His wife
d. Sept. 12, 1813, a. 61ys. Ch. bp: Johannes, Nov. 13, 1774; Catarina, July
5, 1777; Catarina, Dec. 13, 1778; Elisabeth, April 23, 1780; Johannes, Aug.
19, 1781, d. Dec. 28, 1865; Angnietje,
Nov. 2, 1783. Ch. b: William Page,
Sept. 11, 1786; Isaac, April 3, 1789, d.
Sept. 5, 1823; his widow, Jane Swits,
d. Nov. 29, 1839, a. 46ys., 5m., 14d.;
Catharina, July 6, 1791.

DE GOLIER.

JAMES, and Maria Palmontier. Ch.
bp: Joseph, May 14, 1781; John, Mar.
20, 1785; Ch. b: Anthony, February 9,
1787; Isaac, April 10, 1789.

JOSEPH, and Cornelia Boon, both of
the Woestyne, m. April 17, 1789. Ch.
b: James, July 13, 1789; Catharina,
April 5, 1792.

ANTONY, of Montgomery county, m.
Patty Willis of Schenectady, July 23,
1792.

DE GARMO.

MATTHIAS, son of Johannes of Albany, m. Margarita, dau. of Albert Van-
derwerken of Albany. Ch. bp: Albertus,
Feb. 6, 1782; Johannes, Aug. 15, 1784;
Rebecca, b. Dec. 1, 1788.

JOHANNES, and Margarietje ...... Ch:
Annatie, bp. Nov. 15, 1784.

DE GRAAF.

ANDRIES DE GRAAF was a citizen of
New Amsterdam in 1661. Jan Andriese
De Graaf, brickmaker, was in Albany as
early as 1655. Claas Andriese De Graaf,
an early settler at Schenectady, lived in
Glenville at the *Hoek* (lately owned by D.
F. Reese). There was another "Claas
Graven's Hoek" on the north bank of
the Mohawk, just west of the bounds of
Schenectady county, lying in Cuyler's pat-
ent. He m. Elisabeth, dau. of Willem
Brouwer of Albany. She d. Nov. 18,
1723. Ch: *Abraham*, b. Nov. 14, 1688,
d. March 27, 1731; Isaac, bp. in Albany,
August 4, 1691; Antje, bp. in Albany,
Aug. 27, 1693, m. Cornelis Christiaanse;
Sara, bp. in Schenectady, Jan. 8, 1696,
m. Johannes Marselis; Elisabeth, m.
Nicolaas Stensel; Eva, m. Jacob Van
Olinda; Margarita, m. Robert Yates;

Arnout; Jesse; Andries; Rebecca, b. Feb. 29, 1701; Claas, b. Aug. 4, 1709.

JESSE, son of Claas, m. Aaltie Hennions (Henmon, Ackermans) in New York, Oct. 20, 1705. It is said he was carried away captive, to Canada by the French and Indians, but afterwards returned. Ch. bp: *Claas*, Dec. 25, 1706; *Daniel*, May 26, 1708; Elisabeth, bp. in Albany, April 30, 1710, m. Pieter Van Slyck; Anna, Nov. 13, 1712; Aaltie, bp. in Albany, Oct. 31, 1714; Marytje, Dec. 8, 1716, m. Jeronimus Barheit; Catharina, Jan. 10, 1719, m. Adam Condè; Saartje, Jan. 14, 1721, m. Harmanus Peek; Alida, June 8, 1723; Eva, b. April 27, 1725, m. William Schermerhorn; Rachel, bp. June 29, 1729, m. Abraham Groot

ARNOLD (Arnout), son of Claas, m. Ariaantje, dau. of Claas Vander Volgen, May 13, 1715. He d. March 27, 1731, after which his wid. m. Harmanus Vedder. Ch. bp: Claes, March 24, 1716; Maritje, Feb. 8, 1718, m. Harmanus A. Vedder; Elisabeth, March 10, 1720; Neeltje, Aug. 24, 1722, m. Takerus Van der Bogart; Annatje, October 4, 1724; *Claes*, Jan. 7, 1727; Elisabeth, March 27, 1731.

ABRAHAM, son of Claas, m. Rebecca, dau. of Abraham Groot, Aug. 17 (27), 1725. He lived in the old Red House, standing on the Sacandaga turnpike, near the residence of P. Riley Toll, Esq., and his burying ground lies just back of the house. From his family Bible, still in tolerable preservation, are translated the following entries on the fly leaf. "1746, Oct. 30, Abraham De Graaf and his son Willem were taken captive to Canada." "1747, June 12, Abraham De Graaf d. at Quebec, in Canada, and was buried there." "1748, July 18, Nicolaas (Claas) De Graaf and 20 others were murdered at *Beukendal* by the Savage Indians." Ch: *Claas*, b. May 26, 1726; Hester, b. April 8, 1728, m. Philip Ryley; Elisabeth, b. Sept. 1, 1731 (Bible), bp. Aug. —, 1729 (Church record), d. Feb. 28, 1732; *Abraham*, b. Aug. 24, 1732; Wilhelmus (Willem), b. Nov. 20, 1734; *Cornelis*, b. Nov. 23, 1738.

ISAAC, son of Claas, m. Debora, dau. of Jeremia Thickstone, Aug. 18, 1725. He was a carpenter, and lived on the north side of Front street, a little east of Church street. Ch: Elisabeth, b. between the 14th and 15th of Jan. 1726, m. Frederic Clute; *Jeremias*, b. Oct. 21, 1727; Claas, bp. March 6, 1732; Rachel, bp. July 7, 1734; Jesse, bp. Oct. 8, 1737; *Johannes*, bp. April 13, 1740.

ANDRIES, son of Claas, m. Neeltie, dau. of Daniel Van Antwerpen. Ch: Lysbet, b. Feb. 5, 1726, m. Philip Groot.

ANDRIES, same as the last, m. Margarietje, dau. of Fredericus Clute, June 29, 1728. She again m. Arent Laneyn, Dec. 26, 1736. Ch. bp: Claas ...... 1729 (?); *Fredericus* ......, 1729.

DANIEL, son of Jesse, m. Gezina, dau. of Simon Swits, June 26, 1735. He d. March 12, 1790, a. 81ys., 10 m., 15d.;

she d. Jan. 22, 1801, a. 88ys. Ch. b:
a dau. who d. unbaptised in 1735; Susanna, May 8, 1737, m. Andreas Truax;
Jesse, July 21, 1739, d. Sept. 25, 1740;
Gezina, Sept. 3, 1741, m. Frederic Visscher; a son Feb. 8, 1744, d. unbaptised;
Jesse, Jan. 13, 1745; Gezina, Nov. 6,
1747; Alida, March 9, 1750, m. Johannes Vedder; *Simon*, April 6, N. S.,
1753; Elisabeth, Sept. 6, 1755, d. May
27, 1756; *Isaac*, Nov. 16, 1757.

NICOLAAS, son of Jesse, of the *Hoek*,
m. Ariaantje, dau. of Johannes Schermerhorn. He made his will Dec. 28,
1790, proved Jan. 18, 1797; wife not
mentioned, but sons Jesse and Johannes,
and dau. Anneke, widow of Gerrit Veeder, and her ch. Wilhelmus, Nicolaas
and Catharine. Ch. bp: Jesse, Oct. 23,
1743; Engeltie, Oct. 14, 1746; Engeltie,
Feb. 25, 1750; Alida, April 5, 1752;
Johannes, Sept. 3, 1754; Anneke ......,
m. Gerrit Veeder.

CLAAS, son of Arnold, carpenter, m.
first, Lea Gonzalus; secondly, Caty, dau.
of Abraham and Christina Truex, Feb.
1, 1754, in Albany. Ch. b: *Manuel*, son
the first wife, bp. Feb. 10, 1751; Elisabeth, b. June 26, 1754, d. July 29, 1755;
Elisabeth, Dec. 22, 1755, m. Jacob T.
Ten Eyck; Arnout, bp. Oct. 30, 1757;
Abraham, b. April 28, 1759; Jannetje,
Dec. 7, 1760; Johannes, April 16, 1762;
Christina, Oct, 22, 1763, m. Lourens
Myndertse; Maria, April 5, 1765; Neeltje, Aug. 9, 1768; Nicolaas, April 15,
1770; Andreas, bp. May 31, 1772.

ABRAHAM, son of Abraham and Rebecca, m. Rachel dau. of Johannes Clute,
Aug. 4, (July 17), 1753. He d. Jan.
19, 1756. Ch: *Abraham*, b. April 20,
1754.

CLAAS, son of Abraham, and Bata
Quackenbos, dau. of Johannes, both of
De Willegen (below Port Jackson), Sept.
29, 1759. Ch. bp: Margarita, Jan. 23,
1763; *Johannes*, Dec. 1, 1765; Nicolaas,
Aug. 11, 1771.

JOHANNES, son of Isaac, m. Rebecca,
dau. of Gerrit Van Vranken of "Onestoungjoone," Nov. 12, 1763. Ch. bp:
Debora, April 14, 1765; *Gerrit*, Sept.
21, 1766.

FREDERIC, son of Andries, and Sarah
G. Marselis, both of *De Willegen*, m.
Sept. 28, 1765. Ch. bp: Andreas, Sept.
21, 1766; Catarina, Oct. 11, 1767; Claas,
April 16, 1769; Margarita, March 31,
1771; Gerrit, July 25, 1773; Frederick,
March 3, 1776; Pieter, Sept. 13, 1778;
Johannes, Sept. 7, 1783.

JOHANNES, son of Isaac, m. Annatje,
dau. of Harmanus Peek, July 1, 1769.
She again m. Abraham Truax, Jan. 9,
1785. Ch. bp: *Isaac*, July 22, 1770;
Harmanus, July 26, 1772.

JEREMIA, son of Isaac, m. Annatje,
dau. of Johannes Quackenbosch. Ch.
bp: Isaac, b. July 10, 1770, d. June 5,
1851; Helena, bp. March 8, 1772; Claas,
April 17, 1774; Debora, Feb. 25, 1776;
Francyntje, April 19, 1778; Johannes,
Feb. 6, 1780; Elisabeth, Dec. 30, 1781;

Bata, Feb. 11, 1784; Jesse, b. Dec. 17, 1787.

CORNELIS, son of Abraham, m. Rebecca, dau. of Frederic Van Petten, Sept. 16 (10), 1769. He was for 32 years *Voorlezer* of the Dutch Church; lived in a house on south side of State street, next west of Abel Smith's house; about 1800 he removed to Glenville, where he d. July 11, 1830, a. 91ys., 7mo., 7d. His wife d. Jan. 6, 1812, a. 62ys., 2m., 30d. Ch: Eva b. Nov. 7, 1770; Elisabeth, bp. April 24, 1774; Elisabeth, bp. May 17, 1775, d. Oct. 19. 1796; Rebecca, bp. Jan. 31, 1779; Abraham, b. Oct. 10, 1782; Frederick, b. Sept. 28, 1786; Willem, b. Nov. 16, 1791, d. Nov. 6, 1793.

ABRAHAM, son of Nicolaas, of Glenville, m. Margarita, dau. of Willem Schermerhorn, Jan. 29, 1775; made his will June 1, 1810, proved June 24, 1811, spoke of his wife and children; Abraham to have the homestead. He d. June 1, 1810, a. 56ys., 1m., 11d.; she d. July 11, 1825, in her 74th yr. Ch. bp: Elisabeth, July 23, 1775; Tanneke, Nov. 1, 1778, m. Cornelis Viele; Rachel, March 11, 1781; Jacob, Aug. 24, 1783; Ch. b: Charles, Feb. 5, 1786; William, Jan. 10, 1787; Abraham, Dec. 16, 1790; Lourens, May 25, 1793.

JOHANNES N. (D., C.), m. Eva, dau. of Petrus Van Driessen. Ch. bp: Engeltie, April 7, 1776; Alida, March 22, 1778, m. Philip A. Truax; Nicolaas, July 16, 1780; Maria, Sept. 21, 1783. Ch. b: Petrus Van Driessen, Feb. 13,

1786; Jesse, Dec. 25, 1788; John, May 27, 1791; Annatie, March 18, 1794; Simon, Feb. 23, 1798.

ANDREAS, m. Eva, dau. of Esaias Swart. Ch. bp: Elisabeth, Feb. 25, 1777, m. John S. Veeder; Margarita, Nov. 7, 1779; Sarah, b. July 19, 1785; Esaias, b. April 11, 1790.

MANUEL, son of Claas, m. Rebecca Gonzalus. He was one of the first settlers of Amsterdam; his farm was 2 miles east of the village. He has been succeeded in the same place by his son and grandson of the same christian name. He m. Annatje Swart of *de Woestyne*, Jan. 5, 1795, she being his second wife. Ch. bp: Lea, April 27, 1777; Joseph, May 2, 1779; Margarita, Jan. 19, 1782; Nicholas, Feb. 11, 1784; Elisabeth, b. Sept. 11, 1786; Manuel, b. Jan. 24, 1789, d. in Amsterdam, July 1, 1844.

ISAAC, son of Daniel, m. Susanna, dau. of Jan Baptist Van Eps, Dec. 19, 1779. He d. Dec. 21, 1844, a. 87ys., 1m., 5d.; she d. March 14, 1829, a. 67ys., 2m. 23d. Ch. b: Daniel, June 16, 1780; Annatje, Oct. 6, 1781; Johannes, Oct. 2, 1783, for many years a successful merchant, served two terms in Congress, was several times Mayor; d. July 26, 1848; Jesse, May 20, 1786; Gezina, Jan. 13, 1788, m. Abraham Oothout; Neeltje, Jan. 7, 1790; Susanna, Feb. 12, 1792; Susanna, March 29, 1793, m. Pieter Bancker, d. June 29, 1855; Annatie, March 10, 1795; Annatje, Sept. 18, 1797; Jesse, Jan. 9, 1801.

8

SIMON, son of Daniel, m. Annatie, dau. of Simon Schermerhorn, Dec. 6, 1779. Shed. Sept. 21, 1783. Ch: Gesina, b. Aug. 17, 1784, d. May 15, buried 17th, 1785.

SIMON, same as last, m. Jannetie Bratt, dau. of Harmanus, April 12, 1787. Ch. b : Daniel, Aug. 11, 1788; Harmanus, Jan. 8, 1791; Annatje, Aug. 23, 1794. [A Simon De Graff d. in Albany, March 31, 1842, a. 85ys.]

JESSE, son of Daniel, m. Rachel, dau. of Abraham Fonda, Nov. 19, 1774. He d. August 30, 1812, a. 67ys., 7m., 17d. Ch : Daniel, b. Oct. 22, 1784, d. April 12, 1794.

JESSE, same as last, m. Rebecca Quackenbos. Ch : Nicolaas, b. May 11, 1788.

JOHN, son of Nicolaas, m. Annatje, dau. of Louis Groot. She d. June 12, 1829 (?). Ch. b : Nicholas, Sept. 12, 1787; Lewis, Oct. 9, 1790; Abram, Oct. 26 (Oct. 24, Bible), 1793; Elisabeth, June 24, 1796; Maria, Aug. 14, —; John G., July 11, 1804.

ABRAM, son of Nicolaas, m. Christina La Grange. Ch. b: Eyda, Oct. 16, 1790; Sarah, Jan. 28, 1793; John, Jan. 22, 1809.

WILLIAM, m. Annatie Truex, Aug. 7, 1794. Ch : Rebecca, b. June 7, 1798. [A William De G. was buried Sept. 22, 1803.]

GERRIT, son of Johannes, and Elisabeth Duryee, both of New Amsterdam;

banns proclaimed in Schenectady, Dec. 15, 1794.

ISAAC, son of Johannes, m. Sarah, dau. of Johannes Toll, Jan. 16, 1791. She was b. May 18, 1773, and d. Dec. 3, 1814, in Glenville. Ch. b : Johannnes, July 11, 1791; Simon, Oct. 30, 1793 ; Harmanus, June 9, 1796; Arent, March 5, 1799; Catharina, Dec. 20, 1801, d. Feb. 8, 1802; Annatje, Jan. 31, 1803, d. June 15, 1806; Daniel Toll, Oct. 17, 1805; Isaac, Sept. 12, 1808, d. at West Glenville, Dec. 2, 1854; Abraham, May 15, 1812.

HARMANUS, son of Johannes, m. Jane Kinsley, June 8, 1794. Ch. b : Johannes, Sept. 5, 1794 ; Margarieta, May 14, 1796; Annatje, June 11, 1799 ; Catharine, May 28, 1801, d. Nov. 20, 1864.

JOHANNES, son of Claas, m. Catharina, dau. of Seth Vedder of Rosendal, Feb. 3, 1793. Ch : Seth Vedder, b. Nov. 8, 1795.

GIDEON, and Margariet Teerpening, both of Clifton Park, m. July 6, 1796.

ADAM, and Margarieta Schermerhorn. Ch : Rachel, b. Dec. 7, 1795.

NICHOLAS, and Sarah Schermerhorn, both of Montgomery county, m. Dec. 31, 1796.

DE LA GRANGE.

JELLIS, son of Christiaan Johannese of Bergen, N. J., m. Jannetje Molenaar. Ch. bp : Chrystyntje, in Albany, Sept. 24, 1693; Elisabeth, in Albany, Oct. 6,

1695; Anna, in Schenectady, Dec. 29, 1700; Christiaan, in Albany, July 25, 1703. [*See Albany Families.*]

JACOBUS, son of Omy, of the Normanskil, m. Engeltie, dau. of Johannes Veeder, Oct. 24, 1717. Ch. bp: Susanna, Sept. 25, 1719; Barnardus, May 11, 1721; Susanna, Sept. 15, 1723; Antie, in Albany, April 21, 1728; Debora, August (?), 1729, m. Philip Teunise; *Myndert.* [*See Albany Families.*]

MYNDERT, son of Jacobus, of the Normanskil, m. Helena, dau. of Abraham Swits, March 5, 1769. Ch. bp: Engeltie, Jan. 14, 1770, m. Arent N. Van Petten; Neeltie, June 16, 1771; Jacobus, Jan. 19, 1777. [*See Albany Families.*]

ARIE, of Normanskil, and Maria Van Antwerpen of Schenectady, m. Feb. 18, 1762.

CHRISTIAAN, and Elisabeth Freeman. Ch. bp: Antje, March 8, 1779; Engeltje, March 2, 1782; Engeltie, b. Dec. 11, 1785, bp. in Albany; Jannetie, b. May 25, 1790, bp. in Albany.

DE LANY.

PATRICK, and Barbara Cunningham. Ch: Anneke, bp. Oct. 4, 1760.

DE LA WARDE.

JAN, came over from Antwerp in 1662; besides a lot in Albany, and land in Niskayuna, he owned an island in the Mohawk river between Claas Graven's Hoek and Schenectady, for which in 1698 he acknowledged to have received satisfaction from Joris Aertse Van der Baast some years previously. He d. in Albany Jan. 28, 1702.

DELAMONT.

JACOB, of Albany, d. March 14, 1719, a. 81ys., leaving two sons, *Jan* or Johannes, who settled in Schenectady, and *Marten* of Schaghticoke.

MARTEN, son of Jacob, of "Schadthooke," m. Lybeth Viele, Nov. 14, 1702, in Albany. Ch. bp. in Albany: Pieter, Oct. 1, 1703; Catharina, April 20, 1707; Catharina, Oct. 31, 1708; Pieter, Oct. 7, 1711; Abraham, Feb. 10, 1717.

JAN or JOHANNES, son of Jacob, m. first Johanna Clara Kleyn, widow of N. N. Metselaer, May 4, 1707, in Albany; and secondly, Eva, dau. of Hendrick Brouwer. He was b. July 30, 1684, d. Dec. 20, 1766. In 1710 he was High Constable of Albany; in 1735 *Voorlezer* of the church in Schenectady. His wife Eva, d. Oct. 2, 1747, a. 45ys., 6m., 3d. Ch. b: Jacob, July 7, 1723, "murdered by the hands of the enemy and buried in Stillwater, Oct. 24, 1746" [Bible]; Maria, May 9, 1725, m. Abraham Christianse; Hendrik, Feb. 25, 1727, d. Aug. 21, 1743; Catrina, May 6, 1728, m. Henricus Volkertse Veeder; *Abraham*, b. July 25, 1730 [Bible], bp. July 19, 1729 [Church record]; Elisabeth, Dec. 16, 1732, m. Jacobus Bratt; Margarieta, Jan. 26, 1735, m. Abraham Swits; Jannetje, Feb. 26, 1737, m. Johannes Teller; Annatie, May 4, 1739, m. Christoffel Felthousen; Eva, Nov. 10, 1741, m. Claas Vedder; Henrik, Oct. 24, 1745.

ABRAHAM, son of Jan, m. first, Annatje, dau. of Alexander Vedder, Dec. 4, 1766. She d. July 21, 1779, and he m. secondly Volkie Wemp, June 30, 1782; he d. Dec. 23, 1792. Ch. b: Jacob, Jan. 13, 1768, d. March 19, 1768; *Jacob*, Dec. 30, 1768; Maria, Aug. 7, 1771, d. May 16, 1780; *Johannes*, Feb. 25, 1774; Alexander, July 9, 1779, d. Aug. 11, 1779.

HENDRICK, son of Jan, m. Elisabeth Van Dyck. In 1781 he owned the lot in Union street where the Court House now stands, beginning 100ft. Amst. meas. west from Ferry street; made his will Nov. 9, 1808, proved Oct. 25, 1820; wife *Margaret*, but no ch. mentioned. Ch: John, b. Jan. 29, 1787.

JACOB, son of Abraham, m. Debora, dau. of Johannes Bratt, April 5, 1789. She d. in Rotterdam, Nov. 5, 1844, a. 73ys. Ch: Annatje, b. May 21, 1789.

JOHANNES, son of Abraham, m. Rebecca De Graaf, Nov. 23, 1799. She d. Oct. 13, 1837. Ch. b: Maria, June 27, 1800; Cornelius, July 31, 1802, d. Jan. 18, 1837; Annatie, Sept. 25, 1806; Rebecca, Oct. 12, 1809, d. March 9, 1839; Eva, Sept. 24, 1812, d. April 7, 1834; a son unbaptised, Oct. 31, 1815, d. Dec. 22, 1815; Volkie Eliza, April 3 1817, d. Dec. 5, 1842; Debora Ann and Abraham Henry, twins, Feb. 25, 1821.

DELLOE.

WILLIAM H. and Annatie Merkle. Ch: David, b. Feb. 28, 1799.

DEMOREST.

GULIAAN, and Lea Goetschius.   Ch: Elsje, b. June 14, 1794.

PETER, m. Francyntje, dau. of Willem Van Ingen, August 4, 1794.   Ch: William Van Ingen, bp. August 28, 1796; James Van Ingen, b. May 20, 1798; Margarietje Elisabeth, b. Feb. 27, 1801.

ABRAHAM, and Tannitje Brouwer. Ch: Jacob, b. Oct. 11, 1796.

SAMUEL, and Maria ...... Ch: Samuel, bp. Feb. 25, 1798.

DE NIE (DENNY ?).

LOWIS, and Maria Janse. Ch: John, bp. March 1, 1782.

DENNISTON.

CHARLES "VAN IRELAND," m. Catrien, dau. of Johannes Barheyt, Nov. 20, 1762. Ch. bp: Sarah, Jan. 22, 1764; Cornelia, May 26, 1765; Mary, Jan. 12, 1767; Ezekiel, May 7, 1769; Cornelia, May 5, 1771; *Ezekiel*, April 28, 1773; Jacomyntje, Oct. 10, 1775; Jane, Aug. 30, 1778; Robert, Aug. 31, 1782.

EZEKIEL, son of Charles, and Margarieta Pulver, both of Duanesburgh, m. May 31, 1792. Ch. b: Jemima, Oct. 6, 1792; Christina, Sept. 11, 1795; Charles, Nov. 28, 1797.

DENNY.

JOHN, m. Penelope (Eleanor) Lidde (Leede), Oct. 7, 1770. Ch: Margariet, bp. Sept. 14, 1789; Alexander Alexander, b. May 19, 1791.

DE SPITZER.

ERNESTUS, and Barbara Welfon (Wilfelin). He was a clergyman before coming to this country; the following is a translation of a license given him: "Wc give to the bearer of this paper, Rev. Ernest Spitzer of the Diocese of Vienna, permission to say mass during four days in all the churches in and outside the city, if he, according to the rules of the church, in honest priestly clothing, will appear before the rectors and trustees of the church."

"Beben Bratz, the 25th March, 1745.
LOUIS BERTHOLDO,
Archdeacon."

He was surgeon to the garrison at Oswego from Oct. 28, 1753, to May 22, 1755, and perhaps longer. After the French war, he settled in Schenectady, and practiced medicine. He had a farm in Glenville, about 7 miles above the city, where there is a family burying ground. Ch. bp: Elisabeth, May 18, 1755, m. Aaron Potman; *Gerrit*, July 2, 1758; Ernestus, Sept. 27, 1761.

GERRIT, son of Ernestus, m. Annatje, dau. of Nicolaas Sixbury. Ch: Ernestus, bp. Aug. 12, 1781; Nicholas, bp. Dec. 27, 1783. Ch. b: Jeremiah, Aug. 7, 1786; Susanna, Feb. 4, 1789; Peter Sixbury, June 12, 1791; Johannes, May 28, 1794; Barbara, Jan. 13, 1797.

DEVOE.

JOHN, and Margarita Reddely. Ch: Annatje, bp. Dec. 14, 1781. [*See Albany Families.*]

WILLEM, *van de Halve maan*, m. Sara Van Vorst, Aug. 23, 1745.

SAMUEL, and Polly Crown. Ch: Maritje, b. Sept. 19, 1788.

DE WINTER.

BASTIAAN, a native of Middleburgh, Holland, came to Schenectady about 1662. Falling sick, in 1670 he sold his house lot, 200ft square, on the south corner of Church and Union streets, together with his bouwery on the *Groote Vlachte*, to Joris Aertse Van der Baast, Jan Labatie and Elias Van Guysling, with the intention of returning to Holland, but d. before doing so. In 1678 the Dutch church of Albany claimed, and probably obtained his property for the use of the poor. He d. about Aug., 1678, leaving no heirs in this country.

DE WITT.

JOHANNES, and Rachel Wemple. Ch: Andreas, bp. March 24, 1782.

DEYER (DYER).

JONATHAS, bricklayer, from Wales, England, m. Maria Dirkse, widow of Harmanus Hagedorn, Nov. 21, 1695, in Albany. In 1714 he conveyed the 6th Flat to Reyer Schermerhorn. Ch. bp: Robert, Sept. 29, 1696; Anna, Oct. 19, 1698; Sara, Sept. 28, 1701; Jannetje, Jan. 2, 1704; Henderick, Apr. 14, 1706; Henderick, Feb. 8, 1708.

DEYGART.

WILLIAM, and Catharina Head. Ch: Alexander, b. Dec. 15, 1798.

DINGMAN.

JACOB (Petrus in the *Trouw Boek*), and Maria Krankheyt, both of *de Willege*, m. Nov. 9, 1765. Ch. bp: *Samuel*, Aug. 28, 1763; Sarah, Aug. 4, 1765; Eva, June 4, 1769; Abraham, Aug. 18, 1770.

JOHANNES, m. Margarita, dau. of Harman Philipse. Ch: *Gerardus*, b. Oct. 1, 1764; Maria, bp. Sept. 21, 1766, m. Samuel Dingman.

SAMUEL, son of Jacob, m. Maria, dau. of Johannes Dingman. Ch. b: Jacob, Nov. 30, 1785; John, Sept. 26, 1788.

GERARDUS, son of Johannes, and Catharina Hendricksen. Ch: Annatje, b. May 17, 1791.

DIRKSE (VAN VECHTEN).

TEUNIS, of Loonenburgh, now Athens, m. Catalina, dau. of Claas Van Petten of Schenectady, Nov. 28, 1694, in Albany. Ch: Jannetje, bp. May 24, 1702. They were both deceased in 1707. [*See Albany Families.*]

(DOXIE).

SAMUEL, and Elisabeth ......; Abraham and Isaac, bp. July 8, 1716. [*See Albany Families.*]

DIXON.

JOSEPH, and Cornelia Bratt. Ch: Joseph, b. May 21, 1794.

DOD

JOHN, of New York, and Catlyntje, dau. of Johannes Schermerhorn, both dwelling at Schenectady, m. Sept. 29, 1745. Ch: Bartholomew, bp. May 18, 1746.

(DODGE ?).

BARTHOLOMEW, and Marytje Doremus. Ch. b: Jacob, April 21, 1787; Rachel and Engeltie, Dec. 16, 1789.

JOHN, and Elisabeth Mandeville. Ch. b: John, Dec. 27, 1792; Antje, Nov. 9, 1795; David Mandeville, Aug. 27, 1798.

DODDS.

CORNELIUS, and Mary Glen. Ch: Maria, b. May 7, 1797.

DOINE.

MARTIN, and Nancy Barry, m. March 29, 1797.

DOKSTADER.

JOHANNES, and Catarina Bellinger. Ch: Catarina, bp. Nov. 26, 1780.

DONALDSON.

WILLIAM, from Killysandry, Ireland, and Sara Goff of Schenectady, m. Jan. 22, 1743, both then living in Schenectady.

DOOLITTLE.

THOMPSON, m. Nancy Bonney, Aug. 9, 1789. Ch. b: Joseph, Feb. 15, 1791; Margriet, Jan. 13, 1793.

DOORN.

ALEXANDER, m. Rachel, dau. of Jacob Egmond of Albany. Ch: Maria, bp. Jan. 29, 1780; Maria, b. March 31, 1786; Lea, b. April 10, 1788; Eleanor, b. Nov. 22, 1790.

JOHN, Jr., and Mary Van Aken. Ch. b: Petrus, March 27, 1791; Charles, June 27, 1793; Sullivan, May 27, 1797

DORN (DOORN).

JOHN and Maria Sullivan. Ch: Abraham, bp. Oct. 11, 1783; Jacob, b. Feb. 3, 1786.

DOWLAND.

JAMES, and Elisabeth Bradford. Ch: John, b. Oct. 31, 1785.

DOYLE.

CHARLES, tavern keeper, 52 Union street in 1765–1772; wife Jean.

DUDLEY.

STEPHEN, and Cornelia Post, m. April 15, 1764.

DUNBAR (TUMBARR).

JOHN, m. first, Bata Winne of Albany, and secondly, Maria Van Hoesen, dau. of Johannes, April 1, 1724. He was b. Aug. 31, 1670, and d. in Schenectady, May 7, 1736. In 1714 he was associated with Rev. Thomas Barclay and Col. Peter Matthews in building the Episcopal church in Albany. About 1730 he removed to Schenectady, where he resided on the south corner of Church and Front streets. He made his will April 13, 1736; wife not living; and spoke of the following ch: Robert, John, Mary, Catharine, Willempie and Alexander. He was a Vintner or " taffering ceeper." Ch. bp. in Albany: Robert, Nov. 20, 1709; Jannetie, May 17, 1724; in Schenectady, Anna, Jan. 7, 1733; *Alexander*, Nov. 17, 1734. His dau. Mary m. Joseph R. Yates; Willempie, m. Abraham Groot; the former inherited her father's house and lot corner of Church and Front

streets; the latter a parcel of ground on the west corner of Union and Canal streets. The remainder of his ch. settled in Albany. [*See Albany Families.*]

ALEXANDER, son of John, and Susanna Warmoet. Ch: Elisabeth, bp. Dec. 11, 1775.

DUNCAN.

JOHN, merchant, had a house and farm called the " Hermitage," now owned by Hon. Charles Stanford. He d. May 5, 1791, a. 69ys. His wife was Martha March. Ch. bp: George, Oct. 14, 1779; Mary, Aug. 31, 1784; *Richard*.

RICHARD, son of John, was a Capt. in the British army, under Sir John Johnson. Had a dau. Mary Ann, who d. in Schenectady, Jan. 8, 1816, a. 23ys. His wife Mary d. Sept. 8, 1815, a. 45ys. Capt. Duncan d. Feb. —, 1819.

DUNLAP.

JAMES, and Catrien McDarmon Ch. bp: James, Dec. 25, 1767; William, December 31, 1770.

DUPUYS.

JACOB, and Catharina Cantine. Ch: Johannes Cantine, bp. Aug. 21, 1785.

DURKEE.

ASA, and Cornelia Vosburgh. Ch: Catharina, b. Sept. 19, 1793.

DURYEE.

GEORGE, of New Amsterdam, m. Elisabeth Rynex, Dec. 10, 1793. Ch. b: John Van Leuren, March 3, 1794; William Rynex, June 25, 1796; Geertruy, June 28, 1798; James, Feb. 13, 1802.

DU TRIEUX.

See Truax.

EADES.

JOSEPH, and Grace ...... Ch. bp: Ann, Aug. 4, 1765; Joseph, Aug. 23, 1768.

EASTERLY.

MARTINUS, of Clifton Park, m. Ruth, dau. of Jillis Van Vorst, Jr., Feb. 5, 1793.

EBERHART.

JOHAN, and Maria Johnson. Ch: Johan Frederick, bp. Jan. 2, 1782.

ECKER.

JACOB, and Neeltje, dau. of Johannes Fort. Ch: Rebecca, bp. Jan. 20, 1773.

JOHANNES, of Helderbergh, and Dirkje Vrooman. Ch. bp: Jacob, July 29, 1779; Barent, Feb. 16, 1781; Nicholas, June 2, 1783; Adam Vrooman, b. June 9, 1785.

WILLIAM, and Hester Snyder. Ch: Catrina, bp. Nov. 1, 1784.

ADAM, m. Jannetie, dau. of David Frank of Schenectady, Oct. 30, 1785.

ADAM, and Elisabeth Fetherly, both of the Helderbergh, m. July 13, 1791.

ECKERSON.

JAN, of Schoharie, m. Maritje, dau. of Cornelis Slingerland. Ch: Thomas, b. July 14, 1725; Aegie, b. Nov. 9, 1726.

He m. secondly, Margarietje, dau. of Cornelis Viele, June 3, 1733. Ch: Margarietje, bp. July 21, 1734, m. Aarmanus Brouwer.

THOMAS (perhaps son of Jan), and Elisabeth Ecker. Ch: Willem, bp. Jan. 25, 1783.

CORNELIUS, and Rebecca, dau. of Staats Van Santvoord of Albany. Ch: Staats Van Santvoord, bp. Jan. 10, 1785.

EDICH.

HANS MICHAEL, and Eva ...... Ch: Margariet, bp. Feb. 1, 1713.

JACOB, and Catrina Frank. Ch: Elisabeth, bp. May 28, 1758; Annatje, bp. June 1, 1760.

EENKLUYS.

HANS JANSE, is worthy to be remembered as the donor of the Poor Pasture to the poor of Schenectady. In 1632 he was one of the Dutch West India Company's officers, who erected the Arms of the States General at a spot called *Kievit's Hoeck* (Saybrook), at the mouth of the Connecticut river. In July, 1648, on the occasion of Gov. Stuyvesant's visit to Rensselaerswyck, he was employed to clean the Heer Patroon's cannons, and to fire the salute. He was an ancient man in 1680, and apparently without relations in this country, and made the Deacons of the church his administrators and legatees, on condition that he should be supported in his old age and weakness. After his decease in 1683, the deacons applied to the Court of Albany for power to administrate upon his estate, saying that Eenkluys had been weakly for 13 years since 1670; that they had supported and buried him: the Court referred the matter back to the Court of Schenectady. The original quantity of land was 18 morgens, being that portion lying west of, or above the *Hansen* kil (now College brook); that portion lying east, or below the creek, called the *Boght*, was bought of Harmanus Van Slyck in 1806, for $1,750. The whole was sold in 1863 for about $10,000 to pay the debts incurred in building the present church edifice.

EGLINTON.

JOHN, and Catlyntje Dodd, both of Remsenbos, m. Nov. 29, 1790. Ch. b: Bartholomeus, Sept. 29, 1792; Thomas, July 14, 1796; Annatje, July 17, 1798.

ELLICE.

JAMES, Thomas, Alexander and Robert, merchants from London, were in business in Schenectady as early as 1768.

JAMES, m. Ann Adams. After his death she m. Joseph C. Yates, late Gov. of the State. Ch : Catharine Adams, b. Dec. 24, 1786.

ELLIS.

THOMAS, and Maria Van Driessen, m. April 1, 1764.

EMAN.

JOHN, and Margaret Dederick. Ch. b : Catharina, June 28, 1797; Margarieta, Oct. 20, 1799.

9

EMPIE.

ADAM, m. first Catrina Barber, dau. of Adam Smit (?), Feb. 5, 1727; secondly, Anna Maria Saltsman; made his will in 1782, then of "Stoneraby;" proved Dec. 8, 1783; spoke of wife Anna Maria, sons Johannes, Adam, step-son Willem Saltzman, and of his father Johannes. Ch. bp : Maria, b. May 17, 1727, m. Christoffel Felthousen; Anna, bp. July 27, 1729; *Johannes*, Oct. 3, 1731; Adam, May 5, 1734; Hendrik, Sept. 12, 1736.

JOHANNES, son of Adam, brewer, had a brewery on west corner of Union and Maiden Lane; moved to Montgomery county; m. first, Catrina, dau. of Henricus Wempel, Nov. 27, 1756, and secondly, Annatie Quackenbos, Dec. 9, 1768. Ch. bp : Annatie, May 29, 1757 ; Catrina, Jan. 21, 1759; Adam, March 30, 1760; Catarina, Sept. 24, 1769; Adam, March 10, 1771; Maria, Dec. 20, 1772; Elisabeth, Nov. 27, 1774; Johannes, May 27, 1776; Elisabeth, March 15, 1778; Adam, b. Sept. 5, 1785, graduated at Union College, and for many years rector of a church near Richmond, Va.

ERICHZON.

REINHARD, the fourth minister of the Dutch church of Schenectady from 1728 to 1736, came from Groningen, North Holland; d. in Freehold, N. J., 1764. He m. Maria Provost. Ch : Anna, bp. July 13, 1729; Engelina, (?), who m. Pieter Van Slyck.

GERARD, m. Anna, daughter of Owen Owens of Albany, Aug. 12, 1732. Ch.

b: Wilko, Sept. 13, 1733; Henrikus, Jan. 26, 1736; Annatje, Sept. 5, 1738, m. Charles Adams; *Johannes,* bp. Jan. 14, 1741.

JOHANNES, son of Gerard, and Annatje Van Antwerpen. Ch: Annatje, bp· May 30, 1773, m. Abraham Van Dyck.

JOHANNES, perhaps same as last, m. Willemptje Vrooman, widow, daughter of Abraham Groot, Oct 21, 1787. She d. April 2, 1832, a. 73ys., 2d. Ch. b: Gerrit, December 12, 1788; Willemptje, April 14, 1792; Catharina, June, 4, 1793; Gerrit, d. Sept. 22, 1836, a. 37ys., 10m., 20d.

JOHN, and Elisabeth Combs. Ch: William, b. Feb. 3, 1805.

ERNEST.
WILLIAM, and Lena Shutes. Ch. b: Elisabeth, Aug. 26, 1793; Mary, April 26, 1795.

ESLAN.
PRISKS, and Maria Lowisa Robeers. Ch: Lowis, bp. Aug. 17, 1778.

ESSELSTEYN.
See Ysselsteyn.

EVANS.
BENJAMIN, and Mary Beam (Behm). Ch: Mary, bp. Feb. 22, 1781; John, b. Jan. 4, 1790; Nathan, b. Dec. 5, 1795.

EBENEZER, and Sarah Nobel. Ch: Sarah, bp. Feb. 22, 1781.

NATHAN, and Catharina, Fulmer, Ch: John, b. May 30, 1789.

So. (Solomon?), an inhabitant of Schenectady in 1754.

EVERTSON.
JOHANNES, and Eleanor Krankheyt. Ch: Marytje, b. April 11, 1787.

EWING.
WILLIAM, had a lot on south side of Union street, east of Ferry street in 1765.

EZABEL.
CATRINA, (perhaps a colored woman) purchased a lot of the Dutch church in Front street, part of the burying ground, which she sold to Nicolaas Speck; this lot passed to Jno. McKinzie, to Ann McGregor, to William McGill, and in 1785 to Lewis Barhydt, in whose family it still remains.

FAIRLY.
JOHANNES, m. first Metje, dau. of Jan. Pieterse Melbie, July 2, 1724; and probably a dau. of Caleb Beck for his second wife. He had a lot in 1766, on the east side of Church street, south of Union street, adjoining his father-in-law Beck's lot, and opposite Jonathan Ogden's inn. Ch: Annatje, b. Oct. 15, bp. Nov. 6, 1724; Engeltie, b. May 25, bp. June 19, 1726, m. Philip Truax. Ch. bp: Maritje, April 4, 1728; *John;* Maria, May 28, 1732; Jacob, June 2, 1734; Caleb, Dec. 7, 1735; Margarietje, Oct. 9, 1737.

JOHN, son of Johannes, m. Elisabeth, dau. of Simon Toll. He made his will Sept. 8, 1815, proved July 8, 1816; spoke of wife and children, but only of Margaret Groot and Maria Young by name. Ch. bp: Hester, Dec. 18, 1757, m. Hendrick Van Petten; Annatje, Aug. 21, 1760, m. Nicolaas S. Van Petten; Maria, m. Benjamin Young; Alida, Feb. 17, 1765, m. Frederic S. Van Petten; Margarita, Sept. 2, 1766, m. first, Samuel Clement, and secondly, ... Groot.

FAIRMAN.
JOHN, and Elisabeth Robertson. Ch: Hugh, bp. Nov. 7, 1781.

FAULKNER.
JEREMIAS, and Hannah Richard. Ch: Samuel, bp. Aug. 18, 1766.

FARLOW.
CHARLES, and Mary Farlow. Ch: Elisabeth, bp. Nov. 15, 1757.

FARNSWORTH.
AARON, m. Catlyntje Veeder, Dec. 24, 1797. She d. Dec. 25, 1842, a. 72ys. Ch. b: John, June 1, 1798; Nancy, June 15, 1800.

FARQUASON.
MICHAEL, and Ann Little. Ch. bp: *Little*, Oct. 30, 1768; Eleanor, Feb. 9, 1784.

LYTLE, son of Michael, m. Maria Magdalena Pulver. Ch. b: Michael, April 15, 1789; Lidia, July 15, 1792.

FARREL.
JOHN, trader, had house and lot in 1771, on west side of Ferry, between Liberty and Union streets, m. Rachel, dau. of Isaac Vrooman, Nov. 19, 1767. Ch. bp: *Kennedy*, Oct. 9, 1768; Dorothea, Sept. 23, 1770, m. William Van Vredenbergh.

KENNEDY, son of John, m. Anna, dau. of Johannes Peek. She d. Dec. 13, 1832, a. 61ys.; he d. a little before Oct. 23, 1796. Ch: Rachel, bp. Nov. 12, 1786. Ch. b: Eva, Aug. 13, 1789; Johannes, Sept. 25, 1791; Isaac Vrooman, May 3, 1793, d. in Dover, O., June 26, 1842; Sarah, April 18, 1795; Kennedy, Oct. 5, 1796.

FARSEY (FERRY).
THOMAS, and Hanna, dau. of Daniel Toll. Ch: Daniel, bp. April 14, 1751.

FELING (FELINCK).
PIETER, widower, m. Eva, dau. of Cornelis Viele, June 12, 1724. He was the schoolmaster of the village and had a house and lot on north side of State street, about midway between Ferry and Church streets. Ch: Debora, b. May 5, 1725; Elisabet, b. April 24, 1727, m. Joseph Flansburgh; Wilhelmus, b. June 1, 1729; Anna, bp. Nov. 28, 1731, m. Pieter Warmoet; Catharina, b. Jan. 26, 1734, m. Arent Smith (Arrowsmith); *Wilm*, b. Aug. 13, 1736; *Cornelis*, bp. April 29, 1739; Nicolaas, bp. June 21, 1741; Jannetje, b. Feb. 24, 1746, m. Jacobus Van Gyseling.

WILLEM, son of Pieter, m. Jannetje, dau. of Johannes Van Vranken of "Nistoungjoone," Dec. 3, 1762. He settled in Clifton Park. Ch. bp: Annatje, May 22, 1753, m. Dirk Van Vranken; Eva, May 19, 1765, m. Jonathan Powell; Pieter, May 20, 1768.

CORNELIS, son of Pieter, of Clifton Park, m. Susanna Ted (Teed, Tid). Ch. bp: Jannetje, Aug. 22, 1779; Elisabeth, Feb. 17, 1781; Pieter, Jan. 19, 1783; Keziah, b. Sept. 28, 1787, m. John Clark of Niskayuna, d. Jan. 16, 1867; Hannah, b. Jan. 3, 1794.

FELTER.

PHILIP, and Margarita Schoein. Ch: Philip, bp. Aug. 23, 1763.

FELTHOUSEN (FELDHAUSEN).

CHRISTOFFEL, from Hamburgh, m. Maria, dau. of Adam Empie, April 3, 1757. In 1790 he owned a lot on west side of Maiden Lane, between Union and Liberty streets. He d. in 1799; his wife d. May 2, 1760, a. 32ys., 10m., 16d. Ch. bp: Catarina, Oct. 8, 1758; Maria, April 27, 1760.

CHRISTOFFEL, (same as the last), m. Annatje, dau. of Jan Dellamont, June 4, 1763. Ch. bp: Johannes, Jan. 15, 1764; *Jacob Delamont*, July 28, 1765; Maria, June 14, 1767, m. Thomas Wilkie; Hendrick, June 18, 1769; Catarina, Nov. 1, 1772, m. Willem Pieterse.

CHRISTOFFEL, (same as last), m. Sarah Hoogteling, May 28, 1775. Ch. bp: An-

natje, Aug. 25, 1776; *Daniel*, Oct. 18, 1778; Geertruy, July 29, 1781; Jacobus Hoogteling, b. April 25, 1785.

JACOB, son of Christoffel, m. Cathlyntje Young, April 28, 1787. Ch. b: Annatje, Dec. 21, 1787; Annatje, Dec. 9, 1788; Jacob Dellamont, Jan. 11, 1793; Christoffel, April 13, 1795; Rebecca, Sept. 1, 1797; John, Aug. 11, 1799; William, Nov. 5, 1801; Hendrick, Jan. 10, 1804.

DANIEL, son of Christoffel, m. Rachel Whittaker, Aug. 24, 1799.

FERGUSON.

JOHN, and Jannet McGue (McKown, McGowen, McCoun). Ch. bp: James, Nov. 17, 1779; Catrien, June 5, 1782; John, Feb. 2, 1784; Catharine, b. April 2, 1786; Elisabeth, b. Feb. 7, 1793.

FERO.

WILHELMUS, and Geertruy Van Vranken. Ch. b: Margarieta, Nov. 12, 1794; David, Feb. 28, 1796; Francyntje, Sept. 5, 1799.

FERRIO.

ALEXANDER, and Maria Marcot. Ch: Catrien, bp. Jan. 31, 1779.

FERRIS.

LEWIS, and Prudence Pangburn. Ch. bp: John, Feb. 6, 1779.

FETHERLY.

JOHANNES, of Helderbergh, and Maria Paapsteyn. Ch: Margariet, b. Feb. 5, 1786.

PHILIP, and Rebecca Ramsey. Ch: Rebecca, b. Feb. 8, 1787.

FILKINS.

JAMES, and Anna Brown. Ch: Benjamin, b. March 19, 1796.

FILLEBAGH.

BALTUS, and Elisabeth Smith. Ch: Daniel, b. Feb. 10, 1787.

FISHER.

JOHN, and Molly Keely. Ch: John, b. Oct. 7, 1790. [*See also Visscher.*]

FITSGERALD.

THOMAS, and Elisabeth Conklin. Ch. b: William, Aug. 26, 1774; Jannetje, Oct. 16, 1775; Mary, Nov. 1778.

JOHN, and Sarah Rutherford. Ch: Nelly, bp. Oct. 27, 1781; Catarina, Oct. 18, 1783. Ch. b: John, July 11, 1786; James, April 23, 1793; Eleanor, March 25, 1798.

FLAGG.

JOHANNES, and Catarina Creemer. Ch: Maria Susanna, bp. Oct. 22, 1781.

FLANDER.

JACOB and Elisabeth Louer. Ch. bp: Ernest, Feb. 12, 1764; George Wolfgang, Jan. 26, 1765.

FLANSBURGH.

JOSEPH, son of Mattheus of Albany, widower, m. Elisabeth, dau. of Pieter Feling, Nov. 8, 1749. Ch. bp: *Dirk; Willem,* Jan. 16, 1757; *Anthony,* Jan.

4, 1759; Eva, Nov. 22, 1761; Mattheus, March 27, 1763; *Nicolaas,* June 17, 1764; Maria, Feb. 9, 1766; Cornelis Sept. 11, 1774.

DIRK, son of Joseph, and Alida Vanderheyden. Ch. b: Joseph, Nov. 15, 1781; Frans, May 15, 1785, d. March 11, 1850.

ANTHONY, son of Joseph, m. Susanna Van Alen, March 2, 1788. Ch. b: Jannetje, Nov. 7, 1788; Maria, April 16, 1790.

WILLEM, son of Joseph, and Annatje Luke (Loap). Ch. b: Elisabeth, Oct. 28, 1788; Johannes, April 21, (*sic*), 1790.

NICOLAAS, son of Joseph, and Sophia Schermerhorn. Ch: Joseph, b. April 23, 1794; Jannetje, bp. May 1, 1796.

MATTHEW, and Maria Clute, both of Normanskil, m. Sept., 1792.

FLINN.

JOHN, and Catarina Geyselbergh. Ch: James, bp. Oct. 18, 1775.

FLOOD.

PATRICK, from Clonmel, Ireland, and Eleanor Mahar, from Cork, Ireland, both living in Maquaasland, were m. Sept. 25, 1743. Ch: Mary, bp. Feb. 24, 1745.

FODDER.

ISAAC, from Philipstown, m. Eva Buchanan, April 2, 1794. Ch. b: Margariet, Jan. 27, 1795; John, Aug. 4, 1796; Stephen, June 7, 1798; Polly Buchanan, Sept. 20, 1805 (4 ?).

FOLGER.

THOMAS, b. in Islington, Old England, dwelling in Currysbosch, and Abigail Folger, b. in Nantucket, were m. at Saratoga. Ch : Benjamin, b. Oct. 28, 1785.

FOLMER.

JOHANNES, Jr., and Catarina Straat. Ch : Annatje, bp. Feb. 6, 1778; Catharina, b. Aug. 26, 1802.

FONDA.

JILLIS DOUWESE, was in Beverwyck as early as 1654; his wife was Hester. In 1664 Hester Douwese, assisted by her son *Douw Jillise,* and dau. Greetien Jillise, sold to Jan Coster Van Aecken two distiller's kettles for 400 guilders seewant. She was then probably a widow. In 1666 she was the widow of Barent Gerritse.

•DOUW JILLISE, son of the last, m. Rebecca. He owned land at *Lubberde land* (Troy), in 1676; d. Nov. 24, (27), 1700. Ch : Jan, b. 1668; *Jillis;* Isaac, bp. March 9, 1684; Rebecca, bp. March 17, 1786; Anna, bp. Feb. 2, 1690; Claas (?). [*See Albany Families.*]

JILLIS, son of Douw Jillise of Albany, m. Rachel, dau. of Pieter Winne of Albany, Dec. 11, 1695. He removed from Albany to Schenectady about 1700; was a gunstocker; made his will Sept. 8, 1737, his wife then living, and the following Ch : Douw, Pieter, Abraham, Jacob, Eva, wife of Joseph Yates, Tanneke, wife of Johannes Clute, Lena and Re-

becca. Ch. bp : Douwe, in Albany, Aug 23, 1696; Tanneken, in Albany March 9, 1698, m. Johannes Clute; *Douw,* Sept. 1, 1700; Rebecca, Dec. 25, 1702; Lena, April 22, 1705, m.;Pieter Brouwer; Eva, Oct. 16, 1707, m. Joseph Yates; *Pieter,* March 6, 1711; Sara, May 3, 1713, m. Jacobus Van Vorst; *Abraham,* July 17, 1715; Rachel, March 28, 1719; *Jacob,* Feb. 11, 1722.

DOUW, son of Jillis, m. Maritje Vrooman, dau. of Adam, October 29, 1725. " He removed from Schenectady, and settled at Caughnawaga about the year 1751 (the same year in which Harmen Visscher settled below); he was an aged widower (May 22, 1780), and resided at this time in a large stone dwelling. His three sons, John, Jillis (major) and Adam lived in the neighborhood. He was slain by Sir John Johnson's Indians, May 22, 1780, and his house plundered and burned. John and Adam were made prisoners and carried to Canada; their houses were burnt." *Simm's Hist. Schoharie county.* Ch. bp : *Jillis,* b. March 24, 1727; Adam, bp. Nov. (?), 1730; Adam, Oct. 29, 1732; Margrietje, Nov. 10, 1734, m. Barent M. Wemple; Adam, Dec. 26, 1736, d. Nov. 8, 1808; Pieter, Jan. 1739; Johannes, March 8, 1741, d. Feb. 19, 1815.

DOUWE, (probably the last), widower, and Debora, dau. of Johannes Veeder, and widow of Reyer Wemple, both dwelling in Maquaasland, were m. Aug. 19, 1757.

PIETER, son of Jillis, m. Maria, dau. of Daniel Van Antwerpen, June 27 1735. Ch : Rachel, bp. Oct. 19, 1735.

ABRAHAM, son of Jillis, carpenter, m. first, Maria, dau. of Abraham Mebie, July 30 (31), 1746; secondly, Susanna, dau. of Alexander Glen, Feb. 22, 1755; and thirdly, Rachel Vrooman, widow Wimp, Nov. 22, 1774. His first wife d. May 8, 1753; the second wife d. March 21, 1773, a. 49ys., 6m.; the third wife d. Aug. 5, 1791, and he d. Feb. 13, 1805, aged 89ys., 7m., 27d. (22). Abraham Fonda lived in house No. 27 Front street, built in 1752, and now occupied by his great grandson, Nicholas Yates. Ch. b : Rachel, Sept. 14, 1748, m. Jesse De Graaf; Johannes, Nov. 8, 1750, d. Dec. 2, 1751; Annatje, Oct. 18, 1752, d. May 13, 1753; Jellis, Oct. 20, 1755, d. Aug. 31, 1756; Rebecca, June 7, 1757, m. first, Nicholas Yates, secondly, Cornelis Van Vranken, d. Mar. 7, 1846, a. 89ys.; *Jellis*, Oct. 25, 1759 ; *Jacob Glen*, Aug. 29, 1761 ; Alexander, Sept. 12, 1763, d. Aug. 24, 1776; Maria, Nov. 15, 1765, d. Jan. 19, 1772.

JACOB, son of Jellis, m. first, Maria, dau. of Nicolaas Van Petten, April 29, 1748; secondly, Margarieta, widow of Pieter Bosie, Nov. 4, 1758. He made his will May 1806, proved Nov. 9, 1813, then spoke of son Jellis and dau. Rebecca and Rachel. Ch. bp: Rachel, Oct. 10, 1748, m. Philip Viele; *Jillis*, Jan. 13, 1751; Rebecca, Dec. 26, 1753, m. Gerrit Van Antwerpen.

Maj. JELLIS, son of Douw, early settled at Caughnawaga, m. Jannetie, dau. of Hendrick Vrooman, the banns having been proclaimed Jan. 16, 1750. He d. June 23, 1791; she d. Feb. 2, 1804, a. 77ys., 3m., 23d. Ch. bp: Margarita, Dec. 12, 1756; Douwe, d. Sept. 11, 1815, a. 30ys.; Henry, d. April 4, 1832, a. 49ys., 16d.; Margarita, b. 1764, m. John R. Yates. *

PIETER, son of Jellis, m. Alida, dau. of Matthys Nak of Albany, and widow of J. A. Truax, Aug. 10, 1757. He was a tanner, lived on the southerly corner of State street and Mill lane, and had his tan vats on the rear of his lot; made his will 1771, proved Sept. 25, 1775, and spoke of his wife Alida, son Jellis, dau. Angenetie, and step-dau. Janneke Truex. Ch. bp: Gillis, July 2, 1758, d. May 4, 1830; Angenetie, March 30, 1760, m. Robert H. Wendell, d. April 1, 1828.

ISAAC H. (son of Hendrick, of Albany ?), and Susanna Van Den Bergh. Ch. bp: Henderick, Oct. 10, 1771; Cornelis, Jan. 11, 1775. [*See Albany Families*].

Capt. JELLIS, son of Jacob, m. first, Maria Mynderse, Nov. 5, 1774; secondly, Catrina, dau. of Hendricus Veeder, about 1783. Ch. b : Jacob, bp. Sept. 5, 1784 ; Jacob, b. March 22, 1786; Hendricus, Aug. 20, 1788; Gerrit, Nov. 5, 1790 ; Christoffel, March 15, 1793; Christoffel, Aug 28, 1795; Maria, June 11, 1798.

JACOB, son of Abraham, m. Aletta Willet, April 4, 1784, in Albany. He d. in West Glenville, Dec. 8, 1859, a. 98ys.; she d. Dec. 10, 1838, a. 82ys. Ch: Abraham, bp. Jan. 30, 1785; Elbert Willet, b. March 4, 1794; Susanna, bp. Sept. 18, 1796.

ISAAC, of Fonda's bush, and Catharina Vedder of Niskayuna, m. Feb. 12, 1796.

JELLIS, son of Abraham, m. Elisabeth, dau. of Christoffel Yates. He d. Aug. 27, 1834; She d. Jan. 23, 1824. Ch. b: Alexander Glen, Aug. 17, 1785, graduate of Union College, and for many years a physician of this city d. Mar. 4, 1869; Jannetie, Oct. 28, 1786; Susanna, Sept. 23, 1788; Christopher Yates, a doctor of medicine, d. in Claiborne, Ala., Aug. 26, 1845; Jane Helen, May 4, 1793; Jane Helen, March 1, 1795, m. Rev. Nathan N. Whiting, d. at Williamsburgh, N. Y., April 30, 1852; Catharina, Sept. 27, 1796; Annatje, June 11, 1798; James, Nov. 1, 1800; Eliza, Feb. 2, 1803; Mary Austin, Sept. 12, 1804.

DOUWE JACOBSE, and Machtelt Lansing, both of the *Boght*, m. Sept. 20, 1788. [*See also Albany Families.*]

FORT (LA FORT, VANDERVORT, LIBERTEE).

JAN, and Margriet Rinckhout. He made his will Nov. 3, 1706, proved Oct. 3, 1707, in which he made mention of the following Ch: *Isaac*, bp. in Albany, Sept. 3, 1699; *Johannes*, eldest son; Anna, bp. April 5, 1702; *Abraham;*

Daniel, bp. in Albany, Sept. 11, 1687; *Nicolaas;* Jacob; Maria, wife of Johannes Vedder.

JOHANNES, son of Jan, of Niskayuna, m. Rebecca, dau. of Daniel Van Antwerpen. Ch. bp : Johannes, in Albany, Oct. 12, 1713; Johannes, Feb. 10, 1717; Maria, in Albany, April 7, 1715, m. Gerrit Van Vranken; *Daniel*, May 1, 1719; Abraham, May 27, 1721; Annatje, Aug. 31, 1723; Annatje, b. June 7, 1725, m. Johannes Van Vranken; Margarita, in Albany, Jan. 21, 1728; Neeltje, —, 1730, m. Jacob Ecker; Elisabeth, May 21, 1732.

ABRAHAM, son of Jan, freeholder of "Schaatkooke" in 1720, m. Anna Barber, dau. of Frederic Clute. Ch. bp : Johannes, April 27, 1717; Francyntje, Jan. 10, 1719; Frederick, in Albany, April 9, 1721; Eva, Jan. 25, 1724, m. Jacob Viele; Jacob, b. March 30, 1727. [*See Albany Families.*]

NICOLAAS, son of Jan, of Niskayuna, and Maritie, dau. of Daniel Van Antwerpen of the *Woestine*, m. Feb. 11, 1720. Ch. b : Johannes, bp. May 25, 1723; *Johannes*, b. June 14, 1725; Daniel, Mar. 13, 1727; Margarieta, May 15, 1729, m. Pieter Bosie; *Simon*, April 24, 1734.

ISAAC, son of Jan, of "Schaatkooke," m. Jacomyntje Viele, daughter of Lewis. Ch : Margarieta, bp. Feb. 13, 1732. [*See also Albany Families.*]

DANIEL, son of Johannes, of "Genistagione," m. Sara Reyly of New York, now residing in Schenectady, May 20, 1749. Ch: *Johannes*, bp. April 1, 1750.

SIMON, son of Nicolaas, of "Onestoung-joone," m. Annatje Van Vranken of the same place, October 22, 1762. Ch. bp: Ryckert, b. Aug. 12, 1766; Johannes, bp. Aug. 6, 1769, d. Dec. 14, 1838, in Niskayuna. His wife Gertrude d. Jan. 17, 1856, in her 80th year; Maria, Sept. 16, 1772; *Daniel*, Feb. 18. 1776, d. Jan. 15, 1839, in Niskayuna; His wife Eleanor, d. Dec. 6, 1856, in her 77th year.

JOHANNES, son of Nicolaas, and Marytje, dau. of Claas Van Vranken, both of Genistagioene, m. Nov. 24, 1750. Ch. bp: Maria, July 7, 1751; *Nicolaas*, in Albany, Jan. 14, 1753; Daniel, Feb. 16, 1755; Daniel, Aug. 7, 1757; Geertruy, July 22, 1759, m. Eldert Visscher; Simon, March 14, 1762; Elisabeth, Jan. 22, 1764.

HARMEN, son of Jacob, of Albany, and Rebecca Van Woert. Ch : Margarita, bp. Sept. 4, 1768. [*See Albany Families.*]

JOHANNES, son of Daniel Janse, m. Dorothea Hagedoorn, May 7, 1773. Ch. bp: Abraham, Nov. 14, 1773; Jannetje, Jan. 7, 1776, m. Jacob Stiers.

NICOLAAS, (son of Johannes ?), and Catarina Van den Bergh. Ch : Maria, bp. May 18, 1781; Abraham, b. Ap. 18, 1783.

DANIEL, (son of Simon ?) and Annatje Visscher, both born and living at "Nestigaune," m. Jan. 28, 1787.

FRANK.

DAVID, m. Margarita Carol, Dec. —, 1762. Ch. bp : Maria, June 10, 1764;

Jannetie, Apr. 17, 1768, m. Adam Ecker; *Martinus*, Sept. 9, 1770; Susanna, May 9. 1773, m. Frederic Reese.

MARTINUS, son of David. m. Rebecca, dau. of Jillis Van Vorst, Feb. 20, 1796. He d. Dec. 1, 1852. Ch. b : Margarieta, Jan. 29, 1796; David, Dec. 29, 1797; Jellis, Oct. 18, 1799; Abraham, Aug. 18, 1801; Abraham Volleweyser, May 12, 1803; Ann, April 27, 1805; Adam, March 3, 1807.

FRANSIKKEL.

PHILIP, m. Annatje, dau. of Arent Stevens. Ch. bp : John, Sept. 8, 1776; Mary, Oct. 18, 1778; Catarina, Feb. 18, 1781; Fanny, Aug. 23, 1783. Ch. b : Margarietje, Aug. 31, 1785; Geertruy, Sept. 30, 1787; Willem, Oct. 22, 1789; Joan, May 6, 1792; Margarita, bp. Oct. 4, 1794; Arent, b. July 26, 1796.

FRAZIER.

WILLIAM, and Mary Long. Ch : John Long, bp. Nov. 24, 1781; William, b. June 27, 1785.

JOHN, and Maria Scherp. Ch : Elisabeth, bp. May 20, 1782.

GEORGE, and Anna McPherson. Ch : Mary, bp. Nov. 1, 1781; George b. Jan. 29, 1786.

FREANOR.

JOHN, and Martha Springer. Ch : Catharine, b. Nov. 12, 1786.

FREDERICK.

JACOB, and Margaret Jong. Ch : Pieter, bp. March 12, 1770.

10

MICHAEL, and Catarina Wagenaar. Ch: Catarina, bp. Oct. 27, 1779.

THEWALD, and Margarita Merkle. Ch: Catarina, bp. Feb. 25, 1780.

FRANCIS, of Remsenbos, and Susanna Gresaart. Ch: Catharina, b. June 27, 1785.

PETER, and Elisabeth Marlet. Ch: Francis, b. July 20, 1788.

FREEMAN.

ROBERT, and Maritie Leleyn (Le Nain, Olin). Robert Freeman and wife, of Schoharie, joined the church in 1756. Ch: Neeltie, bp. Nov. 10, 1722, m. Andreas Ward; Soffia, b. July 7, 1726; Richard, bp. ——, 1730; *John.*

JOHN, from Dublin, m. Engeltie, dau. of Daniel Van Antwerpen, Nov. 4, 1748. Ch. bp: Elisabet, May 4, 1749; Maria, Dec. 23, 1750; John, Nov. 17, 1754; Daniel, Dec. 19, 1756.

JOHN, son of Robert, and Rebecca Vine, both of Rensselaerswyck, m. June 3, 1768. Ch. bp: Maria, April 11, 1769; Elisabeth, Jan. 24, 1771; Robert, March 3, 1773; Robert, March 3, 1774; Sarah, July 5, 1775; Engeltie, April 22, 1778; Rebecca, Jan. 8, 1781; John, Jan. 11, 1784.

JOHN, and Annatje Bratt. Ch: Daniel, bp. Sept. 2, 1781.

RICHARD, and Hanna Lighthall. Ch. bp: Ann, July 1, 1783; Sara, Jan. 16, 1785. Ch. b: Mary, July 25, 1786;

Elisabeth, May 20, 1788; Catharine, June 25, 1790; James, Sept. 15, 1791; Richard, May 14, 1793; Abraham, Dec. 31, 1795; Ann, April 10, 1801.

FREEMEYER.

MICHAEL, and Jane Patty (Jenny Potter). Ch. b: John, March 15, 1790; Maria, May 12, 1794; Debora, April 20, 1798.

FREER.

CORNELIUS, and Rachel Weller. Ch: Sarah, b. Oct. 16, 1798.

FREERMAN.

BARNHARDUS, the second minister of Schenectady, was born at Gilhuis, Holland, served the church 1700–1705, then removed to Flatbush, L. I., where he was minister of the church until his death in 1741. He m. Margarita Van Schaick in New York, Aug. 25, 1705.

FRELIGH.

JACOB, and Christina Dillenbach. Ch: Lena, bp. Feb. 29, 1790.

HENRY, a citizen of Schenectady in 1791.

FRIES.

JOHN, and Catarina Coens. Ch: Nicholas, bp. March 3, 1782.

FRISBIE.

NATHANIEL, and Sally Herrick. She d. about Jan. 24, 1790. Ch: Sally, b. Jan. 8, 1783.

FRITSCHER.

COENRAAD, and Elisabeth Loucks. Ch.

bp: Catharina, Dec. 21, 1746; Elisabet, Feb. 19, 1749; *Adam,* Jan. 6, 1751.

ADAM, son of Coenraad, and Martha Witon. Ch: Elisabeth, bp. Ap. 21, 1776.

FRYER.

THOMAS, and Brydged .... Ch: Jane, bp. Jan. 22, 1758.

FULLER.

SAMUEL, b. in New England, m. Annatje, dau. of Willem Hall, December 7, 1763. Ch: Annatje, b. April 8, 1771; *Jeremiah.*

JEREMIAH, son of Samuel, m. Mary Kendall, Jan. 23, 1791. Ch. b: Samuel, Nov. 20, 1791; William Kendall, Nov. 24, 1792; Samuel, April 16, 1795; Ann, May 8, 1797, d. June 27, 1798; George Kendall, Jan. 29, 1799; Amelia Ann, March 13, 1801, d. Oct. 27, 1871; Ann, April 21, 1803; Richard, Oct. 28, 1804, d. May 15, 1837; Edward, February 19, 1807; Charles, April 1, 1809; Henry, Feb. 2, 1811; James, July 24, 1814; Elisabeth, June 11, 1816; Robert, Feb. 14, 1822.

GADDES (GEDDES?).

JOSEPH, and Ann Glen. Ch: Johannes Sanderse, bp. Dec. 17, 1769.

GAEF.

JAN, and Emmetje Bosie. Ch: Sarah, April 24, 1720.

GARDINIER.

JACOB, and Dirkje Van der Werken. Ch: Rachel, bp. March 4, 1755.

JAMES, and Anna Proper. Ch: Andries, b. Sept. 28, 1784.

SAMUEL, and Rebecca Van Deusen. Ch: Melchior, b. Aug. 17, 1785.

GARDENER..

SOLOMON, an inhabitant of Schenectady in 1754.

GALLY (GAWLEY).

ROBERT, m. Catharina, dau. of Jellis Yates. Ch. b: Adriana, April 30, 1798; George Brekey, Feb. 10, 1800; Elisabeth, Dec. 30, 1801; Jellis Yates, June 21, 1803; Hellen, Sept. 28, 1804; Rebecca, Nov. 3, 1806; Christopher Jellis, Sept. 9, 1809; Cathaline, Dec. 15, 1812; Harriet, Jan. 17, 1814.

GERRITSE.

FREDERICK, yeoman, and Elisabeth Carstense were residents of Schenectady in 1687. On Sept. 13, 1689, he conveyed to Myndert Wemp 8 or 10 acres of land at *Maalwyck* and *Benten* Island, formerly belonging to Benjamin Roberts.

GILBERT.

JOHN, and Ann Cox. Ch: William, bp. August 3, 1793, at which date the mother was dead.

ABIJAH, and wife Mary, inhabitants of Schenectady in 1795.

GLASSFORD.

WILLIAM, and Sarah Little. Ch: John, bp. July 15, 1783.

GLEN.

SANDER LEENDERTSE, a Scotchman, was in the service of the West India Company at Fort Nassau, on the Delaware, in 1633; received a grant of land there, and prepared to build in 1651, but was prevented by the violence of the Sweeds; 1646 received patent for a lot in Smit's valley, New Amsterdam; also sold his *huysing ende erve gelegen in de Smits Valey opt Eyland Manhatans daer tegenwordig lauris Cornelise Van Welin woont*..... *voor de somme van twee duysent gul.*; was then called *Coopman Van Beverwyck*; owned lands, house and cattle at Gravesend in 1664; obtained patent for lands in Schenectady 1665, which he called *Scotia*, and became his future residence; he likewise owned real estate in divers parts of Albany, and was a considerable trader with the Indians. His wife was Catalyn Dongan, (Doncassen) sister of Willem Teller's first wife, and perhaps of Pieter Lookerman's wife. He d. Nov. 13, 1685; his wife d. Aug. 12, 1684. Ch: *Jacob; Sander*, b. 1647; *Johannes*, b. Nov. 5, 1648.

JACOB, eldest son of Sander Leendertse, trader, settled in Albany. In 1680 he owned a house lot on the south side of State street, west of Pearl street, which afterwards passed to Harmanus Wendel, who m. his dau. Anna. He d. Oct. 2, 1685, as appears by the following entry in the deacon's book: "*In Albanie, Oct. 2 anno 1685, is myn broeder* Jacob Sanderse [Glen] *dieiaken in den here ontslapen s'naghs ontrent een winnigh naer 2 uren*

tussen Vridag en Saterdagh." His wife Catharina, dau. of Jan Thomase Van Witbeek, after his death, m. Jonas Volkertse Douw, April 24, 1696   Ch: *Johannes*, b. 1675, d. 1707; Anna, b. 1677, m. Harmanus Wendel; Jacob, b. 1679; Helena, bp. Nov. 21, 1683, living unmarried in 1707; Sander bp. Nov. 15, 1685.

Capt. SANDER, son of Sander Leendertse, settled at Schenectady; made his will July 19, 1690, and letters of administration were issued to Antje his widow, Feb. 20, 1696; left his linen and woolen clothes and weapons to the sons of his two brothers Jacob and Johannes; to Sander, son of his brother Johannes, his gun; if his wife marry again, she was to have half the property, the other half to go to his brothers children, &c., from which it would seem that Capt. Glen left no children, and that his death occurred about the year 1695. He was Justice of the Peace for Albany County. His wife was Antje, dau. of Jan Barentse Wemp; after his death, she m. Abraham Groot, April 15, 1696.

Capt. JOHANNES, son of Sander Leendertse, settled in Schenectady; m. first, Annatie, dau. of Jan Peek, May 2d, 1667. She d. Dec. 19, 1690 (1689 ?); he m. 2dly, Diwer, dau. of Evert Janse Wendel, and widow of Myndert Wemp, June 21, 1691, in Albany. She d. April 10, 1724; he d. Nov. 6, 1731. " He built the present Sanders mansion in Scotia, in 1713 and occupied the same until his death. His property was spared when Schenectady was burned, by order of the Governor of Canada, for kindness shown to French prisoners captured by the Mohawks." [Hon. John Sanders.] Ch. b : Catrina, March. 23, 1672, d. Feb. 15, 1731 ; Jacquemina, May 9, 1674, m. Jacobus Van Dyck, d. Feb. 6, 1731 ; Sander, Nov. 30, 1676, is said to have d. at Madagascar, Dec. 17, 1696, a surgeon on shipboard ; Maria, March 21, 1678, m. Albert Vedder; Helena, Nov. 2, 1681, m. Jan Baptist Van Eps; Johannes, Nov. 28, 1683, d. Dec. 5, 1709 ; Jacob Sanderse,* Feb. 27, 1686 ; Anna, Dec. 19, 1688 ; *Jacob*, Dec. 29, 1691, d. Aug. 15, 1762 ; *Abraham*, bp. April 11, 1694 ; Margarietje (Maria ?) bp. July 1, 1696 ; Ephraim Wemp, b. Sept. 2, 1709, d. same day ; Susanna Wemp, b. Jan. 12, 1712, d. same day.

JOHANNES, son of Jacob, of Albany, m. Jannetie, dau. of Jan Janse Bleecker, Dec. 11, 1698, in Albany. He made his will in 1706, proved Oct. 4, 1707, spoke of wife Janneke, two sons Jacob Sanderse and Johannes, and dau. Catharina; also of younger brother Sander. Ch. bp : Catharina, Sept. 8, 1699, in Albany. m. Johannes Cuyler ; *Jacob Sanderse,* Oct. 17, 1703; Johannes, —, 1706, in Albany, a merchant; made will Sept. 20, 1769, proved March 31, 1770, gave half his estate to the four children of his late brother Jacob, viz : Johannes, Hendrick, Cornelis, and Jannetie Cuyler, wife of Abraham Cuyler ; and the other half to the four children of his sister Catharina, late wife of Johannes Cuyler, viz : Elsie, wife of Barent Ten Eyck, Jo-

* See Appendix.

hannes Cuyler, Jr., Cornelis Cuyler, Jr., and Jacob Cuyler.

SANDER, son of Jacob Sanderse, settled in Schenectady. He made his will May 3, 1750, his wife Rebecca then living, also Ch. Isaac, Catharina, Susanna, wife of Abraham Fonda, and Annatie. He m. Rebecca, dau. of Isaac Swits, Dec. 18, 1714, in Albany. He d. Nov. 2 (3), 1763 ; she d. Nov. 28, 1775. Ch. bp : Katrina, Oct. 16, 1715 ; *Jacob*, Dec. 8, 1717 ; Isaac, March 19, 1720 ; Susanna, Aug. 4, 1722, m. Abraham Fonda; Isaac, b. Jan. 10, 1725 ; Ariaantje, b. Nov. 17, 1727 ; Anna, bp. July 10, 1729.

JACOB, son of Johannes, Jr., of Albany, m. Elisabeth Cuyler, Dec. 29, 1732. He had a lot on the west corner of Steuben and Chapel streets, was buried in the church, April 16, 1746. Ch. bp. in Albany : Jannetie, Nov. 11, 1733 ; *Johannes*, July 2, 1735 ; Elsie, April 8, 1737 ; *Hendrick*, July 13, 1739 ; *Cornelis*, b. Nov. 1, 1741 ; Jannetie, bp. Oct. 27, 1743, and was buried in the church, Jan. 27, 1755.

JACOB, son of Alexander, m. Volkie, dau. of Jan Barentse Wemple, and widow of Barent H. Vrooman. He was recently deceased April 16, 1749. Ch : Jacob, bp. April 16, 1749.

Col. JOHANNES, son of Jacob Glen, and Elisabeth Cuyler, was quartermaster in the French and Revolutionary wars, stationed at Schenectady; in 1775 bought lands on the Hudson above Fort Edward, of Daniel Parke, which tract was afterwards called *Glen's* Falls. He built and occupied the house now owned by Mr. Swortfiguer in Washington street. He m. Catharina, dau. of Simon Johannese Veeder. She d. Oct 22, 1799, a. 57ys., 9m., 26d.; he d. Sept. 23, 1828, a. 93ys. Ch. bp: *Jacob*, Jan. 25, 1761; Simon, Feb. 26, 1764; Catarina, Sept. 22, 1765, m. John J. Van Rensselaer; Johannes, July 22, 1770; *Simon*, Nov. 3, 1773; Elisabeth, June 15, 1777.

HENDRICK, son of Jacob Glen and Elisabeth Cuyler, m. Elisabeth, dau. of Johannes Vischer, Dec. 9, 1762. He d. January 6, 1814; she d. May 17, 1809. Henry Glen was for some years a trader in company with his brother Johannes, and Jacobus Teller. During the Revolutionary war he was deputy Quartermaster General, stationed at Schenectady, and member of Congres 1794–1802. In 1800 he lived on the south corner of Washington and Union streets; about 1802 this property was sold to James Murdoch to pay his debts, and he removed to a house then standing on lot No. 5 Front street, where he died. Ch. bp: Elisabeth, Aug. 6, 1763, m. Willem Van Ingen of Albany; Catarina, Aug. 17, 1766, d. Sept. 10, 1766; Catarina, March 6, 1768, m. Rev. Jacob Sickles, d. about Nov., 1797; Jannetie, May 12, 1771; Jacob Sanderse, Aug. 22, 1773; Johannes Vischer, Jan. 8, 1775, an officer in the U. S. army, d. June 19, 1831; *Cornelius*, b. June 5, 1785, d. Ap. 25 (?), 1822.

CORNELIUS, son of Jacob Glen and Elisabeth Cuyler of Watervliet, m. Eli-sabeth ......; made his will Aug. 28, 1809, spoke of wife Elisabeth, brothers John and Henry, sister Jane, wife of Abraham Cuyler, nephews and nieces, but not of his own children. He d. Mar. 21, 1810, leaving considerable estate to his relatives above mentioned; his widow d. Nov. —, 1812.

JACOB, son of Col. John Glen, in 1795 was in business at, and owned the Glens falls; removed to Chambly, Canada, as early as 1806, where he d. Nov. 27, 1843, a. 82ys., 10m., 4d. He m. Francis Stenhouse. Ch. b: Catharine Francis, bp. June 25, 1785; John, b. Sept. 28, 1786; Jane Anna, b. Dec. 21, 1804.

SIMON, son of Col. John Glen, m. Margariet Muire, d. in Albany, May 1, 1841. Ch. b: Catharine, July 3, 1799; Christiana Margariet, Feb. 15, 1801; John, Ap. 7, 1803; Alexander Hamilton, Feb. 20, 1805, d. in Albany, Jan. 12, 1832.

CORNELIUS, son of Hendrick, m. Rebecca Humphreys, b. July 10, 1792. He d. April 25, 1822. Ch. b: Elisabeth, Aug. 17, 1812; Isabella, Oct. 29, 1814; Jane, March 12, 1818; Henry, b. Nov. 12, 1821.

Col. JACOB, son of Johannes Sanderse of Scotia, m. Sara, dau. of Capt. Johannes Wendel, merchant of Albany, Dec. 15, 1717. He occupied the ancient Sanders mansion in Scotia; d. Aug. 15 1762; she d. Aug. 19, 1762. Ch: Debora, b. June (July) 9, and bp. June 10, 1721, m. Johannes Sanders of Albany; d. Mar. 8, 1786.

ABRAHAM, son of Johannes Sanderse of Scotia, occupied the wooden house standing easterly from the Sanders mansion, in Scotia; was member of the New York Assembly in 1743; married Maritje, dau. of Johannes Teller, July 11, 1724. Ch. bp: Susanna, b. Aug. 16, 1725; Debora, b. August 22, 1727, m. first, Jan Viele, secondly, William Kirkpatrick; Susanna, bp. —— 1730, m. Abraham Van Eps; Margarietje, Aug. 26, 1733; *Johannes Sanderse*, Jan. 25, 1733; Annatje, Sept. 3, 1738; Sarah, Nov. 30, 1740.

JOHANNES SANDERSE, son of Abraham, m. his cousin Sarah, dau. of Johannes Sanders of Scotia, Sept. 11, 1762. She d Aug. 31, 1788, a. 46ys., 5m., 28d. Ch. bp: Abraham, June 19, 1763; Sarah, Nov. 9, 1765; Maria, Dec. 26, 1770; Jacob Sanderse, June 27, 1773, settled in, and gave name to the town of Glen; m. first, Catharina, dau. of Col. Frederick Visscher, and secondly, Maria Van Rensselaer of Bethlehem, d. April 21, 1859 *sine prole;* Elisabeth, Mar. 31, 1776; Abraham, Feb. 25, 1778; Maria, June 15, 1783.

GLOVER.

THOMAS, and Eleanor Smith. Ch. b: Nancy, May 12, 1785; John, Feb. 8, 1788; Eleanor, Dec. 24, 1790; Henry, Aug. 26, 1793.

GOLDTHUIT (GOLDTHWAITE).

MICHAEL BURRILL of Boston, m. Margarita Farley, Feb. 3, 1761.

GONZALUS.

See Consaulus.

GORDON.

CHARLES, citizen of Schenectady, 1779.

WILLIAM, and Elisabeth, dau. of Cornelis Van Seyssen. Ch: Rebecca, bp. March 3, 1782.

WILLIAM, and Christina Frazier. Ch. b: George, March 18, 1786; Elisabeth, March 3, 1793.

JOSEPH, and Eyke Hoogteling. In 1783 his house and lot was in Church street, next north of the church lot. Ch: Neeltje, b. Sept. 2, 1786.

GRAHAM.

CORNELIUS, and Jane McFaterick (Kitterick). Ch: William, bp. May 7, 1782; Cornelius, b. April 4, 1787.

GRAVENBERG.

JOHANNES, and Maria Willems. Ch. bp: Francyntje, Nov. 19, 1775; Johannes, April 5, 1778; Hendrick, Nov. 3, 1782. Ch. b: Frederick, March 27, 1785; Maria, Sept. 19, 1787; Lena, Nov. 5, 1789.

GRAVES.

JOSIAH, and Mary Beard (Maria Magdalena Baard). Ch. b: Henry, Dec. 9, 1786; Lena, August 15, 1788; Maria, July 27, 1792.

GRAY.

ARCHIBALD, and Elisabeth Greenham. Ch: Catharine, bp. Aug. 11, 1751.

GREADY.

DARBY, and Ariaantje, dau. of Johannese Simonse Veeder. Ch: Ariaantje, bp. Nov. 20, 1743.

GREEN.

WILLEM, and Cathlyntje Borns. Ch: Samuel, b. Dec. 22, 1773; Andreas, bp. Feb. 11, 1784; Symon S. b. Jan. 28, 1784.

PETER, m. Elisabeth Sacia, March 30, 1796. Ch. b: Richard, Nov. 17, 1796; David, April 24, 1798.

GRIER.

JOHN, and Jannet Clerk. Ch: Jane, b. May 31. 1787.

GRIFFITHS.

THOMAS, and Mary Blank. Ch: Cornelius, b. July 27, 1780.

GROESBECK.

WILLEM, and Catarina Van Deusen. Ch. bp: Willem Van Deusen, June 5, 1774; Cornelius, Oct. 22, 1775.

GROENENDYCK.

JOHANNES, son of Pieter of New York, was sheriff of Albany County 1698-9; later, trader in Schenectady, where he was buried in the church Dec. —, 1739; his wife continued his business there some years longer. He married Delia Huylers (Childers) in New York, Sept. 19, 1694. Ch. bp: Maria, in New York, Sept. 16, 1696; Sara, April 28, 1700, in Albany; *Pieter*, Sept. 7, 1701, in Albany; Henrik, Sept. 19, 1703, in Albany; Anna.

PIETER, son of Johannes, trader, m. Margarita ......; made his will 1740, proved March 17, 1760, spoke of his wife and sisters Mary, Anna and Sara, wife of ...... Stevenson of Albany, nephews John and James Stevenson, and niece Sara Stevenson; left "my house and lot wherein I now live" to his three sisters above mentioned. [P. Groenendyck, m. N. (Margarita ?) Van Iveren in Albany, Jan. 15, 1734.]

GROOT.

SYMON SYMONSE, the first settler, came early to New Netherland in the service of the West India Company, as boatswain of the ship Prince Maurice. In 1645 he bought a house and lot of Jacob Roy, in New Amsterdam. Soon after he came to Beverwyck, where he purchased or built a house, which in 1654 he offered for sale. He had lately withdrawn from the service of the West India Company, against whom he then held a claim for services of 834 guilders. In 1662, being about to remove to the Esopus, he empowered Johannes Withart to sell his house and lot; but it is evident that he changed his purpose, for in 1663 he hired a bouwery of 25 or 30 morgens, of Gerrit Bancker and Harmen Vedderen, at Schenectady, and still retained possession of his house in Albany as late as 1667. His house and lot in Schenectady, was on the north side of Union street, 100 Amsterdam feet westerly from Church street, running through to Front street, and remained in the family more than a hundred years. He m. Rebecca, dau. of

Philip Du Trieux (Truax), court messenger of New Amsterdam, and had the following children : *Symon; Abraham; Philip; Dirk;* Cornelis; Claas; Susanna, who m. Isaac Cornelise Swits; Maria, who m. Daniel Janse Van Antwerpen; Rebecca, who m. Claas Cornelise Vander Volgen; Sara, who m. Arent Vedder. On the sad night of the 8th of Feb., 1690, his five sons, Symon, Abraham, Philip, Dirk and Claas were taken captive by the French and Indians, and carried to Canada; the following year they were redeemed.

SYMON, Jr., eldest son of the first settler, owned a lot on the north side of State street, from Jan Baptist Van Eps's lane (now Jay street) to a point 250 feet eastwardly from the "*Lange gang*" (now (Centre street). His dau., Susanna Bragham, inherited one-third of this lot. He m. Geertruy, dau. of Jan Rinkhout of Albany, and had the following children : Rebecca, bp. in Albany, July 3, 1692, m. Nicolaas Van Petten; Eve, bp. in Schenectady, Jan. 3, 1695; Susanna, bp. in Albany, March 21, 1697, m. Joseph Bragham; Simon, bp. in Schenectady, Sept. 29, 1700; Johannes, bp. in Schenectady, Dec. 13, 1702; *Nicolaas;* Lysbeth, bp. in Albany, Feb. 24, 1706, m. Juriaan Siverse; *Cornelis.*

ABRAHAM, son of the first settler, m. first, Antje Wemp, widow of Sander Glen, April 15, 1696; and secondly, Hestertje Visscher, dau. of Harmen Visscher, of Albany, July 9, 1699, by whom he had the following children, all bp. in Sche-

nectady, except Harmanus and Cornelis (he was not living in 1737); Rebecca, bp. May 5, 1700, m. Abraham De Graaf; Hester, bp. April 7, 1701, m. Frans Van de Bogart; Maria, bp. Jan. 24, 1703, m. Jacob Vrooman; Geertruy, bp. April 30, 1704, m. David Marinus; Simon, bp. Oct. 28, 1705; Harmanus, bp. July 13, 1707; Cornelis, bp. Oct. 23, 1709; *Abraham*, bp. Oct. 21, 1711.

PHILIP, son of the first settler, settled on the north side of the Mohawk at Crane's village. He was drowned in the river in 1716. His lands were inherited by his three sons. He m. Sara, dau. of Jacobus Peek, and had the following children : Simon, b. Sept. 5, 1702, d. Nov. 10 (15), 1732; Jacobus, b. Sept. 18, 1707, d. Feb. 18, 173½; Rebecca, b. June 25, 1710, d. Feb. 13, 173½; *Ludovicus,* (*Lewis*), b. Nov. 28, 1712; Elisabeth, b. Sept. 16, 1715, m. Frederic Van Patten.

DIRK, son of the first settler,* m. Lysbeth, dau. of Claas Lourense Vander Volgen, and had the following children all bp. in the Schenectady church, save the second and fourth : Simon, Oct. 16, 1707; *Nicolaas,* Oct. 23, 1709; Rebecca, Feb. 13, 1712, m. Isaac Quackenboss; *Symon,* May 2, 1714; *Philippus,* May 10, 1716; *Cornelis,* June 2, 1718; Maria, June 18, 1720; *Abraham*, Jan. 26, 172¾; Isaac, b. Jan. 28, 1725; Neeltje, b. May 6, 1726, m. Pieter Van Vranken.

SIMON, son of Dirk, m. first, Maria Truex, Nov. 5, 1732, and had a dau. Re-

* Supposed to have settled in Niskayuna.

11

becca, who was bp. April 8, 1733. She
m. Benjamin Smit, and afterwards Volkert Vedder. Simon Groot, m. secondly,
Bata Clute, and had the following children bp. in Schenectady, save the first who
was bp. in Albany: Elisabeth, Feb. 20,
1739, m. Gerardus Clute; Dirk, May 17,
1741; Jacob, Oct. 30, 1743; Geertruy,
April 6, 1746; Geertruy, Oct. 11, 1747;
Rebecca, Dec. 8, 1751, m. Dirk Hagadorn; Isaac, Sept. 3, 1754; Isaac, Nov.
13, 1757; Abraham, July 6, 1766.

NICOLAAS, son of Dirk, was member
of the assembly from Albany county in
1761. He m. Maritje Tymessen, dau.
of Eldert Tymessen of Connestagioene,
Dec. 16, 1732, and had the following
children bp. in the Schenectady church:
Elisabeth, June 10, 1733, m. first, Arent
Van Antwerpen, and secondly, Jan Baptist Wendell; Rebecca, m. Robert Smit;
Eldert, Dec. 21 (?), 1737; Hester, Dec.
28, 1740, m. Joseph Consaulus; ·Dirk,
May 24, 1747.

ABRAHAM, son of Abraham, m. Willempie, dau. of John Dunbar, Nov. 29,
1736, and had the following children bp.
in Schenectady: Jan, April 9, 1738;
Hester, Aug. 23, 1741; Hester, Dec.
12, 1742, m. Cornelis Mebie; Tannetje,
Feb. 17, 1745, m. Johannes L. Peek;
Rebecca, Oct. 6, 1748, m. Volkert Veeder; Maria, April 21, 1751, m. Johannes Hall (?); Catarina, April 28, 1753;
Simon, Oct. 31, 1756; Willempje, April
8, 1759, m. Johannes Erichzon; Abraham, Aug. 6, 1763.

NICOLAAS, son of Simon, m. Agnietje
...... He d. in 1741. Ch: Elias (?);
Simon, bp. Oct. 14, 1738; Nicolaas, bp.
May 24, 1741.

LEWIS (LODOVICUS), son of Philip,
lived at Crane's village; was taken captive by the French and Indians and carried to Canada; d. Jan. 27, 1794, a. 81ys.
He m. first, Annatie, dau. of Pieter Van
Antwerpen, Dec. 6, 1738, who d. June
30, 1750; he m. secondly, Elizabeth,
dau. of Johannes Van Eps, Jan. 14, (21),
1760. She d. Aug. 22, 1794. Ch. by
the first wife: Philip, b. Oct. 18, 1739,
d. Nov. 17, 1769; Engeltie, b. May 27,
1741, d. May 2, 1759; Petrus, b. March
7, 1744; Simon, b. Dec. 20 (?), bp. Dec.
17 (?), 1749. Ch. by second wife: Annatie, b. Sept. 2, 1761, m. Johannes N.
De Graaf; Johannes, b. June 6, 1763,
d. near Crane's village, Jan. 20, 1845;
Jacobus, bp. March 1, 1767.

CORNELIS, son of Simon, Jr., m. Elisabeth, dau. of Cornelis Pootman (now
Putman), Sept. 7, 1739, in Albany.
Ch: Abraham; Jacomyntje, bp. March
20, 1743, m. Jesse Van Slyck; Simon,
bp. Nov. 17, 1745; Hester, bp. Nov. 24,
1751, m. Harman Campbell; Eva, bp.
Sept. 3, 1754; Cornelis, bp. Jan. 23,
1757.

PHILIP, son of Dirk, m. Elisabeth, dau.
of Andries De Graaf of the Woestyne,
June 20, 1747. Ch: Dirk, bp. May 22,
1748; Andries De Graaf, bp. Oct. 15,
1749; Nicolaas, bp. Sept. 22, 1751;
Neeltje, bp. Sept. 3, 1754, m. Petrus

Groot; Nicolaas, bp. June 19, 1757; Elisabeth, bp. March 15, 1761; Nicolaas, bp. Dec. 1, 1765; Rebecca, bp. Aug. 27, 1768.

ABRAHAM, son of Dirk, of Niskayuna, m. Rachel, dau. of Jesse De Graaf of Schenectady, April 4, 1752. Ch: Dirk, bp. April 29, 1753, d. March 15, 1811; Jesse, bp. April 20, 1755; Cornelis, bp. Nov. 5, 1758; Elisabeth, bp. Sept. 21, 1766.

CORNELIS, son of Dirk, m. Maria, dau. of Evert Van Vranken, Nov. 24, 1752, in Albany. Ch: Dirk, bp. in Albany, Sept. 29, 1753; Maritie, bp. in Schenectady, March 16, 1755, m. Jacobus Van Vranken; Elisabeth, bp. in Albany, Jan. 9, 1757, m. Johannes I. Quackenbos; *Dirk,* bp. in Albany, Dec. 31, 1758; Evert, bp. in Schenectady, Feb. 7, 1762; Rebecca, b. Feb. 11, 1771.

ELIAS, son of Nicolaas (?), m. Geertruy Hagadorn, Feb. 20, 1762. Ch: Nicolaas, bp. Dec. 12, 1762, d. Jan. 27, 1813; *Hendrick,* bp. Nov. 18, 1764; Elisabeth, bp. Dec. 21, 1766, m. Jonathan A. Stevens; *Harmanus,* bp. Jan. 27, 1770; Isaac, bp. Nov. 28, 1773.

ABRAHAM, son of Cornelis, m. first, Catarina Kittel, Sept. 25, 1762; and secondly, Elsje, dau. of Daniel McKinney. He made his will Aug. 27, 1803, proved July 25, 1818. Ch. by first wife: Harmen, bp. July 3, 1763; Eva, bp. Dec. 16, 1764, m. Hendrick Van Dyck; Elisabeth, bp. May 15, 1768; Annatje, bp. Sept. 13, 1772, m. Henry Corl, Jr.; Ja-

comyntje, bp. Dec. 25, 1774, m. Valentine Ryncx. Ch. by second wife: Cornelis, bp. April 1, 1781; Sara, bp. Oct. 12, 1784; John Beekman, b. June 3, 1792, d. April 25, 1828.

JACOB, son of Simon (?), of Watervliet, m. Maria, dau. of Abraham Van Vranken. He made his will Oct. 8, 1809, proved June 17, 1814, in which he spoke of his wife Maria, and Claas, Abraham, and dau. Getty, wife of Amos Babcock. Ch: Simon, bp. May 18, 1766; Geertruy, bp. June 5, 1768; Abraham, bp. Sept. 11, 1771; Isaac and Jacob, bp. October 27, 1776; Isaac, bp. May 15, 1778; Bata, bp. Jan. 14, 1781.

JACOB, perhaps the same as the last, and Maria Clute, both of Niskayuna, m. Nov. 29, 1765.

SIMON C., Jr., son of Cornelis, m. Annatie, dau. of Isaac Abrahamse Truax, Sept. 3, 1769. He d. in West Glenville, Feb. 10, 1832, a. 86ys.; she d. April 10, 1834, a. 83ys. Ch: Elisabeth, b. Dec. 4, 1771, m. Isaac J. Vrooman, and d. in Glenville, June 13, 1843; Engeltie, b. May 15, 1774, m. Cornelis Clute; Eva, b. Oct. 16, 1777, m. Adam J. Vrooman; Isaac, b. Jan. 2, 1780, lived and d. in Glenville; Cornelis, b. Aug. 31, 1783, merchant of Schenectady; Sarah, b. July 12, 1786; Jacomyntje, b. Dec. 2, 1788, m. John Dawson of Glenville; Abram, b. Sept. 17, 1794.

PETRUS, son of Lewis (Lodovicus), m. Neeltje, dau. of Philip Groot. Ch: Annatje, bp. Oct. 17, 1773, m. Benjamin

Van Olinda; Philippus, bp. July 29, 1776. The following advertisement was published by the late Judge Sanders, Sen., in the *Albany Gazette* :

" On Thursday, the 4th instant, about four miles from the city of Schenectady, aside the Mohawk turnpike, sitting under a tree, I discovered Petrus Groot, who was supposed to have been slain in the Oriskena battle under General Herkimer on the 6th of August, in the year 1777. I immediately recognized him, and on conversation with him, he confessed himself to be the person I took him to be. I then carried him to the nearest tavern,* where I left him to be sent to his children and brothers, from whence, however, he departed before day the next morning, and was seen in Albany on Friday. His mental faculties are much impaired, supposed to have been occasioned by a wound of a tomahawk near the fore part of his head, though he is at most times tolerably rational. His head is bald ; the circle or scar of the scalping knife is plainly to be seen on it, and a stab on the side of his neck near his shoulder ; has a small scar near his ancle ; is a middle sized man, has blue eyes, a long countenance, and stoops much in the shoulders. He speaks English, French, Dutch and Indian, and says he has been last a prisoner among the Indians north of Quebec ; had on an old dark grey coat and old brownish pantaloons ; has a large pack with him. He refused to go home, as one of his former neighbors whom he saw, would not recognize him, he was fearful his children and brothers would not. He said he would go to the governor's. Being at times deranged, it is feared he will

* The house to which he was taken, was occupied by Simon Van Patten, better known as Cider Simon, from the circumstance of his manufacturing large quantities of cider annually. Van Patten identified him by a mark on his leg, occasioned by the bite of a rattlesnake, which he remembered from the circumstance of its having been cured by an Indian applying a leaf through which he sucked the poison with his mouth, leaving it perfectly free from soreness.

stray too far away for his friends to find him. He is of a very respectable family and connexions. Any person who will take him up and bring him to the subscriber, at Schenectady, shall be well compensated for his care and trouble, and will receive the sincere thanks of his children and relatives, and be the means of relieving this poor unfortunate man from distress by restoring him to his family and friends.

JOHN SANDERS.

SCHENECTADY, June 8, 1807.

N. B. The printers in this and the neighboring states are requested to give the above a few insertions in their respective papers, to aid in restoring a poor sufferer to his children and friends, who has been thirty years a prisoner among the Indians. He is now 63 years of age. He was a lieutenant in the militia at the time he was supposed to have been slain."

ELDERT, son of Nicolaas, m. Alida Gerritse. Ch : Hester, bp. in Schenectady, Dec. 25, 1774 ; Nicolaas, bp. in Schenectady, Sept. 21, 1777 ; Hendrick, bp. in Albany, April 26, 1780 ; Hendrick, bp. in Schenectady, Dec. 28, 1784.

DIRK, son of Philip, m. Ariaantje Wemple, Dec. 10, 1773. Ch : Elisabeth, bp. April 23, 1775, m. Jacobus Van Sice ; Barent, bp. Dec. 19, 1779 ; Neeltje, bp. Feb. 3, 1782.

SIMON, son of Lewis, m. Annatje, dau. of Jeremiah Swart. Ch : Philippus, bp. May 4, 1775 ; Jeremiah, bp. Jan. 4, 1778 ; Annatje, bp. July 22, 1781 ; Louis, bp. Dec. 28, 1783 ; Maria, b. Jan. 24, 1786 ; Elisabeth, b. Nov. 3, 1788 ; Lewis, b. April 15, 1794.

JOHN L., son of Louis, of Crane's village, m. Sarah, dau. of Jeremiah John

Miller, June 26, 1791. She d. Jan. 30, 1812, a. 42ys., and 6d. Ch: Lewis, b. May 8, 1793 [1792 (?)]; Elisabeth, b. March 3, 1794, d. March 21, 1795; Sarah, b. Feb. 26, 1795; Elisabeth, b. April 21, 1796; Maria, b. Sept. 10, 1798; Anna, b. March 30, 1802, m. Walter Conkling, d. May 12, 1841; Elisabeth, b. May 1, 1808; Jeremiah, b. June 8, 1815.

JOHN, son of Abraham, m. Engeltie, dau. of Philip Van Petten, June 12, 1762. Ch: Abraham, bp. Dec. 18, 1763; Philip, bp. August 24, 1766; John, bp. Jan. 15, 1768; Magdalena, bp. May 5, 1771; Willempie, bp. June 13, 1773; Geesje, bp. July 3, 1775; Hester, bp. March 1, 1778; Arent, bp. May 21, 1780; Simon, bp. Sept. 15, 1782.

DIRK, son of Nicolaas, m. Maria, dau. of Reuben Hosford, Dec. 7, 1774. Ch: Nicolaas, bp. Oct. 3, 1775; Ariaantje, bp. July 19, 1778; Maria, bp. Feb. 11, 1781, m. ...... Duncan, and d. Oct. 13, 1852; Neeltje, bp. June 6, 1784; Reuben, b. May 4, 1787; John Hosford, b. April 13, 1790; Cornelius, b. May 13, 1796.

CORNELIS C., son of Cornelis, m. Maria Bastiaanse. Ch: Elisabeth, bp. Aug. 24, 1782; Johannes Bastiaanse, b. Jan. 12, 1786; Eva, b. March 8, 1789; Catharina, b. June 6, 1792; Cornelius, b. Feb. 4, 1796; Abram, b. Nov. 20, 1798; Henrikus, b. Feb. 23, 1802; Maria, b. May 2, 1805.

HENDRIK E., son of Elias, m. Sophia Chase. Ch: Geertruy, b. Feb. 1785, bp. Feb. 2, 1786; Mille, b. Nov. 28, 1788; Antje, b. July 19, 1791; Elisabeth, b. July 4, 1793; Elisabeth, b. Aug. 4, 1795.

SIMON, son of Abraham, m. Rebecca, dau. of Arent Vedder, Sept. 17, 1785. He d. March 4, 1838, a. 81ys., 3m., and 20d.; she d. March 25, 1845, a. 78ys. Ch: Abraham, b. Jan. 31, 1786; Cathârina, b. Jan. 7, 1789; Willempie, b. Oct. 20, 1791, m. Harmanus Swart of *Woestyne*, and d. April 17, 1840; Maria, b. March 1, 1794; Johannes, b. Sept. 15, 1796; Arent, b. Nov. 18, 1799; Esther, b. Sept. 9, 1802; Simon, b. April 12, 1808.

HARMANUS, son of Elias, m. Lois Pitcher. Ch: Geertruyd, b. March 19, 1797.

JEREMIAH, son of John, of Crane's village, m. Sally Swart. Ch: John, b. Aug., 1813.

DIRK, son of Cornelis, m. Jacomyntje, dau. of Bastiaan Tymessen, all of Niskayuna, Dec. 1797. He d. June 26, 1847, in his 89th year; she d. July 29, 1826, in her 67th year. Ch: Cornelis, d. Jan. 31, 1838, in his 38th year.

ANDRIES DE GRAAF, son of Philip, m. Maritie Hagedorn, June 3, 1787. Ch: Philip, b. July 29, 1789.

ANDRIES, perhaps same as the last, m. Maria Murray. Ch: Elisabeth, b. June 15, 1792.

JESSE, m. Geertruy, dau. of Johannes Van Vranken. Ch : Johannes, bp. June 1, 1783; Marytje, b. Feb. 2, 1786; Elisabeth, b. Jan. 15, 1789.

JOHN J., and Elsje Van Bunschoten, both of the Hellenbergh, m. Dec. 25, 1793.

ABRAHAM, and Esther J. Toll, m. Sept. 14, 1787.

DIRK, and Eve Vrooman. Ch : Rachel, b. Nov. 23, 1804. He made his will Nov. 9, 1811, proved Nov. 29, 1811, spoke of dau. Rachel, brother's dau. Alida, brother Cornelius S.

JOHN L., m. Margaret Van Kegen (?), Feb. 28, 1814. Ch. b : Margaret, April 30, 1815; Catrina, Mar. 12, 1817; Jane Ann, Feb. 28, 1819; Lewis, Aug. 16, 1821; Eastean, (dau.), March 24, 1826.

ISAAC, and Nancy Chase. Ch : Geertruy, b. Jan. 15, 1798.

ISAAC, and Melicent (Malissa) Collins. Ch. b : Sally, Aug. 1, 1805; Cornelius, March 26, 1809.

JEREMY, and Elisabeth Van Wormer, Ch : Annatie, b. Oct. 28, 1797.

WILLEM, m. Catharina Flagg, June 12, 1791. Ch : John, b. Oct. 5, 1791.

GYSBERTSE.
See Van Brakel.

GYSELING.
See Van Gyseling.

HACKNEY.
GEORGE and Mary Yule. Ch : John, b. July 7, 1791.

HAEFE.
DIRK and wife, residents of Schenectady in 1697.

HAGE (HAGEDORN ?).
HARMANUS, perhaps son of Hendrick Hagedorn, m. Maria Hall, April 26, 1746, both of Schenectady.

HAGEDORN.
HENDRICK, of the Aalplaats, m. Anna, dau. of Jonathan Stevens, Oct. —, 1716. Ch. bp : Maria, Aug. 31, 1717; Harmanus, July 25, 1719; Jonathan, Sept. 17, 1721; Nicolaas, March 23, 1723; Lea, Dec. 27, 1724; Samuel, b. Sept. 20, 1726; Dina, bp. ——, 1729, m. Samuel Murray; Dirk, June 10, 1733; Arent, Aug. 3, 1735; Geertruy, July 9, 1737; Robert.

JONATHAN, m. Lea Hagen, Oct. 30, 1742. Ch. bp : Samuel, Nov. 25, 1744; Henrik, Jan. 19, 1746.

SAMUEL, and Diana, dau. of Jonathan Stevens, both of the Aalplaats, m. Feb., 1717. Ch. bp : Maria, March 3, 1718; Jonathan, April 16, 1720; Geertruy, Oct. 7, 1722; Lea, March 21, 1725; Harmanus, ——, 1730; Anna, July 9, 1732.

DIRK, of Albany, m. Maritie Matyssen, Aug. 28, 1714, in Albany. Ch. bp. in

Albany : Anna, April 24, 1715 ; Johannes Appel, June 30, 1718 ; Hans Hendrickse, Sept. 18, 1720 ; Maria, Jan. 6, 1723 ; Catharina, Feb. 3, 1725.

ROBERT, son of Hendrick, m. Margariet, dau. of Dirk Van Vorst, April 19, 1760. Ch. bp : Annatie, Jan. 18, 1761, m. Nicolaas Smith ; *Hendrick*, Jan. 24, 1762 ; Dirk, May 20, 1764 ; Immetje, Jan. 14, 1766, m. Peleg Stevens ; Maria, Sept. 18, 1768 ; Jillis, June 4, 1770 ; *Harmanus*, April 19, 1772 ; Sarah, Jan. 30, 1774 ; Jillis and Jonathan, April 7, 1776 ; Hester, Feb. 1, 1778 ; Robert, Oct. 31, 1779 ; Pieter, Dec. 30, 1781.

HARMANUS, son of Samuel, and Catarina .... Ch. bp : *Samuel*, Jan. 24, 1762 ; Maria, Oct. 30, 1763 ; Dina, Mar. 1, 1767 ; Annatje, Sept. 16, 1770, m. Petrus Staats ; *Dirk*, b. Sept. 19, 1773.

HARMANUS, perhaps same as the last, m. Nabby York. Ch. b : Samuel, Sept. 2, 1793 ; Charlotte, June 30, 1795.

DIRK, son of Hendrick, m. Jannetie Van Alstyne, May 24, 1768. Ch : *Hendrick*, bp. Oct. 29, 1769.

DIRK, perhaps same as the last, m. Rebecca, dau. of Simon Groot. Ch. bp : Jannetje, Sept. 6, 1778, m. Reyer Murray ; Simon, Nov. 23, 1780 ; Harmanus, Sept. 19, 1782.

SAMUEL, son of Jonathan, and Sophia Rees. Ch : Jonathan, b. Oct. 8, and bp. in Albany, Nov. 4, 1770 ; Lea, b. April 11, and bp. in Albany, May 8, 1774 ;

Maria bp. in Schenectady, May 4, 1782 ; Samuel, bp. May 28, 1784 ; Margarietje, b. June 9, 1790.

SAMUEL, son of Harmanus, m. Judy, dau. of Abraham Christiaanse. Ch. b : Catharina, Mar. 4, 1785 ; Abraham, Oct. 28, 1786 ; Harmanus, Aug. 28, 1788 ; Jacob, July 9, 1800.

DIRK, son of Harmanus, of Glenville, m. Maria, dau. of Willem Stevens. He d. Dec. 4, 1828 ; she d. June 6, 1853, a. 82ys. Ch. b : Robert, June 31 (*sic*), 1792 ; Catharina, July 8, 1795, d. May 6, 1863 ; William, Oct. 18, 1798, d. May 17, 1851 ; Harmanus, Dec. 25, 1800, d. Feb. 28, 1838 ; Nicholas, March 1, 1803, d. October 14, 1843 ; Jonathan, July 6, 1805, d. Aug. 11, 1859.

HENDRICK, son of Jonathan (?), m. Elisabeth Murray. Ch. b : Jonathan, April 28, 1794 ; Dina, Feb. 11, 1797.

HARMANUS, son of Robert, m. Sarah Symons. Ch. b : Robert, April 23, 1796 ; Pieter, Jan. 24, 1799 ; Margariet, Aug. 22, 1800.

HENDRICK, son of Dirk, m. Jacomyntje Wyldy (Wilds). Ch. b : Thomas, July 19, 1797 ; Cornelia, Nov. 25, 1799 ; Derick, April 18, 1804.

HAGGENBACH.

PIETER, and Annatie Sitlie (Zittle), both of Rensselaerswyck, m. Jan. 21, 1766. Ch. bp : Anna Christina, Feb. 25, 1767 ; Catarina, May 29, 1768 ; Elisabeth, Oct. 14, 1769 ; Maria Barbara,

May 7, 1771; Margarita, April 1, 1773;
Maria, April 26, 1776; Johan Petrus,
Mar. 17, 1778; Coenraat, Feb. 21, 1780.

HAIR.

WILLIAM, m. Elisabeth Clement, Oct.
9, 1758. Ch. bp: John, Feb. 27, 1760;
Pieter, Jan. 1, 1762.

HALE (HALL ?).

JOHANNES, of Niskayuna, m. Maria
Hage of Schenectady, Jan. 6, 175$\frac{9}{1}$.

HALL.

WILLIAM, m. Tryntje Claese, widow
of Elias Van Guysling, April 13, 1695.
Ch. bp: *William*, Jan. 8, 1696; Mary,
April 27, 1698, m. Arent Stevens; *Claas*,
Sept. 1, 1700; *Johannes*, Jan. 24, 1703.

THOMAS, m. Cornelia, dau. of Christiaanse (?). Ch: Maritie and Elisabet,
bp. Dec. 30, 1721; Johannes, b. Nov.
22. 1724; Maritie, b. Nov. 28, 1726, m.
Dirk Van Vorst; Christiaan, bp. June
21, 1729 (?).

NICOLAAS, son of William, m. Maria,
dau. of Johannes Van Antwerpen, July
11, 1724. Ch. b: *William*, January 17,
1725; Johannes, Sept. 30, 1726; Agnietje, Nov. 6, 1733.

WILLIAM, son of William, and Anna
Cowper of New York, m. April 10, 1730.
Ch. bp: Catharina, ——, 1729 (?); Jo-
hannes, March 4, 1733; *Willem*, Dec. 1,
1736; Antje, June 14, 1740, m. Samuel
Fuller; Johannes, May 8, 1743; *Johan-*

nes, July 6, 1746; Maria, Dec. 31, 1749,
m. Thomas Beth.

JOHANNES, son of William, m. Gellesje,
dau. of Claas Fransen Van der Bogart,
Sept. 30, 1743. Ch. bp: Catharina,
April 8, 1744, m. Jacob Vedder; Maria,
July 27, 1746; *Claas*, July 27, 1748;
Maria, Dec. 1, 1751; Maria, Sept. 12,
1753, m. James McMichael.

THOMAS, of Philadelphia, and Susanna
Wendell, both now living in this place,
m. April 15, 1748.

WILLIAM, son of Nicolaas, m. Maria,
dau. of Pieter Veeder, Feb. 13, 1762.
Ch. bp: Willem, Aug. 30, 1762; Maria,
March 31, 1765; Pieter, Oct. 18, 1767;
Johannes, June 24, 1770; Nicolaas, Aug.
9, 1772.

JOHANNES, son of William, m. Catarina, dau. of Abraham Groot (?), Sept.
16. 1770. Ch. bp: Willem, February 9,
1771; Jannetje, May 23, 1773; Abraham, Aug. 6, 1775; Johannes, July 25,
1779; Annatje, Dec. 2, 1781; Cornelis,
b. Feb. 1, 1791. [Johannes Hall bought
a lot on the west side of Church street,
next south of the Fuller lot of Johannes
Van Dyck for £95 New York currency.]

WILLIAM, son of William, m. Annatje,
dau. of Johannes Barheyt. Ch. bp: Annatje, Sept. 4, 1771; Cornelis, Feb. 15,
1778; Allia (Alida ?), Nov. 21, 1779;
Lowis, Nov. 18, 1781; James, Sept. 7,
1783. Ch. b: John, Oct. 14, 1785;
Catharina, July 15, 1788; Alexander,
Nov. 6, 1793.

CLAAS, son of Johannes, m. Hester (Suster), dau. of Isaac Swits. He d. April 17, 1828 : she d. Dec. 8, 1833, in her 80th year. Ch. b : Catarina, March 15, 1778, d. Dec. 10, 1784; Isaac Swits, Dec. 2, 1780, d. June 22, 1789 (?); Isaac, Dec.—, 1782, d. Dec. 15, 1786 (?); Johannes, Nov. 26, 1784; Debora, Jan. 4, 1786, m. James Rosa; Catharina, March 15, 1789, d. June 1, 1789; Gezina, April 30, 1792, d. June 16, 1823; John, Oct. 15, 1795; Maria, April 15, 1797, d. Dec. 10, 1799.

GEORGE, and Maria Veeder. Ch : Maria, b. Nov. 25, 1798.

HALLENBECK.
MACHIEL, and Mary Heans. Ch : Johannes, bp. Feb. 15, 1769.

ALBERT, and Sarah Slingerland. Ch : Jacob, bp. March 14, 1780.

CORNELIUS, and Margaret Freeligh. Ch. b : Johannes, March 20, 1788; Francis, June 10, 1790; Maria, Nov. 16, 1793.

CASPAR, m. Rachel Van Wormer, Ap. 19, 1793. Ch. b : Margarietje, July 2, 1794; John Caspar, July 13, 1797.

HALLENDYCK.
CASPARUS, and Marytje Evertse. Ch : Engeltje, bp. Jan 2. 1725.

HALLIDAY.
See Holoda.

HALLING.
WILLIAM, and Susanna Hallenbeck. Ch : Sarah, b. Jan. 7, 1797.

12

HALSTEAD.
TIMOTHEUS, and Keziah Tid. Ch : Jehilda, b. May 6, 1776; Elisabeth, bp. July 5, 1779; Samuel, b. March 12, 1786.

JAMES, and Elisabeth Tid (Teed). Ch : Abia, bp. July 5, 1779.

JAMES, and Susanna Miller. Ch. bp : James, Dec. 26, 1779; Amos, Dec. 26, 1781.

HAMILTON.
JAMES ALEXANDER, and Jane Atkinson. Ch : Mary, bp. Nov. 3, 1776.

HANNA.
ALEXANDER, and Mary Barnhart. Ch : Mary, bp. Jan. 12, 1785.

JACOBUS, [see Jacobus Hans below] and Rebecca Buys. Ch : William, b. Dec. 18, 1787.

WILLIAM, and Jane Roberson. Ch : George, bp. March 6, 1785.

HUGH, and William, of Albany, in 1797, bought the tannery on east corner of Jay and State streets.

HANS (HINNES, HENNES).
JACOBUS, and Rebecca Buys (Buyn), Ch : Annatje, bp. Jan. 16, 1774; Hendericus, May 3, 1783; Jacobus, bp. Nov. 10, 1785.

JOHAN JURRY, and Martha Heggins. Ch : Catarina, bp. July 5, 1776; John George, b. March 29, 1778.

HANSE.

HENDERICK N., and Catarina Potman. Ch : Debora, bp. Oct. 21, 1760.

HANSEN.

NICOLAAS, son of Hendrick, of Albany, m. Engeltie, dau. of Barent Wemp of *Dorp,* ——, 1722 (?). Ch. bp : Hendrik, June 24, 1722; Barent, ——, 1730; *Pieter,* Feb. 11, 1733.

GERRIT, member of the church 1693.

PIETER, son of Nicolaas, and Alida Scheerman. Ch : Catalyntje, bp. Sept. 13, 1775.

HANSINGER.

FREDERIC, and Rachel Walker. Ch : Isaac, b. July 30, 1794.

HARDENBERGH.

LOUIS, and Cornelia Waldron. Ch : Johannes, bp. Nov. 3, 1754.

PETRUS, and Catalyntje Schermerhorn, both of Caughnawaga, m. July 20, 1794.

HARPER.

GIDEON, and Jennet Craigh. Ch : Sarah, bp. Dec. 7, 1746.

HARRGGROSS.

HUMPHREY, and Jane Wat. Ch : Elisabeth, bp. Sept. 26, 1779.

HARRING.

CORNELIUS, of Fonda's Bos, and Annatje Ary Jansen. Ch. b : Abraham, Jan. 21, 1789 ; Maria, May 19, 1792.

HARRINGTON.

PHILIP, and Rachel Ostrander, m. Aug. 30, 1794.

HARRIS.

PHILIP, and Annetje Tjerkse, widow of Frans Harmense Van de Bogart, m. in Albany, March 25, 1692.

PIETER, and Catharina Nobel. Ch : Samuel, bp. Oct. 25, 1747.

THOMAS, m. Jannetje, dau. of Arent Potman, Jan. 1, 1729. Ch : Francyntje, bp. Feb. 10, 1748.

JACOB, and Elisabeth Pootman, both of Sacondaga, m. Nov. 2, 1767.

(HARRISON).

HENRIK, of "Genistagioene," and Maria, dau. of Harmen Philipse of the *Maquaasland,* m. Jan. 8, 174$\frac{8}{9}$. Ch. bp : Margareta, Aug. 13, 1749 ; Maria, Aug. 11, 1751; Thomas, Ap. 28, 1753; Harmanus, May 4, 1755 ; Petrus, Aug. 28, 1757 ; Philip, July 1, 1760.

WILLIAM, and Jemima Berrit. Ch : Richard, bp. April 29, 1781.

WILLIAM, and Elisabeth Teerpenning. Ch. b : James, Dec. 18, 1791; Elisabeth, July 15, 1795 ; Margariet, July 3, 1797 ; John, Dec. 31, 1799.

HART.

HENDERICK, and Maria Christina Laner. Ch : Johan Daniel, bp. March 5, 1754.

NICHOLAS, and Maria Haynes. Ch. bp : Jacob, Feb. 3, 1771; Margarita, May 3, 1773; Catarina, Oct. 18, 1775; Barent, Nov. 6, 1779.

DANIEL, and Elisabeth Little, m. Nov. 29, 1789.

HASLIP.

JOSEPH, and Anna Haslip. Ch : Caty, b. April 22, 1788.

HAVER.

ABRAHAM, and Geertruy Ostrander. Ch : Abram, b. March 30, 1794.

HAVERLY.

JOHANNES, lived at the Fourth Flat in 1792, on land bought of Teunis Swart; m. Annatje Adams. She d. Dec. 2, 1813. Ch. bp : Maria, Dec. 5, 1774; Christiaan, June 22, 1777.

HAZARD.

JASON, and Lois Jones. Ch. bp : Ells, (*sic*) Nov. 29, 1767; Robert, Dec. 31, 1770.

HEANS.

JAMES, and Phebe Gardinier. Ch. bp : Maria, Aug. 19, 1772; Phebe, Jan. 14, 1782.

HEEMSTRAAT.

JOHANNES, son of Dirk Takelse, and Bata, dau. of Johannes Quackenbos, both of "Connestigioune," m. Feb. 8, 1730. He m. secondly, Geertruy Bosie, widow of Johannes Marinus of Schenectady, March 3, 175⁹⁄₇. Ch. bp: Dirk, b. April 13, bp. May 9, 1731; *Johannes*, bp.

Nov. 19, 1732; Clara, July 6, 1735, m. Nicolaas Clute; Annatje, Dec. 21, 1737, m. Dirk Clute; Bata, Aug. 31, 1740; *Jacob*, May 15, 1743; Gerardus, Dec. 8, 1745; Machtelt, Oct. 11, 1747, m. Johannes Consaulus; *Philippus*, Sept. 22, 1751.

TAKEL DIRKSE, son of Dirk Takelse, of Connestagioune, m. Maria Marinus, dau. of Willem, Oct. 10, 1734. Ch. bp : Machtelt, Aug. 15, 1736, m. Pieter Ouderkerk; Magdalena, Sept. 3, 1738; *Dirk*, Dec. 14, 1740; *Willem*, Jan. 16, 1743; Margareta, Dec. 26, 1745; *Isaac*, Oct. 29, 1749.

JACOB, son of Dirk Takelse of Albany, m. Hesther, dau. of Jacob Vrooman, May 6, 1749. Ch. bp : Dirk, Aug. 13, 1749; Maria, May 5, 1751, m. Abraham Van Vorst.

JACOB, perhaps same as the last, m. Hester, dau. of David Marinus, Jan. 1, 1757. Ch. bp : Hester, Nov. 13, 1757; David, Feb. 1, 1761; Hester, March 31, 1765.

JOHANNES, son of Johannes, m. Elisabeth, dau. of Teunis Van der Volgen. Ch. bp : Teunis, Sept. 3, 1754; Ariaantje, Oct. 17, 1756, m. Nicholas Avery; Sarah, Nov. 12, 1758, m. Isaac Le Roy.

WILLEM, son of Takel Dirkse, and Martha, dau. of Richard Oliver, both of Rensselaerswyck, m. June 9, 1768. Ch. bp: Maria, March 6, 1769; Richard, March 13, 1771; Takel and Thomas, July 4, 1773; Dirk, May 18, 1776;

John, Aug. 30, 1778; Johannes, Jan. 16, 1782; Carel, Dec. 5, 1784.

JACOB, son of Johannes (?), m. Catarina De Ret (Dret), in Albany, Nov. 5, 1763. Ch. bp: Clara, July 22, 1772, m. Samuel S. Bratt; Teunis, Sept. 1, 1778. [*See Albany Families.*]

JOHANNES, of Niskayuna, m. Elisabeth Bovie, in Albany, Dec. 30, 1757. Ch: Annatje, bp. Nov. 4, 1773. [*See Albany Families.*]

DIRK, son of Takel Dirkse, and Eva Paford. Ch: Takel, bp. March 15, 1778.

PHILIP, son of Johannes, m. Dina (Blandina) Van Vliet. Ch: *Johannes*, b. March 20, 1780; Benjamin, bp. July 26, 1783; Geertruy, b. July 22, 1787.

CAREL, son of Dirk of Albany, m. Geertruy Van der Werken, in Albany, Aug, 15, 1779. Ch: Arent, b. March 8, 1784. [*See Albany Families.*]

ISAAC, son of Takel Dirkse, m. Maria Teerpenning, both of the Hellenbergh, Oct. 25, 1788. Ch. b: Bregje, Sept. 12, 1789; Annatje, June 15, 1793.

JOHANNES, son of Jacob of Albany, m. Catharina Weever. Ch. b: Catharina, May 11, 1792; Rachel, Dec. 16, 1793; Jacob, March 30, 1795; Marytje, Feb. 7, 1797.

JOHANNES, son of Philip, m. Catlyntje Turk. Ch. b: Blandina, July 22, 1801; Petrus, Jan. 24, 1802; Philip, March 13, 1804.

JOHN D., and Christina Ries, both of the Maquaasland, m. Sept. 18, 1794. Ch: Maria, b. Aug. 15, 1795.

RYKARD, and Hannah Nostrand. Ch. b: Mary, Jan. 29, 1797; Martha, April 8, 1798.

HEERMANCE.

JACOB, and Jenny Bailey. Ch: Maria, b. Aug. 12, 1786.

HEGEMAN.

CHRISTOPHER, and Elisabeth Cooper. Ch: Johannes, bp. Jan. 12, 1777.

JOHANNES, and Immetje Farquarson. Ch: Jannetje, bp. Oct. 30, 1774.

NICHOLAS, and Maria Peltz. Ch. b: Jannetje, March 25, 1786; Sarah, Sept. 11, 1790; Joseph, Sept. 5, 1792.

HENRY, and Dina (Blandina) Oostrum. He d. before Feb. 15, 1790. Ch. b: Roelif, June 6, 1788; Hendrikus, July 16, 1789.

ADRIAN, and Catarina Jansen. Ch: Eva, bp. Jan. 3, 1782.

EVERT, and Maria Wyser. Ch. b: Sarah, Oct. 26, 1793; Elisabeth, April 15, 1796.

HEGER.

JOHANNES, and Maria Swart. Ch: Henderick, b. Aug. 26, 1780.

HELLING.

WILLIAM, and Tanneke Edwards. Ch: Josias, b. April 6, 1727.

HENDRIKSE.

JOHANNES, and Margareta Philipse.
Ch: Annatje, bp. July 10, 1774.

HENDRIKS.

JOHANNES, of the *Willigen*, and Anna
Bailey. Ch. b: Abigail, Dec. 30, 1784;
Margariet, Feb. 21, 1787; Peter, March
16, 1790; Jacob, Sept. 4, 1791; Elisabeth, Dec. 11, 1793; Jacob, March 4,
1796; Elisabeth, June 10, 1798; Anna,
Feb. 26, 1801.

CORNELIUS, and Mary Jones. Ch:
John, bp. Dec. 28, 1784; Catharina, b.
Mar. 3, 1788; Hendrik, b. Feb. 26, 1790.

·HENNEKE.

EMANUEL, and Hanna Hoener. Ch:
John, b. May 23, 1793.

HENNING.

PHILIP, and Catarina Adams. Ch:
Isaac, bp. Oct. 2, 1763.

HENNION.

PETER and Elisabeth Scherp. Ch. bp:
Margarita, May 12, 1775; Daniel, Nov.
13, 1776.

HENRY.

JOHN, hatter, m. Elisabeth, dau. of
Jan Baptist Van Vorst, June 11, 1763.
In 1784 he owned Nos. 147 and 149,
north side of State street, now Van
Horne Hall. Ch. bp: *John*, Feb. 26,
1764; Jan Baptist, Oct. 27, 1765; Catarina, Sept. 14, 1766; Annatie, May 29,
1768; *Jan Baptist*, March 4, 1770; Elisabeth, Nov. 3, 1771, m. Jacobus Johan-

nes Van Eps; Sarah, Aug. 29, 1773;
Sarah, April 2, 1775, m. Gerrit Van Eps;
Geertruy, Feb. 2, 1777; Maria, Nov. 22,
1778; Maria, Aug. 18, 1782, m. John
Van Eps, Jr.

JAN BAPTIST, son of John, m. Martha
Smith, May 26, 1793. Ch. b: John,
July 31, 1794.

JOHN, JR., son of John, and Maria
Bratt Ch. b: Elisabeth, Ap. 13, 1795;
Daniel, Dec. 9, 1797; Catrina, April 28,
1804; Rebecca, March 30, 1806; Gerrit,
April 5, 1810; Eleanor, May 4, 1812.

HERDER.

HENDERICK, and Catarina Peyper.
Ch: Christina, bp. May 25, 1760.

HERMAN.

COENRAAT, and Christina Bonnum.
Ch: Elisabeth, bp. Nov. 19, 1766.

HERRISON.

THOMAS, and Margariet Davids, both
of Maquaasland or above the *Willigen*
(Willows, a little below Port Jackson).
m. Dec. —, 1717. On March 18, 1723,
she m. William Kelly of Maquaasland.
Ch: Hendrik, bp. Sept. 3, 1720.

HESS.

PETER, and Sarah Harris. Ch: David, b. Dec. 25, 1797.

HESSELINGH.

DIRK, was in Albany in 1666, subsequently at Schenectady where he bought
in 1671 a bouwery of Jurriaen Teunise

Tappan, which he sold the following year to Harmen Vedder. He also bought land at Lubberde's land [Troy]. In 1667 he m. Eytje Hendrickse, who, with her three sisters, had been taken prisoners by the Indians at Yonkers in 1655. Her sister Albrechtie was rescued in 1667 and brought into New Haven. Eytje Hesselingh was a resident of Schenectady in 1697.

ROBERT, was killed in Schenectady by the French and Indians in 1690.

HETHERINGTON (HADINGTON).
JOSEPH, and Sarah Palmontier. Ch: Joseph Haddington, b. Jan. —, 1786.

JOSEPH, and Sarah Ladd. Ch. b: Christopher, Sept. 10, 1790; Ann, June 10, 1792, m. Nicolaas G. Veeder; William Aug. 23, 1793; Joseph, Jan. 10, 1795; John, Nov. 21, 1796; Mary, June 12, 1803.

HEWS.
HERBERT, and Susan Johnson, m. Aug. 12, 1798.

HEYDENRY.
HENDRICK, and Ruth Weetz. Ch: Mary, bp. May 14, 1779.

HEYSEL (HEYSER).
JOHANNES, and Maria Ostrander. Ch. b: Elisabeth, July 12, 1785; Willem, Dec. 18, 1787.

HICKS.
WILLIAM, and Maria Arden. Ch: John, b. Oct. 2, 1796.

HICKSON.
JOHN, m. Catharina Van Sice, Aug. 16, 1789. Ch. b: Joseph, Sept. 12, 1790: Rykard, Sept. 5, 1793.

HIERLY.
EDWARD, m. Sarah T. Marselis, Dec. 14, 1768.

HILL.
RICHARD, a citizen in 1713.

HENRY, and Martha Forsee (Foresn). Ch. bp: Adam, Dec. 10, 1764; Sarah, Nov. 23, 1777.

HILLEN.
JOHN, and Annatje Whyton. Ch: Jane, bp. April 13, 1784.

HILT.
JOHN, a resident of the *Woestyne* in 1690.

HILTON.
PIETER, and Judy Berrit. Ch: Jacobus, bp. Jan. 11, 1775.

(HYLTEN).
ADAM, of the Normanskil, and Annatje Price. Ch: Maria, b. Oct. 7, 1785.

HOCK.
FRANK, and Elisabeth Enger. Ch: Barent, bp. January 1, 1724; Peggy, b. April 7, 1726.

HODGES.
DAVID, and Eva Dingman. Ch: Anna, b. July 27, 1787.

HOFFMAN.

CAREL, and Nancy Ferguson. Ch: Maria, b. Nov. 14, 1785.

HOLODA.

MATTHIAS, m. Judy Van Wormer, Jan. 29, 1794. Ch: James, b. May 29, 1796.

HOOF.

HENRY, citizen of Schenectady in 1713.

HOOGEBOOM.

PIETER, and Neeltje Vroom. Ch. bp: Catarina, Feb. 8, 1767; Jacob, March 4, 1770.

PIETER, and Ann Taylor. Ch: Neeltie, bp. Dec. 10, 1783, m. James Bradford; Mary and Elisabeth, b. March 14, 1786; Robert, b. July 12, 1788.

DIRK, and Maria Buys. Ch: Debora, bp. Jan. 19, 1780.

CHRISTIAAN, and Antje Wirts. Ch. b: Petrus, Nov. —, 1786; Matthys, Aug. 26, 1794.

JOHN, and Lena Spoor, both from Remsen's bos, m. Sept. 20, 1786. Ch. b: Dirk, Feb. 23, 1788; Nicolaas, Nov. 28, 1790.

HOOGSTRASSER.

BALTUS, b. in "Duytsland," and Catharina Aghenbagh, both now living in Rensselaerswyk, m. March 12, 1781. Ch. b: Catharina, Nov. 20, 1791; Annatie, Nov. 21, 1795; Peter, Dec. 10, 1797.

HOOGETELING.

JACOBUS, and Neeltie Palmontier. Ch: Jacobus, bp. Feb. 29, 1784. Ch. b: Charity, Sept. 24, 1790; Willem, Dec. 25, 1793; Angenietje, Feb. 12, 1798.

HOOPOLE (HAPPOOL).

JURRY, and Margarita McKelvy. Ch. bp: Elisabeth, June 2, 1782; Catharina, Jan. 23, 1785. Ch. b: Margarieta, Sept. 7, 1789; Helena, Mar. 19, 1792; Lena, June 11, 1794; John, Dec. 28, 1795; Daniel, July 13, 1802.

FRANS, and Geertruy Winne, wid. of John Ouderkerk, both of Hellenbergh, m. Feb. 12, 1790. Ch. b: John, June 5, 1790; Hendrik, April 23, 1797.

HOPPE.

JACOB, and Elisabeth Tyce. Ch: Hendrik, b. March 6, 1796.

HOSFORD.

REUBEN, of Farmington, New England, hatter, and Ariaantje, dau. of Daniel Van Antwerpen, m. Dec. 8, 1748. Ch. bp: Eliza, Sept. 16, 1750; Daniel, Oct. 27, 1751; Maria, May 7, 1754, m. Dirk Groot; Neeltie, Jan. 2, 1757, m. Samuel J. Pruyn of Albany; *John*, Nov. 4, 1759; Daniel, Oct. 14, 1764; Ariantje, Aug. 16, 1767; Daniel, Oct. 29, 1769.

REUBEN, same as last, m. Anna Glen, Feb. 6, 1775. Ch. bp: Sarah, Sept. 24, 1774; Ariaantje, March 8, 1777.

JOHN, son of Reuben, and Margaret Geddes. Ch. bp: Reuben, April 22,

1781; Joseph, Oct. 24, 1783; Ariaantje, b. April 24, 1786; Annatie, b. Feb. 3, 1788.

HOUSE.

JOHN, and Elisabeth Hicks, m. April 12, 1785.

HOUSWAALD.

SAMUEL, and Mary ...... Ch: Elisabeth, bp. May 30, 1756.

HOVER.

HENRY, and Geertruyd Bohannan, m. Sept. 17, 1798.

HOW.

BENJAMIN, and Neela Cassada, both of Normanskil, m. March 1, 1795.

HUDSON.

JOHN, the well known proprietor and keeper of the "Schenectady Coffee House," next east of the Court House, and owner of a line of coaches between Schenectady and Albany. His son Robert sold this tavern to Resolved Givens in 1814.

HUGENOT.

DAVID, and Batje Clute. Ch: Annatje, bp. Feb. 2, 1784.

HUGH.

ANDRIES, of Hoghatok, and Rebecca Quackenbos of Schenectady, m. Aug 11, 1787.

HUGHS.

JEDIAH, and Elisabeth Van Antwerpen, m. Feb. 26, 1797.

THOMAS, and Dorothea Ernist. Ch: Peggy, b. Oct. 4, 1784.

GEORGE, and Gracy Moore, m. Sept. 20, 1792.

HULL.

JOHN, and Susanna Hicks, m. June 8, 1791.

HENRY, born at Killingworth, Conn., and residing at Nobletown, and Rebecca Waterhouse, residing at Schenectady, m. Feb. 6, 1785.

HUMPHREY.

JAMES, and Margaret Hurd (Stuart). Ch: Willem (?), bp. April 23, 1784; Benjamin, b. Feb. 5, 1786; Samuel, b. April 14, 1787.

BENJAMIN, and Polly Cantler. Ch: John, b. July 20, 1797.

HUSTON.

GEORGE, and Annatie Wemple. Ch: Maria, b. Aug. 14, 1796.

HUTTE.

JAN CHRISTOPHER, and Catarina Staark. Ch. bp: Johannes, Jan. 11, 1755; Maria Barbara, March 12, 1758.

HUTTON.

TIMOTHY, and Elisabeth Olin. Ch: Willem, bp. Jan. 10, 1784.

HUYK.

CORNELIS, widower of Geertruy Vosburgh, dwelling at Hoosack, and Hillegonda Erichzon, widow of Joseph Dance, m. Aug. 20, 1750.

JURRY, and Lena Beekman. Ch: Petrus, bp. Feb. 17, 1782.

PETER, of Albany, and Machtelt Quackenbos of Schenectady, m. Sept. 17, 1785. Ch: Nicholas, b. July 10, 1799.

INGERSON (INGERSOLL ?).

JAMES, and Catharine Hudson (Edsel). Ch. b: John, Oct. 29, 1787; James, May 18, 1792.

ISING.

THOMAS, and Elisabeth Palmontier. Ch. bp: Petrus, Aug. 10, 1777; Frans, June 9, 1782.

ISSELSTEYN.

See Ysselteyn.

IVEREN.

REYNIER, and Elisabeth Cornu. Ch: Johannes, bp. June 23, 1782. See Myndertse in *Albany Families*.

JACOBS.

JOHN, and Margaret Merkle. Ch: Rachel, b. Jan. 18, 1795.

JACOBSEN.

JACOB, and Maria Evertsen. Ch. bp: Hendericus, Feb. 13, 1757; Evert, June 4, 1759; Jannetje, May 24, 1762; Jannetje, Jan. 23, 1765; Johannes, July 4, 1767; Maria, Jan. 27, 1770; Hendricus and Simon, Feb. 28, 1773.

JACOB, perhaps same as last, and Maria Jansen. Ch: Folkert, June 2, 1776.

JACQUES.

JOHN, and Catarina Whiton. Ch: John, bp. Nov. 11, 1781.

JAMES.

WILLIAM, and Rachel Ellin (Allen). Ch. bp: Annestis (Ernestus ?), Feb. 28, 1779; John, Feb. 3, 1782.

JANSEN.

ANDREAS, and Jannetje Burger. Ch: James, bp. March 6, 1768.

ANDRIES, b. in New Jersey, and Margariet Service, both living in Warrensburgh, m. Jan. 31, 1786. Ch: Clara, b. April 27, 1788.

JACOBUS, and Rebecca Buys. Ch: Rachel, bp. March 11, 1770.

EVERT, and Antje La Grange. Ch: Maria, bp. Sept. 18, 1774.

NICOLAAS, and Elisabeth Way. Ch: Maria, bp. March 4, 1780.

JOHANNES, and Susannah ...... Ch: Moses, bp. Aug. 23, 1780.

JAN, and Mary ...... Ch: Johannes, bp. May 9, 1781.

PAULUS, sold to Christiaan Christiaanse his land at Schenectady, in 1671. Arnout, son of Paulyn Janse, was carried away captive by the French and Indians, Feb. 9, 1690.

JOHNSON.

EDWARD, and Rebecca Harris (Nobel). Ch. bp: Maria, Feb. 8, 1783; Benjamin, Feb. 20, 1785.

13

JOSEPH, merchant of Schenectady, 1790.

NICHOLAS, and Hanna ...... Ch: Charles, bp. Jan. 23, 1785.

JOHN, of Remsenbos, and Catharina Pruim. Ch: Andrew, b. July 27, 1785.

JOHN, of Remsenbos, probably same as the last, m. Mary Taylor of the *Woestyne*, May 1, 1788. Ch. b: Amy, April 13, 1789; William, July 7, 1795.

WILLIAM, and Debora Ayres. Ch: James, b. Jan. 26, 1787.

JOHN, and Margariet Hallenbeck. Ch: Robert McMath, b. Oct. 16, 1790.

JOHN, and Maria Teerpenning, both of Clifton Park, m. July 4, 1790. Ch. b: John, Aug. 28, 1792; Peter, Aug. 16, 1795; Elisabeth, Jan. 24, 1798; James, Dec. 20, 1800; Lucas, Oct. 29, 1801.

DAVID, and Jane Lydle. Ch. b: David, March 12, 1793; Jane Eliza, March 12, 1806.

JOICE.

DARCY, in Schenectady before 1800, d. March 28, 1848, a. 76ys., 8m., 7d.

JONCKERS, *alias* VAN ROTTER-DAM.

JAN JANSE, one of the early settlers of Schenectady. His lot was on the east side of Church street, next north of the church. Letters of administration on his estate were issued Feb. 23, 170¾, to his sons-in-law. He had three daughters:

Feitje, wife of Benjamin Lenyn; Pieter-tje, wife of Manasseh Sixberry; Rachel, wife of Willem Boin or Bowing.

JONES.

JAMES, from London, and Catarina Philipse from the *Willigen*, m. April 27, 1757. Ch. bp: Harmanus, Dec. 14, 1760; Maria, March 18, 1764; Anga-nieta, March 22, 1767.

SAMUEL, and Cornelia Simson. Ch: Samuel, bp. Aug. 15, 1784.

SAMUEL, and Ann Buchanan, m. Nov. 30, 1785. Ch. b: William Buchanan, Oct. 8, 1786; Nathaniel Merriam, June 24, 1791; Frederic Stack, August 24, 1793; Nancy, Dec. 4, 1795.

DIRK, and Elisabeth Moulter, both of Warrensburgh, m. Jan. 25, 1786. Ch. b: James, July 26, 1787; Peter, Aug. 10, 1788; Peggy, Jan. 2, 1790.

JOUTES (YOOTIS, YOUTIS).

JOHAN MICHAEL, m. Elisabeth Van Vorst. Ch. bp: Johannes, Dec. 21, 1766; Dirk, March 27, 1768; Pieter, Nov. 19, 1769; Immetje, April 28, 1771; Maria, May 9, 1773; *Philip*, b. Feb. 5, and Eli-sabeth, b. Feb. 6, both bp. April 9, 1775; Johannes, Nov. 15, 1777; Albert, Oct. 17, 1779; David, May 9, 1781.

PHILIP, m. Jacomyntje, dau. of Cor-nelis Christiaanse, July 11, 1796. Ch. b: John, July 14, 1797; Maria, June 22, 1799; Jacobus, June 6, 1801; Cor-nelis, Sept. 15, 1802; Elisabeth, Sept.

25, 1804; Jane Anna Van Gyseling, May 13, 1806; Peter, Dec. 1, 1807; Sarah Emily, Sept. 30, 1810.

KACHEL.

JURRY, and Elisabeth Schwer. Ch: Jurry, bp. Nov. 6, 1771.

KANNERLY.

WILLIAM, and Elisabeth Kelly. Ch: Jacob, bp. Aug. 18, 1765.

KEELY.

CHRISTIAAN, and Margareta Wilkeyser. Ch: *Adam*, bp. Sept. 20, 1769.

ADAM, son of Christiaan, and Margarita Bragham, both of the Noorman's Kil, m. Feb. 22, 1795. Ch: Annatie, b. Nov. 9, 1796.

KEHRLACH.

THEWALT, and Anna Katrina Volmer. Ch: Anna Katrina, b. June 22, 1726.

KELLY.

ALEXANDER, citizen of Schenectady before 1800.

KENDALL.

GEORGE, and Anna Fuller, m. Dec. 8, 1788; Anna Hall, wid. of George K., b. April 26, 1749, d. Jan. 13, 1833, in her 93d year.

KENNEDY.

JOHN, and Lena Vedder. She d. Mar. 30, 1787. Ch. b: James, May 25, 1785; Simon, March 26, 1787.

JOHN, JR., and Nancy Wasson, both of Currybos, m. Feb. 7, 1788. Ch: Andrew Moore, b. Feb. 25, 1792; Dorothea, bp. June 22, 1794; Dorothea Wasson, b. April 9, 1798.

KERCKASSEL.

CASPAR, and Elisabeth Van Vliet. Ch: Isaac, bp. Oct. 28, 1788.

KERN.

VALENTINE, and Maria Margareta Smith. Ch: Sarah, bp. Dec. 25, 1765.

KERNS (CARNES).

WILLIAM, and Susanna Parleman. Ch. b: Isaac, Dec. 10, 1797; Sarah, Jan. 15, 1802; Stephen, Oct. 26, 1806.

KESSELAAR.

THOMAS, and Margariet Kremer. Ch: Maria, bp. Oct. 29, 1780.

KETELHUYN (KETELHUN, KETELHEUM, KITTLE).

JOACHEM, from Cremyn, early settled in Albany. [*See Albany Families.*]

DANIEL, son of Joachim of Albany, m. Debora, dau. of Cornelis Viele, Aug. 16, 1695, in Albany. He settled in "Schaatkooke" as early as 1708. The following Ch. were bp. in Albany save the third, Cornelius: Anna, Sept. 13, 1696; Greetie, March 16, 1698; Cornelis, Nov. 3, 1700; Cornelis, Dec. 6. 1702; Suster, Jan. 30, 1704; *Joachim*, Aug. 12, 1705; Cornelis, bp. in Schenectady, March 6, 1711; Douw, Oct. 5, 1707; Douw, Dec. 19, 1708; David, Oct. 19, 1712; Grietie, April 24, 1715; Margarita, Jan. 24, 1722.

JOACHIM, son of Daniel, of "Schagh-kook," and Eva, dau. of Adam Vrooman of Schenectady, m. June 25, 1730. Ch. bp: Anna, Feb. 20, 1732; *Daniel,* Sept. 23, 1733; Margarieta, July 30, 1735, m. Gerrit Van Ness; Daniel, Jan. 5, 1737, in Albany; Debora, Sept. 10, 1738, in Albany, m. Cornelis Lansing; Maria, June 14, 1740, m. Johannes Lansing; Sara, Jan. 29, 1744, m. Johannes Van Vorst; *Adam,* Dec. 1, 1745.

(KETTEL).

DAVID, son of Douw, of Albany, re-siding at "Schenknick," and Debora, dau. of Nicolaas Viele of Schenectady, m. May 13, 1761. Ch. bp: Catalyntje, Oct. 4, 1761; Catalyna, Mar. 13, 1763, m. Albert A. Vedder; *Douwe,* Nov. 10, 1765; Nicolaas, May 21, 1769; Neeltje, Jan. 5, 1772; Willem, April 17, 1774; Arent, Oct. 31, 1776; Maria, Dec. 26, 1779, m. Albert Vedder.

(KITTEL).

DANIEL, son of Joachim, and Sarah, dau. of Sybrant van Schaick of Albany, m. July 11, 1761. She d. Aug. 4, 1842, in her 102d year. Ch. bp: Jannetje, Oct. 17, 1762, m. Abraham Brown: Eva, Jan. 1, 1764; Joachim, b. July 20, bp. Aug. 11, 1765, in Albany; David; Catalyntje, July 10, 1771; Catalyntje, March 28, 1773; Sybrant Van Schaick, Jan. 8, 1775, d. in Albany, March 1, 1844, a. 68ys., 2m., 4d.; Ann, his wid., d. May 19, 1830, a. 52ys.; Maria, July 6, 1778; Douwe, Nov. 5, 1780; Anna, Feb. 20, 1783.

ADAM, son of Joachim, m. Margarita, dau. of Harmanus Van der Bogart. He d. a little before Oct. 7, 1781, said to have been killed in the Revolutionary war. She was living in 1840 in Mari-poosa Upper Canada, having m. one Wil-liams. Ch. bp: Joachim, Oct. 12, 1777; Annatie, Dec. 19, 1779; Eva, Oct. 7, 1781.

DOUWE, son of David, and Catharina Minkelaar, both of the Noormanskil, m. Feb. 1, 1789. Ch. b: David, Jan. 8, 1790; William, April 6, 1798.

DAVID, perhaps son of Daniel, d. Sept. 3, 1848, in his 73d year; Ann O'Neil, his wife, d. May (4) 5, 1854, a. 73ys.

NICOLAAS, and Elisabeth Cass, both of Normanskil, m. May 13, 1793.

KIDD.

SAMUEL, and Mary Reneaux. Ch: Solomon, b Nov. 13, 1788.

KIERSTED.

HENDRICK, and Sarah Slot. Ch: Sa-rah, b. Sept. 27, 1797.

KIMMER.

HARMANUS, and Esther Groot. Ch: Teunis, b. Sept. 9, 1787.

KING.

Lieut. ......, and Molly ...... Ch: Sa-rah, bp. Dec. 14, 1764.

KINSELA.

JOSEPH, b. at Lisburn, Ireland, in 1749, d. April 15, 1816, a. 67ys. He made his will March 30, 1816, proved April 22, 1816 ; spoke of youngest son George, sons Thomas and William, of his wife Margaret, dau. Jenny, wife of Jacob Lyons, Catharine, wife of Rev. James Murphy, Francis Mary Ann, wife of James Delvin, 4 grand dau., the dau. of Jenny, wife of Jacob Lyons, viz : Margaret De Graaf, Ann De Graaf, Catharine De Graaf and Mary Jane Lyons, also of my grandson John De Graaf.

THOMAS, son of Joseph, made his will June 7, 1822, proved Oct. 14, 1822; spoke of wife Catharine, two dau. Margaret Jane and Rebecca, brother George and sister Caty, wife of Rev. James Murphy. He was b. Feb. 26, 1776, d. Oct. 11, 1822. The Kinsela lot was on north side of State street, from Wall street to the Canal.

KIRKPATRICK.

WILLIAM, of Ireland, m. Debora, dau. of Abraham Glen, Dec. 11, 1763. Ch. bp : Sarah, Jan. 25, 1764; Abraham, Dec. 15, 1765 ; William, May 1, 1768.

KITTLE.

See Ketelhuyn.

KLEYN.

JOHANNES, m. a dau. of Lodovicus Cobes, Secretary of Schenectady. In 1684, in company with his father-in-law, he bought the fourth flat on the north side of the Mohawk river. Ch. bp. in Albany : Weyntje, Jan. 23, 1684 ; Bata, April 2, 1686, m. Willem Marinus ; Clara.

CATHARINA, *abiit cum testimonio Schonegtady*, 1701. *Albany Church Records.*

KLEYNE.

JOHANNES, and Maria Powell, both of Kachnawage, m. Nov. 2, 1767. Ch : Johannes, bp. March 7, 1770.

KNAPTON.

WILLIAM, and Nina Moon, m. Sept. 10, 1797.

KNOWLES.

JEREMIAH, cabinet maker, resident of Schenectady about 1800.

KNOX.

JOHN, m. Elisabeth, dau. of Pierre Cornu, Jan. 19, 1765. Ch : Elisabeth, bp. Dec. 22, 1765.

KOEN.

VELT, and Anna Katarina ...... Ch : Samuel, bp. June 14, 1718.

KOGH.

SOPHRYNUS and Elisabeth Hull. Ch : Maria, b. June 9, 1793.

KORTRIGHT.

HENDERICK, and Jannetie Steen. Ch. bp : Rachel, May 24, 1777 ; Willem, May 13, 1779.

KRANKHEIT.

PIETER, and Mary Humphry. Ch : Joseph, bp. Oct. 6, 1780.

KREDENWYS.

HENDERICK, and Rachel Campbell. She was b. Nov. 22, 1742, and bp. Nov.

8, 1767. Ch. bp: Catarina, June 10, 1764; Johannes, Jan. 24, 1767; Harmanus, April 5, 1769; Isaac, Oct. 27, 1771; Annatje, Nov. 2, 1777. Rachel, b. July 5, 1781.

KYPSE (KIPP).

LEWIS, and Margarietje Kellogg. Ch: Annatje, bp. Sept. 12, 1783.

KULERNAN.

GERRIT CLAAS (alias *Culis* or Van Vranken, which see) in 1670 bought a garden in Schenectady of Bastiaan De Winter.

LABATIE (LABADDIE).

JAN, a native of France, came to Beverwyck previous to 1634, was subsequently *commissaris* of the Patroon of Rensselaerswyck, afterwards held a like office at Fort Orange under the West India Company. He bought and sold various lots and parcels of land in Albany and Schenectady. His wife was Jillesje Claase (Swits) aunt of Claas and Isaac Cornelise Swits and wid. of surgeon Harmen Myndertse Van der Bogart. It is not known that he left any descendants.

LA GRANGE.
See De La Grange.

LAMBERT.

JOHAN, schoolmaster, lived on east side of church street, about midway between Union and State street; made his will July 8, 1809, proved Aug. 30, 1809, d. July 26, 1809, a. 56ys. He m. first, Geertruy, dau. of Cornelis Van Slyck about

1779, and secondly, Geertruy,dau. of Johannes Steers about 1790. Ch. bp: Philip, Nov. 7, 1779; Jannetje, July 22, 1781; Jannetje, May 25,1783; Cornelis Van Slyck, March 20, 1785. Ch. b: Maria Dorothea, June 2, 1787; Abram, Nov. 19, 1788; Maria Dorothea, Feb. 12, 1791; Clara, April 19, 1793; Geertruy, March 21, 1795; John, Nov. 18, 1796; Getty, July 19, 1798; David Campbell, Jan. 11. 1802, d. Dec. 5, 1821; Catharina, March 12, 1805.

LANSING.

SANDER, carpenter, son of Gerrit of Albany, made his will 1769, proved Dec. 31, 1790; spoke of his then wife Neeltie, sons Cornelis, Johannes, Harmanus and dau. Jannetie, wife of Johannes Van Eps, also of his step-dau. Geertruy Van Eps. He m. first, Engeltie, dau. of Harmen Van Slyck, Sept. 23, 1725, and secondly, Neeltje, dau. of Johannes Van Eps, wid., Oct. 9, 1763. Ch. bp: Catrina, b. Oct. 30, bp. Nov. 5, 1727; Cornelis ——, 1729; Gerrit, April 10, 1732; Gerrit, April 21, 1734; Catharina, June 13, 1736; Jannetje, Oct. 14, 1738, m. Johannes Baptist Van Eps; Elsje, Sept. 5, 1742; *Johannes*, March 17, 1745; Harmanus, Jan. 29, 1749.

GERRIT A., son of Abraham of Albany, d. Oct. 6, 1789, a. 83ys., 9m., 27d.

GERRIT G., son of Gerrit of Albany, cooper, m. Anneke Yeats, (Yates) of same county, Dec. 14, 1744.

EVERT, son of Gerrit of Albany, m.

Annatje Cooper. Ch: Alexander, bp. Dec. 25, 1744. [*See Albany Families.*]

CORNELIS, son of Sander, m. first, Catharina, dau. of Johannes Vrooman, Jan. 5, 175$\frac{9}{7}$, and secondly, Debora, dau. of Joachim Kittel, Oct. 28, 1757. Ch. bp: *Alexander*, Sept. 8, 1751; *Johannes*, March 7, 1754; Gerrit, Dec. 21, 1755; Joachim, April 16, 1758; Joachim, Mar. 16, 1760; Engeltie, Aug. 4, 1766; Joachim, Oct. 4, 1771; Harmanus, July 3, 1774.

GERRIT, son of Johannes of Albany, m. Elsje Lansing. Ch. bp: Johannes, July 29, 1753; *Gerrit*, Feb. 8, 1756. [*See Albany Families.*]

JOHANNES, son of Alexander, m. Maria, dau. of Joachim Kittel. Ch. bp: Johannes, Aug. 17, 1771; Jannetje, May 30, 1773; Joachim, Dec. 9, 1774; *Alexander*, March 23, 1777.

ALEXANDER C. son of Cornelis, m. Sarah Van Antwerpen. Ch. bp: Catarina, Oct. 29, 1780; Neeltje, Sept. 29, 1782. Ch. b: Engeltie, July 25, 1785; Elisabeth, June 18, 1790; Cornelius, June 15, 1792.

ALEXANDER, son of Johannes (?), m. Elisabeth Huyk. Ch: John C., b. Feb. 17, 1805.

JOHANNES, son of Cornelis, m. Maria Folmer. Ch: Catarina, bp. March 2, 1783. Ch. b: Margarieta, Jan. 4, 1786; Johannes, April 17, 1790; Cornelius, July 8, 1799.

GERRIT, son of Gerrit, m. Susanna, dau. of Isaac Swits, March 17, 1785. She d. March 31, 1787. Ch: Isaac Swits, b. March 26, 1787.

ISAAC, and Catharina Peek, m. March 25, 1799.

LANTMAN.

MICHIL, m. Maria, dau. of Willem Brouwer. Ch: Petrus, bp. Aug. 8, 1756.

LANYN (LENYN).

ARENT, and Margarita Clute, wid. of Andries De Graaf, m. Dec. 26, 1736.

LARAWAY.

See La Roy.

LA ROY.

ISAAC, m. Sarah, dau. of Johannes Heemstraat. He was aged 72 ys. in 1828. Ch. bp: Lydia, Feb. 6, 1780; Elisabeth, June 5, 1783. Ch. b: Simon, Dec. 27, 1785; Jannetje, June 22, 1788; Maria, June 16, 1793. [*See Albany Families.*]

(LARAWAY).

NICHOLAS, and Neeltie Truax, both dwelling at the Noomanskil, m. May, 17, 1786. Ch: Maria, b. Nov. 8, 1786.

LATA.

WILLIAM, and Ann Jackson. Ch: Margariet, bp. June 24, 1778; Nancy, b. March 9, 1796.

LEACH.

PHINEAS, and Maria Groot. Ch. bp: Joseph, Dec. 23, 1770; Hester, Sept. 19, 1773.

LE CLERCQ.

See De Clerk.

LEE.

BENJAMIN, of Noormanskil, and Maria Leenhart. Ch: Nancy, b. Nov. 28, 1785.

LEENDERSE (LENS).

JAN, m. Magdalena Berrit, Feb. 5, 1727. Ch. bp: Johannes, b. Dec. 8, bp. Dec. 30, 1727; Timotheus, bp. Sept. 3, 1731; Robert, Aug. 26, 1733; Maria, Feb. 23, 1735; Margarita, July 9, 1737; Rachel, Feb. 15, 1741; Magdalena, Feb. 15, 1747.

JOHANNES, and Annatje, Stanhouse. Ch: Weyntje, bp. Feb. 16, 1769.

LEENHART.

MICHAEL, and Maria Woester. Ch. bp: Hendrik Rudolf, May 5, 1779; Elisabeth, June 16, 1781.

SIMON, and Margarita Aghenbagh, both of the Hellenbergh, m. Sept. 19, 1790. Ch: Michael, b. Jan. 26, 1791.

LENNOX.

SAMUEL, and Elisabeth James. He d. shortly before July 20, 1761. Ch: Mary, bp. July 20, 1761.

JAMES, m. Catarina Farenkrog, Dec. 31, 1763. Ch: John, b. Oct. 13, 1764; Anna, bp. July 7, 1784.

LENS (LENSH, LINS).

JAN, and Eliana Janse. Ch. bp: Johannes, Aug. 11, 1700; Maria, April 14, 1706.

LENYN (LINNE, LA NOY).

BENJAMIN, from Picardy, m. Feitje, dau. of Jan Janse Jonkers, March 15, 1699. He settled first on the south side of the Mohawk river, in the *Woestyne*, removed farther west into the Maquas country, where he was living as late as 1736. Ch. bp: Arent, June 8, 1701; Maria, Jan. 31, 1703; Lysbeth, April 14, 1706, m. Joshua Perry; Folkje, March 6, 1711; Cornelius, Dec. 18 (?), 1714; Aeltje, Aug. 11, 1716; Engeltje, Oct. 18, 1718.

LE TONNELIER.

JOHN LOUIS VICTOR, m. Maria Dorothea, dau. of Domine Barent Vrooman. After his death she m. Hendrick Ten Eyck. Ch: John Samuel, b. Aug. 20, 1788, a physician now (1872) living in New York.

LEVENSTEYN.

PIETER, and Maria Bekker. Ch: Maria, bp. Sept. 8, 1773.

PIETER, JR., and Maria Wurmer. Ch: Johannes, b. April 23, 1791.

LEVI.

MICHAEL and Bata Heemstraat. Ch. b: Jacob, Jan. 30, 1789; Catharina, April 11, 1791; Samuel, Jan. 1, 1793; Johannes, June 5, 1795; Teunis, Sept. 15, 1797; Philip, Feb. 6, 1800; Abram, May 29, 1802; Willem Teller, Feb. 16, 1805; Cornelius, May 21, 1809.

LEWIS (LEWES).

DAVID, innkeeper, came to Schenectady as early as 1713; m. Maria Philipse, wid. of Jacob Cromwell. Ch. bp: Willem, Nov. 5, 1720; Sander, Oct. 26, 1722.

PIETER, and Lena Lhar. Ch: Eva, Jan. 22, 1749.

JOHN, and Annatje Hendrikse. Ch: Annatje, b. March, 3, 1776.

HENDRICK, and Maria Davis. He was aged, 76ys. in 1834. Ch: Elisabeth, bp. Feb. 8, 1778.

(LOUES).
JOHANNES, of Helderberg, m. Margaret Sparbeck. Ch: Andreas, bp. Nov. 4, 1784; John, b. Jan. 15, 1786.

ABRAHAM, and Margariet Peek. Ch. b: Isaac, April 24, 1786; Leonard, Feb. 15, 1788; Angenietje, Sept. 14, 1791.

JACOB, and Cornelia Ostrander. Ch. b: Johannes, August 27, 1793; Sarah, Sept. 23, 1796.

WILLIAM, m. Francyntje, dau. of Johannes Gonzalis of the Lysjes kil, March 10, 1791. Ch: Joseph, b. Aug. 28, 1797.

LEYB.
JURRIE, and Engeltie Truex. Ch: Elisabeth, b. Feb. 20, 1798.

LEYBHERTS (LEPHERTZ, LYPHART).
JOHAN TOBIAS, and Anna Catarina Crusenen (Roesgang, Rousinger). Ch. bp: Johan David, Dec. 11, 1757; Jacob, Dec. 28, 1760; Maria Magdalena, Oct. 16, 1767.

14

LEYKEN.
HENDRIK, and Catarina Ronkle. Ch. b: Margarita, March 29, 1785; Elisabeth, July 5, 1790.

LEYNS.
JAMES, and Phebe Gardener. Ch: Sarah, bp. Nov. 6, 1779.

LIGHTHALL.
ABRAHAM, m. Anna, dau. of Claas Van der Bogart. Ch. bp: Anna, June 18, 1720; *Willem*, Feb. 3, 1722; *Claes*, b. March 7, 1724; *Jacobus*, b. Jan. 3, 1726.

WILLEM, son of Abraham, m. Elisabeth, dau. of Johannes Marselis, Nov. 20. 1748. Ch. bp: Abraham, May 7, 1749; Sarah, June 17, 1750; Sarah, Aug. 25, 1751, m. Dirk Van Vranken; *Abraham*, Sept. 12, 1753; Anna, Oct. 26, 1755, m. Adriaan Van Slyck.

JACOBUS (James), son of Abraham, m. Margaret, dau. of Pierre Benoit (Binneway) of Albany. Ch: Anna, bp. March 24, 1751.

JAMES (Jacobus), same as last, widower, m. Sara, dau. of Johannes Van Vorst, Nov. 10, 1752. He d. July 19, 1791; she d. March 14, 1807. Ch. b: *Abraham*, July 9, 1753; Johannes, Feb. 12, 1755; Johanna, April 9, 1756; Margarita, bp. Nov. 20, 1757; *Johannes*, Feb. 18, 1759; Margarita, b. June 13, 1761, m. Pieter Van Slyck; Willem, Dec. 4, 1762; Jilles, Aug. 20, 1765; *Nicolaas*, May 19, 1767; *Jillis*, May 13,

1769; Willem, April 5, 1771; Annatje, April 5, 1774.

CLAAS, son of Abraham, m. Margaret Idich, Jan. 14, 1748–9. Ch. bp: *Jacobus*, May 14, 1758; Lancaster, May 10, 1761; Frans, Feb. 3, 1765; *Willem.*

ABRAHAM, son of Willem, m. Annatje, dau. of Claas Van der Bogart. Ch. bp: Willem, Oct. 18, 1778; Claas Frans, May 20, 1781; Elisabeth, Aug. 3, 1783. Ch. b: Sarah and Rachel, Feb. 12, 1786; Christopher Yates, April 7, 1788; Annatje, July 13, 1790; Eva Van Patten, May 5, 1794; Joseph, Jan. 1, 1797.

NICOLAAS, son of James, m. Elisabeth Wageman. He kept an inn in Water street, on the river bank in 1813; d. Jan. 27, 1838, in his 88th year; she d. Oct. 20, 1836, in her 87th year. Ch. bp: Margareta, Oct. 21, 1776, in Albany; Elisabeth, m. Peter Colson; Nicolaas, April 8, 1781; Willem, b. Aug. 4, 1791.

ABRAHAM, son of James, m. first, Ann Freeman. Ch: Sarah, bp. Nov. 10, 1781; he m. secondly, Catharina C. Cuyler. Ch. b: Sarah, May 16, 1788; Annatie, March 13, 1790; Jacobus, April 24, 1792; Cornelius, March 9, 1794; John, May 25, 1796; Jacob Wendell, July 5, 1798; Jane, Oct. 12, 1800; Catharine Maria, Feb. 11, 1803.

JAMES, son of Claas, sexton of the Dutch Church 1799–1829, m. Charity Page. He d. April 22, 1829, a. 71ys.; she d. May 1827, a. 70ys. Ch. b: Nicholas, April 14, 1785; Elisabeth, July

30, 1787; William, Oct. 3, 1789; Maria, Feb. 13, 1794.

WILLIAM, son of Claas, m. Sarah, dau. of Ahasuerus Marselis. He d. Oct. 5, 1822; she d. Nov., 1828. Ch. b: Maria, Dec. 4, 1786; Margarieta, Sept. 12, 1788; Engeltie, Sept. 21, 1790; Anna, July 31, 1793; Nicholas, Dec. 23, 1793; Ahasuerus, Feb. 12, 1797; Ahasuerus, March 12, 1799, m. Margaret Peek, Sept., 1820; Abraham, Nov. 30, 1800; Ann, April 30, 1804.

LANCASTER, son of Claas, m. Hester Kittle. Ch. b: Nicholas, Nov. 29, 1788; Douwe, Oct. 16, 1790; Abraham, April 22, 1793; Anneke, March 2, 1796.

JOHN, son of James, m. Annatje, dau. of Cornelis Van Slyck, April 23, 1793. He d. in Glenville, Aug. 4, 1835, a. 78ys. Ch. b: Hesje, Jan. 14, 1794; Cornelius, Aug. 16, 1795; James, May 12, 1797; Catharina, May 2, 1799; Abraham and Sarah, Aug. 14, 1801; Sarah, Sept. 12, 1803; Abraham, Jan. 25, 1806, d. Oct. 16, 1830; Peter, July 1, 1807; Hannah, March 8, 1811.

JELLIS, son of James, m. Celia Jenny (Jane Seely), Dec. 25, 1793. Ch. b: Sarah, June 10, 1794; Hanna, Jan. 19, 1796; James, Jan. 12, 1798; Gideon, Sept. 11, 1800.

LITTLE.

DAVID, and Ann Nedham. Ch: John, bp. Dec. 10, 1769.

THOMAS and Lucencea Crawford. Ch: John, bp. Feb. 9, 1784.

LLOYD.

EDWARD, and Maria Young. Ch: Henderick, bp. March 22, 1765.

LOAGUE.

ROBERT, made will July 9, 1818, proved July 25, 1818, spoke of wife Elisabeth, and of dau. Elisabeth, wife of Col. Zeger Van Santvoord, and of the Ch. of said dau.

LOCKWOOD.

HENRY, b. in Fairfield county, Conn., and Letitia Patterson, b. in Massachusetts Bay, both residing in Curry's bos, m. Jan. 13, 1785. Ch. b: Thomas, Jan. 12, 1786; Jeremiah, Oct. 25, 1787; Elisabeth, Sept. 3, 1789; Henry, Sept. 25, 1791; Eleanor, Oct. 7, 1793; Abigail, Sept. 16, 1795; Benjamin, July 27, 1797.

LOORM.

ALEXANDER, and Rachel Egmont. Ch: Annatje, bp. July 9, 1784.

LOUKS.

DIRK, and Dorothea Fox. Ch: Annatje, bp. Nov. 8, 1780.

LOW.

JOHN R., and Abigail Hopkins. Ch: Ann, bp. Sept. 13, 1791.

LULARAN.

JACOB, and Angenieta Doorn. Ch: Jacob, bp. Jan. 22, 1779.

LOSEE.

JOSUA, and Geertruy Moxon. Ch. bp: Robert, Sept. 11, 1771; Geertruy, May 23, 1780.

LUYKASE WYNGAART.

JAN, son of Lukas Gerritse Wyngaart of Albany. His wife was Caatie ......; had a son Luykas Johannese. [*See Albany Families.*] In 1690 he was driven from his land above Schenectady, near Hoffman's Ferry, by the Indians; the same year being about to engage in an expedition against the French and Indians in Canada, he made his will; spoke of wife Catharyna. In 1705 he sold his land to Carel Hansen Toll. He had a lot also in the village, on Front street. His son Luykas, in 1757, owned a lot on south side of State street, 51ft. front, beginning 118ft. west from Mill Lane.

LUYPARD.

JOHAN DAVID, m. Immetje, dau. of Jillis Van Vorst. Ch: Johan Tobias, bp. Nov. 9, 1783; Catharina, bp. Nov. 5, 1785; Jellis Van Vorst, b. Dec. 24, 1787; Lena, b. April 8, 1789; Elisabeth, bp. Feb. 19, 1792. Ch. b: Margarieta, May 28, 1793; Eva, March 17, 1795; Maria, Dec. 5, 1796; Baata, March 1, 1801; David, Mar. 5, 1804; Arme Ann, Oct. 20, 1806; Nancy, Sept. 12, 1808.

JACOB, m. Elisabeth, dau. of Jillis Van Vorst. Ch. b: Tobias, Sept. 24, 1786; Catharina, Sept. 17, 1789; Maria, Aug. 12, 1792; Arent, bp. April 17, 1796; Elisabeth, b. Sept. 23, 1801; Sarah, Aug. 1, 1804.

LYNE (LYON).

MATTHEW, a schoolmaster in Scenectady 1760-6, m. Helena Lansing.

LYSENPAGH.

CHRISTIAAN, and Jane Hammon. Ch: Annatje, b. Jan. 28, 1797.

MACAMNSCH.

JOHN, and Elisabeth Lennox. Ch: Jane, bp. Oct. 8, 1772.

MAC BEEN.

JOHN, and Isabel Grant. Ch: Daniel, bp. March 15, 1779.

MAC BRAID.

JEEMS, and Jannetje ...... Ch: Maria, bp. Dec. 25, 1736.

McCALL.

ALEXANDER, and Catrien Campbell. Ch. bp: Ann, Dec. 9, 1781; Caty, Dec. 12, 1783.

McCALLUM.

ALEXANDER, and Mary Lyde. Ch: Alexander, bp. Jan. 9, 1782.

JOHN, and Jannet Stuart. Ch: Peter, b. April 7, 1792.

McCARTY.

DENNIS, and Nancy ...... Ch: Margariet, bp. Oct. 7, 1777.

McCLELLAN.

JOHN, m. Eleanor Morrison, July 31, 1794. Ch: Ann, b. July 25, 1795.

McCLOUD.

NORMAN, from Scotland, m. Elisabeth, dau. of Douwe Van Vorst, March 16, 1760. Ch: Maria, bp. March 23, 1760.

McCLYMON.

WILLIAM, jeweller, in Schenectady about 1800.

McDANIEL.

ALLEN, and Hester ...... Ch: John, bp. Nov. 15, 1757.

MICHAEL, and Sarah Dubois. Ch. bp: Margarita, Aug. 21, 1763; Catarina June 23, 1765; Jesse, April 25, 1767.

JOHN, and Christina Pater. Ch: Catrina, b. Oct. 5, 1784.

McDONALD.

NICHOLAS, and Mary ...... Ch. b: Margariet, March 4, 1762; Nicholas, Oct. 25, 1764; Daniel, Jan. 26, 1766: these Ch. were bp. March 3, 1767.

JAMES, tailor, m. Annatje Erichzon, Dec. 22, 1768. Ch: James, bp. Nov. 19, 1769.

ALEXANDER, and Catarina Campbell. Ch. bp: James, May 24, 1778; James, Sept. 26, 1779.

JOHN, and Nancy Thompson. Ch. b: John, Sept. 25, 1786; Mary, Dec, 31, 1792.

JAMES, and Mary Vining, m. Feb., 1790.

JOHN, and Maria Minklaer. Ch. b: Elisabeth, Nov. 23, 1797; Isaiah, Sept. 1, 1800; Nancy, Jan. 25, 1802; David, Sept. 17, 1803.

McDOUGALL.

JOHN, and Ann Elisabeth Kennedy. Ch. bp: John, Feb. 17, 1780; Elisabeth, Feb. 18, 1781; Hugh, Oct. 13, 1783; Mary Kennedy, b. Jan. 26, 1786; Joseph, Nov. 20, 1792.

PETER, and Mary Man. Ch: Esther Man, bp. May 18, 1781.

JOHN A., and Maria, dau. of Dirk Van Vranken. Ch. b: Nancy, April 22, 1800; Dirk Van Vranken, Jan. 8, 1802; Margaret Ann, May 2, 1804; Sarah, March 13, 1808.

ALEXANDER, and Mary Wesley. Ch: Ralph, June 19, 1785.

DUNCAN, and Ann Wever. Ch. b: Daniel, March 5, 1786; Margarieta, Jan. 22, 1791; Margariet, Sept. 29, 1794.

ALEXANDER, (Duncan ?), and Ann Wever. Ch: Sarah, b. Dec. 16, 1792.

McEWEN.

JAMES, and Engeltie Peek. Ch. b: Catharina, July 28, 1785; Cornelius, Sept. 3, 1787; Edward, Jan. 6, 1793; Sarah, May 9, 1795; Jannetie, June 28, 1800.

McFARLANE.

ANDREW, merchant as early as 1767, resided in the house, still standing, on west corner of Church and Water streets; m. Annatie, dau. of Willem Pieterse, Feb. 11, 1764. He d. July 17, 1805, a. 72ys.; she d. Oct. 20, 1809, a. 66ys. Ch: Robert, bp. Sept. 30, 1764, m. Elisabeth ......, who d. Nov. 4, 1843, a.

74ys., 4m., 23d.; Helen, b. Nov. 22, 1766, d. Nov. 10, 1850; Ann, bp. Nov. 16, 1768, d. Feb. 21, 1833; William; Henry; Andrew; James.

NORMAN, and Margariet McLaan. Ch: Malcolm, bp. Nov. 17, 1778; Caty, b. Feb. 24, 1787; Isabel, March 8, 1792.

McFARLAND.

JOHN, and Jannet McIntosh. Ch. b: Mary, Dec. 13, 1784; Alexander, Dec. 18, 1787.

McFARLIN.

MALCOLM, and Caty Stuart. Ch. b: Anna, April 23, 1788; Alexander, Sept. 2, 1793; Norman. March 11, 1796; Daniel, April 14, 1798; Jame (Jane ?), June 4, 1800.

McGINNIS.

Capt. WILLIAM, with 89 men of Schenectady was at the battle of Fort George Sept. 7, 1755, where he was killed with Capt. Jonathan Stevens of the same place. According to Sir William Johnson's report "they fought lions." He m. Margareta Veeder, Feb. 21, 175⁹⁄₉, and left an only child, Alexander, who d. Feb. 13, 1770.

McGOWAN.

GEORGE, blacksmith, a citizen of Schenectady about 1800. He owned the land on Nott Terrace and Amanda street, lately sold by his heirs.

McGREGOR.

MALCOLM, and Margery Shaw. Ch: Malcolm, b. April 27, 1785.

ALEXANDER, and Elisabeth McAfee (McWie). Ch. b: Alexander, Feb. 24, 1786; Gregor, March 3, 1788; Catharine, Jan. 12, 1795.

McGRAW.

CHRISTOPHER, and Maria Conner. Ch: Christopher, bp. Jan. 26, 1763.

JOHN, and Margariet Kleyn. Ch: William, b. Sept. 22, 1795.

McGUE (McGEE).

JOHN, and Annatje Quackenbosch, both of the Normanskil, m. June 18, 1763. Ch. bp: Johannes, December 25, 1763; Bata, Aug. 4, 1765; Catharina, Mar. 1, 1767; Abraham, Feb. 11, 1769; Alida, March 13, 1771; Appolonia, Dec. 5, 1775; Thomas, April 29, 1778; Elisabeth. July 17, 1780; Andreas, June 26, 1783.

(McCUE, McKERR).

JEMES, and Engeltie Peek. Ch: John, bp. July 5, 1774; Robert, bp. July 19, 1778; Hendrick, b. Sept. 22, 1789.

McGUFFY.

SAMUEL, and Susan Hoffman. Ch. b: Mary, March 26, 1785; John, April 16, 1786; Joseph Dawson, Feb. 11, 1788; Mary, Jan. 20, 1793; Edward Nelson, June 14 (6 ?), 1794; Christina, Nov. 31 (*sic*), 1796; Samuel, Nov. 22, 1798; James, Feb. 8, 1801.

McINTOSH.

CHARLES, and Susanna Marschalk. Ch: Susanna, bp. April 26, 1747.

JOHN, and Maria Smith. Ch. bp: Gerrit, May 30, 1779; Nicolaas, June 13, 1781; Neeltje, Feb. 8, 1783; Nicholas, Aug. 23, 1784; Elias, b. June 19, 1786; Daniel, b. Nov. 10, 1803.

PHINEAS, and Elisabeth Smith, both of Corry's Bos, m. June 14, 1791. Ch: John, b, Jan. 19, 1792.

WALTER, and Eleanor Frazier. Ch: Isabel, b. April 22, 1793.

McINTYRE.

JOHN, and Maria Idesen, widow of Jorges Rinkhout, m. June 17, 1704.

WILLIAM, trader in 1774, on the north corner of State and Ferry streets, m. Catarina Colon, Feb. 3, 1765. Ch: Robert, bp. Dec. 11, 1767.

McKABB.

OWEN, and Mary Luypard. Ch: Catharine, b. July 23, 1798.

McKAN.

SAMUEL, and Sarah Johnston. Ch: James, b. March 13, 1795.

MACKANS.

ANDREW, a citizen of Schenectady in 1713.

McKELVY.

NEIL, m. Catarina, dau. of Tjerk Van der Bogart, and wid. of Dirk Vergern. Ch. bp: Margariet, Sept. 27, 1761; Catarina, June 12, 1763; Daniel, June 2, 1765; Tjerk, July 27, 1768.

ARCHIBALD, and Mary Young. Ch: Margaret, bp. Dec. 19, 1783; Agnes, b. Oct. 1, 1785.

MACKENZIE.

HECTOR, and Elisabeth Pool. Ch: Daniel, bp. April 15, 1759.

McKINNEY.

DANIEL, m. Margaret Stanhouse, Sept. 7, 1753, in Albany. He d. Aug. 1, 1802, a 77ys.; she d. Nov. 5, 1815. Ch. bp: Margarita, April 10, 1757, m. Robert Bett; Elsje, Jan. 20, 1760, m. Abraham Groot; John, July 25, 1762; Annatje, Nov. 18, 1764, m. Jacob Beekman; Maria, June 7, 1767; Robert, March 6, 1769; *Matthew*, May 12, 1771; *James*, March 13, 1774; Maria, March 30, 1777, m. Archibald H. Adams, M.D.

ALEXANDER, and Margarita Bath. Ch: Elsje, bp. Oct. 22, 1758.

JAMES, and Jane Concord. Ch: Elisabeth, bp. Oct. 18, 1775.

MATTHEW, son of Daniel, m. Elisabeth, dau. of Peter Clute, Nov. 2, 1786. Ch. b: Stanhouse, Jan. 25, 1787; Daniel, Jan. 12, 1790; Catharina, Dec. 13, 1791; John, Feb. 19, 1795; Richard Clute, Aug. 21, 1797; Robert, June 9, 1800; Jacob, Aug. 24, 1802; James, Aug. 2, 1804; Frederic Clute, June 17, 1806.

JAMES, son of Daniel, m. Alida, dau. of Myndert Wemple, Feb. 3, 1793. He was not living in 1811; she made her will April 22, 1818, proved May 2, 1822. Ch: Myndert Wemple, b. June 5, 1796;

John, bp. Jan. 27, 1799, not living in 1811,

ROBERT, son of Daniel, (?), m. Maria De Graaf, Nov. 17, 1786. Ch. b: Margarietje, Jan. 12, 1787; Margarita, Nov. 12, 1788; Nicolaas, April 16, 1790; Christina, Sept. 7, 1791; Alexander, Aug. 25, 1793; Sarah, Jan. 27, 1795; John, Dec. 18, 1796; Andries, March 18, 1798; Matthew, April 28, 1800; Mary Adams, June 26, 1802.

McLEOD.

ALEXANDER, and Eva Wearly of Noormanskil. Ch: Aeneas, Feb. 22, 1785.

McMARLAN.

DAVID, of Corrysbos, and Margarieta Bratt of Noormanskil, m. Sept. 5, 1790. Ch: William, bp. May 22, 1791. Ch. b: Samuel, Dec. 4, 1792; Joseph, July 17, 1796; Lena, Sept. 3, 1799.

McMASTER.

JAMES, and Rachel Teller. Ch: Catrina, bp. Sept. 5, 1784; Ann, b. Oct. 4, 1787.

ROBERT, and Ann Buys. Ch: Robert, bp. Sept. 5, 1784.

THOMAS, of Remsenbos, and Susanna Patterson. Ch: Hugh, bp. March 19, 1785; Catharine, b. Oct. 9, 1789.

HUGH, of Remsenbos, and Rebecca Patterson. Ch: Hugh, b. May 9, 1789.

DANIEL, m. Sarah Marselis, June 12, 1748. Ch. bp: John, May 7, 1749; Elisabet, September 30, 1750; *Daniel;*

Alexander Van Eps, January 22, 1758; *James*.

DANIEL, son of Daniel, m. Barber, dau. of Albert Vedder. Ch. bp : Daniel, Nov. 18, 1781; Hester, Nov. 30, 1783; Sarah, Feb. 12, 1786; Albert, June 1, 1788; Annatje, March 9, 1794.

JOHN, a trader, resident at Schenectady, was killed in 1758 at Fort Stanwix, by a Cayuga Indian.

HUGH, m. Sophia, dau. of Willem Peters. Ch : Helena, bp. July 4, 1782.

SANDER (Alexander), son of Daniel, m. Engeltje, dau. of Dirk Van Patten. Ch. b : Maria, bp, July 18, 1784, m. Philip Ramsey; Rebecca, b. Jan. 24, 1786, m. Gershom Volk ; Sophia, Sept. 15, 1790, m. Helmus Becker; Daniel, Dec. 5, 1792; Margarietje, b. May —, 1795, m. John Realey ; Elisabeth, Feb. 5, 1799, m. Adam Realey; Dirk, Dec. 29, 1800. All the above mentioned Ch. were living April 17, 1818, when the father made his will, which was proved June 9, 1816.

JAMES, son of Daniel (?), m. Maria, dau. of Johannes Hall, Dec. 29, 1774. He d. Nov. 17, 1828, in his 78th year. Ch. bp : Daniel May 25, 1777 ; Sarah, Feb. 11, 1781 ; Johannes, Oct. 12, 1783 ; Nicholas, b. Sept. 25, 1785 ; *Richard*.

McMICHAEL.

RICHARD, son of James, m. Maria, dau. of Henry A. Marselis, Dec. 13, 1812. Ch. b : Henry M., Dec. 17, 1813, d. Sept. 17, 1852; Sarah Maria, Feb. 28, 1816;

John, Jan. 26, 1818, d. May 7, 1872; Cornelia Elisabeth, March 31, 1820, d. Sept. 10, 1822; Cornelia Elisabeth, b. March 1, 1822, d. Sept. 7, 1825; Richard, Dec. 8, 1824; Catharine Louisa, Dec. 15, 1826 ; Cornelia, July 27, 1829.

McNUTT.

JAMES, merchant in 1763, owned a lot on south side of Union street, east of Ferry street.

Mrs. ALICE, made her will Jan. 26, 1814, proved March 7, 1816, bequeathed her lot on north side of State street to her sister Isabella Nixon. This lot was lately owned by Charles Matthews.

McQUEEN.

WILLIAM, and Janet Adair. Ch : Sarah, b. Nov. 30, 1785; James Ellice, b. Nov. 20, 1786.

MADEAL.

WILLIAM, and Mary Tint. Ch : William, b. July 16, 1778, bp. June 12, 1781.

MAGINNIS.

DANIEL, mason, resident in Schenectady 1765.

MAIN.

WILLIAM, citizen of Schenectady, 1790.

MAKELYK.

Alias SOEGEMAKELYK, wid., an inhabitant of Schenectady 1697.

MALCOLM.

HUGH, and Margaret ...... Ch. bp : Hugh, Feb. 21, 1782; Margaret, June 15, 1784.

MALDRUM.

DAVID, m. Annatie Nickson, Sept. 28, 1761.

MAN.

JOHAN, member of the church in 1756.

MANBRUT.

JOHANNES, and Hester Visscher. Ch. bp: Sarah, Sept. 3, 1731; Wilm, Nov. 7, 1731; Margarieta, m. Carel Marinus.

(MOMBRUIT).

JOHN, and Christina Hugenot. Ch: Marytje, b. June 31, (*sic*), 1794.

MANDEVILLE.

DAVID, and Dina Vanderhoef. Ch. b: Maria, March 4, 1794; Sarah, March 28, 1796; Hendrik, Dec. 12, 1797.

HARMANUS, from "Charston," m. Annatie Bodine from Remsenbos, April 22, 1795 (?). Ch. b: Maria, Nov. 22, 1795; Elisabeth, Oct. 9, 1797.

MANGELSE.

PIETER, son of Jan of Albany, m. Jannetie Du Scheen. Ch. bp: Maria, Sept. 1, 1700; Fransyna, Oct. 18, 1702.

MANNING.

EDWARD, and Debora Vroom. Ch: Debora, bp. May 12, 1768.

CHRISTIAN, m. Susanna, dau. of Simon Van Antwerpen, Jan. —, 1788. Ch. b: Edward, Feb. 2, 1789; Rebecca, Oct. 7, 1791; Simon, Dec. 5, 1794; Simon, Aug. 4, 1797.

15

JOHN, of Curry'sbos, m. Catlyntje Truex *van het 'kreupel boss*, Aug. 10, 1786. Ch. b: Debora, Nov. 4, 1787; Maria, Feb. 1, 1790; Catlyntje, Jan. 15, 1792; Isaac Vroom, Jan. 15, 1795; Edward, July 30, 1797; John, Nov. 1, 1799; Elisabeth, March 16, 1802.

MANNY.

GABRIEL, Jun., and Elisabeth Paltz (Pels). Ch. b: Henry, Nov. 8, 1793; Mary, Sept. 1, 1795; James, March 31, 1798.

MANS.

JACOB, and Catarina Smitt. Ch. bp: Annatje, March 13, 1771; Jannetje, Aug. 27, 1777.

JACOB, and Lidia Aarsen. Ch: Cornelius, b. Sept. 9, 1785.

MARCH.

EPHRAIM, and Eva ...... Ch: Ephraim, bp. Aug. 31, 1784.

MARINUS.

DAVID, a citizen of Schenectady before 1684, m. Rachel Hanse. Ch: David, bp. Jan. 8, 1696; Neeltie, m. Pieter Quackenbos; *Willem;* Catarina, m. Thomas Nobel.

WILLEM, son of David, m. Baata, dau. of Johannes Klein. Ch. bp: *David,* April 30, 1707; Maria, June 19, 1709, in Albany, m. Takel Dirkse Heemstraat; *Johannes,* Feb. 13, 1712; Rachel, Oct. 19, 1717; Klaertje, Oct. 2, 1720, m. Daniel Wever; Jeremias, b. May 15, 1727; *Carel* (?).

DAVID, son of Willem, *geboren op de willigen*, m. Geertruy, dau. of Abraham Groot, Jan. 24, 1732. He was a carpenter; his house lot on south side of Union street, is now included in Canal street. Ch: Wilm, b. Aug. 31, 1732. Ch. bp: Hester, Feb. 17, 1734, m. Jacob Heemstraat; Abraham, Jan. 18, 1736; Bata, July 9, 1737; Abraham (?), Oct. 21, 1739; Maria, March 14, 1742; Geertruy, Dec. 9, 1744; Rebecca, Jan. 18, 1747.

JOHANNES, son of Willem, m. Geertruy Bosie, dau. of Philip. The banns were proclaimed June 15, 1735. He d. shortly before Jan. 8, 1749. Ch. bp: Wilm, April 30, 1736; Margarieta, Dec. 21, 1737, m. Jan Baptist Van Vorst, Jr.; Baatje, April 13, 1740; Claartje, May 23, 1742, m. Jacobus J. Van Vorst; Willem, Sept. 2, 1744; Margarietje, Dec. 14, 1746; Johannes, Jan. 8, 1749.

CAREL, son of Wilm, m. Margarietje, dau. of Johannes Mambrut. Ch. bp: Baata and Hester, twins, Jan. 23, 1746; *Willem*, Jan. 15, 1749, in Albany; Johannes, Feb. 18, 1763.

WILLEM, son of Johannes, m. Margariet Truex. Ch: Annatje, b. May 19, 1793.

MARKEL.

WILLIAM, and Rachel Bakker. Ch. bp: Matthias, July 14, 1774; Lourents, July 27, 1780; Elisabeth, March 28, 1783. Ch. b: Petrus, Jan. 15, 1786; Willem, Dec. 2, 1789; Catharina, Sept. 12, 1792.

MATTHIAS, and Elisabeth Gonzalus. Ch. bp: Margarita, Feb. 6, 1778; Maria, Dec. 24, 1779; Margarita, Jan. 19, 1782. Ch. b: Elisabeth, July 3, 1787; Lourens, Nov. 12, 1789.

DIRK, and Catrina Snell. Ch: Delia, bp. Aug. 17, 1783.

LOURENS, and Rachel Kiersted. Ch; Luke, July 22, 1792.

MARORY.

FLORENCE, and Jane Dickie. Ch: Catrien, bp. Nov. 16, 1777.

MARSELIS (MARCELUS).

MARSELIS JANSE, b. at Bommel in Guilderland, Holland, came early to Beverwyck where for many years he was an innkeeper and farmer of the burger and tapster excise of beer, wine &c. He seems to have been a man of good capacity and large business. His children settled in Albany, except Ahasuerus and Gerrit, who removed to Schenectady. He made his will June 11, 1690, proved in Kingston, May 22, 1722, and d. before 1700. His wife was Annatie Gerritse. Ch. Gysbert; Huybertje, m. Joseph Yates; Sytje, m. Joseph Janse Van Santen (*Van Judith*, m. Lucas L. Hooghkerk; *Ahas-Zandt); uerus; Gerrit.* [*See Albany Families.*]

AHASUERUS, cordwainer, son of Marselis Janse Van Bommel, m. Sara, dau. of Takel Heemstraat of Albany. He removed to Schenectady about 1698. Ch. bp. in Albany; *Johannes*, June 26, 1698; *Dirk*, Jan. 5, 1700; Johanna, Jan. 26, 1701, m. Johannes Van Vorst; *Gysbert*,

June 4, 1704; *Takel*, Jan. 1, 1709; Annatje, March 6, 1711, in Schenectady, m. Thomas Christiaanse; Maritie, March 8, 1713, in Albany; Trientien, July 31, 1715, m. Jan Baptist Van Vorst; Ahasuerus, Dec. 15, 1717; Abraham, July 8, 1721; *Isaac*, June 29, 1723.

GERRIT, son of Marselis Janse Van Bommel, m. Bregie Hanse in 1687, and with his wife and one child was killed in the massacre Feb. 9, 1690. One child, Myndert, was saved, and was living in Schenectady in 1709.

JOHANNES, son of Ahasuerus, merchant, made his will Feb. 2, 1732; owned house and lot No. 23 Front street, which, in 1753, his wid. occupied. He m. Sara, dau. of Claas De Graaf, Jan. 12, 1725. Ch : *Ahasuerus*, b. June 26, 1726. Ch. bp: Elisabeth, Aug. (?), 1729, m. William Lighthall; Sara, June 25, 1732; Maria, Nov. 25, 1733, m Dirk Van Vranken; *Claas.*

DIRK, son of Ahasuerus, m. Lysbet, dau. of Jan Baptist Van Eps, July 29, 1726. Ch : Sara, b. Feb. 24, 1727. Ch. bp: Helena, May 30, 1731; Helena, March 4, 173¾, m. Claas Marselis; Catharina, Feb. 15, 1736, m. Pieter Clute; Jan Baptist, Sept. 19, 1739.

GYSBERT, son of Ahasuerus, m. Elisabeth, dau. of Arent Van Antwerpen, May 31, 1730. Ch. bp: *Arent*, Nov. 26, 1732; Sara, June 9, 1734, m. Jacobus Van Sice; Catharina, Feb. 27, 1737; *Ahasuerus*, April 12, 1740.

TAKEL, son of Ahasuerus, m. Jacomyntje, dau. of Jan Baptist Van Eps, March 16, 1738. Ch : *Johannes*, b. Dec. 16, 1738; Helena, Jan. 4, 1741; Sara, June 10, 1743; Annatje, Dec. 8, 1745, m. Jacobus Mills; Alexander, Sept. 20, 1747; Maria, March 11, 1750, m. Cornelis Christiaanse.

GERRIT, son of Ahasuerus, m. Catharina Tyger. Ch: Willem, bp. Nov. 22, 1747.

ISAAC, merchant, son of Ahasuerus, m. Sara, dau. of Wouter Swart, Aug. 5, 1748. She d. in 1805. Ch. bp : Elisabet, April 16, 1749, m. Claas Van der Bogart; Sarah, June 4, 1758.

AHASUERUS, son of Johannes, m. Maria, dau. of Hendrick Vrooman, Jan. 1, 17⁴⁹⁄₅₀. Ch. bp: Johannes, Sept. 30, 1750; *Hendrik*, b. May 25, bp. July 19, 1753; Engeltie, m. Harmanus H. Van Slyck; Sarah, March 23, 1759; Johannes, Aug. 21, 1760; Sarah, Oct. 9, 1763, m. Willem Lighthall; *Nicolaas*, b. Aug. 15, bp. Aug. 17, 1766, d. Aug. 12, 1848; Johannes, Sept. 7, 1769; Jannetje, Oct. 14, 1770; *Johannes*, June 8, 1777.

CLAAS, cordwainer, son of Johannes, m. Lena, dau. of Dirk Marselis, April 30, 1757. He is said to have been killed by lightning in 1766, while crossing the Mohawk river in a canoe. Ch. bp : Sarah, April 9, 1758, m. Maas M. Marselis; *Johannes*, b. Jan. 27, bp. July 6, 1760; Dirk, July 11, 1762; Elisabeth, March 10, 1765, m. Jacob J. Clute; *Nicolaas*, Sept. 14, 1766.

ARENT, son of Guysbert, m. Rebecca, dau. of Jacob Vrooman, Dec. 23, 1758. Ch. bp: Geysbert, Dec. 23, 1758; Geysbert, Nov. 9, 1760; Maria, July 29, 1764; Isaac, July 17, 1768; Jacob, Jan. 17, 1773.

Capt. AHASUERUS, son of Gysbert, m. Hester, dau. of Nicolaas Visscher of Nestoungjoone, Sept. 1, 1765. Ch. bp: Elisabeth, April 20, 1766; Elisabeth, May 22, 1768, m. Gerrit Connor; Nicolaas, Feb. 18, 1770; Gysbert, May 3, 1772; Nanning, June 12, 1774, d. in Amsterdam, April 18, 1854; his wid. Debora, d. Aug. 24, 1869, in her 94th year, at her son's at Hagaman's Mills; Arent, Sept. 1, 1776; Catrina, May 23, 1784.

JOHANNES, son of Takel, m. Annatje, dau. of Johannes Van Antwerpen, Dec. 6, 1767. Ch. bp: Johannes, b. July 16, bp. 17, 1768; Takerius, May 1, 1770; Jacomyntje, Dec. 22, 1771, m. Jacob P. Bovie; Helena, April 24, 1774, m. Isaac A. Truax; Sarah, April 26, 1776; Arent, June 7, 1778; Susanna, Aug. 16, 1782; George Washington, July 12, 1784. Ch. b: Ahasuerus, April 30, 1786; Elisabeth, Sept. 3, 1788; Maritje, Dec. 23, 1790; Alida, Feb. 13, 1795.

JOHANNES, son of Claas, m. Catharina, dau. of Isaac Vrooman. He lived in Ferry street, opposite the Episcopal church; d. Dec. 15, 1833; she d. July 13, 1845, in her 82d year. Ch. b: Elisabeth, Nov. 27, 1785, m. Jacob I. Clute; Isaac Vrooman, Feb. 18, 1788, m. Catharine, dau. of Ezra Cady of Columbia

County, and subsequently settled in Onondaga County; Lena, Dec. 11, bp. Nov. 20, 1789 [*Church Records,*] m. Silas Andrus, publisher, of Hartford, Conn., both now dead; Nicholas, March 12, 1792, graduate at Union College; minister in Dutch Church; m. Jane, dau. of Col. Henry R. Teller; Dorothea and Lourens, Feb. 23, 1795. She d. unmarried, at Freeport, N. J., Feb. 16, 1871; he is now (1872) living in Montgomery county; Sarah, Sept. 12, 1800, m. Rev. Aaron A. Marselis.

EVERT, son of Gysbert m. Catalina Wendell of Albany, m. Sarah Van Benthuysen, both of Albany, the banns were proclaimed in Schenectady, August 13, 1786.

NICOLAAS, son of Ahasuerus, m. Machtelt, dau. of Isaac Rosa, Sept. 14, 1788. He d. Aug. 12, 1848, a. 82ys.; she was b. April 20, 1772, and d. March 20, 1852. Ch. b: Ahasuerus, Dec. 28, 1788; Isaac Rosa, Aug. 9, 1790; Maria, May 13, 1792; Annatje, July 14, 1794; Jannetje, Nov. 3, 1796; Cornelia, July 6, 1799; Isaac, March 21, 1801, a physician in Philadelphia; Cornelia, March 12, 1804; Henry, May 29, 1806; Nicholas, Aug. 6, 1808; Angelica Matilda, Nov. 17, 1811; Sarah Margaret, Dec. 23, 1813.

NICHOLAS, son of Ahasuerus, m. Sarah Vedder. He settled in Amsterdam, where he d. Oct. 4, 1853, a. 83ys. Ch: Ahasuerus, b. Oct. 9, 1792.

JACOB, son of Arent, m. Eva Carol (Corle), June 20, 1794. Ch. b: Aaron, Jan. 20, 1795; Marytje, Oct. 3, 1798; Isaac, May 10, 1801.

HENRY, son of Ahasuerus, m. Cornelia Pootman, Dec. 1, 1793. He was b. May 25, 1753, and d. Aug. 12, 1821; she was b. Dec. 6, 1754, and d. Jan. 3, 1837. Ch : Maria, b. Feb. 24, 1795, m. Richard McMichael, and d. Sept. 7, 1854.

GYSBERT, son of Ahasuerus G., of *de Willegen*, m. Maria Clauw of the Noormanskil, Jan. 26, 1794. Ch. b: Annatje, July 12, 1795; Annatje, July 3, 1796; Esther, Jan. 8, 1799.

JOHN, JR., son of Johannes T., m. Elisabeth, dau. of Abraham Truex. Ch. b: Annatje, July 24, 1795; Abram, Oct. 1, 1797; John, Feb. 19, 1800; Takerus, Feb. 28, 1803; Takerius, Feb. 10, 1805.

NICHOLAS, son of Claas, m. Sarah, dau. of Petrus Clute, April 17, 1795. He d. Nov. 28, 1845, a. 79ys.; she d. March 28, 1872, a. 94ys., 5m., 21d. Ch. b: Dirk, May 6, 1797, d. Sept. 11, 1832; Petrus, June 3, 1801; Helena, Nov. 8, 1804; Helena, Aug. 22, 1806; Jacob, April 18, 1809; Catharine, Jan. 22, 1811, d. April 12, 1846.; John, Nov. 2, 1816.

JOHN A., son of Ahasuerus, m. Catharine, dau. of Jacob Schermerhorn, Jan. 5, 1800. He d. Oct. 12, 1845, a. 68ys.; she d. Feb. 14, 1859, a. 76ys. Ch : Henry, who d. Aug. 17, 1802, a. 18m.

ISAAC, son of Nicolaas, m. Rachel Knorr in Philadelphia, Sept. 20, 1824.

She was b. Oct. 30, 1802. He is a physician in Philadelphia. Ch. b: Maria Mariel, Jan. 8, 1830; Henry Nicholas, Dec. 31, 1831; Rachel Anna, June 19, 1839; Rosa, June 27, 1842; Helen, Aug. 13, 1845.

MARSCHEL.

MARGARITA, member of the church in 1764.

MARTE.

JOHANN, weaver, lived on the *Warme Killetje* in 1761.

MARTENSE (VAN BENTHUYSEN ?).

JACOB, a citizen of Schenectady in 1703.

MARTIN.

ALEXANDER, and Annatje Philipse. Ch : Robert, bp. Dec. 2, 1758.

CHARLES, and Jane Robertson. Ch : George, bp. Oct. 3, 1783.

MASCRAFT (MATHERCRAFT).

DANIEL, and Jonathan Stevens leased Lysbeth Brouwer's land at the *Hoek* in Scotia in 1697.

MASTEN.

EZEKIEL, and Pieternella Viele. Ch : Ezekiel, bp. Jan. 29, 1706.

DIRK, and Mary Simson. Ch. bp: Maria, May 23, 1775; Elisabeth, Oct. 13, 1777.

MAURITS.

MARTEN, the owner of one-half of what is commonly called "Van Slyck's Island," lying immediately west of Schenectady, in the Mohawk river. He d. in the fall of 1662, and his brother Jacques Cornelise Van Slyck inherited his property. The island was at first called "Marten's Island," and was owned by Marten Maurits and Jan Barentse Wemp in Common.

MAXWELL.

WALTER, and Agnes Stuart, both of Corry's bos, m. May 18, 1786. Ch: James, b. March 23, 1787.

MEAD.

Doct. WILLIAM, m. Geertruy Myndertse. He was a surgeon in the Revolutionary war, and settled in Schenectady. Ch. bp: Catarina, March 21, 1780; Benjamin, Dec. 7, 1783.

JOHANNES, m. Margarietje De Mot. He d. in West Glenville, March 13, 1818, a. 74ys., 6m., 12d.; she d. Sept. 12, 1817, a. 68ys., 10m., 17d. Ch: Anna, b. Nov. 11, 1788.

MEAL.

CAREL, and Maria Van Tassel. Ch. bp: Elisabet, Sept. 28, 1779; Abraham, March 10, 1782; Neeltje, June 20, 1784.

MEB.

ROBERT, and Elisabeth Allen. Ch. bp: Annatie, Aug. 6, 1769; Jannetje, Aug. 4, 1771; Thomas, Jan. 28, 1776; Rachel, July 12, 1778; Catarina, Jan. 28, 1781; Sarah, Oct. 13, 1783.

MEBIE.

JAN PIETERSE, of the *Woestyne*, m. Anna Pieterse, dau. of Pieter Jacobse Borsboom. His home lot in the village, was on the east side of Church street, next door north of the Dutch church; he also had land on the Third flat on south side of the Mohawk, eight miles above Schenectady, and in 1697, Rode, a Mohawk sachem called by the Christians Dirk, with consent of all the other Indians, granted a piece of ground (80 acres), on both sides of Tionnondorogoes (Schoharie) creek, commonly known by the name of Kadarodae, to Jan Pieterse Mebie, in consideration that his wife "is something related to the Christian Castle." He made his will April 3, 1725, proved Sept. 13, 1725, and d. April 8, 1725. Ch. bp: *Pieter*, Jan. 20, 1686, in Albany; Catharina, m. Arent Samuelse Bratt, d. 1773, a. 82ys., 2m., 17d.; Annatje, April 16, 1693, in Albany, m. Helmers Veeder; *Abraham*, June 26, 1695; Engeltie, Nov. 10, 1697, m. Pieter Danielse Van Antwerp; *Jacob*, b. March 1, 1698 (?), bp. May 5, 1700, d. April 18, 1755; Maritje, m Cornelis Van Dyck; Meittje, Oct. 7, 1704. m. Johannes Fairly; Margaret.

ABRAHAM, son of Jan, m. Annatje, dau. of Albert Vedder, June, 1718; he m. secondly, Catalina Roseboom, wid., of Albany, March 30, 1752. He was a blacksmith, and lived on the lot next northerly of the Dutch church. Ch. bp: Catharina, Aug. 6, 1720, m. Johannes Volkertse Veeder; Anna, Sept. 1, 1722, m. Adam Hendrickse Vrooman; Maria, b. Nov. 23, bp. Nov. 29, 1724, m. Abraham Fonda; Eva, b. April 24, bp. April 30, 1727, m. Gerrit Van Antwerpen;

Albert, Feb. 20, 1732; Engeltje, July 22, 1733; Engeltje, April 13, 1735, m. Hendrick Van Dyck; *Albert*, May 14, 1738; Margrietje, Aug. 23, 1740, m. Johannes R. Wemple; Abraham, March 27, 1743; Abraham, Aug. 26, 1744.

PIETER, eldest son of Jan, and Susanna, dau. of Arent Vedder, both of the *Woestyne*, m. Nov. 12, 1721. He settled on the north side of the Mohawk river, on "Arent Mebie's kil," just north of the stone bridge on the New York Central railroad. Ch. bp: Anna, Oct. 26, 1722, m. Abraham Van Antwerpen, was buried on the Fifth flat; Sara, b. Feb. 2, bp. March 21, 1725, m. Abraham Yates; *Johannes*, b. Jan. 10, bp. Jan. 19, 1728; *Arent*, bp. ——, 1729; Margarieta, b. March 19, bp. April 15, 1733; Marrieta, bp. Oct. 13, 1734; *Harmanus*, Oct. 9, 1737; Maria, April 13, 1740; *Petrus*, Nov. 14, 1742; Rebecca, Oct. 6, 1745, m. Simon Van Antwerpen.

PIETER, (1731, Jan), and Dorothea Pikkert. Ch. bp: Achien, ——, 1730; Jacobus, Oct. 3, 1731. [There seems to be an error in the record here.]

JACOB, son of Jan, and Catrina, dau. of Hendrick Vrooman, m. Aug. 7, 1725. By his father's will, he received one-half of the Third flat on south side of the Mohawk — 63 acres, 79 rods — between lands of Jacobus Peek and Pieter Vrooman, Jr. His house, still standing, is occupied by one of his descendants. He made his will April 25, 1755, spoke of his eldest son John, wife Catrina, Anna,

wife of Thomas Brouwer Bancker, sons Cornelis and Petrus, and dau. Geesie; he d. April 18, (28 ?), 1755. Ch. b: Anna, July 26 (27), 1726; Geesie, Jan. 26, 1728; Margrieta, Feb. 23, 1730, m. Joseph Wheaton; Anna, Oct. 4, 1732, m Thomas Brouwer Bancker; Geesie, Oct. 24, 1734, m. Richard Smith; Gesina, Nov. 19, 1735; *Jan*, May 1, 1738, d. July 11, 1763; *Cornelis*, March 18, 1741, d. May 10, 1789; Petrus, July 28, 1744, d. Dec. 6, 1771, and buried in the *Woestyne*.

THOMAS, m. Sara Cowper, in New York, Oct. 11, 1730. Ch. bp: Margarieta, March 12, 1732; Johannes, Aug. 18, 1734; Robert, Dec. 25, 1736.

JAN, son of Pieter, m. Alida, dau. of Simon Toll, Dec. 13, 1755. He d. Nov. 24, 1796, and was buried in the Fifth Flat. Ch. bp: Susanna, May 29, 1757; Simon, Aug. 2, 1761; Pieter, Aug. 5, 1764, "a practitioner of physic;" Hesje, Nov. 9, 1766; Simon, Aug. 13, 1769, in 1799 a resident of Charlestown with his wife Gezina.

ALBERT, son of Abraham, m. first, Engeltie, dau. of Bartholomeus (?) Vrooman, Dec. 20, 1760; secondly, Maria Hogen of Albany, Nov. 16, 1773. His last wife was a wid. in 1799, and living in Canajoharie. Ch. bp: Annatje, Nov. 8, 1761; Johannes, Nov. 13, 1763; Catarina, Jan. 20, 1765; Eva, Aug. 23, 1767; Abraham, Feb. 25, 1770; Jacob, Aug. 14, 1774; Johannes, Feb. 4, 1776; Engeltie, Aug. 3, 1777; Rachel, Oct. 10, 1779; Rachel, Nov. 7, 1781.

JOHANNES, son of Jacob, m. Cornelia Hagedoorn, Dec. 25, 1760. He d. July 11, 1763 in the *Woestyne.*

HARMANUS, son of Pieter, m. Susanna, dau. of Barent Wemple, Jan. 8, 1761. In 1780 he was living at the junction of Schoharie creek and Mohawk river, and to avoid the Indian incursions, removed his family to the *Woestyne* in Rotterdam. Ch. bp: Pieter, Oct. 3, 1762; Debora, Dec. 22, 1765; Margarita, Oct. 8, 1769.

JAN, J., and Maria Mebie. He d. a little before March 4, 1764. Ch: John, bp. March 4, 1764.

ARENT, son of Pieter, m. Sarah, dau. of Josias Swart, Dec. 22, 1764. Ch. bp: Pieter, Nov. 17, 1765; Josias, May 21, 1775; Susanna, June 28, 1778.

LOUIS, and Nancy Pouwel, both of Maquaasland, m. Dec. 20, 1767.

PIETER, son of Pieter, m. Alida, dau. of Harmanus Peek, July 11, 1767. He d. before the baptism of his last child Maria. In 1780 he was living at the junction of Schoharie creek and the Mohawk river, but removed his family to Rotterdam or the *Woestyne* to avoid the incursions of the Indians. Ch. bp: Susanna, March 6, 1767; Harmanus, April 15 1770; Sarah, Sept. 26, 1779; Maria, April 17, 1782.

CORNELIS, son of Jacob, m. Hester, dau. of Abraham Groot, Nov. 19, 1767. She was b. Dec. 9, 1742, and d. April 19, 1822, a. 79ys. She made her will Aug. 10, 1816, proved July 1, 1822;

spoke of one son and 6 dau. He lived in the *Woestyne;* by his father's will, made April 25, 1755, he received a lot on the east side of Ferry street between Union and State streets. Ch. bp: Catarina, July 17, 1768, m. Nicolaas J. Van Petten; Willempie, July 15, 1770; Jacob, May 31, 1772; Willempie, b. Feb. 4, 1774, m. Johannes A. Bratt, and d. Jan. 4, 1762, in the *Woestyne;* Margarita, March 3, 1776, m. Nicolaas A. Bratt; Abraham, Jan. 4, 1778, made will Sept. 10, 1803, proved Sept. 21, 1810, gave his property to his mother and sisters, all of whom were then living, d. Nov. 23, 1807; Annatje, Feb. 20, 1780, m. Nicolaas P. Van Petten; Hester, May 9, 1782, m. Jellis Swart; Gezina, Dec. 26, 1784; Rebecca, b. July 27, 1787, d. Jan. 28, 1816.

JOHN, JR., son of Jan J. (?), m. Lena Palmontier, Nov. 3, 1791. Ch. b: Arent, Jan. 15, 1792; Isaac, Oct. 18, 1794; Maria, July 5, 1797.

Maj. JACOB C., son of Cornelis, m. Eva, dau. of Simon Van Patten, Jan. 19, (20), 1793. He lived in the *Woestyne,* and was killed Dec. (4), 1823, "by his waggon passing over his body, on his way to Albany." His wife d. June 7, (8), 1862, a. 91ys., 2m., 8d. Ch. b: Cornelius, May 10, 1794, d. July 8, 1822; Jannetje, Sept. 4, 1796 (1797); Esther, Sept. 11, 1799, Sept. 21, 1800 [*Family Record*]; Engeltie, March 28, 1802, d. May 4, 1822; *Simon,* Aug. 31, 1805; Catharine, March 3, 1807; George C., Dec. 3, 1809, d. July 23, 1853, or July

29, 1852, both dates from *Family Record;*
Nicholas, March 29, 1813; —— a son,
June 1, 1815, d. June 11, 1815; Margaret, April 14, 1816.

SIMON, son of Maj. Jacob C., m. Hannah Marlett, May 7, 1827. Ch. b: Eve,
June 29, 1829; Maria, March 7, 1831;
Jacob, Oct,. 7, 1834; Katharine Eliza,
Nov. 1, 1837; John Alexander, Feb.
20, 1840, d. March 16, 1871; Margaret
Ann, Feb. 18, 1844; Hester Jane, Aug.
17, 1846; Rachel Frances, Aug. 20 (30),
1849.

(MABB).

JOHN, b. in Manor Livingston, m. Seneth Cromwell, b. at Horseneck, Conn.,
Jan. 9, 1785, both living at Schenectady.

MEIER.

JOHN HARDENBURGH, Minister of the
Reformed Dutch church of Schenectady
1803–6, was b. Oct. 19, 1774, made his
will Aug. 2, 1806; spoke of his wife
Mary, but of no children. He m. Mary
Lansing of Albany, March 18, 1806, d.
Sept. 11, 1806, a. 31ys., having been
engaged in the ministry almost eight
years, of which more than three years
were spent in Schenectady.

MERCER.

ALEXANDER, JR., m. Elisabeth, dau.
of Dirk Van Ingen, Feb. 5, 1792. He d.
January 18, 1798 (?), in his 66th year.
(grave stone). Ch. b: James Van Ingen,
Sept. 25, bp. 23 (*sic*), 1792, d. Oct. 3,
1809; Dirk Van Ingen, May 11, 1794;
William, April 15, 1798; William Van
Ingen, Dec. 17, 1799.

16

MESGRAFT.

DANIEL, from New England, and Maria Pieterse, wid. of Willem Nobel, m.
Sept. 30, 1696.

MEYER.

JURRY, and Lena Robin (Ruben), both
of Rensselaerswyck, m. Feb. 5, 1765. Ch.
bp: Pieter, August 4, 1765; Elisabeth,
April 16, 1769.

MICHAEL, m. Eliza Emmerin (Eva
Siverse in *Trouw Boek*), May 19, 1767.
Ch: Philip, bp. Dec. 21, 1769.

JOHANNES, m. Maria Righter. Ch.
bp: Anna Dorothea, Feb. 22, 1780;
Maria Trina (?), Oct. 8, 1782; Christina,
June 15, 1784.

ANDRIES, m. Catarina Ronkel. Ch:
Elisabeth, bp. March 17, 1780.

ADAM, m. Maria Ouderkerk. Ch. b:
Jurrie, Sept. 14, 1793; John, May 8,
1797.

ANDREAS, m. Eleanor Southland, Oct.
14, 1762.

PETER, of Hellenbergh, and Maria
Kraushorn of Schenectady, m. July 1,
1793.

MIAN.

WILLIAM, and Ann Boman. Ch: Jannetje, bp. July 8, 1781.

MICHELS.

JACOB, from Maquaasland, m. Margarieta Van Slyck, Dec. 29, 1725. Ch:
Johannes, b. April 28, 1726.

MIDDLETON.

THOMAS, and Nellie Middleton. Ch:
Catharina, bp. Dec. 25, 1736.

MILLER.

DIRK, a citizen of Schenectady in
1713.

JACOB, and Dina Roos. Ch. bp: Susanna and Helena, March 10, 1762; Jeremia, b. Jan. 7, 1764.

JACOB, of Helderbergh, and Eve
Smith. Ch: Maria, b. March 23, 1786.

JACOB (or John), and Anneke Ostrander. Ch: Susanna, b. May 5, 1796;
Lea, b. Jan. 11, 1799.

JACOB, and Margariet Brown. Ch:
Abram Brown, b. Dec. 9, 1801.

CHARLES, and Hanna Jones. Ch. bp:
John, Aug. 7, 1768; Elisabeth, Sept.
23, 1770.

JOHAN FREDERICK, and Lena Weber.
Ch: Johan Frederick, bp. Aug. 11, 1780.

MILLES.

JOHN, and Elisabeth Murhaus. Ch:
Hendrik Hoff, bp. Sept. 25, 1780.

MILLET.

GIDEON, and Maria Quackenbosch.
Ch: Abraham, bp. Oct. 14, 1781.

MILLS.

JAMES, and w. Engeltie Darby in 1761.

JACOBUS, m. Annatie, dau. of Takel
Marselis, Nov. 9, 1765. Ch: Johannes,
bp. Sept. 21, 1766; Takerius, b. Dec. 30,
1768; Jacomyntje, bp. Jan. 1, 1772.

MITCHELL.

ANDREW, merchant in 1765.

JOHN, m. Catharina Ostrander, June
14, 1791. Ch: Ann, b. Nov. 18, 1791.

HUGH, m. Sophia Pieterse, Jan. 30,
1769. He d. Feb. 21, 1784, in his 43d
year; she d. Oct. 4, 1798.

MOER.

See Philipse.

MOKELWORTH.

THOMAS, and Anastasia Willet. Ch:
William Johnson, bp. Dec. 25, 1763.

MONK.

WILLIAM, and Sarah Waard. Ch. bp:
Johannes, May 17, 1771; Neeltje, Feb.
17, 1773.

CHRISTOFEL, and Christina Flag. Ch.
b: Sarah, Feb. 26, 1793; Catharina,
Aug. 24, 1796.

MONTOUR.

MICHAEL, and Hester (an Indian).
Ch: Seth, bp. June 1, 1747.

MOON.

JACOB, m. Elisabeth, dau. of Hendrick
Brouwer. Ch. b: Hendrick, Feb. 29,
1796; Martin, March 15, 1798.

MOOR.

FREDERIC, and Maria Steler. Ch. bp:
Johannes, Jan. 27, 1760; Elisabeth, Nov.
22, 1761; Frederic, Jan. 1, 1764.

MOORE.

WILLEM, and Maria Zeyn. Ch. bp: Maria, Feb. 8, 1775; John, June 19, 1778; Philip, Aug. 7, 1780.

WILLIAM, and Margariet Barr. Ch: Andrew, b. May 1, 1786.

JACOB, and Rachel Zeyn. Ch. bp: Isaac, Nov. 6, 1779; Maria, Aug. 21, 1781.

RICHARD, and Margariet Setterling. Ch: Maria, bp. Jan. 25, 1783.

JOHN, kept an inn on east corner of Liberty and Ferry streets; m. Dorothea Little, made will March 12, 1821, proved April 10, 1821, d. April 7, 1821 in his 70th year. Ch: Ann, bp. Feb. 16, 1784; Susan, wife of ...... Bullock; Dorothy, wife of ...... Mouncey.

(MUIR).

JOHN, m. Christina McKennel. He d. Feb. 17, 1817, a. 83ys.; she d. March 23, 1794, a. 48ys., 9m., 19d. Ch: James, bp. June 4, 1787.

MORPHY.

PIETER, and Margariet ...... Ch: Daniel, bp. June 21, 1758.

JOHN, and Margariet Costrey. Ch: James, bp. Nov. 13, 1781.

MORREL.

WILLEM, and Johanna Elisabeth ...... Ch: Johannes, bp. Oct. 5, 1755.

JOHN, and Mercy Pander. Ch: Hester, b. Oct. 24, 1774.
t

THOMAS, merchant, in 1794 owned a lot on north side of State street, 93 feet westerly from Maiden lane. He m. Engeltie Van Deusen. Ch: Thomas, bp. March 20, 1783; Abraham, graduated at Union College, d. March, 1864; John, b. Jan. 24, 1788; Neeltje, Dec. 8, 1789; Esther, Aug. 23, 1795.

MORRINGS.

WILLIAM, and Sara ...... Ch: William, bp. April 29, 1739.

MORRIS.

CHARLES, m. Catharina Van Antwerpen, July 31, 1791. Ch. b: Lewis, July 8, 1793; Abraham Van Antwerp, March 17, 1796; Robert, Oct. 7, 1798; Isaac, Jan. 7, 1801; Jacob, April 2, 1803.

MORRISON.

ALEXANDER, m. Abbe Magee. Ch: William, bp. May 16, 1784.

JOHN, and Elisabeth De Voe. Ch: Mary, b. Nov. 26, 1796.

JOHN, and Hanna Humphreys, both born in Londonderry, N. H., dwelling in Currysbush, m. March 16, 1785. Ch. b: David, Dec. 9, 1785; Martha, April 9, 1787; Mary, Dec. 24, 1793; Jenny, Sept. 19, 1794; Margaret, April 15, 1797.

JOHN, m. Catharina Franse Van der Bogart Ch: Maria, b. Oct., 1754, d. June 19 (25), 1840, a. 87ys.; Johannes, bp. Jan. 16, 1757.

MOSER.

JOHANN, m. Margarita Henning, April 14, 1765.

MOSHER.

THOMAS, m. Cornelia, dau. of Teunis Barheyt. Ch. b: Jacomyntje, Sept. 12, 1785; Johannes, Jan. 27, 1787.

MOYSTON.

ROBERT, m. Christina, dau. of Isaac Abrahamse Truex. He d. Aug. 3, 1798, a. 53ys., 3m., 9d.; she d. Oct. 2, 1804, a. 59ys., 8m., 1d. Ch: *John Hugan*, b. Aug. 24, 1772.

JOHN HUGAN, son of Robert, m. first, Nancy, dau. of Albert Vedder of Schenectady, Nov. 11, 1792, who d. May 2, 1795, a. 19ys., 8m., 3d.; secondly, Hannah Searing about 1797; and thirdly, Ann Lytle, March 25, 1799. He d. in Albany, Dec. 23, 1844, in his 73d year. Ch. b: Robert Patterson, Oct. 19, 1794; Daniel, Oct 12, 1798, d. Sept. 3, 1798; Hanna Searing, April 11, 1801; Jane, d. Nov. 9, 1811, a. 2ys., 11m., 7d.; Jane, March 3, 1817; Ann, May 18, 1720; David, d. Dec. 6, 1817, a. 8ys., 6m., 28d.

MUNROE.

ALEXANDER, a Revolutionary soldier, d. April 21, 1823, a. 80ys.

MUNRO.

JOHN, "son of Hugh Munro of Fyrish (Fowlis ?), in the parish of Alness, in the shire of Ross, Scotland," m. Maria, dau. of Cornelis Brouwer, April 5, 1760. In 1765 he was a merchant in Albany, and elder in the Presbyterian church. "On the 16th October, 1780, a party of 400 Regulars and Indians from Canada, under Maj. Munro, a tory from Schenectady, made their appearance in the Ballston settlement. They designed to attack Schenectady, but returned without effecting this object. They pillaged several houses and took 24 prisoners. Ch: Cornelius, bp. Oct. 16, 1768.

MURRAY.

JAN, m. Judickje Jacobse. Ch: *Thomas*, b. Jan. 29, 1727; *Samuel* (?).

THOMAS, son of Jan (?), m. Maria Adams, Oct. 10, 1761.

THOMAS, (perhaps same as the last), m. Maria J. Truex, about 1763. Ch. bp: John, Feb. 26, 1764; Elisabeth, Jan. 5, 1766; Samuel, Oct. 16, 1768.

SAMUEL, son of Jan, m. Dina, dau. of Hendrick Hagedorn, and wid. of ...... Sixberry of the *Aalplaats*, May 25, 1751. Ch. bp: *John*, April 5, 1752; Anna, Dec. 26, 1753; Judy, Sept. 7, 1755; Maria, Feb. 12, 1758; Catharina, Dec. 23, 1759; Geertruy, July 11, 1762; Elisabeth, Dec. 23, 1764; Debora, Aug. 31, 1766; *Hendrik*, April 16, 1769; *Reyer*.

JOHANNES, son of Samuel, m. Martha Buckley (Bokketon, Bokly). Ch: Samuel, bp. June 21, 1778; Pieter, b. Oct. 9, 1782; Elisabeth, March 14, 1785; Johannes, Aug. 3, 1787; Antje, b. Mar. 26, 1790; Catharina, Nov. 27, 1792; Susanna, Aug. 9, 1795; Samuel, April 8, 1799.

JOHN, and Polly Jackson. Ch. b: Hanna, Oct. 27, 1794.

JAMES, and Jane Humphrey. Ch. b: Benjamin, Nov. 20, 1783; William, June 11, 1786; Paris, Jan. 29, 1788.

ALEXANDER, and Isabella Duguid. Ch : William, bp Dec. 29, 1784.

JAMES, and Alida Teller, both of Currysbush, m. March 7, 1786. Ch : William b. Aug. 28, 1786.

WILLIAM, of the *Willigen*, m. Kezia Hilton. Ch: Ann, b. Feb. 22, 1787.

JOHN, m. Geertruyde Murray, Feb. 3, 1785.

HENDRICK, son of Samuel, m. Maria Youtis. Ch: Annatie, b. Sept. 26, 1796.

REYER, son of Samuel, and Jannetje, dau. of Dirk Hagedorn, both of the *Aalplaats*, m. March 17, 1798. Ch. b: Samuel, April 6, 1799; Rebecca, Sept. 16, 1800; John, July 11, 1802; Richard July 8, 1804.

MYNDERTSE.

Two brothers, Myndert and Carsten Frederickse, smiths, were among the early settlers of Beverwyck. They came from Iveren. Among other real estate in the village, they owned the north corner of State street and Broadway, and had their smith shop without the south gate, on the north corner of Broadway and Spanish (now Hudson) street. They were members of the Lutheran church of which Myndert was elder and Carsten deacon in 1680. The latter died probably about 1690, leaving four children. Myndert Frederickse was armorer to the fort in 1697; made his will March 21, 170$\frac{4}{5}$, proved May 1, 1706, in which he spoke of "my house hard by the church in *Cow* street" (now Broadway), and of "my (Lutheran) church book with silver clasp and chain." He m. first, Cathalyn Burchhard (Burger) in New Amsterdam, Aug. 5, 1656; and secondly, Pietertje Teunise Van Vechten in 1663. At the date of his will he had five Ch. living: Frederick, b. in 1657; Burger, b. in 1660; Neeltie, m. Hendrick Douw; Reinier and *Johannes*. [*See Albany Families.*] The unsettled condition of the early Dutch family names is well shown by the descendants of Myndert Frederickse who follow : Some took the surname of *Myndertse*, his christian name, whilst others took that of *Van Iveren*, the place from whence he came in Holland.

JOHANNES, son of Myndert Frederickse of Albany, came to Schenectady about 1700; by trade he was a blacksmith and armorer to the fort, and like most other inhabitants of the village, an Indian trader. In 1723 he was arrested by the sheriff of Albany county, and brought before the common council for having, contrary to the ordinances of the city of Albany received into, and harbored in his house, Indians with beaver and other peltry. Whereupon he was fined £10, and in default of payment the sheriff was ordered to keep said Myndertse safely in the common jail, from whence, however, he shortly after escaped. To punish the sheriff for his negligence or connivance, the common council resolved that he should pay Myndertse's fine and costs. To obtain a fair and impartial verdict in his case, Myndertse appealed to the supreme court of the province sitting in New York, and gained his case; the common council was mulcted in damages, fees and costs in the sum of £41, 9, 3. It is believed this decision effectually established the rights of citizens of Schenectady to the same privileges of trade as the citizens of Albany. Johannes Myndertse made his will May 4, 1754, proved Sept. 7, 1757, in which he spoke of his three sons Myndert, Jacobus and Reynier, and distributed his estate between them. He then owned property on the west corner of Mill lane and State street, also on the north side of State street at No. 93, and east of it, where he had a blacksmith shop and a bolting house. He m. Geertruy, dau. of Jacques Cornelise Van Slyck, and had the following Ch : *Myndert*, bp. Jan. 29, 1706 ; Margaret, bp. in Albany, June 8, 1707, m. Pieter Groenendyk ; *Jacobus*, bp. in Albany, April 22, 1709 ; *Reynier*, Oct. —, 1710 ; Petrus, April 19, 1718.

MYNDERT, son of Johannes, blacksmith, m. Maria, dau. of Jan Barentse Wemp, Jan. 15, 1736. His father, by will, gave him lot No. 93 State street, and blacksmith shop next east of it. He made his will in 1756, proved July 18, 1763, and spoke of his wife Maria, sons Johannes, Barent and Harmen, dau. Geertruy, Margarita and Sarah. He gave to his son Johannes his blacksmith shop and house. This house lately occupied by Mr. John Gilmour as a book store, is now removed. Ch. bp : Geertruy July 11, 1736, m. Petrus Van der Volgen ; Parach, Jan. 7, 1739 ; Margareta, Sept. 28, 1740 ; *Johannes*, Oct. 18, 1741 ; Margareta, May 27, 1744, m. Teunis A. Swart ; *Barent*, Feb. 8, 1747 ; Herman, July 2, 1749 ; Sara, Dec. 26, 1752.

ANDRIES, son of Frederick of Albany, m. Anna Elisabeth Smith, Oct. 15, 1742. Ch. bp : Frederick, August 28, 1743 ; Bregie, Nov. 17, 1745 ; Sara, March 20, 1748. [*See Albany Families.*]

REINIER, son of Johannes, merchant, m. Çatharina, dau. of Lourens Claese Van der Volgen, Mar. 25, 1743. He d. Aug. 6, 1788, a. 77ys., 8m. ; she d. Aug. 31, 1796, a. 72ys , 2m., 6d. His father gave him a bolting house and lot next east of his brother Myndert's shop, also a lot on the west corner of State street and Mill lane, on which stood his dwelling house in 1781. He made his will April 7, 1784, spoke of sons Johannes and Lawrence, wife Catrien, dau. Susanna, wife of Volkert Veeder, and Geertruy, wife of William Mead. Ch. bp : *Johannes*, Dec. 25, 1743 ; Susanna, April 13, 1746, m. Volkert Veeder ; Geertruy, Nov. 27, 1748, m. Dr. William Mead ; *Lawrence ;* Lewis, b. October 12, [grave stone,] bp. October 6, [*Church Record*] ; Petrus, Nov. 3, 1754 ; Nicolaas, August 21, 1757 ; Margarita, Nov. 18, 1759 ; Nicolaas, June 26, 1763.

JACOBUS, son of Johannes, merchant, m. Sara, dau. of Robert Yates, April 27, 1743. He was member of the Provincial Assembly in the years 1752, 1768 and 1769. He owned the lot next west of his brother Reiniers, which was on the west corner of State street and Mill lane; this he sold May 6, 1757, to James Wilson, merchant, for £240. He also owned the house and lot opposite the Court House in Union street, which perhaps came from his father-in-law, Robert Yates. Ch. bp : Geertruy, Sept. 8, 1745, m. Myndert Wemple; Maria, Oct. 20, 1748; Maria, July 14, 1751; Maria, Dec. 26, 1753; Maria, March 28. 1756; Margarita, May 24, 1759, m. Johannes C. Yates.

JOHANNES, son of Reinier, m. Catarina, dau. of Joseph Robertse Yates, March 15, 1768. He d. Sept. 6, 1819, a. 75ys., 8m., 7d.; she d. Oct. 13, 1821, a. 78ys., 6m., 24d. Ch. bp : Reinier, Dec. 18, 1768, d. young; Joseph, Sept. 23, 1770, d. Sept. 17, 1830, a. 60ys.; Catarina, Sept. 6, 1772, m. Henricus Yates; Maria, Sept. 8, 1776, d. young.

BARENT, son of Myndert, m. Jannetje Van Vranken, Dec. 2, 1770. He was b. Feb. 6, 1747, and d. Aug. 30, 1815. Ch. b : Maria, Aug. 23, 1771, m. Pieter C. Veeder; Nicolaas Van der Volgen, Oct. 9, 1773, d. Feb. 22, 1805; *Myndert*, Mar. 22, 1776; Annatje, May 16, 1779; Abraham, March 14, 1782; Sarah, Oct. 26, 1787.

Col. JOHANNES, son of Myndert, m. Annatje, dau. of Simon Vedder. He d. Oct. 29, 1815, a. 74ys., 4d.; she d. March 9, 1825. Ch : Simon, bp. Jan. 23, 1785; Simon, b. June 10, 1787; Barent, b. July

17, 1790, d. March 8. 1860; his wife, Catharina Douw Ten Eyck, d. Dec. 14, 1852, in her 61st year; Arent, b. Nov. 3, 1793, d. Sept. 14, 1834; Maria, b. Jan. 8, 1797, d. Oct. 25, 1805.

LOURENS (Lawrence), son of Reinier, m. Christina, dau. of Nicolaas De Graaf, Dec. 8, 1785. He was b. Oct. 12, 1751, and d. Aug. —, 1789; she made her will April 8, 1790, spoke of her two daughters mentioned below, of her mother Catalyntje De Graaf, and sisters Elisabeth, Mary and Neeltie; she was b. Oct. 2, 1763, and d. April 11, 1790. Ch. b : Margarieta, Aug. 2, 1786; Catalyntje, Sept. 13, 1789.

MYNDERT, son of Barent, m. Elisabeth Veeder, Nov. 22, 1806. Ch. b : Jane, Sept. 14, 1807; Enland (?), Aug. 12, 1810; Maria, June 9, 1813.

NAK.

JOHANNES and Andries, sons of Matthys, of Albany, members of the church 1731-5.

NEELY.

MATTHERS, and Elisabeth Johnson. Ch. b : Frances, Sept. 15, 1785; Dorothea, July 11, 1787.

JOHN, of Remsenbos, and Elisabeth McMasters. Ch. b : Eleanor, May 23, 1786; Sarah, May 20, 1790.

NEILSON.

THOMAS, and Catharina McDonald. Ch : Elisabeth, b. Sept. 14, 1787.

NEP.

ISAAC, and Lena Bertely. Ch. bp: Jacob, June 12, 1775; Elisabeth, March 31, 1777.

NESBIT.

JOHN, and Engeltie Ryan. Ch: John, b. Nov. 12, 1785.

JOSEPH, of Schenectady, served through the Revolutionary war, after which, in 1783, he sold his bounty land to John Ogden.

NESTEL.

MARTEN, and Anna Maria Zeel. Ch: Anna Maria, bp. May 28, 1758.

NESTLE.

GEORGE, and Rebecca Blackwood. Ch: George, b. June 8, 1789.

NIEUWKERK.

JOHANNES, Indian trader, m. Rachel Clute, Jan. 9, 1759. Ch. bp: *Gerrit*, Feb. 3, 1760; Tanneke, May 24, 1762; William, Feb. 3, 1764; Johannes, Sept. 20, 1767.

JACOB, and Pietertje Philips. Ch. bp: Annatje, Aug. 23, 1763; Sarah, Oct. 6, 1765.

GERRIT Cornelise, and Neeltje Quakkenbosch. Ch: Johannes, bp. Oct. 17, 1767.

GERRIT, son of Johannes, m. Maria Vedder. Ch: Rachel, bp. Dec. 29, 1782; Neeltje, b. Nov. 21, 1794; Johannes, b. Jan. 18, 1797.

NIXON.

THOMAS, m. Antje (Anganieta) Van der Bogart. Ch. bp: Sibby, Dec. 6, 1741; Alice, m. James McNutt; Helena, Nov. 9, 1755; Helena, Jan. 23, 1757; Isabella, Oct. 1, 1759; Josua, Nov. 22, 1761. Alice (McNutt) bequeathed to her sister Isabella, a house and lot on north side of State street.

JOHN, and Elisabeth Nellinger. Ch: Maria, bp. July 22, 1764.

NOBEL.

THOMAS, m. Catarina, dau. of David Marinus, Sept. 28, 1701. Ch. bp: Anna, May 24, 1702; David, in Albany, March 8, 1704; Marten, Jan. 29, 1706; Johannes, May 26, 1708; Thomas, in New York, Oct. 30, 1717; Anthony, in New York, Jan. 20, 1720. In 1706 Thomas Nobel occupied lot No. 36 Washington street, and the lot next north of it. He refused to pay for a license to sell strong liquors in 1706.

WILLEM, m. Maritje Pieterse. He d. before Sept. 30, 1696; his wid. m. Daniel Mesgraft. In 1686 she, being then 40ys. old, with her family, lived in the fort.

NORRIS.

JOSEPH, from New Jersey, m. Sarah McLean from Gosin (Goshen), March 30, 1760. Ch: Elisabeth, bp. Sept. 23, 1764.

O'BRIAN.

MICHAEL, m. Sarah Kirkpatrick, April 8, 1790. Ch: John, bp. Dec. 8, 1790; John, b. Feb. 15, 1792.

THOMAS, and Elisabeth Bonny. Ch. b: Mary, Jan. 18, 1788; Elisabeth, Feb. 1, 1791; Margariet, April 11, 1793; Thomas, May 2, 1795.

ODUNAINE.

PATRICK, and Maria Buys. Ch: Rachel, b. Sept. 3, 1778.

OESTERHOUT.

LOURENS, and Rebecca Rosa. Ch: Arien, bp. Feb. 21, 1705.

OFMULDER.

DIRK, m. Alida Pieterse, wid. of Ludovicus Cobes, and in 1698 lived on the Fourth flat on the north side of the Mohawk river; this property having been owned by said Cobes previous to his death. Ofmulder and wife, in 1698, gave Thomas Smit, Cobes's son-in-law, a life lease of the same.

OGDEN.

JONATHAN, *capiteyn van het Nieuw Yorksche regement Van Westchester*, m. Rachel, dau. of Joachim Vander Heyden of Albany, Dec. 10, 1758. He was an inn keeper, and occupied lot No. 24 Church street, next south of the Tomlinson lot. Ch: Susanna, bp. Aug. 3, 1764.

JOHN, (perhaps son of the last), m. Alida Nesbit, and was buried Aug. 23, 1801. Ch: Joseph, bp. July 25, 1784; Timothy, b. Sept. 19, 1786.

OHLE.

JOHAN CHRISTOFFLE, and Anna Geertruy Ohle. Ch: Anna Geertruy, bp. April 25, 1756.

OHLEN.

HENRY GEORGE, b. in London, and dwelling in Albany, m. Catharine Henry, April —, 1785. He was b. Sept. 16, 1758, and d. Oct. 1, 1837; she d. Nov. 25, 1839, a. 73ys., 2m., 23d. He served in the Revolutionary war as Sergeant. Ch. b: Elisabeth, Sept. 7, 1786; Mildred, June 11, 1795.

OIRENDORPH.

HENDRIK, and Anna Margaret....... Ch: Jannetje, bp. May 3, 1713.

OKEY.

JOHN, m. Jane Williams, Dec. 24, 1795.

OLIVER.

JOHN, m. Clara Sybert (Sybel). Ch. bp: Martha, b. July 4, bp. Sept. 6, 1769; Adam, May 13, 1772; Richard, May 25, 1776; Richard, Dec. 19, 1781; Clara, b. June 22, 1791.

RICHARD, of Albany, m. Bata Quackenbos of Niskayuna, Sept. 24, 1763.

OLSAVER.

THOMAS, and Christina Sittle. Ch: Mary, b. Aug. 28, 1798.

NICHOLAS, m. Eva Van der Bogart, Feb. 4, 1798. Ch. b: Jannetje, Sept. 4, 1799; Rachel, Feb. 9, 1802; Christiana, ..., 1807.

O'NEIL.

JAMES, from Duanesburgh, m. Elisabeth Bratt, Nov. 6, 1791. Ch. b: Peter, March 24, 1792; Elsje, Aug. 15, 1795.

17

JAMES, and Rebecca Harris. Ch:
John, b. July 7, 1777.

JOHN, and Catharina Van Valkenburgh. Ch. b: Johannes, July 3, 1791;
Elisabeth, Aug. 2, 1793.

OORLOFF.

WILLEM, and Maria Hartman. Ch.
bp: Bastian and Elisabeth, Sept. 6, 1769.

OOSTRANDER (VAN OOSTRANDER).

HENDRICK, and Elisabeth Scheffel
(Schoufelt). Ch. bp: Rachel, Sept. 23,
1772; Annatje, April 10, 1774; Elisabeth, July 22, 1776; Petrus Wilhelmus,
Oct. 6, 1781; Michael, Nov. 9, 1783.

TEUNIS, and Maritie Van Vliet. Ch.
bp: Johannes, Dec. 23, 1779; Machtelt,
Oct. 7, 1781. Ch. b: Solomon, Sept.
20, 1789; Elisabeth, Aug. 22, 1793;
Arie, Oct. 29, 1795; Catharina, Sept.
4, 1797; Johannes, Dec. 14, 1799;
Geertruy, Nov. 20, 1801.

PETRUS, and Antje Deenmark. Ch:
Elisabeth, bp. July 4, 1780.

WILLEM, and Elsje Van Pelt. Ch:
Engeltie, b. Sept. 25, 1786.

OSTRANDER.

JOHN, and Maritje Heemstraat, both
of Noormanskil, m. Jan. 27, 1791. Ch.
b: Elsje, Feb. 10, 1792; Willem, Jan.,
1794; Martha, May 4, 1796; Samuel,
Aug. 14, 1798.

PETER, and Christina Hoogteling.

Ch. b: Magdalena, Feb. 20, 1792; Margariet, April 27, 1794.

JOHN, and Rachel ...... Ch: Hendrick, b. Sept. 21, 1792.

SOLOMON, and Hannah Tuttle (Turtle),
both of Noormanskil, m. Oct. 19, 1794.
Ch. b: Petrus, Sept. 8, 1795; Maria,
Nov. 18, 1796; Isaac, Aug. 14, 1798;
Lea, Dec. 20, 1803; Rachel, Oct. 30,
1805; Stephen, Aug. 2, 1809; Solomon,
Aug. 11, 1811.

OOSTRUM.

HENDRICK, m. Abigail Danford (Davenport). He d. Feb. 22, 1826, a. 85ys.,
2m., 27d.; she d. March 19, 1819, a.
73ys., 10m., 7d. Ch: Abigail, bp. Feb.
10, 1782; Hendrick, b. Oct. 10, 1784;
David, b. Feb. 17, 1787; Oliver, b. Nov.
8, 1789.

ANTHONY, m. Sarah Hegeman. Ch.
b: Elisabeth, Aug. 21, 1790; Joseph,
June 15, 1794; John, Oct. 14, 1796.

JOSHUA, m. Jannetje Hall. Ch: Hendrick, b. April 16, 1792.

JOHN, m. Esther Hegeman, Jan. 31,
1788. Ch: Roelif, bp. Sept. 14, 1794.

JOHN, and Catharina Bratt, both of
Duanesburgh, m. Dec. 23, 1793.

OOTHOUT (OOTHOET).

JAN JANSE, brewer, in Greenbush as
early as 1660; made his will March 13,
168⅞, letters of administration issued to
his sons Hendrick and Jan, Jan. 3, 169⅝;
gave to son Johannes a red mare; to

Hendrick 3 or 4 years after "my decease," a young horse or an old one; Arien, aged about 12yrs., to have two years schooling and a trade, and a red stone horse with a star in his forehead; when 20 years of age a new suit of clothes; the remaining property then to be divided equally among his six children; his Ch. were Johannes, eldest son; *Hendrick;* Arien; Mayke, wife of Capt. Johannes Thomase Mingael; Antje; and Jannetje, m. Hendrick Van Ness. [*See Albany Families*].

HENDRICK, son of Jan Janse, m. Caatje, dau. of Volkert Douw, April 30, 1684. He was a brewer, also surveyor of the city of Albany; made his will Oct. 11, 1738, proved April 26, 1740, in which he mentioned the following Ch., save Maritie. He was buried July 15, 1739. Ch. bp: Volkert, March 1, 1685; Hendrick, March 10, 1686; Dorothea, Dec. 18, 1687, m. Cornelis Bogard; Maritie, d. before 1738; Volkert, Oct. 23, 1692; Jan, April 7, 1695; Henderickje, May 2, 1697; Henderickje, Sept. 3, 1699, m. Isaac Bogard; Margariet, July 13, 1701, m. Domine Johannes Van Driessen; Anna, Dec. 15, 1703, m. Pieter Wouterse Quackenbos; *Jonas,* Dec. 9, 1705. [*See Albany Families.*]

JONAS, son of Hendrick, m. first Elisabeth Lansing, March 30, 1741; secondly, Elisabeth Vinhagen, April 13, 1756. The tradition is (not strictly true) that the first child bp. in the old church was Elisabeth Vinhagen, wife of Jonas Oothout, and that the church bell tolled the last time for her burial, she having

d. March, 1806, in her 92d year. His first wife was buried March 11, 1754. His father bequeathed him a farm and *Groenen Island.* Ch. bp. in Albany: Hendrick, May 16, 1742; *Abraham,* May 27, 1744; Volkert, Dec. 26, 1747; Volkert, Sept. 2, 1750; Magdalena, July 8, 1753; Johannes, Feb. 6, 1757; Catarina, May 7, 1758. [*See Albany Families.*]

Gen. ABRAHAM, son of Jonas, early settled in Schenectady. During the Revolutionary war he was Capt. of a company in Col. Abraham Wemple's regiment, and was afterwards for many years prominent in the civil and military affairs of the city. He m. first, Margarita, dau. of Gerrit Janse Lansing of Albany, Nov. 27, 1767; she d. May 31, 1786; and he m. secondly, Lena Lansing, wid. of John Zabriskie of Hackensack, N. J., Nov. 14, 1787; she d. April 26, 1826, a. 75ys., 6m., 3d. Gen. Oothout made his will Jan. 12, 1811, proved July 18, 1822, spoke of his wife Lena, sons Gerrit, Henry, Abraham, and grand dau. Elisabeth Craig, and of the fact that he was then building the house which he afterwards occupied in Washington street, now the residence of Hon. Samuel W. Jackson. Ch. b: Jonas, Jan. 11, 1769, d. Jan. 13. 1787; Magdalena, Sept. 9, 1770, d. May 12, 1788; Elisabeth, Aug. 29, 1772, d. Feb. 26, 1786; Gerrit, Jan. 14, 1776, d. June 19, 1832; Elsje, Jan. 28, 1778, d. Oct. 17, 1786; *Henry,* June 30, 1780, d. June 27, 1846; Margarita, Aug. 28, 1782, m. Archibald Craig, Aug. 7, 1804, and d. Oct. 12, 1810, leaving one dau. Elisabeth, who m. Julius Rhodes of Albany; *Abraham*, April 29, 1785, d. May 20, 1840.

VOLKERT, son of Hendrick and Lydia, of Albany, m. Debora, dau. of Isaac Swits. Ch. b : Isaac Swits, Feb. 15, 1794; Isaac Swits, Feb. 6, 1795; Abraham, Dec. 25, 1796; Lidia, May 27, 1798; Hendrick, May 12, 1800.

ABRAHAM, son of Gen. Abraham, m. Gezina, dau. of Isaac De Graaf, Nov. 12, 1808. He d. May 20, 1840; she d. Jan. 14, 1861. Ch. b : Gerrit Lansing, Sept. 12, 1809, graduated at Union College, 1829; Margaret, June 7, 1811, m. Hon. Peter J. Wagner.

HENRY, son of Gen. Abraham, m. Eliza Ann Nicoll. He d. June 27, 1846; she d. in Rochester, Jan. 22, 1872, in her 85th year. Ch. b : Samuel Nicoll, Aug. 25, 1810, graduated at Union College, 1830, now an attorney-at-law in Rochester.

ORINGER.

MARTINUS, and Christina Scherrer. Ch. bp: Petrus, July 2, 1769; Maria, Jan. 25, 1780.

OSBURN.

FRANCIS, m. Anganieta Van Antwerpen, Nov. 15, 1761. Ch. bp: Neeltje, May 30, 1762; William, March 8, 1768; Jacob, Dec. 26, 1770; Neeltje, Aug. 21, 1774; Maria, Feb. 20, 1780; Robert, April 11, 1784.

WILLIAM, son of Francis, m. Annatje

Henry, June 22, 1793. Ch. b : Francis and Elisabeth, April 13, 1795; Anganietje, Nov. 20, 1796.

OTTEN.

HELMER, from Isens (Essen ?), baker, was in Beverwyck from 1663 to 1676, when he died. Among other property owned by him in Albany, was the lot on the north corner of Pearl and State streets, which he conveyed to Domine Nicolaas Van Rensselaer in 1675; Aug. 13, 1670, he bought of Pieter Adriaense Soegemakelyk 26 morgens of land, including the Schermerhorn bouwery in Rotterdam, and a village lot in Schenectady on the west corner of Church and Union streets. His wife was Ariantie, dau. of Arent Bratt, by whom he had one dau. Tryntje, who m. Gerrit Symonse Veeder. After Otten's death, his wid. m. Reyer Schermerhorn.

OUDERKERK.

JAN JANSE, cooper, in Beverwyck as early as 1664; in 1692 lived on the north side of Yonker (State) street, and was commonly called *Smalle Cuyper*. He was the earliest settler of this name in or about Albany.

PIETER, (perhaps son of the last), m. Alida, dau. of Johannes Clute, June 13, 1704, in Niskayuna. He was a freeholder of Half Moon in 1720. Ch. bp: Johannes, Feb. 11, 1705; *Johannes*, Jan. 19, 1707, in Albany; Bata, Jan. 30, 171⅚, m. Abraham Quackenbos; *Pieter*, May 8, 1720, in Albany.

JOHANNES, (perhaps son of Jan Janse), m. Neeltie Claese, wid. of Hendrick Gardenier, May 20, 1695. An inventory of Gardenier's property was made in 1695; at the time of his death he was an inhabitant of *Shotac*, previously he had resided in Schenectady, where he owned a lot of 100ft. front on the north side of Union street, one-half of which is now included in the Dutch church lot, and the other half is owned by Mr. Aaron Barringer. This whole lot was then appraised at 15 beavers seewant or 48 dolls. Gardenier left four Ch : Claes, Andries, Josina and Hendrick. Ouderkerk had the following Ch. bp. in Albany : Maria, June 21, 1696 ; Annetie, Oct. 30, 1698, d. 1706 ; Ariaantje, June 1, 1701 ; Neeltje, July 11, 1703. [*See Albany Families.*]

JOHANNES, son of Pieter, born and dwelling in Konnestagioune, m. Wyntie, dau. of Arent Van Petten, Dec. 24, 1731. Ch. bp : *Petrus*, Sept. 10, 1732 ; Jannetje, March 24, 1734 ; *Jacob ;* Arent, July 9, 1737 ; Myndert, March 4, 1739 ; Nicolaas, April 12, 1741 ; Johannes, b. April, 1743 ; Frederick, bp. ——, 1745 ; *Johannes*, May 20, 1750, was living in 1837 in the town of Glen.

ISAAC, miller, m. Mary Foster, Oct. 13, 1750. [*See Albany Families.*]

PIETER, son of Pieter, m. Machtelt, dau of Takel Heemstraat, June 18, 1755. Ch. bp : Alida, April 25, 1756 ; *Takel*, June 11, 1758 ; Maria, Nov. 3, 1760 ; *Petrus*, April 10, 1763 ; Anna, Sept. 20,

1769, m. Johannes G. Bancker ; *Johannes*, May 13, 1772 ; *Isaac.*

JACOB, son of Johannes, and Maria, Freeman, both of the manor Rensselaer, m. Dec. 30, 1762. Ch. b : *Johannes*, Dec. 29, 1763 ; Maria, Jan. 25, 1768 ; Wyntje, Dec. 18, 1770.

PETRUS, son of Johannes, and Maria Seybert, both of the manor of Rensselaerswyck, m. Jan. 16, 1762. Ch. bp : Johannes, July 13, 1765 ; *Frederick*, Feb. 9, 1769 ; Adam, Oct. 22, 1772 ; Wyntje, Oct. 11, 1776 ; Maria, Dec. 21, 1778 ; Jannetje, Jan. 18, 1781.

PIETER, m. Machtelt Marinus. Ch : Lena, bp. March 22, 1766.

TAKEL, son of Pieter, of Helderbergh, m. Maria Ramsey. Cb. bp : Pieter, June 19, 1779 ; Frederick, Dec. 13, 1781 ; Jacob, Jan. 17, 1784 ; Rebecca, b. April 1, 1786 ; Magdalena, April 24, 1788 ; Maria, Sept. 17, 1790.

JOHANNES, son of Johannes, m. Rebecca Groot. Ch. bp : Bata, June 19, 1780 ; Arent, July 27, 1782.

JOHN, son of Jacob, m. Geertruy Winne. Ch : Maria, bp. Feb. 14, 1784.

PETER J., m. Jannetje Winne. Ch : Peter, bp. Dec. 24, 1783 ; Rebecca, b. Oct. 11, 1785.

ROBERT, d. March 1, 1844, a. 65ys., 4m., 12d. ; Susan Van Slyck, wife of Robert Ouderkerk, d. July 20, 1846, a. 63ys., 3m., 10d.

PETRUS, son of Pieter, of Helderbergh, m. Marytje Syver. Ch: Jacob, b. July 4, 1785.

JOHN, son of Pieter, and Elisabeth Clute, both of Helderbergh, m. Dec. 7, 1793.. Ch: Machtelt, bp. Nov. 24, 1794; Maria, b. May 28, 1801.

OUGHST.

ADAM, and Anna Barbara Reght. Ch: Catharina, bp. March 11, 1744.

OWEN.

BENJAMIN, and Mary Boesboth from England, but living in Schenectady, m. Nov. 20, 1749.

OX.

MELCHIOR, and Susanna Serserbach. Ch. bp: Elisabeth, March 1, 1773; Elisabeth, March 3, 1774.

MELCHIOR, and Engelina Bekker. Ch: Maria, b. Jan. 7, 1786.

PAAPS.

ADAM, and Eva Maria Hamin. Ch.: Daniel Frederick, bp. May 17, 1771.

PALMONTIER.

ISAAC, and Neeltie Van der Bogart. Ch: Hildegonda, bp. June 12, 1775.

DAMON, and Elisabeth Bertely. Ch: Maria, b. Feb. 11, 1776; Damon and Ariaantje, bp. May 25, 1778; Pieter, b. Nov. 22, 1782.

JOHN, and Catarina Kip. Ch: Maria, bp. Sept. 8, 1781.

MICHAEL, and Geertruy Hegeman. Ch: Elisabeth, b. Aug. 19, 1797.

PANGBURN.

EDMOND, and Mary Ostrander. Ch: Elisabeth, bp. June 30, 1778.

RICHARD, and Catalyntje Van Etten. Ch. bp: Thomas, June 25, 1780; Mary, Oct. 14, 1781; Jacobus, b. May 13, 1789.

RICHARD, m. Hetty (Esther) Wilson, Feb. 11, 1796. Ch. b: Moses, Feb. 16, 1797; Nancy, Feb. 17, 1799.

BENJAMIN, m. Maria Vrooman, ——, 1798. Ch. b: Christina, March 11, 1799; Weyntje, July 14, 1804; Richard, Feb. 7, 1807.

PARKER.

RICHARD, m. Mary Frank, Dec. 14, 1785. Ch: John and Margaret, b. April 14, 1787.

PARTORT.

MARTEN, and Maria Elisabeth ...... Ch: Credelis, bp. June 14, 1718.

PARYS.

JACOB, and Gouda Ennet. Ch: Maria, bp. June 12, 1784.

PASSAGE.

GEORGE, JR., and Lea Ostrander, both of the Noormanskil, m. Feb. 10, 1788. Ch. b: Mary, Oct. 6, 1788; George, Oct. 14, 1790; Johannes, Feb. 23, 1793; Lea, Jan. 21, 1795; Eva, June 15, 1797; Elisabeth, Aug. 20, 1799; Margarieta, Jan. 5, 1802.

PATTERSON.

JAMES, and Cornelia Brouwer. Ch:
Willem, bp. Jan. 10, 1779.

WILLIAM, and Mary McArthur. Ch:
Robert, bp. June 20, 1780.

SAMUEL, and Christina Mitts. He d.
before the baptism of his last child. Ch.
bp: Elisabeth, Oct. 21, 1781; Mary,
Dec. 11, 1783; John, b. May 17, 1786;
Elsje, b. Sept. 14, 1787.

OLIVER, b. in New England, and
Nancy Doorn, wid. of Jacob Sullivan, b.
in Claverac, — both dwelling in Corrysbos,— m. Jan. 27, 1785. Ch. b: Mary,
Aug. 3, 1785; Charles, June 15, 1787;
Eleanor, July 19, 1789.

BENJAMIN, and Magdalena Truex.
Ch. b: Maria, July 11, 1790; Eleanor,
March 17, 1792; Isaac, March 4, 1794;
Elisabeth, June 20, 1796; Adam, Sept.
9, 1798; Charlotte, November 2, 1800;
Maggy, Oct. 10, 1802; Isaac, Dec. 19,
1803; Jacob Benjamin, Oct. 25, 1807.

JOHN, and Mary Fenton. Ch: Thomas, b. Dec. 22, 1792.

PAUL.

JACOB, and Annatje Van Vorst. Ch:
William Berrit, bp. May 7, 1779.

PAULDING.

ABRAHAM, m. Catharine McKelvy,
May 9, 1790. Ch. b: Eliza, Nov. 4,
1790; Catharina, Aug. 6, 1794; Eleanor, May 10, 1798; Margariet, Nov. 20,
1802 (1801 ?); Jane, Oct. 29, 1804.

PAWLING.

HENRY, and Nancy Brown. Ch. bp:
Levi, Nov. 9, 1783; John, March 10,
1786; Henry, b. Dec. 8, 1787; Abram
Brown, July 22, 1790.

PEARSE.

JACOB, of Nistagioene in 1720, m.
Jannetie ...... Ch. bp. in Albany: Annatie, April 20, 1712; Geertruy, April
5, 1719; *Johannes,* Nov. 27, 1720, Elisabeth, Oct. 7, 1722. This family settled
on the north side of the Mohawk river at
and above Fort's ferry.

JOHANNES, son of Jacob, m. Alida,
dau. of Ryckert Van Vranken, Nov. 8,
1745. He was buried Oct. 26, 1756.
Ch. bp. in Albany except Maria: Ryckert, March 24, 1751; Abraham, Jan.
17, 1753; Johannes, Aug. 5, 1754; Maria, March 6, 1757, in Schenectady; Jacob; Annatie. [*See Albany Families.*]

RYCKERT, son of Johannes, m. Esther,
dau. of Bastiaan Tymensen. He d. May
24, 1835, a. 84ys.; she d. April 23, 1814,
a. 59ys. Ch. b: Mayeka, June 9, 1788;
Bastiaan, Feb. 26, 1790. The late Judge
Pearse of Niskayuna was a son of Ryckert.

PEEK.

JAN, an early settler of New Amsterdam, where for many years he and his
wife kept an inn. Frequent prosecutions
were instituted against them for selling
spirits without license, and for selling to
the Indians. In 1664 Maria Peeck was
called "one of the oldest inhabitants of
New Amsterdam." In 1655 he sold two

houses in Fort Orange to Johannes Dyck-
man for 1627 guilders. The creek at
Peekskill takes its name from him. He
m. Maria (De Truy) Volchers, wid. of
Cornelis Volkertse, in New Amsterdam,
Feb. 20, 1650, and had the following
Ch. bp. in N. A.: **Anna**, Oct. 15, 1651;
Johannes, Oct. 12, 1653, settled in New
York; *Jacobus*, Jan. 16, 1656; Maria,
March 6, 1658; Maria Peek, wife of
Jan, late in life resided in Schenectady,
perhaps with her son Jacobus.

JACOBUS, son of Jan, took up land on
the Second flat, south side of the Mohawk
river, about five miles above the village.
He settled on this land as early as 1670,
in company with his kinsman Isaac De
Trieux (Truax). The patent for the same
was confirmed by Gov. Andross on the
29th Oct., 1677. He m. Elisabeth Teunise. Ch. bp: Sarah, m. Philip Groot;
Maria, m. Simon Danielse Van Antwerpen; Lodovicus July 14, 1686, in Albany; Annatje, m. Joseph Clement;
Margariet, March 27, 1692, in Albany;
Elisabeth, March 27, 1695, m. first, Cornelis Vander Volgen; secondly, Joost
Van Sice; *Jacobus*, Dec. 28, 1698; *Johannes.*

JOHANNES, son of Jacobus, m Annatje,
dau. of Harmanus Vedder. Ch: Margarietje, bp. May 3, 1713; *Jacobus*, bp.
May 28, 1716; *Harmanus*, b. Dec. 5,
1718; Lowys, bp. Sept. 30, 1721; Margariet, b. March 12, 1726; Johannes,
June 27, 1729.

JACOBUS, son of Jacobus, of the *Woes-
tyne*, m. Margarita, dau. of Cornelis Van
Slyck, Jan. 1, 1721. His will was made
June 22, 1759. His land on the Second
flat was divided among his three sons,
Jacobus, Cornelis and Hendrick. His
wife and all the following Ch. were then
living except Nantje. Ch. bp: *Jakus*,
April 15, 1721; *Jacobus*, Oct. 20, 1722;
Lysbet, Nov. 3, 1723, m. Arent Pootman;
Claartje, b. March 21, bp. April 4, 1725,
m. Abraham Schermerhorn; Saartje, b.
Feb. 1, bp. Feb. 26, 1727; *Cornelis*, b.
Dec. 1, 1729; *Lodovicus*, b. April 28,
bp. May 21, 1732; *Hendrick*, bp. Sept.
15, 1734; Margarieta, March 7, 1736,
m. Harmanus Pietersen; Nantje, July
6, 1738; Lena, Oct. 26, 1740, m. Johannes Barheit.

JACOBUS, son of Johannes, m. Rebecca,
dau. of Arent Schermerhorn. Ch. bp:
Margarietje, May 31, 1741; *Arent*, Dec.
25, 1743; *Johannes*, Sept. 13, 1747; Annatje, July 19, 1753.

JACOBUS, JR., son of Jacobus and
Margarita, m. Maria, dau. of Pieter Van
Antwerpen, June 30, 1749. Ch: *Jaco-
bus*, July 13, 1760.

LOWIS, son of Johannes, m. Jannetie,
dau. of Daniel Van Antwerpen, May 16,
1741. Ch. bp: Antje, Nov. 15, 1741;
Daniel, June 30, 1745; *Johannes*, Mar.
22, 1747.

HARMANUS, son of Johannes, m. Sara,
dau. of Jesse De Graaf, Dec. 1, 1740.
He was a wheelwright, and lived in an
ancient Dutch house built in 1723, standing on the south side of Union street,
west of the Court House. He d. Aug.

29, 1781, a. 61ys., 7m., 24d.; she d. Feb. 2, 1810, a. 89ys., 28d. Ch. bp: Annatie, March 28, 1742; *Johannes*, May 13, 1744; Annatje, April 13, 1746; Annatje, Dec. 13, 1747, m. first, Johannes De Graaf, and secondly, Abraham Truex; Alida, June 16, 1751, m. Pieter Mebie; *Jesse*, Feb. 9, 1753; Margarita, March 21, 1756, m. Jan Baptist Van Eps; *Harmanus*, Jan. 14, 1759; Sara, March 15, 1761, m. Wouter Swits; *Jacobus Vedder*, Jan. 29, 1764.

JACQUES, son of Jacobus, m. first, Susanna, dau. of Samuel Bratt, June 24, 1743; and secondly, Eva Vrooman, wid., Oct. 6, 1750. Ch. bp: Margrietje, Jan. 15, 1744, m. Simon H. Vrooman; Eva, July 18, 1745, m. Daniel Peek; Susanna, Sept. 15, 1751, m. Jacob S. Bratt; Lena, June —, 1757; Catarina, July 31, 1763, m. Jacobus A. Schermerhorn; Jacobus, June 8, 1766.

CORNELIS, son of Jacobus, m. Catlyntje, dau. of Joseph Yates, April 4, 1752. He made his will Jan. 16, 1800, proved Dec. 6, 1809; his wife and children were then living except Hendrick. Ch. bp: *Jacobus*, Nov. 10, 1752; *Joseph*, Nov. 30, 1755; Margarita, May 29, 1757, m. Abraham P. Truax; *Christoffel*, April 15, 1759; Eva, June 7, 1761, m. Nicolaas Van Vranken; *Cornelis*, Aug. 21, 1763; Sara, Nov. 17, 1765; Sarah, May 8, 1768; Hendrik, Aug. 5, 1770; Hendrik, June 16, 1773.

HENRICUS, son of Jacobus, hatter, m. Elisabeth, dau. of Willem Bancker, Nov.

30, 1757. Ch. bp: *Jacobus*, Aug. 20, 1758; Evert, Aug. 9, 1760; Henderick, July 25, 1762; *Henderick*, April 22, 1764; *Willem*, Feb. 23, 1766; Margarita, Jan. 3, 1768, m. Bartholomeus Clute; Thomas, Dec. 10, 1769; Annatje, Jan. 19, 1772; Annatje, Jan. 3, 1773, m. Ryckert Rosa; Clara, June 23, 1776.

LOUIS, son of Jacobus, m. Annatje Peek. Ch. bp: Jacobus, Sept. 11, 1763; Helmer, Jan. 30, 1766; Jacobus, July 3, 1768; Lowis, Dec. 16, 1770; Cornelis, Nov. 7, 1773; Cornelis, Oct. 22, 1775; *Johannes*, Aug. 2, 1778; Acus, Sept. 14, 1781.

JOHANNES, son of Harmanus, m. Eva, dau. of Joseph Yates, Feb. 20, 1762. He made a codicil to his will, May 22, 1812; spoke of dau. Nancy Farrel, Tanneke, wife of Sybrant Van Schaick, and Sara, wife of James Peek, to whom he gave a farm in Charlton; also of his son Joseph Yates, and dau. Eva Wendell. He d. May 27, 1812; she d. Sept. 1, 1807. Ch. bp: Sara, Sept. 26, 1762, m. Jacobus H. Peek; *Harmanus*, May 20, 1764; Eva, March 22, 1767, m. Ahasuerus Wendell; *Joseph*, October 9, 1768; Annatje, July 1, 1770, m. Kennedy Farrel.

DANIEL, son of Louis, m. Eva, dau. of Jacques Peek, Aug. 16, 1764. Ch. bp: Louis, Feb. 3, 1765; Jacques, July 27, 1766; Johannes, Oct. 9, 1768; Susanna, July 4, 1773, m. Jacob Bodyne; Jannetje, Nov. 27, 1774; Catarina, Feb. 21, 1779; Margarita, Oct. 27, 1782.

18

JOHANNES, son of Louis, m. Jannetje, dau. of Abraham Groot, March 21, 1768. Ch. bp: Lowis, Oct. 15, 1769; Willempie, Nov. 24, 1771, m. James Wiley; David, Feb. 6, 1774; Lowis, April 21, 1776; Rebecca, Nov. 22, 1778; Abraham, July 28, 1782; Johannes, Feb. 14, 1785; Jannetje, b. Sept. 11, 1787; Cornelis Mebie, b. April, bp. April 18, 1791.

JOHANNES, (probably same as last), m. Elisabeth Johnson. Ch: Lewis, b. Oct. 7, 1800.

LEWIS D., son of Daniel, m. Margarita Van Antwerpen, Sept. 10, 1786. By will Johannes Danielse Van Antwerpen left her all his estate Nov. 3, 1812. Ch: Daniel, b. Jan. 22, 1787.

ARENT, son of Jacobus, of the *Woestyne*, m. Rebecca Groot, Dec. 4, 1768. Ch. bp: Margarita, Jan. 14, 1770; Willempie, Feb. 2, 1772, m. Reyer Wemple; Annatje, May 22, 1774, d. August 15, 1844; Abraham, Aug. 4, 1776; Jacobus, April 18, 1779; John, Oct. 14, 1781. Ch. b: Rebecca, March 2, 1785; Arent, Sept. 30, 1789; Arent, April 25, 1791.

JOHANNES, son of Jacobus, m. Suster Bratt, July 16, 1769. Ch. bp: Jacobus, Feb. 25, 1770; Catarina, Sept. 22, 1771; Arent, Aug. 1, 1774; Susanna, Dec. 21, 1777.

JOSEPH YATES, son of Johannes, m. Anne Moore. Ch: Joseph, b. Sept. 23, 1789; Anne Peek, the wife of Joseph Yates Peek, d. May 28, 1845, in her 72d year.

JACOB (Jacobus ?), son of Cornelis, m. Annatje, dau. of Jan Baptist Van Vorst. Ch. bp: Catalyntje, Sept. 13, 1772; Catarina, Sept. 25, 1774; Cornelis, Dec. 1, 1776, d. March 22, 1833; Elisabeth, Dec. 6, 1778; Henderick, Dec. 24, 1780; Jan Baptist, May 4 1783; Joseph, b. Nov. 2, 1786.

JESSE, son of Harmanus, m. Geertruy, dau. of Pieter Bosie, May 7, 1775. He d. June 3, 1810, a. 58ys., 4m., 6d.; she d. May 13, 1832, a. 78ys., 7m., 8d. Ch. bp: Margarita, July 6, 1775; Harmanus, June 10, 1781, d. Sept. 27, 1838.

HARMANUS, son of Harmanus, (?), m. Annatje Peek. Ch: Harmen, bp. Jan. 11, 1777.

HARMANUS, son of Johannes, m. Lena Ouderkerk of Noormanskil, August 27, 1785. He made his will March 3, 1809, proved June 28, 1809; spoke of wife Helena, and Ch. John, Matilda, Eva, Harmanus, Alida and Pieter. Ch. b: John, Sept. 11, 1786; Machtelt, March 4, 1789; Machtelt, June 11, 1790; Eva Yates, Sept. 16, 1793; Harmanus, Feb. 9, 1798; Alida, May 17, 1800; Peter Van Vranken, Jan. 23, 1803, d. Nov. 20, 1853, a. 51ys., (*Reflector*) d. Dec. 10, 1853, a. 52ys. (grave stone).

JACOBUS, son of Jacobus (?), m. Rebecca Quackenbosch. Ch: *Abraham*, bp. Nov. 1, 1778.

HARMANUS, son of Harmanus, m. first, Ellice Lloyd about 1778, and secondly, Nelly, dau. of Abraham Van Antwerpen,

July 5, 1787. Ch: Lydia, bp. June 6, 1779. Ch. b: Harmanus, March 11, 1782; Hannah, July 15, 1785; Abram, Dec. 26, 1787; Peter, March 1, 1792; Margarita, June 3, 1794; Jesse, Jan. 2, 1798; Arent Vedder, June 16, 1800; Johannes, May 20, 1802.

JACOBUS VEDDER, son of Harmanus, m. Catarina Mebie, Oct. 29, 1780, in Albany. Ch: Sarah, bp. Feb. 18, 1781. Ch. b: Albert, Jan. 15, 1790; Johannes, Aug. 5, 1792; Abram Mabie, Sept. 10, 1795; Jesse, Aug. 12, 1800.

JACOBUS, m. Susanna Peek. Ch: Jacobus, bp. Dec. 29, 1783.

JOSEPH, son of Cornelis, m. Catlyntje Van Vleck. In the Revolutionary war he served as Captain of a company of bateau men; d. May 24, (25), 1842, in his 87th year; she d. Feb. 1, 1834, a. 76ys., 3m. Ch. b: Catalina, Oct. 10, 1782, m. Richard Waldron, and d. June 18, 1805; a son, b. Sept. 11, and d. Sept. 17, 1784; Jannetie, July 29, 1786; Margarietje, Feb. 16, 1789, m. Capt. Jonas Holland, and d. Feb. 14, 1864; Susanna, Aug. 12, 1791; Eva, Sept. 2 (Aug. 31), 1794, m. William McCamus, and d. Nov. 4, 1828; Teunis, Oct. (Nov.) 24, 1796, d. Dec. 31, 1828.

JACOBUS, son of Hendricus, m. Sara, dau. of Johannes H. Peek. He d. Sept. 23, 1835, a. 77ys, 1m., 7d.; she d. Jan. 27, 1840, a. 77ys., 4m., 7d. Ch. b: Elisabeth, Nov. 6, 1783, m. first, Cornelius Van Antwerp, and secondly, Peter V.

De Graaf of Herkimer, d. Oct. 10, 1848; Johannes, July 29, 1785, d. Jan. 14, 1834, a. 48ys., 7m., 14d.; Eva, Nov. 22, 1790; Sarah, July 20, 1793.

CORNELIUS, son of Cornelis, m. Neeltie, dau. of Thomas Brouwer Bancker. She d. Feb. 16, 1832, a. 65ys., 21d. Ch. b: Thomas Bancker, April 28, 1785; Thomas Bancker, Sept. 15, 1786, d. Aug. 7, 1853; Jacobus, May 26, 1789, d. Jan. 15, 1831; Christoffel, March 24, 1793, d. April 28, 1839; Evert, Aug. 10, 1795; Annatie Bancker, bp. Dec. 14, 1800, d. Aug. 10, 1872; Margarieta Truex, b. Dec. 10, 1799, bp. Dec. 14, 1800; Henry Dellamont, Sept. 27, 1807.

CHRISTOFFEL, son of Cornelis, m. Debora, dau. of Johannes Wemple, Feb. 14, 1785. She d. in Watervliet in 1840. Ch. b: John Wemple, Jan. 31, 1786; Christopher Yates, July 29, 1787, d. in the *Woestyne*, June 20, 1861; Cornelius, July 13, 1789; Nicolaas, Aug. 2, 1791; Jacobus, March 6, 1793; Myndert, Nov. 15, 1797; Joseph, May 4, 1800; Marytje, April 8, 1802; Catlina who m. ...... Oothout of Watervliet.

HENRICUS, son of Hendricus, m. Susanna, dau. of Cornelis Van der Volgen, Nov. 11, 1787. Ch. b: Jannetie, Jan. 6, 1788; Cornelius, June 8, 1791.

WILLIAM, son of Hendricus, m. Judith Hicks, Sept. 22, 1788. Ch. b: Evert, April 23, 1790; Sarah, Sept. 22, 1792; Susanna, Oct. 3, 1794; Susanna, Feb. 5, 1796.

DANIEL, JR., and Jannetje Peek, m.
June 5, 1796.

ABRAM J., son of Jacobus and Geertruy Van Valkenburgh of the *Woestyne,*
m. Jan. 17, 1799.

PELS.

JOHN E., and Eleanor Freer. Ch :
Johannes, b. Dec. 22, 1796.

PEMBERTON.

WILLIAM, m. Mary, dau. of Johannes
Van Sice, Sept. 30, 1796. Ch : Margarieta, b. Jan. 12, 1797.

PENNET.

PETER, from Philadelphia, merchant
in Schenectady, 1783.

PEPSTON.

THOMAS, and wife, members of the
church in 1793.

PERRY.

JOSHUA, m. Lysbet, dau. of Benjamin
Lenain. Ch : Maria, b. Aug. 24, 1727.

PESINGER.

SAFRINUS, and Mary Young. Ch :
Hendrick, bp. July 28, 1782.

PETENGILL.

JOSEPH, and Margariet Cooley. Ch.
b : Margary, Sept. 20, 1794; Peter, Oct.
8, 1796.

PETERS (PETERSE, PETERSEN).

WILLEM, m. Sophia, dau. of Harmanus Vedder, Nov. 25, 1725, and secondly,
Helena, dau. of Jan Baptist Van Eps,
Nov. 27, 1742. His first wife d. May
10, 1741, in her 41st year ; the second
d. May 1, 1751, a. 37ys. Ch. bp : Joan,
May 1, 1726; Harmanus, March 21,
1731; *Harmanus,* Nov. 5, 1732; Margariet, Oct. 8, 1737; *Jacobus,* April 26,
1741; Anna, Oct. 9, 1743 m. Andrew
McFarlane; Sophia, Sept. 28, 1745, in
Albany, m. Hugh McMichael; Maria,
Aug. 3, 1755.

PETERSEN.

HARMANUS, son of Willem, m. Margarita, dau. of Jacobus Peek, Nov. 4,
1761. She made her will May 20, 1811,
proved March 11, 1817; spoke of her
sons Harmanus, Willem, James and dau.
Lydia and Sophia. Ch. bp : Sophia,
June 18, 1762; *Harmanus,* May 24,
1764; Sophia, Dec. 5, 1765, m. Nathan
Clark; Margarita, June 20, 1768, m.
Dirk Van Vranken; Jacobus, Jan. 7,
1770; Lydia, Nov. 24, 1771; *Willem,*
May 29, 1774; Lydia, April 14, 1780,
m. Jan Baptist Van Petten.

PETRUS, and Rebecca De la Montagne.
Ch. bp : Sarah, Sept. 9, 1764; Isaac, Jan.
10, 1767; Annatje, Jan. 22, 1769, m. Cornelis Bratt; Rebecca, May 10, 1772.

JAMES, son of Willem, m. Mary ......
Ch. bp : Sarah, July 24, 1765; Jane,
July 13, 1769.

JOSEPH, and Mary Lad. Ch. bp : Maria, Dec. 13, 1767; John, Jan. 5, 1770.

FRANS, m. Susanna, dau. of Cornelis
Van Slyck. Ch : Jannetje, bp. Jan. 10,
1779.

THOMAS, and Sarah Dennison. Ch: Thomas, bp. Oct. 15, 1784; Catharina, March 29, 1786; Susanna, b. March 30, 1788.

HARMANUS, son of Harmanus, m. Polly (Maria) Rykman, Sept. 9, 1785. Ch. b: Catharine, Jan. 30, 1786; John, Jan. 14, 1788; Margarietje, Jan. 28, 1789; Johannes, Dec. 12, 1790; Harmanus, Eunice and Sophia, all b. Oct. 23, 1792; Cornelius, Aug. 5, 1794.

WILLIAM, m. Catharina, dau. of Christoffel Felthuysen, Sept. 5, 1795. He d. "28th of 2d month," 1846; she d. July 22, 1854. Ch. b: Annatje, Feb. 24, 1796; Harmanus, June 17, 1797, d. Dec. 6, 1870; Christoffel, March 8, 1800; William, Aug. 20, 1802; Annatje Velthuysen, Feb. 20, 1805, d. Sept. 4, 1805; Andrew McFarlin, July 16, 1806; Henry Velthuysen, March 19, 1810; John Broderick, Sept. 19, 1814, d. May 28, 1815.

PETIT.

JONATHAN, and Elisabeth Van Etten. Ch. b: Nathaniel, Oct. 19, 1799; Mary Ann, May 20, 1801.

PHILIP (PHALIP).

ASA, and Ann Schadik. Ch: Oliver, bp. Dec. 14, 1764.

JOHN, and Maria Middleton. Ch: Jane, bp. April 25, 1777.

PHILIPS.

JOHN, and Elisabeth Zitterly, both of the Hellenbergh, bans, January 8, 1791.

She d. Aug. 18, 1858. Ch. b: Catharina, March 1, 1792; Eva, Sept. 12, 1793; Elisabeth, Aug. 4, 1797; Johannes, Aug. 7, 1800; Peter, Feb. 19, 1803; Margaret, Sept. 6, 1805; Mary Ann, April 4, 1808; Jacob, May 9, 1810.

JOHN, and Isabella Phinney. Ch. b: Mary, Feb. 13, 1790; Sytje, June 12, 1793; Elisabeth, June 20, 1796, all bp. Feb. 26, 1797.

ROSELL (Roswell), and Lena Simons. Ch. b: Elisabeth, March 13, 1799; David, May 22, 1800; John, Dec. 18, 1803.

PHILIPSE (DE MOER).

PHILIP, m. Elisabeth, dau. of Harmen Gansevoort of Albany (?). He owned the sixth flat, which he contracted to exchange, in 1689, with Claes Willemse Van Coppernol for the *Willigen Vlachte*, which willow flat lies on the south side of the Mohawk river, about one mile above Crane's village. The family still reside there. Ch. bp: Sander, Jan. 24, 1686, in Albany, living with wife Margaret in the "Mohax contray" in 1730; Jacob, August 27, 1693, in Albany; Jacob, April 6, 1697; Claes, May 5, 1700; *Harmen.*

HARMEN, son of Philip, m. Maritje Ursula Lappien, April 18, 1712. Ch. bp: *Philip,* May 3, 1713; Anganietje, Dec. 18, 1714, m. Jan Philipse Cromwell; Lysabet, May 21, 1716; Maritje, Jan. 9, 1720, m. Henrik Harris; Abraham, March 31, 1722; Anna, Nov. —, 1723; *Johannes,* b. Oct. 15, bp. Nov. 6,

1726; Jacobus, July 18 (?), 1731; Margarieta, June 3, 1733, m. Johannes Dingman.

WILLEM, and Maria Sixberry. Ch. bp: Pietertje, Sept. 8, 1734; Willem, July 9, 1737.

PHILIP, son of Harmen, and Elisabeth Wanel (Wanner). Ch. bp: *Lodewyck*, June 7, 1741; Harmen, April 24, 1743; Philip, Jan. 1, 1747; Abraham, Dec. 8, 1751.

JOHN, son of Harmen, m. Mary Middleton, Feb. 9, 1752, in Albany. Ch. bp: Annatje, May 4, 1755; Mary, April 2, 1758.

LOWIS, son of Philip, m. Margarita Headcock. Ch: Margarieta, bp. Jan. 25, 1781.

PHYN.

JAMES, of the firm of Phyn, Ellice & Co., merchants in Schenectady as early as 1768.

PICKEN.

ROBERT, m. Jane Lennox (Macowley, *trouw-boek*), May 11, 1768. Ch: Robert, bp. April 5, 1769.

PIKARD.

JOHN, and Eva Haverman. Ch: Henderick, bp. June 26, 1781.

PIKKERT.

BARTHOLOMEW, and Eva Claese. In 1717 he had a grant of land on the plain between Schenectady and Albany at a place called *Verrebergh*. Ch. bp: Bartholomew, Jan. 9, 1700, m. Anna Catharine ......, Aug. 3, 1722, being then a resident of "Scoharry;" Nicholas, Feb. 23, 1701; Dorothea, July 28, 1703; Rachel, ——, 1706, in Albany.

PITTINGER.

JOSHUA, and Elisabeth Slover. Ch: Isaac Wimple, b. Oct. 31, 1797.

PLATTO.

ALEXANDER, and Barbara Ramsey, both of Normanskil, m. July 17, 1787. Ch. b: Maria, Sept. 6, 1793; James, March 2, 1798.

PLOMADO.

LOWIS, and Maria Louisa Plomado. Ch: Pierre, bp. Oct. 12, 1777.

JOSEPH, and Maria Labrusch. Ch: Maria Theresia, bp. Feb. 10, 1779.

POLHEMUS.

HENRY, member of the church in 1795.

POLL.

JURRIE, and Catharina Shaver. Ch: Abraham, b. Jan. 7, 1799.

POOTMAN (PUTMAN).

JOHANNES (Jan), sixteen years of age in 1661, was apprenticed by Jan Hendrickse Van Bael for three years to Philip Hendrickse Brouwer for his food and clothes. He m. Cornelia, dau. of Arent Andriese Bratt and Catlyntje De Vos. His home lot, in the village, was on the north corner of Union and Ferry streets, having 100ft. frontage on the former street; later he purchased the 100ft. lot next west, of Jan Roeloffse, son of the celebrated Anneke Janse. On the fatal night of the 8th of Feb., 1690, both Pootman and his neighbor Roeloffse with their wives, were slain by the French and Indians. The following Ch. were living in 1715, when they received their mother's portion of her father's estate (£101, 13, 4): *Arent;* Maritie, m. Stephen Bedeut; *Victoor;* David; *Cornelis;* Catalyntje, m. Cornelis Post.

ARENT, eldest son of Jan, inherited his father's home lot on the north corner of Union and Ferry streets. He moved to the Maquaas country with his family, where he was living as late as 1754. He m. Lysbet Akkerman. Ch. bp : Jannetie, in Albany, June 12, 1709, m. Thomas Harris ; Johannes, October 21, 1711; *Lodewyck,* Nov. 14, 1713; David, Oct. 3, 1715, is said to have been taken prisoner by the forces of Sir John Johnson and held three years in Canada ; Cornelia, Oct. 12, 1717, m. Jeronimus Barheit or Stephen Cromwell ; Maritie, July (?) 15, 1719 ; Victor, April 29, 1721 ; Sara, July 5, 1724.

VICTOOR, son of Jan, m. Grietje, sister of Jan Pieterse Mebie (?), in Albany, Dec. 13, 1706. Ch. bp : Cornelia, in Albany, Aug. 3, 1707 ; Antje, in Albany, April 25, 1709 ; Johannes, Oct. 21, 1711 ; Pieter, Feb. 1, 171⅔ ; Maritie, Dec. 18, 1714 ; Jacob, March 23, 171⅚ ; *Arent,* Feb. 14, 1719 ; Catharina, Feb. 18, 1721 ; Cornelis, b. Dec. 17, 1724.

LODEWYCK, son of Arent, of Johnstown, m. Elisabeth Soets. Ch : Elisabeth, bp. in Albany, Aug. 29, 1754. May 21, 1780, a party of Sir John Johnson's regiment " proceeded directly to the " house of Lodowyck Putman, an honest " Dutchman living two miles and a half " from the Johnstown Court House. Put- " man had two daughters and three sons ; " two of the sons were absent ; the old " man and his son Aaron were killed ; " the old woman and her dau. Hannah " were spared ; the latter afterwards m. " Jacob Shew ; the other dau. was m. " to Amasa Stevens whom the savages " killed." [*Simms's History of Schoharie Co.*]

CORNELIS, son of Jan, m. Jacomyntje, dau. of Teunis Viele. Ch. bp : Cornelia, Nov. 14, 1713 ; *Teunis,* March 31, 1716 ; Elisabeth, Dec. 30, 1717, m. Cornelis Groot ; Johannes, Mar. 18, 1720 ; *Lowys,* Dec. 1, 1722 ; Maritie, March 14, 1724, m. Johannes C. Van Vranken ; Catalyntje, b. May 4, bp. May 5, 1726 ; Jacob, July 6, 1729 ; Margarita, b. Jan. 13, bp. Jan. 30, 1732, m. Jacob Van Vranken ; Eva, b. Dec. 16, bp. Dec. 22, 1734 ; *Arent,* July 31, 1736 ; Gysbert, June 28, 1741.

ARENT, son of Victor, m. Elisabeth, dau. of Jacobus Peek, Aug. 5, 1743. Ch. bp : Margrietje, Feb. 26, 1744 ; Jacobus, Jan. 19, 1746 ; Victoor, May 20, 1748 ; Margarita, b. Oct. 20, 1749, m. Simon H. Vedder ; Cornelis, bp. May —, 1758 ; Maria, Jan. 21, 1763.

LOUIS, son of Cornelis, m. Sara, dau. of Arent Van Antwerpen, Jan. 3, 174⅔. Ch. bp: Cornelis, June 14, 1747; Sara, Dec. 24, 1749; *Arent*, July 10, 1751; Jacomina, Dec. 26, 1753; *Johannes*, Oct. 7, 1756; Sara, Oct. 21, 1759.

TEUNIS, son of Cornelis, m. Rebecca, dau. of Arent Van Antwerpen, Oct. 20, 1750. Ch. b: Sara, May 3, 1751; Jacomyntje, April 23, 1753, m. Alexander Van Eps; *Cornelis*, b. May 15, [*Family Record,*] bp. April 20, 1755 [*Church Record*]; Daniel, b. June 15 [*Family Record,*] bp. May 21, 1758 [*Church Record*]; Johannes, b. Oct. 2, 1760; Johannes, bp. May 20, 1762, made will Feb. 13, 1821, proved March 6, 1821; spoke of sister Jemima Van Eps, and brother Cornelis; Arent bp. March 10, 1766.

ARENT, son of Cornelis, m. Clara (Catarina), dau. of Harmanus Vedder of Nestoungjoone, April 18, 1763 (?). Ch. bp: Cornelis, April 15, 1764; Cornelis, Jan. 25, 1767; Catarina, April 16, 1769; Jacomyntje, Aug. 18, 1771; *Christiaan*, Dec. 25, 1774.

ARENT, son of Louis, m. Rebecca De Garmo, Feb. 28, 1772. Ch. bp: Sarah, Oct. 17, 1773; Johannes, Aug. 6, 1775; Lowis, Nov. 23, 1777; Annatje, April 9, 1780; Matthias, Nov. 4, 1781; Cornelis, April 18, 1784; Mattheus, b. Jan. 18, 1787.

ARENT, perhaps son of Johannes, who was son of Arent and Lysbet Akkerman; m. first, Elisabeth De Spitzer (Spitser),

dau. of Doct. Ernestus De Spitser, Feb. 21, 1772; secondly, Catalina Van Schaick. He d. Aug. 1, 1830, a. 85ys., 1m., 18d.; his first wife d. May 18, 1796, a. 42ys., 25d; his second wife d. Dec. 22, 1836, in her 87th year. Ch. bp: Geertruy, Nov. 21, 1773; *Ernestus*, b. Oct. 27, bp. Nov. 3, 1776; Johannes, Feb. 7, 1779; *Johannes*, Sept. 10, 1780; Barbara, March 2, 1783, m. Oliver Springer.

CORNELIUS, son of Teunis, of Glenville, m. Maria, dau. of Jan Baptist Van Vorst. He made his will July 20, 1824; in a former will made Jan. 22, 1822, he spoke of wife Maria, son Jan Baptist, and dau. Rebecca, wife of Thaddeus Bolt. Ch. bp: Jan Baptist and Daniel, Dec. 22, 1782; Jan Baptist, Sept. 29, 1784; Rebecca, b. July 19, 1787.

JOHANNES, son of Louis, m. Elisabeth, dau. of Harmen Vedder. Ch. bp: Jacomyntje, Aug. 17, 1783; Harmen, June 10, 1787. Ch. b: Sara, Dec. 9, 1788; Isaac, March 17, 1796.

JOHN, son of Arent and Elisabeth De Spitser, m. Magdalen, dau. of Hendrick Vrooman. He d. May 1, 1851, in Rotterdam. She d. Dec. 16, 1830, a 43ys., 8m. 25d. Ch b: Aaron, Nov. 10, 1805, of Rotterdam; Henry Vrooman, Dec. 29, 1807, of Niagara county; Ernestus, of Schenectady; John, of Niagara county; Andrew Y., of Rotterdam; Sebastian, of Rotterdam; Oliver, of Rotterdam; Sarah, m. Joseph Levy of Niagara county; Clarissa, of Rotterdam.

DAVID S., m. Annatje Van Antwerpen. Ch: Maria, b. June 5, 1794.

ARENT, m. Cathlyntje Stevens, Jan. 21, 1798.

CHRISTIAAN, son of Arent, m. Catalina Peek. Ch. b: Arent, Dec. 22, 1796; Arent, Jan. 28, 1799.

CHRISTIAAN (probably same as last), m. Catlyntje Bratt. Ch: Jacomyntje, b. Oct. 23, 1801.

ERNESTUS, son of Arent and Elisabeth De Spitser, m. first, ..., and secondly, Elisabeth Gray, in Shepardstown, Va., March 24, 1814. He settled in New Madison, O., in 1819, where he resided 38 years; removed in 1857 to Winchester, Ind., where he d. Oct. 20, 1865; his wife d. Feb. 15, 1864. Ch. b: Aaron, —— 1811; Ann Elisabeth, 1815, d. 1816; Jane G., 1816; John G., 1818; Elisabeth S., 1819; David, 1821; Barbara, 1823, d. two months old; Mary J., 1824; Ernestus J., 1826; Thomas C., 1828, d. 1848; James, 1830; Nancy C., 1833.

PORTEOUS.

JOHN, merchant in Schenectady 1774; of Herkimer 1794; not living 1801.

PORTER.

THOMAS, m. Sophia Nickson, Feb. 2, 1762.

POST.

CORNELIS, perhaps son of Elias, of New York, m. Catalina, dau. of Jan Pootman

in New York, Dec. 11, 1704. Ch: *Elias*, bp. in New York, Jan. 7, 1708.

ELIAS, son of Cornelis, m. Maria, dau. of Jan Baptist Van Eps, Nov. 7, 1730. He was a gunsmith, and in 1760 had a house and lot on the south side of State street, 75 to 80 feet easterly from Washington street, which house and lot in 1775 belonged to Hugh Mitchell. Ch. bp: Cathlina, Oct. 31, 1731; Cathlyn, June 3, 1733, m. Zeger Van Santvoord; Jan Baptist, Oct. 12, 1735; Cornelis, July 6, 1738; Helena, June 14, 1741; Anna, Sept. 18, 1743; Cornelia, April 13, 1746; *Johannes*, Jan. 1, 1749.

JOHANNES, son of Elias, m. Margarietje Bellinger. Ch. bp: Maria, Jan. 2, 1785. Ch. b: Maria, Jan. 8, 1786; Frederick, August 9, 1787; Catharina, Oct. 17, 1788; Elisabeth, Aug. 18, 1795.

ABRAHAM, and Maria Zabriskie. Ch: John, b. Dec. 25, 1798.

POWELL.

JONATHAN, and Eva, dau. of Willem Feeling, both of Clifton Park, m. "in the middle of Dec.," 1786. Ch: Willem Feeling, b. July 23, 1787.

WILLEM, and Charity (Geertruy) Brouwer. Ch. b: Mattheus, Nov. 3, 1791; Catharina, Aug. 5, 1793; Hanna, June 25, 1795; Jonathan, April 12, 1797.

PREVOOST.

AUGUSTUS, and Susanna Croghan. Ch: George William Augustus, bp Sept. 4, 1767.

JOHN, and Annatje Prevoost. Ch:
Nicholas, bp. Nov. 7, 1784.

PRICE.

DANIEL, Voorlezer in the Dutch
church in 1768.

JESSE, carpenter, m. Ann Forris
(Smith), Aug. 4, 1765. Ch. bp: Sarah,
March 23, 1766; John, June 20, 1768;
David, March 4, 1770.

JONATHAN, waggon maker, of Schenectady 1798, d. May 7, 1832, a. 67ys.

PRINCE.

JOHN, m. Elisabeth, dau. of Pieter Van
Gyseling, Nov. 2, 1790. He was a mer-
chant, at one time member of assembly.
The town of Princetown was named for
him. His residence was No. 3 Front
street. He d. in 1801; his wife was b.
Feb. 14, 1775, and d. August 8, 1825.
Ch: Ann, b. Jan. 29, 1794.

PROKTER.

JOSEPH, and Mary Fenning. Ch. bp:
Hester, April 23, 1764; Margariet, April
28, 1768.

PRUYN.

SAMUEL I., of Albany, m. Neeltje, dau.
of Reuben Hosford, June 11, 1775.
Ch: Reuben, bp. Jan. 25, 1778. [See
Albany Families].

DAVID, m. Rebecca, dau. of Carel
Hanse Toll, Oct. 29, 1796. He d. in
Glenville, Oct. 17, 1856, a. 84ys. Ch.
b: Annatie, Oct. 26, 1797; Carel Hansen, May 22, 1800; Margarieta, Jan.

13, 1803; Francis, June 15, 1805;
John Toll, Feb. 17, 1808; Hester, July
25, 1810; David, July 23, 1812; Philip,
July 21, 1815; Simon Edwin, Dec. 13,
1817.

PULVER.

MARTINUS, and Margarita Poplar
(Pepler). Ch. b: Christina, Dec. 10,
1785; Catryntje, May 16, 1788; Jacob,
Nov. 20, 1792; Solomon, Oct. 24, 1794;
Annatje, Nov. 25, 1797.

SOLOMON, and Maria Denniston, both
of Duanesburgh, m. Oct. 22, 1787. Ch:
Sarah, b. July 11, 1795.

JACOB, and Catharina Bowman. Ch:
John, b. July 24, 1797.

PURDY.

WILLIAM, m. Folkje, dau. of Barent
Veeder. Ch. b: Jannetje, Sept., 1791;
Margarieta, July 14, 1793; Marytje,
Feb. 13, 1796; Jannetje, July 12, 1798.

PURMERENT.

See Vander Volgen.

PUTMAN

See Pootman.

PUTNAM.

CALEB, tanner, from Bolton, Mass.,
m. Elisabeth Rynex, May 31, 1794.

QUACKENBOS.

PIETER, brick maker, in 1668 bought
Adriaen Van Ilpendam's brickyard in
Albany. He probably had the following

sons: Wouter; Reinier; Pieter; *Jo-hannes.* [*See Albany Families.*]

JOHANNES, son of Pieter, of Niska-yuna, m. first, Magtelt Janse Post, and secondly, Anna, dau. of Johannes Clute, Oct. 20, 1700. He and his brother Rei-nier owned farms on the north side of the Mohawk river, in the present town of Clifton Park, which were extended north one mile by patent of date April 22, 1708. Ch. bp. in Albany: *Pieter*, (?); Geer-truy, May 10, 1684; Magtelt, Feb. 13, 1687; Abraham, March 23, 1690; Isaac, Feb. 19, 1693; Jacob, Nov. 17, 1695; *Johannes*, in Schenectady, Jan. 4, 1702; Bata, in Schenectady, Feb. 6, 1704. Ch. bp. in Albany: Bata, Dec. 7, 1707, m. Johannes Heemstraat; *Abraham*, Nov. 3, 1710; *Isaac*, Jan. 25, 1713; Jacob, Oct. 30, 1715. Ch. bp. in Schenectady: Machtelt, March 9, 1718, m. Frederick Clute; *Gerardus*, March 11, 1721; Anna Barbara, Sept. 29, 1723.

PIETER, m. Neeltie, dau. of David Ma-rinus, Nov. 1, 1701, in Albany. In 1733 he bought lands on the Mohawk river, of Edward Collins; was buried July 20, 1748. Ch. bp. in Albany: *David*, June 21, 1702; Abraham, Nov. 19, 1704; Maghtelt, Dec. 30, 1705; Abraham, Sept 19, 1708; Jeremias, Oct. 26, 1713; Rachel, Jan. 22, 1716; Johannes, in Schenectady, March 15, 1718; Geertruy, in Schenectady, July 17, 1720.

DAVID, son of Pieter, m. Annatje, dau. of Capt. Scott, of Scott's Patent, May 11, 1723, in Albany. [See an account of his courtship in Simms's *History*.] Ch. bp:

Jan (John Scott), June 14, 1724; Neeltje, Oct. 15, 1725; Lena, Sept. 21, 1727; *Abraham*, Feb. 5, 1732, in Schenectady.

JOHANNES, son of Johannes Pieterse m. Helena, dau. of Frederick Clute, both of Konnestegioune, banns June 26, 1731; secondly, m. Lena, dau. of Jacob Van Olinda, Feb. 12, 1755. He d. be-fore the baptism of his last child. Ch. bp: Annatie, May 21, 1732; Francyna, Dec. 25, 1733, m. Isaac Van Vranken; Bata, Oct. 19, 1735, m. Claas De Graaf; *Fredericus*, Dec. 21, 1737; Johannes, May 16, 1742; Johannes, Jan. 20, 1745; Walran, Dec. 28, 1746; Annatje, July 24, 1748, m. Jeremiah De Graaf; Eva, July 18, 1756; Lena, Aug. 21, 1757; Elisabeth, Oct. 29, 1758; Jacobus, Feb. 17, 1760 (Jan. 30, 1784, letters of admin-istration were issued to John Q. on the estate of Jacobus Q., Corporal in Col. Seth Warner's regiment); Elisabeth, Aug. 2, 1761.

ISAAC, son of Johannes Pieterse, m. Rebecca, dau. of Dirk Groot, Oct. 27, 1737, in Albany. Ch. bp: Annatje, July 6, 1738, m. Albert H. Vedder; Elisabeth, April 13, 1740; Rebecca, April 25, 1742; Rebecca, July 8, 1744; Bata, Aug. 2, 1747, m. Frederic Bratt (?); *Johannes*, and Maria, b. Aug. 9, bp. Aug. 12, 1750; Maria, July 19, 1753.

ISAAC, and Geertruy ...... Ch: Ra-chel, bp. April 13, 1740.

JACOB, of Niskayuna, and Catharina Huyk of Kinderhook, m. in Schenectady, Feb. 25, 174⅘. [*See Albany Families.*]

ADRIAAN, son of Adriaan, of Albany, m. Elisabeth, dau. of Jacob Clute. Ch. bp: Catharina, Jan. 7, 1739; Geertruy, Dec. 20, 1741.

PIETER, JR., m. Sarah, dau. of Pieter Conyn of Albany. Ch. bp: Alida, Oct. 12, 1740; Meindert, Oct. 1, 1746; Abraham, Feb. 28, 1748.

ABRAHAM, son of Johannes Pieterse, of Niskayuna, m. Bata, dau. of Pieter Ouderkerk, Jan. 11, 1740, in Albany. He d. before the baptism of his last child. Ch. bp: Annatje, Dec. 14, 1740; Anna, June 27, 1742; Elisabet, Feb. 3, 1745; Alida, Dec. 6, 1747; Johannes, Feb. 11, 1750, d. July 28, 1839, a. 89ys.; Bata, Jan. 5, 1752; Susanna, Nov. 28, 1756; Rebecca, Jan. 14, 1758; Machtelt, Aug. 29, 1761, m. John Wood.

GERRIT (Gerardus), son of Johannes Pieterse, of Genistagioene, m. first, Elisabeth Van Vorst, April 25, 1747. She was buried March 17, 1805. Ch. bp: Anna, Oct. 16, 1748; Johannes, March 3, 1751; Bata, Feb. 9, 1753; Jacobus, March 30, 1755; Machtelt, April 3, 1757; *Johannes*, September 9, 1759; Sara, Feb. 7, 1762, m. Richard Van Vranken, jr.; Machtelt, Sept. 30, 1764, m. Pieter Huyck; Maria, Feb. 28, 1767; Rebecca, August 6, 1769, m. Andrew Huyck; Engeltie, Dec. 27, 1771, m. Joseph Carley.

ABRAHAM, son of David, of Kachnawage, m. Maria Bratt, October 8, 1762. Ch: John Schot (Scott), bp. Jan. 3, 1768.

FREDERICK, son of Johannes and Helena Clute, and Maria Schitterlin (Sitterlin), both of Rensselaerswyck, m. Dec. 1, 1768. Ch. bp: *Johannes*, Dec. 22, 1771; Catarina, Sept. 8, 1773; *Isaac*, Jan. 30, 1777; Jacob, May 12, 1779; Jacob, May 15, 1781; Lena, Aug. 6, 1783.

JOHANNES G., son of Gerrit, m. Annatje Shannon. Ch. bp: Elisabeth, June 22, 1782; Benjamin, Nov. 16, 1783; Annatje, b. Sept. 13, 1785.

JOHN, son of Isaac, m. Elisabeth, dau. of Cornelis Groot of Nestigaune, Dec. 8. 1793. He lived at the junction of Lafayette and Liberty streets, and d. July 28, 1839, a. 88ys., 11m., 9d.; she d. May 11, 1835, in her 79th year. Ch. b: Isaac, Sept. 8, 1797; Maria, March 18, 1799, m. Abraham O. Clute, and d. Feb. 26, 1855, a. 55ys., 10m., 8d.

JACOBUS, and Maria Leenhart, both of Helderbergh, m. April 24, 1791.

ISAAC A., and Catharina Bancker. Ch: Magdalena, b. Aug. 5. 1789, d. Jan, 21, 1790.

ABRAM, and Jannetje De Noe, both living in the *Halve Maan*, m. May 18, 1786.

DAVID, and Catlyntje Hoevener, both of Cagnawago, were m. at that place, banns May 10, 1787.

JOHN, son of Frederick, of Albany, m. Catharina, dau. of Arent S. Bratt, July 26, 1796. Ch. b: Johannes, Nov.

22, 1796; Arent Bratt, May 28, 1799,
d. March 21, 1846.

PETER, widower, of Canajoharie, m.
Marytje Rosa, widow, of Schenectady,
March 5, 1792.

ISAAC F., of Noormanskil, m. Engeltie
Erichzon, Oct. 29, 1798.

QUANT.

FREDERICK, of the Hellenbergh, m.
Maria Seger, Feb. 19, 1786. Ch: Elisabeth, b. May 31, 1797.

QUINEZ.

PIETER, in Schenectady, 1715.

RADLEY.

PHILIP, and Susanna Seger. Ch: Gerrit, b. Dec. 18, 1796.

RAL.

PIETER, member of the church in 1700.

RAMSAY.

DAVID, and Ann Lovell. Ch: Lovel,
b. May 6, 1777.

FREDERIC, and Catharine Quackenbos,
both of the Noormanskil, m. June 17,
1794. Ch. b: Maria, Feb. 1, 1800:
Catharina, Jan. 31, 1802.

REAGLES (RIGEL).

CORNELIUS, m. Maria, dau. of Gillis
Van Vorst, Aug. 25, 1788. Ch. b: Annatie, June 8, 1789; Cornelius; James,
who d. Dec. 21, 1870, a. 70ys.

REDDILY.

JOHANNES, and Maria Egmont. Ch:
Maria, bp. Sept. 4, 1784.

REESE (RIES).

FREDERICK, of Albany, m. Susanna,
dau. of David Frank, August 1, 1790.
Ch. b: Margaret, March 17, 1792, m.
Isaac G. Yates, and d. Sept. 22, 1850.
Annatie, Sept. 25, 1794; David Frank,
Dec. 16, 1796; Elisabeth, Dec. 12, 1800;
Janneke, May 18, 1802; Elisabeth, Mar;
28, 1805; Maria, April 10, 1807; Rebecca, March 14, 1808 (1809?), bp. Jan.
14, 1810; Susan Catharine, January 20,
1811; Caty Beekman, Sept. 7, 1814.

MARKUS, and Maria Heemstraate, both
of Montgomery county, m. Mar. 29, 1794.
Ch: Nicholas, b. July 17, 1795.

GEORGE, and Anna Bullock. Ch. b:
Martinus, Feb. 17, 1799; Anna, Nov.
19, 1802.

PHILIP, and Eleanor Callener. Ch.
bp: Elisabeth, March 2, 1782; Robert,
Oct. 10, 1784; Anna, b. March 20, 1801.

REILMAN.

JURRY, and Dorothea ...... Ch: Elisabeth, bp. Feb. 1, 1756.

RELDER.

BARENT, and Catarina Pellin. Ch:
Elisabeth, bp. Sept. 8, 1765.

RELYEA.

DENNIL (Daniel), of the Noormanski.
m. Annatje, dau. of Nicolas Van Petten

Ch. bp: David, July 18, 1779; Nicolaas, Dec. 1, 1780; Sarah, Feb. 22, 1785; Petrus, b. Oct. 19, 1790; Annatje, b. June 12, 1793.

PIETER, of the Noormanskil, and Neeltie Seybert. Ch. bp: Daniel, Jan. 29, 1770; Maria, May 3, 1783; Annatje, Feb. 22, 1785.

REYM.

JOHAN ERNST, and Wilhelmina Catharina Brouwn. Ch: Sebastian, bp. Oct. 30, 1779.

REYNEX.

ANDREAS, b. at Maastricht, m. first, Anna Symons, and secondly, Maria Smitt, Jan. 29, 1769. Ch: James, b. May 14, 1766. Ch. bp: Willem, July 29, 1770; Elisabeth, Sept. 15, 1771; *Valentyn*, June 13, 1773; Maria, Dec. 25, 1775, m. Jacob G. Van Antwerpen; Andreas, Feb. 13, 1778; Andreas, Sept. 2, 1780.

JOHANNES, b. in Duytsland, m. Sarah Smitt, July 16, 1769. Ch. bp: Susanna, Sept. 9, 1770, m. Abraham Buys Walker; Elisabeth, April 19, 1772; *Willem*, April 10, 1774; Ephraim, April 28, 1776; Sarah, May 21, 1777, m. Pieter S. Van Antwerpen; Andreas, Oct. 19, 1778; Maria, May 5, 1780; Dorothea, b. May 20, 1786.

VALENTINE, son of Andreas, m. Jemima, dau. of Abraham Groot, April 22, 1797. Ch. b: Maria, March 30, 1798; Abram Groot Andrew, Oct. 24, 1800.

WILLEM, and Esther Templer, both of Schenectady Patent, m. Nov. 16, 1797.

Ch. b: John, Jan. 21, 1799; Elisabeth, Aug. 13, 1800; Valentine, Jan. 22, 1802.

ANDREW, m. Sara Sanders, Oct. 11, 1795.

REYNOLDS.

JOHN, m. Eva Schermerhorn, Nov. 2, 1799.

RICHARDSON.

JONATHAN, and Elisabeth Bonn (Bow). Ch. bp: Catrien, May 29, 1782; Han, Sept. 12, 1784; Elisabeth, b. April 14, 1787; Ebenezer, Oct. 14, 1788.

JOHN, merchant in 1786.

PARIS (Parys), and Delia (Dinah) Humphreys. Ch: Elisabeth, bp. Sept. 9, 1783. Ch. b: Sarah, Nov. 16, 1785; Martha, Sept. 10, 1787; Zachariah, Jan. 20, 1792; Eleanor, Sept. 6, 1794; Hanna, March 18, 1797.

RICKEY.

Capt. JOHN, from New Jersey, m. Catharina Van Antwerpen, Nov. 17, 1759.

RICKY.

JOHN, (perhaps same as the last), and Catarina Brouwer. Ch: Cornelia, bp. June 2, 1765.

RIDDER.

ANDREAS, and Maria Hanin. Ch: Johannes, bp. March 14, 1762.

EVERT, and Jacoba Lewis. Ch: Rachel, bp. Nov. 21, 1774.

RIGHTER (RICHTER).

MICHAEL, and Elisabeth Weller. Ch. bp: Anna, March 18, 1783; Anna Maria, March 29, 1785; Eva, b. March 16, 1788.

NICHOLAS, and Catrina Doonok (Cook). Ch: Maria, bp. Feb. 10, 1784; Jenny, b. July 17, 1788.

JOHANNES, and Maria Tits (Tidd). Ch: John, bp. Feb. 26, 1784.

MICHAEL, and Dorothea Weynigen. Ch: Johannes, bp. Feb. 9, 1755.

RINCKHOUT.

JAN, baker, of Albany, hired Bent Bagge's house and lot at Schenectady for one year. He owned a bakery in Albany, which in 1670 his wife Elisabeth Drinckvelt rented to Antony Lespinard.

JURRIAN (Jorgen), and Maria Idesèn. He made his will Feb. 2, 1703, and letters of administration were issued to his wife March 30, 1704; spoke of his father Jan, and Ch. Teunis, a. 17ys.; Eefje, a. 12ys.; Jan, a. 9ys.; Daniel, bp. in New York Sept. 11, 1698; Jannetie, bp. in New York Sept. 22, 1700; Ide, bp. in Schenectady Feb. 28, 1703; gave to his wife the use of his real and personal property here in Schenectady and New York, during her life time, his father Jan to be maintained out of the estate; son Teunis to have the farm at Schenectady at a fair price; Ida, when he comes of age, to have the farm near New York as made over by his father-in-law Teunis

Idesse. After Jurriaen Rinckhout's death, his wid. m. John McIntyre, June 17, 1704.

MARGARITA, member of the church in 1700.

ROBERSON.

DANIEL, and Elisabeth Slingerland. Ch: Antony, bp. June 25, 1771.

(ROBINSON).

JOHN, and Jane Thompson. Ch: John, bp. Oct. 20, 1780; Nancy, b. July 30, 1786; Alexander, b. Feb. 14, 1793.

JOHN, and Geertruy Van Petten. Ch: Susanna, bp. Feb. 17, 1782.

......, and Susanna Hoffman. Ch: Elisabeth, bp. July 2, 1783.

ROBERTS.

BENT, an early settler in Schenectady before 1669, at which time he released his house and lot to Jan Rinckhout, and perhaps removed to his farm at *Maalwyck*, where he received a grant of 76 acres opposite to Arent the Noorman's [Bratt] as conveyed to him by the Indians. He made his will June 28, 1706, and gave his property to his wife Maria, and in case of her remarriage, to his stepsons Peter and Joseph Clement In 1710 Peter Clement sold his half of the farm to Cornelis Viele, together with half of *Benten* island for £445, and on March 17, 1712, his brother Joseph sold the other half to Carel Hansen Toll for £400.

ROBINSON.

CALEB, and Geertruy Bragham, both of the Noormanskil, m. Aug. 17, 1795. Ch. b: Robert, Nov. 16, 1795; John, May 22, 1798; Margariet, Nov. 3, 1801.

ANTHONY, and Annatie Vlack, m. Oct. 30, 1794.

ROEF.

CHRISTIAAN, of Duanesburgh, and Eva Beerop of Noormanskil, m. Sept. 1, 1789. Ch: Johannes, b. Sept. 9, 1790.

ROELOFFSEN.

JAN (*De Goyer*), son of the famous Anneke Janse, removed from Albany to Schenectady about 1670, in which year he accidentally killed Gerrit Verbeeck in the former place, for which he was pardoned by the Governor. His lot in Schenectady, was on the north side of Union street 100 Amst. ft. west of Ferry, the same lot now owned by Mr. Giles Y. Van der Bogart; this he sold to Jan Pootman, his neighbor on the east, reserving a life interest in the same for himself and wife. On the fatal night, Feb. 8, 1690, both were slain with their wives. Roeloffse left no children.

LOURENS, and Elisabeth Bernhart. Ch: Carel, bp. Feb. 13, 1785; Cornelius, b. Nov. 25, 1786.

ROGERS.

WILLIAM, JR., and Geertruy, dau. of Philip Ryley. Ch. bp: Eva, May 25, 1777; Maria, June 25, 1780.

JAMES, and Anne Cuyler. Ch: Mary, b. June 23, 1796.

JAMES, and Anna Lighthall, both of the *Aalplaats*, m. July 7, 1795.

ROJEMAN.

JOHAN, and Maria Ries. Ch: Johan Jacob, bp. July 20, 1766.

ROMEYN, D.D.

Rev. DIRK, minister of the Dutch church 1784–1804; was b. at New Barbados, N. J., Jan. 12, 1744 O. S.; installed at Schenectady, Nov., 1784. He had two Ch: Rev. John B., pastor of the Cedar street church, New York, where he d. Feb. 22, 1825, in his 47th year; and Catharina Theresa, who m. Caleb Beck. Doct. Romeyn d. April 16, 1804; his wife Elisabeth, d. Jan. 27, 1815, a. 74ys., 7m., 11d.

Rev. JACOBUS VAN CAMPEN, m. Susanna Van Vranken of Schenectady, May 24, 1788.

RONDO.

MICHAEL, and Johanna Roos. Ch: Elias Cornelius, bp. May 23, 1767.

RONKEL.

CORNELIUS, and Elisabeth Rafein (Raaf). Ch. bp: Catarina, April 12, 1761; Johannes, March 13, 1763.

JOHANNES, and Barbara Neer. Ch. bp: Elisabeth, June 18, 1762; Maria, July 6, 1765.

ROSA (Roos).

GYSBERT, and Margarieta Bondt. Ch: Geesje, bp. Feb. 21, 1705.

SAMUEL, and Elisabeth Ries. Ch. bp: Johannes, Dec. 15, 1768; Anna, March 31, 1782.

JOHN, and Elisabeth Lennox. Ch: Mary bp. May 18, 1778.

ISAAC, m. Maria, dau. of Ryckert Van Vranken, Nov. 22, 1763, in Albany. Ch. b: Johannes, Aug. 13, 1764; Annatie, Aug. 18, 1766, m. Joseph Yates; *Ryckert*, Dec. 11, 1769; Machtelt, April 20, 1772; *Jacobus*, bp. May 28, 1778; Maas Van Vranken, b. Sept. 20, 1780.

RYCKERT, son of Isaac, m. Annatje, dau. of Hendericus Peek. Ch. b: Maria, Nov. 6, 1793; Hendrik, Aug. 17, 1795; Isaac, Sept. 8, 1797; Elisabeth, Oct. 13, 1799; John, May 28, 1801; James, Aug. 10, 1803; Martin, July 30, 1805.

JAMES, (Jacobus), son of Isaac, m. first, Margariet Mills, secondly, Sarah, dau. of Claas Van der Bogart, and thirdly, Debora Hall. Ch. of first wife : William, b. Jan. 1, 1792. Ch. of second wife, who was buried Jan. 24, 1804; Isaac, b. July 31, 1802; Nicholas Van der Bogart, b. Jan. 16, 1804. Ch. of third wife, who d. July 26, 1853 : Isaac Swits, b. Oct. 6, 1805; John, May 10, 1807, d. April 8, 1841; Sarah, April 18, 1809; Nicholas May 9, 1811, d. March 5, 1847; Maria, April 22, 1813; James, March 19, 1815, d. Dec. 5, 1837; Catharine

Geziah, July 14, 1817; Richard, Nov. 27, 1819; Henry, Oct. 28, 1821; Edward.

ROSEBOOM.

JOHANNES H., son of Hendrick Myndertse of Albany, m. Susanna Veeder. She d. Jan. 26, 1812, a. 67ys., 9m., 6d. Ch. bp: Henderick, Sept. 18, 1764; Meyndert, Aug. 4, 1766, d. Feb., 1788, a. 21ys., 6m., 16d.; Elisabeth, Dec. 26, 1768; Barent, June 23, 1771; Johannes, Oct. 30, 1774; Abraham, Aug. 17, 1777; Maria, Feb. 23, 1783.

BARENT, of Canajoharie, perhaps son of the last, m. Ruth Schermerhorn, of Schenectady, April 7, 1796.

ROWE (Rouw).

WILLEM, and Ariaantje Wessels. Ch. b: John, April 3, 1791; Elisabeth, Feb. 12, 1798; Joseph, May 2, 1800.

PETER, and Amy Hicks. He d. before April 20, 1806; she afterwards m. Johannes Jacobse Vrooman, and d. Dec. 18, 1869, in her 91st year. Ch. b: Catharine, Oct. 9, 1804; Peter, March 10, 1806, late member of Congress from this district.

ROWLAND.

ISAIAH (Cyrus), and Maria Wiest. Ch: Henry, b. Oct. 26, 1792; Maria, bp. March 15, 1795; John, b. July 6, 1796, bp. Feb. 28, 1796 (*sic*). [*Church Record.*]

RUFF.

JONATHAN, and Sarah Price. Ch. bp: Jesse, March 19, 1785; Daniel, July 9, 1788; Ann, b. July 8, 1789.

20

RUNJANS.

JOHN, and Lena Van Vliet. She d. between March 20, 1793, and June 29, 1794. Ch: Lena, b. March 20, 1793.

HENRY, and Machtelt Van Vliet, both of Fort Hunter, m. Feb. 18, 1788. Ch. b: Maria, May 23, 1792; Machtelt, Jan. 25, 1794; Henry, July 7, 1795.

RUNKEL (RONKEL).

CORNELIUS, citizen of Schenectady 1763.

RUSSELL.

BENJAMIN, and Rachel Banks (Bags). Ch. b: George Young, July 11, 1791; Petrus, Aug. 6, 1793.

RUTHERFORD.

WILLIAM, and Annatie Hanse. Ch : Elisabeth, b. Jan. 20, 1792.

WILLIAM, perhaps the same as the last, m. Elisabeth (Nancy, *trouw-boek*), Sept. 24, 1799. Ch. b: Robert, Oct. 13, 1800 ; Lea, May 2, 1802; Peter, Feb. 4, 1804; Nelly, Feb. 16, 1806.

RUYTER.

JOHAN JURRY, and Anna Aplie. Ch : Margariet, bp. July 5, 1779.

RYAN (ROYAL).

THOMAS, and Maria Kittel. Ch. bp : Dorothea, Dec. 11, 1763; Engeltie, March 10, 1766; Catarina, Oct. 16, 1768.

RYKER.

PETER, and Alida De Remer (Doremus). Ch. b: Johannes, May 7, 1795;

Jacob, Dec. 21, 1796 ; Susanna, Dec. 9, 1798.

RYKMAN.

WILHELMUS, eldest son of Pieter of Albany, m. Anna, dau. of Albert Wyngaart of Albany. Ch. bp : Cornelia, Jan. 29, 1723; Sara, Dec. 25, 1723 ; Albert, b. March 11, bp. March 14, 1725; Hester, b. Aug. 13, bp. Aug. 21, 1726 ; Pieter, bp. ——, 1730; Gerrit, July 5, 1733; Tanneke, Jan. 30, 1737; Gerrit Lucasse, Jan. 7, 1739.

JOHANNES, son of Johannes of Albany, m. Maria, dau. of Cornelis Van Slyck, June 13, 1729. He was a barber or "perukemaker," and in 1753 lived in New York. Ch. bp: Johannes, b. Dec. 14, bp. Dec. 20, 1730; Cornelis, March 26, 1732; Cathrina, Sept. 23, 1733; Clara, March 23, 1735; Cathrina, March 29, 1737; Susanna, Feb. 14, 1739; Maria, March 8, 1741.

TOBIAS, son of Johannes of Albany, m. Maria, dau. of Evert Van Eps, July 7, 1734. In 1755 he was a resident of Hackensack, N. J. Ch. bp: Catharina, Jan. 19, 1735, m. Johannes Van Zeyl; Aafje, Jan. 12, 1737, in Albany; Johannes, Sept. 3, 1738; Evert, Jan. 4, 1741 ; Nelletie, Dec. 11, 1743.

JOHANNES, J. or Jr., m. Eunice Ward in New York, May 30, 1754. Ch. bp : Rachel, Oct. 8, 1758, m. Andries Bratt; Cornelis, Oct. 19, 1760; *Cornelis*, Nov. 6, 1763; *Albert*, Aug. 24, 1766; Sarah, Nov. 20, 1768; Harmanus, May 19,

1771; Clara, Sept. 18, 1774; Samuel, July, 1777.

CORNELIS, son of the last, and Margaritje Bratt   Ch: Cornelis, bp. Nov. 14, 1784.

ALBERT, son of Johannes J., m. Annatje Van Etten, Jan. 25, 1791. Ch: Marytje, b. Nov. 14, 1791.

RYLEY.

PHILIP, "*van Nieuw York*," m. first, Eva, dau. of Lourens Vander Volgen, Dec. 3, 1742 O. S.; secondly, Hester, dau. of Abraham De Graaf, Feb. 17, 174⅔ O. S.; and thirdly, Jannetje, dau. of Jacobus Van Slyck, Oct. 11, 1755. His first wife d. May 3, 1746; the second, Sept. 28, 1754, a. 26ys., 5m., 20d.; and the third, Aug. 1, 1824, in her 89th year. Philip Ryley was b. in New York, April 29, 1719 O. S.; in 1757 he was *voorlezer* for the church in Albany. Ch. b: Alida, July 15, 1743, m. Gerrit R. Van Vranken; Geertruy, Oct. 3, 1744, m. William Rogers, Jr.; Elisabeth, Nov. 27, 1749, "at Bloemendal;" Eva, May 26, 1751, d. June 9, 1751; Eva, Sept. 17, 1752, d. April 30, 1769; Philippus, Sept. 4, d. Sept. 17, 1756; Philippus, Jan. 7, 1759; *Jacobus Van Slyck*, Oct. 23, 1761, in Albany.

JACOBUS VAN SLYCK, son of Philip, m. Jannetie, dau. of Isaac Swits, Aug. 19, 1792. He d. Jan. 8, 1848, a. 86ys.; she d. Oct. 24, 1838. Ch. b: Catlyntje Van Slyck, May 8, 1797; Folkje Ann, Dec. 13, 1804, d. Dec. 7, 1844, a. 39ys.; Jane Helen, June 23, 1807.

SACIA.

DAVID, m. Susanna Bratt. In 1778 his house stood north of the junction of the *Poonties kil* and *Davidtjes Gat*, which latter stream received its name from him. Ch. b: Margarieta, Nov. 3, 1786; Debora, Dec. 30, 1788; David Frederic, bp. March 4, 1792.

SAINT JOHN.

THADDEUS, and Elisabeth Mackie. Ch: Mary, bp. Sept. 11, 1783.

SALSBURY.

JOSEPH, and Neeltie Buys.   Ch: Joseph, bp. Aug. 13, 1769.

SAMMONS.

JACOB, and Eva Veeder.   Ch: Simson, bp. July 12, 1778.

SAMPLE.

SAMUEL, and Sarah Lenox (Rynex). Ch: Jacob, bp. Dec. 19, 1783; Alexander, b. April 20, 1789.

SANDERS.

THOMAS, of Amsterdam, m. Sara Cornelise Van Gorcum, in New Amsterdam, Sept. 16, 1640. She d. in Albany in Dec. 1669. He received a patent from Gov. Kieft for a house and 25 morgens of land on Manhattan island. In 1654 he owned a house and lot in Beverwyck, which he sold to Jan Coster Van Aecken. He probably returned to New York. Ch. bp. in New Amsterdam: *Robert*, Nov. 10, 1641; Cornelis, Nov. 25, 1643; Cornelis, Nov. 17, 1644; Thomas, July 14, 1647.

Robert, son of Thomas, settled in Albany, and became a trader. In 1691 he and Harmanus Myndertse Van der Bogart received a patent for a mile square of land in Dutchess county, including the site of the city of Poughkeepsie. His wife was Elsie Barentse, b. Aug., 1641, d. Dec. 30, 1734, a. 93ys., 5m.; Robert Sanders and his wife Elsie, made a joint will, April 19, 1673, in which the first four Ch. below written, were mentioned, they being the only ones then born. The birth years of all their Ch., save those of Barent and Effie, are unfortunately erased from the family record; those given below are conjectural. Ch. b: Elisabeth, April 11, 1666 (?); Maria, Aug. 28, 1668 (?), m. Gerrit Roseboom, Nov. 24, 1689 ; Sarah, Feb. 5, 1670 (?), m. Henricus Greveraad of New York; Anna, Nov. 15, 1672 (?); Barent, March 11, 1674 (?); Thomas, Sept. 24, 1675 (?); Barent, Dec. 9, 1676 (?); *Barent*, May 8, 1678; Amelia, May 16, 1680 (?); Helena, Jan. 22, 1682 (?), m. Johannes Lansing, Sept. 20, 1704; Effie (Elsie), July 8, 1683, bp. July 13, 1683, buried Dec. 31, 1732.

Barent, son of Robert, m. Maria, dau. of Evert Wendel, Sept. 19, 1704. He was mayor 1750–4; was buried in the church, Nov. 21, 1757; she was buried in the church, June 22, 1738. Ch. bp: Robert, July 15, 1705; Maria, Dec. 3, 1707; *Johannes*, July 12, 1714.

Johannes, son of Barent, of Albany, m. Debora, dau. and only child of Col. Jacob Glen of *Scotia*. In 1765, by the purchase of the interest of John Glen of Albany, and John Glen Jr., of Schenectady, for £4000 ($10,000), Johannes Sanders and wife became sole owners of the Glen estate in the present town of Glenville. He made his will Jan. 27, 1779, proved Feb. 11, 1783; in it he mentioned his only son Johannes, wife Debora, and dau. Maria, Sarah, Elsje and Margaret. He d. Sept. 13, 1782; his wife d. March 8, 1786. They were m. Dec. 6, 1739, in Albany. Ch. b. (and bp. in Schenectady): Maria, May 21, 1740, m. Johannes J. Beekman of Albany, Nov. 22, 1759; Sarah, Feb. 20, 1743, m. her cousin John Sanderse Glen of Scotia; Barent, Aug. 6, 1744, d. Nov. 21, 1746; Elisabeth, Sept. 19, 1746, d. Sept. 19, 1747; Elisabeth, Dec. 5, 1748, d. Feb. 5, 1776; Barent, Dec. 22, 1750, d. Sept. 5, 1758; Elsje, March 14, 1752, m. Myndert Schuyler Ten Eyck; Jacob Glen, April 5, 1755, d. Sept. 18, 1765; *Johannes*, Oct. 2, 1757, m. his cousin Debora, dau. of Robert Sanders of Albany, Feb. 24, 1777; Barent, Dec. 26, 1759, d. Dec. 30, 1759; Margarita, bp. June 24. 1764, m. Kilian K. Van Rensselaer of Claverack, Jan. 27, 1791.

Johannes, son of Johannes, m. first, Debora, dau. of Robert Sanders of Albany, Feb. 24, 1777; and secondly, Albertina Ten Broeck of Clermont, Nov. 30, 1801 (?). His first wife d. Nov. 28, 1793; the second d. July 30 (23), 1840, a. 79ys.; he d. March 30, 1834. He inherited his father's estate, and resided in the ancient Glen house at Scotia.

Ch. b: Elisabeth, Dec. 20, 1777, m. Doct. William Anderson, and d. June 21, 1850; *Barent*, January 12, 1779, d. June (4) 5, 1854; Robert, Sept. 8, 1781, d. Oct. 25, 1783; Sarah, Aug. 28, 1783, m. Peter S. Van Rensselaer, and d. Aug. 13, 1869; Catharina, Oct. 10 (11), 1785, m. Gerard Beekman of New York, April 9, 1810; child, Hon. James W. Beekman, New York, b. Nov. 24, 1815; Robert, July 18, 1787, d. Nov. 5, 1840; *Jacob Glen*, April 20 (22), 1789; *Peter*, Feb. 17, 1792, d. May 12, 1850; *John*, Dec. 27, 1802; *Dirk Wessels*, Oct. 20, 1804.

BARENT, son of Johannes, m. Catalina Bleecker, dau. of James Bleecker of Albany, June, 1810; he d. June 5, 1854, a. 75ys. Ch: John B., b. Feb. 1, 1812, d. July —, 1866; Deborah S., b. Feb. 12, 1814, d. June 28, 1872, m. Philip W. Groot; Gerrit V. S., b. November 8, 1816; James Bleecker, b. Feb. 6, 1819, m. Elisabeth S. Bleecker, Dec. 24, 1845; Barent B., b. May 15, 1821, m. Louisa P. Read, June —, 1855; Robert, b. Aug. 15, 1823, d. March 3, 1863; Sarah E., b. Feb. 12, 1828.

JACOB GLEN, son of Johannes, m. Catharine Mary, dau. of Isaac B. Cox and Cornelia Beekman, June 30, 1847. He d. in Albany, March 26, 1867. Ch: Jacob G., b. April 27, 1850, m. Janie, dau. of Hon. John C. Ten Eyck of Mount Holly, New Jersey, Oct. 11, 1870.

PETER, son of Johannes, m. Maria, dau. of Peter E. Elmendorf of Albany,

Feb. 3, 1824. Ch: Charles P., b. Nov. 26, 1824, m. Jane L., dau. of Leonard W. Ten Broeck of Livingston, Columbia county, Sept. 15, 1846; Peter E., b. April 2, 1827.

JOHN, son of Johannes, m. Jane, dau. of Walter T. Livingston of Clermont, Columbia county, Oct. 2, 1826; she d. Oct. 27, 1871 Ch: Albertina, b. Dec. 22, 1828, d. Nov. 19, 1834; Walter T. L., b. Sept. 7, 1832; Eugene L., b. Nov. 1, 1835, m. Lizzie A., dau. of David Passage of Glenville, Schenectady county; Mary Elizabeth, b. January 8, 1841, m. Harold Wilson of Clermont, Columbia county.

THEODORE W. (or DERRICK WESSELS), son of Johannes, m. first, Margaret N., dau. of William N. Sill of Bethlehem, Albany county, June 20, 1829; and secondly, Rachel B. Winne, dau. of Gerrit V. S. Bleecker of Albany, Jan. 29, 1867. Ch. b: Elizabeth N. Sill, Dec. 22, 1829; Catharine M., b. Dec. 7, 1831, m. William J. Mott of Gt. Neck, Long Island, June 17, 1854; Margaret Mather, Feb. 5, 1834; Albertina, April 26, 1836; William N. Sill, Aug. 24, 1838, m. Catharine V. R. Osborn, dau. of James Osborn, Feb. 3, 1864; Alexander Glen, Oct. 29, 1840; Lydia Mather, Dec. 19, 1842; Lindsay Glen, Feb. 23, 1853.

SANDERSE.

ANTONY, and Margaret Leen. Ch: Petrus, bp. Feb. 7, 1762.

SANDERSON.

WILLIAM, and Rebecca Reyk. Ch: Elisabeth, bp. May 20, 1774.

SANSON.

NICHOLAS, and Elisabeth Way. Ch: Elisabeth, b. Feb. 19, 1783.

SCHAETS.

REYNIER, " chyrurgion," eldest son of Domine Schaets of Albany, was an early settler of Schenectady, where he was appointed justice of the peace by Leisler in 1689. He and a son were killed on the 9th of Feb., 1690, at the massacre and burning of the village by the French and Indians. His wid., Catrina Bensing, m. Jonathan Broadhurst, in Albany, April 23, 1696. Two of Schaets' Ch. survived him, a son Gideon, and a dau. Agnietje, who m. Matthys Nak of Albany.

SCHARP.

JOHANNES, and Ariaantje Short. Ch: Philip, b. Sept. 2, 1785.

JACOB, and Lea Dingman. Ch: Johannes, b. Dec. 16, 1786.

SCHEER.

JOHANNES, and Catarina Quackenbosch. Ch: Elisabeth, bp. Sept. 12, 1781.

SCHEFFER (SCHEFFEL, SCHOFFELAAR)

CHRISTIAAN, m. first, Sara Starenbergh. Ch: Anna, bp. May 14, 1758; secondly, Catarina Beck, Nov. 17, 1759; thirdly, Magdalena Corpman. Ch: Johannes, bp. July 12, 1777.

SCHELD.

JOHANNES COENRAD, member of the church 1758.

SCHELL.

JACOB, and Martha Elkins. Ch. bp: Martha, Feb. 22, 1766; Maria, Sept. 20, 1769.

PHILIP, and Jannetje Seger. Ch: Maria, April 27, 1799.

SCHELLY.

WILLIAM, and Maria Bouman. Ch: Christina, bp. Aug. 30, 1775.

SCHERMERHOOREN (SCHERMERHORN).

JACOB JANSE, was born in 1622, in Waterland, Holland, it is said; though in 1654 his father was living in Amsterdam. He came to Beverwyck quite early, where he prospered as a brewer and trader. In 1648 he was arrested at Fort Orange by Governor Stuyvesant's order, on a charge of selling arms and ammunition to the Indians. His books and papers were seized, and himself removed a prisoner to Fort Amsterdam, where he was sentenced to banishment for five years with the confiscation of all his property. By the interference of some leading citizens, the first part of the sentence was struck out, but his property was totally lost. These proceedings against Schermerhorn formed subsequently a ground of complaint against Stuyvesant to the States General. [*O'Callaghan's Hist. N. Y.* I., 441.] He made his will May 20, 1688, and soon after died at Schenectady. His estate was large for the times, amounting to 56,882 guilders. His wife was Jannetie Segers, dau. of Cornelis Segerse Van Voorhoudt. The following Ch. are mentioned in his will: *Reyer;* Symon; Helena, m. Myndert Harmense Van der Bogart; Jacob; Machtelt, m. Johannes Beekman; Cornelis; Jannetie, m. Caspar Springsteen; Neeltie, m. Barent Ten Eyck; Lucas. [*See Albany Families*]

REYER, son of Jacob Janse, m. Ariaantje, dau. of Arent Arentse Bratt, and wid. of Helmer Otten of Albany, in July, 1676, at which time, in anticipation of this marriage, she made a contract with the guardians of her dau. Catharine Helmerse Otten, by which she mortgages her farm at Schenectady, for the payment of 225 beaver skins to said dau., when she arrived at mature age or married, also to give her one-half of her late husband's property in Holland. The dau. subsequently m. Gerrit Symonse Veeder. Reyer Schermerhorn settled in Schenectady; was one of the five patentees of the patent granted in 1684, and was the sole surviving patentee of the township in 1705, when he was complained of as exercising arbitrary power over the town affairs and rendering no accounts of his proceedings. In 1690 he was member of the Provincial Assembly from Albany county, and Justice of the Peace. In 1700 he was appointed assistant to the Judge of Common Pleas. Bouwery No. 4, together with the mills, heretofore called "Schermerhorn's Mills," after belonging to this family nearly 200 years,

has lately passed into other hands; this property came to Reyer Jacobse through his wife Ariaantje, whose first husband, Otten, purchased it of the original proprietor, Pieter Adriaense Soegemakelyck. He made his last will April 5, 1717, and d. Feb. 19, 1719; his wife d. in 1717. The following Ch. are mentioned in his will: Catalina, wife of Johannes Wemp; Janneke, wife of Volkert Simonse Veeder; *Jan*, eldest son, b. Oct. 4, 1685; *Jacob; Arent*, b. Jan. 1, 1693.

JOHANNES, eldest son of Reyer, inherited the homestead at the *Schuylenbergh;* m. Engeltie, dau. of Jan Hendrickse Vrooman, Apr. 8 (28), 1711. He made his will Oct. 28, 1752, proved Aug. 22, 1767; spoke of wife Engeltie, and all the following Ch. save Bartholomeus. He d. in 1752, and his wife in 1754. Ch. b: Ariaantje, June (?), 1712, m. Nicolaas De Graaf; Gesina, Dec. 9, 1713, m. Philip Van Petten; *Reyer*, Sept. 24, 1716; Catalyntje, Nov. 13, 1718, m. John Dodds; *Johannes*, Nov. 24, 1720; *Simon*, Jan. 22 (23), 1723; Neeltje, May 26, 1725, m. Claas Viele; Bartholomeus, Nov. 11, 1727, d. 1742; *Jacob*, Nov. 21, 1729; Barnhardus Freerman, June 25, 1732; Magdalena, Jan. 9, 1734; Jannetie, Nov. 21, 1736, m. Barent Veeder; *Barnhardus Freerman,* Oct. 14, 1739.

JACOB, son of Reyer, m. Margarieta, dau. of Johannes Teller, Oct. 20, 1712. He d. July 4, 1753; she d. May 22, 1741. Ch. bp: Reyer, Feb. 28, 171$\frac{3}{4}$; *Johannes*, June 22, 1717; *Jacobus*, Jan. 31, 1720; *Willem*, Nov. 10, 1722; *Arent*,

April 10, 1725; Andries, July 1, 1727, d. May 25, 1742; _Simon_, b. Sept. 19, 1730; Susanna, bp. Jan. 5, 1735, m. John Visger, July 27, 1759.

ARENT, son of Reyer, m. Annatje, dau. of Douw Jillese Fonda, April 16, 1714. He inherited from his father the easterly half of the Second flat on the north side of the Mohawk river, lived at "the mills." Ch. bp: Catalyntje, Oct. 10, 1714, in Albany, m. Nicolaas Viele; Rebecca, Dec. 23, 1716, m. Jacobus Peek; Ariaantje, Mar. 1, 1719 ; _Abraham_, Oct. 22, 1721; Jannetje, August 24, 1723; Helena, b. Jan. 8, bp. Jan. 30, 1726; Jannetje, Nov. 7, 1731; Alida, June 9, 1734; _Reyer_.

JOHANNES, son of Jacob Reyerse, m. Magdalena, dau. of Arent Bratt, Dec. 12, 1744. Ch. bp: Jacob, May 19, 1745; Margrietje, March 15, 1747; Jannetje, Jan. 29, 1749; Jacob, Jan. 13, 1751; Arent, July 19, 1753.

JOHANNES, son of Johannes, of Pompton, N. J., m. Eva, dau. of Nicolaas Van Petten, March 2, 174⅘. Ch : Jan, bp. Oct. 20, 1745.

JOHANNES, probably the last, m. Sarah Teller, Aug. 2, 1765. Ch. bp: Margarita, Sept. 26, 1766; Susanna, Aug. 16, 1767.

WILLEM, son of Jacob Reyerse, m. first, Elisabet, dau. of Lourens Van der Volgen, June 17, 1745, and secondly, Eva, dau. of Jesse De Graaf, about 1766. He made his will June 28, 1809, proved

May 6, 1811; spoke of wife Eva, and sons Lawrence and Nicolaas &c. Ch. bp : Jacob, Dec. 1, 1745; _Lourens_, Feb. 12, 1749; Margarieta, Sept. 29, 1751, m. Abraham De Graaf; Nicholas, March 23, 1755; Nicholas, June 18, 1758; _Claas_, Aug. 21, 1760; Elisabeth, Oct. 18, 1767.

RYER, son of Johannes, m. first, Maria, dau. of Corset Vedder, June 8, 1746, and secondly, Maria, dau. of Ryckert Van Vranken, June 8, 1750. He lived at the _Schuylenbergh_, d. March 6, 1795; his second wife d. Feb. 18, 1799, a. 73ys., 6m., 3d. Ch. bp: Johannes, May 24, 1747; Johannes, March 31, 1751, d. Jan. 18, 1797; Maria, Nov. 10, 1752, m. Pieter Van Gyseling; _Richard_, March 9, 1755; _Bartholomeus_, August 24, 1757 ; Engeltie, m. Claas Schermerhorn; _Gerrit_, Oct. 23, 1763.

SIMON, son of Johannes, m. Hillegonda, dau. of Maas Van Vranken. He was b. January 23, 1723, and d. May 6, 1808, a. 85ys., 3m. 3d.; she was b. May 30, 1726, and d. Nov. 28, 1807, a. 81ys., 4m., 26d. Ch : Isaac, Oct. 21, 1750, d. Sept. 21, 1776; _Maas_, bp. April 29, 1753; Engeltie, bp. Nov. 30, 1755, m. Adam S. Vrooman; Anna, b. July 6, 1759, m. Simon De Graaf; _Johannes_.

RICHARD, son of Reyer, m. Annatje Van Vechten. Ch. bp: Maria, July 18, 1779, m. Douwe J. Clute; Helena, Nov. 8, 1781, m. Nicolaas P. Clute.

ABRAHAM, son of Arent, m. Clara, dau. of Jacobus Peek, Sept. 8, 1750.

He made his will July 7, 1810, proved August 26, 1811; mentioned three sons, Jacobus, Reyer and Abraham. He lived near Haverly's, in Glenville, until about his 90th year. Ch. bp: Antje, Feb. 24, 1751; Margaritje, Nov. 10, 1752, m. Thomas Shannon; Catalyna, Nov. 3, 1754, m. John Crawford; Elisabeth, m. John Shannon; Rebecca, February 9 (?), 1759, m. Adam Van Petten; *Jacobus,* Jan. 18, 1761; Arent, Dec. 12, 1762; Claartje, Nov. 11, 1764, m. Abraham Buys; Reyer, Feb. 8, 1767; *Abraham,* May 28, 1769.

ARENT, JR., son of Jacob Reyerse, m. first, Jacomyntje, dau. of Myndert Van Gyseling, Nov. 8, 1751; and secondly, Annatje Dellamont Teller, wid., Nov. 9, 1786. His last wife d. Sept. 19, 1823, a. 86ys., 6m., 13d. Ch. bp: Jacob, Dec. 20, 1752; Meyndert, July 27, 1755; Suster, March 26, 1758; Meyndert, Jan. 20, 1760; *Andreas,* July 11, 1762; Margarita, Nov. 10, 1765, m. Gerrit Schermerhorn; Bregje, April 24, 1768.

JACOBUS, son of Jacob Reyerse, m. Annatje P. Vrooman, Sept. 4, 1762. He d. July 28, 1782; she d. Sept. 7, 1770. Ch. b: Jacob, July 21, 1763, d. April 26, 1787; *Johannes,* Jan. 29, 1765.

MAAS, son of Simon, m. Catharina, dau. of Abraham Swits, April 12, 1786. He was b. March 9, 1753, and d. Jan. 26, 1830; she was b. May 1, 1764, and d. Aug. 20, 1829. Ch. b: Annatje, July 13, 1786; Isaac, Jan. 2, 1790, d. Jan 30, 1849; Elisabeth C., wid. of Gen.

Isaac M. Schermerhorn, d. in New York, Sept. 12, 1862; Abram, Dec. 12, 1791, of Rochester, d. ——— 1855; Margarieta, May 14, 1795; Simon, Nov. 28, 1798, d. Jan. 15, 1800; Simon, Feb. 23, 1801, d. July 26, 1805; Jacob, Nov. 12, 1804, of Homer.

JACOB, son of Johannes, of Normanskil, m. Maria, dau. of Arent Vedder, Nov. 13, 1762. Ch. bp: John, Feb. 5, 1764; *Arent,* Oct. 6, 1765; Engeltie, m. Hendrick Banta; Sarah, Jan. 27, 1770, m. Gerrit Van Vorst; Catalyntje, Feb. 23, 1772; Catarina, April 23, 1775; Maria, June 22, 1777; Catrina, June 1, 1783, m. Johannes A. Marselis.

JACOB L., and Maria Vedder. Ch: Catharina, b. Feb. 28, 1815.

BARNHARDUS FREERMAN, m. Ariaantje, dau. of Takerus Van der Bogart, May 9, 1767. She was b. Sept. 15, 1745, and d. Oct. 29, 1827. Ch. bp: John, Oct. 4, 1767; Neeltje, April 16, 1769, m. Thomas Barton Clinch; Engeltie, March 13, 1774, m. Lourens Van der Volgen; Margarita, Dec. 21, 1777, m. Henry Frey Yates; John, b. Sept. 24, 1786, grad. of Union College, minister in the Dutch church, m. first, Kitty Yates, and secondly Mrs. Spottiswood of Virginia, d. at Richmond, Va., March 16, 1851.

REYER, son of Arent, m. Maria Teller. Ch. bp: *Arent,* Nov. 1, 1772; Alida, July 19, 1778; Annatje, Aug. 31, 1783; Jeremiah, b. Nov. 6, 1792.

21

SIMON J., son of Jacob Reyerse, m. Sarah Vrooman. She d. Sept. 16, 1795, a. 34ys., 3m., 15d. He lived upon the *hindermost* lot of the Bouwland, originally patented to William Teller, probably inherited from his mother Margaret, dau. of Johannes Teller. The brick house built upon this lot is now (1872) occupied by Simon S., his grandson. He d. Jan. 13, 1793, a. 62ys., 3m., 24d. Ch. b : *Johannes* (?) ; *Jacob*, Dec. 30, 1773 ; Sara, Sept. 1775, m. Barent Roseboom of Canajoharie.

GERRIT, son of Reyer, m. Margarietje, dau. of Arent Schermerhorn jr., May 18, 1787. He d. in Rotterdam, March 24, 1848, in his 85th year. Ch. b : Maria, August 27, 1788 ; Jacomyntje, Aug. 10, 1790 ; Maria, March 27, 1792 ; Jacob, May 28, 1794 ; Catharina, Sept. 27, 1796.

LOURENS, son of Willem, m. Geesie, dau. of Nicolaas Viele. He d. in Rotterdam, March 26, 1836 (1837), a. 88ys., 1m. ; she d. Sept. 26, 1847, aged 87ys. Ch : *Claas*, b. Oct. 21, 1776 ; Elisabeth, bp. Jan. 1, 1779 ; Neeltje, bp. April 29, 1781.

ABRAHAM, son of Abraham, m. first, Catlyntje Clement, dau. of Johannes, May 11, 1786; secondly, Maria, dau. of Nicolaas Sixberry, Aug. 10, 1790. His wife Maria, d. Dec. 24 (?), buried Dec. 26, 1803. Ch. b : Claara, Aug. 17, 1786 ; Johannes, Oct. 25, 1787 ; Abram, Jan. 14, 1791 ; Susanna, Dec. 4, 1792 ; Clara, Dec. 24, 1794 ; Nicolaas, Feb. 16, 1797 ;

Catlyntje Clement, Oct. 20, 1799 ; Annatje, July 26, 1802.

CLAAS, son of Willem, m. Engeltje, dau. of Reyer Schermerhorn. She d. Oct. 6, 1834, a. 73ys., 1m., 25d. Ch. b : Willem, bp. Nov. 8, 1781 ; Maria, b. March 14, 1784 ; Reyer, Dec. 3, 1786 ; Jacobus, Dec. 26, 1788 ; Lourens Claessen, Aug. 30, 1792 ; Elisabeth, July 24, 1795 ; Elisabeth, Oct. 29, 1799.

JACOBUS, son of Abraham, m. Catarina, dau. of Jacques Peek. Ch. bp : Eva, June 2, 1782 ; Caatje, March 20, 1785. Ch. b : Lena, Nov. 28, 1787 ; Abram, Jan. 12, 1791 ; Aakus, July 6, 1793 ; Arent, Dec. 6, 1795 ; Antje, Jan. 3, 1799 ; Jacobus, Aug. 14, 1801 ; Maria, May 8, 1804.

BARTHOLOMEW, son of Reyer, m. Annatje, dau. of Johannes Teller, July 10, 1785. He d. in Rotterdam, July 16, 1845, a. 87ys. ; she d. May 4, 1844, in her 77th year. Ch. b : Reyer, Dec. 8, 1785, a printer, d. Nov. 11, 1850, Gertrude, his wife, d. April 10, 1830, in her 43d year, at her brother's, Henry Abel's, 10 Orange street, Albany ; *Johannes*, Oct. 12, 1787, d. Feb. 29, 1872 ; Bartholomew, Dec. 8, 1789 ; Jannetje, April 16, 1792, m. Nicolaas Viele, d. Nov. 17, 1860 ; Maria, July 26, 1794, d. April 5, 1816 ; William, Oct. 25, 1796, d. Nov. 21, 1871 ; Annatje, Aug. 14, 1799, m. Jacob De Foreest jr., of Rotterdam, and d. April 27, 1851, a. 52ys. ; Bernardus Freerman, Dec. 22, 1801, d. suddenly, Aug. 25, 1871, at a religious meeting in the First Dutch church, and was buried on the 27th; Catharine, Oct. 29, 1804; Simon, June 23, 1810; Eliza Margaret, Oct. 13, 1811.

ANDRIES, son of Arent jr., m. Nancy Clyde, June 14, 1787. He made his will June 13, 1809, proved March 8, 1816; spoke of wife Nancy, and the following children. Ch. b: Aaron, Feb. 28, 1788, d. in Rotterdam, May 8, 1870, in his 83d year; Catharina, Nov. 19, 1789; Jacomyntje, Dec. 3, 1791; Jennet, Aug. 3, 1798; Myndert; Jacob; Ann; Rebecca.

JOHN, son of Jacobus, m. Catharina, dau. of Jacobus Bratt, Nov. 13, 1788. He d. Jan. 7, 1814, a. 48ys., 11m., 8d.; she made her will Sept. 8, 1817, proved Feb. 5, 1820; spoke of her father, Jacobus Bratt, and mother, Elisabeth, and of her Ch. Jacob, Jacobus Bratt, Annatje, Simon, Arent and Peter Vrooman. She was b. June 29, 1764, d. Sept. 13, 1817, a. 48ys., 2m., 20d. Ch. b: Jacob, March 26 [*Church Record*], Feb. 28 [Bible], 1789, d. April 20, 1849, in his 61st year, his wife, Maria Vedder, d. Aug. 19, 1832, aged 44ys., 1m., 9d.; Elisabeth, Dec. 3, 1790, d. Feb. 24, 1797; Annatje, June 16, 1792, d. July 4, 1794; Eva, Feb. 23, 1794, d. October 4, 1796; Jacobus Bratt, April 20, 1796; Annatje, July 7, 1798, m. Anthony Van Slyck; Elisabeth, May 10, 1800, d. June 9, 1801; Simon, April 23, 1802; Arent Bratt, May 4, 1804; Peter Vrooman, May 11, 1806, m. Catharina Clute, who d. ———, a. 34ys., 9m., 14d.; he d. Feb. 26, 1853,

a. 46ys., 11m., 13d., both buried in the *Woestyne.*

JOHN J., m. Jenny Clyde, Jan. 18, 1789.

ARENT, son of Jacob, m. Geertruy, dau. of Arent Potman, Oct. 20, 1791. Ch. b: Jacob, June 8, 1792; Jacob, Feb. 18, 1794; Arent Potman, April 10, 1796; Ernestus, March 21, 1802; Elisabeth, Dec. 24, 1803.

WILLIAM J., m. Annatje Wesselse, Aug. 18, 1792. She was buried Jan. 6, 1804. Ch. b: Sarah, Aug. 12, 1793; Ariaantje, Sept. 5, 1795; John, April 8, 1798; James, Sept. 9, 1801.

JEREMIAH, m. Annatje Ostrander. Ch. b: Reyer, Aug. 11, 1793; Elisabeth, Sept. 11, 1797; Petrus, Aug. 25, 1805; Magdalen, Oct. 15, 1809.

ARENT J., m. Jannetje Jacobusse. Ch: Cornelius, b. Sept. 11, 1793.

HENDRICK, probably son of Jacob jr., of manor of Livingston, m. Cornelia Lansing, Dec. 17, 1762. He d, August 27, 1794. Ch. b: *Jacob*, Sept. 10, 1763; Annatie, Sept. 10, 1764 (?), m. Benjamin Springsteen, and d. Jan. 27, 1796; Catelyntje, Feb. 10, 1768; Catrina, Feb. 9, 1770, d. Sept. 8, 1795; *Evert*, Aug. 17, 1772; Catelyntje, Sept. 15, 1775; Cornelia, June 21, 1778; Cornelius, Aug. 31, 1781.

JACOB, son of Hendrick, m. Antje Schermerhorn, 1782. Ch. b: Cornelia,

April 15, 1783; Reyer, Nov. 1, 1786; Ariaantje, June 7, 1788; Hendrick, Jan. 25, 1791; Daniel, Aug. 27, 1793; Evert Lansing, Dec. 13, 1796; Cornelius, Aug. 4, 1799; Pieter H., Feb. 3, 1802.

EVERT, son of Hendrick, of Caughnawago, m. Elisabeth Schermerhorn of Schenectady, January 5, 1795. He d. April 26, 1849, a. 76ys., 9m., 15d.; she d. Jan. 13, 1852, a. 73ys., 1m. Ch. b: Annatje (Nancy), March 4 (5), 1796, d. Jan. 14, 1812; Giney, Aug. 29, 1798; Cornelia, Dec. 4, 1800; Gezina, May 9, 1804; William Henry, May 8, 1807, d. Feb. 2, 1852; Eleanor, June 27, 1809; Nancy, Aug. 4, 1812; Clara, March 17, 1815; Jacob E., March 13 (30), 1819.

NICHOLAS, son of Lourens, m. Maria Schermerhorn. He d. Nov. 29, 1821. Ch. b: Lourens, Dec. 31, 1796; Claas Viele, Jan. 20, 1798; Jacob, June 17, 1800; William, Oct. 26, 1802.

JOHN S., son of Simon, m. Susanna, dau. of Petrus Van der Volgen. He d. March 11, 1846, a. 83ys., 10m., 25d.; she d. Aug. 26, 1828, a. 57ys., 6m., 22d. He lived in the house now owned and occupied by Doctor Harmen Swits (218 220 State street), and his brother Maas lived next east. The Schermerhorn property extended southeast to, or beyond Veeder avenue, and southerly to Oothout street, including the greater part of what is now called the *Bouwery.* Ch. b: Engeltie, Oct. 11, 1797; Simon, May 22, 1800, d. Feb. 6, 1830; Gertrude, Sept. 11, 1803, m. Col. Stephen Yates, and d.

—— 1867; Peter, Dec. 12, 1807, d. Sept. 2, 1808; Peter Van der Volgen, Aug. 2, 1809.

JACOB S., son of Simon, m. Engeltie dau. of Jacobus Bratt. She d. Nov. 17, 1843, a. 68ys., 8m., 27d. Ch. b: Simon, Oct. 14, 1797, d. in Rotterdam, Dec. 8, 1872; Jacobus Bratt, Sept. 16, 1799; Jacobus Bratt, April 5, 1801, d. July 16, 1842; his wife Catharine, d. Jan. 22, 1838, a. 33ys., 2m., 23d.; Daniel David Campbell, March 10, 1803; John, June 13, 1806; Elisabeth, Jan. 15, 1809; Sarah Maria, Sept. 10, 1810.

ARENT R., son of Reyer, m. Elisabeth, dau. of Marten Van Slyck, Dec. 23, 1797. He d. Nov. 2, 1837; she d. in Glenville, March 19, 1845, in her 69th year. Ch. b: Maria, May 18, 1799; Maria, June 1, 1801, m. John James, and d. at Mills corners, Fulton county, Nov. 3, 1845; Lena, March 3, 1803; Reyer, June 17, 1805; Helen Jane, Sept. 1, 1807; Alida Margaret, June 26, 1809; Rachel, Aug. 8, 1813; Susan Eliza, April 20, 1815.

SIMON N., m. Elisabeth Bratt. Ch: Frederick, b. Sept. 30, 1799.

JOHANNES, son of Bartholomew, m. Gitty, dau. of Andries Van Patten, Apr. 3, 1806. He d. Feb. 29, 1872; she d. Nov. 20, 1844. Ch. b: Bartholomew Teller, March 26, 1807; Andrew Vedder, April 18, 1809; Ann Maria, Dec. 18, 1811; William, June 30, 1814, d. March 6, 1869; Angelica, Feb. 25, 1819; Barnardus Freerman, February 4, 1821;

Abraham Van Patten, July 9, 1823, d. Sept. 13, 1823; Simon, Oct. 4, 1824; James, Jan. 17, 1827.

JOHN J., m. Maria Vedder. Ch: Catharine, b. Feb. 28, 1815.

SCHERP.

JOSEPH, m. Sarah Marselis. Ch: Magdalena, bp. March 3, 1781.

SCHLAUT.

PHILIPPUS, and wife Anna Maria were members of the church in 1737.

SCHOCH.

ANDREAS, and Catarin Meyer. Ch: Anna Maria, bp. Dec. 30, 1765.

SCHOEVER.

JOHANNES, and Christina Bouman. Ch: Maria, bp. July 4, 1779.

SCHOOLCRAFT.

JACOB, and Magdalena ...... Ch: Astien (Augustine), bp. April 2, 1720.

CHRISTIAAN, and Elisabeth Margaret Becker. Ch. bp: Christiaan, Sept. 25, 1759; Jacobus, Feb. 19, 1762; Martinus, Feb. 6, 1764.

JOHANNES, and Anna ...... Ch: Jacob, bp. Jan. 25, 1768.

JOHANNES, m. Maria, dau. of Isaac Jacobse Truax. Ch: Annatje, bp. Mar. 6, 1785; Isaac, b. Dec. 29, 1786; Johannes Wyngaart, b. June 14, 1790.

LOURENS, of Noormanskil, and Margaret Row. Ch: Lourens, b. May 2, 1786, d. in Schenectady, July 28, 1851, a. 63ys.

JOHANNES, m. Mary Catharine McKinney. Ch: Frances, b. April 20, 1801.

SCHRAM.

VALENTINE, m. Catharina Hughs, March 8, 1795.

SCHREFFER (SCHREPPER).

CAROL, and Anna Maria Spel (Spetler). Ch. bp: *Jurry*, Nov. 30, 1760; Eva, July 28, 1765.

(SCHAFFORD).

JURRY, son of Carol, and Rosina Keeley. Ch. bp: Carol, July 15, 1780; Margarita, Dec. 14, 1781; Mattheus, Nov. 2, 1783; Christiaan, Nov. 8, 1785; Andries, Dec. 29, 1787; Adam, April 18, 1789.

SCHRETER.

BASTIAAN, and Annatje Richter. Ch. bp: Anna Dorothea, June 22, 1780; Michael, Aug. 29, 1782.

SCHULER.

JURRY, and Barbara Ratlena. Ch: Lena, bp. Jan. 14, 1784.

JACOB, and Elisabeth Hazzard. Ch. b: Lourens, March 19, 1789; Jacob, Oct. 6, 1797.

LOURENS, and Lena Service. Ch. b: Peter, April 11, 1788; Catharina, Sept. 11, 1789; Levi, Nov. 14, 1797.

PETRUS, and Maria Sixberry.   Ch. b :
Annatje, Oct. 18, 1789; George, Jan.
22, 1794; Barbara, June 20, 1796.

SCHURMAN.

JOHAN, and Catarina Merlelie.   Ch :
Michael, bp. Oct. 2, 1779.

SCHUYLER.

NICOLAAS, Indian trader, son of Philip
of Albany, m. Elsie, dau. of Harmanus
Wendell of Albany. He was a member
of the Provincial Assembly in 1727. Ch.
bp : Ariaantje, March 6, 1720; Harmanus, Jan. 28, 1722; Cathrina, Aug. 11,
1723, m. John Jacobse Lansing, gentleman, of Albany, Dec. 12, 1747 ; Harmanus, b. April 2, bp. April 3, 1727 ; Johannes, Feb. 4, 1733. [*See Albany
Families.*]

Rev. JOHANNES, of Schoharie, m.
Anna, dau. of Pieter Symonse Veeder
of Schenectady, June 19, 1743.

LOURENS, and Sarah Dubois. Ch : Johannes, Dec. 24, 1769.

JOHN S., and Catharine Cuyler, both
of Albany flat, m. Feb. 21, 1793.

JOHANNES, and Margarita Veeder.
Ch : Jannetje, bp. May 20, 1781; Gerard, b. Nov. 13, 1785.

SCHWAHN (ZERHN).

CHRISTOFFEL, and Geertruy Leven-
steyn. Ch. bp : Pieter, Oct. 18, 1769;
David, Nov. 18, 1770; Pieter, Dec. 12,
1779.

SCOTT.

Capt. JOHN, and Magdalena ...... Ch :
Magdalena, bp. Oct. 21, 1721.

JOHN, and Anna Kip.   Ch : Helena,
bp. March 5, 1754.

SCRIBNER.

SOLOMAN, and Helena Van Winkelen.
Ch : Helena, b. Aug. 3, 1798.

SECKER.

LODOVYK, and Christina Fritz.   Ch :
Elisabeth, bp. May 14, 1780.

SEGE.

PIETER, and Frederica Elisabeth ......
Ch : Abraham, bp. June 3, 1762.

(SIEGE).

DAVID, m. Susanna, dau. of Ephraim
Bratt. Ch. bp : Ephraim, Sept. 5, 1773 ;
Elisabeth, March 19, 1775; Philip, Sept.
8, 1776 ; Pieter, April 4, 1779 ; Johannes, July 29, 1781; Susanna, Sept. 21,
1783; Geertruy, b. June 3, 1785.

SEGER (SEGERS).

GERRIT, and Maritje ...... Ch. bp :
Frederic, Nov. 2, 1717 ; Johannes, Mar.
30, 1719 ; Lydia, Jan. 1, 1721.

ALEXANDER, and Mary Potter.   Ch :
Mary, bp. Jan. 8, 1776.

PIETER, and Maria Hoogteling.   Ch.
bp : Maria, Feb. 25, 1776 ; Johannes
Hoogteling, Sept. 23, 1778. Ch. b :
Moses, Oct. 28, 1789; Ida, March 26,
1792; Gerrit, Sept. 30, 1794.

GERRIT, and Maria Pangburn. Ch. bp: David, Aug. 10, 1777; Moses, June 25, 1780.

JOHANNES STAATS, and Sarah Pangburn. Ch. bp: William and Maria, June 19, 1779.

JOHN, and Catrina Whiton. Ch: Margarita, bp. April 13, 1784.

HENDRIK, JR., and Catharina Ronkle. Ch: Cornelius, b. Oct. 31, 1787.

FREDERIC HANS, and Rachel Walker. Ch. b: Sally, May 8, 1793; Frederic Elphenton, March 8, 1797.

JOHN, and Maria Schermerhorn. Ch. b: Maria, Sept. 15, 1799; Engeltje, Oct. 23, 1801.

SERVOSS (SERVIS, CERVUS).
FREDERICK, and Aefje Jansen. Ch: Andreas, bp. Feb. 1, 1775.

CHRISTIAAN, and Catarina Overbach. Ch. bp: Sarah, May 4, 1775; Jacob, Jan. 7, 1783.

GEORGE, of Remsenbos, and Mary Overbagh. Ch: Solomon, b. Feb. 9, 1790.

WILLIAM, of Remsenbos, and Sophia Young. Ch: Rachel, b. Oct. 10, 1789.

SETTER.
PHILIP, and Margarita Schoeman. Ch: Elisabeth, bp. Nov. 6, 1771.

JOHANNES, and Maria Paaps. Ch. b: Johannes, June 26, 1779.

SEYBERT.
JURRY ADAM, and Sophia Freeman. Ch. bp: Neeltie, July 18, 1756; Margarita, June 8, 1765.

MARTINUS (Normanskil), and Maria Bell, both of Rensselaerswyck, m. Oct. —, 1768. Ch. bp: Adam, Feb. 21, 1770; Philip, Nov. 18, 1773; Jacob, April 17, 1778; Margarita, Sept. 15, 1780; Joseph, Nov. 6, 1782; Maria, Feb. 22, 1785.

......, and Catarina Sneyder. Ch: Elisabeth, bp. June 30, 1780.

SHANKLAND (SHANKLIN).
WILLIAM, and Margariet Henry. Ch: Anna Nichols, b. June 4, 1797.

THOMAS, and Rachel Terneur. Ch. b: Alexander, Apr. 19, 1796; William, Dec. 7, 1798 (1797 ?).

ROBERT, and Sally Clarke, m. Oct. 29, 1796.

SHANNON (CHANON, SHENNEL).
ROBIN, from Scotland, and Elisabeth Bowel of New York, m. May 28, 1750. Ch. bp: *George*, March 17, 1751; *Thomas*, Dec. 20, 1752; *Alexander*; *Michael*; Margarita, May 14, 1758, m. Simon B. Veeder; *John*; *William*; *Robert*.

THOMAS, son of Robert, m. Margarita, dau. of Abraham Schermerhorn. Ch. bp: Robert, Nov. 29, 1780; Claartje, Dec. 4, 1782; Abraham, Feb. 18, 1787; George, April 8, 1790; Abram, July 15, 1792; Arent, April 26, 1795; Elisabeth, May 27, 1798.

GEORGE, son of Robert, and Sarah Smith. Ch. bp: Elisabeth, August 17, 1782; Eleanor, March 17, 1784. Ch. b: George, July 2, 1786; Jannetje, Nov. 21, 1788; John, April 8, 1791; Robert, May 9, 1793. [George Shannon, a Revolutionary soldier, d. Jan. 8, 1829, a. 80ys.]

JOHN, son of Robert, m. Elisabeth, dau. of Abraham, about July 4, 1781. He served in the Revolutionary war, lived at Normanskil, and d. April —, 1821. Ch: Claartje, bp. Nov. 15, 1784. Ch. b: Elisabeth, July 6, 1786; Abram, June 15, 1788; John, April 24, 1790; Arent, April 11, 1792; William, Nov. 5, 1794; Margrieta, Sept. 20, 1796; Annatje, May 15, 1799.

WILLIAM, son of Robert, m. Jenny Smith. Ch. b: Robert, Oct. 22, 1785; Nelly, April 22, 1788 ;Elisabeth, Oct. 1, 1790; Annatje, Jan. 25, 1793.

ROBERT, JR., son of Robert, m. Nancy McGregor; and secondly, Eva Weller, about 1805. Ch. b: Elisabeth, Jan. 12, 1788; Catharina, Dec. 5, 1789; Peggy, Dec. 4, 1791; Annatje, July 19, 1793; John, Aug. 22, 1795; Elisabeth, April 1, 1797; Jenny, Feb. 1, 1799; Robert, Nov. 23, 1800; Elisabeth, May 17, 1806.

ALEXANDER, son of Robert, and Elisabeth, dau. of Joseph Bragham, both of Normanskil, m. April 20, 1788. Ch. b: Margrietje, Nov. 21, 1788; Robert, Dec. 18, 1789; Annatje, Sept. 2, 1791; Joseph, July 19, 1797; George, Aug. 13, 1799.

MICHAEL, son of Robert, and Susanna, dau. of Joseph Bragham, both of the Normanskil, m. Aug. 29, 1789. Ch. b: Margarita, Jan. 31, 1791; Robert, May 31, 1793; Joseph, April 23, 1795; John, Sept. 19, 1797.

SHARE.

SYLVANUS, and Elisabeth Connor. Ch: Elisabeth, b. Sept. 25, 1799.

SHARPENSTEYN.

JACOB, of Remsenbos, and Sarah Barnhart. Ch: Antje, b. May 2, 1785.

MATTHIAS, of Remsenbos, and Percy Kenny of Warrensburgh; banns, June 12, 1789, m. at Remsenbos. Ch. b: Jacob, Feb. 16, 1790; Robert, Jan. 18, 1793.

SHARTS.

JOHN, and Elisabeth Thomas. Ch: Jacob, b. May 25, 1796.

SHEA.

JAMES, and Annatje Vedder, m. Feb. 12, 1765.

SHELLY.

SAMUEL, and Rebecca Ledies, m. Oct. 24, 1773.

SHEARER (SHERWOOD).

Revolutionary soldier, d. Dec. 31, 1818, a. 62ys.

SHERRER.

JAMES, perhaps same as the last, m. Mary Man. Ch: Annatje Bratt, b. Oct. 1, 1786.

SHERWOOD.

SAMUEL, and Elisabeth Mitts. Ch: Luana, b. Dec. 22, 1786.

SHURTLEFF.

JOSEPH, m. Annatje Beck, dau. of Johannes Van Vorst. He was the first postmaster of the village of Schenectady, made his will Dec. 2, 1814, proved Dec. 6, 1814; spoke of wife Olive, Elisabeth, wid. of my deceased son Clark, Angelica, dau. of my deceased son Hezekiah; Mary, Sally and Mary Ann, dau. of my deceased son Joseph; Hezekiah and Joseph Clark, sons of my deceased son Joseph. His wife Annatje, b. Feb., 1768, d. Oct. 5, 1855. Ch: *Joseph;* Clark; Hezekiah, b. Feb. 7, 1775, d. June 1, 1802.

JOSEPH, son of Joseph, m. ...... Ch: Mary; Sarah, b. Dec. 20, 1802, d. Oct. 16, 1822; Mary Ann; Hezekiah, b. Feb. 26, 1804, d. Sept. 27, 1833; Joseph, b. June 23, 1807, d. March 30, 1847.

SICKLES.

WILLIAM, and Marytje Pels. Ch. b: Robert, Oct. 13, 1795; Jane, July 6, 1797.

Rev. JACOB, m. Catharina, dau. of Hon. Henry Glen, Aug. 1, 1797. She d. before the baptism of her child. He was associate pastor with Dr. Romeyn, 1796–7; accepted a call from the church of Coxsackie; removed from thence to Kinderhook, where he d. in March, 1846, a. 72ys. Ch: Nicholas Glen, b. Nov. 7, 1797.

22

SIMON.

ANTONY, m. Catarina Bastiaan, June 18, 1775.

SIMONDS.

REUBEN, inn keeper in 1785, kept a public house on the west side of Church street, on what is now number 24. This was a popular resort, at which public meetings were held. His house was burned on Pinxter day, 1803: the fire having commenced in a hatter's shop, standing next south, burned thence to State street. Tradition has it, that Burr's carpenters, then at work upon the Mohawk bridge, gave each one day's work towards rebuilding Simonds's house, which was framed, raised and boarded in one day, and that he moved in the next day. He made his will Dec. 8, 1809, proved June 27, 1810; spoke of wife Elisabeth and Reuben Simonds Blood, but mentioned no children. He d. May 5, 1810, a. 74ys.

SIMONSE.

See Veeder.

SIMPSON.

JOSEPH, and Mary Ferguson. Ch: William, bp. Feb. 19, 1785.

SIMSER.

NICHOLAS, and Margariet Beemmer. Ch: Martinus, bp. Aug. 25, 1781.

SITTERLY (SITTERLIN).

JOHANNES, of Helderbergh, and Catharina Sittel. Ch. bp: Johannes, Feb. 9, 1766; *Isaac* Frederic, Sept. 20, 1769;

Petrus; Abraham, July 4, 1777; Jurry Hendrick (*George*), Jan. 6, 1779; Rudolf, Feb. 15, 1781; Martinus, Nov. 4, 1784; Catharina, b. March 19, 1786.

JOHANNES, perhaps same as the last, and Anna Roef. Ch :. Johannes, Dec. 29, 1787.

JACOB, and Appolonia Conterman. Ch : Catrina, bp. March 9, 1784; Maria, b. Nov. 2, 1785.

ISAAC, son of Johannes, of the Hellenbergh, and Elisabeth Shannon of the Normanskil, m. Nov. 16, 1788. Ch. b : Johannes, Sept. 26, 1790 ; Elisabeth, bp. Nov. 11, 1792; Abraham, b. Sept. 21, 1794; Catharina, Oct. 25, 1796; Maria, March 15, 1801; Isaac, May 4, 1803.

PETRUS, son of Johannes and Debora Schermerhorn. Ch : Catharina, bp. Aug. 7, 1797; Arent, b. July 13, 1799.

GEORGE, son of Johannes, and Debora Hoogeboom, both of Corrysbush, m. May 1, 1798. Ch. b : Maria, Aug. 27, 1798; Jacob, April 16, 1804.

SIVER (SIVERSE, SIBERSE, SEBER, SIVERT).
JURRIEN, and Elisabeth, dau. of Simon Groot, m. Feb. 5, 1727. [*See Albany Families.*]

JOHANNES, and Maria Wormer, both of Rensselaerswyck, m. Dec. 13, 1764. Ch : Jurry, b. April 24, 1766. Ch. bp : Nicolaas, Dec. 17, 1769 ; Cornelius, Jan. 7, 1777 ; Abraham, May 26, 1779.

CAREL, and Celia Reddely (Radley). Ch : Annatje, bp. Jan. 7, 1777 ; Margarita, b. Feb. 16, 1790 ; Hendrick, b. Dec. 13, 1792.

ADAM, and Annatje Blessin. Ch : Philip, b. Sept. 15, 1789.

ADAM, perhaps the same as the last, and Annatje, Staley, both of the *Woestyne,* m. Sept. 17, 1793. Ch. b : Elisabeth, Oct. 21, 1794; Jacob, June 16, 1796; George, May 20, 1798.

ROBERT, and Catharina Siver. Ch : George or Jurry, b. Nov. 17, 1789.

JACOB, and Martha Radley. Ch : Peter, b. May 1, 1790.

SIXBERRY.

MANASSEH, young man from London, and Pietertje, dau. of Jan Janse Jonkers of Schenectady, m. March 15, 1699. He owned a part of the "First flat," about four miles above Schenectady, on the south side of the river; being sick at Fort Nicholson, Sept. 23, 1709, he made his will. Ch. bp : Johannes, January 9, 1700 ; *Wilhelmus,* July 13, 1701; Mary, living in 1709.

WILLEM, son of Manasseh, of Maquaasland, and Maria Catharina Smit of "Dorp," m. 1722 (?). Ch : Anna Lysbet, bp. Jan. 19, 1724 ; Manasseh, b. Sept. 23, 1725 ; *Adam,* bp. May 21, 1732.

......, and ...... Jurriaanse. Ch : Catharina, b. Feb. 15, 1730.

ABRAHAM, and Eva Ekkerson. Ch. bp: Johannes, Aug. 9, 1752.

NICHOLAS, m. Susanna, dau. of Pieter Clement, March 20, 1756. Ch. bp: Nicholas, April 17, 1757; Pieter, Dec. 17, 1758; Annatje, June 15, 1760, m. Gerrit De Spitzer; Maria, Jan. 16, 1763, m. Abraham Schermerhorn jr.; Pieter, Dec. 25, 1764; Arent, July 10, 1768.

ADAM, son of Willem, m. Annatje Olin. Ch. bp: Maria, Feb. 1, 1769; Alida, Dec. 19, 1770; Annatje, Jan. 20, 1780.

CORNELIS, m. Maria Olin. Ch. bp: Alida, Dec. 23, 1769; Benjamin, Oct. 25, 1775.

WILLIAM, m. Annatje Hendrickse. Ch: Peggy, b. May 19, 1796.

JOHN, m. Sarah Dingman. Ch : Jane, b. June 19, 1797.

ABRAHAM, m. Maria Zeeger, Nov. 11, 1799.

SLINGERLAND.

CORNELIS, son of Teunis Cornelise of Albany, m. Eva, dau. of ...... Mebie, May 28, 1699. Ch. bp: Engeltie, Jan. 9, 1700, m. Hendrick Janse Vrooman; Anna, Oct. 3, 1703, m. Johannes Slingerland of Albany; Maria, August 25, 1705, m. Jan Ekerson; Lysbeth, April 30, 1707; Catharina, April 28, 1710, in Albany, m. first, Hendrick Van Slyck, and secondly, Bartholomeus Vrooman; Eva, July 12, 1714, in Albany; Lena, Oct. 6, 1716; Grietje, March 22, 1718; Rachel, Dec. 24, 1720; Teunis, May 18, 1723,

settled in Albany. [A Cornelis Slingerland d. at Niskatha, Sept. 3, 1753.]

ANTHONY, son of Teunis of Albany (?), m. Claartje Clute. Ch. bp : Teunis, Oct. 31, 1756; Maritje, Oct. 29, 1769. [*See Albany Families.*]

SLOT.

BENJAMIN, and Sarah Demara. Ch : Benjamin, bp. Jan. 5, 1766.

SLOVER.

DANIEL, m. Maria Van Eps, Feb. 7, 1796. Ch. b : Ann, March 17, 1797; Engeltie, July 16, 1798.

SLUYTER.

NICHOLAS, and Catarina Redderford. Ch. bp : Nicholas, Oct. 19, 1778; John, Nov. 27, 1783; Sarah, b. Nov. 18, 1785.

PETER, and Ann Johnson. Ch : Ann, bp. Dec. 8, 1783.

CORNELIUS, and Lydia Ostrander. Ch : Magdalena, bp. July 4, 1784.

ROBERT, cooper, of the Hellenbergh, m. Catharina, dau. of Johannes Clute. He d. in Rotterdam, April 4, 1839, a. 83ys.; she d. March 11, 1822, a. 60ys. Ch. b : Maria, May 18, 1785; William, Apr. 19, 1797; Geertruy, Aug. 30, 1798.

SMITH (SMITT, SMIT).

TAM, from New England, m. Maria Cobes, dau. of Ludovicus Cobes (?), and wid. of Gerrit Janse, Sept. 30, 1696. He lived on the south side of the Mohawk, opposite the Fourth flat. Ch : Anna, bp. July 28, 1700.

ADAM MICHAEL, and Breggje Smit.
Ch. bp: Willem, December 18, 1714;
Ephraim, Sept. 15, 1717; Anna Elisa-
beth, Nov. 5, 1720; Catrina Barber, m.
Adam Empie.

CORNELIUS, b. in the county of Bergen
(N. J.), and Sara, dau. of Arent Vedder,
b. in this place, m. Sept. 19, 1730. Ch.
bp: *Benjamin*, May 30, 1731; Anna,
Nov. 25, 1733; Arent, Oct. 15, 1738.

EPHRAIM, son of Adam Michael, mason, and Elisabet, dau. of Robert Yates,
m. in Albany, June 28, 1739. Ch. bp:
Maria, Jan. 15, 1744; Brechtje, June
29, 1746; *Adam;* Brechtje and Sarah,
twins, Jan. 28, 1750; *Robert*, April 4,
1752; Elisabeth, Nov. 3, 1754.

BENJAMIN, son of Cornelius, m. Rebecca, dau. of Simon D. Groot, Nov. 29,
1754. She again m. Volkert Vedder,
Nov. 26, 1763. Ch: Cornelius, May
28, 1756.

ARENT, and Catarina, dau. of Pieter
Veling (Feling), m. Oct. 2, 1762.

ROBERT, from New Jersey, m, Rebecca, dau. of Nicolaas Groot, April 18,
1756. Ch. bp: Nicolaas, July 16, 1758;
Maria, July 15, 1759; *Nicolaas*, Dec.
20, 1761; Elias, Jan. 8, 1764; Elisabeth,
Sept. 22, 1765; Anganieta, July 4, 1767;
Dirk, March 7, 1771.

RICHARD, m. Geesie, dau. of Jacob
Mebie. Ch. bp: John, May 13, 1766;
Jacob, May 15, 1768; Willem, April 8,
1770.

ADAM, son of Ephraim, cordwainer,
m. Frances Borris (Burris), Sept. 17,
1763. She d. May 29, 1808, a. 77ys.
Ch. bp: Thomas, August 16, 1767, d.
April 26, 1812; Ephraim, May 5, 1778.

HARMANUS, and Maria Wemple, of
Kachnawaga, m. Feb. 7, 1768.

MOSES, and Anna Sengh (Zeyn). Ch.
bp: Samuel and Maria, Sept. 16, 1772;
Elisabeth, May 21, 1779.

JOHANNES, and Elisabeth Pesinger.
Ch. bp: Catarina, March 3, 1774; Dorothea, May 10, 1775; Maria, Oct. 27,
1779; Hans, March 27, 1785.

ALEXANDER, and Rachel Reddely.
Ch: Rachel, bp. May 18, 1775.

JOSEPH, and Mary Gyet (Jollie). Ch.
bp: Joseph, Oct. 5, 1777; Lowis, June
25, 1779.

JOHANNES, and Mary Anselaar. Ch:
Bastiaan, bp. June 24, 1781.

ROBERT, son of Ephraim, and Graec
Brave (Brevit, Braithwate, Brasitt).
Ch. bp: Robert, Nov. 11, 1781; Elisa-
beth, Jan. 9, 1785. Ch. b: William,
Oct. 20, 1787; Abram, July 30, 1791;
Isaac, May 29, 1794.

NICHOLAS, son of Robert, m. Annatje,
dau. of Robert Hagedorn. Ch. bp: Rebecca, June 15, 1783; Robert, Sept. 29,
1784. Ch. b: Derick, Aug. 18, 1786;
Harmanus, Sept. 4, 1788; John, April
11, 1790; Margarita, May 16, 1792;
Dirk, April 3, 1794, bp. Feb. 22, 1795.

ABRAM, and Rebecca Van Huysen. Ch. b : Harmanus Van Huysen, Nov. 7, 1790; William, Sept. 23, 1792; Roedolph, Oct. 3, 1803.

JACOB, of Corrysbos, and Maria Weller of Normanskil, m. Dec. 4, 1791. Ch. b : Willem, June 18, 1792; Annatje, Jan. 6, 1794; Jacob, Sept. 28, 1796 ; Maria, Aug. 13, 1799

HENDRIK, and Alida Van Vranken, both of Nestigaune, m. June 28, 1789. Ch : Maria, b. Sept. 18, 1790.

JACOB, of Corrysbos, and Effie (Elsje) Bratt of Normanskil, m. in May, 1789. Ch : John, b. Jan. 24, 1790.

JOSEPH, and Alice Grantshorn, m. July 16, 1786.

THOMAS, and wife Rebecca, in. Schenectady about 1800. She d. Feb. 22, 1819, in her 52 year.

JOHN CAREL, and Fanny Hoogteling, m. March 23, 1789.

THOMAS, and Agnes Smith. Ch. b : Daniel, Dec. 8, 1794; Rebecca, Dec. 2, 1796 ; Simon, Jan. 28, 1801 ; William, June 8, 1802 ; Nelly, April 12, 1804.

SNELL.

MAJOR (his christian name), merchant, m. Elisabeth Gill. He was a native of Yorkshire, England ; made his will Mar. 7, 1809, proved Nov. 7, 1818; spoke of wife Eliza, dau. Elisabeth, wife of Helmus Veeder, sons John, Robert and Major ; Major L., son of my son John ;

my dau. Ann, wife of Robert Buchanan, Sarah, wife of John Smith, Maria, wife of Peter Truax, and Margaret. He d. Sept. 24, 1818, a. 98ys , 4m., 29d. Ch. bp : Elisabeth, wife of Wilhelmus Veeder ; Robert, June 13, 1779 ; *Major*, May 2, 1784 ; Sarah, Feb. 28, 1787.

MAJOR, son of Major, m. Elisabeth Reese. Ch : Elisabeth, b. July 8, 1801.

JOHN G., son of Major, m. Maria Lytle, July 12. 1794.

ROBERT, son of Major, m. Margaret Bohannan, June 11, 1796.

SNEYDER (SNYDER).

JURRY, and Maria Ecker. Ch. bp : Nicholas, Sept. 16, 1780 ; Johannes, Dec. 15, 1783.

JURRY, perhaps same as the last, and Annatje Paaps. Ch : Lodowyck, b. Oct. 8, 1786.

PHILIP, and Mary Mackitrik. Ch. bp : William, May 29, 1781 ; Catrina, March 5, 1783 ; Henry, b. Sept. 6, 1791.

JACOB, and Elisabeth Man. Ch : Johannes Ingold, Aug. 24, 1782.

LODOWYCK, and Louisa Stoffman. Ch : Catrina, bp. March 27, 1784.

SOEGEMAKELYK.

See Adriaanse.

SOUTHARD.

JOHN, and Elisabeth Teerpenning of Clifton Park, m. September 11, 1792.

Ch. b: Mary, July 14, 1793; Margariet, August 12, 1795; Jonas, Jan. 30, 1798; Peter, Nov. 2, 1800.

SPAARBECK.

ANDRIES, and Eva ...... Ch: Coenraadt, b. Sept. 20, 1788.

MARTINUS, and Barbara Sitterling. Ch: Johannes, bp. March 24, 1785.

COENRAAT, and Annatje (Christina in the *Trouw-boek*) Achenbagh, both living in the Hellenbergh, m. Aug. 16, 1786. Ch. b: Hendrik, May 26, 1788; Jacob, Dec. 15, 1790.

SPECK.

SYMON, in 1725, lived in a house on south side of Front street, 125 feet west of the burial ground.

NICOLAAS, in 1766, had a lot at the north corner of the burial ground in Front street.

SPEYER.

FREDERICK, and Anna Felte. Ch. bp: Maria, June 9, 1765; Maria Magdalena, Oct. 20, 1767.

SPICER.

JABEZ, and Elisabeth Van Deusen. Ch. b: Sarah, April 10, 1786; Elisabeth, Nov. 6, 1787.

SPITSER.

See De Spitser.

SPOOR.

ANTJE, dau of Jan Spoor *alias* Wiebese of Niskayuna, was killed at Sche-nectady, Feb. 9, 1690, by the French and Indians.

CLAAS, and Maria Van Vechten. Ch: Catarina, bp. Oct. 19, 1777.

JOHANNES, and Elisabeth Van Wormer. Ch. b: Rachel, Feb. 6, 1793; Johannes, Sept. 11, 1795.

ABRAM, and Maria Wells. Ch: Annatje, b. Jan. 23, 1793.

SPOTTER.

JACOBUS, and Rachel Lewis. Ch: Jacobus, bp. Aug. 24, 1735.

SPRINGER.

DAVID, and Margaret Oliver. Ch. bp: Marytje, 1761, m. Willem Carol; Dannis, Jan. 15, 1764; Martha, April 6, 1766; Rachel, Sept. 4, 1768; John, March 13, 1771; Henderikje May 10, 1775; Cezia, May 13, 1777.

BENJAMIN, and Hendrikje Olivier. Ch. bp: Maria, May 18, 1770, m. Samuel Bratt; Dannis, Jan. 11, 1775; Oliver, b. Feb. 22, 1778, d. Sept. 15, 1831.

VINCENT, and Sarah Howe, both of Noormanskil, m. Dec. 4, 1787. Ch. b: Sarah, June 20, 1791; David, March 11, 1798.

DANIEL, m. Margaret Vrooman, Oct. (?) 18, 1798.

SPRINGSTEEN.

CASPARUS, miller, m. Jannetje, dau. of Jacob Janse Schermerhorn, July 28, 1695, in New York, Ch. bp: Abraham,

Sept. 19, 1703; Jannetje, Oct. 28, 1705; Ryer, April 30, 1707.

SPROUT.

JAMES, and Geertruy Lansing. Ch: James, bp. June 2, 1784.

STAATE.

HENDRIK, and Elisabeth Allebragh. Ch: Philip, b. Feb. 3, 1793.

STAATS.

JOCHIM, son of Barent of Albany, and Elisabeth Schuyler. Ch: Gerrit, bp. March 2, 1746. [*See Albany Families.*]

PETRUS, of Schoharie, and Annatie, dau. of Harmanus Hagedorn of Schenectady, m. April 20, 1794.

STAF (STOFF).

HENDRICK, and Maria Jones (Janes). Ch. bp: Joseph, Sept. 28, 1779; Abraham, Jan. 25, 1783; Johannes, b. Aug. 7, 1785.

STAFFORD.

ANNANIAS, and Susanna De Groot, both of Duanesburgh, m. July 14, 1791.

STALEY.

JACOB, and Susanna Reynex. Ch. bp: Susanna, Dec. 28, 1775; Maria, April 17, 1778. Ch. b: Hendrik, October 17, 1788; Uldrik, July 5, 1797.

HARMANUS, and Maria Hoogeboom. Ch. bp: *Hendrick*, Dec. 28, 1775; Pieter, January 19, 1780; Maria, May 24, 1783. Ch. b: Catharina, March 22, 1785; Rachel, Sept. 29, 1789.

JURRY (George), of Princetown, and Jane (Jannette) Mackall. He d. June 7, 1832; she d. July 5, 1846. Ch. b: Anna, Sept. 21, 1775; *Hendrick*, May 13, 1777; Oliver, July 4, 1781, living in 1848; Jacob, Aug. 16, 1783; Jenny, Jan. 15, 1786, living in 1848; Maria, June 12, 1788, living in 1848; Betsey, March 18, 1791, living in 1848; Susan, Aug. 4, 1793, living in 1848; George, Jan. 13, 1796.

HENDRICK, and Rachel Van Hoesen. Ch. bp: Abraham, Jan. 5, 1779; Jacob, March 19, 1784. Ch. b: Susanna, Jan. 22, 1786; Maria, March —, 1788.

HENDRICK H., son of Harmanus, and Elisabeth Van Hoesen. Ch. b: Eleanor, Nov. 25, 1797; Harmanus, Apr. 26, 1800.

HENDRIK, son of George and Sally Dods. Ch. b: Jenny, Aug. 21, 1798; Mary, Dec. 5, 1799.

RULOFF (Rudolf), and Elisabeth Crawford. Ch: Anna, bp. June 26, 1784. Ch. b: Margarieta, Oct. 10, 1786; Joseph, April 7, 1788; Mary, October 2, 1791; Harmanus, Feb. 5, 1794; Catharine, Sept. 2, 1797.

MATTHIAS, and Susanna Sattn. Ch: Elisabeth, bp. Oct. 15, 1784.

STANLEY.

DAVID, and Anna Lighthall, m. Jan. 14, 174⅞.

STANSBURY.

ELIAS, and Judith Deval. Ch. bp:

Elias, Jan. 15, 1749; Willem, May 12, 1751.

STATEN.

FREDERIC, and Margariet Tigert. Ch : Maritje Eva, bp. June 30, 1722.

STEELE.

HARMANUS, and Maria Hoogeboom. Ch : Abram, b. May 18, 1787.

STEERS (STIERS).

ST. JAN, soldier, and Trientje McGregor. Ch : Samuel, bp. Oct. 26, 1722 ; Fil, b. May 15, 1725 ; *Johannes*, bp. Oct. 15, 1732 ; *Pieter*, Jan. 7, 1739.

JOHN, son of St. Jan, m. Clara, dau. of Pieter Van Slyck, Nov. 3, 1759. His father had a grant of a lot in Green street, near the fort, in 1756. John inherited it, and Cornelius, his son, possessed it until his death in 1863. John Steers, d. Feb. 12, 1811 ; his wife was b. July 4, 1738, and d. Aug. 3, 1812. Ch. bp : Catarina, Dec. 7, 1760 ; Engeltje, May 19, 1765 ; Geertruy, Aug. 16, 1767, m. John Lambert ; *John*, Oct. 8, 1769 ; *Petrus*, July 19, 1772 ; Margarita, Oct. 16, 1774, d. Nov. —, 1840 ; Cornelius, Aug. 17, 1777, d. Nov. 21, 1863 ; Samuel, Apr. 14, 1780.

PETER, and Catarina Rykeman, m. March 6, 1762.

PIETER, son of St. Jan, m. Geesje, dau. of Jacob Vrooman, Oct. 25, 1764. Ch. bp : Catarina, Sept. 29, 1765 ; Jacob, August 23, 1767 ; *Jacob*, Nov. 19, 1769 ; Maria, May 3, 1772 ; John, July 5, 1778 ; Philip, May 17, 1782.

JOHN, and Elisabeth Groot. Ch : Gezina, b. Feb. 6, 1792.

JACOB, son of Pieter, m. Jannetje, dau. of Johannes Fort. Ch. b : Sarah, Oct. 25, 1795 ; John, Nov. 30, 1797, d. perhaps Jan. 5, 1852 ; Gezina, June 27, 1800 ; Sarah, January 22, 1803 ; James Ryley, June 13, 1809.

PIETER, son of John, m. Lydia, dau. of Gerrit Van Schaick, Dec. 5, 1795. Ch. b : John, June 20, 1796 ; Elisabeth, July 5, 1798 ; Clara, April 18, 1801 ; Clara, Sept. 28, 1802 ; Harmanus, Nov. 8, 1804 ; Gerrit, Oct. 11, 1807.

JOHN, son of John, m. Annatje Nesbit, August 17, 1795. Ch. bp : Claara, June 10, 1796 ; John, June 13, 1802.

STEIN.

COENRAADT, and Eva Wirts. He d. before the baptism of his child. Ch : Coenraadt, b. Dec. 24, 1798, bp. Jan. 20, 1799.

STEINBERG.

ELIAS, and Catharina Hoffman. Ch : Catharina, b. Nov. 24, 1785.

JOHANNES, and Lidia Griffith. Ch : Esther, b. July 15, 1795.

JONATHAN, and Elisabeth Reis. Ch : Jacobus, b. Nov., 1795.

STEL.

RUDOLF, and Margarita Wierts. Ch : Rebecca, bp. March 3, 1782.

STENNER.

ANGUS, and Mary ...... Ch: Thomas, bp. May 4, 1775.

STENSEL.

NICOLAAS, m. Elisabeth, dau. of Claas De Graaf. Ch: Catharina, b. March 15, 1712 *op de Pootenhoek* in the county of Albany, and bp. in Klinkenberg (near Athens) *aan Domin: palm:* [Lutheran church records, Athens;] Nicolaus, b. *op de Groote Nooten Hoek* Jan. 3, and bp. at Klinkenberg, Jan. 17, 1714 [Lutheran church records, Athens.] Ch. bp. in Schenectady: Jesse, June 8, 1717; Lysabet, Dec. 24, 1718; Eva, April 2, 1721; Saartje, March 16, 1723; Wilhelmus (?); Thomas (?), Sept. 30, 1725.

STERLING.

JAMES, and Catharine Staley. Ch: William, b. Feb. 16, 1798.

STERNBERG (STAUNBERGH).

ADAM, and Jannetje McCready. Ch: Rebecca, bp. March 13, 1784.

STEVENS.

JONATHAN, from New England, m. Lea, wid. of Claas Willemse Van Coppernol, July 24, 1693. He was b. in 1675; Lea, his wife, a Mohawk woman, often acted as interpreter. Besides a home lot in the village, he owned a farm on the north side of the river, about 3½ miles east of the town. Ch. bp: Annatje, March 27, 1695, m. Hendrick Hagedorn; Henricus (*Nicholas*), Nov. 10, 1697; Dina, May 5, 1700, m. Samuel Hagedorn; *Arent*, July 26, 1702.

23

ARENT, son of Jonathan, m. first, Maritie, dau. of Willem Hall, Feb. 3, 1726; she d. Dec. 23, 1739, in her 42d year; he m. secondly, Mary Griffiths, wid. of Lieut. Thomas Burrows, Feb. 4, 17⁴⁸⁄₅₀; she d. July 2, 1794, a. 75ys.; he d. May 15, 1758. Arent Stevens, for more than 20 years before his death, acted as an Indian interpreter, and was often employed by Sir William Johnson in negociations with the different tribes. He owned lands, and for some time resided at Canajoharie. Ch. b: Jonathan, Dec. 1, 1726, killed at the battle at Lake George, Sept. 8, 1755; Catrina, bp. Aug. 1, 1729, d. Aug. 27, 1790; *Wilm*, bp. Sept. 10, 1732; *Nicolaas*, b. Nov. 14, 1734; Johannes, b. July 21, 1736; Jacobus, b. Dec. 13, 1739; Maria, b. Oct. 20, 1750, m. John Stuart; Richard, b. Dec. 10, 1752, d. 1800; Lea and Anna, b. April 22, 1755, the former d. July 11, 1756, the latter m. Philip Fransikkel.

NICOLAAS (Henricus), son of Jonathan, and Maria Phoenix, b. in New York, and residing in this place, m. May 29, 1730. Ch. bp: Jonathan, May 21, 1732; Sander, Dec. 2, 1733; *Arent*, Sept. 21, 1735; Hester, Dec. 21, 1737; Cornelia, June 14, 1741; Lea, July 3, 1743; *Johannes*, March 31, 1745; Annatje, Mar. 6, 1748; Maria, April 5, 1752; Diana, living in 1747, when her father made a will; all d. young and unmarried, save Arent and Johannes.

NICOLAAS, son of Arent, m. Margarita Mebie, April 10, 1761. He d. Sept. 19, 1788; she d. August 4, 1764. Ch. b:

Arent, Sept. 18, 1762; Johannes, June 26, 1764, d. Sept. 30, 1787.

ARENT, son of Nicolaas (Henricus), m. Jannetje De Spitser, Nov. 20, 1768. He made his will 1783, proved June 6, 1784; spoke of wife and children, save Nicolaas. Ch. bp: *Jonathan*, Jan. 27, 1770; Thomas, b. and bp. March 22, 1772; Nicolaas, April 24, 1774; Margarita, May 18, 1777; Maria, Dec. 31, 1780; Hendericus, April 27, 1783; Nicolaas, b. after his father's will was made, d. in Schenectady, 1863.

WILLEM, son of Arent, m. Geertruy, dau. of Alexander Van Eps, Sept. 25, 1770. He made his will Nov. 6, 1793, and spoke of his wife and the following Ch., save William, who was not then b. d. Dec. 7, 1793. Ch. b: Maria, May 3, 1771, m. Dirk Hagedorn; Neeltje, Apr. 30, 1773, d. August 10, 1853; Arent, April 5, 1775, d. June 28, 1853; Alexander, Jan. 11, 1777, m. Mary Clement, July 17, 1810; Catarina, April 11, 1779, d. April 17, 1794; Jonathan, Aug. 8, 1782 (3); Jan Baptist, Feb. 23, 1785; Nicholas, March 11, 1787; Richard, March 5 (6), 1789; Lourens, Dec. 20, (21), 1791, d. Nov. 1, 1807; William, Jan. 27, 1794.

JOHANNES, son of Nicolaas (Henricus), m. Catalyntje Van Schaick, Feb. 9, 1771. Ch. bp: Catarina, June 27, 1773; Catarina, Nov. 13, 1774, m. John S. Barheit; Jonathan, Sept. 7, 1777; Jannetje, Jan. 2, 1780; Gerrit, Nov. 4, 1781; Arent, March 20, 1785.

JONATHAN, son of Arent, m. Elisabeth, dau. of Elias Groot. He d. in Glenville, Sept. 3, (4), 1844; she d. March 11, 1856, a. 89ys., 2m., 19d. Ch. b: Maria, April 9, 1788; Geertruy, April 26, 1790, d. Aug. 6, 1852; Arent, June 16, 1792, d. in Glenville, June 20, 1850; Jannetje, Feb. 15, 1796.

ARENT, son of Nicolaas, m. first, Maria Crysler in 1785; secondly, Maria Van Sickler, about 1803. He d. June 13, 1838. Ch. b: Nicholas. Dec. 28, 1785; Johannes, Oct. 30, 1787; Adam Crysler, Sept. 11, 1789; William Alexander, Sept. 30, 1804; Lawrence, March 21. 1809.

PELEG, m. Emmetje, dau. of Robert Hagedorn. Ch. b: Henry, February 25, 1794; Margarietje, Feb. 3, 1796; Marytje, July 1, 1798.

STEWART.

See Stuart.

STEYMER.

CASPARUS, and Annatje Weytman. Ch. bp: Annatje, July 23, 1763; Catarina, March 22, 1765.

STISSER.

CHRISTIAAN, and Margariet Ray. Ch: Maria, bp. Jan. 23, 1785. Ch. b: Catharina, Nov. 1, 1786; August Anthoon, Dec. 8, 1788; Margariet, Nov. 9, 1791; Christiaan, b. Feb. 17, bp. Feb. 16 (*sic*), 1794.

STOCK.

GEORGE CHARLES, m. Mary Simpson, March 5, 1786.

STOUWT.

DIRK, and Eva, dau. of Isaac (?) Truax. Ch : Elisabeth, bp. Aug. 25, 1722

STRAIL.

JOHN, from Remsenbos, and Catharina Sullivan of Corrysbos, m. Oct. 8, 1794. Ch : Mary, b. Aug. 28, 1797.

HENDRIK, and Elisabeth Beman. Ch. b : Margariet, June 21, 1801; Daniel, Oct. 5, 1802.

STRANG.

WILLIAM, and Jane Strang. Ch : Isabella, b. May 12, 1795.

STUART (STEWARD).

JOHN, m. Maria, dau. of Arent Stevens. Ch. bp : *James*, Jan. 17, 1773; Catarina, Oct. 30, 1774; Arent, August 31, 1777; Abraham, Dec. 16, 1781; Judith, Nov. 9, 1783; Nicolaas Stevens, b. Jan. 25, 1789.

WILLIAM, and Mary ...... Ch : Pieter, bp. Nov. 2, 1778; William, b. Sept. 19, 1785.

DANIEL, and Nancy (Agnes) Frazer. Ch : Duncan, bp. Feb. 21, 1782; Mary, b. Jan. 28, 1787.

JAMES, and Jane Adair. Ch : John, bp. June 15, 1783; Mary, b, May 4, 1785; Agnes, bp. June 10, 1791; Elisabeth Yates, b. April 18, 1792; Jane, b. March 10, bp. March 9 (*sic*), 1794.

GEORGE, and Elisabeth Ferguson. Ch : Anna Ferguson, bp. March 10, 1785.

JOHN, from Chalotsbos, and Sarah Sample of Warrensbos. Banns, June 1, 1794. Ch. b : William, Aug. 8, 1795 ; Catharine, Jan. 13, 1800; Sarah, Dec. 28, 1801.

JAMES G., and Eleanor Blakely. Ch : George Hulse, b. May 11, 1797.

STYLES.

MOSES, of Remsenbos, and Catharina Strail. Ch : Margariet, b. March 13, 1785.

SULLIVAN.

JOHN, and Elisabeth Cooper. She d. before the baptism of her last child. Ch. b : Agnes, Oct. 26, 1786; Elisabeth, Feb. 9, bp. Feb. 14, 1789.

SUPPLISOO.

JACOB, and Eytje Hendrickse, wid. of Dirk Hesselingh, both dwelling in this place, m. Oct. 24, 1693, in Albany.

SWANN.

GEORGE, and Eva Mackintee. Ch : Isabel, bp. Jan. 26, 1779.

SWART.

Two brothers of this name were early settlers at Schenectady ; —Frederic Cornelise Swart, who was proposed by Secretary Ludovicus Cobes in 1676, as one of the magistrates of the village, and Teunise Cornelise Swart, from whom all the families in this vicinity are descended. The latter, as one of the original proprietors of Schenectady, received allotment No. 10 on the *Groote Vlachte*, comprising 48 acres lying over, or westward of the *Third* or *Poenties* kil, and a village lot on the east corner of State and Church streets 200×170 feet. After his death, about 1686, his wife, Elisabeth Lendt or Van der Linde, m. Jacob Meese Vrooman of Albany. He d. about 1690, and October 14, 1691, she again m. Wouter Uythoff of Albany. Teunis Cornelise Swart had the following : *Cornelis*, eldest son, b. 1652 ; *Esaias*, b. 1653 ; Teunis ; Frederic ; *Adam ;* Marytje, m. Claas Lourense Van der Volgen ; Jacomyntje, m first, Pieter Viele ; secondly, Bennony Arentse Van Hoeck ; and thirdly, Cornelis Vynhout of Ulster county.

CORNELIS, eldest son of Teunis, early settled in Ulster county. April 25, 1692, he conveyed the lot on the east corner of Church and State streets, 200×170 feet, inherited from his father to his brother-in-law Claas Lourense Van der Volgen, reserving for his brother Esaias, a lot fronting on Church street; and Feb. 3, 171⅚, he released to Jan Mebie a parcel of pasture land, for which he had received a patent in 1670 from Gov. Lovelace. He had the following Ch. bp. in Albany : Abigail, Sept. 16, 1685 ; Elisabeth, Nov. 13, 1687 ; Geertruy, April 27, 1690. [*See Albany Families*]

ESAIAS, son of Teunis, m. Eva, dau. of Teunis Van Schoenderwoert *alias* Van Woert of Albany. In 1686 he received conveyance of part of bouwery No. 10 over the *Poenties* kil from his mother, also a release in 1716 from his brother Cornelis, of a lot on the east side of Church street, 200 feet north of State street. His descendants now, or lately owned the *Sixth flat* on the north side of the Mohawk, bounded west by Taquatsera creek. Ch. bp : *Teunis ;* Sara, Dec. 16, 1691, in Albany, m. Jan Barentse Wemp ; *Wouter*, April 11, 1694 ; Elisabeth, Dec. 30, 1696 ; Maria, January 9, 1700 ; Esaias, Feb. 27, 1704 ; Jacobus, April 30, 1707 ; *Jesaias*, Oct. 30, 1709, in Albany.

TEUNIS, son of Esaias, m. Christina, dau. of Adam Vrooman, Oct. 30, 1710. Ch. bp : *Jesaias*, May 3, 1713, settled in Schoharie ; Engeltie, Dec. 17, 1715, m. Barent Vrooman ; *Adam*, July 12, 1718 ; Jacobus, Jan. 1, 1722 ; *Dirk* (?).

WOUTER, son of Esaias, m. Elisabeth, dau. of Jeremie Thickstone. He lived near Towereune ; 1736 bought of Grace Cosby 120 acres of land on the south side of the Mohawk, 2 miles west of Towereune; 1737 purchased of Jan Wemp three islands in the Mohawk. Ch. bp : Jesaias, Feb. 20, 1720 ; Jeremias, July 15, 1721 ; Jesaias, March 30, 1723 ; Saartje, March 16, bp. April 4, 1725. m. Isaac Marselis ; Willem, b. Dec. 18, 1727, bp. Jan. 19, 1728 ; Eva, bp. ——, 1730 ; Rachel, Aug. 13, 1732 ; Jesaias, Feb. 23, 1735 ; Elisabeth, March 17, 173⅞ ; *Teunis*.

JESAIAS, son of Esaias, m. Elisabeth, dau. of Arent Vedder, Dec. 13, 1731. Ch. bp : Jesaias, May 28, 1732 ; Arent, April 13, 1735 ; Elisabeth, July —, 1739 ; *Jacobus*, Oct. 19, 1740 ; Sara, Nov. 28, 1742, m. Arent Mebie ; Eva, Jan. 26,

1746; Eva, March 27, 1748, m. Andries De Graff; Jesaias, Aug. 13, 1749; Anna, Dec. 8, 1751; *Jesaias,* July 29, 1753; Annatje, March 2, 1755.

JEREMIE, son of Wouter, m. Maria Van Vlek, Apr. 15, 1748. Ch. bp: *Jesaias,* Oct. 30, 1748; *Benjamin,* Nov. 4, 1750; *Wouter,* April 29, 1753; Annatje, Jan. 18, 1756, m. Simon L. Groot; Elisabeth, Feb. 26, 1758; *Johannes,* Mar. 23, 1760; *Willem,* June 14, 1767.

ADAM, son of Teunis, dwelling at Schoharie, m. Catharina, dau. of Nicolaas Van Petten, Dec. 23, 1742. She m. Arent Vedder, April 4, 1758. He removed from Schoharie, and settled in Glenville near the Fourth flat on the north side of the Mohawk. His son Nicolaas inherited the homestead and built the brick house standing there, in 1792. Teunis settled on *Tincker-Hooghten,* south of his brother Nicolaas, on the bank of the river; his house was called the "Old Fort;" it is not standing now. Ch. bp: *Nicolaas; Teunis,* eldest son; Geertruy, m. Albert A. Vedder; Jacob, April 8, 1752, d. before he arrived at maturity; Adam, Jan. 19, 1755.

ADAM, and Francis Borris. Ch: Elisabeth, bp. Aug. 19, 1764.

TEUNIS, son of Wouter, m. Sarah, dau. of Jan Baptist Van Vorst, Nov. 26, 1763. Ch. bp: *Wouter,* Sept. 18, 1764; *Jan Baptist,* Nov. 2, 1766; Elisabeth, b. Nov. 4, bp. Dec. 4, 1768; *Jeremia,* bp. September 16, 1770; Elisabeth, June 21, 1772; Catarina, Apr. 24, 1774; *Jesaias,*

April 7, 1776; Jillis, May 18, 1781; Elisabeth, June 8, 1783.

DIRK, son of Teunis, m. Jannetie Vanderzee in Albany, July 22, 1758. Ch: Teunis, bp. in Albany, Jan. 4, 1760.

ADAM, son of Teunis, m. Metie Willemse Van Slyck of New Albany, Jan. 15, 1690. He was of Schenectady 1690, of Kinderhoek 1706. Ch: Johanna, bp. Jan. 13, 1706, in Albany.

TEUNIS, son of Adam, m. Margarita, dau. of Myndert Myndertse, Sept. 22, 1767. He settled at *Tincker Hooghten,* near the "Fourth flat," south of his brother Nicolaas; built a brick house upon the bank of the river, which was stockaded and called, latterly, the "Old Fort;" it is now removed. Ch. bp: *Adam,* Sept. 18, 1768; *Myndert,* April 28, 1771; *Jacob,* Dec. 19, 1773; Johannes, Dec. 22, 1776; Arent, June 30, 1780; Barent, Jan. 4, 1784.

BENJAMIN, son of Jeremia, of *de Willege,* m. Catalyntje Wemp, Oct. 25, 1772. He lived on Jeremiah Thickstone's farm, on north side of the river, near Hoffman's Ferry. Ch. bp: *Jeremia,* May 30, 1773; *Benjamin;* Isaac, Sept. 15, 1776; Isaac, Dec. 20, 1778; Reyer, Jan. 28, 1781; Jesaias, March 19, 1784. Ch. b: Walterus, March 18, 1787; Elisabeth, Oct. 8, 1789; Johannes, Aug. 23, 1793.

NICOLAAS, son of Adam, m. Anganietje, dau. of Simon Vedder. He lived in Glenville, five miles above Schenectady, near the Fourth flat; his house built in

1792, is still standing   He d. March 1, 1825, and was buried near his house; his wife d Sept. 19, 1817, a. 65ys., 7m. Ch. bp: Adam, April 10, 1774; Simon, Oct. 6, 1776; Catarina, Aug. 8, 1779; Maria, April 17, 1782. Ch. b: Simon, Feb. 18, 1787, d. in Glenville, Aug. 7, 1851; Adam, Oct. 8, 1789, d. Sept. 30, 1872; Harmanus, March 23, 1792; Jacob, Oct. 25, 1794.

JACOBUS, son of Jesaias, m. Sarah, dau. of Harmanus Vedder. He made his will Nov. 30, 1802, proved Feb. 9, 1813; spoke of wife Sarah, sons Josias, Harmanus, Arent, Arnout, also of dau. Maria, Elisabeth, Anna and Sarah. Ch. bp: Maria, Aug. 4, 1776; Jesaias, Mar. 26, 1779, d. October 3, 1841, near the "Sixth flat," Glenville; his wife, Elisabeth De Graaf, d. Nov. 11, 1810, a. 24ys., 1m., 29d.; Harmanus, b. Aug. 22, 1781, d. in the *Woestyne*, Jan. 7, 1823, Wilmet Groot, his wife, d. April 17, 1840, a. 49ys.; Arent, bp. November 2, 1783. Ch. b: Arent, Oct. 11, 1784, d. Sept. 18, 1854; Elisabeth, May 2, 1787; Annatje, Jan. 15, 1790; Sarah, Nov. 2, 1792, d. Sept. 20, 1816; Arnhout, Dec. 22, 1796.

WOUTER, son of Jeremias, of *de Willegen*, m. Eva Quackenbosch. He lived on Jeremiah Thickstone's old place on the north side of the Mohawk river, near Hoffman's Ferry, opposite three islands, which formerly belonged to Thickstone, afterwards to the Swarts. Ch. bp: Maria, June 7, 1778; Johannes and Jeremia, Sept. 26, 1779; Johannes, April

3, 1781; Maria, Sept. 1, 1782; Helena, May 8, 1784. Ch. b: Jeremiah, Oct. 31, 1785; Jacob, May 9, 1787; Annatje, Jan. 19, 1789; Elisabeth, Feb. 6, 1790; Machtelt, Sept. 2, 1795; Esaias, Nov. 9, 1798.

JESAIAS, son of Teunis and Christina Vrooman, m. Geertruy, dau. of Pieter Vrooman of Schoharie. He resided in Schoharie; made his will Feb. 21, 1781, proved June 14, 1782; mentioned his wife and the following children : *Teunis*, eldest son; Bartholomew, youngest son ; Geertruy, m. ...... Clerk, deceased, in 1781; Sarah; Steyntje; Maria; Susanna, deceased in 1781 leaving Ch.; Engel; Eva, youngest dau.

TEUNIS, son of Jesaias and Geertruy Vrooman, m. Annatje, dau. of Peter Ziellie, Nov. 17, 1770. He resided in Schoharie. Ch. b: *Jesaias*, July 10, 1771; *Pieter*, Jan. 7, 1773; David, April 10, 1777; Bartholomeus, bp. in Schenectady, Jan. 21, 1781.

JAN BAPTIST, son of Teunis, of *de Willege*, m. Catharina, dau. of Coenraad Wiest of Duanesburgh; banns, May 2, 1790. She again m. Simon H. Vedder, April 28, 1799. Ch. b: Sarah, August 30, 1790; Coenraet, Dec 31, 1791; Catharina, Jan. 5, 1794, m. Cornelis Mebie, and d. Dec. 12, 1816; Teunis, Aug. 25, 1796.

PIETER, son of Teunis and Annatie Ziellie of Schoharie, m. Margaret Ingold, March 27, 1792. Ch. bp: Johannes Ingold, b. June 21, and bp. Aug. 9, 1795;

Johannes Ingold, bp. March 21, 1804; Annatie and Elisabet, Jan. 21, 1807.

JESAIAS, son of Jeremia, m. Neeltje Groot. Ch. bp: Jeremias, Feb. 2, 1783; Jeremias, May 9, 1784.

MYNDERT, son of Teunis A., m. Lena, dau. of Abraham Van Eps, January 17, 1797. Ch. b: Margarieta, Sept. 4, 1797; Debora, Sept. 12, 1799; Teunis, Aug. 7, 1801; Abraham, Aug. 4, 1803.

JOHN, son of Jeremia, and Neeltje Van Eps, both of *de Woestyne*, m. Sept. 3, 1786. He d. May 18, 1826, a. 66ys., 2m., 16d., and was buried at West Glenville; she d. April 20, 1846, a. 82ys., 11m., 18d. Ch. b: Maria, March 12, 1787, m. Abraham A. Truax, and d. Sept. 20, 1821; Johannes, Nov. 6, 1788.

JACOB, son of Teunis A., m. Neeltje, dau. of Myndert Wemple. Ch. b: Teunis, May 14, 1798; Myndert, Jan. 4, 1801; Sarah, April 20, 1805.

ESAIAS, son of Jesaias, m. Susanna, Vedder. Ch. b: Neeltje, Feb. 19, 1788; Elijas, (Esaias?), March 8, 1790; Maria, October 26, 1792; Maria, July 10, 1794; Annatje, Feb. 16, 1796.

WOUTER, son of Teunis W., m. Catharina, dau. of Martin Van Olinda. Ch. b: Sara, Oct. 8, 1789; Martinus, Feb. 8, 1794; Martinus, April 1, 1796, d. Jan. 4, 1852, and was buried in the *Woestine*; Elisabeth, Aug. 1, 1799.

WILLEM, son of Jeremiah, and Marytje, both of "Cagnawago district," m.

at Cagnawago; banns, June 12, 1789. Ch. b: Marytje, Jan. 9, 1793; Annatje, Feb. 16, 1795.

JEREMIAH, son of Teunis W., and Cornelia Van Vleck, both of the *Woestine*, m. at "Galloway;" banns, August (?), 1793. Ch: Sarah, b. Oct. 16, 1794.

JEREMIAH, perhaps the same as the last, of Remsenbush, and Margaritje Veeder, of the *Woestine*, m. Sept. 3, 1796.

JEREMIAH, son of Benjamin, and Lena, dau. of Jan Baptist Van Eps, both of the *Woestine*, m. Oct. 8, 1796. She d. Nov. 28, 1855, a. 79ys., near Hoffman's Ferry. Ch: Maria, b. July 6, 1800.

ADAM, son of Teunis A., m. Margarieta, dau. of Abraham Truax. Ch. b: Teunis, Dec. 21, 1796; Sarah, April 18, 1799; Abram Truex, Nov. 9, 1800; Maria, July 30, 1803.

BENJAMIN, son of Benjamin (?), m. Helena Van Eps. Ch: Benjamin, b. April 8, 1798.

JESAJAS, son of Teunis and Sarah, and Elisabeth Peek, both of the *Willegen*, m. June 23, 1798. Ch. b: Teunis, Nov. 8, 1798; Annatje, Dec. 16, 1799.

JESAIAS, son of Teunis and Annatje Zielie, m. Alida, dau. of Adam Vrooman. He lived in the house (still standing) which he built in 1803, on the east corner of Front and Ferry streets; d. in Schenectady, April 25, 1843; she d. March 30, 1852. Ch. b: Margarieta, Oct. 31, 1798; Elisabeth, Aug. 9, 1801;

Teunis Josias Pieter Ziele, Dec. 15, 1804; Alida Maria, Jan. 11, 1809; Maas Simon Schermerhorn, Dec. 5, 1812.

SWEETMAN.

JOHN, m. Margarieta Van Aelstyn, Oct. 3, 1762. Ch. bp: Isaac, April 10, 1763, living in Canajoharie 1788, m. Sarah Smith of Hellenbergh, March 13, 1788; Nicholas, March 10, 1765; Abraham, March 17, 1767.

SWITS.

CORNELIS CLAESE, resident in New Amsterdam as early as 1639, received Dec. 13, 1645, a patent for bouwery No. 5, on Manhattan island, comprising 25 morgens, 296 rods of land, which he sold March 22, 1653, to Willem Beeckman, [*Patents* G G 129 and H H 23.] Feb. 7, 1664, Ariaentje Cornelissen, wid. of Cornelis Claese Swits, and wife of Albert Leenderts of New Amsterdam, presented a petition to the governor and council, praying, that as her farm had been cut up into lots and distributed among the settlers in Harlem, she may be released from a debt due the West India Company by her late husband, who had been murdered by the Indians in 1655; granted. *Dutch MSS.* x³, 37. Cornelis Claese Swits had, by his wife above mentioned, the following children, all bp. in New Amsterdam (New York): *Claes Cornelise;* Apolonitje, Feb. 17, 1641; Jacob and *Isaac,* Oct. 5, 1642; Jacob, Feb. 5, 1645; Abraham, March 10, 1647; Appolonia, Oct. 25, 1648; Cornelis, July 9, 1651; Pieter, Oct. 12, 1653; Cornelia, Oct. 31, 1655.

CLAES, son of Cornelis, was hired Jan. 13, 1663, by Willem Teller of Beverwyck as his *bouw-knecht* to work his bouwery at Schenectady; during the summer following, while at work on Teller's land on the *Groote Vlachte,* he was accidentally killed by Philip Hendrickse Brouwer with a gun, for which offence Brouwer was acquitted both by the governor and by the friends of the deceased. *Notarial Papers* I, 410.

ISAAC, *alias Kleyn* Isaack, son of Cornelis, settled in Schenectady in 1664, in which year he and Claes Frederickse Van Petten hired Willem Teller's bouwery, *gelegen op* Schanechtede *bestaende in woonhuys, Schuer-bergh en bouwlant in twee parcelles genomeneert van den lant meter No. 5 &c.* His village lot was on the west side of Washington street opposite the west end of State street. At the destruction of the town, Feb. 9, 1690, he was carried away captive with his eldest son, but returned the following July. During his absence, a parcel of land owned by him, probably near the junction of Green and Ferry streets, was taken by order of the governor for the erection of a new fort. He repeatedly petitioned the governor and council, once Nov. 2, 1704, and again Oct. 21, 1706, for remuneration in money (£30), or for a land grant. On the 16th of April, 1707, the Indian proprietors gave him a deed for 1,000 acres of land lying along the south side of the Mohawk river, extending from the *Aalplaats* to *Rosendal,* a patent for which was granted to Isaac Swits's son, Cornelius, October 2, 1708.

(*Council Minutes* x 62, *Land Papers* IV, 28, 120). On the 7th day of July, 1702, Isaac Swits bought of Evert, son and heir of Gerrit Bancker, his bouwery on the *Groote Vlachte*, and his village lot about 200ft. square on the south corner of Union and Washington streets, all for £183, 12s; the bouwery remained in possession of the family more than 100 years; the village lot was sold soon after its purchase. He made his will April 1, 1701, proved Oct. 4, 1707, then his 8 children were all living. He m. Susanna, dau. of Simon Groot. Ch. bp: *Cornelis;* Simon, b. January 10, 1680; Abraham; *Isaac*, bp. in Albany, July 28, 1691; Jacob, Oct. 29, 1693, in Albany; *Jacob*, June 26, 1695; Nicolaas, Nov. 10, 1697; Ariaantje, m. Johannes Wemp; Rebecca, m. Alexander Glen.

CORNELIS, eldest son of Isaac, *geboren en wonende tot Schenechtade*, m. Hester Visscher in Albany, Oct. 9, 1702. In 1690 he was carried away to Canada with his father, when Schenectady was burned by the French and Indians; on his marriage he took up his residence in Albany. His wife was buried November 14, 1757. Ch. bp. in Albany: Isaac, July 2, 1703; Femmetje, Jan. 13, 1705, buried June 8, 1725; *Isaac*, Sept. 22, 1706; Tjerk, Feb. 29, 1708; Anna, Oct. 19, 1712, m. Hendrick Beeckman; Tjerk Harmense, Aug. 14, 1714; buried, Aug. 25, 1740; Ariaantje, April 15, 1716; Cornelis, Aug. 30, 1790. [*See Albany Families.*]

ISAAC, son of Cornelis, m. Maria, dau. of Hendrick Vrooman of Schenectady,

Feb. 25, 1728, in Albany. Ch. bp. in Schenectady: Cornelis April 4, 1731; Femmetje, March 11, 1733. Ch. bp. in Albany: Femmetje, August 22, 1735; *Cornelis*, April 23, 1738; Geertruy, Jan. 10, 1742; Catharina, January 10, 1746. Col. Isaac Swits and his wife Maria were living in Albany as late as 1773. [*See Albany Families.*]

CORNELIS, son of Col. Isaac Swits and Maria Vrooman, m. Catharina, dau. of Brandt Schuyler (?), Jan. 15, 1762, in New York. Ch. b. in Albany: Maria, Aug. 7, 1763; Margarita, Sept. 20, 1765; Isaac, Oct. 19, 1767; Johanna, Jan. 2, 1771; *Brandt Schuyler*, Sept. 11, 1772; Femmetje, Aug. 17, 1774; Catharina, Aug. 21, 1776. [*See Albany Families.*]

BRANDT SCHUYLER, son of Cornelis Swits and Catharina Schuyler, m. Alida, dau. of Col. Goosen Van Schaick, Oct. 13, 1797, in Albany. She d. April 1, 1823, a. 52ys., then a wid. Ch: Schuyler, b. Aug. 15, 1798, d. April 15, 1799. See *Albany Families.*]

SIMON, son of Isaac and Susanna Groot, m. Gezina, dau. of Martin Beeckman (?) of Albany, Oct. 29, 1712. She was b. Nov. 25, 1685. He inherited his father's village lot opposite the west end of State street with other real estate upon the *Groote Vlachte.* Ch. b: Gesina, April 20, 1713, m. Daniel De Graaf; Susanna, Nov. 24, 1715; *Isaac*, August 2, 1717; Susanna, Sept. 4, 1719.

JACOB, son of Isaac and Susanna Groot, m. Helena De Witt. Ch. bp: *Isaac*, b.

24

May 17 (*Bible*), bp May 7, (*Church Record*), 1720, d. April 4, 1790, a. 69ys., 11m., 21d.; Jannetje, bp. March 24, 1722; *Andries*, Nov. 24, 1723; Susanna, May 29, 1726, m. Adam W. Vrooman; Jannetje, b. Oct. 25, bp. Oct. 28, 1727, m. Johannes H. Vrooman; *Abraham*, b. Oct. 1, 1730; Cornelis, bp. June 3, 1733; Maria, July 8, 1737.

ISAAC, son of Jacob, m. Volkie, dau. of Hendrick Vrooman, March 11, 174⁷⁄₈. He d. April 4, 1790; she d. March 8, 1804. Ch. bp: Helena, May 24, 1750, m. Jacob A. Vrooman; Maria, April 4, 1752, m. Johannes J. Wemple; Susanna, m. Daniel Toll; Engeltje, Oct. 17, 1756; Jacob, June 22, 1760, d. Sept. 13, 1786; Henderick, Oct. 34, 1762; Jannetje, Feb. 17, 1764, m. Jacobus V. S. Ryley.

HENDERICK, son of the above, d. unmarried, Sept. 18, 1825. His house stood on what is now White street, near State; he left to his next of kin 2½ morgens of land comprehended between the east side of Barret street and the *Cowhorne* kil.

Major ABRAHAM, son of Jacob, m. first Neeltje, dau. of Pieter Van Antwerpen, Feb. 24, 17⁴⁹⁄₅₀; secondly, Elisabeth, dau. of Wouter Vrooman, Dec. 26, 1753; and thirdly, Margaret, dau. of Jan Delamont, Nov. 22, 1760. Major Swits served in the Revolutionary war; owned a house and lot on the north corner of Maiden lane and State streets, extending to Liberty street; d. Aug. 17, 1814, a. 83ys., 10m., 17d.; his last wife, b. Feb. 7, 1735, d. Dec. 23, 1810. Ch. bp: Helena, child

of the first wife, July 15, 1750, m. Myndert De La Grange, " 1789, Oct. 29, *is myn dogter Helena overlede gestorve in de cram;*" Ch. of second wife: *Walterus*, Nov. 10, 1754; Maria, Sept. 18, 1756, "1790, June 6, *is myn docter Marya overlede in sik geweest 5 weke in3dage in de cram gestorve;*" Susanna, May 13, 1759. Ch. of the third wife, born; Eva, July 24, 1761, m. Cornelis Zeger Van Santvoord, d. June 8, 1835; *Jacob*, Nov. 3, 1762; Catarina, May 1, 1764, m. Maas Schermerhorn, d. Aug. 20, 1829; Susanna, b. June 12, (*Bible*), bp. June 11, (*Church Record*), m. Nicolaas F. Clute; Johannes, March 21, 1768, d. Sept. 18, 1774; Jannetie, Aug. 23, 1770, d. Jan. 30, 1774; Elisabeth, March 12, 1772; *Andries*, Nov. 8, 1773; *Johannes*, Dec. 1, 1775, d. March 9, 1827.

Lieut. WALTERUS, son of Abraham, m. Sarah, dau. of Harmanus Peek. He lived on a lot of 60ft. 6in. front on west side of Ferry street, 205ft. 6in. north of Union street, and his blacksmith shop was near the old market, then on the west corner of Front and Ferry streets; he served as lieutenant in the Revolutionary war, and d. Oct. 31, 1823, a. 69ys.; his wid. d. July 18, 1843, a. 82ys., 4m., 6d. Ch: Elisabeth, b. Nov., 1778, m. Frederick P. Clute, d. October 23, 1840; Annatie bp. Dec. 31, 1780, d. Jan. 22, 1862; Margaarita, bp. Nov. 17, 1782. Ch. b: Harmanus, Jan. 20, 1785; Sarah, Nov. 1, 1787; Abram, Apr. 22, 1790, d. at Rockford, Ill., in 1856, a. 65ys.; Jacob, June 15, 1792; Alida, Oct. 11, 1794; Isaac,

Jan. 4, 1797, d. April 30, 1839; John Peek, Jan. 11, 1799; Mary Magdalena, Jan. 9, 1801.

Gen. JACOB, son of Major Abraham Swits. m. Margarieta, dau. of Capt. Abraham Van Eps, Jan. 22, 1791. In the Revolutionary war Gen. Swits served in Capt. Johannes Myndertse's company. In 1810 he was made Maj. General of the state militia; d. Nov. 21, 1835; his widow, b. Jan. 25, 1763, d. April 12, 1839, a. 76ys., 2m., 18d. Ch. b : Catharina, Jan. 10, 1792; *Abraham*, June 3, 1794; Margarieta, April 21, 1796, m Bartholomew Schermerhorn, d. Oct 29, 1864; *Nicholas*, January 5, 1798; Eva, June 10, 1800, d unmarried, Feb. 23, 1872 ; Maria, Oct. 7, 1803, d. Sept. 24, 1856; Jane Helen, October 18, 1805, m. Augustus Elmendorf of Redhook; Jacob, July 27, 1808, d. Sept. 4. 1836; Sally Ann, March 10, 1811.

ANDRIES, son of Major Abraham, m. Maria Hicks. Ch. b : Jannetje, August 5, 1798; John, Oct. 24, 1800; John, Nov. 28, 1802; Abraham, Oct. 13, 1805; Eliza Ann, June 23, 1808 ; Jacob, Nov. 25, 1810.

JOHANNES, son of Major Abraham, m. Maike, dau. of Teunis T. Visscher, Aug. 25, 1803, at the *Boght.* He d. March 9, 1827, a. 51ys., 3m., 9d. ; she d. April 21, 1851, a. 69ys. Ch. b : Margaret, July 21, 1804 ; Teunis, April 12, 1806, d. May 22, 1852, a. 47ys., 1m., 10d. ; Maria, April 29, 1810; Abraham, Nov. 26, 1812; Sebastian, April 12, 1815;

John, May 11, 1817; Catharine Sept. 6, 1820, d. July 27, 1829 ; a dau., Oct. 16, 1823.

ABRAHAM J., son of Gen. Jacob, m. Eveline, eldest child of Jacob L. Viele, Esq., of the " Viele Homestead," Hoosick, N. Y., May 27, 1823. He graduated in the class of 1817, in Union College, and at the Seminary of the Dutch Reformed church, at New Brunswick, N. J., in 1820; became pastor of the Reformed Dutch church, of Schaghticoke, 1823–9, Warwarsing, 1829–35 and Glenville, 1837–42. Ch : John Livingston, b. July 26, 1825, graduated in class of 1846, in Union College, now attorney in Davenport, Iowa.

NICHOLAS, son of Gen. Jacob, m. Angelica C., dau. of Simon P. Vedder of West Milton. He d. in Schenectady, Sept. 18, 1872. Ch. b : Elisabeth Vrooman, June 1, 1825, d. Nov. 27, 1853; Simon Vedder, Nov. 24, 1828, graduated in the class of 1849, Union College ; Jacob N., April 23, 1831, d. May 8, 1868; Charles N., May 24, 1834, d. August 20, 1863 ; Catharina Cecilia, Dec. 4, 1839, m. John L. Hale of Brooklyn ; Mary Augusta, Dec. 17, 1845, m. Rev. Gansevoort D. Consaul of Herkimer.

TAIT.

ROBERT, and Elisabeth McLogan. Ch : Robina, b. Feb. 19, 1791.

TANNAHILL.

JOHN, merchant in 1793. Isabella

Grier, wife of John T., d. March 9, 1846, in her 82d year.

ROBERT, probably son of the last, m. Griselda Donnan, Sept. 22, 1792; in 1813 she had a store on the east side of Church street, second door from Union street, and d. Oct. 5, 1839, in her 88th year. Ch : John, b. April 1, 1793; Mary, bp. Nov. 9, 1794.

TAYLOR.

DANIEL, and Molly Bettys. Ch: Molly Betteys, bp. Oct. 12, 1780.

WILLIAM, from Sligo, Ireland, and Sarah, widow of Patrick More, both of Schenectady, m. Nov. 17, 1745.

SOLOMON, m. Jerusha Smith, 1785.

WALTER, m. Annatje, dau. of Samuel Bratt and Hubertje Yates, •August 19, 1787. She d. about 1856, at the house of her son Walter, in Geneva. Ch. b : Samuel Bratt, Nov. 10, 1788; Sarah, Feb. 21, 1791; Eva Yates, Feb. 25, 1794; Hubertje Yates, July 3, 1797; Anna-Maria, March 1, 1800; Walter Teller, 1802, d. in Geneva, 1856; Joseph Giles Yates, May 25, 1806.

CHARLES, m. Catharina, dau. of Adam Condè. Ch. b : Carel Hanse, Aug. 21, 1799; Cornelius Van Santvoord, Dec. 13, 1801.

GEORGE, of Neskatha, and Baata Clute of Normanskil, m. 1793.

JAMES, and Catharina Browad, m. Mar. 6, 1794.

TEERPENNING.

ELIAS, and Rachel ...... Ch : Maria, bp. Nov. 7, 1784; Sophia, b. Dec. 17, 1786.

PETRUS, and Maria Terwillegen Ch. b : Marytje, Feb. 14, 1786; Rachel, April 14, 1788.

PETRUS, and Margarieta Reneaux, both of Clifton Park, m. Jan. 23, 1790. Ch. b : Jacob, July 2, 1792; Catharina, Oct. 6, 1795; Maria, Jan. 3, 1799; Petrus, July 29, 1801; Sarah, March 25, 1804.

JOHN, JR., and Juliana Halstead, both of Clifton Park, m. Mar. 4, 1790. Ch. b : Timothy, Aug. 16, 1791; John, Dec. 9, 1793; James, July 28, 1796; Keziah, Aug. 4, 1798.

PETRUS, and Elisabeth Brown. Ch : Johannes, b. July 2, 1795.

LUCAS (Lewis), and Jane Vieling, both of Clifton Park, m. Nov. 8, 1797. Ch : Elisabeth, b. Jan. 21, 1798.

JOHN, and Phebe Southard of Schenectady, m. Dec. 25, 1799. Ch : Freelove, b. Nov. 15, 1800.

TELLER.

WILLEM, the first settler of the name in New Netherland, was b. in 1620. In a deposition made July 6, 1698, he stated that he arrived in the province in the year 1639, was sent to Fort Orange by Gov. Kieft, served there as corporal in the West Iudia Company's service, was then advanced to be *Wachtmeester* of the fort; that he had continued his residence at Albany from 1639 to 1692, with some small intermissions upon voyage to New York, Delaware, and one voyage to Holland. He was a trader about 50 years in Albany, from whence he removed to New York in 1692, with his sons. He was one of the earliest proprietors of Schenectady in 1662, though probably never a permanent resident there, and one of the five patentees mentioned in the first patent of the town granted by Gov. Dongan in 1684. His allotments on the *bouwlandt* were numbered five, the foremost lot lying on the west side of, and separated by the *Teller's killetie*, from Elias Van Gyseling's *plantasie;* and his village lot, 200 feet square, was on the east corner of Union and Washington streets. All his real estate in Schenectady was given, in 1700, to his son Johannes, who alone remained behind when the family removed to New York. He made his will Mar. 19, 1698, proved in 1701, and though a prosperous merchant, the inventory of his property amounted to only £910, 10*s.*, 6*p.*; there is reason to believe, that as in the case of his Johannes, he had distributed most of his property among his children before his death. His first wife was Margaret Donchesen; she died before 1664, in which year he made a marriage contract with, and (April 9) m. Maria Varlett, wid. of Paulus Schrick; she d. in 1702, the year after the death of her husband; the inventory of her estate amounted to £1,275, 12*s.*, 9*p.* Ch. b: Andries, b. 1642, m. Sophia, dau. of Oloff Van Cortlandt of New York, May

6, 1671; Helena, 1645, m. first, Cornelis Bogardus, son of the noted Anneke Janse; secondly, Francois Rombouts; Maria, 1648, m. first, Pieter Van Alen, secondly ...... Lookerman's; Elisabeth, 1652, m. first, Abraham Van Tricht, and secondly, Melgert Wynantse Van der Poel; Jacob, 1655, m. Christina Wessells of New York, Oct. 24, 1683; Willem, 1657, m. Rachel Kiersted in New York, Nov. 19, 1686; *Johannes*, 1659, settled in Schenectady; Jannetie, m. Arent Philipse Schuyler; Caspar. [*See Albany Families.*]

JOHANNES, son of Willem, m. Susanna, dau. of Capt. Johannes Wendel of Albany, August 18, 1686. In 1700 his father, "in consideration that his son Johannes was much reduced in property at the burning of Schenectady in 1690," conveyed to him his bouwery and village lot. He was carried away to Canada by the French in 1690; made his will May 15, 1725, and spoke of sons Johannes, Willem, Jacob, and dau. Margareta, wife of Jacob Schermerhorn; Maria, wife of Abraham Glen; and Annatie, wife of Harmanus Vedder; d. May 28, 1725. Ch. bp: Johannes; Margareta, Feb. 19, 1693, in Albany, m. Jacob Schermerhorn; *Willem*, Oct. 4, 1695, in Albany; Jacobus, July 15, 1698, in Albany; Maria, Dec. 25, 1700, m. Abraham Glen; Anna, February 20, 1704, m. Harmanus Vedder.

WILLIAM, son of Johannes, b. in Albany, and Catharina, dau. of Willem Van Alen of Albany, were m. March 5, 1731. He lived on the Teller bouwery

No. 5, next west of Teller's *killetie*; made his will April 9, 1752, proved Nov. 6, 1764, all his Ch. then living, also a stepson, Johannes Schoonmaker, son of his second wife; d. in 1757 ; his first wife d. April 25, 1732, and was buried in Albany. Ch : *Johannes*, child of the first wife, b Nov. 24, 1732; Ch of second wife, bp : *Jacobus*, March 17, 1738; *Willem*, June 14, 1740 ; Gerrit Teunise, June 30, 1745.

JOHANNES, son of Willem, m. Jannetje, dau. of Jan Delamont, Oct. 8, 1761. He d. Mar. 5, 1784. Ch. b : Catarina, Sept. 4, 1762, m. Alexander Kelly, d. Nov. 12, 1817 ; *Johannes*, May 18, 1765 ; Annatje, bp. May 1, 1768, m. Bartholomew Schermerhorn ; Eva, bp. March 20, 1774, m. Johannes Clute, and d. April 29, 1853, a. 80ys. ; Willem, bp. Jan. 5, 1777, m. Margareta Peek, lived in Schoharie.

WILLEM, son of Willem, m. first, Helena, dau. of Jacobus Van Eps ; and secondly, Esther Hederington, March 15, 1789. By his father's will, he became possessed of bouwery No. 5, next west of Teller's *killetie*. Ch. bp : Annatie, Feb. 14, 1768 ; Susanna, Oct. 31, 1773, m. Joshua Burnham ; *Jacobus*, July 21, 1776 ; Willem, b April 30, 1779 ; Margarita, bp. Dec. 16, 1781 ; *Johannes*, b. July 15, 1784; Engeltie, b. June 8, 1787.

JACOBUS, son of Willem, m. Maria, dau. of Joseph R. Yates, Nov. 20, 1762. In 1764 he was an Indian trader in company with John and Henry Glen ; from his father, inherited part of the Teller lot on the east corner of Washington and Union streets ; made his will July 4, 1783, proved Feb. 12, 1785 ; killed by the Indians, Sept. 27, 1784. Ch. bp : Annatie, m. John Bonney ; *Willem*, June 4, 1775.

JOHANNES, son of Johannes, m. Esther, dau. of Carel Hansen Toll, May 15, 1787. He d. March 29, 1790, a. 25ys., 10m., 11d. ; she afterwards m. Frederic Van Petten, and d. Jan. 10, 1812. Ch. b : Jannetie, March 7, (Feb. 28), 1788, m. Emmanuel De Graaf of Amsterdam ; Elisabeth, Feb. 20, 1790.

Col. HENRY REMSEN, and Maria Terwilleger, both of the *Boght*, m. Aug. 11, 1788. He d. Feb. 28, 1829, in his 64th year ; she d. March 8, 1813, aged 44ys. Ch. b : Rebecca, Sept. 18, 1789 ; Jannetje, June 27, 1792, m. Rev. Nicholas Marselis ; John Remsen, Sept 11, 1795 ; James, Oct. 21, 1798 ; Mary, July 18, 1801.

WILLEM, son of Jacobus, m. Cornelia, dau. of Pieter Yates of Albany (?). He was an attorney-at-law ; the first surrogate of the county of Schenectady ; lived on north side of Union street, near Washington street ; d. July 19, 1815, a. 40ys. ; she d Jan. 12, 1837, in her 62d year. Ch. b : Mary, July 16, 1796 ; Anna Maria, March 16, 1798 ; Jacobus, March 2, 1800 ; Peter Yates, May 31, 1802 ; Joseph Yates, Aug. 25, 1804, d. July 11, 1815 ; Magdalena, Aug. 14, 1809 ; Catharine, Oct. 20, 1812.

Jacobus, son of Willem, m. Catharine Stuart, Nov. 24, 1797. Ch. b: Lena, Aug. 14, 1798; John, Aug. 18, 1800, d. Oct. 8, 1855; Maria, March 1, 1804; William James, March 13, 1807, d. Sept. 3, 1851; Levi Willard, Nov. 1, 1809.

Remsen, m. Catharina McDonald Ch. b: Nancy, April 10, 1793; Isaac, May 29, 1796; Michael, May 29, 1798; John, Feb. 15, 1800; Henry, Jan. 1, 1802; Mary, Sept. 9, 1804; Gitty Caroline, March 19, 1806; Lucina, May 13, 1808.

John, son of Willem, m. Catharine Clute. He d. July 14, 1852. Ch. b: William Alexander, March 15, 1805; Jacob, April 19, 1807; James Edward, June 24, 1809, d. Jan. 31, 1834; Maria Eliza, Dec. 2, 1811; Susan, March 3, 1814; Sally Anne, Aug. 23, 1816; Helen Margaret, Dec. 2, 1818; John Edward, Nov. 20, 1820; Catharine Jane, Oct. 7, 1822.

TEMPLE.

Alexander, of Ballston, and Maria Flansburgh of Schenectady, m. April 16, 1786.

TEMPLETON.

Thomas, and Margaret Stewart. Ch. bp: Margary, Oct. 22, 1781; William, Sept. 14, 1783.

John, and Barbara Black. Ch. b: John, Oct. 16, 1790; Mary, March 23, 1792.

TEN EYCK.

Coenraad, of New Amsterdam, tanner and shoemaker. Ch. bp. in N. A.:

Margariet, Aug. 20, 1651; Tobias, Jan. 26, 1653; Coenraad, November 22, 1654; Hendrick, Apr. 30, 1656; Matthys, Mar. 20, 1658; Margriet, Oct. 22, 1659; Andries, Jan. 15, 1662; Metje, April 11, 1664; *Jacob;* Dirk. [*See Albany Families.*]

Jacob, son of Coenraad, shoemaker, of Albany, m. Geertje, dau of Barent Pieterse Coeymans, the miller; she was b. April 23, 1654, and d. Feb. 2, (27), 1736; made her will Sept. 6, 1716, proved July 10, 1736, then a wid., and spoke of the following Ch., except Andries; Coenraat, b. April 9, 1678; Barent; Mayken, b April 2, 1685, m. Andries Van Petten of Schenectady, Dec. 26, 1712; Andries, bp. March 25, 1688; Anneken, bp. Aug. 20, 1693, m. Johannes Bleecker, and d. Dec. 9, 1738; *Henrik.* [*See Albany Families.*]

Henrik, son of Jacob, of Albany, baker, m. Margarita Bleecker, Nov. 28, 1706. Ch. bp. in Albany: Jacob, Jan. 25, 1708; Johannes, October 28, 1710; Geertie, Jan. 18, 1713; Margarita, May 10, 1715; *Tobias,* b. Aug. 15, and bp. Aug. 18, 1717; Henrik, May 8, 1720; Barent, Sept. 9, 1722; Hendrik, Sept. 5, 1725. [*See Albany Families.*]

Tobias, son of Henrik, of Albany, m. Rachel, dau. of Johannes De Peyster of Albany, Sept. 7, 1750. He was a merchant; settled in Schenectady about 1750; built and lived in the house, now owned and occupied by Mr. Nicholas Cain, in Front street; made will 1774, proved May 24, 1785, wife and all his Ch. then living; d. Feb. 9, 1785; she d. April 6, 1787, a. 58ys., 11m., 19d., and was buried in the church at Albany. Ch. bp: *Myndert Schuyler*, Feb. 9, 1753; *Hendrick*, July 27, 1755; Johannes De Peyster, d. April 9, 1798, in Albany; Jacob, July 29, 1759; *Jacob*, Feb. 15, 1761; Tobias, b. Sept. 12, 1763, d. Feb. 9, 1785; Barent, bp. Nov. 2, 1766, d. Jan. 31, 1796.

MYNDERT SCHUYLER, son of Tobias, m. first, Elsje, dau. of Johannes Sanders, Oct. 20 (27), 1774; and secondly, Margareta, dau. of Harmanus F. Visscher, and wid. of John C. Van Everen, Dec. 30, 1797, in Caughnawaga. In 1794, and previously, he was a merchant in Schenectady; removed to Caughnawaga, where he d. Oct. 4, 1805. His first wife d. Feb. 12, 1797, a. 43ys., 11m. Ch: Tobias, bp. May 5, 1776; *Johannes Sanders*, b. Sept. 3, 1778; Anna, b. Feb. 20, 1780, m. Nicolaas S. son of Henry H. Van Rensselaer, Jan. 16, 1802; Debora, b. Aug. 20, 1782; Rachel, b. Aug. 22, 1785; Tobias, b. May 6, 1787; Jacob Glen, b. Feb. 14, 1789, d. April 4, 1791; Elsie Sanders, dau. of the second wife, b. Sept. 9, 1799.

JACOB, son of Tobias, m. Elisabeth De Graaf, dau. of Nicolaas De Graaf. He was a merchant in Schenectady. Ch. bp: Tobias, July 16, 1780; Nicolaas, Dec. 30, 1781; Rachel, Oct. 5, 1783; Catlyntje, b. May 14, 1786; Elsje, Aug. 6, 1788; Elisabeth, bp. Jan. 19, 1794.

Capt. HENDERICK, son of Tobias, m. first, Antje, dau. of Jan Baptist Van Eps;

and secondly, Maria Dorothea, dau. of Domine Barent Vrooman, and widow of John L. V. Le Tonnelier. He was captain in the Second Connecticut regiment in the Revolutionary war, and at the storming of Stony Point was wounded in the arm; retired from the service about 1783, on account of sickness, and in 1807 received a pension of 120 dollars; made his will July 18, 1814, proved June 29, 1816; spoke of wife Maria, and children Tobias and Maria. Ch: Tobias, bp. July 18, 1784, followed the sea for some years; Maria, b. April 11, 1787.

COENRAAT, m. Jane Thompson. Ch. bp: John Thompson, Sept. 6, 1795; Elsje Schenck, June 3, 1798.

JOHN SANDERS, son of Myndert Schuyler, m. Eliza, dau. of Ephraim Wemple of Florida, July 20, 1799, at Caughnawaga. He d. July 15, 1838. Ch. b: Myndert Schuyler, in Florida, April 3, 1800, d. July 3, 1801; Angeneitie, Oct. 20, 1801, in Charlestown, Montgomery county; Elsie, Nov. 10, 1803; Rebecca, Aug. 8, 1805; Margaret Ann, Nov. 1, 1808, in Scotia, m. Peter Vrooman of Schenectady.

TERWILLEGER.

HARMANUS, from Ulster county, m. Magdalena, dau. of Simon Veeder, Dec. 22, 1748. Ch. bp: *Salomon*, March 26, 1749; Margrieta, May 5, 1751; Simon, Sept. 12, 1753; Catarina, Jan. 11, 1756; Jannetje, Dec. 13, 1761; Barent Veeder, Dec. 15, 1765.

DIRK, m. Sarah Le Roy. Ch. bp: Catarina, Oct. 30, 1757; Simon, March 23, 1760; Jannetje, Feb. 27, 1763.

SALOMON, m. Geertruy, dau. of Frederic Van Petten. Ch. bp: Harmanus, Dec. 31, 1780; Elisabeth, May 9, 1784. Ch. b: Frederick, Dec. 9, 1786; Lena, Oct. 15, 1789; Margarieta, Dec. 16, 1792.

THOMAS, m. Christina Van Olinda. Ch: Jacobus, b. July 30, 1795.

TEUNISSE.

PHILIP, m. Debora, dau. of Jacobus La Grange. Ch: Cornelis, bp. March 24, 1751.

JURRIAEN, sold a lot of land to Dirk Hesselingh before 1672.

SWEER, see Van Velsen.

THESSCHENMAECKER.

PETRUS, first minister of the church in Schenectady, officiated in Kingston in 1676, and gained the esteem and respect of the people of that place to such a degree that they petitioned for his continuance as their minister; in 1679 ordained in New York by a classis comprising the ministers then settled in this province, as minister of the church at New Castle, on the Delaware; 1684 settled at Schenectady as pastor of this church; 1690 in the destruction of the village, burned in the parsonage house then standing upon the present church lot.

THOMAS.

JOHN, m. Catharina Speck. Ch: Johannes, bp. Jan. 20, 1760.

STEWBREY (Abrie), in Schenectady 1754, m. Lena Van Eps.

DAVID, m. Nancy Smith. Ch: Judy, b. July 14, 1796.

SUSANNA, member of the church in 1701.

THOMPSON.

THOMAS, m. Catharina ...... Ch: Rachel, b. May 5, 1785.

AARON, and Margariet Davidson (Wilson), both of Corrysbosch, m. Dec. 6, 1785. Ch: Margariet, b. Jan. 14, 1787.

JAMES, and Esther Harrison, m. Aug. 1, 1797.

THOMSON.

ELIAS, m. Rhoda Nichols. Ch: Mary, b. Sept. 19, 1778, bp. May 18, 1781.

JOHN, m. Mary Lyell. He d. July 11, 1850, a. 71ys. (Schenectady *Reflector*), or July 11, 1851, a. 72ys. (gravestone); Ch: Thomas Lyell, b. March 20, 1799.

THORN.

Lieut. SAMUEL, m. Helena, dau. of Adam Van Slyck. Ch. bp: Jonathan, Jan. 10, 1779; Adam Van Slyck, Aug. 13, 1780; Robert Livingston, March 24, 1782. Ch. b: Jacobus Van Slyck, Aug. 28, 1785; Jannetje, Jan. 13, 1790; Jan Baptist Van Eps, June 25, 1794; Elisabeth, March 28, 1796; Helena, May 28, 1798; Gilbert, May 26, 1800; Samuel, June 16, 1801.

THORNTON.

JAMES, m. Antje Schermerhorn. Ch; Dorcas, bp. June 2, 1770. Ch. b : Mary, Sept. 9, 1785; William, Feb. 17, 1793; Margarieta, April 14, 1795.

MATTHEW, m. Mary Crafford. Ch : Dorcas, bp. June 12, 1770.

THOMAS, m. Elisabeth Richardson. Ch. bp: William, March 4, 1780; Juratta, Oct. 23, 1782; Elisabeth, March 20, 1785. Ch. b; John, Dec. 20, 1787; Thomas, Nov. 23, 1792; Charles, bp. June 12, 1796; George b. Jan. 2, 1799.

SAMUEL, and Engeltie Peek, m. July 8, 1798.

JOHN, m. Ann (Adelia) Clyde. Ch. b : John Clyde, July 28, 1793 ; John Clyde, Nov. 24, 1795; Adelia, Aug. 27, 1797; William Anderson, Aug. 30, 1801 ; Caty Agnes, Oct. 30, 1804.

ABRAHAM, and Margaret Peek, both of the *Woestyne,* m. Oct. 9, 1796. Ch. b : Jacobus, June 28, 1797 ; Arent, Dec. 17, 1799.

TIBER.

JOSEPH, m. Debora Smitt. Ch : John, bp. Jan. 25, 1775.

TICKSTON (THICKSTONE).

JEREMI, m. Rachel, sister of Carel Hanse Toll, and wid. of David Wilemse, in 1697. He lived near and above Hoffman's Ferry on a farm received from his brother-in-law, Carel Hanse Toll. The Swarts afterwards owned his farm ; it was first patented to Johannes Luykasse.

Ch. bp : Elisabeth, October 19, 1698, m. Wouter Swart; Debora, Oct. 30, 1701, m. Isaac De Graaf.

TIDD.

SAMUEL, m. Maria Reneaux. Ch : Jesse, bp. Feb. 14, 1784; Samuel, b. Feb. 12, 1786.

JEREMIAH, m. Ariaantje Fouler, July 8, 1798.

TIETSOORT.

CLAES WILLEMSE, in Schenectady in 1681, afterwards in Dutchess county.

TILGHMAN.

RICHARD, m. Sarah Morell. Ch : Angelica, b. Nov. 10, 1794.

TILLENBACH.

MARTINUS, m. Elisabeth Casselman. Ch : Martinus, b. Nov. 12, 1726.

TILLEY.

SAMUEL, and Ann Gilland, m. Sept. 9, 1764.

TIMMERMAN.

JACOB, m. Margaret Schitzen. Ch : John Jurriaan, bp. Jan. 20, 1734.

TINKENHOWER.

JACOB, m. Maria Rysenberg (Rypenberger). Ch : Jurry, bp. April 22, 1764; Elisabeth, b. Feb. 6, 1766.

TITHSOART.

WILLEM, m. Catharina Yong. Ch : Elisabeth, bp. Aug. 19, 1772.

TITLY.

JOHN, m. Catrien Titly. Ch: Eloner, bp. Aug. 3, 1764.

TOBI (TOBEY ?).

MARIA, member of the church 1719.

TOLES.

ELIJAH, m. Helena Bear. Ch. b: Christina, March 24, 1792; George William, Aug. 15, 1793.

TOLHAMER.

DAVID, m. Anna Teller. Ch. b: Barent, June 1, 1791; Barent (?), b. June 1 (*sic*), bp. Sept. 4, 1791 (?).

TOLL.

CAREL HANSEN, first settled on land near, or at Hoffman's Ferry, which he bought of Hendrick Cuyler and Geraldus Cambefort on the north side of the river, and of Johannes Luykasse on the south side; which latter parcel he conveyed to his brother-in-law, Jeremiah Tickstone, who m. his sister Rachel. His lands on the north side extended from *Taquaatsera* or *Droybergh* kil, the boundary between the 6th and 7th flats westwardly, to the lands of heirs of Philip Groot, i.e. to about " Swarts Ferry." In 1712 he purchased a parcel of land at *Maalwyck*, from Joseph Clement, to which he removed. About this time he also owned the lot in the village of Schenectady on the south corner of Union and Church streets, extending eastwardly along the former street, and including the Court House lot, which latter lot, 100ft. front by 210ft., he sold in 1712 to Isaac Van Valken-

burgh for £53 ($132.50). Carel Hansen, m. Lysbet, dau. of Daniel Rinckhout of Albany; d. March, 1737 or 1738. Ch. bp: Eva, m. Evert Van Eps; Neeltje, June 20, 1786, in Albany; *Daniel*, b. July, bp. Aug. 11, 1691, in Albany, m. Margarita Bratt; Neeltje, bp. July 7, 1695, m. Johannes Van Eps; *Simon*, May 8, 1698, in Albany; Abraham, July 28, 1700, in Schenectady; Bregje, April 18, 1703, in Schenectady, m. Adriaan Van Slyck; Lysbeth, Jan. 29, 1706, m. Pieter Cornu. [*See Albany Families.*]

Capt. DANIEL, son of Carel Hansen, m. Grietje, dau. of Samuel Bratt, Sept. 8, 1717. She was b. March 24, 1686, and d. March 22, 1743; he made his will 1747, proved Oct. 18, 1748, in which he mentioned his dau. Susanna, Hannah and Geertruy, and son Johannes, then deceased. " Capt. Toll d. July 18, 1748, having been found barbarously murdered by a party of French Indians, at a place (in the present town of Glenville) called the *Kleykuil*, a short distance, less than half a mile north of *Beukendaal*, accompanied by Dirk Van Vorst." Ch. b: Susanna, Feb. 12, 1718; *Johannes*, Aug. 13, 1719, d. Dec. 31, 1746;. Elisabeth, b. Jan. 19 (Bible), bp. Jan. 14 (*Church Record*), 1721, m. Rev. Cornelis Van Santvoord, d. Oct. 14, 1746; Anna or Hanna, Sept. 6, 1722, m. Thomas Ferry, d. Sept. 30, 1751; Samuel, Jan. 31 (30), 1725, d. Jan. 14, 174⅚ *sine prole;* Eva, Dec. 11, 1726, d. January 14, 174⅚ *sine prole;* Geertruy, Aug. 7 (10), 1729, m. Jillis Clute, d. Aug. 12, 1756.

SIMON, son of Carel Hansen, b. on Roeloff Jansen's kil, m. Hester, dau. of Jesse De Graaf, June 13, 1731. He made his will Mar. 7, 1776, proved June 28, 1782, in which he spoke of wife Hester, then living, and all his children. He is said to have d. in 1777, and his wife in 1793. Ch. bp: Elisabeth, Oct. 31, 1731, m. John Fairly; *Carel Hansen*, Sept. 2, 1733, m. Maria Kittle; Alida, Feb. 23, 1735, m. Johannes Mebie; Anneke, Dec. 21, 1737, m. Willem Kittle; Aeffie, 1739 (?); Jesse and *Johannes*, July 24, 1743; *Jesse*, May 18, 1746, m. Maritie Viele; Eva, Jan. 15, 1749, m. Lodovicus Viele; *Daniel*, Oct. 27, 1751, m. Susanna Swits; Sarah, July 25, 1756, m. Stephanus Viele.

JOHANNES, son of Daniel, m. Eva Van Petten, Dec. 23, 1742, d. Dec. 31, 1746. Ch. b : Carel, Oct. 11, 1743, d. Oct. 31, 1743; Carel, Nov. 4, 1744, d. Jan. 10, 174⅘; *Carel Hansen*, Feb. 10, 1746, m. Elisabeth Ryley.

CAREL HANSEN, son of Simon, m. Maria Kettel, Oct. 2, 1759. Ch. bp: Neeltje, January 20, 1760; Hester, July 11, 1762; Simon, Jan. 1, 1763; Elisabeth, May 14, 1769; Maria, b. Oct. 5, and bp. Nov. 3, 1771, in Albany.

JOHANNES, son of Simon, m. Catarina, dau. of Arent Vedder and Sarah Van de Bogart, Dec. 22, 1764. Ch. bp : Hester, June 23, 1765, m. Abraham Groot; *Simon*, April 10, 1768, m. Maritie Vedder; Arent, Aug. 18, 1770, d. Dec. 7, 1787, of hydrophobia, caused by the bite of a rabid dog; Sarah, May 30, 1773, m. Isaac De Graaf; *Johannes; Daniel*, March 3, 1776; Maria, Nov. 22, 1778, m. Nicolaas V. Wemple; Carel Hansen, Oct. 14, 1781, d. young.

CAREL HANSEN, son of Johannes, m. Elisabeth, dau. of Philip Ryley, Jan. 10 (11), 1768. He d. Aug. 26, 1832; she d. Oct. 25, 1839. Ch. b : Hester, July, 24, 1768, m. first, Johannes Teller, May 15, 1787; secondly, Frederic Van Petten, d. at Amsterdam, Jan. 10, 1812; Eva, Oct. 5, 1771, m. Johannes C. Veeder; Johannes, Jan. 23, 1775, d. Sept. 22, 1776; Rebecca, April 1, 1778, m. David Pruyn, and d. Dec. 25, 1867; *Johannes*, Sept. 13, 1780; Sara, Sept. 21, 1783, m. Arent Marselis of Amsterdam, d. April 9, 1827; Hanna, Mar. 17, (18), 1788, m. Simon P. Van Patten; Philip, May 10, 1793, m. Nancy, dau. of Isaac De Graaf, d. Aug. 17, 1862.

DANIEL, son of Simon, m. Susanna, dau. of Isaac Jacobse Swits, July 2, 1775. She d. in Glenville about Jan. 1, 1831, "at an advanced age." Ch. bp: Hester, April 28, 1776, m. Albert Condè; Volkje, May 3, 1778, m. Pieter F. Veeder; Simon, May 6, 1780; Isaac, May 19, 1782; Carel Hansen, October 17, 1784, d. in Memphis, Onondaga county, July 1869; Helena, b. July 27, 1786; Elizabeth, b. March 2, 1789; Maria, bp. August 14, 1791; John, b. August 3, 1793; Jacob Swits, b. March 2, 1797.

JOHANNES, son of Johannes (?), m. Elisabeth W. Rynex. He was buried

Sept. 12, 1804; she d. Jan. 2, 1831, in her 72d year. Ch. b: Letty, June 5, 1793; Rachel, July 30, 1794; Catharine, April 3, 1796.

JESSE, son of Simon, m. Maritie Viele. He lived in Saratoga. Ch: Anna, b. Dec. 31, 1786, bp. in Albany, Feb. 19, 1787.

SIMON, son of Johannes, m. Maritie Vedder. Ch. b: John Symon, Sept. 18, 1794; Catharina, Mar. 29, 1796; Esther, Nov. 18, 1798; John, Apr. 26, 1800; Maria, Nov. 26, 1801; Jacob, Dec. 2, 1807.

DANIEL, son of Johannes, m. Catalyna Wemple, June 20, 1801. He was a physician and d. in Schenectady, April 20, 1849; she was b. Jan. 15, 1777, and d. Feb. 16, 1812.

JOHANNES, son of Carel Hansen, m. Nancy, dau. of Barent Mynderse, Jan. 31, 1802. She was b. May 16, 1779, d. Oct. 9, 1859. He graduated at Union College in 1799, entered the ministry of the Reformed Dutch church, d. Oct. 21, 1849. Ch. b: Carel Hansen, April 8, 1804; Nicholas Mynderse, June 7, 1806, d. Aug. 29, 1847; Philip Ryley, Feb. 8, 1811; Jane Sarah, Sept. 8, 1815, d. 1863.

TOMLINSON.

DAVID, came from Connecticut about 1798, for many years a merchant on the west corner of Union and Church streets.

TONELLIER.

See Le Tonellier.

TOOLE.

JOHN, from Ireland, and Mary Moore from New York, both residing here, m. May 13, 1750.

TOOPER.

WILLIAM, and Polly Hilton. Ch: Christiaan, b. Nov. 28, 1788.

TOTTEN.

SAMUEL, and Frances Hopson. Ch: Sophia and Elisabeth, b. April 23, 1789.

JOSEPH, and Anna Van Leuren. Ch: Leffert, b. July 26, 1796.

TOURNEUR.

JACOBUS and Jacomyntje De Grauw. Ch. bp: Johannes, March 5, 1774; Rachel, b. March 27, bp. May 3, 1776; Petrus, July 4, 1780; Margarita, Aug. 8, 1782; Effe and Lena, Oct. 23, 1784.

TRAINER.

JOHN, and Martha Springer. Ch: Margarieta, b. July 30, 1788.

TROWBRIDGE.

STEPHEN, and Isabella Frazier. Ch William Frazier, bp. Jan. 23, 1785.

TRUAX (DU TRIEUX, DU TRUY).

PHILIP DU TRIEUX, a Walloon, born in 1585, was in New Amsterdam during Minuit's administration 1624–29; was appointed court messenger in 1638; in 1640 received a patent for land in "Smits valley;" his wife was Susanna De Scheene who was living as late as 1654. Ch: Rebecca, m. Simon Simonse Groot; Sara, m.

Isaac De Foreest in New Amsterdam, June, 1641; Susanna, m. Evert Janse Wendel of Beverwyck, July 31, 1644; Rachel, m. first, Hendrick Van Bommel in New Amsterdam, Sept. 3, 1656, and secondly, Dirk Janse De Groot, Aug. 8, 1677; Abraham was in Beverwyck in 1656; *Isaac,* bp. in New Amsterdam, April 21, 1642; Jacob, bp. in New Amsterdam, Dec. 7, 1645, m. Lysbeth Post in New York, Sept. 26, 1674.

ISAAC, son of Philip, m. Maria, dau. of Willem Brouwer of Albany. He settled upon the " Second flat," on the south side of the Mohawk, in the present town of Rotterdam, as early as 1670 with his cousin (?) Jacobus Peek, as appears by a petition to, and grant from Gov. Andros. Ch. bp: *Abraham;* Eva, m. Dirk Stouwt; Sarah, m. Gillis Truax; *Isaac,* March 2, 1690, in Albany; Lysbeth, July 3, 1692, in Albany, m. Evert Van Eps; *Jacob,* Oct. 9, 1694; Johannes, Dec. 11, 1696, in Albany.

ABRAHAM, son of Isaac, m. Christina, dau. of Gillis De La Grange of Albany. He d. March 16, 1770; she d. Jan. 7, 1773. Ch. b : Maria, *geboren op de Normanskil,* April 2, 1712, and bp. in the Lutheran church in Albany, m. first, Johannes Bratt of Schenectady, and secondly, Evert Wendel of Albany; Jannetie, Aug. 11, 1713, m. Cornelis Van Slyck; *Isaac,* Jan. 13, 1715; Annatie, April 10, 1717, m. Ryckert Van Vranken jr.; *Johannes,* March 24, 1718; *Jillis,* July 7, (Family Bible), bp. June 11, 1719 (*Church Record*); *Philip,* Nov. 5,

1720; *Andries,* Aug. 21, 1722; *Christiaan,* Feb. 17, 1724; Elisabeth, May 19, 1725, m. Caleb Beck; Susanna, Nov. 7, 1726, d. March 4, 1805, a. 78ys., 4m.; her portrait is in possession of Doctor Andrew Truax; Abraham, Feb. 8, 1728; Sarah, Sept. 20, 1729, m. Nicolaas Van der Volgen; Cathlyntje, Feb. 28, 1731, m. Nicolaas De Graaf.

ISAAC, son of Isaac, m. Catalina, dau. of Martin Van Benthuysen, October 23, 1719. He owned a lot on the east side of Washington street, third from Front street, inherited probably by his wife. In 1782 he is said to have been the oldest man in the town. Ch : Maritje, bp. Sept. 11, 1720, m. Jan Baptist Van Eps; *Pieter,* b. Aug. 27, 1723; *Isaac,* b. May 14, 1726. Ch. bp : Philip (?), d. in Wilmington, Del., 1795, a. 64ys.; Sara, March 26, 1732; Sophia, July 20, 1735, m. Andries Truex; Martinus, May 14, 1738; Margrietje, Nov. 30, 1740, m. Johannes Van Driessen.

JACOB, son of Isaac, m. Lysbet, dau. of Gillis De La Grange of Albany, July 11, 1724. He lived 7 miles south of Schenectady on the old Albany road. His wife d. May 10, 1788. Ch. b : *Isaac,* May 8, 1726 *des morgens vroes; Jillis,* November 12, 1727 *omtrent middernagt;* Maria, June 15, 1729. m. Emmanuel Adams; *Christiaan De La Grange,* Feb. 10, 1731; Willem, Sept. 15, 1732, m. Ann Eliza Zebel, April 17, 1760; Johannes, Nov. 1, 1734; *Jacob* and *Abraham,* April 4, 1737; *Andries,* bp. April 29, 1739.

ISAAC, son of Abraham, m. Engeltie, dau. of Caleb Beck, July 24, 1742. She d. June 27, 1758. Ch. b: *Abraham*, Jan. 2, 1743; Anna, July 8, 1744, d. Feb. 7, 1745; Christina, Feb. 1, 1746, m. Robert Moyston; *Caleb*, Nov. 19, 1747; *Johannes*, Aug. 29, 1749; Anna, Aug. 8, 1751, m. Simon C. Groot; Sarah, Dec. 11, 1753; *Isaac*, July 16, 1756, d. Dec. 21, 1854, a. 98ys., 7m., 5d.

JOHANNES, son of Abraham, m. Alida, dau. of Matthys Nak of Albany. In 1757 she m. Pieter Fonda. Ch: Agnietje, bp. Nov. 1, 1744; Jannetie, m. Arent S. Vedder.

GILLIS, son of Abraham, m. first, Dorothea, dau. of Wouter Vrooman, Oct. 27, 1744, secondly, Sarah, dau. of Isaac Truex, March 17, 174⅜. Ch: Wouter Vrooman, b. Dec. 18, 1745. Ch. bp: Abraham, Oct. 15, 1749; Isaac, Oct. 20, 1751; Dorothea, Sept. 3, 1754.

GILLIS, son of Jacob, m. first, Ariaantje Jansen, and secondly, Engeltie Evertsen. Ch: Jacob, ch. of the first wife, bp. in Albany, June 26, 1755; Jacob, ch. of the second wife, bp. in Schenectady, May 3, 1761.

ISAAC, son of Isaac, m. Susanna, dau. of Hendrick Roseboom of Albany, April 26, 1755. She d. July 7, 1819, a. 80ys., 23d. Ch. bp: Hendrick, April 4, 1756; Hendrick, Oct. 23, 1757; *Isaac*, May 3, 1759; *Hendrick*, Oct. 4, 1761; Pieter, Dec. 23, 1764; Pieter, Dec. 25, 1766; Cathalyna, b. Nov. 9, 1770; Cornelis, b. April 9, 1773.

JACOB, son of Jacob, m. Catharina Dochsteder. Ch. b. (bp. in Albany): *Jacob*, January 8, 1780; Caty, July 23, 1783; Elisabeth, Dec. 16, 1786; John, Dec. 28, 1790.

PIETER, son of Isaac, m. Jacoba, dau. of Domine Cornelis Van Santvoord, *van Staten Eiland*, Feb. 26, 174⅜. He made his will April 12, 1796, proved Aug. 21, 1822; spoke of son, Isaac P. and 6 dau., Catalina, Nancy, Sophia, Mary, Sarah, Willempie, also of Cobatie, dau. of Adam Condé, Cobatie, dau. of Harmen Wessels and Cobatie, dau. of Isaac Truex; he was b. Aug. 27, 1725, d. Aug. 29, 1797. His wife d. March 24, 1794, a. 65ys., 3m., 10d. Ch. bp: Catlina, July 2, 1749; Cornelis, Feb. 17, 1751; Catalina, April 5, 1752, m. Adam Condé; Anna, Sept. 3, 1754; Sophia, Dec. 25, 1756; Sophia, July 1, 1759, m. Harmanus Wessels; Maria, Nov. 22, 1761; Sarah, Sept. 18, 1764, m. Jacobus J. Van Vorst; Willempie, March 1, 1767, m. Jacobus J. Van Vorst, d. in Glenville, Sept., 1855, in her 98th year; *Isaac*, May 5, 1771.

ISAAC, son of Jacob, m. Marytje, dau. of Johannes Wyngaard of Albany, June 16, 1750, in Albany. He lived 7 miles south of Schenectady; d. April 17, 1808, a. 81ys., 10m., 27d. Ch. b: Jacob, April 16, 1751, made will Dec. 31, 1814, proved May 10, 1816, spoke of brothers and sisters, but not of wife or ch. Ch. bp: *Johannes Wyngaard*, Oct. 7, 1752; Elisabeth, Oct. 28, 1754; Pieter and Isaac, Dec. 28, 1756; *Isaac*, Oct. 26, 1759;

Petrus, bp. March 19, 1762, in Albany; Abraham, bp. July 1, 1764; Maria (Polly), Oct. 8, 1766; Catalyntje, Nov. 4, 1768; David, ——; Machtelt, bp. April 20, 1771; Lena.

PHILIP, son of Abraham, m. Engeltie, dau. of John Fairley, Nov. 29, 1747. Ch. bp: *Abraham*, April 28, 1753; *Johannes*, July 27, 1755

ANDRIES, son of Abraham, m. first, Elisabeth, dau. of Ryckert Van Vranken, Feb. 4, 1758; she died Dec. 15, 1777; secondly, Susanna, dau. of Daniel De Graaf, Sept. 20, 1778, who d. March 25, 1807, a. 69ys., 10m., 14d. ; he d. Sept. 6 (Oct. 11), 1804, a. 82ys., 1m., 8 (10) (20), d. Ch: Abraham, bp. September 24, 1758; *Abraham*, b. June 29, 1779, d. May 26, 1862.

CHRISTIAAN LA GRANGE, son of Jacob, m. Elisabeth Quackenbos, July 18, 1761. Ch. bp: *Abraham*, July 15, 1764; *Jacob*, July 5, 1766.

CHRISTIAAN, son of Abraham, m. Catrien Bel. Ch. bp: Philip, Nov. 6, 1771; Isaac, Jan. 7, 1781.

ANDRIES, son of Jacob, m. first, Sophia, dau. of Isaac Truex, May 10, 1755, and secondly, Catalyntje, dau. of Johannes Wyngaard of Albany. Ch. bp: Gillis, son of the first wife (?) ——; Jacob, September 27, 1772; Maria, m. Abraham Truex; Andries, July 20, 1777; Elisabeth, b. March 4, bp. in Albany, April 16, 1780.

GILLIS, son of Andries (?), m. Nancy McKinney. Ch: Andries, b. Nov. 2, 1775, bp. in Albany.

ABRAHAM, son of Jacob, m. Elisabeth, dau. of Harmanus Van Antwerpen, Mar. 27, 1761. Ch. bp: *Harmanus*, Aug. 19, 1764; Isaac, Dec. 14, 1766; Neeltie, May 14, 1769; Johannes, September 13, 1772; Elisabeth, Jan. 29, 1775, m. Johannes Marselis jr.; Rebecca, Sept. 21, 1777; Abraham, June 16, 1782.

CALEB, son of Abraham Isaacse, m. Sophia, dau. of Philip Van Patten jr., Aug. 11, 1770. Ch. bp: Isaac, July 29, 1771; Geesje, Sept. 5, 1773; Philip, Apr. 14, 1776; Abraham, Feb. 15, 1778 (1775); John, July 4, 1780; Arent, Aug. 20, 1783; Engeltie, b. March 18, 1787.

ABRAHAM, son of Isaac Abrahamse, m. first, Sarah, dau. of Alexander Vedder, April 28, 1770, and secondly, Annatie, dau. of Harmanus Peek, and wid. of Johannes De Graaf. He d. June 27, 1833, a. 91ys.; his second wife d. Oct. 2, 1834, a. 87ys. Ch. bp: *Isaac*, Oct. 6, 1771; Margarita, June 5, 1774, m. Adam Swart. Ch. b: Sarah, April 3, 1787, m. Cornelis S. Condé; Engeltie, Dec. 27, 1790, m. Samuel Hays; Johannes, Aug. 10, 1793.

JOHANNES, son of Isaac, m. Annatje, dau. of Dirk Jochemse Van der Heyden. Ch. b: Engeltie, Apr. (May?) 19, 1773; Dirk, Jan. 5, 1775; Isaac, Feb. 17, 1778; Christina, July 20, 1780; Margarita, Aug. 29, 1782; Abraham, August 12, 1784;

Jochim Van der Heyden, July 17, 1787 (Bible), July 25, 1788 (*Church Record*); David, July 6, 1790 (*Church Record*), July 6, 1789 (Bible); Engeltie, May 4, 1793 (*Church Record*), May 12, 1792 (Bible); Caleb, March 13, (*Church Record*), March 21 (Bible) 1795; Daniel and Elisabeth, July 30, 1798.

ABRAHAM, son of Philip, m. first, Margarita, dau. of Cornelis Peek; secondly, Alida Quackenbos, Nov. 17, 1799. He was of Guilderland in 1804, d. March 13, 1822; his first wife d. June 11, 1792, in her 37th year; his second wife died March 5, 1841, a. 83ys., 11m., 5d. Ch. bp: *Philip*, Jan. 28, 1776; Cornelis, Apr. 12, 1778; Engeltie, Sept. 17, 1780; Engeltie, Jan. 25, 1783, m. Peter Walker. Ch. b: Catlyntje July 14, 1785; Eva, Jan. 31, 1788, m. R. Walker; Sarah and John, May 12, 1791; Sarah, m. John Mesick of Guilderland.

WILLIAM, son of Jacob and Annatje Sybel, m. April 17, 1760. Ch: Engeltie, bp. Sept. 18, 1779.

JOHN, son of Philip, m. Cornelia, dau. of Cornelis Barheyt. He was of Charlestown, Montgomery Co., in 1805; made his will June 26, 1817, proved Sept. 18, 1817; spoke of wife Cornelia, and dau. Angelica, Rachel, Cornelia and Eve; d. Aug. 12, 1817, a. 62ys., 17d.; his wid. d. March 15, 1827, a. 67ys. Ch. bp: Engeltie, Feb. 18, 1781; Cornelius, Mar. 20, 1783, d. June 13, 1855, a. 72ys. Ch. b: Engeltie, July 9, 1785; Cornelius, Aug. 6, 1787; Rachel, March 29,

1789, m. Cornelius Van Petten; Philip, April 30, 1791; John Fairly, Nov. 26, 1794; Philip, Feb. 14, 1797; Cornelia Ann, Jan. 4, 1799; Eva Helen, Dec. 7, 1800, m. first, ... Clews, secondly, Henry Phillips.

JOHN W., son of Isaac, m. Magdalena Huysen. She d. May 23, 1812, in her 57th year. Ch. b: Isaac, bp. in Albany, June 13, 1779, d. Aug. 25, 1800 *sine prole;* Pieter, b. Aug. 26, 1782, d. Oct. 12, 1855; Christiaan, Oct. 9, 1783; Maria, Aug. 22, 1784, m. Robert William Bohannan, d. Oct. 1866: Magdalena, Mar. 22, 1786, m. James Hall, d. a wid., April 14, 1858, a. 72ys.; *John Wyngaard*, March 20, 1788, died March 28, 1855; Catharina, March 25, 1790, m. William Clark, died in Albany; Jacob, Feb. 16, 1792, d. Oct. 24, 1815; *Abram*, Dec. 27, 1794, d. in Adrian, Mich., Dec. 3, 1862; David Campbell, Oct. 16, 1797.

ABRAHAM (son of Christiaan), and Maria Ouderkerk, both born and dwelling in Rensselaerswyck, m. Feb. 21, 1786.

JACOB, son of Jacob, m. Catharina Dochsteder. Ch. b. (and bp. in Albany): *Jacob*, January 8, 1780; Caty, July 23, 1783; Elisabeth, Dec. 16, 1786; John, Dec. 28, 1790.

ISAAC, son of Isaac and Marytje Wyngaard, m. Catharina Dochsteder. He d. Oct. 9, 1814, a. 54ys., 11m., 13d.; she d. August 6, 1836, a. 70ys., 10m., 30d. Ch. b: Maria Magdalena, Apr. 28, 1785; Isaac, Nov. 8, 1786, d. March 17, 1811;

26

Johannes Wyngaart, Nov. 9, 1788; Maria, July 15, 1790; Hendrik, Feb. 22, 1792; Jacob Winne, January 16, 1794; Cathlyntje, Jan. 22, 1796; John Schoolcraft, Feb. 2, 1798, d. June 1, 1811; Adam, March 5, 1800; Francis Patterson, May 14, 1802; Susanna, Feb. 17, 1804; Caroline, 1807; Robert, 1809.

PIETER, son of Isaac Jacobse, and Christina Scharp *geboren in Claverack en wonende te Sappamith*, m. June 5, 1785. Ch. b: Maria, June 2, 1791; Catharina, May 14, 1793; Elisabeth, Nov. 16, 1797; Peter Scharp, Jan. 31, 1799; John Scharp and Philip Scharp, May 22, 1803; Magdalena Susanna, May 14, 1805.

ISAAC, son of Pieter, m. first, Anna De Riemer, and secondly, Anna Bevier. He d. Sept. 21, 1852, a. 82 ys. Ch. b: Jacoba Van Santvoord, March 12, 1794; Catlyntje, Feb. 17, 1796; Peter, May 14, 1798; Elisabeth, April 17, 1800, m. James Van Vorst; Jacob, Oct. 21, 1802; Ch. of the second wife, bp. in Albany, and b. as follows: Sarah Ann, Oct. 24, 1805; Isaac Van Santvoord, April 17, 1808; Cornelius Van Santvoord, 1810; Ezekiel Van Santvoord, Jan. 4, 1812; Elisabeth Maria, June 5, 1816; Alida Mead and George Mead, 1819; Alida, m. George Griswold.

JACOB, son of Christiaan, of Noormanskil, and Sophia Ouderkerk of Hellenbergh, m. March 31, 1789. Ch. b: Elisabeth, Sept. 8, 1789; Petrus, Jan. 9, 1792.

JACOB, son of Jacob and Catharina Dochstcder, m. Cornelia Cromwell, Sept. 16, 1802. Ch. b: Jacob, Oct. 19, 1805; Jacob, Feb. 8, 1807; Stephen, Dec. 1, 1809; Eleanor Maria, March 2, 1811; Robert Yates, Aug. 5, 1813, d. in Utica, Dec. 1, 1872; Rachel, Jan. 3, 1816; Eliza Willet, July 10, 1821.

JACOB, son of Willem, and Barbara Bell, both of Hellenbergh, m. March 18, 1788.

ISAAC, son of Abraham, m. Lena, dau. of Johannes Marselis, Feb. 20, 1793. Ch. b: Abram, July 20, 1795; John Marselis, Aug. 24, 1797; Jacob, Feb. 12, 1801.

JACOB C., son of Gillis, and Martha Oliver, both of Hellenbergh, m. at Hellenbergh, banns March 4, 1789, m. Mar. 31, 1789.

ISAAC, son of Isaac Abrahamse, and Baata Clute, both of Normanskil, m. Jan. 1, 1794. Ch: Engeltie, b. February 13, 1796, m. Cornelis P. Clute, April 16, 1828; Clara, bp. Jan. 26, 1800, m. Jacob P. Clute; Isaac, b. March 31, 1802.

ISAAC, son of Isaac and Susanna Roseboom, m. Jenneke, dau. of John Bleecker of Albany, March 16, 1788. He d. Oct. 12, 1812, a. 53ys., 5m., 9d.; she d. Mar. 26, 1811, a. 47ys., 5m., 11d. Ch. b. (and bp. in Albany): Hendrick Roseboom, March 30, 1789; Ann Bleecker, April 7, 1791; Isaac, July 21, 1793; Gerritje, Aug. 29, 1795; John Bleecker. Dec. 14, 1798, d. May 9, 1817. [*See Albany Families.*]

PHILIP, son of Abraham P., m. Alida, dau. of Johannes De Graaf, Oct. 1, 1796. She d. Sept. 4, 1845, in her 69th year. Ch. b: Abraham, June 26, 1797; Eva, March 9, 1799, m. Josiah Hoskin; Johannes De Graaf, March 30, 1805; Mary Ann, March 8, 1808, m. Robert Miller; Catalina, Sept. 18, 1810, m. Henry Playford; Alida, April 13, 1813; Cornelius.

ABRAHAM, son of Andries, m. Maria, dau. of John Swart. She d. Sept. 20, 1821; he d. May 26, 1862. Ch: Eleanor; Andrew; Anna Maria; Catharine J.

HENRY (Hendrik), son of Isaac and Susanna Roseboom, m. Ann Yates in Albany, Nov. 9, 1789. He d. Dec. 15, 1834, in his 74th year; she d. Nov. 23, 1845, in her 77th year. Ch. b. (and bp. in Albany): Catharine Waters, July (June) 26, 1791, d. August 15, 1791; Catharine Waters, July 25, 1792, d. May 19, 1794; Susanna, b. Oct. 15, bp. Sept. 18 (*sic*), 1795; Catharine Waters, Feb. 28, 1800, d. July 21, 1826. [*See Albany Families.*]

JOHN W., son of John W., m. Ann Nancy D. Wilkie, Oct. 4, 1812. He d. on the 28th day of March, 1855, aged 67ys. and 8d.; she d. Aug. 28, 1867, a. 72ys., 3m. and 20d. Ch. b: Hellen Magdaline, July 18, 1813, m. George L Houston; Jacob, Oct. 15, 1815; *John I.*, Oct. 16, 1817; Sabra Maria, Feb. 17, 1820, m. first, Lawyer Stanford, second, Stephen Harris; Thomas Wilkie, June 20, 1822; William Wallace, March 30, 1825; Catharine Ann, Dec. 29, 1829, m.

first, John Middlewood, secondly, Alexander Morrison; Minerva Blanchard, April 1, 1831; Abraham, Jan. 26, 1833; Isaac M. S., Sept. 26, 1836; Daniel David Campbell, Jan. 16, 1838.

ABRAHAM, son of John W., m. Minerva Blanchard, Feb. 3, 1817. She d. May 17, 1862, a. 62ys. and 23d.; he d. Dec. 3, 1862, a. 67ys. and 11m. Ch. b: Harriet Eveline, Feb. 13, 1818; Perry Blanchard, June 17, 1820; Eliza, July 16, 1822; William P., Nov. 24, 1824, d. Feb. 3, 1837, a. 12ys., 2m. and 10d.; Edmund Armstrong, August 10, 1827; David Anson, May 14, 1829; Abraham jr., March 28, 1831, d. July 26, 1832, a. 1yr., 3m. and 28d.; Sarah Ann, April 23, 1833; Minerva M., July 15, 1835; Marshall Spring Bidwell, May 18, 1837; Louisa Minerva, March 6, 1841.

JOHN I., son of John W. m. Margaret Ann Deal, Sept. 24, 1838. Ch. b: John J., Jan. 30, 1840, d. July 12, 1840, a. 5m. and 12d.; Theodore T., April 15, 1842; John J., Aug. 21, 1845; Alfred D., Jan. 10, 1847; Margaret Ann, Sept. 28, 1849, d. Feb. 12, 1854, a. 4ys., 4m. and 15d.; Colinda, April 4, 1852, d. April 28, 1853, a. 1yr. and 24d.; Margaret Colinda, Jan. 18, 1855, d. Jan. 18, 1857, a. 2ys.; Elizabeth E., Aug. 29, 1857; Charles B., March 3, 1860.

TRUMBULL.

JOHN, m. Agnes McCoul. Ch. b: Charles, Feb. 16, 1776; Mary, Jan. 1, 1778; George bp. Feb. 18, 1782.

TUTTLE.

EZRA, m. Hanna McGraw. Ch: Mary, bp. March 9, 1782·

TURK.

ANTONY, m. Rachel Van Aken. Ch: Sophia, bp. June 1, 1783.

ABRAM, m. Maria, dau. of Andries Truex. Ch: Andries Truex, b. April 28, 1794.

TYCE (TEYS).

GEYSBERT (Gilbert), of New Jersey, m. Christina, dau. of Cornelis Van Slyck, May 30, 1761. Ch. bp: Jannetje, Mar. 21, 1762; David, May 6, 1764.

TYMENSEN.

ELDERT, m. Hester, dau. of Bastiaan Visscher of Albany, Nov. 7, 1709, in Albany. He settled in Niskayuna. Ch. bp. in Albany: Marytje, Oct. 30, 1710; Dirkie, April 20, 1712; Cornelis, July 26, 1713; Anna, Jan. 5, 1715, m. Nicolaas Visscher. Ch. bp. in Schenectady: *Bastiaan* and Pieter, twins, Feb. 1, 1718; Petrus, June 30, 1722. [*See Albany Families.*]

BASTIAAN, son of Eldert, m. Mayke Ouderkerk in Albany, July 7, 1743. Ch: *Eldert*, bp. July 1, 1747. [*See Albany Families*]

ELDERT, son of Bastiaan, of " Nistoungjoone," m. Catalyntje, dau. of Jan Baptist Van Eps, Dec. 10, 1774. Ch. bp: Bastiaan, d. in New York, March 24, 1825, in his 50th year ; Jan Baptist, Nov.

30, 1777; Mayke, March 13,1780; Isaac, Sept. 8, 1782; Maria, b. Jan. 18, 1789 ; Peter, Feb. 1, 1794.

PIETER, son of Cornelis, of Albany, and Geertruy, dau. of Martinus Cregier, both of " Canastagajoone," m. June 21, 1771. Ch: Martinus Cregier, bp. Nov. 5, 1776.

ELDERT, son of Cornelis, of Albany, m. Elisabeth, dau. of Pieter Van Vranken. Ch. bp: Neeltje, March 5, 1780; Cornelius, April 7, 1782, d. Jan. 4, 1842; his wife, Elisabeth Clute, d. Aug. 3, 1844, a. 53ys.. 8m., 12d. ; Petrus, b. Nov. 16, 1789.

TYMS.

SAMUEL, m. Jannetie, dau. of Nicolaas Van Petten. Ch. bp: *Michael*, Sept. 18, 1763; Ariaantje, Nov. 25, 1764. Mrs. Jane Tyms, d. Jan. 13, 1769, a. 23ys., 3m., 1d.

MICHAEL, son of Samuel, m. Catharina, dau. of Johannes Visscher (Visger); after his death she m. Barent Roseboom, and survived both him and her ch. and died about 1852. Michael Tyms was appointed English teacher in the Schenectady academy, April 29, 1785, and was still teaching there March 1, 1790; made his will Aug. 7, 1804, spoke of wife Catie and son Samuel, d. Aug. 28, 1804. Ch. b: Harriet Jane, May 15, 1799, d. Oct. 9, 1800; Ariaantje Jane, Oct. 30, 1801 d. July 27, 1802; Samuel John, July 29, 1803, d. Aug. 8, 1804.

TZIDEL.

HENDRICK, m. Maria Barbara Kersimer. Ch: Johannes, bp. May 26, 1765.

VAN AAKEN.

JOHANNES, m. Maria Masten. Ch. bp: Johannes, May 4, 1777; Aart, May 21, 1779; Catarina, Sept. 8, 1781.

HENDERICUS, of Helderbergh, m. Maria Teerpenning. Ch. bp: Jacob, Jan. 1, 1778; Jeremia, July 2, 1780; Maria, Jan. 13, 1783; Elisabeth, b. March 20, 1786.

LEVI, of Helderbergh, m. Elisabeth Teerpenning, Ch. bp: Maria, March 1, 1778; Jacobus, July 2, 1780; Levi, Nov. 5, 1782; Teunis, b. Jan. 28, 1786.

PETER, m. Sarah Kip. Ch: Jeremiah, b. April 6, 1788.

VAN AALSTYNE.

JACOB, of Canajoharie, and Eva Van Eps, m. June 15, 1750.

JOHN, m. Rachel Vanderbergh. Ch: Johannes, bp. Jan. 24, 1780.

JOHN, m. Magdalena Springsteen. Ch: Johannes, bp. May 29, 1784. Ch. b: Catharina, July 5, 1786; Simon, March 22, 1788; Abram, June 18, 1792.

ABRAHAM, m. Margarita Van den Bergh. Ch: Bartholomeus, bp. May 29, 1784.

ABRAHAM, and Marytje Winne, both of Noormanskil, m. September 4, 1789. Ch. b: Rebecca, Oct. 20, 1791; Anthony, Aug. 12, 1793.

FREDERICK, of Helderbergh, and Rebecca ...... Ch: Mattheus, b. Jan. 22, 1786.

PETER, m. Alida Peek. Ch: Margarita, b. March 31, 1794.

LAMBERT, m. Elisabeth Lee. Ch. b: Maria, June 15, 1796; Thomas, July 11, 1797.

VAN ALDYN.

JOHANNES, m. Magdalena Spitzer (?). Ch: Johannes, bp. June 8, 1784.

VAN ALEN.

PIETER, m. Maria Ellwood. Ch. bp: James, June 27, 1782; Isaac, May 23, 1784. Ch. b: Frans, April 9, 1786; Abram, Oct. 5, 1788.

PETER, m. Christina Mets (Patterson *trouw-boek*), March 11, 1795. Ch. b: Hendrik, Aug. 30, (bp. Sept. 20), 1795; Bartholomeus, June 4, 1797; Benjamin, May 12, 1800.

PETER, m. Margarieta Springer. Ch: Vincent, b. Dec. 16, 1798.

VAN AMSTERDAM.

See Yoncker or Joncker.

VAN ANTWERP (VAN ANTWERPEN).

DANIEL JANSE, born in 1635, was in Beverwyck in 1661, when he agreed to serve Adriaan Appel for one year, for 35 beavers (112 dollars), and found. Soon after Schenectady was settled, he became possessed of the Third flat on the south side of the Mohawk river, about 8 miles above Schenectady; in 1706 he sold the west half of his bouwery (63a., 79 rods) his neighbor Jan Pieterse Mebie. His village lot was on the east side of Church street, next north of the present church lot, and was 108 feet wide in front, and 206 feet deep, *wood* measure. In 1676 he was one of the five magistrates; in 1701 supervisor of the town. His wife was Maria, dau. of Simon Groot. Ch: *Jan; Simon; Arent; Daniel; Pieter;* Neeltje, bp. July 27, 1690, m. Andries De Graaf; Rebecca, bp. Dec. 25, 1692, m. Johannes Fort; Maria, bp. Jan. 3, 1695, m. Nicolaas Fort.

JAN, son of Daniel, m. Agnieta, dau. of Harmen Albertse Vedder, Nov. 24, 1700. [A Jan Danielse m. Jannetie Paulusse, wid. of Simon Janse Post, Mar. 9, 1692, in Albany.] He d. Jan. 26, 1756; she d. April, 1756. Ch. bp : Maria, Mar. 2, 1701, m. Nicolaas Hall; *Harmanus,* Jan. 17, 1703; Anna, April 29, 1705; *Daniel,* Oct. 16, 1707; Neeltie, April 28, 1710, in Albany; Sara, June 21 (?), 1712; Rebecca, March 2, 1715, in Albany, m. Daniel Simonse Van Antwerpen; *Abraham,* b. April 10, 1717; Arent, bp. May 7, 1719; *Arent,* June 9, 1722; Anna, Dec. 20, 1724.

SIMON, son of Daniel, m. Maria, dau. of Jacobus Peek, Dec. 22, 1706, in Albany. He bought land and settled in Schaghticoke in 1710; Oct. 13, 1718, "the commonalty (of Albany) have granted unto Simon Danielse, his heirs and assigns forever, a certain small creek on the south side of his land, to build a

grist-mill thereon, provided he grinds no wheat for boulting except ye same be boulted within the city of Albany, for which he is to pay yearly, after January, 1724, six skeple wheat yearly." Ch. bp : Maria, Nov. 9, 1707; Lysbet, Jan. 15, 1710, in Albany; Rebecca, June 21 (?), 1712; Daniel, Dec. 18, 1714; Sara, May 13, 1716, in Albany; *Daniel,* Jan. 10, 1719; the following were bp. in Albany : Margarita, Oct. 1, 1721; Jacobus, May 17, 1724, settled in New York (?); *Johannes,* Jan. 22, 1727; *Lewis,* Feb. 25, 1731.

ARENT, son of Daniel, m. Sara, dau. of Johannes Van Eps. Ch. bp : Maria, Dec. 25, 1706, in Albany; Lysbeth, Oct. 10, 1708, m. Gysbert Marselis; Neeltie, April 28, 1710, in Albany, m. Harmanus Van Antwerpen; Anna, Oct. 21, 1711, m. Dirk Groot; Daniel, Nov. 14, 1713; Maria, April 22, 1716, m. Wessell Wessells; *Johannes,* Feb. 8, 1718; Rebecca, Aug. 18, 1721, m. Teunis Pootman; Sara, Sept. 29, 1723, m. Louis Pootman.

DANIEL, son of Daniel, m. Ariaantje, dau. of Gerrit Simonse Veeder. He was not living March 12, 174⅚, when Gerrit Simonse made his will. Ch. bp : *Wilhelmus;* Maritje, May 3, 1713, m. Pieter Fonda; *Gerrit,* Dec. 18, 1714; Catharina, Jan. 28, 1716; Jannetje, Nov. 8, 1717, m. Lewis Peek; Abraham, Dec. 31, 1719; Helmer and Engeltie, Jan. 13, 1722; Engeltie, Aug. 30, 1724, m. John Freeman; Catrina, b. Feb. 12, bp. Feb. 18, 1727, m. Harmanus Franse Van de Bogart; Ariaantje bp. Sept. 19, 1731, m. Reuben Hosford.

PIETER, son of Daniel, m. Engeltie, dau. of Johannes Mebie. Ch. bp: Annatie, March 8, 1718, m. Louis Groot; *Daniel*, April 2, 1720; *Johannes*, Nov. 11, 1721; Maria, Dec. 25, 1723, m. Jacobus Peek jr.; *Abraham*, b. Nov. 12, bp. Dec. 19, 1725; Neeltie, b. Dec. 16, 1727, bp. January 7, 1728; Achien, bp. ——, 1730; Rebecca, Feb. 6, 1732, m. Dirk Van Petten; Catharina, Oct. 13, 1734, m. Willem Boon; Petrus, Oct. 24, 1736; *Simon*, Dec. 7, 1738; Margrietje, Sept. 12, 1742.

HARMANUS, son of Jan, m. Neeltje, dau. of Arent Danielse Van Antwerpen, Dec. 5, 1730. His house lot was on the east side of Washington street, 190 feet north of State street. Ch. bp: *Johannes*, Feb. 6, 1732; Daniel, b. Dec. 22, bp. Dec. 23, 1733: *Arent*, bp. Aug. 15, 1736; *Abraham*, Feb. 14, 1739; Elisabeth, May 3, 1741, m. Abraham J. Truax; Agnietje, Nov. 13, 1743; Agnietje, Aug. 2, 1747; Harmanus, Jan. 1, 1749.

DANIEL, son of Simon, m. Rebecca, dau. of Jan Danielse Van Antwerpen, Oct. 21, 1738. Ch. bp: *Symon*, Jan. 1, 1741; Johannes, Jan. 9, 1743; *Johannes*, Feb. 3, 1745; Angenietje, Dec. 2, 1750, in Albany; Annatie, January 23, 1757, in Albany.

JOHANNES, son of Simon, m. Catharina, dau. of Johannes Vedder, Aug. 11, 1750. He made his will 1757, proved Sept. 12, 1763, spoke of wife and two

ch. Ch. bp: *Symon*, March 24, 1751, in Albany; Engeltie, April 15, 1753, in Albany; Johannes and Daniel, Dec. 25, 1754; Engeltie, January 11, 1756, m. Richard Bond (?).

ABRAHAM, son of Harmanus, m. Sarah, dau. of Johannes Van Antwerpen, June 13, 1761. Ch. b: Johannes, Oct. 12, 1763; Elisabeth, July 26, 1764; *Harmanus*, Aug. 7, 1767; Johannes, Oct. 15, 1772; Daniel, Aug. 26, 1774 (*Church Record*), 1775 (*Family Record*).

GERRIT, son of Daniel Danielse, m. first, Maria, dau. of Robert Yates, Nov. 30, 1736; secondly, Eva, dau. of Abraham Mebie, May 4, 1746, and thirdly, Catharina, dau. of Cornelis Brouwer, Nov. 10, 1752. He made his will in 1747, proved Oct. 25, 1753, spoke of dau. Ariaantje and Maria, son Daniel, and wife Catharina. His house lot, in 1747, was on the west side of Church street, 231ft. north of Union street. Ch. bp: Ariaantje, m. Lancaster Conner; Maria, Oct. 10, 1742; Daniel, Dec. 2, 1744; *Daniel*, May 31, 1747; Anna, Oct. 15, 1749, *Gerrit*, b. Oct. 15, 1753.

ABRAHAM, son of Jan Danielse, m. Anna, dau. of Pieter Mebie, Aug. 21, 1742. He d. March 7, 1792 (old Bible), June 14, 1795, a. 64ys., 4m. (grave stone in Glenville), the latter date wrong; she d. Aug. 15, 1810, a. 89ys., 6m. (grave stone on the "Fifth flat"). Ch. b: Johannes, Dec. 22, 1743, d. Feb. 17, 1746; Susanna, April 6, 1745, d. Dec. 29, 1746; Susanna, Nov. 29, 1747, d. January 22,

1748 (?); Johannes, Nov. 22, 1749, d.
Jan. 19, 1750; Johannes, Nov. 22, 1751,
d. Aug. 21, 1759; Susanna, Dec. 1, 1753,
m. Nicolaas Barheit; Pieter, Dec. 4,
1755; Anganietje, Nov. 20, 1757, d.
Dec. 2, 1829, a. 72ys., 13d.; Maria, Nov.
3, 1759; Sarah, Dec. 29, 1761, m. first,
Johannes G. Becker, secondly, Gilbert
Van Sice.

DANIEL, son of Jan Danielse, m. Helena, dau. of Cornelis Van Slyck, Oct.
17, 1736. She d. Feb. —, 1794, in her
88th year. Ch: Johannes, bp. May 29,
1743.

SWERUS (Ahasuerus), son of Johannes,
m. Margaret Rightmeyer. Ch. b: Helena,
Nov. 18, 1783; Johannes, Nov. (Oct.) 17,
1785; Geertruy, Jan. 31, 1788.

DANIEL, son of Gerrit, m. Dirke Winne,
in Albany, Dec. 5, 1766. Ch. b: Gerrit, Dec. 11, 1767; Willem, January 23,
1770. [*See Albany Families.*]

DANIEL, probably the same as the last,
m. Gerritje Witbeck, Oct. 27, 1772, in
Albany. Ch: Andries Witbeck, b. Jan.
30, 1774. (Daniel Van Antwerpen and
wife Gerritje lived in Coeymans in 1794).
[*See Albany Families.*]

JOHANNES, son of Arent, m. first, Lena
(Helena) Wendell, dau. of Ahasuerus,
Nov. 5, 1743, secondly, Maria, dau. of
Jan Viele, April, 1773. Ch. b: Sara,
July 16, 1744, m. Abraham Van Ant-
werpen; Daniel, Nov. 28, 1748; Anna,
June 11, 1751, m. Johannes T. Marselis;
Daniel, Oct. 29, 1754; Arent, Aug. 2,

1756; Ahasuerus, March 25, 1761; Elisabeth, Aug. 30, 1765. Ch. bp: Arent,
Sept. 19, 1773; Johannes, Dec. 24, 1775;
Elisabeth, Dec. 21, 1777; Debora, Feb.
20, 1780; Guy Jong, Feb. 8, 1782.

WILHELMUS, son of Daniel Danielse,
skipper of Albany, m. Hilletje Van Vranken of " Ganestagioene," March 6, 1744¾.
He made will 1781, proved Nov. 6, 1783,
spoke of wife, but of no ch. Ch: Adriaantje, bp. Dec. 26, 1744.

SIMON, son of Pieter Danielse, m. Rebecca, dau. of Pieter Mebie of the *Woestine.* Ch. bp: Margarita, June 14, 1767;
Susanna, Oct. 8, 1769, m. Christiaan
Manning; *Petrus,* March 22, 1772; Johannes, Aug. 28, 1774; Abraham, b.
Dec. 3, 1777 (grave stone in the *Woestine*), bp. Jan. 5, 1777, d. Aug., 1778;
Annatje, Aug. 30, 1778; Neeltje, Aug.
26, 1781; Abraham, July 18, 1784;
Sarah, b. April 7, 1787.

DANIEL, son of Pieter, m. Elisabet
Keizer. He lived in "Corrysbush" in
1794. Ch. bp: *Petrus,* Dec. 15, 1745;
Johannes, July 29, 1753; Annatje, Feb.
1, 1761, m. John Bond.

PETER, son of the last, m. Susanna,
dau. of Richard Bond. He lived in
"Corrysbush." Ch. b: Polly, July 25,
1787; Daniel, May 11, 1791; Sara, Sept.
25, 1793; Engeltie, February 21, 1795;
John, Feb. 14, 1798; Richard May 14,
1800.

JOHANNES, son of Pieter Danielse, m.
Eva, dau. of Hendrick Vrooman, Jan. 29,
1744⅝. Ch: Johannes, bp. Oct. 6, 1748.

ARENT, son of Harmanus, of "Nisthigioone," m. Hester, dau. of Samuel Cregier, Nov. 29, 1764, in Albany. Ch. bp. in Albany: Geertruid, Oct. 6, 1765; Neeltie, Feb. 26, 1767; Harmanus, Apr. 18, 1770. [*See Albany Families.*]

ARENT, son of Jan, of Schenectady, and Elisabeth, dau. of Nicolaas Groot of Nistagioene, m. Nov. 24, 1752, in Albany. Ch. bp: *Johannes*, Sept. 12, 1753; Nicolaas, Dec. 7, 1755; Hester, Jan. 2, 1756.

ARENT, son of Johannes, m. Elisabeth Laping (Lappens). She was b. Dec. 25, 1759. (Arent V. A. d. in 1805). Ch. b: Lena, April 11, 1782; Daniel, Dec. 3, 1783; Sarah, Oct. (Dec.) 22, 1785; Johannes, Nov. 12, 1787; Annatie, April 13, 1790; Ahasuerus, Oct. 2, 1792; Abram, June 16, 1795, d. Dec. 11, 1860; William, May 6 (16), 1798; Maria Brouwer, Sept. 18, 1801; Wendel, Mar. 16, 1804.

ABRAHAM, son of Pieter Danielse, m. Margarita Kaljer. Ch. bp: Anna, Nov. 10, 1754; Isaac Kaljer, Oct. 31, 1756; Maria, Jan. 14, 1759, m Daniel Van der Heyden; Petrus, Sept. 26, 1762; Volkje, Dec. 23, 1764, m. Pieter Van Petten; Neeltie, Sept. 28, 1766, m. Harmanus H. Peek; Margarita, May 28, 1769.

LEWIS, son of Simon, of Schaghticoke, and of *Halve Maan* in 1771, m. Hendrikje Fonda (Van Buren), Nov. 27, 1754, in Albany. Ch. bp. in Albany: Simon, March 30, 1755; Douwe, July 24, 1757; Johannes, b. Jan. 12, 1760;

Alida, b. March 16, 1762; Louys, b. Aug. 17, 1771. [*See Albany Families.*]

JOHANNES, son of Harmanus, m. Annatie Veeder, March 4, 1755. Ch. bp: Neeltie, Feb. 22, 1756; Johannes, Mar. 4, 1759.

HARMEN, son of Abraham, of "Nestigaune," m. Annatie Van Eps, Nov. 30, 1787. Ch. b: Sarah, Dec. 25, 1788; Geertruy, July 18, 1794.

SIMON, son of Daniel, m. Maria Dunbar, Nov. 20, 1761, in Albany. She d. April 11, 1826, a. 87ys., 11m. Ch. b: (and bp. in Albany): Rebecca, Sept. 19, 1762; Cornelia, Jan. 30, 1764; Saartje, Jan. 4, 1771; Sara, Jan. 27, 1774. [*See Albany Families.*]

SIMON, son of Johannes, m. Magdalena, dau. of Henricus Veeder. "This venerable couple died on the same day, Sept. 11, 1834, he a. 84ys., and she 82ys. of age." Ch. bp: Johannes, August 16, 1772; Judith, March 17, 1776. Ch. b: Philip, Feb. 25, 1787, d. May 28, 1841; Hendrikus, June 5, 1791, a captain in the war of 1812, d. Sept. 8, 1834.

GERRIT, son of Gerrit, m. Rebecca, dau. of Jacob Fonda, March 12, 1774. He made his will Feb. 22, 1807, proved Aug. 20, 1810, spoke of wife and ch. Jacob, Cornelis, Catarina, Maria, Gerrit and Jellis; d. May (10 ?), 1809; she d. Aug. 5, 1828, a. 74ys., 7m., 20d. His grandfather Brouwer bequeathed him a house and lot in the village in 1765. Ch. bp: *Jacob*, Dec. 11, 1774; Cornelis,

27

July 20, 1777, d. Jan. 29, 1815; Catarina, Sept. 16, 1781; Jilles, Oct. 6, 1782; Catrina, Feb. 11, 1784; Jellis, Jan. 28, 1787. Ch. b: Maria, May 24, 1789; Gerrit, Aug. 5, 1792; Jellis, Dec. 29, 1795.

JOHANNES, son of Daniel (?), m. Catlyna Yates in Albany, Aug. 12, 1778. Ch. b: Catlyna, Jan. 14, 1789; John, Feb. 20, 1806.

JOHN J., m. Abigail Johnson, Oct. 24, 1795.

JACOB, son of Gerrit, m. Maria, dau. of Andreas Rynex, July 17, 1795. In 1807 his father, by will, left him the " house and lot in Schenectady where he now lives," being No. 63 Union street. He ˙d. Sept. 21, 1839; she d. Dec. 3, 1863, in her 88th year. Ch. b: Rebecca, Oct. 26, 1795; Maria, Feb. 24, 1798; Catharina, Oct. 22, 1799; Geertruy, Dec. 14, 1801; Sarah, January 11, 1804; Catharine, Dec. 21, 1805; Susan Elisabeth, Sept. 21, 1808; Harriet, Dec. 31, 1810; Anna, Feb. 19, 1813.

PETER, son of Peter, m. Sarah, dau. of Johannes Rynex, August 28, 1797. Ch. b: Simon, March 1, 1798.

VAN ARNHEM.

JACOBUS, and Catarina, dau. of Willem Bancker, both from colony Rensselaerwyck, m. Nov. 26, 1757. Ch. bp: Johannes, July 23, 1758; *Willem*, Oct. 1, 1759; *Evert*, Nov. 1, 1761; Annatie, Oct. 23, 1763; Henderick, March 10, 1766; Elisabeth, Dec. 20, 1767; Hester,

Sept. 20, 1769; Thomas, Feb. 9, 7774; Helena, June 19, 1779.

JOHANNES, JR., and Geertruy Siversen, both of Rensselaerswyck, m. Oct. 25, 1755. Ch. bp: *Johannes*, Nov. 21, 1756; Elisabeth, Dec. 16, 1759; Jurry, Dec. 22, 1765.

JOHANNES, son of Johannes, m. Jannetje Van Loon. Ch. bp: Geertruy, June 19. 1779; Petrus, Dec. 11, 1780; Jacob, Nov. 5, 1782; Jannetie, Jan. 11, 1785; Catalyntje, b. July 25, 1789.

ISAAC, of Helderbergh, m. Catharina Van Wie. Ch. b: Helena, May 28, 1785; Helena, Oct. 11, 1789.

WILLEM, son of Jacobus, of Normanskil, m. Helena, dau. of Abraham J. Wemple (?). Ch. b: Catharina, Sept. 7, 1785; Rachel, Oct. 13, 1789; Elisabeth Wemple, May 10, 1796.

EVERT, son of Jacobus and Lena, dau. of Johannes Hendrickse Vrooman, both of Rensselaerswyck, m. June 16, 1786. Ch : Johannes Vrooman, b. March 17, 1787.

VAN BENTHUYSEN.

MARTIN son of Paulus Martense of Albany, m. Feitje, dau. of Pieter Jacobse Borsboom, June 2, 1696, in Albany. Ch. bp: Pieter, Nov. 10, 1697; Catalyntje, May 5, 1700, m. Isaac Truex; Pieter, April 22, 1705.

MARTIN, perhaps son of Pieter last written, m. Cornelia, dau. of Ephraim Bratt. Ch. bp: Margarita, Feb. 27,

1780; Clara, Dec. 2, 1781; Peter, Aug. 31, 1783; Pieter, b. March 2, 1785; Petrus, b. March 11, 1787, not living 1801; Sophia, bp. April 30, 1789; Ephraim, b. Nov. 25, 1790.

VAN BOEKHOVEN.

CLAES JANSE, an early settler in Albany, in 1662 owned a lot on the *Vossen kil;* 1672-7, in company with Ryck Claase Van Vranken, bought land over the river at Niskayuna, afterwards inherited by his step-son, Dirk Bratt; 1683 his wife was Volckertje Janse; about 1691 he m. Catalyntje, dau. of Andries De Vos, and wid. of Arent Andriese Bratt, after which time he became a resident of Schenectady; made his will Jan. 11, 1698; Ryer Schermerhorn and Dirk Arentse Bratt administered on his estate April 3, 1712, which estate passed equally to his six step-children (the Bratts).

VAN BOSKERK.

LOURENS, m. Catharina Terhune. Ch : Peter, b. Dec. 17, 1796.

VAN BRAKEL.

GYSBERT GERRITSE, an early settler of Schenectady, made his will Dec. 10, 1709; gave to his son Gerrit the lot where Gerrit's house now stands, lying next to Jan Vroomans and Arent Danielse (Van Antwerpen's) lots, also his piece of land named *Juffrouw's* Land and half of the pasture, &c. His pasture of 5 morgens, bought of the patentees of Schenectady Feb. 11, 170⅔, extended along the south side of Union street,

from Ferry street to Maiden Lane, and south about half way to State street. In 1699 he bought the island west of *Spuyten Duyvel,* in the Mohawk river. His first wife was Reyntie Stephense; he m. secondly, Lysbet, wid. of Jan Van Eps, July 23, 1693, in Albany. Ch : Sander, killed by the French and Indians, Feb. 9, 1690; Stephen, carried away captive at the same time; Anneke, bp. in Albany, Dec. 6, 1685; *Gerrit,* eldest son, bp. in Albany, July 15, 1688; *Gysbert,* bp. in Schenectady, Jan. 3, 1695.

GERRIT, eldest son and heir of Gysbert, m. Catryntje, dau. of Claas Lourense Van der Volgen, Oct. 15, 1704. In 1754 he resided in the *Maquaas land,* lately of Schenectady. Ch. bp : *Gysbert,* Oct. 28, 1705; Maria, Feb. 15, 1710, in Albany; Claas, Oct. 12, 1712, in Albany; Sander, June 13, 1715; Reyntien, Sept., 1717; Claes, July 9, 1720; Neeltje, March 8, 1723.

GYSBERT, son of Gysbert, m. Marytje, dau. of Jan Hendrikse Vrooman, Jan. 1, 1717.

GYSBERT, son of Gerrit, and Maria Van Antwerpen, both born and dwelling in this place, m. July, 5, 1730. Ch. bp : Catharina, May 30, 1731, m. Johannes Van der Heyden; Elisabeth, Dec., 1733; Rebecca, Sept. 28, 1745, in Albany; Neeltie, July 16, 1749, in Albany; Sara, Aug. 5, 1753, in Albany.

VAN BUREN.

GOOSE, m. Baata Van Valkenburgh. Ch : Elisabeth, b. Jan. 27, 1799.

HENDRIK, m. Marytje Van den Bergh. Ch: Aaltie, b. March 10, 1785.

THOMAS, m. Catharine Van Dyck. Ch: Letty, b. Feb. 11, 1796.

PETER, m. Abigail Mudge. Ch. b: Catalina, Oct. 22, 1798; Jarvis, August 7, 1801; Catalina, April 9, 1804.

VAN COPPERNOL.

See Coppernol.

VAN CURLER.

ARENT, was one of those characters who deserve to live in history. His influence among the Indians was unlimited, and in honor of his memory, these tribes addressed all succeeding governors of New York by the name of "Corlaer." He possessed feelings of the purest humanity, and actively exerted his influence in rescuing from the savages such Christians as had the misfortune to fall into their hands, of whose danger he might receive timely notice. On his marriage with Antonia Slaghboom, the widow of Jonas Bronck, about 1643, he visited Holland, and on his return, moved to the *Flatts* above Albany, where he had a farm. He was proprietor of a brewery in Beverwyck in 1661. Being a cousin of the Van Rensselaers, he had considerable influence in the colony, where he was a magistrate to the time of his death. He was one of the leaders in the settlement of Schenectady in 1661-2, and on the surrender of New Netherland, was specially sent for by Governor Nicoll to be consulted on Indian affairs and the interests of the country generally. He was highly respected by the governors of Canada, and the regard entertained for him by M. De Tracy, viceroy of that country, will be best judged of by the following extract of a letter which that high personage addressed him, dated Quebec, April 30, 1667:

"If you find it agreeable to come hither this summer, as you have caused me to hope, you will be most welcome, and entertained to the utmost of my ability, as I have great esteem for you, though I have not a personal acquaintance with you. Believe this truth and that I am, sir, your affectionate and assured servant, TRACY."

Having accepted this invitation, Mr. Curler prepared for his journey. Gov. Nicoll furnished him with a letter to the viceroy. It bears date 20 May, 1667, and states that "Mons. Curler hath been importuned by divers of his friends at Quebec to give them a visit, and being ambitious to kiss your hands, he hath entreated my pass and liberty to conduct a young gentleman, M. Fontaine, who unfortunately fell into the barbarous hands of his enemies, and by means of Mons. Curler obtained his liberty." On the fourth of July following, Jeremias Van Rensselaer writing to Holland, announces that "our cousin Arendt Van Curler proceeds overland to Canada, having obtained leave from our general, and being invited thither by the viceroy, M. De Tracy." In an evil hour he embarked on board a frail canoe to cross Lake Champlain, and having been overtaken by a storm, was drowned, I believe, near Split Rock. In his death this country experienced a public loss, and the French of Canada a warm and efficient friend. [O'Callaghan's *Hist. N. Netherland*, I, 322.] Van Curler's village lot in Schenectady was probably on the north corner of Church and Union streets, and his bouwery, after his death called *Juffrouw's Landt*, comprised 114 acres lying immediately southwest of the village. After his death this farm was sold in parcels to divers individuals. His wid. continued to reside in Schenectady until her death, Jan. 15, 167$\frac{7}{8}$. In consideration of the loss of her husband in public service, and of her house, barn and corn by fire, she received a license from Gov. Lovelace in 1672 to trade with the Indians. It was thought also, that her license would stop the quarrels of the other two tapsters, Cornelis Cornelise Viele and Akes Cornelise Gautsh (Van Slyck), the Indian. [Orders in Council, p. 127.] Mrs. Van Curler's will was admitted to probate in New York, and letters of administration issued to Willem Beeckman, Jan. 15, 1676. He reported April 5, 1681, the proceeds to be 10,805 guilders, 17 stivers in beavers, debts 21,171 guilders, 7 stivers. [Court Proceedings, Albany, I 20, 51.] Mr. Van Curler probably left no children.

VAN DALSEN.

HENDRICK, m. Neeltie Zabriskie. Ch. b: Willem, Dec 3, 1788; Henry, Dec. 6, 1790.

VAN DEN BERGH.

NICOLAAS, m. Ariaantje Schermerhorn, Jan. 9, 174$\frac{7}{8}$.

CORNELIS, m. Anne Van Vranken. Ch: *Maas*, bp. Dec. 25, 1744.

EVERT, m. Annatje Lansing. Ch: Lena, bp. Sept. 28, 1760.

ABRAHAM, m. Rachel, Siverse. Ch: Rachel, bp. Jan. 29, 1764.

WYNANT, and Francyntje Clute, both of Rensselaerswyck, m. Sept. 20, 1767.

MAAS, son of Cornelis, m. Catarina Schier. Ch: Anneke, bp. Oct. 18, 1775.

PETRUS, m. Maria Fort. Ch: Petrus, bp. Nov. 12, 1775.

EVERT, m. Jannetje, dau. of Sybrant Van Schaick. Ch. bp: Eva, June 15, 1777; Sybrant Van Schaick, Sept. 29, 1782; Catrina, May 30, 1784.

NICHOLAS, m. Annatje, dau. of Gerardus Clute. Ch: Cornelius, bp. Sept. 13, 1781; Gerhardus, b. Oct. 8, 1785.

DANIEL, m. Ann Maemolem. Ch: Willem, bp. March 26, 1784.

JOHANNES, m. Eva Van Alstyne. Ch: Antje, b. June 24, 1787.

MATTHIAS, m. Catharina Ray. Ch: Ryckert, b. Oct. 15, 1796.

GYSBERT, of Stillwater, m. Sarah Van Schoonhoven of Schenectady, March 7, 1795. Ch: Hendrik, b. Jan. 22, 1797.

VAN DER BAAST.

JORIS AERTSE, surveyor, and in 1689 clerk or secretary of Schenectady. He called himself an "Amsterdam boy;" in

1670 bought of Bastiaan De Winter a house and lot on the south corner of Union and Church streets, where he was killed on the night of Feb. 8, 1690, by the French and Indians. Feb. 27, 169⅝, the trustees of Schenectady, united with Pieter Bogardus, attorney for the heirs of Joris A. Van der Baast, in a conveyance to Gysbert Marselis of Albany, of Joris's Great island in the Mohawk river, between Scotia and Claas Graven's Hoek, and of the adjacent small islands except *Kruisbessen* and *Spuyten Duyvel* islands; said lands comprising 15 morgens, having been bought by Joris, of Jan De La Warde; also a house and lot in Schenectady and three morgens of land for a *hofstede* near land of wid. of Claas Graven.

VAN DER BOGART.

HARMEN MYNDERTSE, b. in 1612, came to New Netherland in 1631 as surgeon of the ship *Eendracht*, and continued in the West India Company's service until 1633, after which he resided in New Amsterdam until appointed commissary to Fort Orange. He was highly respected, though from all accounts, he appears to have been of an irascible temper. An instance is mentioned of his having attempted, in the excitement of a high quarrel, when both appear to have been in a violent passion, to throw the director general out of a boat in which they were sailing on the river; he was with difficulty prevented from accomplishing his purpose. He came to a violent death, I believe, in 1647 or 1648, and Carl Van Brugge succeeded him as commissaris at

Fort Orange. [O'Callaghan's *Hist. New Netherland.*] Surgeon Van Der Bogart made his will in 1638, and left his property to his wife, Jillisje Claese Schouw of Zierickzee in Holland. After his death his wid. m. Jan Labbadie of Beverwyck. Ch : *Myndert*, bp. in New York, May 3, 1643; *Frans*, bp. Aug. 26, 1640, in New York; Lysbet, m. Harmen Janse Knickelbacker.

MYNDERT, son of Surgeon Van der Bogart, m. Helena, dau. of Jacob Janse Schermerhorn. He was a very active partisan in Leisler's time, by whom he was appointed justice of the peace in 1690. In company with Robert Sanders he obtained a patent, in 1686, for 12,000 acres of land in Dutchess county, including the site of Poughkeepsie, and soon after removed from Albany with his family, upon it. Ch. bp. in Albany; Jacobus; Myndert; Johannes, Jan. 18, 1685; Cornelis, Dec. 15, 1686; Elisabeth, Sept. 30, 1688; Catarina, Aug. 10, 1690; Reyer and Francis, June 5, 1692.

FRANS, son of Surgeon Van der Bogart, m. Annetje Tjerkse, and settled in Schenectady before 1684, where he was killed Feb. 9, 1690, by the French and Indians. His wid. afterwards m. "Fil Harrits," March 25, 1692. Ch : *Claes : Tjerk.*

CLAES, son of Frans, m. Barber, dau. of Takel Heemstraat of Albany, Dec. 31, 1699. Ch. bp : Anna, Nov. 10, 1700, m. Abraham Lighthall; *Frans*, Aug. 22, 1703; Maria, Oct. 28, 1705, m. Pieter Veeder; Grietje, Feb. 9, 1709, in Albany, m. Alexander Vedder; Jillisje, March 6, 1711, m. Johannes Hall; Sara, Feb. 28, 1714, m. Arent A. Vedder; *Takerus*, March 23, 1717.

TJERK FRANSEN, son of Frans, m. Grietje, dau. of Harmanus Vedder. She made her will July 19, 1777, proved May 1, 1781, and spoke of the following Ch. as then living except Margariet and Geertruy. Ch. bp: Frans, Jan. 13, 17$\frac{16}{17}$; Margariet, March 29, 1718; *Harmanus* and Helena, July 21, 1721, she m. Richard Collins; *Nicolaas*, May 11, 1723; Catrina, b. Feb. 3, and bp. Feb. 27, 1725, m. ...... Calvin; Feytje and Agnietje, b. and bp. Dec. 24, 1726, the first m. Voorhis, of New Jersey, the second m. ...... Nixon; Geertruy, July 19, 1729; Annatie, m. ...... Nixon.

FRANS, son of Claes Fransen, m. Hester, dau. of Abraham Groot, Nov. 8, 1726. He d. May 19, 1775, in his 73d year. Ch. bp: *Claes*, b. June 6, bp. June 11, 1727; Abraham and Hester, Dec. 17, 1732, she m. Albert Vedder.

TAKERUS, son of Claes Fransen, m. Neeltje, dau. of Arnout De Graaf, Feb. 2, 174$\frac{4}{5}$. He lived on the north side of Front street, opposite the north end of Church street; d. in 1799. Ch. bp: Adriana, Sept. 15, 1745, m. Bernard F. Schermerhorn; *Nicolaas*, Feb. 14, 1748; Margriete, July 15, 1750, m. Philip Vedder; Johannes, April 30, 1753.

HARMANUS FRANSE, son of Tjerk, m. Catharina, dau. of Daniel Danielse Van Antwerpen, May 18, 1745. Ch. bp: Mar-

griet, Sept. 22, 1745; Margriete, Dec. 21, 1746; Margrieta, October 29, 1749; Adriana, July 14, 1751; Ariaantje, Aug. 8, 1752; Margarieta, July 6, 1755, m. first, Adam Kittle, who was killed in the Revolutionary war, and secondly, one Williams, and was living in 1840 at Maripoosa, Upper Canada; Nicholas, Dec. 11, 1757.

CLAAS, son of Frans, m. Rachel, dau. of Joseph Yates, Aug. 8, 1752. He was dead at the baptism of his last child. Ch. bp: Anna, Sept. 12, 1753, m. Abraham Lighthall; Frans, Feb. 23, 1755; *Joseph*, Nov. 21, 1756; Claas Fransen, March 4, 1759.

NICOLAAS, son of Tjerk, m. first, Ariaantje Schermerhorn, Jan. 9, 174$\frac{7}{8}$, and secondly, Anna Van Vorst, July, 1753. He was dead at the baptism of his last child. Ch. bp: Tjerk, March 5, 1754; Frans, May 4, 1755; Rachel, Feb. 6, 1757; Margarita, July 16, 1758.

NICHOLAS, and wife Margaret were living in Albany county 1784; 1795 he lived in Jerico, in said county, " late corporal " in the First New York regiment, having faithfully served 7ys. and 3 m., received 600 acres of land as a bounty, which he sold to John McMillan.

CLAAS, son of Takerus, m. Elisabeth, dau. of Isaac Marselis, Sept. 16, 1769. Ch. bp: *Johannes*, Jan. 27, 1770; Isaac, Jan. 17, 1773, d. March 10, 1845, in his 73d year; Neeltje, April 21, 1776; Sarah, March 26, 1780, m. Jacobus Rosa; Takerus, Oct. 3, 1784; Frans, b. Nov. 11, 1787, d. Nov. 22, 1824.

JOSEPH, son of Claas, m. Rachel Pietersen. He served in Capt. Fonda's and Capt. Peek's companies in the Revolutionary war. Ch. bp: Eva, Sept. 26, 1779; Claas Fransen, April 11, 1784. Ch. b: Petrus, June 18, 1786; Johannes, Nov. 13, 1788; Rachel, Sept. 18, 1793; Huybertje Yates, March 14, 1796.

JOHANNES, son of Claas, m. first, Annatje Van Vorst, Aug. 2, 1789, and secondly, Neeltje or Eleanor Osburn about 1801. He d. Sept. 8, 1846, in his 76th year. His second wife was b. July 30, 1775, and d. Nov. 1, 1834. Ch. b: Nicholas, Jan. 10, 1789 (grave stone), 1790 (*Church Record*), d. Jan. 11, 1850; Margarit, April 23, 1792; Elisabeth, May 5, 1796; Annatje, July 16, 1802; Francis, Feb. 28, 1806; Sarah, Sept. 2, 1809; John, Dec. 14, 1811; John, April 1, 1814.

VAN DER HEUVEL.

CORNELIS W., m. Remptje Speeleveld. He was a druggist in partnership with Doctor Dirk Van Ingen, and professor of mathematics and natural philosophy in Union College in 1798; died in 1799. He owned the lot on the south corner of Union and Ferry streets, which was sold by his executors in 1802, to Richard Cook, his wife being about to return to Holland. Ch. b: Alida, June 9; 1794; Maria, Feb. 18, 1796; Cornelius Willem, June 6, 1798.

VAN DER HEYDEN.

JOACHIM, son of Dirk, of Albany, widower of Anna, dau. of Daniel Ketelhuyn of Albany, m. Bata, dau. of Johannes Clute of " Konnestagioone," banns, July 10, 1730. Ch. bp: Bata, April 13, 1740, m. Maffhias Bovie; Matthys, March 7, 1742; Abraham, Oct. 28, 1744. [*See Albany Families.*]

JOHANNES, son of Joachim above, m. Catarina, dau of Gysbert Van Brakelen. Ch. bp: Maria, June 26, 1757; Rachel, May 31, 1761. [*See Albany Families.*]

JOHANNES, "*advocaat van Albany,*" and Mary Butler of Schenectady, m. Aug, 1758.

DAVID, son of Dirk, of Albany, m. Emmetje Van Vorst. He served in Capt. Willem Pieters company in the Revolutionary war, d. July 9, 1840, in his 82d year; she d. July 8, 1805, a. 59 ys. 3m., 3d. Ch : Margarita, bp. July 8, 1781. Ch. b : Maria, Jan. 3, 1784, d. Dec. 24, 1805; Annatje, Feb. 24, 1786; Johannes, April 31 (*sic*), 1787 (?); Evah, Jan. 25, 1789; Cornelius, Nov. 27, 1791; Elisabeth, May 8, 1793; Elisabeth, Dec. 10, 1795; Dirk, Sept. 19, 1798; Daniel, Nov. 4, 1800; Debora, Nov. 17, 1801. David Van der Heyden was an Indian trader, travelling as far west as Detroit; his village lot was on the north corner of Union and College streets. Gitty Thalimer, consort of David Van der Heyden, d. June 23, 1822, in her 69th year.

DANIEL, son of Dirk, of Albany, m. Maria, dau. of Abraham Van Antwerpen.

Ch. b : Dirk, bp. July 11, 1784; Margarietje, b. Oct., 1786; Annatje, March 30, 1790; Engeltje, June 15, 1792; Eva, Dec. 2, 1794; Abraham, Aug. 21, 1797; David, April 21, 1800.

VANDERKAR.

DIRK, m. Jannetje Van der Werken. Ch : Abraham, b. Oct. 20, 1783.

VAN DER MERKEN.

JOHN, m. Cornelia Van Den Bergh. Ch. b : Sylvester, Dec. 15, 1798; Jacob, Aug. 28, 1802.

VAN DER VOLGEN (VAN PURMERENT).

CLAAS LOURENSE, one of the early settlers of Schenectady, m. Maritie, dau. of Teunis Cornelise Swart. His house lot, in the village, comprised the lots on which the Myers stores and Van Horne Hall now stand. At the burning of Schenectady, his son Lourens was carried away prisoner to Canada. Ch. bp. in Albany : Lysbeth, May 9, 1686, m. Dirk Groot; Claas, Aug. 7, 1687; Ariaantje, May 18, 1690.; Ariaantje, Feb. 12, 1693, m. first, Arnout De Graaf, and secondly, Harmanus Vedder; Neeltje, m. Pieter Simonse Veeder; *Cornelis; Lourens Claese; Teunis;* Catryntje, m. Gerrit Gysbertse Van Brakel.

CORNELIS, son of Claas Lourense, m. Elisabeth ......; made his will March 24, 173½, proved Dec. 30, 1735, spoke of his wife, brothers, sisters, &c., but not of any children. His wife, after his death,

m. Joseph Van Sice. He lived on the Van Horne Hall lot, which he left to his wife. His brother Lourens lived on the lot next east, Nos. 153 and 155, now the Myers house lot.

TEUNIS, son of Claas, m. Sara Harmens Freer. Ch. bp: Claas, June 26, 1709, in Albany; Jannetje October 21, 1711; Marigien, Oct. 9, 1715; Neeltje, Oct. 12, 1713, in Albany; Catrina, Mar. 1, 1718; Jacomyntje, July 3, 1720, m. Arent Slingerland of Albany; Lysbet and Ariaantje, Aug. 31, 1723, the former m. Johannes Heemstraat.

CLAAS, son of Claas, m. Rebecca, dau. of Simon Groot. Ch : Frederic, bp. March 6, 1711.

LOURENS CLAESE, son of Claas, m. first, Geertruy, dau. of Claas Van Petten, and secondly, Susanna Welleven, Sept. 18, 1722. At the destruction of Schenectady, Feb. 8, 1690, he was carried away captive to Canada, by the Indians, with whom he remained several years, as late as 1699, acquiring a perfect knowledge of their language. After his return he was appointed interpreter of the province for the Five Nations, which office he held till his death about 1740. In 1701 Abraham Gouverneur, speaker of the provincial assembly, prayed Governor Nanfan to use no interpreter for the Indians but Lawrence Claessen, the sworn interpreter. His salary was £30 till 1724, when it was raised to £60. He made his will Aug. 30, 1739, proved Oct., 1742; spoke of his second wife as then

28

deceased, and of his ten children then living, viz : Neeltie, wife of Sander Van Eps; Eva and Maritie, ch. of his first wife; and the seven by his second wife. Ch. bp : Neeltie, May 3, 1713, m. Sander Van Eps; Eva, August 27, 1715; Eva, Nov. 30, 1717, m. Philip Ryley; Marytje, March 5, 1720, m. Simon Johannese Veeder; Lourens Claesse (or *Claes Lourense* by his father's will), Sept. 1, 1722; Catrina, June 21, 1724, m. Reinier Meyndertse; Elisabeth, b. Sept. 7, bp. Sept. 12, 1725, m. Willem Schermerhorn; Ariaantje, b. July 11, bp. July 16, 1727, m. Maas M. Van Vranken; Geertruy, Aug. 2, 1729; *Cornelis*, July (?) 25, 1731; *Petrus*, June 10, 1733.

CORNELIS, son of Lourens Claese, m. Rebecca Fort, April 22, 1756. She d. April 17, 1791, a. 55ys., 17d ; he made his will May 14, 1782, proved Jan. 24, 1787 ; spoke of wife Rebecca, and of ch. Susanna, Elisabeth and Lourens, of his brother-in-law, Johannes Fort, and of his brothers Claes and Petrus. He d. January 16, 1786, a. 55ys., 6m., 6d. Ch. bp : Susanna, March 29, 1761; Susanna, April 28, 1764; Lourens, Aug. 4, 1766; Susanna, July 16, 1769, m. Henry H. Peek, d. June 1, 1792; Johannes, Dec. 2, 1771 ; Elisabeth, b. Aug. 10 (grave stone), bp. Aug. 9 (*Church Record*), 1773, d. Aug. 11, 1792; *Lourents*, bp. May 5, 1776.

PETRUS, son of Lourense Claese, m. Geertruy, dau. of Myndert Myndertse, Nov. 7, 1761. Ch. bp : Lourens, Dec. 23, 1764; Lourens, Jan. 11, 1767; Sus-

anna, February 4, 1770, m. Johannes S. Schermerhorn; Myndert, Oct. 18, 1772, m. Eleanor Voght, d. in Princetown, Oct. 14, 1843, a. 71ys.

NICOLAAS, son of Lourens Claese, m. Sarah, dau. of Abraham Truex; banns, Sept. 16, 1749. He was a merchant and lived upon the lot on which the Myers house stands. He gave to the Dutch church £150 for the purchase of an organ, which was burned with the church in 1861. He d. May 21, 1797, a. 74ys., 9m.; his wife d. Aug. 1, 1795, a. 65ys., 10m., leaving no ch. living. Ch. b : Susanna, b. July 12, bp. July 17, d. July 27, 1768; Lourens Claessen, April 1, 1771, d. Aug. 1, 1791.

LOURENS CLAESSEN, son of Cornelis, m. Engeltie, dau. of Barnhardus F. Schermerhorn, May 24, 1794. Ch. b : Rebecca, Dec. 13, 1794; Freeman Schermerhorn, Nov. 18, 1796; Susanna, Sept. 28, 1799 ; Margaret; Cornelis; John; Peter, living in Albany; Eleanor.

VAN DER WERKEN.

BARENT, m. Molly Barted (Barten). Ch : Margarita, bp. Feb. 1, 1780; Elisabeth, b. July 10, 1781; Barent, May 31, 1783.

VAN DER WERVEN.

MARTINUS, m. Margarita Oyens, Feb. 19, 1727.

VAN DER ZEE.

WOUTER, m. Maria Berger. Ch : Maria, b. Jan. 17, 1797.

VAN DEUSEN.

ABRAM, m. Elisabeth Ostrander, Nov. 1795. Ch: Catharine, bp. December 11, 1796; Thomas, b. April 5, 1802.

MELGERT, m. Neeltje Quackenbos. Ch: Abraham, bp. Feb. 6, 1759.

VAN DE WATER.

MICHAEL, m. Catharina Pulver. Ch: Jacob, b. June 8, 1787.

VAN DITMARS.

BARENT JANSE, in Schenectady as early as 1670, m. Catalyntje De Vos, wid. of Arent Andriese Bratt; owned land on the south side of the Mohawk, near the *Steene kil;* he had a son Cornelis, who m. Catharina Glen, dau. of Sander Leendertse (?); after his death she m. Gerrit Lansingh jr. Both father and son were killed by the French and Indians, Feb. 9, 1690.

VAN DRIESSEN.

PETRUS, son of Domine Petrus Van Driessen of Albany, m. Engeltie Vrooman. He made will in 1751, proved April 19, 1762, then called trader, spoke of wife Engeltie and ch. Johannes, Petrus, Mary and Anna. Ch. bp: *Johannes,* March 11, 1744; Petrus, Oct. 26, 1746; *Petrus,* Oct. 18, 1747; Anna, Dec. 2, 1750; Eva, Sept. 3, 1754, m. Johannes De Graaf.

, JOHANNES, son of Petrus, m. Margarita, dau. of Isaac Truex, June 22, 1770. Ch. bp: Catalyntje, Jan. 20, 1771; Hen-

derick, March 21, 1773; Annatje, Sept. 10, 1775; Sarah, Jan. 4, 1778.

HENDRICK, son of Petrus, m. Hanna Johnson. He was deceased at the baptism of his last child. Ch. bp: Petrus, May 9, 1773; Willem, Oct. 20, 1776; Hendrick, May 2, 1779.

VAN DYCK.

HENDRICK, came from Utrecht in 1645. He was *schout fiscaal* under Stuyvesant who dismissed him from office, on which account he appealed to the States General for redress. In 1652 he stated that he had served the West India Company and the States General thirteen years, as ensign commandant and as *fiscaal;* and at this time was burthened with a wife, Duvertje Cornelise, and four children of whom two were *Cornelis;* and Lydia, wife of Nicolaas De Meyer. He d. in 1688.

CORNELIS, son of Hendrick, received a chirurgeon's certificate in 1661, from Jacob D'Hinsse of Albany, with whom he studied medicine four years. He practiced his profession in Albany until his death in 1686. His first wife was Elisabeth Lakens; the second, Elisabeth Beck, wid. of Capt. Sylvester Salisbury; after Van Dyck's death, she m. Capt. George Bradshaw, Oct. 29, 1691; in 1692 she was again a wid., and was deceased in 1701. Ch: Hendrick, chirurgeon, settled in Albany; *Jacobus;* Alida, bp. Apr. 20, 1684, in Albany; Elisabeth, bp. Aug. 22, 1686, in Albany. [*See Albany Families.*]

JACOBUS, son of Cornelis, chirurgeon, settled in Schenectady, where he practiced his profession until his death. For many years he was surgeon of the fort at one shilling a day. His house lot was on the west side of Church street, about 50 feet north of State street. He m. Jacomyntje, dau. of Johannes Sanderse Glen, Oct. 25 (Nov. 9), 1694. Ch. bp: Elisabeth, June 30, 1697; *Cornelis,* Aug. 28, 1698.

CORNELIS, son of Jacobus, m. first, Maritje, dau. of Jan Pieterse Mebie of the *Woestine,* November 12, 1721, and secondly, Margarita, dau. of Arent Bratt, March 16, 1738. He was a physician; made his will 1758, proved February 15, 1759, when the following ch. were living, except Arent, Andries, Elisabet and Annatje. Ch. bp: Elisabet, Sept. 8, 1722, m. Harmanus Bratt; Johannes, May 24, 1724, of Canajoharie, 1771; Jacobus, b. March 17, bp. Mar. 20, 1726; Annatje, b. Dec. 27, bp. Dec. 30, 1727; *Hendricus,* Aug. 29, 1731; Jacomina, Sept. 16, 1733, m. Johannes Baptist Wendel; Arent, Feb. 14, 1739; *Cornelis,* Oct. 8, 1740; Andries, Sept. 22, 1745.

Col. CORNELIS, son of Cornelis, m. Tanneke, dau. of Joseph Yates, Feb. 20, 1762. In the Revolutionary war he was Lt. Col. of the First New York regiment, commanded by Col. Goose Van Schaick, and d. June 9, 1792. His wife made her will Aug. 4, 1812, proved July 2, 1813, by which she left her real estate to Eva, wife of Ahasuerus Wendel; spoke of Henry, Cornelis and Abraham, sons of Hendrick Van Dyck, and of "my father, Joseph Yates," but not of any children.

HENDRICK, son of Cornelis, m. Engeltje, dau. of Abraham Mebie, June 8, 1753, in Albany. In 1766 he was of Corrysbush. Ch. bp: Anna, March 23, 1759, m. Ephraim S. Bratt; Elisabeth, Feb. 8, 1761, m. Hendrick Delamont; *Cornelis,* Feb. 27, 1763; Margarita, Mar. 3, 1765, m. Jeronimus Van Valkenburgh; Jacomyntje, Nov. 15, 1767, m. Frederic D. Van Petten; *Abraham,* Dec. 2, 1769; Johannes, Dec. 22, 1771; Eva, b. May 26, 1774 (5), bp. June 25, 1775, m. Caspar Van Wormer, and d. Dec. 26, 1851, a. 76ys., 6m., 30d., buried in West Glenville.

PIETER, son of Henricus of Albany (?), m. Alida, dau. of Johannes Barheit. She d. June 10, 1839, a. 80ys., 15d. Ch. bp: Catarina, Nov. 7, 1779; Johannes, Sept. 23, 1781;. Lena, April 11, 1784. Ch. b: Petrus, Sept. 22, 1785; Maria, Oct. 16, 1787; Joseph, April 12, 1789; Alida, Apr. 9, 1791; Margarietje, June 9, 1794.

CORNELIS, son of Henricus of Albany (?), m. Elisabeth Rikkert. Ch: Johannes, bp. Feb. 26, 1781.

CORNELIS, son of Hendrick, m. Marytje, dau. of Dirk Van Petten, March 11, 1787. She d. June 20, 1861. Ch. b: Hendrick, Sept. 7, 1787; Rebecca, Dec. 21, 1789; Engeltie, March 6, 1793; Catharina, August 20, 1796; Elisabeth, Dec. 23, 1798; Dirk, Feb. 6, 1801, d.

Nov. 11, 1853; Abraham, Apr. 2, 1803; Sophia and Annatje, twins, Oct. 11, 1806.

JACOB, m. Charlotta Lawrence. Ch: Johannes, bp. June 1, 1782.

PIETER, m. Margarita Thompson. Ch: Johannes, bp. Aug. 18, 1784. Ch. b: Gerrit, April 4, 1786; Cornelia, June 16, 1791; Aaron Thompson, March 2, 1794; Jacob, Oct. 23, 1796; Maria, Aug. 2, 1802.

HENDRICK, m. Eva, dau. of Abraham Groot. Ch. b: Cornelis, March 30, 1785; Abram, Dec. 23, 1786; Abram, Dec. 16, 1787.

ABRAM, son of Hendrick, and Annatje, dau. of Johannes Erichzon, both of Normanskil, m. September 25, 1792. Ch. b: Engeltie, Sept. 29, 1793; Annatje, Oct. 30, 1796.

PETER, of *Sink-Hoik*, and Margarita Staats of *Hoogebergh*, m. Sept. 28, 1796.

VAN ERDE.

WILLIAM, a refugee from Schenectady after the massacre of 1690.

VAN EPS.

DIRK, m. Maritie Damen, and had two children, *Johannes*, and Lysbet who m. Gerrit Bancker of Albany. After Van Eps death his wid. m. Hendrick Andriese Van Doesburgh, and had a dau. Jannetie b. in 1653, who m. Martin Cregier, and settled in Niskayuna. Van Doesburgh was a considerable dealer in real estate in Beverwyck, and d. about 1663. His wid. m. Cornelis Van Nes in 1664. She received a patent May 8, 1668, for a parcel of land at Canistigioone, opposite the "Great Island," and between the two creeks, which land passed to her dau. Jannetie, wife of Martinus Cregier jr., on her death; Jannetie, by will, gave her son Martinus, vintner of New York, the east half and the house, which his wid. and ch. conveyed to Eldert Tymesen in 1741 for £750. Maritie Damen also owned a house and lot in North Pearl street, Albany, which fell to her dau. Jannetie; she was not living in 1682.

JOHANNES, son of Dirk, m. Elisabeth Janse. His mother purchased for him a bouwery on the *Groote Vlachte* and a house and lot in the village in 1664. His lot, about 200ft. square, was on the north corner of State and Church streets. In the massacre of 1690 he was killed with two of his children. His wid., after-' wards, July 23, 1693, m. Gysbert Gerritse Van Brakel. Ch: *Johannes Baptist*, eldest son, b. 1673; *Evert;* Sara, m. Arent Danielse Van Antwerpen; Elisabeth, m. first, Teunis Viele, and se_ condly, Jillis Van Vorst; Maria, m. Dirk Bratt; Anna, m. Coenraat Ten Eyck.

JAN BAPTIST, son of Johannes, m. Helena, dau. of Johannes Sanderse Glen, July 9, 1699. He was taken captive by the French and Indians when Schenectady was burned, Feb. 9, 1690; and after remaining with them three years effected his escape in the following manner: "169¾, Feb. 8, Wed., about 2 o'clock afternoon, we had the alarm from Schenectady, that the French and their Indians had taken the Maquas castles; soon after we had the news that a young man named Jan Baptist Van Eps (taken at Schenectady 3 years ago) was run over from the French, as they were to attack the first castle of the Mohogs, and came to Schenectady, who related that the French were 350 Christians and 200 Indians," &c. [*Colonial Documents*, IV, 16.] During his captivity he acquired a knowledge of the Indian language, and was subsequently often employed as interpreter and embassador to the Five Nations. In 1701 the sachems say, " Wee have a small right in the Maquase river att Canastagiowne, to witt, five small islands containing about five or six acres between *Rosendael* and Cornelis Tymesen's, which wee give to Jan Baptist Van Eps and Lourens Claese (Van der Volgen), the two interpreters, to be equally divided between them; Jan Baptist to have the uppermost halfe, and Lawrence the lowermost, and that in consideration because they take much pains in interpreting." [*Colonial Documents*, IV, 906.] In 1706 Jan Baptist lived upon the east corner of State and Jay streets, the latter being his private lane leading to his land in the rear and along Cowhorne creek, upon which he had a corn mill situated a few rods below the present tan works. Isaac Quackenbos became possessed of a portion of his land extending east and north to Prospect hill and Union street, which land passed to his son, Johannes Quackenbos, whose dau. Maria, late wife of Mr. Abraham O. Clute, inherited the same

Jan Baptist's house lot on State street, extended from the west side of Jay street to Cowhorne creek. Ch. bp : *Johannes*, May 5, 1700; Anna, March 22, 1702, m. Ahasuerus Wendel; Elisabeth, May 14, 1704, m. Dirk Marselis; *Sander*, July 2, 1706; Maria, Oct. 9, 1708, m. Elias Post; *Jan Baptist*, Sept. 27, 1713, in Albany; *Jacobus*, Nov. 26, 1715; Jacomyna, March 29, 1718, ·m. Takel Marselis; Helena, May 28, 1721, m. Willem Pieterse; Catarina, b. Nov. 16, 1723, m. Adam Van Slyck.

EVERT, son of Johannes m. first, Eva, dau. of Carel Hanse Toll, July 8, 1705, and secondly, Elisabeth, dau. of Isaac Truex, July 19, 1729. In 1704 he owned the lot in Washington street, on which stands the house of the late Hon. Alonzo C. Paige. Ch. bp : Johannes, April 14, 1706; Lysbeth, Feb. 8, 1708, m. Hendrick Brouwer; *Johannes*, Apr. 28, 1710, in Albany; Marytje, June 21 (?), 1712; Neeltje, Dec. 18, 1714; Mary, ——, 1716, m. Tobias Ryckman; Abraham, May 18, 1717; *Abraham*, Jan. 2, 1720; Neeltje, Dec. 22, 1722; Carel, July 3, 1724; Annatje, b. June 7, 1727, m. Christiaan Christiaanse; Isaac, ——, 1730.

JOHANNES, son of Jan Baptist, m. Neeltje, dau. of Carel Hansen Toll, Oct. 28, 1720. He lived on the north side of the Mohawk, near Hoffman's Ferry, on land received from his father-in-law, Carel Hansen Toll. Ch. bp : Helena, June 2, 1722; Carel Hansen, Feb. 16, 1724; Elisabeth, b. Sept. 10, bp Sept. 17, 1725, m. Louis Groot; Eva, Sept. 25, 1728,

m. Hendrick Wemple; *Jan Baptist,* May 30, 1731; Catharina, February 25, 1733, m. Claas Veeder; Neeltje, Feb. 15, 1736, m. Alexander Lansing; *Abraham,* Oct. 15, 1738.

ALEXANDER (*Sander*), son of Jan Baptist, m. Neeltje, dau. of Lourens Claese Van der Volgen, March 8, 1731. He made his will 1756, proved Aug. 3, 1758, and spoke only of four ch. Jan Baptist, Jacobus, Lourens and Geertruy. Ch. bp: Helena, April 30, 1732; Lourens, Sept. 23, 1733; Helena, June 13, 1736, m. ...... Thomas; *Jan Baptist,* April 29, 1739; Jacobus, February 28, 1742; *Jacobus,* March 31, 1745; *Lourens,* Jan. 1, 1748; Geertruy, Dec. 23, 1750, m. Willem Stevens.

JOHANNES, son of Evert, m. Anna Van Vechten, wid. of Pieter Winne of Koksaggie, Dec. 29, 1733. In 1769 he resided in Caughnawaga. Ch. bp: Antje, Jan. 5, 1735; Evert, Jan. 28, 1741.

JACOBUS, son of Jan Baptist, m. Catharina, dau. of Helmigh Veeder, March 18, 174⅔. He was an Indian trader in 1744; in 1759, trading with the Chenussio Indians (Senecas) at Irondequoit. Ch. bp: Jan Baptist, Dec. 18, 1743; Helmich, Nov. 17, 1745; Lena, Nov. 16, 1746, m. Willem Teller; Anna, Aug. 27, 1749; *Jan Baptist,* Nov. 10, 1751; Margarita, Nov. 3, 1764.

JACOBUS, son of Alexander, m. Engeltje, dau. of Johannes Wendel, Dec. 6, 1764. He lived in *Swagertown,* made his will June 16, 1820, proved Feb. 18, 1822, then had sons Alexander and Law. rence, &c. Ch. bp: Neeltje, Oct. 5, 1766, m. Isaac Vedder; Annatje, Jan. 15, 1769; Alexander, Dec. 9, 1770; *Johannes Wendel,* Oct. 16, 1774; *Lourents,* June 8, 1777; Maria Catarina, May 9, 1779.

JAN BAPTIST, son of Jan Baptist, m. Maria, dau. of Isaac Truex, Nov. 19, 1743; an Indian trader, was taken prisoner 1763 by the Ottawas on Lake Erie, but escaped and reached Detroit in safety; was at Oswego 1748 in some public capacity, perhaps resident commissioner Ch. bp: Helena, Dec. 26, 1744, m. Arent N. Van Petten; Catlina, May 13, 1750, m. Eldert Tymessen; Jan Baptist, b. June 2, bp. June 17, 1752, d. Oct. 28, 1821; Sarah, Nov. 3, 1754; Isaac, July 10, 1757; Isaac, Sept. 9, 1759; Anna, Sept. 20, 1761, m. Hendrick Ten Eyck.

ABRAHAM, son of Evert, m. Susanna, dau. of Abraham Glen, Nov. 3, 1750. He made his will 1760, proved May 16, 1775, spoke of wife Susanna, and ch. Maria and Effie. Ch. bp: Effie, Aug. 9, 1752; Maria; Effie, Aug. 24, 1756; Abraham, March 18, 1759; Evert, Jan. 10, 1762; Abraham, b. Sept. 20, bp. Sept. 23, 1764; Debora, bp. March 10, 1771.

JAN BAPTIST, son of Johannes, m. Annatje, dau. of Harmanus Vedder, May 2, 1761. He inherited a portion of his father's property at Hoffman's Ferry; made his will Sept. 9, 1809, proved Dec. 24, 1814, spoke of wife Annatje, sons

John, Harmanus, Albert and Carl, and dau. Susanna De Graaf, Jannetie Veeder, Agnes Vedder, Nelly Swart and Lena Swart. Ch. bp: Susanna, Jan. 24, 1762, m. Isaac De Graaf; Johannes, Feb. 10, 1764, d. Aug. 29, 1847, a. 82ys., 9m. 2d., buried at West Glenville; Jannetje, b. April 16, bp. May 18, 1766, m. Peter V. Veeder, d. March 13, 1848; Harmanus, Jan. 14, 1768; Anganietje, Oct. 6, 1771, m. Arent Albertse Vedder; Elisabeth, May 22, 1774; Harmanus and Helena, Sept. 8, 1776; she m. Jeremiah B. Swart; Maria, Dec. 27, 1778; Maria, Oct. 5, 1780; Neeltie, m. ...... Swart; Carel, May 11, 1783; Albert, b. May 18, 1785, d. March 17, 1831, buried near Hoffman's Ferry.

JAN BAPTIST, of Glenville, son of Alexander, m. Jannetje, dau. of Sander Lansing, Dec. 20, 1760. He made his will Oct. 3, 1813, proved Mar. 27, 1815, spoke of sons Alexander, Gerrit, James, John, and dau. Nelly and Angelica, wife of Abraham Cole. Ch. bp: *Alexander*, February 28, 1762, resided in Charlton; *Gerrit*, b. Jan. 30, bp. Feb. 5, 1764; Neeltje, March 1, 1767; Engeltje, June 25, 1769, m. Abraham Cole; *Jacobus*, Oct. 8, 1772; Harmanus, June 12, 1775; *Jan Baptist*, Oct. 19, 1777.

ABRAHAM, son of Johannes, m. first, Margarita Veeder, Nov. 15, 1761, and secondly, Debora, dau. of Jan Viele, Oct. 11, 1768. He had a farm at the *Aalplaats*. His first wife d. about Feb. 7, 1763. Ch. bp: Margarita, Feb. 7, 1763, m. Jacob Swits; Neeltje, b. August 12,

bp. Sept. 11, 1769; Debora, bp. Dec. 29, 1771, m. Hillebrant Banta (?); Catarina, June 19, 1774, m. Arie Banta (?); *Johannes*, Sept. 1, 1776; Helena, Sept. 6, 1778, m. Myndert Swart; Elisabeth, January 28, 1781; Eva, May 11, 1783. Ch. b: Maria, August 7, 1785; Carel, Dec. 9, 1787; Abraham, Dec. 8, 1793.

JAN BAPTIST, son of Jacobus, m. Margarita, dau. of Harmanus Peek. He d. June 6, 1839; she d. Sept. 14, 1820. Ch. bp: *Jacobus*, April 24, 1774; Harmanus, Feb. 11, 1776; Margarita, Mar. 22, 1778; Johannes Peek, August 13, 1780; Jesse, Jan. 25, 1783, d. Feb. 28, 1851. Ch. b: Henricus Veeder, June 29, 1785; Alexander, April 14, 1789; Sarah, June 19, 1792, m. Jerome N. Barhydt, and d. July 31, 1872; Abram Truex, Jan. 25, 1799, d. May 19, 1833.

LOURENS, son of Alexander, m. Margarita Folmer. Ch. bp: Alexander, May 17, 1775; Neeltje, Oct. 5, 1777; Debora, April 30, 1780; Catarina, Oct. 27, 1782; Geertruy, b. May 11, 1786; Johannes, Sept. 24, 1791.

LOURENS, son of Jacobus, of *Swagertown*, m. Neeltje, dau. of Cornelis Van Slyck. Ch. b: Jacobus, Sept. 8, 1800; Cornelius, March 4, 1803; Anna Maria, June 1, 1805; Peter Cornelius, Feb. 5, 1807; Robert Smith, October 6, 1811; Alexander, Feb. 28, 1814.

GERRIT, son of Jan Baptist, m. first, Geertruy Clute, and secondly, Sarah, dau. of John Henry, in 1795. He d. in Glenville, May 19, 1844, in his 81st year; she

d. in 1854. Ch. b: Susanna, March 12, 1785; Gerardus, Dec. 23, 1788; Jan Baptist, March 18, 1797, d. 1867; Elisabeth, May 25, 1801; Jane, Nov. 4, 1803, d. 1872; Maria, Jan. 30, 1807; James, June 21, 1809; Amelia, 1812, d. 1872.

ALEXANDER, son of Jan Baptist, m. first, Jacomyntje, dau. of Teunis Pootman, Nov. 1, 1788; secondly, Margarita Folmer about 1796. Ch. b: Jan Baptist, Jan. 2, 1789; Rebecca, July 29, 1792; Alexander, May 1, 1797.

JACOBUS, son of Jan Baptist, m. Suster, dau. of Pieter Van Gyseling, Oct. 26, 1790. He d. March 2, 1827; she d. March 31, 1859, a. 84ys., 3m. Ch. b: Jannetje, March 31, 1791, m. James F. Bratt, and d. Jan. 28, 1856; John B., July 18, 1793; Jacob, Aug. 11, 1795, d. March 29, 1859, in Rotterdam; Margariet Vedder, June 11, 1800; Eva, June 7, 1802; Cornelius, Sept. 20, 1806; James Alexander, Sept. 13, 1808; Sarah Catharine, Dec. 30, 1817, d. July 17, 1818.

JACOBUS, son of Jan Baptist, m. Elisabeth, dau. of John Henry. Ch. b: Jannetje, May 26, 1798; Henry, Oct. 12, 1800; Cornelius, Oct. 18, 1802; Harmanus, July 4, 1806; Elisabeth, Nov. 9, 1810; Abraham, Oct. 25, 1812.

JOHN, son of Abraham, m. Eva, dau. of Johannes Van Petten. Ch. b: Abram, Feb. 19, 1799; John, Feb. 9, 1804; Carel Hansen, August 11, 1806; Jacob Swits, Aug. 1, 1809.

JOHN, son of Jan Baptist, m. first, (Ann Barnes ?), wid. of Daniel Egan, Nov. 30, 1791, and secondly, Debora Brouwer. His first wife d. about Feb. 3, 1794; his second wife outlived him, and d. May 14, 1843, in her 80th year. Ch. b: Anna Maria, February 3, 1794; Nancy Margaret, Oct. 4, 1805, d. Sept. 23, 1826.

JOHN, JR., m. Polly, dau. of John Henry. He was deceased at the baptism of his last child. Ch. bp: Samuel, June 1, 1800; John Henry, April 18, 1804; Gerrit, April 24, 1806; Elisabeth, Sept. 5, 1808; Harmanus, Jan. 2, 1813; Angelica, Oct. 6, 1814; William, July 11, 1815.

ALEXANDER, of *Swagertown*, son of Jacobus, m. first, Clara, dau. of Cornelis Van Slyck, Aug. 30, 1794. She d. May 18, 1821, a. 49ys., 8m., 28d., and he m. secondly, Eve ......, who d. April 9, 1840, a. 66ys., 1m., 24d. Ch. b: Engeltie, June 17, 1796, m. John L. Van Eps, and d. Sept. 2, 1825; Catharina, Oct. 24, 1799; Neeltje and Maria, Oct. 4, 1802; Jacobus and Neeltje, July 16, 1807.

ABRAM, JR., m. Anna, dau. of Charles and Anna Miller, March 16, 1793. She was b. Feb. 9, 1766, and d. Sept. 20, 1826.

JOHN W., son of Jacobus, m. Mary Slover of New Amsterdam, July 26, 1795. Ch. b, Engeltje, Aug. 29, 1796; Jacob, Sept. 17, 1797; Jacobus, Jan. 24, 1799; Rebecca, Sept. 5, 1800; Neeltje, Dec. 7, 1801; Daniel, May 14, 1803;

29

JOHN, m. Jannetje Van Vleck. Ch. b : John, Aug. 28, 1796; Abigail, June 21, 1798; Agnes, Aug. 4, 1809.

VAN ESS (NESS).

JOHANNES, son of Cornelis of Albany, m. Hester Gerritse of Nestoungjoone, Dec. 5, 1762. Ch. bp : Cornelis, July 3, 1763; Henderick, May 15, 1768; Tjerk, Dec. 22, 1769; Susanna, Jan. 16, 1774.

GERRIT, son of Philip of Albany (?), m. Margarita, dau. of Joachim Kettel (?). Ch. bp : Margarita, Oct. 6, 1771; Eva, Aug. 2, 1773; Sarah, Aug. 20, 1775; Henderick, Dec. 25, 1778.

TJERK, son of Cornelis, of Albany, and Geertruy Clute, both of Nistoungjoone, m. Dec. 18, 1773. Ch. bp : Cornelis, May 23, 1775; Cornelis, Oct. 17, 1779; Gerrit, Feb. 20, 1782.

PHILIP, m. Engeltje Ryan, Aug. 18, 1789. Ch. b : Sarah, Dec. 15, 1790; Gerrit, July 14, 1793.

HENDRIK, m. Maria Ten Eyck. Ch : Andries, b. March 21, 1794.

VAN ETTEN.

JACOBUS, m. Annatje Pangburn. Ch. bp : *Johannes De Hooges,* Jan. 24, 1762; *Abraham,* Oct. 30, 1763; *David,* Sept. 6, 1767; Annatje, January 27, 1770; *Petrus,* July 5, 1772; Rebecca, Feb. 5, 1775; Sarah, March 6, 1778. [*See Albany Families.*]

JOHANNES, m. Annatje Van Vredenbergh, March 23, 1764. Ch. bp : Rebecca, March 3, 1765; Catalyntje, Feb.

8, 1767; Johannes, Nov. 26, 1769; Catalyntje, Oct. 13, 1771; Rachel, April 16, 1775; Elisabeth, May 3, 1778.

BENJAMIN, m. Maria Davis. He d. April 22, 1823, a. 66ys. Ch : John Davis, bp. Jan. 4, 1784; Elisabeth, b. Feb. 15, 1786; Maria, b. Dec. 2, 1790.

WILLIAM, m. Annatie Merkle. Ch : Willem, bp. Nov. 17, 1784. Ch. b : Hannah, Sept. 20, 1786; Catharina, June 4, 1790; Benjamin, June 8, 1794.

ABRAM, son of Jacobus, m. Maria La Roy. Ch. b : Annatje, Oct. 31, 1790; Amelia, Nov. 15, 1792; John La Roy, Nov. 13, 1794; Abraham, June 10, 1797.

JOHANNES, son of Jacobus, m. Geertruy Gerritsen. Ch : Jacobus, bp. Mar. 6, 1785. Ch. b : Gerrit Reyersen, May 1, 1786; Annatje, May 1, 1788; Maria, Sept. 1, 1791; Dirkje, Nov. 7, 1793; Sarah, Dec. 7, 1795.

DAVID, son of Jacobus, and Marytje, dau. of Johannes Van Petten, both of "Galloway," m. May 30, 1793. Ch : Annatje, b. Jan. 23, 1794; John Van Petten, bp. May 1, 1796.

PETER, son of Jacobus, m. Margarieta Springer. Ch : Henrietta, b. Aug. 14, 1797.

VAN GYSELING.

ELIAS, from Zeeland, arrived in New Netherland in 1659 in the ship *Bontè Koe;* settled at first in Beverwyck; and in 1670 bought a bouwery of Bastiaan De Winter at Schenectady, which was afterwards known as *Elias's plantatie.* This farm, situated on the *Bouwlandt* in Rotterdam, remained in the family until the death of the late Mr. Cornelius Van Gyseling in 1865. His wife was Tryntje Claese b. in 1643; after Elias's death she m. Willem Hall, April 13, 1695. " *Sprekende goet Frans,*" he was sometimes employed as an interpreter. Ch. bp : Jacomyntje, April 11, 1686, in Albany; *Myndert,* Oct. 25, 1691; Jacob.

MYNDERT, son of Elias, m. Suster, dau. of Cornelis Viele, April, 1721. He made his will April 2, 1771; proved Sept. 22, 1772, mentioned the following ch. as then living : Catharina, Debora, Elias, Cornelis, Jacomyntje, Jacob and Petrus. He lived upon *Elias's plantatie* which he devised in his will to sons Elias and Jacob. Ch. bp : Catharina, Feb. 3, 1722, m. Samuel Arentse Bratt ; Debora, Jan. 26, 1723 ; Debora, July 5, 1724, m. Isaac Swits ; *Elias,* ———, d. Sept. 5, 1802, a. 75ys, 11m., 23d. ; Cornelis, Nov. 13, 1726 ; Jacomyntje, ———, 1730, m. Arent Schermerhorn ; Jacob, March 6, 1732 ; Jannetje, April 8, 1733 ; Jannetje, July 21, 1734 ; *Jacob,* Jan. 18, 1736 ; Nicolaas, July 9, 1737 ; Suster, March 4, 1739 ; Bregje, May 31, 1741, m. Gerrit Van Vranken ; Nicolaas, June 26, 1743 ; *Petrus,* b. Jan. 22, 1745.

ELIAS, son of Myndert, m. Elisabeth Quackenbos, Sept. 17, 1763, d. Sept. 5, 1802.

PIETER, son of Myndert, m. first, Maria, dau. of Reyer Schermerhorn, about 1770, and secondly, Annatje, dau. of Caleb Beck, about 1773. His first wife, b. Nov. 7, 1752, d. May 26, 1772 ; his second wife d. Nov. 23, 1827, a. 79ys., 3d. ; he d. Nov. 30, 1824. His home lot in the village was on the north side of Front street near Washington street. He made his will Jan. 18, 1814, spoke of sons Myndert, Caleb and Pieter, and dau. Elisabeth and Anna Maria, father Myndert and brother Elias. Ch. bp : Myndert, Sept. 22, 1771 ; Myndert, Oct. 23, 1774, d. Sept. 1, 1846 ; Elisabeth, Feb. 18, 1776, m. John Prince ; Caleb, Jan. 7, 1781, d. March 19, 1835 ; Peter, b. April 11, 1786, d. May 5, 1856 ; Anna Maria, b. Feb. 18, 1791, m. Harmanus Vedder, d. July 9, 1861.

JACOB, son of Myndert, m. first, Jannetje, dau. of Pieter Feling, June 3, 1773 ; secondly, Helena Lansing, July 9, 1790. His first wife d. Dec. 20, 1786, a. 39ys., 9m., 26d. ; his second wife b. Dec. 10, 1740, d. July 20, 1803. He d. Nov. 19, 1803, a. 68ys. Ch. b : Suster, July 13 (*Family Record*), bp. July 10 (*Church Record*), m. Jacobus Johannese Van Eps ; Cornelis, March 5, 1776, the last owner of *Elias's plantasie* of this family, d. Dec. 30, 1865 ; Myndert, Aug. 13, 1778, d. Feb. 13, 1858 ; Eva, Aug. 21, 1780, d. Aug. 17, 1782 ; Eva, Sept. 17, 1782, d. Dec. 7, 1783 ; Eva, May 6, 1785, m. Jacob Van Eps ; a son, Dec. 17, d. Dec. 19, 1786.

VAN HOEK.

BENNONY, son of Arent Isaacse of Beverwyck, m Jacquemina Swart, wid.

of Pieter Cornelise Viele; was killed
Feb. 9, 1690, by the French and Indians.
Ch: Gerritje, bp. in Albany, Jan. 24,
1686.

VAN HOESEN.

ALBERT, m. Sophia Olin. Ch: Jacob,
b. Oct. 9, 1771; Annatje, bp. April 3,
1775; Elisabeth, bp. May 21, 1777;
Cornelis, b. May 22, 1789; Albert, Sept.
5, 1792

VAN HOORN.

CORNELIS, and Eva Frederick, both
of Warrensburgh, m. Feb. 25, 1774.

JOHN, m. Sarah Everett. Ch: John,
b. Dec. 24, 1788.

VAN HOUTEN.

GERRIT, m. Neeltje Wessels. Ch. b:
Annatje, May 19, 1788; Adriaana, July
22, 1790; Sarah, May 14, 1794; Joseph
Wesselse, Feb. 19, 1796.

VAN HYSEN.

RODOLF, m. Sarah, dau. of Dirk Van
Vranken, Feb. 8, 1789. He lived on the
south corner of Union street and Maiden
lane, d. August 30 (31), 1842, a. 78ys.;
his wife d. March 10, 1832, a 66ys.,
1m , 23d. Ch. b: Harmanus, Nov. 19,
1789, d. March 14, 1841; his wife Gezina Clute, d. Feb. 2, 1859; Maria, Nov.
8, 1791; Sarah, Jan. 22, 1794.

VAN INGEN.

Doct. DIRK, from Rotterdam, m. first,
Margariet, dau. of Joseph Van Seysen
(Sice), Sept. 29, 1759, and secondly,
Geertruy Mynderse Wemple, widow of

Myndert Wemple, June 30, 1790. He
lived and d. in the second house north
of the church in Church street; d. Feb.
27, 1814, a. 76ys., 5m., 8d. Ch. bp : *Willem*, b. Nov. 23, bp. Nov. 30, 1760, d.
Jan. 10, 1800; Joseph, bp. Oct. 3, 1762;
Johannes Vischer, b. Nov. 11, bp. Dec.
9, 1764, d. Aug. 30, 1839; *Jacobus*, Dec.
28, 1766, d. in Albany March 1, 1843;
Abraham, May 21, 1769; Francina, Oct.
7, 1770; Elisabeth, Oct. 11, 1772, m.
Alexander Mercer; *Abraham*, b. Nov.
30, 1773 (grave stone), bp. Dec. 5, 1774
(*Church Record*), d. March 18, 1853;
Judith, June 1, 1777, m. ...... Groesbeck of Schoharie, and d. Apr. 26, 1844.

JOHANNES, perhaps brother of Doct.
Dirk, m. Maria Vrooman. Ch: Petrus,
bp. Sept. 15, 1765.

WILLEM, son of Dirk, m. Elisabeth,
dau. of Hon. Henry Glen of Schenectady; made his will December 24, 1799,
proved Feb. 5, 1800, spoke of only one
child, d. in Albany Jan. 10, 1800; buried
in Schenectady. His wife d. May 25 (?),
1816. Ch: Hendrick Glen, b. June 19,
1784, d. Nov. 15 (?), 1817, his wid. Elisabeth, b. May 20, 1784, d. Nov. 8, 1849;
Francyntje, m. Peter Demorest.

JOHANNES V., son of Doct. Dirk, m.
Peggy McKinsey, Feb. 12, 1787. He
was sheriff of Schenectady county, d.
June 9, 1810.

JACOBUS (James), son of Doct. Dirk,
m. first, Catharine Bleecker, who d. April
4, 1798, a. 29ys.; secondly, Elisabeth

Schuyler, who d. Feb. 28, 1801, a. 29ys.; and thirdly, Gertrude ......, who d. Dec. 21, 1825, a. 52ys, He d. Feb. 22, 1843. Ch. b: Catharine, Jan. 26, 1800; Philip Schuyler, Feb. 9, 1801, d. at Bethany, Va., March 20, 1847, a. 46ys.; William Henry, Oct. 9, 1806; Margaret, ——, 1809, d. Sept. 6, 1810, a. 1yr., 1m., 6d.; Harriet, ——, d. in Patterson, N. J., Dec. 28, 1872, in her 55th year.

ABRAHAM, son of Dirk, m. Elisabeth Van Boskerk, Jan. 11, 1796. He was an attorney-at-law in Schenectady, d. at Rahway, N. J., March 18, 1852; his wife b. Dec. 22, 1776, d. Sept. 8, 1849.

VAN IVEREN.

REINIER, of Canajoharie, m. Neeltie Van Eps of Schenectady, Nov., 1761.

VAN LOON.

JOHN, m. Elisabeth Key (Frey). Ch. bp: Dirkje, Jan. 22, 1780; John, Dec. 27, 1781; Catrina, Aug. 10, 1783.

VAN MARCKEN.

JAN GERRITSE, and wife Geertje Huybertse (Gysbertse), sister of Frederick Gysbertse Van Den Bergh, came over in the ship *St. Jacob* in 1654; in 1657 received a patent for a lot at Fort Casimir; banished from New Amstel same year, and came thence to Beverwyck, and for several years was farmer of the excise of wine, beer and spirits; in 1673 was appointed *schout* of Schenectady.

VAN NORSTRAND.

JOHN, m. Marytje Van Etten. Ch: Annatje, bp. Jan. 10, 1779. Ch b: Sarah, Dec. 13, 1793; Rebecca, June 4, 1795; Ariaantje, Feb. 24, 1798.

VAN OLINDA.

PIETER DANIELSE, m. Hilletie Cornelise, sister of Jacques Cornelise Van Slyck. She was a half breed, her mother being a Mohawk woman, her father Cornelis Antonissen Van Slyck. For many years she was employed with Jan Baptist Van Eps and Lourens Claese Van der Volgen as provincial interpreter at a salary of £20. The Mohawk sachems gave her the Great island in the Mohawk river at Niskayuna in 1667, which Van Olinda sold to Capt. Johannes Clute in 1669; they also gave her land at the *Willow flat* (below Port Jackson), and at the *Boght* in Watervliet. She d. Feb. 10, 1707. Van Olinda made his will Aug. 1, 1715, proved Dec. 27, 1716, gave to his eldest son *Daniel* ten shillings, to *Jacob* the use of his land above Schenectady called the *Willow flat*, being land " patented to me and William Van Coppernol till my son Matthys (now *non compos mentis*) shall dye," &c., spoke also of his land at the *Boght*.

DANIEL, son of Pieter, m. Lysbeth, dau. of Martinus Cregier of Niskayuna, June 11, 1696. Ch. bp: Pieter, Nov. 8, 1696, in Albany; Johannes, Sept. 3, 1699; Martinus, Oct. 25, 1702; Maria, ——, 1704. [*See Albany Families.*]

JACOB, son of Pieter, m. Eva, dau. of Claas De Graaf. Ch. bp: Pieter, Feb. 17, 1712, in Albany; Willem, Oct. 13, 1716; *Marten*, Jan. 18, 1718; Nicolaas, May 30, 1719; Helena, Feb. 12, 1721,

m. Johannes Quackenbos; Elisabet, June 16, 1723.

MARTIN, son of Jacob, of the *Willigen*, and Catharina, dau. of Frederic Clute of Ganestagyoene, m. July 25, 1741; he m. secondly, Cornelia, dau. of Benjamin Van Vleck, Dec. 7, 1754. Ch. bp : *Jacob*, June 13, 1742; Francyntje, Jan. 15, 1744; Eva, Nov. 24, 1745; *Pieter*, Jan. 17, 1748; Frederick, May 13, 1750; Catharina, Aug. 10, 1755, m. Wouter Swart; *Benjamin*, Dec. 25, 1757; Willem, April 27, 1760; *Willem*, Feb. 2, 1766; Johannes, Oct. 3, 1768.

PIETER, son of Martin, m. Eva Spoor. Ch. bp : Nicolaas, June 9, 1782; Francyntje, March 7, 1784; Ch. b : Maria, Sept. 15, 1786; Cornelia, Dec. 14, 1788; Martinus, Oct. 27, 1791; Judith, Sept. 27, 1793; Eva, June 16, 1796.

JACOB, son of Martin, and Machtelt Quackenbos, both of the *Willigen*, m. March 12, 1769.

DANIEL, of *Halve maan*, son of Marten Danielse, m. Marytje Van Der Werken, Dec. 1, 1764, in Albany. Ch. b. (and bp. in Albany); Johannes, Nov. 29, 1771; Elisabeth, Jan. 5, 1777; Daniel bp. in Schenectady, April 25, 1783. [*See Albany Families.*]

WILLEM, son of Martin, m. Elisabeth Truex. Ch. b : Martinus, July 21, 1789; Jacob, Dec. 13, 1790; Peter, March 9, 1798.

BENJAMIN, son of Martin, and Annatje, dau. of Petrus Groot, both of the

Willigen, m. Feb. 28, 1790. Ch. b : Cornelia, Oct. 31, 1790; Neeltje, Aug. 27, 1793; Benjamin, June 13, 1797; Peter Groot, July 26, 1805.

TEUNIS, and Catlyntje Peek, both of the *Willigen* m. June 27, 1795.

VAN PELT.

PETER, m. Marytje Van Slyck. Ch : Samuel; Baltus, bp. March 27, 1785; Elsje, b. Feb. 4, 1788; Maria, April 23, 1790.

SAMUEL, m. Elisabeth Westlo, July 1, 1792. Ch : Hannah, b. Apr. 8, 1793.

SAMUEL, perhaps the same as the last, m. ...... McMarlin. Ch. b : William May 1, 1796; Samuel, March 10, 1799.

VAN PETTEN.*

CLAAS FREDERICKSE, m. Aeffie, dau. of Arent Bratt and Catalyntje De Vos. He first came to Schenectady in 1664, and

with Isaac Cornelise Swits hired Willem Teller's *bouwerye gelegen op Schanechtede bestaende in woonhuys, schuerberg èn bouwlant in twee parcelles genomeneert* * * *

* The accompanying cut, purporting to be the arms of the Van Pettens of Holland, was furnished by one of the family.

van de landmeter No. 5, &c. In 1668 he bought, in company with Cornelis Cornelise Viele, the bouwery of Marten Cornelise Van Isselsteyn, lying next west of Reyer Schermerhorn's farm; and this remained in the family for several generations. Schermerhorn was his brother-in-law. In 1683–94 he owned a farm at Papsknee below Albany; 1690 was appointed justice of the peace by Leisler. He was b. May 30, 1641, and d. Oct. 3, 1728, a. 87ys., 5m. His wife d. Jan. 23, 1728, a. 78ys. Ch. bp. in Albany: *Arent;* Diewer, m. Cornelis Viele; Cathlyntje, m. Teunis Van Vechten of Loonenburgh; *Andries,* Sept. 10, 1684; Geertruy, April 17, 1687, m. Lourens C. Van der Volgen; *Claas,* April 6, 1690; Geertruy, July 28, 1692.

ARENT, son of Claas, m. Jannetje, dau. of Philip Conyn of Albany, April 10 (17), 1703. In company with Myndert Schuyler and Jan Dellamont, he received a patent for 500 acres of land on the Normanskil, Nov. 3, 1714. Ch. bp.: Frederick, Aug. 22, 1703; *Philip,* July 9, 1704; Claas, Jan. 29, 1706; Cathlyntje, Oct. 16, 1707, m. Samuel Bratt; Weyntje, Oct. 30, 1709, in Albany, m. Johannes Ouderkerk; *Nicolaas,* Oct., 1710; Eva, Nov. 13, 1712; Feitje, Dec. 18, 1714; Maritje, Jan. 19, 171$\frac{6}{7}$; *Dirk,* Jan. 3, 172$\frac{4}{5}$.

ANDRIES, son of Claas, m. Maieke, dau. of Jacob Ten Eyck of Albany, Dec. 26 (Nov. 25), 1712. He d. Sept. 25, 1748; she d. Jan. 31, 1777, a, 91ys., 9m., 27d. Ch. b: Nicolaas, Oct. 6, 1713,

d. Oct. 4, 1722; Geertruy, Oct. 17, 1715, d. March 22, 1730 (173$\frac{2}{9}$); Catharina, Sept. 13, 1718, m. Simon Veeder, d. Dec. 23, 1741; Jacob, May 30, 1721, d. July 23, 1730; Nicolaas, Oct. 28, d. Nov. 11, 1723; *Nicolaas,* July 23 (24), 1725; Barent, Sept. 12, 1727, d. May 21 (22), 1735.

NICOLAAS, son of Claas, m. Rebecca, dau. of Simon Groot jr. Ch. bp: *Frederick,* April 20, 1712; *Nicolaas,* Dec. 16, 1716; Eva, Sept. 24, 1719, m. Johannes Schermerhorn; *Simon,* March 24, 1722; Catrien, b. Feb. 1, bp. Feb. 21, 1725, m. first, Adam Swart, secondly, Arent Vedder; Maria, b. Sept. 27, bp. Oct. 15, 1727, m. Jacob Fonda; Elisabeth, ——, 1730, m. Harmanus Van Slyck; *Johannes,* April 29, 1739.

PHILIP, son of Arent, m. Geesie, dau. of Johannes Schermerhorn. Ch. bp: Arent, June 14, 1740; *Arent,* July 19, 1741; Engeltje, Dec. 2, 1744, m. Johannes Groot; Fytje, May 24, 1747; *Jan,* March 26, 1749; Fytje, May 12, 1751, m. Caleb Truex.

PHILIP, son of Frederick, m. Debora, dau. of Cornelis Viele, May 4, 1764. He made his will Sept. 2, 1809, proved Dec. 12, 1812, spoke of sons Philip, Simon and John. He d. Sept. 15, 1812, a. 69ys., 7m., 3d.; she was b. July 11, 1743, d. Dec. 13, 1816, a. 73ys., 5m., 2d. Ch. b: Elisabeth, Sept. 12, 1765; *Cornelis,* May 30, 1767; Clara, July 15, 1769, m. Pieter Condè; Frederic, Jan. 8, 1772, d. Dec. 29, 1817, a 45ys., 11m.,

21d.; Nicholas, Nov. 26, 1774; Sarah, August 17, 1776, bp. Sept. 21, 1777; Philippus, June 18, 1780, made will May 26, 1815, proved June 16, 1816, spoke of Polly my wife, brother Cornelis, dau. Debora Ann, Elisabeth and Clarissa; d. June 28, 1815, in Glenville*; Simon, Dec. 14, 1782; Johannes, May 17, 1786.

FREDERIC, son of Claas, m. Elisabeth, dau of Philip Groot, April 10, 1737. In 1770 his house lot was on the south side of Front street, the second west of Church street; d. June 20, 1771. Ch. bp: Sarah, Dec. 21, 1737, m. Abraham Bratt; *Philippus*, b. Jan. 18, bp. Feb. 6, 1743, d. Sept. 15, 1812, a. 69ys., 7m., 3d.; his wife Debora, b. July 11, 1743, d. Dec. 13, 1816, a. 73ys., 5m., 2d.; *Nicolaas*, July 13, 1740; Rebecca, Oct. 11, 1747, m. Cornelis De Graaf; *Simon*, Jan. 6, 1751; Geertruy, June 20, 1756, m. Solomon Terwilliger.

NICOLAAS, son of Arent, m. Ariaantje, dau. of Arent Andriese Bratt. Ch. bp: Arent (?), Oct. 21, 1739; Andries, June 13, 1742; *Arent*, July 1, 1744; Jannetje, Dec. 14, 1746, m. Samuel Tyms; Andries, April 23, 1749; Marytje, Nov. 10, 1752; Catharina, Nov. 22, 1759.

NICOLAAS, son of Nicolaas, m. Sarah, dau. of Pieter Clement, Sept. 19, 1744. Ch. bp: *Nicolaas*, Sept. 23, 1744; *Petrus*, May 5, 1751; *Frederic*, Dec. 26, 1753; Annatje, May 30, 1756; Annatje, Dec. 24, 1758, m. Daniel Relyea; Simon, July 19, 1761; *Arent*, June 17, 1764; *Johannes*, Feb. 8, 1767.

SIMON, son of Nicolaas, m. Jannetje, dau. of Hendrick Vrooman, January 27, 17$\frac{49}{50}$. Ch. bp: *Nicolaas*, Oct. 21, 1750; *Hendrick*, April 2, 1753; *Adam*, Jan. 2, 1757; *Frederic*, Jan. 20, 1760; Engeltie, July 1, 1764; Rebecca, Oct. 9, 1768, m. John Bradford; Eva, b. April 1, 1771, m. Jacob C. Mebie.

DIRK, son of Arent, m. Rebecca, dau. of Pieter Van Antwerpen, June 1, 1750. Ch. b: Sophia, Mar. 9, 1751, m. Arent A. Vedder; *Johannes*, b. Sept. 4, 1753 (Bible), bp. Feb. 9, 1752 (*Church Record*); Arent, b. Sept. 15, 1757 (Bible), bp. March 27, 1757 (*Church Record*); made will March 29, 1810, proved 1813, left real estate to Henry C. Van Dyck and Richard McMichael his nephews, sons of his sisters Mary and Engeltie; *Petrus*, Jan. 17, 1759; *Frederic*, b. Mar. 23 (Bible), bp. Feb. 15, 1761 (*Church Record*); Engeltie, April 1, 1763, m. Alexander McMichael; Maria, Oct. 6, 1766, m. Cornelis Van Dyck; *Dirk*, Nov. 19, 1769; Nicolaas, Dec. 31, 1773.

NICOLAAS, son of Andries, m. first, Catlyntje Wemple, Oct. 24, 1747; and secondly, Susanna, dau. of Harmanus Vedder, June 2, 1749. His last wife, Susanna, m. Johannes Cuyler, July 5, 1763. Ch. bp: Geertje, Aug. 26, 1750; *Andries*, March 5, 1754; *Harmanus*, Aug. 8, 1756.

NICOLAAS, son of Nicolaas, and Margarita Ecker, both of Rensselaerswyck, m. Dec. 19, 1767. Ch. bp: Sarah, Mar. 12, 1769; *Jacob*, Jan. 27, 1771; *Petrus*, Dec. 14, 1777.

JOHANNES, son of Nicolaas, m. Neeltje, dau. of Simon Vedder, July 10, 1762. Ch. bp: Rebecca, March 20, 1763, m. Frans Vedder; Maria, July 27, 1766, m. David Van Etten; *Nicolaas,* Dec. 10, 1769; Sarah, Nov. 1, 1772; *Simon,* Sept. 3, 1775, d. at West Glenville, Dec. 20, 1851, a. 76ys.; Elisabeth, Nov. 8, 1778; Eva, Oct. 14, 1781, m. John A. Van Eps; Arent, b. April 4, 1785.

ARENT, son of Nicolaas, m. Helena, dau. of Jan Baptist Van Eps, July 28, 1765. He made his will 1785, proved Jan. 28, 1786, and spoke of the following ch.: Ch. bp: Nicholas, Aug. 10, 1766; Maria, May 1, 1768; Nicholaas, May 13, 1770; Maria, Oct. 15, 1772; *Jan Baptist,* July 16, 1775; Jannetje, July 25, 1779.

ARENT, son of Nicolaas and Sarah Clement, m. Engeltie, dau. of Myndert LaGrange. Ch. b: Helena, April 26, 1788; Petrus, Aug. 20, 1795.

NICOLAAS, son of Simon, m. first, Engeltje, dau. of Nicolaas Viele, and secondly, Annatje, dau. of John Fairly, July 1, 1792. He d. in Glenville July 15, 1829, in his 80th year. Ch. bp: *Simon,* Nov. 6, 1774; Neeltje, August 3, 1777; Jannetje, Sept. 24, 1780; Nicolaas, Oct. 20, 1782; Hendrick, Dec. 26, 1784. Ch. b: Engeltie, Sept. 13, 1787; John, April 18, 1795; Elisabeth, Oct. 4, 1796; Rebecca, Feb. 6, 1798.

ANDREAS, son of Nicolaas, m. Engeltie, dau. of Caleb Beck. He once lived on east corner of State and Ferry streets;

owned a house and farm northwest of the Schermerhorn mills, which he sold to his son-in-law, John B. Schermerhorn. His wife d. July 13, 1817, aged 56ys. Ch. bp: Nicolaas, Dec. 21, 1777; Caleb, Dec. 10, 1780; Susanna, Nov. 3, 1782; Maria, Nov. 1, 1784. Ch. b: Getty, Aug. 4, 1787, m. John B. Schermerhorn, d. in Rotterdam, November 20, 1844, in her 58th year; Abram, Nov. 13, 1793, d. July 12, 1863, in his 70th year; his wife Sophia, d. June 4, 1848, a. 43ys., 3m., 11d.; Andries Vedder, Feb. —, 1798.

HENDERICK, son of Simon, m. Hester, dau. of John Fairly. Ch. bp: Simon, March 1, 1778; Jannetje, Sept. 2, 1781; Metje, Nov. 2, 1783.

SIMON, son of Nicolaas, m. Elisabeth Bratt, Nov. 12, 1797. Ch. b: Engeltje, Feb. 18, 1798; Bata, Nov. 10, 1801; Claas Viele, Sept. 8, 1803; Gezina, Nov. 27, 1805; John Platt, Oct. 26, 1808.

JAN, son of Philip, m. Margarita Heemstraat of Rensselaerswyck, Jan. 15, 1775. Ch. bp: Maria, March 15, 1778; Dirk, April 14, 1784. Ch. b: Reyer, June 15, 1789; Lena, Nov. 14, 1793; Arent, May 11, 1797.

JACOB, son of Nicolaas, m. Susanna Brooks of Normanskil, Feb. 5, 1796.

SIMON, son of Frederic, m. Maria, dau. of Jan Baptist Wendell. Ch. bp: *Frederic,* Jan. 17, 1779; Jacomyntje, Aug. 19, 1781; Jan Baptist, April 26, 1784. Ch. b: Elisabeth, Aug. 30, 1786;

Ahasuerus Wendell, January 23, 1789; Sarah, Nov. 12, 1791, m. Simon Swart of Glenville, and d. July 19, 1841, a. 50ys., 8m. 7d.; Annatie Wendell, April 20, 1794, d. Sept. 22, 1851, a. 57ys.; Nicolaas, May 24, 1796; Rebecca, Aug. 22, 1798, m. Cornelius J. Bratt, d. Jan. 18, 1822, a. 23ys., 4m., 26d.; Cornelius Jacobus Van Dyck, July 11, 1801, d. in Glenville, April 22, 1854.

ARENT, son of Philip, m. Martha Bucly (Bokly). Ch. bp: Gesina, April 9, 1779; Philippus, Feb. 28, 1781.

DIRK, son of Dirk and Heyltje Pangburn, both of Normanskil, m. Feb. 18, 1793. Ch. b: John, June 24, 1793; Dirk, Oct. 24, 1794; Petrus, May 2, 1796; Catlyntje, April 5, 1798; Arent, Dec. 28, 1799; Rebecca, Oct. 13, 1801; Nicolaas, Nov. 9, 1803; Isaac, March 5, 1806.

JOHANNES, son of Dirk, m. Wyntje Clute. Ch. bp: Dirk, b. Nov. 18, bp. Nov. 29, 1778, in Albany; Johannes, bp. May 28, 1781; Rebecca, June 6, 1784. Ch. b: Jannetje, Sept. 6, 1787; Sophia, Sept. 25, 1789; Sophia and Elisabeth, Oct. 24, 1795.

JOHN, son of Arent, m. Lydia, dau. of Harmanus Pieters, July 30, 1796. Ch. b: Arent, May 3, 1798; Jacob Sanderse Glen, Dec. 22, 1799; Harmanus Peters, Sept. 6, 1801; Arent, March 10, 1803; Helen Maria Van Eps, bp January 13, 1805; Harriet Jane, b. June 19, 1808.

ADAM, son of Simon, m. Rebecca, dau. of Abraham Schermerhorn. In 1838 he was living in Blenheim, a. 81ys. Ch. bp: Simon, Dec. 23, 1781; Abraham, Sept. 24, 1783. Ch. b: Gezina, January 22, 1786; Clara, Oct. 17, 1787; Nicolaas, Sept. 6, 1789; Engeltje, Dec. 9, 1791; Rebecca, Dec. 16, 1793; Adam, Jan. 21, 1796; Eva, Oct. 21, 1797.

FREDERIC, son of Nicolaas, m. Helena Swits. Ch: Sarah, bp. Sept. 22, 1782.

CORNELIUS, son of Philip F., m. Margarieta, dau. of Jesse Van Slyck. He d. March 17, 1845, in his 78th year. Ch. b: Debora, April 30, 1796, m. Nicholas H. Vedder, d. May 29, 1822; Jacomyntje, March 2, 1798; Philip, Feb. 25, 1800, d. Nov. 1, 1836; Jesse, May 27, 1803, d. in Glenville, Aug. 26, 1845, his wife Rebecca, b. Feb. 19, 1811, d. Nov. 20, 1839, a. 28ys., 9m., 1d ; Elisabeth, June 3, 1806.

NICHOLAS A., m. Eva, dau. of Cornelis Barheyt. Ch. b: John, bp. Aug. 3, 1784; Cornelius, August 23, 1786; Cornelius, June 12, 1788; Andries, Oct. 8, 1789.

NICHOLAS, widower, m. Elisabeth Quackenbos, Oct. 30, 1792.

FREDERIC, son of Simon, m. first, Alida, dau. of John Fairly; she d. between Sept. 19, 1792 and Feb 3, 1793; and he m. secondly, Sally Bartlett. Ch. b: Engeltie, bp. Oct. 10, 1784; Elisabeth, b. Aug. 5, 1786; Symon, Dec. 11, 1788; Esther, Oct. 17, 1790; Alida

Fairly, Sept. 19, 1792; Jemima, Aug. 31, 1805.

PETRUS, son of Nicolaas, of Normanskil, m. Annatje Ecker. Ch : Nicolaas, bp. Feb. 22, 1785.

SIMON, son of Johannes, and Eva, dau. of Adam Condè, both of Charlton, m. Dec. 16, 1797. Ch. b : Neeltje, Oct. 15, 1798; Sarah Truex, Feb. 6, 1800; Rebecca, March 9, 1802 ; Catalina, Aug. 10, 1804; George, Oct. 29, 1806; Adam Condè, Jan. 19, 1810; Rebecca Maria, Jan. 31, 1831.

NICOLAAS, son of Frederic, m. Margarita, dau. of Ephraim Bratt. Ch. b : Frederic, April 5, 1785, d. Nov. 4, 1852, in Glenville; Ephraim, Aug. 10, 1786; Elisabeth, Aug. 21, 1788; Philip, Mar. 16, 1790; Simon, Feb. 5, 1792; Clara, Oct. 20, 1793; Nicolaas, Mar. 17, 1795, d. Sept. 27, 1849.

JOHN, and Susanna Brooks, both of Normanskil, m. Feb. 5, 1796.

JOHN, son of Nicolaas A. and Margarita Haverly (Haverling), both of Rensselaerswyck, m. Oct. 25, 1787. Ch. b : Nicholas, July 23, 1788; Annatje, June 24, 1790; Sarah, Aug. 21, 1792; Johannes, July 22, 1794; Catharina Beck, Dec. 13, 1798; Christiaan Haverly, May 30, 1801.

PETER, son of Dirk, m. Volkje, dau. of Abraham Peterse Van Antwerpen, Oct. 26, 1788. Ch. b : Dirk, March 15, 1789; Margarita, Aug. 18, 1791; Annatje, May 3, 1794.

FREDERIC, son of Dirk, m. Jacomyntje, dau. of Hendrick Van Dyck, Nov. 2, 1788. He was living in 1839 in Glenville, then a. 78ys. Ch. b : Nicolaas, March 10, 1789; Hendrick, Aug. 19, 1791; Rebecca, Dec. 28, 1793; Engeltie, June 10, 1796; Sophia, Feb. 23, 1799 ; Maria, Sept. 17, 1803; Jannetje, March 31, 1806; Cornelius, April 2, 1809.

NICOLAAS, son of Johannes, m. Catharina, dau. of Cornelis Mebie, March 12, 1789. (A Nicolaas V. P., perhaps the above, was buried July 19, 1804). Ch. b : Johannes, Nov. 13, 1790; Esther, May 12, 1793; Simon, Aug. 20, 1795; Neeltje, July 27, 1798; Cornelius, April 14, 1803.

FREDERIC, son of Simon, m. Esther, dau. of Carel Hansen Toll, and wid. of Johannes Teller. Ch : Simon, b. Feb. 24, 1797.

VAN RENSSELAER.

HENDRIK, son of Hendrik of Greenbush, m. Elisabeth, dau. of Johannes Van Brugh of New York. Ch. bp : Johannes Van Brugh, Oct. 14, 1738; Jeremia, Aug. 16, 1740. [*See Albany Families.*]

KILIAAN, of Claverak, m. Margarita, dau. of John Sanders of Schenectady, Jan. 27, 1791.

VAN ROTTERDAM.

JAN JANSE, was a landholder in Schenectady before 1678. Ch. bp. in Albany : Rachel, Jan. 20, 1686; Sander, June 8, 1690.

VAN SANTVOORD.

Rev. CORNELIS, the fifth minister of the church in Schenectady, was called from the church on Staten island in 1740. He probably came from Leyden, where he had a sister living at the date of his death, 1752. He was an accomplished scholar, and could preach equally well in the English, French and Dutch languages. His wife was Anna, dau. of Johannes Staats of Staten island, where all his ch. were born; she d. soon after coming to Schenectady, and he m. secondly, Elisabeth Toll, Aug. 19, 1745; she also was deceased at the date of his will, leaving no issue. On the 6th March, 174⁴⁄₅, he made his will, proved Nov. 24, 1752, and spoke of ch. *Cornelis; Staats; Zeger;* Jacoba, who m. Pieter Truex; Geertje, wife of Ryk Van der Bilt on the Raritan; Anne; also of his grand children Antje Veldtman and Anna Wendell, and of his sister and her husband Zeger Hazebroek living at Leyden. He had a dau. Maria Catharina, who m. Johannes E. Wendell. Dec. 25, 1751, Domine Van Santvoord preached his last sermon from the text, Luke II. 13, 14. Seven days after, on New year's day, he again ascended the pulpit, but being too weak to preach, concluded his last service with prayer and the customary New year's blessing; six days after, to wit on the 6th day of Jan., 1752, he died, aged 55yrs. [De Graaf Bible.] He was buried under the church.

CORNELIS, eldest son of Domine Van Santvoord, removed to Albany about 1747, and m. Ariaantje Bratt, Dec. 31, 1747, in Albany. He and his brother Staats m. sisters, dau. of Anthony Bratt, on the same day. In 1761 he lived on the site of the present Delavan House. Ch. bp. in Albany: *Cornelis,* Dec. 31, 1749; Rebecca, Jan. 5, 1752; Antje, April 22, 1754; Anthony, Oct. 16, 1757; Willempie, Nov. 19, 1758; *Antony,* Sept. 20, 1761.

STAATS, second son of Domine Van Santvoord, was a gunsmith, settled in Albany about 1747, and m. Willempie, dau. of Anthony Bratt, Dec. 31, 1747. Ch. bp. in Albany: Antje, May 28, 1749; Rebecca, Jan. 6, 1751; Anthony, Feb. 2, 1752; Rebecca, March 24, 1754; Cornelis, May 22, 1757; Teunis, b. Mar. 10, 1760.

ZEGER, son of Domine Van Santvoord, remained in Schenectady, where he m. Catlyntje, dau. of Elias Post, April 18, 1756. He d. April 18, 1813, a. 79ys., 6m., 6d.; she d. June 17, 1810, a. 71ys., 14d. Ch: *Cornelis,* bp. May 29, 1757.

CORNELIS, son of Cornelis of Albany, m. Cornelia Van Wie of Albany, where he settled. Ch. b. in Albany: Cornelis, April 4, 1776; Hendrik, July 29, 1779; Ariaantje, Feb. 2, 1783; Catharina, Apr. 16, 1786; *Anthony* (?).

Capt. ANTHONY, son of Cornelis and Ariaantje Bratt of Albany, m. first, Maria Roff (Ross, Rhoff), Sept. 15, 1786. She d. Nov. 16, 1800, a. 22ys., 4m., 16d.; and secondly, Rachel Groesbeck, about

1806. She d. in the Middle Dutch church, March 8, 1835, a. 60ys., 2m., 3d.; he d. Feb. (March) 17, 1852, a. 90ys., 5m., 3d. Ch. b: Adriaantje, May 15, 1787; John, Oct. 12, 1788, d. Mar. 1, 1811, a. 22ys., 4m., 16d.; Hadrian, Aug. 23, 1790, d. at Kendall, Sept. 6, 1870, a. 80ys., 14d.; Hosiah, Jan. 16, 1793; Christina Louisa, March 2, 1796; Rebecca, Sept. 7, 1799; Anthony Groesbeck, Oct. 13, 1806.

ANTHONY, son of Cornelis and Cornelia Van Wie of Albany, m. first, Catharine Groesbeck, October 3, 1807, and secondly, Sarah ......, about 1815. Ch. b: Anna Maria, June 12, 1808; Cornelia, March 12, 1810; Cornelius, Mar. 11, 1813; Catharine Groesbeck, Nov. 29, 1815.

CORNELIUS, son of Zeger, of Schenectady, m. Eva, dau. of Abraham Swits. He d. March 12, 1845, a. 87ys., 9m., 21d.; she d. June 8, 1835, a. 73ys., 8m., 14d. Ch. b: Zeger, June 21, 1783, d. Nov. 28, 1824, m. Elisabeth Loague; Abraham, bp. Dec. 26, 1784, m. Sarah Hitchcock; Elias, b. June 23, 1786; Margrietje, April 3, 1788; Staats, Mar. 15, 1790, minister of the Ref. church, m. Margaret Van Hisling; Margarieta, Oct. 30, 1791, d. Dec. 30, 1859; Catlyna, July 6, 1793, m. William Dow; Catharina, Nov. 1, 1795, d. June 28 (30), 1854; Johannes Post, March 2, 1798, d. Aug. 3, 1802; Annatje, Aug. 3, 1800, d. July 26, 1802; Annatje, Dec. 13, 1803, m. Richard Wilson, d. Jan. 10, 1860.

VAN·SCHAICK.

ANTONY, son of Anthony, of Albany, m. Anna Cuyler. Ch: Adam, bp. Nov. 13, 1712. [*See Albany Families.*]

SYBRANT, m. Eva Vrooman. Ch. bp: Jannetje, March 30, 1755, m. Evert Van den Bergh; Eva, Feb. 6, 1756, m. Johannes Bastiaanse.

GERRIT, son of Sybrant of Albany, "VAN Schachtekook," m. Elisabeth, dau. of Harmanus Van Slyck, Dec. 4, 1766. Ch. bp: *Sybrant*, Oct. 11, 1767; Harmanus, June 25, 1769; Sarah, March 10, 1771; Jannetje, Mar. 28, 1773, m. Arent A. Bratt; Lidia, Mar. 26, 1775, m. Pieter Stiers; Catalyntje, July 19, 1778, m. Hendrick Barheit; Harmanus Van Slyck, Aug. 20, 1781.

SYBRANT, son of Gerrit, m. Tanneke Peek, May, 1789. He d. June 15, 1840, in his 74th year; she d. Feb. 9, 1845, a. 74ys. Ch. b: Gerrit, Oct. 21, 1789; John, Dec. 2, 1791; Gerrit, April 18, 1793; Elisabeth, Dec. 17, 1794; Eva Yates, July 9, 1797; Sarah, August 6, 1799; Harmanus, May 10, 1801, d. Apr. 22, 1854; Joseph Yates, Mar. 10, 1803; Sarah Ann, Aug. 9, 1804; Christopher Joseph Yates, Aug. 8, 1806, d. Aug. 30, 1852.

VAN SICE (SEYSSEN).

JOSEPH (Joost), m. first, Helena Magdalena, dau. of Jan Vrooman, and secondly, Elisabeth, dau. of Jacobus Peek, and wid. of Cornelis Van der Volgen, Nov. 8, 1732. In 1735 he lived on lot now occupied by William McCamus & Co.; was a gunsmith and armorer. Ch. bp: *Johannes*, b. Jan. 16, bp. Jan. 23, 1726; Judickje, m. Henricus H. Veeder; *Jacobus*, Aug. 19, 1733; *Cornelis*, March 29, 1737; *Petrus;* Margariet, m. Doctor Dirk Van Ingen.

JAN (Johannes), son of Joseph, gunsmith, m. Margarita Fort, March 11, 174⅞. Ch. bp: Magdalena, October 29, 1749, m. Alexander Campbell; Elisabeth, April 28, 1753; *Joseph*, June 29, 1755; Rebecca, Nov. 6, 1757; Johannes, Aug. 19, 1759; *Cornelis*, Nov. 1, 1761; *Abraham*, Nov. 27, 1763; *Simon*, Sept. 1, 1765; Maria, Oct. 18, 1767; Maria, Jan. 1, 1769, m. Willem Pemberton; Daniel, Aug. 18, 1771.

JACOBUS, son of Joseph, widower, m. Sarah, dau. of Gysbert Marselis, July 16, 1757. Ch. bp: Joseph, June 18, 1758; Joseph, May 24, 1759; Elisabeth, Nov. 9, 1760; *Gysbert*, Oct. 17, 1762; Margarita, Oct. 7, 1764; Catarina, Dec. 7, 1766; *Joseph*, Oct. 9, 1768; Catarina, Sept. 6, 1770; *Jacobus*, Oct. 3, 1772; Ahasuerus, Feb. 5, 1775, d. Oct. 8, 1852.

CORNELIS, son of Joseph, m. Maria, dau. of Alexander Vedder. Ch. bp: Elisabeth, Aug. 9, 1760, m. Willem Gordon; Annatje, Sept. 26, 1762; Margarita, Dec. 9, 1764; Catarina, September 27, 1767; Alexander, Dec. 6, 1772; Joseph, July 23, 1775.

JOSEPH, son of Johannes, m. Elisabeth Krankheyt. Ch: Johannes, b. Jan. 17, 1786.

GYSBERT (Gilbert), son of Jacobus, m. first, Barbara Fyles of Montgomery county, Oct. 22, 1786; and secondly, Sarah, dau. of Abraham Van Antwerpen. Ch. of the first wife : Sarah, b. Sept. 17, 1787. Ch. of the second wife : James, b. Aug. 21, 1797; Annatje, June 7, 1800.

CORNELIS, son of Johannes, and Debora Murray, both of the Hellenbergh, m. Dec. 16, 1787. Ch. b: Simon, May 16, 1791; Margarita, Dec. 25, 1793; Samuel, Nov. 22, 1796; Abram, Sept. 2, 1799; Annatje, Feb. 3, 1803.

SYMON, son of Johannes, m. Annatje, dau. of Teunis Barheyt, March 15, 1789. Ch. b: Margarieta, February 18, 1790; Teunis, Jan. 9, 1792; Jacomyntje, Nov. 9, 1793; Annatje, Apr. 15, 1798; Magdalena, Nov. 15, 1796; Elisabeth, Dec. 25, 1800.

ABRAHAM, son of Johannes, m. Maria Smith, Sept. 20, 1789. Ch. b: Johannes, July 1, 1790; Margarieta, Feb. 10, 1794; Christiaan, May 18, 1798; Hendrik, Feb. 1, 1803.

JOSEPH, son of Jacobus, m. Sarah Hughs. Ch. b: Jacobus, Nov. 8, 1792, d. Sept. 13, 1794; Rebecca, Sept. 18, 1794; Jacobus, Sept. 6, 1796; Maria, April 28, 1798; John Post, July 25, 1800.

JACOBUS, son of Jacobus, m. Elisabeth, dau. of Dirk Groot. He d. Nov. 4, 1841; she d. April 30, 1847, a. 72ys. Ch. b: Sarah, Aug. 6, 1799; Ariaantje, Dec. 25, 1801; Catharine, Feb. 19, 1804;

Derick, Oct. 23, 1805; James, Aug. 29, 1809; Andrew Groot, Oct. 9, 1811; Cornelius, Dec. 26, 1814; Gilbert, Dec. 8, 1816; John Ogden, May 6, 1820.

VAN SLICHTENHORST.

GERRIT, son of Brant Aertse, was one of the magistrates of Schenectady in 1672. [*See Albany Families.*]

VAN SLYCK.

There were two early settlers of Beverwyck of this name; Willem, whose descendants settled below Albany, in Columbia county and elsewhere, and Cornelis Antonissen, *alias* "*Broer* Cornelis," so called by the natives. The latter is said to have married a Mohawk woman by whom he had several children : *Jacques;* Marten Mouris; Hilletie and perhaps Lea. Marten was in Beverwyck in 1661; gave name to the island (now Van Slyck's) lying in the Mohawk, west of Schenectady, and d. probably early in 1662; Hilletie, m. Pieter Danielse Van Olinda, and was often employed as the provincial interpreter for the Five Nations; Lea, m. first, Claas Willemse Van Coppernol, and secondly, Jonathan Stevens. "Broer Cornelis," d. in 1676. By reason of his eminent services rendered in bringing about peace with the natives, he received a patent for a large tract of land at Catskil; he also owned land near Cohoes.

JACQUES, son of Cornelis, was b. in 1640 at Canajoharie; his Indian name was Itsychosaquachka; he was also sometimes called Aques Cornelyssen Gautsh. The Mohawks gave him half of the island

in the Mohawk lying immediately west of the city; also land five miles above the city on the south side of the river. In 1671 he was one of the two licensed tapsters in the village. His wife was Grietje, dau. of Harmen Janse Ryckman of Albany; after his death in 1690, she m. Adam Vrooman, Feb. 21, 169½. His will was made May 8, 1690. The following children were living in 1697; *Harmen,* eldest son; Susanna, m. Samuel Arentse Bratt; Grietje, m first, Andries Arentse Bratt, and secondly, Harmen Vedder; *Cornelis;* Geertruy, m. Johannes Myndertse; *Marten;* Helena; Sytje; Lidia, m. Isaac Van Valkenburgh. Of the above children, Marten and Cornelis lived upon the First flat, on land which was left them by their father, and which is still owned by the family.

CORNELIS, son of Jacques, m. Clara Janse Bratt of Albany, Feb. 10, 1696. He lived upon the First flat. Ch. bp : Margriet, Feb. 12, 1696, in Albany, m. Jacobus Peek; Maria, May 23, 1697, in Albany, m. Johannes Ryckman; Jacques, Oct. 19, 1698; *Johannes,* Jan. 9, 1700; *Adriaan,* Feb. 9, 1701; *Harmanus,* April 19, 1702; *Henderick,* Oct. 24, 1703; Helena, May 6, 1705, m. Daniel Van Antwerpen; *Antony,* Dec. 15, 1706, in Albany; *Albert,* May 26, 1708; Geertruy, Oct. 30, 1709, in Albany; Catharina; *Cornelis,* March 6, 1711; *Petrus,* Feb. 1, 17½⅔; Susanna, March 24, 1716.

MARTEN, son of Jacques, m. Grietje Gerritse (Van Vranken ?), March 23, 1701. Ch. bp : Jacob, Feb. 8, 1702;

Gerrit, Feb. 27, 1704; Margarita, Feb. 16, 1707, in Albany; *Petrus*, Oct. 30, 1709; Ariaantje, June 21 (?), 1712; Susanna, Dec. 18, 1714.

Capt. HARMEN, son of Jacques, m. Jannetie, dau. of Adam (?) Vrooman, March 26, 1704, and Antje Schell about 1726. He was ensign of the company of foot in Schenectady in 1700; captain in 1714; Indian trader in 1724; received a grant of 300 morgens of land at Canajoharie from the Mohawks because "his grandmother was a right Mohawk woman," and "his father born with us in the above said *Kanajoree.*" By his father's will he also received 14 morgens of land on the First flat. He made his will Nov. 1, 1731, and left his sons, Adam and Jacobus of Schenectady, and Harmanus of Canajoharie, half of his 2,000 acres of land at the latter place. He was not living Dec. 20, 1734. Ch. bp : *Jacobus*, May 28, 1704; Engeltie, Jan. 29, 1706, m. Sander Lansing; Margarieta, Nov. 9, 1707, d. Mar. 12, 1787, a. 79ys., 4m.; Helena, Jan. 15, 1710, at Albany; Samuel, d. 1778; Catrina, September 13, 1712, m. Johannes Visger; Jannetje; Adam, Nov. 10, 1716; Geertruy, Jan. 10, 1719; *Adam*, March 5, 1721; *Harmanus*, June 14, 1724; Akers (Jacques), Jan. 7, 1727; Gerrit, Aug. (?), 1729.

HENDERICK, son of Cornelis, m. Catharina, dau. of Cornelis Slingerland, June 6, 1729. Ch : Clara, bp. ——, 1730, m. Johannes J. Vrooman.

ANTHONY, son of Cornelis, m. Mar-garet Van Slyck, Nov. 19, 1730. Ch : Cornelis, bp. April 18, 1731.

ADRIAAN, son of Cornelis, m. first, Jannetje Viele, Oct. 17, 1736; and secondly, Bregie, dau. of Carel Hansen Toll, Nov. 26, 1741. He was killed July, 1748, in the *Beukendaal* massacre. Ch. bp : Jannetje, May 14, 1738; Claartje, Nov. 7, 1742, m. Anthony Van Slyck; *Cornelis*, b. June 3, bp. June 10, 1744; Carel Hansen, March 2, 1746.

HARMANUS, son of Cornelis, m. first, Lydia, dau. of Harmanus Vedder, Aug. 16, 1729 ; secondly, Sara Visscher about 1738. He was an Indian trader. Ch. bp : Margarita, Oct. 12, 1731; *Anthony*, April 29, 1733; Clara, July 27, 1735; ......, July ——, 1739; Maria, Sept. 21, 1740; Johannes, May 9, 1742; Elisabeth, June 10, 1744, m. Gerrit Van Slyck; Annatje, Nov. 9, 1746; Johannes, Sept. 18, 1748; Maria, January 8, 1752, m. Pieter Symonse Veeder; *Harmen*, July 13, 1755.

CORNELIS, son of Cornelis, trader, m. Jannetje, dau. of Abraham Truex *geboren in Albanie*, March 11, 1733. He made his will May 30, 1753, spoke of wife Jannetje and daus. Chistina, Geertruy, Klaartje and Susanna. Ch. b : Abraham, b. "between the 15th and 16th of June," 1736; Clara, Sept. 1, 1737, d. Oct. 31, 1745; Christina, Sept. 21, 1739, m. Gilbert Tice; Geertruy, July 19, 1743, d. Nov. 4, 1745; Abraham, July 29 (Bible), bp. July 21, (*Church Record*), 1745, d. Nov. 12, 1746; Clara and Geertruy,

April 27, 1747, the first d. March 4, 174⁷⁄₈, the second m. Johan Lambert; Clara, Aug. 27, 1749; Susanna, Oct. 13, 1751, m. Frans Pietersen.

ALBERT, son of Cornelis, m. Sara, dau. of Jan Danielse Van Antwerpen, Sept. 17, 1733. Ch. bp: Clara, June 16, 1734; Agnietje, July 9, 1737; Annatje, Dec. 27, 1741; Annatje, Nov. 27, 1743; Lena, Oct. 18, 1747.

Col. JACOBUS, son of Harmen, m. Cathlyna, dau. of Samuel Bratt, Sept. 2, 1732. He was commanding officer at Schenectady in 1754; member of the assembly 1750 and 1771. Ch. bp: *Harmanus*, Aug. 5, 1733; Geertruy, Nov. (?) 1, 1734; Jannetje, June 13, 1736, m. Philip Ryley; Samuel, March 17, 1738.

PETER, son of Cornelis m. Engelina, dau. of Domine Reinhard Erichzon (?), *geboren in Groningen in Europa*, Aug. 30, 1734. Ch. bp: Clara, b. Nov. 15, bp. Nov. 17, 1734; *Cornelis*, Dec. 1, 1736; Claartje, July —, 1739, m. John Steers; Annatje, Aug. 9, 1741, m. Johannes Barheyt; Willem, Dec. 4, 1743; Geertruy, Nov. 30, 1746; Geertruy, Oct. 8, 1749; *Adriaan*, June 23, 1751.

PIETER, son of Marten, m. Lysbetje, dau. of Jesse De Graaf, April 9, 1738. Ch. bp: Marytje, June 14, 1740; *Jesse*, Jan. 29, 1744; *Marten*, Oct. 20, 1748.

JOHANNES, son of Cornelis, trader, m. Lena Van Slyck, Feb. 4, 174⁹⁄₀. He made his will Dec. 10, 1751, proved Nov. 14, 1752; spoke of wife Lena, dau.

of Harmen Van Slyck, as then deceased; no children mentioned; left his property to his brothers and sisters, &c. Ch. bp: Jacobus, July 5, 1741; Cornelis, July 8, 1744.

HARMANUS, son of Jacobus, m. Annatje, dau. of Sander Glen, September 26, 1767. Ch: Cataleyntje, bp. Oct. 12, 1767.

ADRIAAN, son of Pieter, m. Annatje, dau. of Willem Lighthall. Ch. bp: Engelina, Jan. 12, 1777, m. Isaac Ouderkerk; *Willem*, b. Oct. 10, bp. Oct. 18, 1778; Elisabeth, bp. March 25, 1781; Petrus and Abraham, June 1, 1783. Ch. b: Elisabeth, Aug. 26, 1785; Geertruy, Sept. 13, 1787; Cornelius, Aug. 6, 1790; Elisabeth, Aug. 19, 1792; Maria, June 26, 1795; Albert, Jan. 8, 1798; Ahasuerus, Nov. 21, 1799.

ADAM, son of Harmen, m. Catharina, dau. of Jan Baptist Van Eps, Sept. 19, 1747. She was b. Nov. 16, 1723, d. June 30, 1793. Ch. bp: *Harmanus*, June 3, 1750; Helena, Aug. 5, 1759, m. Samuel Thorn.

HARMANUS, son of Harmen, m. Elisabeth, dau. of Nicolaas Van Petten, Jan. 27, 17⁴⁹⁄₅₀. He made his will April 20, 1776, spoke of wife Elisabeth, son Nicolaas, and dau. Rebecca and Engeltie; he then lived at Palatine, Tryon county. Ch. bp: *Nicolaas;* Jannetje, Dec. 11, 1757; Rebecca; Engeltje.

HARMANUS, JR., m. Christina Vrooman, June 4, 1757.

JESSE, son of Pieter, m. Jacomyntje, dau. of Cornelis Groot, Dec. 4, 1762. She d. Dec. 28, 1809, a. 67ys., 2m. He was captain in Col. Abraham Wemple's regiment in the Revolutionary war; made will May 25, 1815, proved Sept. 8, 1815, spoke of ch. Pieter, Elisabeth, Marten, Simon and Lena, and gave Marten his house in Green street. Ch. bp: Pieter, Nov. 20, 1763; Cornelius, Oct. 19, 1766; Margarita, Sept. 11, 1769, m. Cornelis Van Petten; Elisabeth, April 26, 1772; Marten, Feb. 19, 1775; Abraham, April 12, 1778, had a dau. Jemima mentioned in her grandfather's will; Simon, July 8, 1781; Simon, Feb. 1, 1783; Lena, b. Aug. 5, 1786.

CORNELIS, son of Pieter, m. Catarina, dau. of Pieter Veeder, March 30, 1764. Ch. bp: Engelina, Sept. 2, 1764, m. Petrus Clute jr.; Pieter, April 12, 1767; Maria, October 8, 1769, m. Johannes C. Barheyt; Clara, Aug. 23, 1772, m. Alexander Van Eps; Annatje, Oct. 23, 1774, m. Johannes Lighthall; Geertruy, Oct. 12, 1777, m. Pieter Beth; Neeltje, Oct. 22, 1780, m. Lourens Van Eps; Margarita, July 26, 1783; Margarieta, b. May 29, 1786, m. Robert Beth; Adriaan, b. Oct. 20, 1789.

ANTONY, son of Harmanus jr., m. Clara, dau. of Adriaan Van Slyck, April 12, 1767. Ch: Harmanus, b. Dec. 21, 1767, d. April 12, 1769; Harmanus, bp. Jan. 14, 1770; Harmanus, b. Feb. 4, 1777.

PIETER, son of Cornelis, m. Margarieta, dau. of James Lighthall, Feb. 28, 1790.

Ch. b: Cornelius, Aug. 11, 1790; James, Nov. 30, 1791; Catharina, Jan. 6, 1794; Abram, Sept. 3, 1797; Sarah, Aug. 6, 1799; James, Dec. 26, 1803.

HARMANUS, son of Adam, m. first, Maria, dau. of Isaac Vrooman, Dec. 5, 1771. Ch. bp: Adam, Oct. 31, 1773; Adam, March 26, 1775; Jacobus, March 23, 1777; Dorothea, July 18, 1779; Catarina, March 31, 1782. Ch. b; Rachel, Dec., 1784, m. Walter Groesbeck, d. October 9, 1821; Catharina, July 20, 1787; Christina Vrooman, Dec. 17, 1789. Harmanus Van Slyck, m. secondly, Annatje Haverly, Oct. 28, 1798. He d. Dec. 2, 1847, a. 70ys., 9m., 28d.; she d. June 3, 1855, a. 74ys. Ch. b: Anthony, July 25 (June 22 ?), 1800, d. Jan. 6, 1859; John Haverly, Jan. 20, 1809, d. Jan. 30, 1813; Clarissa, Sept. 27, 1810.

MARTEN, son of Pieter, m. Helena, dau. of Adam W. Vrooman, June 6, 1773. Ch. b: Pieter, August 9, 1774; Susanna, April 25, 1776, d. Sept. 1, 1778; Elisabeth, March 10, 1778, m. Arent B. Schermerhorn; Adam, bp. Apr. 2, 1780; Susanna, bp. July 4, 1782; Alida, Jan. 2, 1785; Jacob, b. Jan. 25, 1787; Margarietje, June 11, 1789.

HARMANUS, son of Harmanus m. Engeltje, dau. of Ahasuerus Marselis, June 11, 1775. [A Harmanus V. S. was buried August 8, 185 .] He lived at No. 33 Church street; his wife Angelica, .d Feb. 9, 1841, a. 86ys. Ch. bp: Harmanus, Dec. 10, 1775; Ahasuerus, October 19, 1777; Ahasuerus, Sept. 19, 1779; Johannes, January 1, 1782. Ch. b: Henderick, July 3, 1784; Sarah, June 28, 1787; Cornelius Nov. 10, 1789; Nicolaas, May 19, 1791, d. Nov. 11, 1864, a. 74ys.; Anthony, Dec. 8, 1793; Maria, Nov. 16, 1800.

CORNELIS, son of Adriaan, m. Elisabeth, dau. of Joseph R. Yates. He d. Jan. 27, 1799, in his 55th year; she d. between Jan. 2, 1802, and April 23, 1803. Ch. b: Elisabeth, April 19, 1776, d. Oct. 21, 1778; Maria, Dec. 1, 1777; Adriaan, Jan. 14, 1779; Maria, Jan. 29, 1781, d. Dec. 29, 1793; Joseph, Oct. 26, 1782, d. Jan. 22, 1784; Elisabeth, April 5, 1785.

NICOLAAS, son of Harmanus, m. Geertruy Visscher. Ch: Harmanus, bp. Sept. 23, 1781.

CORNELIS, son of Jesse, m. Ruth Clark. Ch. b: Jesse, Oct., 1794; William, July 7, 1801.

PETRUS, m. Geertruy Van Vorst, Feb. 17, 1788. Ch. b: Jacobus, Feb. 16, 1789; Margarietje, Jan. 1, 1791.

PIETER, son of Marten, m. Rebecca Fairchild. Ch. b: Martinus, March 13, 1797; Maria, Oct. 14, 1799.

MARTEN, son of Jesse, m. Margarietje Olsaver, Feb. 4, 1798. He was b. Feb. 12, 1775, d. May 12, 1817 (grave stone); made his will May 17, 1817, proved June 5, 1817, spoke of wife Margaret and ch. She was b. Feb. 25, 1780, and d. June 1, 1826. Ch. b: Jacomyntje, Dec. 27,

1798; Jannetje, May 2, 1800; Jesse, March 4, 1802; Jemima, Dec. 20, 1803; Sarah, Sept. 20, 1805; Margaret, Dec. 22, 1808; Henry M. July 28, 1815, d. Sept. 27, 1834.

WILLIAM, son of Adriaan, m. Sarah Veeder, Nov. 7, 1799.

VAN VALKENBURGH.

ISAAC, son of Jochem of Albany, m. Lydia, dau. of Jacques Van Slyck, May 12, 1705. On the 6th Sept., 1712, he received a conveyance from Carel Hansen Toll, of a lot on the south side of Union street, including the Court House lot, 100ft. front by 210ft. deep, for the sum of £50. Ch. bp: Jacobus, Oct. 28, 1705; Eva, Oct. 10, 1708; *Isaac*, Feb. 12, 171½; Jannetje, October 28, 1716; Geertruy, July 31, 1720; Lydia, b. Sept. 1, 1725. [*See Albany Families.*]

ISAAC, son of Isaac, m. Jannetje Clement. Ch: Marytje, bp. Jan. 29, 1744.

HENDRIK, from Kinderhook, and Margarieta Clute from "Nistoungjoone," m. Dec. 27, 1765. Ch: Maria, bp. Oct. 29, 1766.

JOHANNES, m. Elisabeth Feek. Ch: Joachim, bp. Feb. 18, 1782.

JACOB, m. Rachel Barheyt. Ch: Margarietje, bp. Nov. 28, 1784.

JERONIMUS, m. Margarieta, dau. of Hendrik Van Dyck, September 2, 1792. Ch. b: Jacob, April 25, 1793; Hendrik, Oct. 16, 1795; Rachel, Jan. 8, 1798.

JOHANNES, m. Cornelia Barheyt, Ch. b : Lucas, Nov. 20, 1796; Jannetje, Sept. 1, 1798; Walter, Sept. 11, 1801; Rachel, Aug. 16, 1804.

VAN VECHTEN.

DIRK, son of Johannes, of Catskil, m. Helena Seulant. Ch : Hubertus, b. Oct. 30, 1725. [*See Albany and Catskil Families.*]

DIRK, son of Hubertus of Catskil, m. Rachel Spoor. Ch. bp : Maria, March 2, 1781; Hubertus, July 14, 1782; Rebecca, July 5, 1784. Ch. b : Teunis, April 23, 1788; Lena, March 20, 1790; Jurrie, March 23, 1792; Isaac, April 14, 1794.

ANTONY, m. Maria Fonda. Ch : Margarita, bp. July 17, 1782.

VAN VLECK.

BENJAMIN, son of Maritie, widow of Hendrick Brouwer, m. Anna Gilbertsen. In 1737 he owned a lot on east side of Church street, next south of the Yates lot, 58ft. wide, also land on the west side of the church burying ground. Ch. bp : Teunis, Oct. 21, 1721; Cornelia, b. Nov. 20, 1722, m. Marten Van Olinda; *Teunis*, bp. April 18, 1731; Marya, b. April 27, 1725; Johannes, bp. April 11, 1737.

TEUNIS, son of Benjamin, m. Jannetje, dau. of Harmanus Vedder. Ch. bp : *Benjamin*, Jan. 11, 1756, living in 1837 in Fowler, St. Lawrence county; Catleyntje, Nov. 20, 1757; *Harmanus*, March 16, 1760; Johannes, May 2, 1762; Susanna, March 4, 1764; Annatje, Jan. 26, 1766;

Johannes, March 6, 1767; Folkert, Sept. 6, 1770; *Pieter*, May 16, 1773; Cornelia, May 21, 1775.

BENJAMIN, son of Teunis, m. Sarah Marselis. Ch : Annatje, bp. Oct. 29, 1777.

JOHN, son of Teunis, m. Judick Spoor. Ch : Teunis, b, Feb. 10, 1789. He m. secondly, Catharina Swart, both then of Remsenbos, May 7, 1790. Ch. b : Teunis, Nov. 1, 1795; John, Dec. 25, 1799.

HARMANUS, son of Teunis, m. Abigail Bettheys (Beatty). Ch. bp : Jannetje, June 6, 1779; Joseph, June 2, 1781. Ch. b : Abigail, June 17, 1785; Catlyntje, Dec. 13, 1797; Mary, Oct. 3, 1799.

PETER, son of Teunis, m. Gezina Van Petten. Ch : Annatje, bp. March 5, 1797; Arent, b. Jan. 22, 1799; Teunis, b. April 9, 1801.

VAN VLIET.

JAN, m. Maria, dau. of Adam W. Vrooman. She d. May 12, 1816. Ch : Machtelt, bp. Aug. 27, 1780, m. Henderick Witman, Feb., 1800; Susanna, bp. Sept. 19, 1783. Ch. b : Geertje, June 20, 1786; Helena, Oct. 16, 1788; Blandina, March 14, 1792.

JACOB, m. Mary Ragan. She d. Sept. 21, 1821, a. 76ys., 4m. Ch : Johannes, b. Aug. 23, 1786.

BENJAMIN, JR., of Fort Hunter, and Annatje Heemstraat of Lysje's kil, m. Feb. 18, 1788. Ch. b : Jacob, April 17, 1791; Johannes, Sept. 20, 1794; Catharina, March 24, 1797; Aarje, April 15, 1798; Baata, April 20, 1799.

VAN VELSEN *alias* VAN WEST-BROEK.

SWEER TEUNISE, one of the five patentees of the town of Schenectady in 1684. In 1664 he m. Maritie Myndertse, wid. of Jan Barentse Wemp, by which marriage he became possessed of the *Poesten* mill at *Lubberde's* land (Troy), and a lot of land in Albany. About this time he removed to Schenectady and built a grist mill on Mill lane; this was carried away by a flood, and rebuilt in 1673. In consideration of his loss, he was allowed to take an eighth instead of a tenth, as toll. In 1676 he was made magistrate of the village. In the massacre of 1690 he was slain, with his wife and four negro slaves, leaving no heirs. Besides half of Van Slyck's island, he owned the land on the south side of State street, from Church street nearly to Cowhorne creek, and extending upon the low land so as to comprehend about 25 acres. Before his death it was understood that he had in his will devised a half or a third of his property to the church, and the remainder to his wife's children by her first husband, but as this will, if it ever existed, was burned in the massacre, the church had no legal claim upon his estate. A compromise was therefore effected in 1696, the church taking that portion of his land lying on the south side of State street, between Church street and Dock street, together with the grist mill, and

his wife's heirs the remainder. [*See Albany Families.*]

VAN VOORT or VAN OORT.

GOOSEN, a resident of Schenectady in 1700.

VAN VORST.

JACOBUS GERRITSE, b. in 1641, was in Albany as early as 1681, when he apprenticed his son *Gillis*, then aged 11ys., to Jeronimus Wendell for 6ys. to learn shoemaking. In 1686 Jacobus Van Vorst was a licensed porter and carman in Albany.

GILLIS, son of Jacobus, came to Schenectady about 1700. In 1702 he bought of Johannes Ouderkerk and Neeltje Claese his wife, the lot on Union street, 100ft. × 200ft., Amst. meas , lying next east of the church lot; the westerly half of this lot last owned by the estate of Isaac Riggs is now included in the church yard, the easterly half now belongs to Mr. Barringer. He m. Elisabeth, dau. of Jan Baptist Van Eps, and widow of Teunis Viele, July 16, 1699. Ch. bp : Jacobus, ——, 1700; *Johannes*, Nov. 9, 1701; *Jacobus*, Dec. 12, 1703; *Dirk*, Aug. 25, 1705; Gerrit, May 26, 1708; Douw, Feb. 15, 1710, in Albany; *Jan Baptist*, Oct. 21, 1711; Sara, Nov. 14, 1713; Elisabeth, Feb. 4, 1716, m. Willem Beth; Gysbert, Jan. 17, 1721.

JOHANNES, son of Gillis, m. Hanna, dau. of Ahasuerus Marselis, Sept. 15, 1726. He inherited the easterly half of his father's lot next to the church in

Union street. Ch. bp: Jillis, b. March 30, bp. April 2, 1727; Sarah, m. Jacobus Lighthall; Elisabeth, bp. Dec. 5, 1731; Elisabeth, June 3, 1733; Ahasuerus, August 24, 1735; *Johannes*, Dec. 21 (?), 1737; Annatje, Aug. 23, 1741; Jacomyntje, Oct. 30, 1743, m. Teunis Barheit; *Jacobus.*

JACOBUS, son of Gillis, m. first, Anna, dau. of Caleb Beck, Feb. 14, 1728, in Albany; and secondly, Sarah, dau. of Jellis Fonda, May 20, 1749. Ch. bp: Margriet Vedder, Sept. 18, 1726; Caleb, ——, 1730; Anna, Oct. 22, 1732, m. Claas Van der Bogart (?); *Jellis*, Feb. 9, 1735; Engeltje, July 6, 1738; *Johannes*, b. Jan. 19, bp. Feb. 8, 1741; *Abraham*, April 3, 1743; *Jan Baptist*, Feb. 23, 1746.

DOUWE, son of Jillis, m. Margriet, dau. of Philip Bosie, August 29, 1735. Ch. bp: Jellis, Jan. 18, 1736; Jellis, Jan. 30, 1737; Elisabeth, July, 1739, m. Norman McCloud (?); Sara, March 8, 1741; Philip, Dec. 22, 1745, d. April 3, 1830, in his 85th year; his wife Angelica, b. Jan. 10, 1756, d. April 10, 1824; Margarieta, Jan. 21, 1750.

DIRK, son of Jellis, m. first, Emmetje, dau. of Philip Bosie, Aug. 5, 1733; and secondly, Maria, dau. of Thomas Hall, wid., June 30, 1758. Ch. bp: *Jellis*, April 15, 1734; Philippus, July 20, 1735; Elisabeth, April 10, 1737, m. Johan M. Youtis; Petrus, February 14, 1739; Johannes, Jan. 11, 1741; Mar-

gareta, Feb. 13, 1743, m. Robert, Hagedorn; *Johannes*, Feb. 23, 1746.

JAN BAPTIST, son of Jellis, m. Catharina, dau. of Ahasuerus Marselis, June 28, 1739, in Albany. He owned the westerly half of his father's lot, late the Rigg's lot, now included in the church yard. Ch. bp: Elisabet, June 7, 1741, m. John Henry; Sara, July 10, 1743, m. Teunis Swart; Annatje, May 12, 1745, m. Jacob C. Peek; *Jillis*, Oct. 14, 1747; Maria, May 6, 1750, m. Cornelis Pootman; Catarina, Aug. 8, 1752; Susanna, July 13, 1755; Susanna, July 23, 1758, m. John Carol.

JAN BAPTIST, JR., son of Jacobus, m. Margarita, dau. of Johannes Marinus. Ch. bp: *Gerrit*, Dec. 14, 1766; Geertruy, March 6, 1769; Annatje, March 31, 1771; Johannes, Aug. 2, 1773; Sarah, Dec. 10. 1775; Bata, Aug. 16, 1778, m. ...... Glen, d. June 1, 1854, a. 75ys; Jacobus, Sept. 5, 1784, d. in Albany March 15, 1844; Johannes, b. Aug. 23, 1791.

JILLIS, son of Jacobus, m. Anna, dau. of Willem Berrit, June 19, 1756. He d. Sept. 4, 1823. Ch. bp: Catalyna, Feb. 6, 1757; Annatje, Dec. 10, 1758; Catleyntje, Aug. 3, 1760, m. Jan Baptist Clute; *Jacobus*, February 14, 1762; Weyntje, June 3, 1764; Maria, Oct. 19, 1766, m. Cornelis Reagles; Sarah, Feb. 26, 1769; Rebecca, March 10, 1771, m. Martinus Frank; Ruth, July 25, 1773, m. Martinus Easterly; Elisabeth, May 5, 1776; Willem, April 9, 1780.

JOCHIM, (Major Gershom), son of Johannes J. and Sarah Kittel, m. Neeltje, dau. of Albert Vedder, Jan. 12, 1789. He lived near the easterly bounds of the city, on the Troy and Schenectady turnpike; was sheriff of the county; d. July 13, 1849, in his 85th year; his wife d. May 30, 1826, in her 59th year. Ch. b: Johannes, April 11, 1790; Esther, Jan. 24, 1792; John, Nov. 14, 1794; Albert, Dec. 16, 1797, d. Aug. 26, 1869; Jacobus, Nov. 4, 1800, d. at Ephratah Sept. 21, 1869.

JOHANNES, son of Jacobus, m. Sarah, dau. of Joachim Kittel, Sept. 11, 1762. He d. in Glenville May 23, 1844, in his 103d year; she d. Feb. 1, 1834, a. 89ys., 9m., 23d. Ch. bp: *Jacobus*, May 23, 1763, d. Aug. 9, 1851; *Joachim*, July 28, 1765; Annatje (Beck), Feb. 13, 1768, m. Joseph Shurtleff; *Caleb*, Oct. 24, 1770; *Adam*, b. Sept. 11, bp Sept. 19, 1773; *Jillis*, Jan. 12, 1777; Johannes, Nov. 12, 1780, d. March 15, 1844.

JACOBUS, son of Johannes, m. Claartje, dau. of Johannes Marinus, Dec. 11, 1762. He d. shortly before the baptism of his last child. Ch. bp: Johannes, Sept. 4, 1763; Geertruy, Aug. 17, 1766.

JACOBUS, son of Jellis, m. Willempie, dau. of Pieter Truex, June 2, 1788. He was living in 1838; she d. in Glenville Sept. 1855, in her 98th year. Ch. b: Jellis, Oct. 9, 1789; Peter, Feb. 1, 1792; Jacobus, Sept. 5, 1795; Annatje, Dec. 9, 1797; Sophia, Feb. 14, 1800; Cat-

lyntje, April 17, 1803; Elisabeth, Nov. 6, 1805.

JACOBUS, son of Johannes, m. Sarah, dau. of Pieter Truex, Jan. 8, 1786.

JILLIS, son of Dirk, m. Catarina Van der Heyden (Brown), Nov. 23, 1764. He d. Aug. 9, 1823. Ch. bp: Emmetje, Sept. 22, 1765; Dirk, Nov. 20, 1768; Elisabeth, April 12, 1767, m. Jacob Luypard; Johannes, Oct. 13, 1776.

JELLIS, son of Jan Baptist, m. first, Catarina Lewis, about 1780; and secondly, Lena Sharp, about 1803. Ch. bp: Catarina, Feb. 12, 1781; Annatje, October 6, 1782; Sarah, June 6, 1784. Ch. b: Johannes, July 22, 1786; Jan Baptist, Aug. 3, 1788; Rachel, Sept. 28, 1790; Isaac, bp. Jan. 6, 1793; Barent, b. Oct. 28, 1795.

JOHANNES, son of Johannes, of Schoharie, m. Mary Adams of Fort Johnson, March 22, 1767. She d. April 8, 1787. He inherited lot, 25 Union street, from his father. Ch. bp: Johannes, March 20, 1768; Robert, Dec. 2, 1770; Jacobus, March 28, 1773; Johanna, Aug. 15, 1784; Mary Anne Adams, b. April 1, 1787.

ABRAHAM, son of Jacobus, m. Maria, dau. of Jacob Heemstraat. He lived and d. at or near "Burnt Hills," in Glenville, a. about 90ys. Ch. bp: *Jacobus*, Jan. 14, 1770; Jacob, June 4, 1772; Hester, Aug. 9, 1773; Jacob, June 16, 1776; Annatje, Mar. 21, 1779; Rebecca, Mar.

15, 1782; Abraham Fonda, b. June 3, 1785, father of A. A. Van Vorst, late mayor of Schenectady, d. in Glenville Dec. 19, 1853; his wife Martha d. Oct. 4, 1862, a. 75ys.; Sarah, b. May 17, 1768.

JOHANNES, son of Dirk, m. Bata Van der Heyden, Oct. 30, 1774. Ch. bp: Dirk, Sept. 17, 1775; Dirk, Nov. 17, 1776, d. Aug. 11, 1857, a. 81ys.; Jane his wife, d. April 10, 1854, a. 80ys.; Catarina, March 1, 1779; Immetje, Sept. 2, 1781; John, June 17, 1784, d. March 15, 1844; Eliza his widow, d. August 1, 1844, a. 56ys. Ch. b : Adam, Oct. 29, 1786; Margrietje, Jan. 5, 1789; Caleb Beck, Feb. 8, 1792, d. in Albany April 4, 1825; Jellis, April 27, 1794.

GERRIT, son of Jan Baptist, m. Sarah, dau. of Jacob Schermerhorn, June 7, 1789. Ch. b : Johannes, Nov. 21, 1789; Jacob, Feb. 13, 1791; Margarieta, April 28, 1793; Jan Baptist, Feb. 9, 1796; Mary, May 31, 1798, in Albany.

JACOBUS, son of Abraham, m. Sarah Bovier. He d. in Glenville, April 11, 1865. Ch. b : Abram, Jan. 3, 1792; Jacob Bovier, Oct. 9, 1794; Maria, Oct. 27, 1796; Antje, Sept. 2, 1799; Nicholas, Dec. 15, 1801; Jacob, June 1, 1804; Isaac, May 21, 1809; Esther, July 24, 1812.

CALEB, son of Johannes J., m. Hillegonda, dau. of Adam Vrooman. She d. March 25, 1858, then a widow. Ch. b : Sara, Dec. 18, 1797; Engelina, July 6, 1800; Sarah, Mar 20, 1803; Angelica

Eve, Oct. 5, 1806; Ann Margaret, Aug. 2, 1809; Adam Vrooman, Dec. 15, 1814; Adam Seth Vrooman, February 4, 1817; Susan Schermerhorn, July 22, 1820.

JELLIS, son of Johannes J., m. Helena Granger, June 15, 1798.

ADAM, son of Johannes J , m. Annatie Vedder, May 20, 1799. He d. in Glenville Feb. 6, 1844; she d. March 21, 1872, a. 92ys., 11m.

VAN VRANKEN.

Two brothers of this name, *Ryckert Claase* and *Gerrit Claase*, early settled in Niskayuna. [*See Albany Families.*]

RYCKERT, m. Hillegonda......; owned a lot in North Pearl street, Albany, and *een sekere stuk landts geleeghen over de rivier aen* Canastagioene, which he purchased in company with Claes Janse Van Boekhoven in 1672 for 550 skiples of wheat. In 1684 he sold his house and lot, in Albany to Johannes Wendel. His ch. were *Maas; Gerrit; Evert; Isaac* and *Margaret.* Of Isaac, it is related that on the 9th July, 1690, " three captives escaped from Canada, arrived at Schenectady, among whom was *Klyn Isac,* son of Ryck Claase." Maas Ryckse, son of Ryckert, m. Annatie, dau of Adam Winnè of Albany. Both Maas and his brother Gerrit owned farms on the north side of the Mohawk, in what is now Clifton Park, but then a part of Niskayuna, to which farms an addition of one mile, extending north, was made by patent of date April 22, 1708. In 1704 Maas

Ryckse built a fort at Niskayuna, probably on or near his own farm for the sum of £12. His wife Annatie was b. Oct. 5, 1687, d. March, 1778. Ch. bp. in Albany: Ryckert, Oct. 7, 1711; Annatie, Oct. 30, 1715; *Adam*, Dec. 8, 1717; *Maas*, November 11, 1722; Hillegonda, b. May 30, 1726, m. Simon Jacobse Schermerhorn.

GERRIT, son of Ryckert, m. Barber Janse in Albany, Sept. 27, 1696. He resided in that part of Niskayuna lying on the north side of the Mohawk; was buried January 13, 1748; his wife was buried Dec. 21, 1747. Ch. bp. in Albany: *Ryckert*, b. Dec., bp. Dec. 12, 1697; Alida, Sept. 3, 1699, buried Mar. 12, 1729; Anna, June 20, 1703; Margarita, Apr. 1, 1705, m Johannes Bratt; Johannes, Oct. 24, 1708; Hillegonda, Oct. 12, 1711; Andries, Aug. 7, 1715.

CLAAS GERRITSE, probably son of Gerrit, brother of Ryckert, m. Geertruy Quackenbos, *in de kerke van Schonegtade*, Dec. 30, 1704. He settled on the south side of the Mohawk in Niskayuna, where he bought land of Johannes Clute March 6, 170$\frac{9}{10}$. Ch. bp. in Albany: Gerrit, Oct. 7, 1705; Lysbeth, Dec. 25, 1706; *Gerrit*, Oct. 3, 1708: Adriantje, Oct. 30, 1710, m. Pieter Clute; Magtelt, April 20, 1712, m. Frans Bovie; Sara, Feb. 21, 1714; Rachel, Dec. 25, 1715; Johannes, Oct. 25, 1719. Ch. bp. in Schenectady: *Petrus*, Dec. 3, 1721; Maria, Dec. 1, 1723, m. Johannes Claase Fort; *Isaac*, b. May 21, bp. June 19, 1726; Jacob, June 22, 1729; *Abraham*.

RYCKERT, son of Gerrit Ryckse, m. Maria, dau. of Dirk Bratt, Feb. 9, 1723. He was b. Dec., 1697, d. April 28, 1746; she was b, Sept. 22, 1698, d. Sept. 27, 1774. Ch. bp: Alida, Dec. 18, 1723, in Albany, m. Johannes Pearse; Maria, b. Aug. 5, bp. Sept. 5, 1725, m. Reyer Schermerhorn; Barber, Sept. 24, 1727, in Albany, m. Pieter Pieterse Bogart of Albany; Baata (?); *Gerrit*; *Dirk*, May 21, 1732; *Richart*, b. Aug. 20, bp. Sept. 15, 1734; Elisabeth, b. July 5, bp. July 31, 1736, m. Andries Truex; Anna, b. Sept. 13, 1739.

EVERT RYCKSE, son of Ryckert Claase, m. Maritje, dau. of Bastiaan Visscher of Albany, Nov. 14, 1709, in Albany. He resided in Niskayuna; was buried May 24, 1748. Ch. bp. in Albany, except Harmen : Richart, Oct. 28, 1710, buried Feb. 9, 1731; Dirkie, May 17, 1713; Bastiaan, Aug. 7, 1715; Nicolaas, Feb. 11, 1719; Harmen, Feb. 18, 1721, in Schenectady; Anna, March 13, 1723; Hilletie, March 21, 1725; Maria, Jan. 29, 1727, m. Cornelis Groot.

GERRIT, son of Claas Gerritse, m. Marytje, dau. of Johannes Fort, July 7, 1738, in Albany. She d. Nov. 16, 1802. Ch. bp. in Albany, except Rebecca and Abraham: Rebecca, b. April 4, 1739, m. Johannes De Graaf; *Gerrit*, May 7, 1741; *Johannes*, b. Oct. 25, 1743; Barber, b. March 13, 1746; *Abraham*, b. July 6, 1750, d. July 31, 1787; Alida, b. Sept. 8, 1753.

ABRAHAM, son of Claas Gerritse, m. Dirkje, dau. of Samuel Crcgier, Nov. 19, 1742, in Albany. Ch. bp: *Claas,* Sept. 4, 1743; Geertruy, Feb. 24, 1745; Maria, August 23, 1747, in Albany, m. Jacob Groot; Samuel, July 23, 1749, in Albany; Samuel, Oct. 13, 1754, in Albany; *Samuel,* Feb. 8, 1761.

ABRAHAM, son of Gerrit, m. Geertruy Groot. Ch: Elisabeth, b. Aug. 2, 1790.

RYCKERT, son of Maas Ryckse, m. Anna, dau. of Abraham Truax, Oct. 14, 1738. Ch: Maria, bp. Oct. 7, 1744, m. Isaac Rosa. [*See Albany Families.*]

RICHARD, son of Ryckert, m. Maria, dau. of Johannes Marselis, April 26, 1760. He d. Sept. 11, 1805; she was b. Dec. 4, 1734, d. Feb. 5, 1813. In 1755 he bought of Tobias Ryckman jr., the land on the south side of Union street, between Centre and Yates streets, and on his death gave it in equal portions to his daus. Maria and Sarah. Ch. b: Maria, May 12, 1761, d. Sept. 27, 1772; *Richard,* Aug. 17, 1763; Sarah, b. Jan. 16 (*Family Record*), bp. January 14, (*Church Record*), 1766, m. Rudolf Van Huysen; John, Feb. 8, 1768, d. Sept. 13, 1772; Elisabeth, Sept. 29, 1770, d. Oct. 2, 1772; *John,* April 17, 1773; Maria, Aug. 9, 1775, m. Gerrit Bensen; Nicolaas, April 12, 1779, d. in Onondaga county, 1863.

PIETER, son of Claas Gerritse of Genistagioene, m. Neeltie, dau. of Dirk Groot, of Schenectadè Mar. 3, 174⅝. He made his will May 3, 1804, proved June 26,

1809, spoke of wife Machtelt, sons Nicolaas, Gerrit, Cornelis and Dirk, and dau. Elisabeth Tymese and Gitty Van Vranken. Ch. bp: *Nicolaas,* Aug. 3, 1749; *Gerrit,* April 2, 1758; *Cornelis,* July 6, 1760; *Dirk,* Jan. 19, 1752, in Albany; Elisabeth, m. Eldert Tymese.

RICHARD, JR., con of Richard, m. Sara, dau. of Gerardus Quackenbos, July 21, 1785. Ch. b: Maritje, Sept. 17, 1788; Rykaart, Jan. 17, 1790; Gerardus John Van Ingen, Jan. 8, 1792; Elisabet, May 24, 1794; Sara, Jan. 21, 1796; Rudolf Van Huysen, April 1, 1801; John, Feb. 4, 1803.

ADAM, son of Maas Ryckse, m. first, Ariaantje Clute, March 8, 1744, in Albany; secondly, Geertruy Van Vranken about 1785. Ch. bp: Maas, April 21, 1745, in Albany: *Rykhart,* Sept. 23, 1750; Geertruy, Sept. 15, 1754, in Albany; Adam, Nov. 23, 1760; Ariaantje, b. Aug. 6, 1786. [*See Albany Families.*]

MAAS, son of Maas Ryckse, m. Ariaantje, dau. of Lourens Van der Volgen, April 15, 1750. He was b. Oct. 18, 1721, d. July 24, 1787. Ch. b: *Lourens,* Sept. 27, 1751, d. April 1, 1800; *Maas,* May 23, 1756; Nicolaas, March 26, 1759, d. August 20, 1760; *Nicolaas,* May 24, 1762, clergyman of the Reformed Dutch church, d. May 20, 1804; Anneke, April 28, 1765, d. Feb. 18, 1831; Susanna, Feb. 9, 1771, d. April, 1826.

MAAS, son of Maas and Ariaantje, m. Sarah, dau. of Claas Marselis, Aug. 11, 1778. He d. July 1, 1833; she d. April

1, 1838. Ch. b : Ariaantje, May 9, 1779, m. Rev. Herman Vedder, d. Sept. 2, 1840; Nicholas, Sept. 11, 1782, d. Nov. 17; 1789; Helena, Nov. 20, 1787, m. Doct. Daniel McDougall, Oct., 1824, and d. Jan. 11 (18), 1850; Nicholas, April 7, 1791, merchant of Schenectady, d. Jan. 29, 1864.

JOHANNES, son of Claas, m. Maria, dau. of Cornelis Pootman, Jan. 18, 1752, in Albany. Ch. bp : *Jacobus*, Feb. 9, 1753, d. Oct. 6, 1812 ; Geertruy, March 21, 1756, m. Jesse Groot ; Jacomyntje, May 14, 1758. [*See Albany Families.*]

JOHANNES, widower, son of Gerrit Ryckse (?), m. Anna, dau. of Johannes Fort, Aug. 4, 1753. Ch. bp : Annatje, Sept. 21, 1755 ; Johannes, Sept. 23, 1759.

ISAAC, son of Claas Gerritse of Nistagioene, m. Claartje Bratt, Feb. 1, 1754, in Albany. Ch : Claas, bp. Nov. 24, 1754. He m. secondly, Francina, dau. of Johannes Quackenbos, Sept. 12, 1757. Ch. bp : *Claas*, Aug. 5, 1759 ; *Johannes*, Jan. 17, 1762 ; Geertruy, Feb. 17, 1771.

ANDREAS, son of Gerrit Ryckse of Albany, and Maria Groot of the same place, m. Aug. 14, 1750. Ch. bp : Gerrit, August 9, 1760 ; Neeltje, May 22, 1763 ; Elisabeth, Dec. 16, 1753, in Albany ; Barber, Sept. 4, 1757, in Albany, m. Ryckert Van Vranken.

JACOB, son of Claas Gerritse of " Onestounghjoone," m. Margarita, dau. of Cornelis Pootman, July 17, 1758. Ch. b : *Claas*, Feb. 15, 1761 ; *Cornelis*, Oct. 11,

1767 ; Petrus, July 18, 1773, d. in Niskayuna, Jan. 13, 1856, a. 81ys., 5m., 25d., his wife, Hester Visscher, d. Sept. 7, 1852, in her 66th year.

GERRIT, son of Ryckert, of Nestoungjoone, m. first, Alida, dau. of Philip Ryley of Albany, February 13, 1765 ; secondly, Brechje, dau. of Myndert Van Gyseling of Schenectady, March 15, 1763 ; Ch. bp : Philippus, April 16, 1769 ; *Dirk*, May 13, 1772 ; Harmanus, Jan. 3, 1779 ; Maria, Dec. 25, 1781.

GERRIT, son of Gerrit, m. Geertruy Visscher, Jan. 9, 1771. He d. Nov. 16, 1785. Ch. b : Maria, July 22, 1772 ; Nicolaas, Nov. 9, 1773, d. Jan. 29, 1792 ; Rebecca, ——, 1775 ; Gerrit, Jan. 19, 1777 ; Annatje, Dec. 22, 1778 ; Barber, Sept. 6, 1780 ; Alida, June 4, 1782 ; Gerrit, April 18, 1784 ; Eldert, Feb. 9, 1786 ; *het kint Eldert is geboren na den doot van Syn vader.*

LOURENS, son of Maas M., m. Engeltie Veeder. " Poor Louw Van Vranken is dead — died very sudden."—*Mrs. Henry Glen's letter dated April 7*, 1800. Ch : Ariaantje, bp. July 5, 1772, d. July 25, 1858, a. 86ys.

NICOLAAS, son of Maas M. (?), m. Ruth Comstock of " Saratoga district," Feb. 11, 1787. Ch. b : Samuel Amasa, April 25, 1788 ; James Romeyn, May 21, 1789 ; Harriet, Oct. 1, 1790.

CLAAS, son of Abraham, m. Geertruy Groot. He lived on his father's farm on

the Consaul road. Ch. bp : Dirkje, Jan.
10, 1773; Abraham, June 8, 1779;
Bata, Feb. 3, 1782; Simon, lived on the
Consaul road.

DIRK, son of Ryckert, m. Sarah, dau.
of Willem Lighthall, Nov. 4, 1774. He
bought a lot on the south side of Union
street, next east of his brother Ryckert's,
extending from Yates street to No. 120,
and southwardly beyond Liberty street.
He d. in 1799. Ch. b : Richard, bp.
March 12, 1775; Elisabeth, b. June 13,
1776, d. April 16, 1854; Richard b.
August 17, 1779 (*Family Record*), bp.
Aug. 23, 1778 (*Church Record*); Maria,
bp. April 1, 1781, m. John A. McDougall; Barber, b. March 5, 1783; Abram,
b. July 3, 1787; Gerrit, Oct. 12, 1788;
Dirk, May 24 (29), 1791; Sara, Dec.
22, 1793.

JOHANNES, son of Gerrit, m. Maria
(Geertruy) Van Vranken, Apr. 16, 1776.
He resided in Clifton Park, d. March 23,
1811; she d. Dec. 1, 1839. Ch. bp : Ma-
ria, Nov. 9, 1776; Adam, Jan. 10, 1779;
Ariaantje, August 19, 1781, m. Andrew
Yates; Abraham; Rebecca, m. John D.
Fort.

JACOBUS, son of Johannes Claese of
Rosendal, m. Geertje Fonda, Nov. 5,
1775, in Albany. Ch : Adam, bp. Jan.
11, 1777; Catharina, b. Aug. 24, 1778;
Alida, b. Sept. 3, 1782. [*See Albany
Families.*]

CORNELIS, son of Jacob and Annatje
Fisher, both of Nestigaune, m. May 8,

1787. Ch. b : Machtelt, Mar. 21, 1794;
Jacob, Apr. 8, 1796; Eva, May 23, 1798.

JACOBUS, m. Maritje, dau. of Cornelis
Groot. Ch. bp : Hilletje, August 16,
1778; Jacomyntje, April 2, 1780; Maria, Feb. 16, 1783. Ch. b : Johannes,
March 29, 1785; Elisabeth, Feb. 1, 1788.

GERRIT P., m. Maria Birch, March 8,
1779, in Albany. Ch bp : Pieter, Apr.
1, 1781; Willem, May 4, 1783.

NICOLAAS P., m. Maria Vedder. He
d. Sept. 10, 1835, a. 87ys.; she d. Feb.
1, 1846. Ch. bp : Pieter, Oct. 8, 1778,
d. March 23, 1833 (1835); Catarina,
Sept. 15, 1782. Ch. b : Neeltje, May
21, 1786; Elisabeth, July 3, 1789.

SAMUEL, son of Abraham, m. Margarita Levy. Ch. bp : Geertruy, April 17,
1782; Jacob, July 7, 1784; Dirkje, b.
Jan. 4, 1789.

JOHANNES, son of Isaac, m. Susanna,
dau. of Jan Vielè. Ch. bp : Lena, Dec.
22, 1782; Johannes Vielè, Feb. 6, 1785;
Isaac, b. Aug. 5, 1787; Margarietje, b.
Dec. 15, 1789.

CLAAS, son of Jacob, m. Eva, dau. of
Cornelis Peek. He d. July 20, 1837,
in his 77th year; she d. Oct. 30, 1837,
in her 77th year. Ch. bp : Jacob, Feb.
23, 1783; Jacob, b. March 15, 1784, d.
May 24, 1861, a. 77ys., 2m., 9d.; Cornelius, b. Oct. 27, 1791; Geertruy, b.
Dec. 15, 1795.

RYCKERT, son of Adam, m. Barbara,
dau. of Andries Van Vranken. Ch. b :

Ariaantje, May 7, 1785; Maria, Aug. 2, 1787; Andries, May 5, 1789.

DIRK, son of Pieter, m. Annatje, dau. of Willem Faling. Ch: Pieter, b. Aug. 13, 1785.

DIRK, son of Gerrit R., m. first, Margarieta, dau. of Harmanus Pieters, and secondly, Elisabeth Bragham about 1805. He was deceased at the baptism of his last child, June 26, 1815. Ch. b: Eva, June 14, 1795; Harmanus, Sept. 1, 1802; Gerrit, March 11, 1806; Dirk, Feb. 1, 1815.

CLAAS, son of Isaac and Rachel Boon, both of Nestigiune, m. Feb. 14, 1785. He lived at Rosendal, d. Sept., 1839, a. 79ys., 10m. Ch: Isaac, b. July 6, 1789, m. Maria Van Antwerp, d. August 30, 1858, a. 70ys.

MAAS A., of Nestigayune, m. Maria Quackenbos, Aug. 2, 1794.

CORNELIS, son of Pieter, of Rosendal, m. Sarah Peek, Feb. 1, 1789. Ch. b: Neeltie, Oct. 25, 1789; Elisabeth May 25, 1793.

JOHN, son of Richard and Maria Marselis, m. Sarah Zabriskie, March 2, 1794. Ch. b: Mary, May 1, 1796; Henry, Sept. 30, 1800.

PETER, and Magtelt Ouderkerk, m. Oct. 15, 1798.

VAN VREDENBERGH.

ABRAHAM, and Eva Van Etten, both born at Rhinebeck, m. Jan. 13, 1764. Ch. bp: Cataleyntje, Oct. 28, 1764; Jo-

hannes, Dec. 14, 1766; Elisabeth, Aug. 26, 1770; Rachel, June 6, 1773; Isabella Mary, Jan. 12, 1777; Rebecca, Aug. 12, 1781.

JOHANNES, m. Geesje Kool. Ch. bp: Johannes, Oct. 23, 1768; Geesje, April 20, 1771.

ISAAC, turner, m. Alida Van Etten. Ch. b: Willem, May 8, 1769; Cataleyntje, Aug. 19, 1774; Johannes, April 4, 1776; Rebecca, Dec. 3, 1777; Isaac, May 14, 1779; Rebecca, May 9, 1782; Rachel, bp. Feb. 27, 1785.

WILLIAM, m. Dorothea, dau. of John Farrel. Ch: Rachel, b. July 11, 1789.

VAN WORMER.

ARENT, m. Maria Van Schaick. Ch. bp: Eva, May 10, 1775; Susanna, May 26, 1779; Isaac, May 18, 1781.

JOHANNES, m. Rachel Ebbertson. Ch. bp: Johannes, Jan. 26, 1777, d. at West Glenville Nov. 14, 1845; Ebbert, March 9, 1779; Maria, June 25, 1784.

PIETER, m. Rachel Van Hoesen. Ch. bp: Maria, March 8, 1777. Ch. b: Rachel, May 10, 1786; Lourens, Sept. 11, 1789; Johannes, April 5, 1793.

PETRUS, m. Susanna Burger. Ch: Cornelius, bp. Aug. 8, 1780.

ABRAHAM, m. Catarina Lanhart. She d. June 7, 1852, a. 105ys. and 5d. (grave stone). Ch: Arent, bp. Nov. 15, 1780; Margarita, b. Oct. 3, 1785; Margarieta, b. April 4, 1791.

CORNELIS, m. Neeltje Brouwer. Ch: Richard, b. Aug. 14, 1790.

CASPAR, m. Eva, dau. of Hendrick Van Dyck, Jan. 29, 1794. He was b. July 16, 1770, and d. at West Glenville Dec. 16, 1859, a. 89ys., 5m.; she d. Dec. 26, 1851, a. 76ys., 6m., 30d. Ch. b: Maria, May 23, 1795; Petrus, Sept. 25, 1797; Engeltje, Feb. 14, 1800, m. John I. Swart, d. Jan. 5, 1851, at West Glenville.

JACOB, m. Maria Kerk. Ch: Rebecca, b. Aug. 22, 1798.

VAN ZEYL.

JOAANNES, m. Catarina, dau. of Tobias Ryckman. Ch. bp: Tobias, August 7, 1768; Johannes, June 18, 1771.

VEDDER.

HARMEN ALBERTSE, the first settler, was a trader in Beverwyck before the year 1657, when he sold to Rutger Jacobsen his house and lot *gelegen in de doorpe beverwyck, breet voor en achter ses en dertich voet, lanch vier en sestich voet en met aen ganch van vyfte`voet end breet lanch tot aen kil welcke gansch is gelegen tusschen goossen gerritsen en den vercooper &c.* This lot was on the south side of State street, between Green and Pearl streets, and extended back only to the *Rutten* kil, now arched over and used as a sewer. The price of this house and lot was 2,325 guilders. In 1660 he returned to Holland; 1661 as agent for Dirk De Wolfe, merchant of Amsterdam, he erected a salt kettle on Coney island, which being claimed by the inhabitants of Gravesend, he brought a suit before the governor and council to make good his claim to it, and being beaten, abandoned the enterprise; 1663 leased his bouwery at Schenectady to Symon Groot for 6ys., at 500 guilders rent; 1664 Harmen Vedder, William Teller and Sander Leendertse Glen petitioned Gov. Stuyvesant to have their lands surveyed at Schenectady; 1668 being in Holland with other merchants from the province of New York, he purchased goods and chartered the ship *King Charles* and petitioned the king of England for permission to send the same to New York, which was granted; 1667 he lived in Albany in a house belonging to Dirk De Wolfe of Amsterdam, who, having returned to Holland, Gov. Nicolls ordered the house and lot to be confiscated; 1672 he bought of Dirk Hesselingh *de bouwery* (*daer den voorz; Dirk Hesselingh op woont op Schenechtede*),*soo het landt, also huys, schuer ende twee berghen, &c., soo als het de voornoemde* Hesselingh *van Jurriaen Teunissen gecocht heeft gehadt*, &c., to be delivered to Harmen Vedder the coming May 1, 1672, together with the seed in the ground; this bouwery, No. 8 on the *Bouwlandt*, comprised 12 morgens and 130 rods of land and now forms the homestead of Col. D. D. Campbell of Rotterdam; 1672 Harmen Vedder and Barent Ryndertsen sold to Claese Janse Van Boekhoven and Ryck Claese Van Vranken *een sekere stuck landts geleeghen over de Rivier aen Canastagioene :* con_ sideration 550 skiples of wheat; 1673 he was appointed one of the three magistrates of Schenectady; 1674 was *schout* of the village, and with the magistrates was reprimanded for not showing due respect for the magistrates of Willemstadt (Albany), and for pretending to the privilege of Indian trade; he was particularly complained of because of his conduct towards Capt. Schuyler and was warned "to regulate himself accordingly." His village lot on the north side of Union street, was the same as occupied by the late Doct. Alexander G. Fonda, 51ft. front and 404ft. deep Amsterdam measure, extending to Front street; he purchased it of the heirs of Reinier, son of Domine Schaets of Albany, after his massacre by the French and Indians in 1690. His son Johannes occupied it after his death, which probably took place about the year 1715, for on the 3d of May that year, Arient Vedder, his brethren and sister petitioned the common council of Albany for the renewal of a release ("burnt at Schenectady when it was cut off") of a lot owned by their late father Harmen Vedder deceased, lying on the south side of the city of Albany. The following Ch. of Harmen Vedder were living in 1715: *Harmanus; Arent; Albert*, b. May 10, 1671; *Johannes; Corset;* Angenietje, wife of Jan Danielse Van Antwerpen.

HARMANUS, son of Harmen, m. first, Grietje, dau. of Jacques Cornelise Van Slyck, and wid. of Andries Arentse Bratt, Dec. 10, 1691, in Albany; and secondly,

Ariaantje, dau. of Claas Lourense Van der Volgen, and widow of Aarnold De Graaf, Dec. 31, 1733. He was an Indian trader. Ch. bp: Antje, March 27, 1692, in Albany, m. Johannes Peek; Margriet, April 11, 1694, m. Tjerk Franse Van der Bogart; Jacobus, b. March 25, 1696, made will 1762, proved Sept. 6, 1762, spoke of wife Maria, but not of any children, d. July 14, 1762; *Harmen*, bp. Jan. 1, 1698, in Albany; Helena and Feitje, *tweling*, May 5, 1700, the latter m. Willem Pieterse; Angenietje, April 19, 1702; Lydia, July 23, 1704, m. Harmanus Van Slyck; Johannes, April 14, 1706, made will 1784, proved Aug. 13, 1785, made no mention of wife or child; Albert, May 26, 1708; Jacomyntje, Oct. 1710.

ARENT, son of Harmen Albertse, m. Sara, dau. of Symon Groot. He settled on land on the south side of the Mohawk river, opposite Hoffmans Ferry, which was called Vedder's Ferry, made his will Aug. 10, 1746, all his ch. then living. Ch. bp: Agnietje, Feb. 11, 1694, in Albany, m. Pieter Janse Vrooman; Rebecca, Oct. 25, 1691, in Albany, m. Willem Brouwer; *Harmen*, b. May 28 (29), 1696; Maria, bp. Sept. 1, 1699; Susanna, July 13, 1701, m. Pieter Mebie; Sara, Jan. 30, 1704, m. Cornelis Swits; Lysbeth, July 20, 1706; *Symon*, b. October 3, 1707, d. May 17, 1791; Antje, m. Pieter Clement; Lysbeth, Oct. 19, 1711, m. Jesaias Swart; *Albert*, b. Nov. 10, 1714.

ALBERT, son of Harmen Albertse, m. Maria, dau. of Johannes Sanderse Glen,

Dec. 17, 1699. He was carried away by the French and Indians, to Canada, Feb. 9, 1690; made his will Feb 8, 175¼, proved Feb. 13, 175¾, spoke of wife and children except Johannes, Catharina and Arent, d. August 1, 1753, a. 82ys., 2m., 21d.; his wife d. March 13, 1753, a. 74ys., less 19d. Ch. bp: Anna, July 28, 1700, m. Abraham Mebie, d. Dec. 22, 1750, leaving no ch.; *Johannes*, b. August 20, 1702; *Harmanus*, Sept. 3, 1704; Catharina, Dec. 25, 1706, in Albany; *Alexander*, Feb. 20, 1709, in Albany; Arnout; *Arent*, Dec. 18, 1714.

JOHANNES, son of Harmen Albertse, m. first, Maria, dau. of Johannes Fort (Van der Vort), July 8, 1705; and secondly, Engeltje, dau. of Gerrit Symonse Veeder, Nov. 25, 1732. He was carried away by the French and Indians to Canada Feb. 9, 1690, d. Aug. 14, 1748. Ch. bp: Harmen, April 14, 1706; Angenietje, Jan. 28, 1716; Hermanus, June 8, 1707, in Albany; Margarita, April 28, 1710, in Albany, m. Reyer Veeder; Anna, June 21, 1713, in Albany; Johannes, Nov. 22, 1718; Arent, June 17, 1721; Maritje, June 18, 1724; Abraham, b. May 14, 1727; Albert, bp. ——, 1729; Catharina, June 3, 1733, m. Johannes Van Antwerpen; Maria, Sept. 22, 1734; Anna, July 8, 1737.

CORSET, son of Harmen Albertse, m first, Margarita Barrith in Albany March 3, 1709. She d. before the baptism of child Anna Margarita, and he m. secondly, Neeltie, dau. of Christiaan Christiaanse of Albany, March 11, 1711. As early as 1708 he was living at "Schaghkook," also in 1720. In 1721 he sold his farm, and moved to Niskayuna; made his will Oct. 25, 1745, not living Sept. 20, 1748. Ch. bp: Anna Margarita, Jan. 8, 1710, in Albany; Isaac, Feb. 10, 1712, in Albany; Anna, Aug. 7, 1713, in Albany; Maria, Oct. 23, 1715; *Harmen*, June 29, 1717; *Christiaan*, Jan. 7, 1720, in Albany; Isaac, June 2, 1722; Neeltje (?), Sept. 5, 1723; Anna, b. Mar. 12, 1726; Maria, b. Sept. 9, 1727, m. Reyer Schermerhorn,

JOHANNES, son of Albert, m. Maria, dau. of Pieter Symonse Veeder, Feb. 21, 1730. She was b. Nov. 29, 1706, and d. March 27, 1731. Ch: *Albert*, b. July 27, 1730.

HARMANUS, son of Harmanus, m. Anna, dau. of Johannes Teller, Oct. 8, 1729. She was b. Feb. 14, 1705, d. Oct. 17, 1761, a. 56ys., 8m. 8d. He made his will 1762, proved June 27, 1763, spoke of his only dau. Susanna, wid. of Nicolaas A. Van Petten, deceased, and of his brother Johannes. Ch. bp: Margarita, Dec. 24, 1730; Susanna, March 25, 1733, m. first, Nicolaas A. Van Petten, and secondly, Johannes Cuyler jr.; Harmanus, July 9, 1737; Margarieta, June 14, 1740; Maria, b. March 12, 1743, d. March 31, 1761.

ALEXANDER, son of Albert, m. Margaret, dau. of Claas Van der Bogart, Dec. 26, 1736. He made his will Jan. 28, 1779, d. Oct , 1780, spoke of sons Albert and Nicolaas, and dau. Anna; left his house and lot in the village to his two sons. Ch. bp: *Albert*, March 17, 1737; Sara, June 14, 1740; Maria, Aug. 14, 1743, m. Cornelis Van Sice; Anna, Oct. 20, 1745, m. Abraham Dellamont; Nicolaas, July 3, 1748, d. Nov. 10, 1808, without issue; Sara, Nov. 17, 1751, m. Abraham J. Truex.

HARMANUS, son of Albert, m. Susanna, dau. of Volkert Veeder, Nov. 16, 1733. He inherited his father's farm at the *Lousen hoek*. Ch. bp: *Albert*, b. Feb. 17, (19), 1734, d. March 20, 1805, in Amsterdam; Jannetje, bp. June·7, 1735, m. Teunis Van Vleck; *Folkert*, April 10, 1737; Maria, Sept. 3, 1738; Catlyntje, March 8, 1741; Anna, Oct. 10, 1742, m. Jan Baptist Van Eps; Agnietje, Dec. 25, 1744; *Johannes*, Sept. 9, 1750.

SIMON, son of Arent, m. Maria Truax, wid. of Simon Groot, Jan. 16, 1735. He lived in the *Woestyne*, and d. May 17, 1791. Ch. bp: *Arent*, b. August 14, 1735; *Philip*, bp. July 9, 1737; *Harmanus*, March 4, 1739; Neeltje, Dec. 6, 1741, m. Johannes Van Petten; Sarah, May 13, 1744, m. Myndert Wemple; Annatje, Sept. 14, 1746; Maria, Oct. 15, 1749; Agnietje, April 5, 1752, m Nicolaas Swart; Susanna, May 18, 1755; Anna, March 12, 1758, m. Johannes Myndertse.

JOHANNES, son of Arent Albertse, m. Alida, dau. of Daniel De Graaf. March 20, 1809, Johannes Vedder *in den Heer gerust gestorven out zynde* 58 *jaer twe maanden* 27 *dagen; begraven March* 23. She d. Jan. 16, 1827, a. 76ys., 10m., 7d.

Ch. b: Arent, March 18, 1778; *Daniel*, Aug. 20, 1780; Sarah, March 20, 1783, d. Aug. 15, 1807; Gezina, Sept. 1, 1785, d. Sept. 29, 1804, Maria, July 10, 1788, m. John I. Schermerhorn, Feb. 5, 1814; Jesse, Feb. 1 (Jan. 31), 1793, d. Aug. 13, 1795; Johannes, May 31, 1795, d. Oct. 4, 1795.

HARMANUS, son of Corset, m. Tryntje, dau. of Dirk Heemstraat of Albany, July 2, 1738. He was the only son of his father living in 1762, lived in Niskayuna, made his will Sept. 14, 1778, proved April 2, 1812; wife then living, and the following Ch.: Isaac, Corset, Jacob, Clara or Caty, wife of Arent Pootman, Elisabeth and Mary; to each dau. £20. On the 14th Sept. 1778, Philip Ryley, sexton of the church, gave notice of Harmen Vedder's funeral to be held on the 16th Sept. Ch. bp: *Isaac*, January 7, 1739; *Corset*, Jan. 4, 1741; Claartje, April 3, 1743, m. Arent Pootman; Dirk, Feb. 17, 1745; Christiaan, July 26, 1747; *Jacob*, January 28, 1750; Maria, Aug. 9, 1752; Elisabeth, Feb. 27, 1757, m. Johannes Pootman.

ARENT, son of Albert, m. first, Sara, dau. of Claas Van der Bogart, and secondly, Catarina, dau. of Nicolaas Van Petten, and wid of Adam Swart, April 4, 1758. Ch. bp: Marytje, Jan. 7, 1739, m. Jacob Schermerhorn; *Albert*, Oct. 5, 1740, d. Aug. 7, 1821, a. 81ys., 1m., 27d.; *Nicolaas*, April 3, 1743; Catharina, Nov. 24, 1745, m. Johannes Toll; Johannes, Oct. 20, 1748; *Johannes*, Dec. 30, 1750, d. March 20, 1809; *Frans*, b. Dec. 14, 1753; Alexander, bp. February 6, 1757;

Harmen, bp. Nov. 19, 1758, d. in Springfield, Otsego county, Feb. 18, 1857, a. 99ys.; *Frederick*, bp. May 3, 1761; Rebecca, May 9, 1764; Rebecca, bp. Nov. 23, 1766, m. Simon A. Groot.

ALBERT, son of Arent, m. Catharina, dau. of Cornelis Viele. In 1746 he lived on the west side of Washington street, on a lot owned by D. Cady Smith and P. W. Holmes, which lot was given to him by his father's will. He d. Jan. 3, 1763. Ch. bp: Arent, May 31, 1741; Debora, b. July 20, 1744, m. Samuel Bragham; *Arent*, b. Sept. 30, 1747; Sarah, bp. April 22, 1750, m. Abraham I. Vedder; Margarita, b. March 5, 1752, m. John Bragham and John Brood; Cornelius, bp. Jan. 19, 1755; *Albert*, bp. Oct. 29, 1759.

ALBERT, son of Albert Albertse, m. Geertruy, dau. of Adam Swart, May 28, 1763. Ch. bp: Sarah, Oct. 30, 1763; *Arent*, Dec. 30, 1764; Catarina, April 12, 1767; *Adam*, Jan. 27, 1770; Sarah, August 9, 1772; Harmanus, Feb. 12, 1775; Rebecca, June 1, 1777.

CHRISTIAAN, son of Corset, of Schackkook, m. Hillegonda Van Vranken of Genistagioene, Sept. 27, 1745, both then living in the latter place.

HARMEN, son of Arent, m. Marytje, dau. of Arnout De Graaf. His father, by his will, gave him a farm, the westerly portion of his land at Hoffman's Ferry, the east bounds of which was the *Kromme kil* above the ferry; he had a house there in 1746. "*Ick*, Harmen Vedder, *out synde* 93 *jaer en* 3 *manten op den dag kore gemayt en gebonde en ok kore gedost*

Aug. 3, 1789 (his Family Bible). He d. Dec. 18, 1795, a. 99ys., 6m., 20d. Ch. bp: *Arnoud*, Feb. 21, 1742; Sara, Nov. 20, 1743; *Simon*, Nov. 11, 1744; Anna, Dec. 28, 1746; Nicolaas, Sept. 18, 1748; Anna, Jan. 26, 1752; Sarah, June 29, 1755, m. Jacobus Swart.

ALBERT, son of Johannes, m. Hester, dau. of Frans Van der Bogart, Oct. 30, 1756. He d. Nov. 18, 1805, a. 75ys.; she d. May 12, 1813, in her 80th year. Ch. bp: *Johannes*, May 15, 1757; Maria, Apr. 8, 1759; Maria, Jan. 18, 1761, m. ...... Newkerk; Hester, March 28, 1762, d. unmarried, Jan. 12, 1812, in her 50th year; *Frans Van der Bogart*, Jan. 1, 1764; Barber, Sept. 29, 1765, m. Daniel McMichael; Neeltje, May 3, 1767, m. Joachim Van Vorst; Engeltje, Sept. 9, 1770, m. Johannes Banta; Claas, Dec. 6, 1772, m. Clara Viele, d. May 23, 1828, a. 53ys., 5m., 17d.; Annatje, May 12, 1776, m. ...... Van Vorst.

ARENT, son of Albert Arentse, m. Sophia, dau. of Dirk Van Petten, Aug. 4, 1770. Ch: Catharine, b. Dec. 1, 1785.

ALBERT, son of Harmanus Albertse, m. Annatje, dau. of Isaac Quackenbos, Jan. 20, 1759. He d. March 20, 1805, a. 71ys., 29d., in Amsterdam; she d. March 6, 1806, a. 69ys., 8m., 27d. Ch. bp: Susanna, February 17, 1760; *Isaac*, Nov. 1, 1761; Rebecca, Jan. 29, 1763, m. Isaac Bovie; Maria, March 31, 1764; Elisabeth, Jan. 4, 1767, m. Abraham Bovie; Elisabeth, Aug. 21, 1768; *Harmanus*, Sept. 9, 1770, d. in Eagle, Wis., Dec. 16, 1852, a. 82ys.; Johannes, Oct.

22, 1772; Folkert, Oct. 23, 1774; Elias, Jan. 16, 1777; Alexander, May 2, 1779, d. in Brooklyn Dec. 13, 1854, a. 76ys.; his wife Agnes, d. Jan. 20, 1855, a. 65ys.; *Albert*, Aug. 10, 1780; Nicolaas, Sept. 12, 1784, m. Charity Esman, who d. Mar. 25, 1813, a. 27ys.

ALBERT, son of Albert Arentse, m. Catlyntje, dau. of David Kittle. Ch. b: Catharina, Feb. 4, 1786; Debora, Aug. 5, 1788; Catlyntje, Aug. 5, 1790; Sarah, Sept. 12, 1796; Albert, Aug. 28, 1802.

ISAAC, son of Harmanus C, of Niskayuna, m. Sara, dau. of William Birch. His father, by will, gave him a farm of 240 acres in Niskayuna. Ch. bp: *Harmen*, July 10, 1763; *Willem*, Oct. 6, 1765; Catarina, Aug. 27, 1768; Maria, Aug. 19, 1772.

ISAAC, son of Albert H., m. Neeltje, dau. of Jacobus Van Eps. Ch. b: Annatje, bp. March 27, 1785; Jacobus, b. Aug. 24, 1786; Albert, Aug. 6, 1788, d. Dec. 12, 1847; Engeltje, Aug. 22, 1790; Alexander, Jan. 25, 1795; Harmanus, July 25, 1797.

CORSET (Seth), son of Harmanus C., of Niskayuna, m. Neeltje, dau. of William Birch. His father, by will, gave him his dwelling house and farm in Niskayuna. Seth made his will Sept. 17, 1822, proved Oct. 2, 1822, and spoke of wife Nelly, son Harmanus, dau.-in-law Mary, wid. of son Dirk, deceased, and dau. of his dau. Catharina. Ch: Harmanus, b. March 1, 1762; Maria, bp. Nov. 13, 1763; Marytje, b. July 13, 1766; Dirk, bp. May 28, 1769;

Catarien, Sept. 15, 1771, m. Johannes De Graaf; Willem, bp. Oct. 24, 1773.

FREDERIC, son of Arent, m. Maria Van Petten. Ch. b: Arent, June 15, 1786; Johannes, June 1, 1789; Nicolaas, July 11, 1792; Simon, Oct. 15, 1796; Albert, May 22, 1799.

ALBERT, son of Alexander, m. Neeltje, dau. of Willem Bancker, May 30, 1761. He d. June 21, 1800. Ch. bp: Margarita, Jan. 10, 1762; *Alexander*, b. Oct. 27, 1764; *Willem*, bp. Jan. 4, 1767; Thomas, July 25, 1773; Annatje, Sept. 3, 1775, m. Robert Moyston.

ARENT, son of Albert, m. Angenietje, dau. of Jan Baptist Van Eps, July 18, 1790. Ch. b: Geertruy, Sept. 15, 1791; John Van Eps, Jan. 9, 1794; Catharina, bp. May 1, 1796; John, b. July 16, 1798.

FOLKERT, son of Harmen Albertse, m. Rebecca, dau. of Simon Groot, Nov. 26, 1763. Through his grandmother, Maria Sanderse Glen, he inherited a farm on the *Lusig hoek*, on the north side of the Mohawk river, next above Freeman's bridge, where he kept a ferry and inn. Ch. bp: Harmanus, May 19, 1765; Simon, Oct. 18, 1767; *Albert*, Nov. 5, 1769; Arent, Aug. 23, 1772; *Cornelis*, Feb. 16, 1777.

CLAAS, son of Arent Albertse, m. Eva, dau. of Jan Dellamont, Feb. 9, 1765. He made his will Aug. 1, 1812, proved Sept. 3, 1819, spoke of wife Eva, dau. Sarah, and son Harmanus. Ch. bp: Sarah, June 2, 1765, m. Johannes Vedder; *Johannes*, Feb. 1, 1767; *Arent*, Aug. 20, 1769; Eva, Jan. 19, 1772; *Harmanus*, July

3, 1774; Maria, Nov. 24, 1776; Catarina, April 24, 1779; Abraham, Dec. 23, 1781.

NICOLAAS, widower, m. Maria Van Petten, March 24, 1790.

SIMON, son of Harmen Arentse, m. first, Margarita, dau. of Arent Pootman, June 1, 1777; secondly, Catharina Wiest, widow of Jan Baptist Swart, and dau. of Coenraad Wiest, April 28, 1799. She was b. Oct. 4, 1768, and d. Oct. 26, ——, a. 81ys., 12d.; he d. May 24, 1821, a. 77ys., 6m., 9d. Ch. b : Mary, Dec. 20, 1778; Cornelis, Oct. 19, 1781; Elisabeth, April 1, 1784, d. June 17, 1811; Harmen, July 19, 1786; Arent, Dec. 22 (23), 1788, d. May, 1789; Margarietje, Jan. 11, d. March 10, 1800; Peggy Ann, June 19, 1806, d. March 9, 1810.

ARENT, son of Simon, of "Mount Hope," Niskayuna, m. first, Jannetje, dau. of Johannes Truex, Dec. 10, 1768. She was b. Nov. $\frac{12}{13}$, 1744, d. April 10, 1780; he m. secondly, Annatje, dau. of Willem Bancker, Feb. 23, 1782; she d. July 14 (18), 1813, a. 72ys., 11m. In his will made Sept. 3, 1811, proved Dec. 31, 1811, his second .wife, Nancy, was living, also ch. Simon, John B., Maria and Alida. Ch. b : Simon, Aug. 22, 1769, d. June 26, 1770; Johannes, Feb. 11, 1771, killed by the falling of a stick of timber, Feb. 17, 1787; Simon, Sept. 1, 1772, d. in Niskayuna, Dec. 22, 1844, a. 72ys., 2 (3) m., 22d.; his wife, Mary Bassett, d. Jan. 17, 1823, a. 40ys., 11m., 17d.; Maria, Feb. 27, 1775, m. John

Cowen, d. April 20, 1837, a. 62ys., 1m., 21d.; Alida, Sept. 12, 1777; Janneke, April 3, d. June 21, 1780; Johannes, April 10, 1787.

JACOB, son of Harmanus C., of Niskayuna, m. Catharina, dau. of Johannes Hall. Ch. bp: Maria, May 24, 1772; *Harmanus*, Dec. 19, 1773; Johannes, Sept. 22, 1776.

WILLEM, son of Isaac, of Nestigaune, m. Catharina, dau. of Johannes S. Vrooman, July 5, 1787. He d. June 23, 1852, in his 87th year; she d. Feb. 18, 1858, in her 95thy ear. Ch. b : Sarah, June 11, 1788; William, ——, 1790, d. Dec. 24, 1831, a. 41ys., 1m., 2d.; Catharina, May 8, 1794; Clara, May 30, 1797; Maria, March 15, 1800; Engeltje, Feb. 27, 1804.

PHILIP, son of Simon, of Rotterdam, m. Margarita, dau. of Takerius Van der Bogart, Dec. 1, 1770. He made his will Aug. 24, 1818, proved May 30, 1822, spoke of two sons Takarus and Simon P., and dau. Mary, wife of Frederic Bratt, and Eleanor, wife of Almon Norton. He d. May 6, 1822, in his 85th year. Ch. bp : *Simon*, Dec. 20, 1772; *Takerius*, March 5, 1775; Maria, July 13, 1777; Neeltje, April 15, 1781.

HARMANUS, son of Claas, m. first, Margarita Van Eps; and secondly, Jacomyntje Van Petten. Ch : Nicolaas, b. May 1, 1797; Maria, child of second wife, b. Dec. 5, 1801, m. Abraham N. Bratt, and d. May 12, 1833, in the *Woestine.*

HARMANUS, son of Simon, m. Annatje Vedder, Nov. 10, 1770. He made his will Oct. 14, 1813, proved May 14, 1816, gave to Arent " my farm in Schenectady where I now live," and to Philip " my farm in Florida," spoke also of son Nicolaas and dau. Maria, also of Ch. of his deceased son Simon, viz. : Harmanus, John, Aaron, Philip, Gertrude and Annatie. Ch. bp : Simon, July 11, 1773 ; Maria, Oct. 13, 1776 ; Maria, Nov. 11, 1781 ; Arent, Nov. 28, 1784 ; Philip, b. Dec. 3, 1788 ; Nicholas, b. Oct. 12, 1794.

JOHANNES, son of Albert, m. Eva, dau. of Jacob Clute, Aug. 22, 1779. [A John A. Vedder, elder of the church, d. between Dec. 3, 1808, and April 6, 1809.] Ch. bp : Albert, April 23, 1780 ; Elisabeth, Sept. 29, 1782 ; Esther, Jan. 23, 1785 ; Johannes, b. Jan. 15, 1787 ; Elisabeth, b. March 18, 1790.

SIMON, son of Philip, m. Eva Bratt. Ch : Margarita, b. July 22, 1798.

ARNOUT, son of Harmen Arentse, m. Ariaantje Wemple. Ch : Rebecca, bp. July 8, 1781.

ADAM, son of Albert A., of the *Woestyne*, m. Annatje Van Vleck of *Remsen's bos*, Nov., 1792 (?). Ch. b : Benjamin, Oct. 14, 1793 ; Sarah, March 10, 1798.

ARENT J., m. Jannetje Hoghing. Ch : Susannah, b. July 31, 1776. [*See Albany Families.*]

FRANS, son of Arent Albertse, m. Rebecca, dau. of Johannes Van Petten. He d. May 20, 1827, a. 73ys., 5m., 6d.

Ch. b : Arent, bp. Nov. 30, 1783 ; Johannes, b. June 3, 1786, d. in Rotterdam, Sept. 5, 1864, a. 78ys. ; Albert, Nov. 1, 1789 ; Nicolaas, Dec. 19, 1792 ; Sarah, Nov. 12, 1796 ; Neeltie, Aug. 20, 1800 ; Frederick, April 1, 1805 ; Sarah Ann, March 19, 1808.

HARMEN, son of Isaac, of Fonda's bos, m. Rebecca Bogart. He d. July 7, 1850, a. 87ys. ; she d. March 2, 1823, a. 58ys., 4m., 7d. Ch. b : Barbara, Feb. 6, 1786 ; Isaac, May 28, 1787 ; Pieter, Sept. 16, 1789 ; Willem, June 2, 1792 ; Rykardt, Feb. 1, 1795 ; Sarah, Nov. 18, 1798.

HARMANUS, of Nestigaune, and Elisabeth Bassett of the Greene Boss, m. at Albany, May 19, 1788. Ch. b : Cornelius Bassett, Sept. 8, 1790 ; Eleanor, June 5, 1796. [*See Albany Families.*]

JOHANNES, son of Harmanus Albertse, m. Sarah, dau. of Nicolaas Vedder, Jan. 29, 1786. She d. Dec. 29, 1850. Ch. b : Harmanus, Feb. 16, 1787 ; Sara, March 25, 1789 ; Nicolaas, Nov. 1, 1791, d. July 29, 1838 ; Susannah, Jan. 13, 1795 ; Johannes, November 7, 1797, d. Nov. 20, 1857 ; Eva, July 8, 1800 ; Elihu, Nov. 13, 1802 ; Levi, May 18, 1805, d. Aug., 1839 ; Uri, April 12, 1808.

ALEXANDER, son of Albert, m. Susanna, dau. of Jacob Vrooman, July 25, 1787. She d. 1832, a. 63ys. ; he d. Mar. 7, 1813 (Dec. 27, 1812 (?)). Ch. b : Maria, Jan. 25, 1788, m. Thomas Tillman, May 27, 1808, d. 1832 ; *Jacob*, Oct. 2 (5), 1789, d. Jan. 22, 1838 ; Elisabeth, his wid., d. Dec. 20, 1870, a. 80ys. ; *Ni-*

colaas, Nov. 27, 1791, d. Oct. 13, 1862; Hendrick Swits, March 2 (3), 1794, d. 1832; Albert, April 30 (May 1), 1796, d. Oct. 28, 1867; Lena, Aug. 13, 1798, m. Frederic B. Allen, d. Sept. 6 (26), 1824; Neeltje, Nov. 20, 1800, m. George Manly, and d. 1862.

ABRAM, m. Annatje Van Vranken. Ch: Albert, bp. May 1, 1796.

DIRK, of Nestigaune, m. Maria Vrooman of the Zandkil, Nov. 27, 1788. Ch. b: Neeltie, Feb. 13, 1789; Maritie, Feb. 9, 1794.

JACOB, son of Alexander, m. Elisabeth, dau. of Christopher Ward, ——, 1809. He d. Jan. 22, 1838; she d. Dec. 20, 1870. Ch. b: Susan, Jan. 26, 1810, m. Peter H. Clute, Aug. 1, 1827. He d. March 13, 1866; she d. Aug. 19, 1860, Margaret, Nov. 14, 1811, m. Henry Fritcher of Canajoharie, Sept. 11, 1830, he d. Dec. 3, 1843; she d. May 22, 1845; Maria, Aug. 16, 1813, m. Isaac Christiaanse, April 19, 1832, he d. April 13, 1864; Christopher, Sept. 9, 1815, d. Nov. 29, 1817; Jane Helen, Aug. 27, 1818, d. Sept. 13, 1819; Eleanor, July 13, 1819, m. Robert Bannard, March 3, 1841, he d. Oct. 11, 1857; Nicholas A., Aug. 13, 1821, m. Fanny M. Thayer of Taunton, Mass., Oct. 16, 1852; Jacob A., Oct. 15, 1823, m. Susan Jane Vrooman, April 17, 1849; Elisabeth, March 7, 1825, m. Philo Timmerman of Medina, Dec. 8, 1847, he d. July 29, 1855. Harmen P., Nov. 3, 1827, m. Mary E. Chap-

man of Rockford, Ill., July 16, 1857; Jane, Oct. 26, 1829, m. Thomas L. Pemberton of Albany, Dec. 30, 1847; Christopher, Oct. 14, 1831, d. July 25, 1838; Rachel, Aug. 23, 1834, m. George Marselis, Sept. 13, 1853, she d. October 13, 1854; Henry, March 28, 1837, d. Aug. 25, 1837.

FRANS VAN DE BOGART, son of Albert, m. Lena, dau. of Thomas Brouwer Bancker, Dec. 15, 1788. He d. April 3, 1811; she was b. May 5, 1769, d. April 7, 1834. Ch. b: Annatie, Nov. 8, 1789, m. John Newkirk; Albert, Jan. 14, 1792, m. Nancy Feling; Jacob, April 30, 1794, m. Elsie Fisher, d. Jan. 17, 1855, a. 59ys., 8m., 17d.; Johannes, Oct. 29, 1796, m. Lucy Ann Norton; Esther, Jan. 4, 1799, m. John F. D. Vedder, Dec. 11, 1821; Margarieta, January 17, 1801, m. Abraham Veeder; Nicholas, Jan. 10, 1804, m. Cornelia Blandina Veeder, Oct. 12, 1836; she was b. May 22, 1801, d. Sept. 12, 1867; Elisabeth Catharine, July 15, 1806, m. Aaron I. Bratt, Feb. 15, 1832; he was b. August 13, 1806, d. March 7, 1861; Francis Van de Bogart, Oct. 4 (5), 1810, m. Grace Bush.

WILLEM, son of Albert A., m. Eva De Graaf, Oct. 16, 1790. He d. in Glenville 1849, a. 82ys. Ch. b: Nicholas, Oct. 29, 1790; Cornelius, Aug. 18, 1792, d. March 16, 1845; Annatje, July 16, 1795, m. John L. Van Eps, d. May 22, 1843; Albert, Jan. 6, 1798; Elisabeth, Aug. 24, 1800; Margarietje, Jan. 1, 1802; Abraham, Feb. 14, 1806; Abra ham De Graaf, Jan. 23, 1809; William Bancker, Oct. 26, 1811.

ARENT, son of Claas, m. Catlyntje Bratt, Sept. 1, 1792. Ch. b : Nicholas, March 6, 1794; Frederic, March 16, 1796; Baata, May 23, 1798.

JOHN, son of Claas, m. Annatie Palmontier, May 28, 1793.

ALBERT, son of Volkert, m. Maria, dau. of David Kittle. [Albert Vedder was buried Nov. 18, 1805.] Ch. b : Rebecca, May 1, 1799; Sarah, Oct. 19, 1802; David, Dec. 3, 1804.

HARMANUS, son of Jacob, and Maritie Wever, both of Rensselaerswyck, m. Sept. 6, 1794.

CORNELIUS, son of Volkert, m. Sarah Van Vorst. She d. 1800. Ch : Rebecca, b. Aug. 16, 1799.

EPHRAIM, of Steen Arabia and Nelly Vreelandt of Remsenbos, m. Oct. (?) 1794.

TAKERUS, son of Philip, m. Eva, dau. of Jacobus Bratt, March 9, 1799. She inherited from her father the ancient brick house and lot of land lying west of the first lock in Rotterdam. He d. Feb. 24, 1836, a. 61ys., 21d.; she d. June 7, 1839, a. 67ys., 8m., 21d.

ALBERT, son of Albert H. and Annatie Quackenbos, m. Maria Rumney, May 8, 1805. She d. July 24, 1821; and he m. secondly, Susan Fulton, Mar.

29, 1823. Ch. b : Benjamin Van Schaick, Feb. 6, 1806; Debora Ann, August 5, 1808; Elisabeth, Sept. 4, 1810, d. June 23, 1843; Madison, February 15, 1813; Maria, June 23, 1815, d. Dec. 16, 1816; Edmund B., Aug. 23, 1817; Sheridan B., July 6, 1820, d. Aug. 15, 1841; Lafayette, July 29, 1824, d. Feb. 10, 1850; Charles, Oct. 7, 1826, grad. Uuion College, 1851; Andrew Jackson, Dec. 8, 1831.

DANIEL, son of Johannes Arentse, m. Mrs. Gitty Swart, Nov. 3, 1804. Ch. b : John, Oct. 12, 1805; Sarah Gesina, June 27, 1808; Agnietie, April 23, 1811; Alida, June 9, 1815; Nicholas Swart, Feb. 17, 1819.

CORNELIUS, m. Caty Duicher. Ch : Peter, b. Oct. 16, 1792. [*See Albany Families.*]

NICHOLAS, son of Alexander, m. Annatie, dau. of Nicholas Marselis, Oct. 24, 1812. He d. ——. Ch. b : Alexander M., graduated at Union College 1833; Prof. of anatomy and physiology 1849–1863; Simon V. ......, merchant in New York; Jacob ......, d. in infancy; Stephen Y. ......, in class 1841, Union College, merchant, d. in Rhinebeck May 11, 1860; Anna M. ......, m. Rev. William H. Ten Eyck, D.D., of Astoria; Henry N. ......, merchant, Rhinebeck; Edward ......, d. in infancy; Joseph H. ......, of class 1851, Union College, Doct. of medicine, d. ——; Maus R. ......, of class 1856, Union College, Doct. of medicine in New York; Susan Gertrude.

VEEDER.

SIMON VOLKERTSE VEEDER, *alias de Bakker*, born in 1624, belonged to the ship *Prince Maurice* in 1644, which ship plied between Amsterdam and New Amsterdam; 1652 he bought a lot and settled in the latter city; sold the same in 1654 for 30 beavers, removed to Beverwyck, and from thence to Schenectady in 1662. He owned a bouwery on the Great flat numbered 9, containing 24 morgens, and a village lot on the north corner of State and Ferry streets. He also owned land on the Normanskil; made his will Jan. 8, 169$\frac{4}{5}$, and spoke of the following Ch: *Pieter; Gerrit; Johannes; Volkert;* Volkie, m. Barent Janse Wemp; Geesie, m. Jan Hendrickse Vrooman; Magdalena, m. Willem Appel.

PIETER, eldest son of Simon Volkertse, m. Neeltie, dau. of Claas Van der Volgen, June 17, 1704. At the date of his last child's baptism, June 26, 1709, he was not living. His father gave him land on the Normanskil. Ch. bp: *Simon*, Dec. 30, 1704; Maria, Feb. 19, 1707, in Albany, m. Johannes Vedder; *Pieter*, June 26, 1709, in Albany.

GERRIT, son of Simon, m. Tryntje, dau. of Helmer Otten, Aug. 3, 1690, in Albany. She was the only child of Otten, who d. in 1675, after which her mother m. Reyer Schermerhorn. Gerrit Simonse owned the land about Veeder's mills early in the 18th century and had a lease from the church of the mill privilege in 1718. Through his wife he obtained possession of lots in the village on the

north and west corners of Union and Church streets; made his will March 12, 174$\frac{4}{5}$, proved July 8, 1755. Ch. b: *Helmers*, Oct. 22, 1690; *Wilhelmus;* Engeltie, in Albany, July 22, 1693, m. Johannes Vedder; Ariaantje, Nov. 16, 1695, m. Daniel Danielse Van Antwerpen; *Hendricus*, Aug. 3, 1698; Simon, Dec. 31, 1700; Annatie, Aug. 16, 1703, m. William Bancker; *Cornelis*, Jan. 27, 1706; Helena (Magdalena), April 2, 1710, m. Johannes Bancker.

JOHANNES, son of Simon, m. first, Susanna, dau. of Myndert Wemp, Nov. 19, 1697, and secondly, Susanna Wendell of Albany, June 3, 1718. She was buried in the church in Albany, Nov. 16, 1739. By his father's will he received land on the Normanskil, he also bought part of Jan Hendrickse Van Bael's patent there; made his will July 15, 1746, and spoke of the following Ch. except Ariaantje, also of his step-son Luykas Johannese Wyngaard: Ch. bp: Debora, June 20, 1698; Engeltie, Oct. 27, 1700, m. Jacobus De La Grange; Debora, Jan. 17, 1703, m. first, Reyer Wemp, secondly, Douwe Fonda; Maria, April 1, 1705; *Myndert*, April 30, 1707; *Simon*, Oct. 30, 1709; Ariaantje, May 31, 1719.

VOLKERT, son of Symon, m. Jannetie, dau. of Reyer Schermerhorn, August 6, 1698, in Albany. In 1719 the sheriff of Albany seized two pieces of *Strouds* in his house and condemned them to be sold and disposed of according to the Albany city charter. By the will of his father he received farm No. 9 on the

Bouwland; he made his will August 4, 1733, d. Aug. 12, 1733. Excepting Engeltje, the following Ch. were then living: Ch. bp: *Simon*, Dec. 28, 1698; Ariaantje, Aug. 18, 1700, m. Willem Daasen; Reyer, Dec. 28, 1701; Engeltie, Nov. 7, 1703; *Reyer*, Oct. 28, 1705; Catalyntje, Feb. 8, 1708; Magdalena, Oct. 30, 1709, in Albany; Susanna, April 20, 1712, in Albany, m. Harmanus Vedder; *Johannes*, May 23, 1714, in Albany; Catalyntje, Jan. 1, 1716, m. Simon Veeder; Hendericus, Oct. 5, 1717; *Hendericus*, July (?) 9, 1719.

HELMERS, son of Gerrit, m. Anna, dau. of Jan Mebie, July 19, 1715. In 1713 he owned a lot 200ft. square on the west corner of Union and Church streets. From his father he received half of the saw mill at "Veeder's mills." Ch. b: *Gerrit*, April 7, 1716; *Johannes*, b. and bp June 2, 1718; Catharina, Aug. 20, 1720, m. Jacobus Van Eps; Anna, Dec. 1, 1722, m. Rev. Johannes Schuyler; *Simon; Hendericus;* Petrus, July 30, 1732; Maria, Oct. 27, 1734.

SIMON, son of Volkert Symonse, m. Margriet, dau. of Barent Wemp, 1719. He d. Sept. 5, 1746; she d. Dec. 9, 1777. Ch. bp: Jannetje, Dec. 3, 1720; Magdalen, April 21, 1723, m. Harmanus Terwilliger; Jannetje, b. and bp. March 14, 1725; Volkje, b. June 5, bp. June 11, 1727; *Barent*, March 26, 1732; Jannetje, Aug. 25, 1734; Volkje, Oct. 17, 1736, d. Jan. 9, 1801; Folkert, Feb. 14, 1739; Engeltje, Jan. 11, 1741, d. Aug. 17, 1827; Volkert, Jan. 15, 1744.

PIETER, son of Pieter Symonse, b. on the Normanskil and residing at Schenectady, m. Maritie, dau. of Claas Van de Bogart, Jan. 21, 1732. Ch. bp: Neeltje, May 25, 1732, m. Hendricus Vrooman; *Claas*, b. Feb. 9 (grave stone), bp. Feb. 3 (Church Register), 1734; Maria, Aug. 17, 1735, m. Willem Hall; Margriet, March 29, 1737; Pieter Symonse, June 14, 1740; Anna, April 25, 1742; Catharina, April 22, 1744, m. Cornelis Van Slyck; *Pieter Symonse*, Dec. 28, 1746; *Frans*, Aug. 27, 1749.

JOHANNES, son of Volkert, m. Catharina, dau. of Abraham Mebie, March 16, 1738. Ch. bp: *Volkert*, Dec. 14, 1740; Jannetie, August 21, 1743; *Abraham*, Nov. 17, 1745; Simon, b. May 31, bp. June 5, 1748; Maria, Dec. 9, 1750; Catalina, Aug. 5, 1753; Eva, April 22, 1756; Catalyntje, Dec. 10, 1758.

CORNELIS, son of Gerrit Symonse, m. first, Elisabeth Visscher, Oct., 1727, in Albany; secondly, Engeltje, dau. of Wouter Vrooman, Jan. 7, 1732. His father gave him a lot 40×100ft., on the west side of Church street, 180ft. northerly from Union street. Ch. bp: Elisabeth, July 6, 1738; Wouter Vrooman, Oct. 5, 1740; Ariaantje, Sept. 23, 1744; Gerrit Symonse, Jan. 17, 1748; Gerrit Symonse, Sept. 30, 1750.

SIMON, son of Johannes, of the Normanskil, m. first, Catharina, dau. of Andries Van Petten, July 10, 1741 (Church Register), June 10, 1738 (Family Record); she d. Dec. 20 (23), 1741; he m.

34

secondly, Maria, dau. of Lourens Van der Volgen, April 7, 1744; thirdly, Geesje, daughter of Hendrick Janse Vrooman; (fourthly, Annatie Bratt, wid., Dec. 24, 1748), and fifthly, Catalyntje, dau. of Volkert Veeder of Normanskil, April 9, 1752, in Albany. In 1756 he was called " merchant of Albany ; " 1761 conveyed to his son-in-law, Johannes Glen, lot 52 Washington street; made his will March 19, 1785, proved Dec. 20, 1786, then of Normanskil, gave to son Wyngaart farm and lands " now in my possession at Normanskil," to Volkert house in Albany; spoke also of dau. Catriena. Ch : Catharina, b. Dec. 15, 1741, m. Col. John Glen, and d. Oct. 22, 1799, a. 57ys., 9m., 26d. ; Susanna, bp. Feb. 24, 1745 ; Susanna, bp. July 26, 1752, in Albany ; Johannes, bp. Dec. 26, 1753 ; *Johannes Simonse*, bp. Mar. 12, 1755, in Albany ; *Lucas Wyngaard*, July 24, 1757, in Albany ; *Volkert*, b. June 14, 1760, in Albany.

JOHANNES, m. Wyntje Veeder. Ch : Annatje, bp. Oct. 14, 1738.

SIMON, son of Helmers, m. first, Elisabeth, dau. of Johannes Bancker, Sept. 25, 1755 ; secondly, Margarita Pootman about 1783. Ch. bp: Helmer, Feb. 1, 1756; Helmer, Feb. 11, 1759 ; Magdalena, March 4, 1764 ; *Johannes*, Oct. 12, 1766 ; Simon, July 10, 1774 ; Elisabeth, b. April 1, 1784.

REYER, son of Volkert Simonse, m. first, Margrieta, dau. of Johannes Vedder, Oct. 13, 1735 ; and secondly, Immetje, dau. of Cornelis Christiaanse of Gen-

istagioene, Nov. 14, 1747; she was buried June 2, 1805. Ch. bp : Volkert, Aug. 14, 1748 ; Cornelis Christiaanse, Jan. 21, 1750; Christiaanse, Oct. 20, 1751; Simon, Feb. 10, 1753; Cornelis Christiaanse, May 4, 1755 ; Henricus, June 14, 1761.

MYNDERT, son of Johannes Simonse, m. Elisabeth Douw in Albany, Dec. 19, 1733. Ch. bp. in Albany: *Johannes*, June 29, 1734 ; Volkert, Oct. 3, 1736 ; Symon, Feb. 20, 1739 ; *Abraham*, Oct. 18, 1741 ; Susanna, April 29, 1744 ; Myndert, Dec. 14, 1746 ; Margarita, Jan. 14, 1753 ; *Jacob*, Jan. 14, 1759.

GERRIT, son of Helmers, m. first, Hester, dau. of Johannes Slingerland of Albany ; secondly, Anneke, dau. of Nicolaas De Graaf about 1761. Ch. bp : Anna, Jan. 22, 1749 ; Maria, May 26, 1751 ; Margarita, April 28, 1753 ; Engeltie, Dec. 25, 1754 ; Johannes, Dec. 3, 1758 ; *Nicolaas*, b. Dec. 25, bp. Jan. 24, 1762 ; Alida, bp. Nov. 4, 1764, m. Pieter Clement; Helmer, May 13, 1770 ; *Wilhelmus ;* Catharine.

WILHELMUS, son of Gerrit Symonse, m. Annatie Mebie. He received from his father half of the saw mill at " Veeder's mills," was not mentioned in his father's will 174$, then probably deceased. Ch. b : *Hendericus*, Feb. 20, 1725 ; Margariet, Aug. 18, 1727.

HENDERICUS, son of Wilhelmus above, m. Elisabeth Bratt, Aug. 18, 1750.

SIMON, son of Pieter Symonse, m. first, Geertruy Kip in Albany, Dec. 17, 1730. She was buried July 20, 1746, and he

m. secondly, Annatie Van Antwerpen about 1749. Ch. bp: Pieter, Sept. 26, 1731; Geertje, Oct. 28, 1733; *Pieter Symonse*, Feb. 10, 1737; Abraham, June 20, 1742; Geertruy, Jan. 14, 1750; Johannes, Jan. 1, 1755; Geertruy, Sept. 10, 1758.

HENRICUS, son of Gerrit Symonse, m. Elisabeth Wemp, Aug. 18, 1750. He received a conveyance of the "Veeder's mills" from his mother July 11, 1752; from his father a lot on the north corner of Union and Church streets, which passed to his dau. Catharina, wife of Jillis Fonda; made his will March 3, 1790, his wife, son Gerrit and dau. Catharina then living. Ch: *Gerrit Symonse*, b. July 4, 1751; Abraham, bp. Dec. 27, 1753; Catharina, bp. June 29, 1755, m. Jillis Fonda; Abraham, bp. April 9, 1758; Volkje, bp. Aug. 5, 1759.

HENRICUS, son of Volkert, m. Catharina, dau. of Jan Dellamont, Feb. 19, 174⅞. He was b. August 17, 1719, d. Aug. 23, 1776; she was b. May 6, 1728, d. Aug. 18, 1802.

JOHANNES, son of Helmer, m. Anna, dau. of Arent Samuelse Bratt, Nov. 24, 1750. He d. August 4, 1794, a. 76ys., 2m., 2d. She was b. Sept. 2, 1721, d. September 1, 1809, a. 87ys., 11m., 30d. Ch. b: Wilhelmus, July 5, 1751, d. Nov. 8, 1751; Wilhelmus, July 21, 1753, d. Dec. 16, 1787, a. 34ys., 4m., 16d.

HENRICUS, son of Helmer, m. Judikje, dau. of Joost Van Sice, Aug. 30, 1752.

In 1762 he owned the lot on west corner of Union and Church streets. Ch. bp: Magdalena, July 29, 1753, m. Simon Van Antwerpen; Annatje, Dec. 1, 1754, m. John Combs; Maria, Dec. 5, 1756; Johannes, Sept. 20, 1767.

CLAAS, son of Pieter, m. Catarina, dau. of Johannes Van Eps, Feb. 5, 1757. He made his will July 26, proved Sept. 1, 1810, spoke of his wife Catharine and sons John and Pieter C., John to have half the farm 6 miles south of Schenectady called "*Het Dunkere Bos,*" 70 acres in all, and Pieter to have pasture land on "Simon Groot's kil" (now College brook), called Teunis Van Vleck's pasture, four acres. His house was on the lot bounded by Front, Green and Ferry streets, which his son Johannes inherited. He was b. Feb. 9, 1734, d. Nov. 11, 1807, a. 73ys., 9m., 2d.; his wife d. October, 1815. Ch. bp: Maria, June 19, 1757; Johannes, Oct. 18, 1761; Pieter, Nov. 17, 1765; *Johannes*, July 24, 1768; *Pieter*, March 26, 1775.

BARENT, son of Simon Volkertse, m. Jannetie, dau. of Johannes Schermerhorn, Oct. 12, 1757. Ch. bp: *Simon*, January 29, 1758; Johannes, April 29, 1759; *Johannes*, Nov. 23, 1760; Engeltje, Sept. 12, 1762, m. Samuel S. Bratt; Folkert Simonse, March 4, 1764; Margarita, July 7, 1765; Volkert Simonse, Sept. 6, 1767; Magdalena, Jan. 1, 1769, m. Johannes A. Bratt; Jannetje, Oct. 14, 1770; Reyer, May 3, 1772; Volkje, July 3, 1774, m. William Purdy; Maria, Nov. 24, 1776.

BARENT (perhaps the same as the last), widower, m. Mathia Peters, widow, Jan. 24, 1790.

FOLKERT, son of Johannes Volkertse, m. Elisabeth Smith. Ch : Johannes, bp. Jan. 2, 1763.

VOLKERT, of Rensselaerswyck, son of Myndert, of Albany, m. Susanna, dau. of Reinier Myndertse, January 6, 1767. Ch. bp : Meyndert, Jan. 3, 1768 ; Reynier, July 15, 1770 ; Elisabeth, Oct. 10, 1773 ; Petrus, April 7, 1776 ; Johannes, Dec. 7, 1783 ; Margarieta, b. May 11, 1788.

VOLKERT SYMONSE, son of Symon Johannese of Albany, and Annatie Spaan of Normanskil, m. Jan. 25, 1786 ; he afterwards, about 1790, m. Ann Quackenbos in Albany. Ch. b. (bp. in Albany) : Catelyntje, March 18, 1791 ; Anna, bp. Feb. 15, 1794, d. Aug. 24, 1797, a. 2ys., 12d. ; Anna, b. Aug. 12, 1795, d. July 9, a. 17m. ; Elisabeth, b. Feb. 16, 1798 ; Maria, b. January 22, 1801, d. June 13, 1803. [*See Albany Families.*]

JOHANNES, son of Myndert of Albany, of the *Woestine,* m. Lena, dau. of Pieter Vrooman, July 6, 1759. He was b. July 29, 1734, d. Sept. 26, 1793 ; she was b. Aug. 18, 1734, d. Dec. 20, 1813. Ch. b : *Pieter Vrooman,* Nov., 1760 ; Margaret, Oct. 22, 1763 ; Myndert, Sept. 14, 1769, d. June 12, 1833 ; Annatie, October 30, 1771, m. Frederic Bratt, d. June 20, 1794 ; Elisabeth, bp. April 16, 1775.

JOHANNES, son of Claas, m. Eva, dau. of Carel Hansen Toll, Jan. 26, 1791. He inherited from his father, the lot bounded by Front, Green and Ferry streets. Ch. b : Maria, Oct. 25, 1792 ; Carel Hansen, Oct. 1, 1795 ; Nicolaas, Jan. 7, 1799 ; Elisabeth, Aug. 15, 1801 ; Elisabeth, Jan. 18, 1804 ; Peter, March 30, 1806 ; Elisabeth, d. Oct. 31, 1808, a. 2m., 3d. ; John James Ryley, March 19, 1809 ; Philip Henry, Sept. 9, 1811.

ABRAHAM, son of Johannes Volkertse, m. first, Sarah. dau. of Albert Vedder, Feb. 14, 1768. She d. about July 19, 1769, and he m. secondly, Annatie Fonda about 1778. Ch. bp ; Albert, July 19, 1769 ; Sarah, June 27, 1779.

ABRAHAM, son of Myndert, of Albany, m. Neeltje Schuyler. Ch : Elisabeth, b. July 6, 1781 ; Simon, bp. Nov. 3, 1782 ; Elisabeth, b. May 28, 1785 ; Geertruy, July 27, 1789 ; Myndert, July 5, 1793. [*See Albany Families.*]

ABRAHAM, m. Sara Hansen. Ch. bp. in Albany : Isaac, Sept. 1, 1775 ; Pieter, July 1, 1787. [*See Albany Families.*]

PIETER SYMONSE, son of Symon Pieterse of Albany, m. Marytje Van den Bergh, March 13, 1762, in Albany. Ch. b : Geertruit, May 26, 1763 ; Cornelis, March 12, 1766. [*See Albany Families.*]

FRANS, son of Pieter, merchant, m. Maria, dau. of Pieter Bosie, Oct. 31, 1772. Ch. bp : *Pieter,* Aug. 2, 1773 ;

Margarita, June 6, 1779, d. in Glenville unmarried, Oct. 15, 1849; Nicolaas, b. July 16, 1792, d. Aug. 4, 1794.

PIETER VROOMAN, son of Johannes, m. Jannetje, dau. of Jan Baptist Van Eps, July 28, 1789. He made his will Dec. 28, 1813, proved Oct. 12, 1814, spoke of his wife Jane, sons John, Harmen and Myndert, and of daus. Helen, Nancy, Margaret, Susanna and Maria. He d. and was buried in the *Woestine*, Oct. 9, 1814. a. 53ys., 10m., 10d.; his wife d. March 13, 1848, in her 82d year. Ch. b: Magdalena, December 17, 1791; Helen; Annatje, May 11, 1794 ; *Johannes*, Feb. 14, 1796; Harmen, Dec. 29, 1797, d. July 31, 1850, a. 52ys., 6m.; Margarieta, Oct. 27, 1799; Myndert; Susanna, Aug. 29, 1802; Maria, Oct. 30, 1808.

VOLKERT, son of Johannes, m. Rebecca, dau. of Abraham Groot. [Volkert Veeder was buried Sept. 9, 1804.] Ch : Johannes, bp. June 5, 1775.

WILHELMUS, son of Gerrit, m. Elisabeth, dau. of Major Snell, July 3, 1791. Ch. b: Gerrit, Jan. 29, 1782, lived on the east corner of Ellis avenue and Jackson place, d. Nov. 10, 1869 ; Eliza Gill, July 4, 1794; Major, Nov. 30, 1796; Nicholas, Nov. 10, 1799; Wilhelmus, March 4, 1803; John Darius Snell, March 27, 1813.

PIETER SYMONSE, son of Pieter, m. Maria, dau. of Harmanus Van Slyck. Ch. bp: Maria, Dec. 29, 1776 ; Sarah,

April 26, 1778; Pieter, Jan. 9, 1780; Harmanus Van Slyck, Oct. 6, 1782.

PIETER, son of Claas, m. Maria, dau. of Barent Myndertse. He made his will August 9, 1811, proved Jan. 24, 1812, spoke of wife Maria and son Nicholas. Ch. b: Nicholas, Jan. 22, 1798; Barent Mynderse, Jan. 20, 1800; John, Sept. 18, 1809.

SIMON, son of Barent, m. Margarita, dau. of Robert Shannon. Ch. bp: Barent, Oct. 19, 1777; Robert, Feb. 20, 1780; Reyer, May 29, 1781; Jannetje, Feb. 16, 1783. Ch. b: Alexander, May 29, 1785; Simon, March 15, 1787; Cathlirra, m. John S. Vrooman; John, Dec. 27, 1794; Elisabeth, Aug. 25, 1798.

LUCAS WYNGAART, son of Simon, of Normanskil, m. Susanna, dau. of Samuel Bratt Ch. bp: Catalyntje, Sept. 1, 1782; Catrina, March 28, 1784. Ch. b: Simon, June 30, 1786 ; Samuel, Jan. 16, 1788; Samuel, Feb. 23, 1790 ; Johannes Symonse, Dec. 16, 1791; Elias, b. Jan. 1, 1794; Volkert, b. July 8, 1796 ; Simon, Aug. 3, 1798.

JOHANNES SYMONSE, son of Symon Johannese, m. Catharina Winne. Ch. b. (and bp. in Albany): Annatie, April 20, 1787; Frans, Jan. 2, 1789; Rebecca and Simon, twins, March 4, 1792; Simon, Oct. 16, 1793; Rebecca, March 10, 1797; Ann, Jan. 28, 1799. [*See Albany Families.*]

VOLKERT, son of Simon Johannese, m. Ann Quackenbush. Ch. b : Cateleyntje, March 18, 1791; Anna, bp. Feb. 15, 1794, d. Aug. 24, 1797, a. 2ys., 12d.; Anne, Aug. 12, 1795, d. Jan. 9, 1797, a. 17m.; Elisabeth, Feb. 16, 1798; Maria, Jan. 22, 1801, d. June 13, 1803. [*See Albany Families.*]

JOHN, son of Simon, and Elisabeth, dau. of Andries De Graaf, both of Corrysbos, m. Dec. 30, 1797. Ch. b : Simon, July 5, 1798; Andries, May 9, 1801; Nicholas, Apr. 7, 1803; Andries, Aug. 8, 1806.

JOHANNES, son of Barent, m. Marytje, dau. of Hubartus Van Vechten of Catskil. He lived in the town of Providence, d. in Monroe county, Aug., 1847. Ch. b : Jannetje, March 23, 1785; Hubattus, Oct. 19, 1786; Barent, Oct. 10, 1788; Reyer, April 16, 1791; Dirk, Jan. 16, 1793; Johannes and Rykard, March 28, 1795; Reyer, Oct. 30, 1797; Maria, Oct. 7, 1801; Barent, July 29, 1803; Annatje, Aug. 22, 1805.

GERRIT, son of Henricus G., m. Janneke Ten Eyck of Esopus, Jan. 12, 1782. He was justice of sessions; lived at and owned "Veeder's mills," d. Feb. 18, 1836, a. 84ys.; his wife, b. May 5, 1759, d. Aug. 31, 1834. Ch. b : Henricus, April 27, 1783; Cornelia, Dec. 12, 1785, d. Dec. 23, 1787; Mattheus Ten Eyck, May 21, 1788, graduate at Union College 1808, d. June 9, 1824; Abram, Nov. 22, 1791; John, Sept. 8, 1794, d. Sept. 23, 1872; Elisabeth, January 26, 1798; Cornelia Blandina, May 22, 1801.

JACOB, son of Myndert of Albany, of the Normanskil, m. Catharina Spaun of Manor of Rensselaerwyck, March 4, 1787, in Albany. Ch. b. (bp. in Albany): Jochum, Oct. 30, 1789; Jochum, April 1, 1791. [*See Albany Families.*]

NICHOLAS, son of Gerrit of Glenville, m. Ann, dau. of Joseph Hetherington. He d. in 1862, a. 100ys. Ch. b : Annatje, Oct. 5, 1790; Jane, Sept. 14, 1794; Gerrit, Jan. 13, 1798; Joseph, April 1, 1801, d. April 24, 1853.

ALBERT F., m. Maria Kittle, June 6, 1798.

PETER, son of Frans, m. Folkje, dau. of Daniel Toll, April 4, 1795. He lived in house No. 40 Washington street, opposite the west end of Union street, still occupied by his dau. ; his wife d. March 5, 1861, a. 82ys. Ch. b : Marytje, Nov. 5, 1795; Nicholas, May 14, 1798; Susanna, June 10, 1801, d. Sept. 18, 1872; Margaret, April 1, 1805, m. G. Lansing Oothout, now deceased ; Elise, June 20, 1807 ; Eleanor, Sept. 30, 1811.

ARENT S., m. Jannetje Hoghingh. Ch : Anna, b. Dec. 10, 1787. [*See Albany Families.*]

MYNDERT, m. Elisabeth Perry. Ch : Reynier, b. Jan. 31, 1797. [*See Albany Families.*]

JOHANNES, son of Pieter Vrooman, m. Rebecca, dau. of Nicolaas Van Petten, Feb. 5, 1819. He d. July 29, 1849.

Ch. b : Jane, Sept. 5, 1820, d. Oct. 5, 1829; Nicholas, Nov. 22, 1822, graduated at Union College 1844, m. Mary Jane Greig, August 7, 1866, resides at Pittsburgh, Penn.; Peter Vrooman, June 23, 1825, grad. Union College 1846, m. Amelia Jack; clergyman of the Pres. church; Prof. of the Japanese College at Jeddo; Anne Elisabeth, Nov. 28, 1827, m. William Augustus Willson, Dec. 14, 1849, d. April 30, 1865; Herman, July 13, 1830, m. April 30, 1857, Hannah Adair, who d. Oct. 24, 1872; Jane Helen, August 5, 1832, m. John Miller Thorp, Feb. 14, 1856; Sylvester, June 13, 1835, d. Aug. 17, 1836.

VENTAN (FENTON ?).

WILLIAM, and Annatje Egmont. Ch : Anna, b. Sept. 24, 1786.

VERGERN.

DIRK, m. Catharina, dau. of Tjerk Van der Bogart. Ch : Libbertje, bp. March 5, 1749. She afterwards m. Neil Mc-Kelvy.

VERWY.

TRYNTJE, a refugee from *Woestine* after the massacre of 1690.

VIELE.

CORNELIS CORNELISE, early settled in Schenectady, where, in company with Claas Frederickse Van Petten, he bought Marten Cornelise Van Isselsteyn's bouwery in 1668; 1670 he sold his moiety consisting of 12 morgens, 130 rods, with house, barn, two ricks and garden to Jurriaen Teunise Tappen of Albany,

taking in exchange a house and lot in Albany on the west corner of State and Pearl streets; three years later he sold this house and lot to Richard Pretty, sheriff; 1671 he was a licensed tapster in Schenectady; 1677 received a grant of 34 acres of land by patent on the *Steene kill*, about four miles west of Schenectady, and on the south side of the Mohawk river. His wife was Suster ...... Ch : *Arnout; Cornelis; Pieter;* Volkert, bp. Dec. 1, 1689; Jannetie, wife of Johannes Dyckman; Debora, wife of Daniel Ketelhuyn.

PIETER CORNELISE, brother of Cornelis, also settled in Schenectady, where, in company with Elias Van Gyseling, he purchased Bastiaan De Winter's bouwery in 1670. His wife was Jacomyntje, dau. of Teunis Swart. Ch : *Teunis; Lowis;* and one or more daus. His wife m. secondly, Benony Arentse Van Hoek, who was killed by the French and Indians in 1690; and thirdly, Cornelis Vinhout of Ulster sounty, where she was living as late as 1700.

ARNOUT, son of Cornelis, lived in Albany; for many years he was the provincial interpreter, attending the yearly gathering of the natives at Albany, and frequently visiting them in the then western wilderness. On account of their high esteem for him, and as a recognition of the value of his services, the Mohawks, in 1683, gave him a parcel of land above Schenectady, on the north side of the river called *Wachkeerhoha*. In 1687 he was taken prisoner by the

French as he was on his way to Ottawa to trade. Espousing the cause of Leisler in opposition to Col. Ingoldsby he was turned out of his office, after which he retired to Long Island, but being held "in great esteem by the Indians," and being "a good and faithful interpreter," he was soon recalled to the office of Indian interpreter. He m. Geeritje Gerritse of Amsterdam in 1677. Ch: Aernout; Wilempie, wife of Simon Jacobse Schermerhorn; Maria, who m. first, Matthys Vrooman, and secondly Douwe Aukes of Schenectady, 1685. His son Aernout was carried away by the Indians Feb. 9, 1690. 169⅔, Feb. 16, "upon which we marched about two miles where a Christian boy, Aernout the interpreter's son, came to us, who had been three years a prisoner among the French."

CORNELIS, son of Cornelis, m. first, Maria Aloff; and secondly, Diwer, dau. of Claas Van Petten, April 1, 1700. His first wife was killed by the French and Indians, Feb. 9, 1690. He settled at *Maalwyck;* in 1710 bought half of Benjamin Robert's property from his step-son Pieter Clement; in 1712 bought *Poversen's landeryen* on the opposite or south side of the Mohawk, of Jan Hendrickse Bout. Ch. b: Suster, June 4, 1700, m. Myndert Van Gyseling; Eva, June 11, 1702, m. Pieter Feling; *Cornelis,* Jan. 21, 1705; Jannetie, Oct. 29, 1707; *Nicolaas,* bp. Oct., 1710; Margarietje, bp. May 3, 1713, m. Jan Eckersen; Catrina, bp. March 31, 1716, m. Albert Arentse Vedder; *Johannes,* bp. Sept. 24, 1719.

PIETER, son of Cornelis, m. Anna Myndertse, March 17, 1704. Ch: Suster, bp. April 29, 1705.

CORNELIS CORNELISE, chirurgeon, m. Catharina Bogardus in New York, April 24, 1693. He was then a widower. In 1698 he was admitted freeman of the city. Ch. bp. in New York: Sara, April 24, 1695; Cornelis, Dec. 16, 1702.

TEUNIS, son of Pieter, m. Elisabeth, dau. of Johannes Dirkse Van Eps, June 16, 1693, in Albany. In 1699 she again m. Jillis Van Vorst. Ch. bp: Jacomyntje, April 11, 1694, m. Cornelis Pootman; Elisabeth, Jan. 8, 1696.

LOWIS, son of Pieter, m. Maria Freer. He settled in "Scaatkooke" as early as 1708. Ch. bp: *Pieter,* Nov. 3, 1700; *Teunis,* Sept. 28, 1702; *Hugus,* Feb. 25, 1705; Jacomyntje, Nov. 9, 1707, m. Isaac Fort; *Isaac,* April 28, 1710; Stephanus, Feb. 1, 171⅔; *Abraham,* Sept. 26, 1715; Jacob, June 21, 1719.

NICOLAAS, son of Cornelis, m. Catlyntje, dau. of Arent Schermerhorn, May 14, 1736. He m. secondly, Neeltje, dau. of Johannes Schermerhorn, March 2, 174⅘. He made his will April 20, 1795, proved Oct. 7, 1820, spoke of wife Neeltje, dau. Gezina, Catalyntje, Jannetje and son Cornelis. Ch. bp: Debora, Oct. 24, 1736, m. David Ketelhuyn; Arent, Dec 7, 1738; Catlyntje, Mar. 21, 1742; Jannetje, Jan. 26, 1745; Engeltje, Jan. 26, 1747; Cornelis, Oct. 8, 1749; Engeltje, Oct. 6, 1751, m. Nicolaas S. Van Petten; Catlyntje, April 28, 1753; Jannetie, Dec. 1, 1754 ; Cornelis, Jan. 11, 1756; Gezina, March 2, 1760, m. Lawrence Schermerhorn, and d. Sept. 26, 1847; Jannetje, May 9,1762, d. Sept. 26, 1841.

PIETER, son of Lowis, m. Catharina Van Schaick, June 23, 1728. Ch. bp. in Albany : Lowys, Jan. 22, 1729; Sara, Aug. 2, 1730 ; Maria, June 4, 1732.

TEUNIS, son of Lowis, m. Maria Fonda in Albany, Oct. 12, 1724. Ch. bp. in Albany : Lowys, Aug. 30, 1725 ; *Johannes*, Sept. 17, 1727 ; Maria, February 1, 1730; Rebecca, Oct. 30, 1732; Stephanus, June 2, 1735; Stephanus, July 1, 1736; Jannetie, Nov. 20, 1737 ; Catharina, Sept. 28, 1740 ; Pieter, Oct. 21, 1744.

HUGUS, son of Lowis, of Schachtekook, m. in Albany, first, Catharina Van Woert, Feb. 13, 1728, and secondly, Elisabeth Van Vechten, widow, Sept. 17, 1752. Ch. bp. in Albany : Lodovicus, April 20, 1729; Jacob, Aug. 2, 1730 ; Maria, May 27, 1733 ; Stephanus, Oct. 26, 1735 ; Maria, May 14, 1737 ; Anna, Feb. 17, 1739 ; Sara, Feb. 14, 1742 ; Pieter, Jan. 12, 1746.

ISAAC, son of Lowis, m. Hendrikje ...... Ch. bp : Maria, July 3, 1737; Lammetje, Jan. 23, 1740 ; Lodovicus Biblicus Jacobus, April 1, 1743.

ABRAHAM, son of Lowis, m. Annatie Quackenbos, Ch. bp. in Albany : Maria, Feb. 24, 1754; Elisabeth, Jan. 30,

1757 ; Teunis, Aug. 5, 1759 ; Teunis, Feb. 14, 1762; Stephanus, b. Feb. 3, 1767.

JACOB, son of Lowis, m. Eva, dau. of Abraham Fort, in Albany, July 4, 1742. Ch. bp. in Albany save the first : *Lodovicus*, in Schenectady, Oct. 17, 1742 ; *Abraham*, Aug. 25, 1745 ; Maria, July 12, 1750; *Stephanus*, Aug. 3, 1753 ; Annatje, May 27, 1756 ; Johannes, June 24, 1759 ; [Jacob Viele and Catarina Coddington were m. in Albany Nov. 10, 1757.]

CORNELIS, son of Cornelis, m. Clara, dau. of Philip Bosie, Nov. 20, 1742. In May, 1751, she m. Ephraim Bratt. Ch. bp : Debora, July 17, 1743, m. Frederic F. Van Petten ; *Philip*, b. July 7, 1745.

JAN, son of Cornelis, m. Debora, dau. of Abraham Glen, April 15, 1749. He made his will 1760, proved June 17, 1770, spoke of wife Debora and of the following dau., but not of the son. Ch. bp : Debora, Jan. 28, 1750, m. Abraham J. Van Eps; Margarita, April 29, 1753, m. Eldert Ament; Maria, Sept. 7, 1755, m. Johannes A. Van Antwerpen ; Cornelis, Dec, 18, 1757 ; Susanna, April 20, 1760, m. Johannes Van Vranken.

PHILIP, son of Cornelis m. Rachel, dau. of Jacob Fonda, Nov. 24, 1770. He d. Aug. 7, 1797, a. 52ys., 1m. ; she d. May 1, 1839, a. 90ys., 6m., 25d. Ch : Cornelis, bp. Feb. 9, 1772 ; *Cornelis*, b. March 4, 1773, d. in Schenectady Aug. 17, 1863, a. 90ys., 5m., 13d. ; Jacob, bp. Nov. 19, 1775; Maria, bp. May 16, 1779, d. Dec. 15, 1788; Margarita, bp. October 21, 1781 ; Rebecca, b. Jan. 28, 1784, d. October 22, 1845; Deborah, b. Nov. 31 (*sic*), 1786, d. Feb. 13, 1790; Nicolaas, b. July 10, 1790, m. Jane Schermerhorn, d. Nov. 24, 1861.

LODOVICUS, son of Jacob, m. Aeffie, dau. of Simon Toll. Ch : Abraham, bp. Jan. 24, 1773.

STEPHANUS, son of Jacob, of Saratoga, m. Sarah, dau. of Simon Toll. Ch : Jacob, bp. Jan. 30, 1774; Lodovicus, b. Oct. 3, 1777, in Albany; Hester, b. June 23, 1789, in Albany

PHILIP G., m. Maria Bratt. Ch. b. (and bp. in Albany): Catharina, April 11, 1773; Barent Bratt, June 7, 1775; Gerrit, Dec. 28, 1777; Rebecca, Aug. 13, 1780; Philip, bp. in Schenectady, Jan. 4, 1783.

CORNELIS, son of Philip, m. Tanneke, dau. of Abraham De Graaf, May 27, 1798.

VINE.

JOHN, m. Elisabeth Bell. Ch. bp : Robert, Feb. 14, 1775; Elisabeth, July 8, 1778; Henry, June 20, 1781 ; John, b. Nov. 20, 1785.

HENRY, m. Maria De La Grange. Ch. bp : Catarina, July 5, 1775; Henry, April 22, 1778.

VINK.

WILLEM, m. Margarita Ball. Ch: Pieter, bp. Jan. 26, 1782.

VINKENOUWER.

JACOB, m. Maria Reydenberger. Ch. bp : Johannes, Sept. 19, 1761; Jacob, June 6, 1768.

VISSCHER (VISGER).

NICOLAAS, son of Nanning of Albany, and Anna, dau. of Eldert Tymessen, both b. in Albany, now dwelling in Connestiagioune, m. January 18, 1734. Ch. bp : Hester, June 16, 1734, m. Ahasuerus G. Marselis; Maria, Sept. 2, 1744, m. Johannes R. Wemp. [*See Albany Families.*]

JOHANNES, son of Johannes and Elisabeth of Albany, m. Catharina, dau. of Harmen Van Slyck, March 29, 1737. Ch. bp: *Johannes*, Oct. 9, 1737, d. in Albany, Oct. 24, 1821, a. 85ys.; Harmen Van Slyck, April 29, 1739; Jacobus, April 25, 1742; Elisabet, Oct. 9, 1743, m. Col. Henderick Glen.

Col. JOHANNES, son of Johannes and Catharina, m. Susanna, dau. of Jacob R. Schermerhorn. He is said to have died about 1822. Ch. bp : Johannes, b. May 8, bp. May 25, 1760; *Johannes*, Oct. 3, 1762; Jacob, Dec. 30, 1764; Catarina, May 22, 1767; *Harmen Van Slyck*, May 22, 1768; Margarita, Nov. 12, 1770; Catarina, Oct. 24, 1773, m. first, Michael Tyms, and secondly, Barent Roseboom ; Elisabeth, Feb. 9, 1777.

HARMEN, son of Frederick of Albany, m. Catharina, dau. of Willem Brouwer. He was among the earliest settlers at Caughnawaga, d. before the Revolution, leaving an aged widow, three sons — Frederic, a colonel of the militia, Johannes a captain, and Harmen, and two dau. Margarita and Rebecca. Ch. bp : *Frederic,* b. Feb. 22, 1741; Johannes; Harmen; Margarietje, bp. Sept 30, 1747; Willem Brouwer, April 30, 1749; Rebecca; Geertruy bp. in Albany, Aug. 30, 1754. [*See Albany Families.*]

PIETER, m. Dorothea Ball. Ch : Maria, bp. July 30, 1763.

NANNING, son of Johannes of Albany, m. Lena Lansing. Ch : Alida, b. April 22, 1769, m. James Welden; Rachel, bp. Oct. 18, 1775; Hester, b. March 27, 1780. [*See Albany Families.*]

TEUNIS, son of Teunis of Albany, m. first, Maria, dau. of Bastiaan Tymesen of Nistoungjoone, Oct. 22, 1767, and secondly, Elisabeth Groot, Nov., 1789. She d. before the baptism of her last child. Ch : Teunis, b. June 26, 1768; Jannetie, b. March 21, 1770; Johannes, Dec. 5, 1771; Bastiaan Tymesen, bp. Oct. 18, 1778; Machtelt, m. Abraham Vrooman; Mayke, bp. Oct. 10, 1782, m. Johannes Swits; Eldert, b. May 31, 1786; Eldert and Esther, b. Aug. 24, 1788; Teunis, b. June 23, 1798; Henry, b. March 12, 1805. [*See Albany Families.*]

ELDERT, son of Nicolaas of Albany (?), m. Geertruy, dau. of Johannes Fort. Ch. b : Elisabeth, Aug. 27, 1781; Elisabeth, Jan. 4, 1786; Johannes, March 8, 1790.

JOHANNES, son of Johannes jr., m. Annatie Ehl (Aele). Ch : Susanna, bp. Jan. 11, 1784; Petrus Aele, b. July 16, 1786; Johannes, Nov. 9, 1788.

BASTIAAN, son of Teunis, m. Catharina Vroom. Ch : Teunis, b. Oct. 23, 1799.

HARMANUS, son of Johannes jr. (?), m. Elisabeth Cowper. Ch : Maria Cowper, b. Jan. 23, 1790.

JOHN, of Fort Hunter, m. Annatje Pearsen (Pearse ?). Ch : Isaac, b. April 19, 1793.

Col. FREDERIC, son of Harmen, m. Gezina, dau. of Daniel De Graaf. May 22, 1780, the Visscher house at Caughnawaga was attacked by Sir John Johnson's party, and Capt. Johannes and Harmen Visscher were killed and Col. Frederic was left for dead, but afterwards he recovered, as also did his mother, who was struck down by a blow from a musket. [*Simms's History.*] Col. Visscher d. June 9, 1809; his wife d. in 1815. Ch. b : Harmen, June 4, 1769; Gezina, July 14, 1771; Daniel, Sept. 2, 1773; Willem Brouwer and Catrina, b. May 19, 1776; Harmen, April 4, 1780; Johannes, Dec. 16, 1784.

VLAAK

HARMANUS, m Rebecca Vries. Ch : Maria, bp. April 8, 1782.

VOE.

JOHN, m. Margarita Redely. Ch : Johannes, bp. June, 29, 1779.

VOLLEWEYSER.

JACOB, m. Maria, dau. of Dirk Bratt. Ch. bp: Abraham, Oct. 19, 1755; Annatje, Dec. 3, 1758; Dirk, April 19, 1761; Maria, March 4, 1764.

ABRAHAM, m. Barber Bratt.

VOORHEES (VAN VOORHEES).

GERRIT, m. Levyntje Francisco. Ch. b: Andries, Sept. 22, 1785; Michael, Jan. 20, 1788.

VOSBURGH.

ISAAC, m. Maria Van Valkenburgh. Ch: Hendrick, bp. Aug. 14, 1784.

HENDRICK, of Normanskil, m. Eetje Van Valkenburgh. Ch: Marytje, bp. May 9, 1786.

ISAAC, m. Annatje Dixon. Ch: Rachel, b. Jan. 26, 1798.

VREDENDAL.

FREDERICK, m. Catarina Courtzinger. Ch: Jurry Matthias, bp. Sept. 5, 1780.

VREELAND.

GERRIT, m. Sarah Wemple. Ch. b: Dirk, Jan. 21, 1790; Sarah, July 4, 1795; Joan, Sept. 2, 1797.

VROOMAN.

There were three early settlers of this name in Beverwyck and Schenectady.

PIETER MEESE, settled in Beverwyck; m. first, ..., and secondly, Volckie Pieterse, widow of Gerrit Jan Stavast. In 1677 he lived in Joncker street near the church; d. in 1684. His widow m. Adriaan Appel, June 28, 1685. Pieter Meese had but one son, Matthys, who with his wife, Maria Arnoutse Viele, made a joint will in 1684, in which they spoke of only one child Geertruy.

JACOB MEESE, carpenter and surveyor of Beverwyck, m. Elisabeth, wid. of Teunis Cornelise Swart of Schenectady. He made his will July 20, 1691, proved Sept. 22, 1691, wife Elisabeth executrix; spoke of no children; his wife was to occupy "my house by the bridge formerly Domine Schaets."

HENDRICK MEESE, the third brother of this name, was living "behind Kinderhook" in 1670; same year leased of Robert Sanders the long island called *Steenraby*, for six years; 1677 moved to Schenectady, where his home lot was on the north side of State street, extending from Centre street to, and including the Central R. R. depot. His *bouwlandt* was a portion of Van Curler's land; the engine house of N. Y. Central R. R. Co. southwest of the city, now stands nearly in the centre of his land; 1678 he mortgaged his house and barn lying *opt voorste ende van t' Dorpe Shaenhechtady*, &c. In the massacre of 1690 he was killed, with his son Bartel and two negroes. He left two sons, *Adam* and *Jan*.

ADAM, son of Hendrick Meese, b. in 1649 in Holland, was naturalized in the province of New York in 1715; in 1670, by consent of his father, he bound himself for two years to Cornelis Van den Burgh to learn the millwright's trade for

80 guilders and a pair of new shoes the first year, and 120 guilders the second year; 1683 built a mill on the *Sand kil* where the Brandywine mills now stand; 1688 bought lands of the Mohawk sachems at Fort Hunter; in 1690, when Schenectady was attacked and burned by the French and Indians, he saved his life by his bravery in defending his house which then stood on the west corner of Church and Front streets; on this occasion his first wife Engeltie, with her infant child, was killed, and his two sons Barent and Wouter were carried away captives to Canada; 1697 went to Canada with an embassy to try to obtain the release of his sons (one of whom had turned Catholic), his brother (Jan ?) and cousin (son of Pieter Meese of Albany), all carried away in 1690; 1703–1708 obtained a patent for the *Sand kil* and adjacent lands for mill purposes; 1714 obtained a patent for lands in Schoharie upon which he settled in 1715; some of the Palatines attempted to drive him off. He commenced a stone house 23ft. square by help of his sons, and had proceeded as far as the second story floor beams, when one night his unruly neighbors, led on by one Conrad Weiser, entirely demolished it. He then retired to Schenectady and petitioned to the governor for redress. The governor commanded the sheriff of Albany to arrest said Weiser, and succeeded, it is presumed, in stopping the opposition to Vrooman's cultivating his land. [*Doc. History,* iii, 412.] In 1726 he received an additional patent for 1,400 acres for his son Pieter; made

his will September 12, 1729, proved June 13, 1730, spoke of the following children, save Christina and Jannetie, d. on his farm in Schoharie Feb. 25, 1730, and was buried in his private burying ground No. 35 Front street. He m. first, Engeltie, secondly, Grietje Ryckman, widow of Jacques Cornelise Van Slyck in 1691; thirdly, Grietje Takelse Heemstraat, Jan. 13, 1697, in Albany. Ch. bp: *Barent,* 1679; *Wouter,* 1680; *Pieter,* b. May 4, 1684; Christina, bp. Oct. 18, 1685, m. Teunis Swart; *Hendrick,* 1687; Johannes or Jan bp. May 30, 1697, in Albany; Maria, Sept. 1, 1699, m. Douw Fonda; *Bartholomeus,* Dec. 22, 1700; Timotheus, Nov. 8, 1702; *Seth,* Jan. 7, 1705; *Jacob Meese,* July 3, 1707, in Albany; Eva, m. Joachim Ketelhuyn; Jannetie, m. Harmen Van Slyck.

JAN, son of Hendrick Meese, m. Geesje, dau. of Simon Veeder, July 4, 1680. He lived on the site of the depot of the New York Central rail road; 1686 bought half of Jan Hendrickse Van Bael's patent on the Normanskil; made his will April 24, 1732. Ch. b: *Simon,* Feb. 25, 1681; Jannetie, July 23, 1682, m. Arent Bratt; Hendrick, March 26, 1684, *anno* 1690 *den* xx8 *Mey is min soon in den Here gervst* Hendrick Jansen Vrooman. Jan Vrooman. Jacob, 1686, murdered in his father's house 1688; *Pieter,* Oct. 1688, killed at the *Beukendaal* massacre 1748; *Hendrick,* Sept. 12, 1690; Engeltje, Dec. 22, 1692, m. Jan R. Schermerhorn; *Johannes,*

Oct. 24, 1694; Maria, Oct. 31, 1696, m. Gysbert Van Brakel; *Jacob*, Dec. 28, 1698, d. April 20, 1774; Catarina, May 12, 1701, m. Jacob Mebie; *Bartholomeus*, Jan. 10, 1703; Magdalena, July 6, 1704, d. April 6, 1732; Cornelis, Dec. 29, 1705, d. Jan., 1733; Helena, m. Joseph Van Sice.

BARENT, son of Adam, m. Tryntje, dau. of Takel Heemstraat of Albany, June 18, 1699. He and his brother Jan had a brewery on north side of Union street, near or upon the crossing of the New York Central rail road; he lived on the north corner of Centre and State streets; buried in Albany Aug. 14, 1746. Ch. bp: Adam, Jan. 9, 1700; Engeltie, March 6, 1711.

PIETER, son of Adam, m. Grietje, dau of Isaac Van Alstyne of Albany, Feb. 2, 1706, in Albany. He settled on what was called *Vrooman's land* in Schoharie, with his father; made his will 1768, proved Dec. 20, 1771. Ch. b : Adam, Sept. 21, 1707; *Barent* and Martynus, twins, Feb. 19, 1709; Cornelis, March 3, 1711; Engeltie, May 18, 1713, m. David Ziele; Abraham, Nov. 15, 1715; Jannetie, Jan. 18 (?), bp. Feb. 6, 1718; Pieter Meese, June 5, 1720; Isaac, Nov. 15, 1722, bp in Albany Jan. 30, 1723; Geertruy, Sept. 3, 1725,.m. Josias Swart; Catarina, March 29, 1728, m. Johannes Lawyer; Lidia, April 18, 1730.

WOUTER,son of Adam,m. Marytje,dau. of Isaac Casparse Hallenbeck of Albany, Sept. 24, 1707. He made his will May 7,

1748, proved April 18, 1757, d. Oct. 26, 1756; she d. Jan. 19, 1748. Ch: Adam, b. 1708 (?); Engeltie, bp. in Albany June 12, 1709, m. Cornelis Veeder; Isaac, b. Oct. 20, 1710; Isaac, bp. Nov. 13, 1712; Dorothea, bp. Oct. 3, 1714, m. Gillis Truex; *Adam*, bp. Feb. 3, 1716; *Jacob*, bp. Aug. 24, 1717; Christina, b. Jan. 19, bp. Apr. 4, 1719; *Isaac*, bp. April 8, 1721, d. June 1, 1807; Christyntje, bp. Jan. 19, 1723; Rachel, bp. May 31, 1724, m. Abraham Wemp and Abraham Fonda; *Barent*, b. Dec. 24, 1725; Elisabeth, b. 1727; Angelica, b. 1729; Nicholas, bp. 1730; Elisabeth, bp. May 7, 1732, m. Abraham Swits.

Capt. HENDRICK, son of Adam, m. first, Geertruy ......, and secondly, Maria, dau. of Barent Wemp. He was constable in Albany in 1705, removed to Schenectady; was *baes* of the carpenters, who built the church in 1732, at seven shillings a day. Ch. bp. in Albany: Engeltie, Feb. 15, 1702; Maria, Oct. 14, 1705, m. Isaac Swits; *Barent*, Jan. 15, 1710; Adam, April 20, 1712; Engeltie, Sept. 27, 1713. Ch. bp. in Schenectady : *Adam*, b. April 1, bp. April 2, 1716; *Johannes*, bp. April 4, 1719; *Hendrick*, Aug. 4, 1722; Volkie, b. March 28, bp. March 29, 1725, m. Isaac Jacobse Swits; Wouter, April 4, 1728; Jannetje, 1729, m. Simon Van Petten.

PIETER, son of Jan, m. Agnietje, dau. of Arent Vedder, Oct. —, 1716, both of the *Woestyne.* He d. July 18, 1748; she d. April 27, 1785. Ch. bp : Sarah, Aug. 3, 1717, d. Feb. 28, 1737; Johannes, April 8, 1721; Geesie, b. Sept. 24, bp. Oct. 22, 1723, d. Oct. 27, 1747; Anna, b. July 24, bp. Aug. 21, 1726; Maria, bp. 1729, d. Sept. 23, 1784; Arent, Feb. 13, 1732, d. March 3, 1737; Magdalena, Sept. 15, 1734, m. Johannes M. Veeder; Rebecca, Feb. 27, 1737, d. Dec. 11, 1747; Sarah, June 28, 1741.

HENDRICK, son of Jan, m. Engeltje, dau. of Cornelis Slingerland, April, 1718. In 1723 he received conveyance from Arent Bratt of a lot 190×45ft. on the east corner of State and Washington streets, which lot passed to his son Cornelis, who conveyed the same in 1746 to Arent Samuelse Bratt. Ch. bp : Gesina, Sept. 7, 1719, m. Simon Johannese Veeder; *Cornelis*, b. Feb. 4, bp. Feb. 10, 1722; Eva, bp. Sept. 27, 1724, m. Johannes Pieterse Van Antwerpen; Jannetje, b. Nov. 3, bp. Nov. 5, 1727, m. Jillis Fonda; Maria, bp. Jan. 30, 1732, m. Ahasuerus Marcelis; Johannes, Dec. 25, 1734, d. Dec. 24, 1810, a. 76ys., 4d.; Anthony, Dec. 21, 1737; Simon (?), b. 1740.

SIMON, son of Jan, m. Eytje, dau. of Jacob Delamont, Oct. 14, 1717. He bought in 1710, of Willem Appel, the lot lying on the west side of the canal between State and Liberty streets, now the property of Hon. Peter Rowe; made his will 1752, gave to son Johannes the " tan pits " near " the City mill " on Mill lane, and to son Jacob the house and lot above mentioned. Ch. bp : *Johannes*, May 23, 1718; Catharina, November 14, 1719; *Jacob*, Nov. 13, 1723; Maria, May 19, 1728.

BARTHOLOMEW, son of Jan, m. Susanna, dau. of Samuel Bratt, March 11, 1726. He d. March 29, 1771. Ch : Margaret, b. Oct. 29, 1726; Maria, bp. July 2, 1732.

BARTHOLOMEUS, son of Adam, m. Catharina, dau. of Cornelis Slingerland, and wid. of Hendrick Van Slyck, Oct. 20, 1738. It is said he was born blind. Ch : Geesie, m. Johannes Clute; Engeltie, bp. Oct. 3, 1742, m. Albert Mebie (?); *Johannes*, bp. Jan. 13, 1745; Gezina, b. April 1, 1746 (?).

BARENT, son of Pieter, of Schoharie, m. Engeltie, dau. of Teunis Swart. He made his will Jan. 23, 1782, proved June 6, 1782. Ch. b : *Pieter*, Jan. 7, 1736; *Teunis*, June 27, 1738; *Adam*, Sept. 25, 1740; Christyntje, May 29, 1743; *Martynus*, Dec. 6, 1744 (1745 ?); Josias, Oct. 11, 1747; Jannetie, Sept. 29, 1750, m. ...... Schuyler; *Barent*, March 10, 1754; Sarah, Nov. 2, 1757.

JACOB, son of Jan, m. Marytje, dau. of Abraham Groot, Oct. 17, 1725. His house lot was on the north side of State street, at the rail road crossing. Being a carpenter, he was sent by Sir William Johnson, in 1756, to Onondaga, to build a fort for the Indians; d. April 20, 1774. Ch. bp : *Johannes*, b. Jan. 8, bp. same day, 1726; Hester, bp. 1730, m. Jacob Heemstraat; Annatie, October 3, 1731; Rebecca, Feb. 17, 1734, m. Arent Marselis; Magdalena, April 11, 1736; Catharina, April 28, 1739; Geesie, May 13, 1744, m. Pieter Stiers.

JOHANNES, son of Jan, m. Maria Magdalena, dau. of Willem Appel, March 8, 1724, in New York. He d. June, 1730. Ch. b: Magdalena, Sept. 22, 1725; Catrina, Dec. 12, 1726, m. Cornelis Lansing; Willem.

ADAM, son of Hendrick, m. Anna, dau. of Abraham Mebie, Feb. 7, 174⁴⁄₇. At the date of his marriage he was living in *Maquaas landt*, i.e. on the Mohawk river above Amsterdam. Ch. bp: Maria, Nov. 15, 1741; Maria, May 22, 1743; Abraham, Nov. 17, 1745; Anna, Jan. 21, 1750; Eva, August 9, 1752; Hendrick, Dec. 29, 1754; Abraham, Aug. 14, 1757; Engeltie, Dec. 2, 1759; Abraham, May 9, 1762.

JACOB MEESE, son of Adam, *van Schonechtade* and Sara, dau. of Myndert Myndertse (?) *van Nieu Albanien, beide in en onder Schonechtade wonende*, m. Oct. 30, 1742.

ADAM, son of Wouter, m. Susanna, dau. of Jacob Swits, Jan. 29, 174²⁄₃. In 1757 he lived in the ancient brick house at the Brandywine mill; sold out his portion of his father's estate to his brother Isaac; made his will 1759, proved May 1, 1760, spoke of wife Susanna and the following ch., d. July 30, 1759, a. 43ys. Ch. bp: Wouter, June 10, 1744; *Jacob*, Dec. 30, 1747; Isaac, March 25, 1750; Maria, April 7, 1751, m. Jan Van Vliet, Aug. 29, 1779; Helena, July 19, 1753, m. Marten Van Slyck; *Isaac*, Aug. 17, 1755; Jannetje, Dec. 11, 1757, m. Johannes Bloemendael, Feb. 13, 1780.

SETH, son of Adam, m. first, Geertruy Van Petten; secondly, Eva, dau. of Jesse De Graaf, Jan. 25, 174⁵⁄₈. Ch. bp: Margariet, Feb. 8, 1747, m. Johannes B. Vrooman; Alida, Nov. 20, 1748; Adam, Dec. 16, 1750; *Adam*, March 5, 1754.

BARENT, son of Hendrick, m. Volkie, dau. of Jan Barentse Wempel. She afterwards m. Jacob Alexander Glen, and lastly, Johannes Simonse Vrooman. He was buried in Albany August 14, 1746. Ch: Alida, bp. June 17, 1747.

·HENDRICK, son of Hendrick, m. Neeltie, dau. of Pieter Veeder. Ch. bp: Pieter, March 7, 1756; Maria, Jan. 15, 1758; Maria, March 4, 1762.

ISAAC, son of Wouter, m. Dorothea Van Boskerken of Bergen, N. J., 1744. She was b. Oct. 12, 1721, d. Aug. 23, 1800. He was a surveyor, justice of sessions, member of the provincial assembly 1759, d. June 1, 1807, on his farm at the Brandywine mills. Ch. bp: Rachel, 1745, m. John Farrell; Maria, 1747, m. Harmanus Van Slyck; Walther, Jan. 21, 1750; Catarina, Jan. 26, 1752; Engeltie, March 30, 1755; *Lourens*, July 26, 1757; Adam, May 25, 1760, was living in 1832; Catarina, Nov. 13, 1763, m. John N. Marselis.

JOHANNES, son of Simon, m. first, Volkje, dau. of Jan Barentse Wemple, Dec. 8, 1750. She d. Feb. 7, 1760, and he m. secondly, Sarah Van Antwerpen, Jan. 31, 1762. Ch. bp: Simon, Sept. 22, 1751; Johannes, March 5, 1754;

Jacob, Nov. 14, 1756; Abraham, Feb. 7, 1760; *Abraham*, Sept. 12, 1762; Catarina, April 28, 1765, m. Willem S. Vedder.

JOHANNES, son of Jacob, m. Clara, dau. of Hendrick Van Slyck. He lived upon a farm 3½ miles south of Schenectady, upon the "Middle road," opposite the "Hermitage," now the property of Hon. Charles Stanford. Ch. bp: Jacob, June 17, 1752; Catrina, Nov. 4, 1753; *Jacob*, March 30, 1755; Hendericus, Oct. 27, 7757; Abraham, Feb. 10, 1760; Catarina, July 15, 1764; *Johannes*, Feb. 1, 1767; Maria, Aug. 6, 1769; Engeltie, Dec. 15, 1771, m. Johannes Bulsen; Bartholomeus, March 13, 1774.

CORNELIS, son of Hendrick, m. Margarita, dau. of Arent Samuelse Bratt, Dec. 16, 1753. She d. May 30, 1790, a. 66ys., 8m., 6d.; he d. in 1806, a. 84ys., 6m., 16d. Ch. b: Henderick, Jan. 21, 1755, d. Jan. 8, 1778; Catharina, Jan. 6, 1757, d. June 20, 1757; Arent, June 14, 1758, d. Feb. 18, 1814.

PIETER, son of Barent, and Sarah, dau. of Josias Swart, both of Schoharie, m. May 15, 1761. Ch. b: Jannetie, Oct. 31, 1764, d. Nov. 13, 1764; Engeltie, May 22, 1766, m. Maj. Pieter Vrooman; Josias, August 19, 1769; Barent, Aug. 22, 1775; Pieter Meese (?), Sept. 29, 1793; Pieter Meese (?), June 19, 1801.

JOHANNES, son of Hendrick, m. Jannetie, dau. of Jacob Swits, Nov. 26, 1757. He d. on the Normanskil, May 1, 1785.

36

Ch. bp: *Henderik*, Feb. 9, 1759; *Jacob*, Sept. 7, 1760; Maria, b. July 12, 1763, m. first, ... Van Alstyne, secondly, John W. Van Aernhem of Guilderland, d. April 28, 1852; Isaac, bp. Feb. 3, 1765; Helena, Aug. 31, 1766, m. Evert Van Aernham; Adam, Aug. 21, 1768; Barent, April 1, 1770.

JACOB, son of Simon, m. Margarita, dau. of Jan Barentse Wemple, Dec, 29 1758. He made his will June 29, 1794, proved May 26, 1820, spoke of wife Margaret, dau. Maria, and sons Simon and Johannes; owned the lot on the west side of the canal, between State and Liberty streets; served in the Revolution as captain of a company of carpenters. Ch. b: *Simon*, Aug. 3, 1760; Johannes, April 5, 1763, served with his brother in Col. Christopher Yates's regiment, d. Nov. 10, 1841; Maria, bp. April 27, 1766.

HENDERICK, son of Johannes H., m Sara, dau. of Johannes Gonzalis. She died July 11, 1849, in her 86th year. Ch. bp: Magdalena, m. Johannes Pootman; Johannes, Dec. 21, 1783; Machtelt, b. March 21, bp. April 30, 1786; Jacob, b. Aug. 16, 1788; Bastiaan, bp. Dec. 26, 1790. Ch. b: Claartje, March 21, 1793; Pieter, Nov. 7, 1795; William, Jan. 14, 1798; Bartholomeus, July 27, 1800; Abraham, March 16, 1803; Joseph, April 16, 1805; Angelica, May 5, 1810.

BARENT, son of Wouter, *predikant*, m. Alida, dau. of David Van Der Heyden of Albany, Jan. 12, 1760. He became minister of the Dutch church in 1754, d. Nov. 13, 1784; she d. in 1833, a. 99ys. Ch. b: David, Oct. 25, 1760; Maria Dorothea, March 27, 1764, m. first, Le Tonnelier, secondly, Henry Ten Eyck; *Walterus*, July 21, 1768.

WALTER, son of Domine Barent, m. Elisabeth Welsh. Ch: Walter, b. Dec. 24, 1786.

SAMUEL, and Catarina Ziellè, both of Schoharie, m. March 6, 1761.

TEUNIS, son of Barent, m. Maria Ecker. Ch: Johannes, bp. Feb. 19, 1766.

LOURENS, son of Isaac, m. Maria, dau. of Harmanus Bratt. Ch: Isaac, bp. Feb. 29, 1784, who had a son named Jacob Swits Vrooman. Ch. b: Dorothy, Dec. 1, 1784; Helena, Oct. 15, 1786; Eva, July 8, 1790; Lourens, Feb. 17, 1793; *Lourens Van Boskerk*, April 6, 1796.

ADAM, son of Barent and Jannetie Ziele, both of Schoharie, m. May 15, 1761. [This marriage is recorded in the Dutch church of Albany as of March 17, 1763.] He d Oct., 1823; she d. Sept. 4, 1811, a. 72ys., 4m., 4d. Ch: Engeltie, m Peter Shaver; Peter; Nancy, m. John Ziele; Jacob; *Barent*, b. July 2, 1771, m. Nancy Becker, May 15, 1790; Jane, m. Christiaan Sternbergh.

JACOB W., m. Rachel Van Woerd. Ch: Jannetie, b. Jan. 31, 1767.

JACOB, son of Johannes, m. Catlyntje,

dau. of Cornelis Bulsen. He inherited his father's farm 3½ miles south of Schenectady. Ch. b: Clara, bp. July 13, 1783; Cornelis, b. March 27, 1785; Annatie, Feb. 8, 1788; Maria, Aug. 14, 1790; Sarah, March 5, 1794; Clara, January 14, 1797; Johannes, April 18, 1799; Francyntje, Jan. 21, 1803.

SIMON, son of Hendrick, m. Margarita, dau. of Jacques Peek, Aug. 14, 1767. He d. March 10, 1814, in his 75th year; she d. Nov. 18, 1823, in her 80th year. Ch. bp: Henderick, Oct. 4, 1767; *Arent Bratt*, March 12, 1769; Cornelis, Aug. 26, 1770; Susanna, Aug. 25, 1774; *Cornelis*, Sept. 3, 1780; *Johannes*, b. July 19, 1783.

WOUTER I., of Normanskil, m. Jacomyntje, dau. of Johannes Barheyt (?). Capt. Wouter Vrooman of Guilderland was taken prisoner in 1780 and held two years. Ch. bp: Rachel, Dec. 6, 1767; Cornelia, Oct. 1, 1796; Jacob, May 29, 1771; Isaac, Jan. 3, 1773; Johannes, Aug. 7, 1774; Alida, May 12, 1776; Margarita, May 10, 1778; Isaac, Sept. 25, 1779; Maria, Oct. 19, 1784; Styntje, b. April 23, 1786.

JOHANNES, son of Bartholomew, m. Margarita, dau. of Seth Vrooman, March 28, 1767. Ch. bp: Bartholomeus, July 3, 1768; Eva, Feb. 17, 1771; Bartholomeus, May 15, 1774; Catarina, Aug. 24, 1777; Adam, Oct. 28, 1780; Seth, June 3, 1781, d. Jan. 1, 1856; Bartholomeus, b. Feb. 28, 1784, d. May 12, 1820; Alida, b Feb. 4, 1786; Engeltie, Jan. 16, 1790.

JACOB, son of Adam W., m. Helena, dau. of Isaac Swits, Dec. 11 (18), 1768. He d. in Glenville July 21, 1831, in his 84th year; she d. Sept. 30, 1827, a. 77ys., 3m. Ch. b: Susanna, Dec. 29, 1769, m. Alexander Vedder; *Isaac*, October 13, 1771; *Adam*, Sept. 18, 1773; Volkie, b. Jan., d. July 19, 1776; Volkie, Feb. 5, 1781, m. ...... Van Etten; Maria, Jan. 27, 1786, m. Isaac De Graaf; *Jacob*, June 29, 1788.

JACOB, JR., and Rebecca Ewing, both of Normanskil, m. June 17, 1792.

ADAM, son of Seth, m. first, Engeltie, dau. of Simon Schermerhorn. She d. June 29, 1799, a. 43ys., 7m., 10d., and he m. Nancy ......, who d. Feb. 10, 1831, a. 70ys.; he d. Aug. 3, 1808, in his 55th year. Ch: Alida, b. Dec. 24, 1774, m. Josias Swart, d. March 30, 1852; Hillegonda, bp. Oct. 27, 1776, m. Caleb Van Vorst, d. March 25, 1858.

ARENT, son of Simon H, m Annatie, dau. of Jan Baptist Wendell. She d. in Glenville, Nov. 3, 1839, a. 75ys., 1m., 25d. Ch. b: Simon, Oct. 19, 1790; Elisabeth, June 2, 1793, d. March 4, 1810; Jan Baptist Wendell, bp. June 12, 1796; Hendrik, b. Nov. 15, 1798; Cornelius, b. April 1, 1804.

WILLEM, m. Isabel Armstrong. Ch: Sarah, bp. July 10, 1775.

ABRAHAM, son of Johannes S. (?), and Machtelt, dau. of Teunis Visscher, both of *Leysjes kil*, m. Nov. 23, 1790. Ch. b:

Teunis, June 13, 1794; Teunis, Dec. 8, 1795; Maria, Sept 20, 1798, m. Jacob Vrooman; John, May 8, 1801; Jannetje, March 30, 1803.

ISAAC, son of Adam W., m. Magdalena, dau. of Gerrit Bancker, Jan. 12, 1778. Ch. b: Adam, Oct. 28, 1778; Hester, Aug. 2, 1784; Susanna, Oct. 2, 1793.

ARENT, and Elisabeth Bratt, wid. of Jacob Schermerhorn, m. Dec. 19, 1790. She d. Oct. 16, 1847, in her 83d year.

PIETER, son of Adam, m. Catarina Hun (?). Ch: Adam, bp. July 23, 1780.

ISAAC, son of Jacob, m. Elisabeth, dau. of Simon Groot, Aug. 4, 1792. He d. March 17, 1816, a. 44ys., 6m., 19d. Ch. b: Adam, Nov. 24, d. Nov. 28, 1792; Isaac, Dec. 11, d. Dec. 12, 1793; a dau., Sept. 20, d. Sept. 28, 1794; Jacob, Nov. 7, 1795; Simon, Nov. 23, 1797; a dau., Dec. 22, d. Dec. 30, 1799.

JOHN JOHANNESE, of *Sandkil*, and Alida, dau. of Cornelis Bulsen of Rensselaerswyck, m. July 24, 1794. Ch. b: Clara, Nov. 13, 1798; Bartholomeus, Aug. 13, 1802; Cornelis, Mar. 24, 1809.

SIMON, son of Jacob, m. Sarah Clark. Ch. b: Elisabeth Wemple, Jan 2, 1796; John, May 22, 1799.

LOURENS VAN BOSKERK, son of Lourens, m. Sarah Truax, Aug. 16, 1821. Ch: Lourens, b. June 11, 1822, (only child).

NICHOLAS, of Normanskil, son of Jacob and Rachel (*See Albany Families*), m. Maria Swits. Ch : Elisabeth, bp. Sept. 29, 1782; Jacob, b. Aug. 24. 1785.

JACOBUS, m. Hanna Watson. Ch : Peter, b. Dec. 4 (?), June 10, 1798.

JOHN, son of Simon, m. Cathalina, dau. of Simon Veeder. He d. July 27, 1834; she d. Sept. 18, 1848, a. 57ys., 6m. Ch. b : Simon V., d. Dec. 28, 1828, in his 12th year; Simon V., b. Jan. 18, 1829, d. April 3, 1829; Cathalina, d. Dec. 4, 1833(?), a. 3ys., 7m.

CORNELIS, son of Simon, was a physician, become the agent of Mrs. Angelica Campbell; made his will Nov. 29, 1810, proved Feb. 14, 1811, spoke of brother Johannes, brother-in-law Tobias Ten Eyck, and of his wife's grandfather, Johannes Baptist Van Eps; d. Jan. 20, 1811. His dau. Angelica died at the house of her step-father, Herman W. Brouwer, in Albany, July 10, 1832.

JACOB, son of Johannes H., and Jannetje Swits, m. Delany Casler. He d. Sept. 7, 1810; she was b. Oct. 26, 1789, and d. Oct. 15, 1871. Ch : *Nicholas*, b. July 31, 1809.

NICHOLAS, son of the last, m. Christina Wright, Dec. 28, 1829. She was b. Feb. 17, 1809. Ch. b : Lena M., Dec. 18, 1830, m. Daniel D. Shoemaker, Dec. 31, 1851; Jacob H., March 3, 1833, m. Mary J. Ford, June 16, 1858; Joseph Aug. 15, 1835, m. Eliza C. Jones, May

30, 1860; John W., March 28, 1844, attorney-at law, m. Bettie A. Ford, Nov. 14, 1867.

ADAM, son of Jacob A., m. Eva, dau. of Simon Groot, Feb. 10, 1798. Ch. b. Jacob, Feb. 7, 1799 ; Annatie, June 10 (May 3), 1801 ; Helen, Dec. 23 (Nov. 22), 1803 ; Simon, June 9, 1806; Susan Maria, Sept. 18, 1808 ; Elisabeth, Sept. 11, 1812; Jacomyntje, Nov. 20, 1813 ; Jannetie (?), Feb. 16, 1816.

PIETER, son of Adam B., of Schoharie, and Anna, dau. of Pieter Meese Vrooman, were m. July 12, 1784. He was b. May 12, 1764; she was b. May 22, 1766. Ch. b : Adam jr., Jan. 12, 1786; Sally, Sept. 11, 1789 ; Jane, Dec. 14, 1792; Christina, May 3, 1794, d. Aug. 1, 1785; Mary, March 8, 1797; Anna, Jan. 2, 1798: Gitty, April 3, 1800 ; Caty, Dec. 10, 1803.

BARENT, son of Barent, m. Catharine Zielè of Schoharie, May 3, 1777. Ch. b : Josias, Feb. 8, 1777 (?) ; Barent, March 24, 1780; Cornelia, bp. Jan. 17, 1781 ; Engeltie, b. July 11, 1786; Annatie, April 1, 1788.

MARTINUS, son of Barent, m. Sautje Swart of Schoharie, January 15, 1769. Ch : Josias, bp. Dec. 26, 1771 ; Josias, b. March 4, 1773 Sara, bp. April 15, 1777.

BARENT, son of Adam and Jannetje Ziele, m. Nancy Becker, May 15, 1790. He resided in Schoharie, where he d. Oct. 25, 1846. Ch. b. Jane, Dec. 7,

1791, m. Elisha Kane Roof, Jan. 16, 1814; Magdalena, Sept. 12, 1794, m. John Enders; Anna, June 16, 1797, m. Daniel Larkin, July 14, 1816; Alexander, July 28, 1801; Gitty, May 28, 1804, m. Joseph Kniskern; *Jacob*, Nov. 28, 1808; Ann Eliza, March 20, 1806, m. Abraham Volwider.

ISAAC L., son of Lourens, m. ...... Ch : Peter, d. Sept. 6, 1830.

PETER, son of Isaac L., m. Margaret Ann, dau. of John Sanderse Ten Eyck, Aug. 6, 1828.

JACOB, son of Jacob, m. Maria, dau. of Abraham Vrooman and Machtelt Visscher, Aug. 8, 1816. He d. June 22, 1860; she d. Jan. 26, 1839. Ch. b : Helena, May 27, 1817, m. Giles Brouwer; *Abraham*, Aug. 9, 1818, m. Sarah White, Sept. 2, 1841; Matilda, July 14, 1820, m. Henry Swartfiguer, July 7, 1840; Maria De Graaf, July 12, 1822, m. Abram De Graaf, May 24, 1838; Clarissa, August 31, 1824, m. John Van Vranken, Oct. 5, 1843; Sarah Ann, July 22, 1826, m. James Peek, March 31, 1845; *Isaac*, Dec. 6, 1828, m. Maria McGugan, Oct. 25, 1853; Teunis, Dec. 25, 1830, d. Jan. 16, 1833; Susan Jane, Jan. 3, 1833, m. Jacob Vedder, April 17, 1849; Rachel, Feb. 22, 1835, m. first, Henry Young, Sept. 19, 1852, and secondly, William Schermerhorn, Feb. 22, 1858; Francis Elisabeth, Jan. 14, 1841, child of wid. Jane Tanner, whom he m. April 21, 1840.

ABRAHAM, son of Jacob and Maria, m. Sarah White, Sept. 2, 1841. Ch : Jacob ; Cornelia.

ISAAC, son of Jacob and Maria, m. Maria McGugan, Oct. 25, 1853. Ch : Alexander B.

JACOB, son of Barent and Nancy Becker, m. Maria Vrooman, May 4, 1827. He resides in Schoharie. Ch. b : Daniel L., May 16, 1828, d. October 9, 1856; *David B.*, Oct. 29, 1829; *Charles*, Sept. 9, 1831; *Lucian*, Oct. 2, 1833; *Cornelius*, Nov. 17, 1835; Christina, March 20, 1838, d. July, 1856; Jacob, April, 1840, deceased; Nancy, April 18, 1842; Henry Egmont, July 24, 1844, deceased; Henry Clay, Aug. 1846, deceased; *Peter C.* and Paul, Nov. 11, 1848; William J., May 1, 1851.

CHARLES, son of Jacob and Nancy Becker, m. ......; resides in Schoharie. Ch. b : Maria, deceased; Daniel J., June 24, 1860; Margaret, March 1, 1863, Edward Everett, June 2, 1872.

LUCIAN, son of Jacob and Nancy, m. ......; resides in Schoharie. Ch. b : Elsworth, Sept. 3, 1861; Jacob, April, 1863; Lala, Feb. 14, 1866; John, July 4, 1868.

CORNELIUS, son of Jacob and Nancy Becker, of Schoharie, m. ...... Ch. b : Maria, Dec. 3, 1859; Eva, May 17, 1861; James, Jan. 20, 1863; Caty, Oct., 1864.

PETER C., son of Jacob and Nancy Becker, of Schoharie, m. ...... Ch. b :

Clara Anita, Feb. 17, 1869; Morris Egmont, Jan. 15, 1872.

DAVID B., son of Jacob and Nancy Becker, of Schoharie, m. ...... Ch. b: Charles, Feb. 19, 1852; Anna Christina, Nov., 1857.

WAGEMAN (WAGONER).

GEORGE, m. Mary Philips. Ch. b: Elisabeth, Aug. 14, 1785; John, July 17, 1787; Neeltje, July 7, 1789; Jane, Nov. 1, 1793.

MANUEL, m. Rachel Herron. Ch: Esther, bp. Oct. 7, 1785; Elisabeth, b. June 28, 1787; David, Sept. 7, 1789.

WAGENAAR.

JOHANN JURRY, and Susanna Mans, both of Rensselaerswyck, m. July 7, 1767. Ch. bp: Anna, Dec. 7, 1769; Pieter, May 13, 1772; Jurry, April 21, 1777; Wilhelmus, Aug. 14, 1780.

JOHANNES, m. Elisabeth Smith. Ch: Henderick, bp. July 11, 1778.

JOHN, and Elisabeth Myer, both of the Hellenbergh, m. September 2, 1787. Ch. b: Jurrie, Dec. 20, 1789; Susanna, Feb. 27, 1792; William, Nov. 9, 1796.

PHILIP, m. Dorothea Kassilman. Ch: Engeltie, bp. Sept. 18, 1780.

WALDRON.

CORNELIUS, and Catharina Merkle. Ch: Cornelius, bp. July 8, 1792.

WILLIAM, son of Cornelis, of Albany,

m. Caty Van der Zee. Ch: Peter, b. Dec. 17, 1797.

WALKER.

JOHN, and Mary Johnson, m. Jan. 31, 1761.

ABRAHAM BUYS, m. Susanna, dau. of Johannes Rynex, March 13, 1792. Ch. b: John Rynex, Nov. 19, 1793; James, April 9, 1796; Ephraim, July 24, 1798.

ISRAEL, of Normanskil, m. Jane Schism. Ch: John and Rebecca, b. Sept. 29, 1785.

BENJAMIN, and Peggy Dixon. Ch. b: John, August 26, 1785; Mary, Aug. 8, 1787; Hannah, April 18, 1791; Abram, May, 1789; Catharine, June 2, 1793; Rachel, July 6, 1795; Elisabeth, Dec. 5, 1798.

WALLACE.

WILLIAM, and Sarah Kennedy. Ch: Polly Hamilton, b. Jan. 30, 1787.

WALSH.

THOMAS, d. April 18, 1806, a. 69ys.

WALTON.

JOHN, m. Susan Mebie, April 28, 1798.

WARD.

ANDREAS, and Neeltie, dau. of Robert Freeman. Ch: *Andreas; Mosis: John; Benjamin*, bp. May 12, 1758.

ANDREAS, JR., and Elisabeth Snyder. Ch. bp: Robert, July 18, 1769; Maria, March 13, 1771; Sarah, July 5, 1775; William, Feb. 11, 1777; Elisabeth, April 22, 1779.

Mosis, son of Andreas, m. Eva Weerly.
Ch. bp: Andreas, March 29, 1775; Johannes, June 26, 1777; Johannes Jacob,
Oct. 27, 1779.

John, son of Andreas, and Wyntje
Redderly, both of Rensselaerswyck, m.
Jan. 19, 1775. Ch. bp: Neeltje, Jan.
1 (?), 1776; Johannes, Nov. 26, 1777;
Andreas, Dec. 28, 1779.

William, of Normanskil, and Elisabeth Wagenaar, both of the Helderbergh,
m. Dec. 29, 1773. Ch. bp: Johannes,
Nov. 8, 1776; Robert, Dec. 4, 1778;
Pieter, May 6, 1782; Aaltje, June 11,
1784; Susanna, b. Dec. 31, 1785.

Richard, and Margarita Sitterlin.
Ch. bp: *Willem*, April 29, 1779; Catrina, Feb. 15, 1781. Ch. b: Robert, Dec.
17, 1789; Margarieta, April 23, 1792.

Benjamin, son of Andreas, of Normanskil, m. Annatje Bratt. Ch. bp:
Christina, Sept. 15, 1780; Neeltje, Aug
16, 1783; Elisabeth, b. Sept. 1, 1785.

William, son of Richard, m. Susanna
Bratt. Ch. b: Maria, May 22, 1800;
Margariet, Feb. 28, 1802.

Christoffel, m. Margarita Casselman.
He d. Nov. 18, 1838, a. 81ys., 3m., 26d.;
she d. July 3, 1816, a. 52ys., 6m., 22d.
Ch. b: Martinus, bp. June 15, 1783;
John, b: July 11, 1785, d. Sept. 29,
1816; Warnaar, Sept. 8, 1787, d. Dec.
12, 1800; Elisabeth, June 20, 1790, m.
Jacob Vedder; Hendrik, May 12, 1792;
Thomas, Oct. 20, 1794, d. Jan. 22, 1803;

Nela, March 8, 1797; Christopher, Mar.
8, 1799; Michael Ferrel, Sept. 26, 1801;
Rachel, d. June 6, 1804, a. 2ys.

WARN.

Samuel, and Catarina Campbell.
Ch. bp: Hanna, March 1, 1780; Catrien, Oct. 14, 1781; Catrina, July 27,
1784; John Shey, b. Aug. 16, 1786.

Samuel, and Catharina Van Antwerpen. Ch. b: Benjamin, April 4, 1790;
Simon, March 20, 1792; Benjamin, Apr.
22, 1795.

Richard, and Mary Hilton. Ch. b:
Thomas, Nov. 24, 1786; Ann, April 17,
1788; Benjamin, Jan. 12, 1790; Ann,
Nov. 28, 1791.

WARMOET.

Pieter, m. Ann, dau. of Pieter Feling.
Ch. bp: Willem, Aug. 12, 1750; Margarita, Jan. 22, 1758.

WARMOUWFF.

Jacob, and Pissilla ...... Ch: Ann
Elisabeth, bp. Feb. 1, 1713.

WARRENT.

Thomas, and Barbara Bouwman. Ch:
Thomas, bp. Dec. 26, 1769.

WASSON.

George, of Remsenbos, and Agnes
Sullivan. Ch: William, bp. Aug. 16,
1785; Agnes, b. June 28, 1787; Mary,
b. Jan. 16, 1790.

James, and Sarah Nile. Ch: Robert,
b. Jan. 30, 1783.

JOHN, and Ann Burdick. Ch. b: Dorothea, Aug. 9, 1786; Thomas, May 10,
1788.

THOMAS, and Sarah Neely. Ch: Matthew Neely, b. April 19, 1786.

THOMAS J., and Helen Bradshaw.
Ch. b: Lydle, Nov. 2, 1791; Lydia, Sept.
8, 1793; Dorothea, Aug. 16, 1795; Elisabeth, Aug. 15, 1798; John, July 29,
1800; Mary, Feb. 3, 1802.

JAMES, and Margarieta Doran, both of
Corrysbos, m. Jan. 23, 1791. Ch. b:
Dorothea, Nov. 8, 1790; John, Sept. 12,
1792; both bp. Aug. 11, 1793.

JOHN T., and Betts Hanna Gibson,
m. 1792.

WATSON.
ABRAHAM, m. Baata, dau. of Jacobus
Bratt, Oct. 9, 1761. Ch. bp: Annatie,
Aug. 5, 1762; Johannes, Nov. 20, 1763;
Jacobus, Nov. 15, 1767.

ALEXANDER, m. Mary Cummins.
Ch. bp: James, March 4, 1778; Margriet, July 23, 1779; Catrina, May 16,
1784; Mary, b. May 6, 1786.

WEBER.
JOHANNES, and Appolonia Levesteyn.
Ch: Pieter, bp. Sept. 18, 1770.

WEETLY.
PIETER, and Maria Smitt. Ch: Johannes Martinus, bp. June 19, 1779.

WELDEN.
JAMES, and Alida, dau. of Nanning
Visscher. Ch. b: Nanning Visscher,
May 26, 1787; Michael, Feb. 23, 1790.

WELLER.
ROBERT, and Catarina Pall. Ch. b:
Johannes, August 25, 1792; Frederic,
July 22, 1794; Peter, Sept. 18, 1796;
Elisabeth, Oct. 13, 1798; Robert, Jan.
14, 1801; Jacob, May 20, 1803; Michael,
March 16, 1805.

WILLIAM, and Peggy Passage, both
of Normanskil, m. May 4, 1786. Ch. b:
Eva, July 25, 1786; Johannes, Sept. 8,
1788; Maria, Aug. 29, 1790; Jacob,
Sept. 5, 1792; George, Feb. 4, 1796;
Margarita, May 4, 1798; Annatje, June
20, 1800; William, July 12, 1803; Elisabeth, Aug. 10, 1805.

JOHANNES, and Anna Mink. Ch: Maria, bp. Dec. 30, 1764.

JOHANNES, and Maria Coeper. Ch. bp:
Elisabeth, Sept. 23, 1772; Lena, Feb.
27, 1777.

FREDERIC, and Elisabeth, dau. of Johann Bastiaanse. Ch. b: Annatje, May
10, 1785; Catharina, June 11, 1788;
Johannes, Dec. 10, 1790.

WELLS.
TEUNIS, and Annatje Van Vliet, both
of Rensselaerswyck, m. Oct. 23, 1785.
Ch. b: Hendrick, Aug. 28, 1786; Machtelt, Dec. 22, 1787; Nelly, March 26,
1789; Geertje, Oct. 22, 1790; Benjamin, May 7, 1792; Lena, May 30, 1801.

WEMPLE (WEMP).

JAN BARENTSE WEMP *alias* Poest (?) arrived in Beverwyck in 1643–5, where he owned several lots; received contract from Madam Johanna De Laet for a bouwery at *Lubberde's Land* (Troy), which his heirs in 1669–72 conveyed to Pieter Pieterse Van Waggelum whom Wemp's son Myndert, sued in 1675 for the fourth payment. This bouwery was on the *Poestenkil*, which was probably named from his *alias*. He also received in 1662 a patent, in company with Jacques Cornelise Van Slyck, for the Great island lying immediately west of Schenectady, and a house lot in the village on the west side of Washington street, a little north of State street. His wife was Maritie Myndertse, who, after his decease in 1663, again married Sweer Teunise Van Velsen, the village miller; both were killed at the massacre of Feb. 9, 1690. Ch. b: *Myndert*, 1649; Grietje, 1651; Anna, 1653, m. Sander Glen; *Barent*, 1656; Johannes; Aeltie, m. Jan Cornelise Van der Heyden of Beverwyck.

MYNDERT, eldest son of Jan Barentse, m Diewer, dau. of Evert Janse Wendel. He was appointed justice of the peace for Schenectady, by Leisler, in 1689; was killed at the massacre of Feb. 9, 1690, and his son Johannes and two negroes were carried away captive. Ch: *Johannes:* Susanna, m. Johannes Simonse Veeder.

BARENT, son of Jan Barentse, m. Folkje, dau. of Symon Volkertse Veeder. He was appointed captain of the company of foot by Leisler in 1690; made his will Jan. 1, 169$\frac{9}{0}$, in Albany. Ch. bp: *Johannes*, Aug. 24, 1684, in Albany; Symon, ——, 1686; Marytje, ——, 1688, m. Hendrick V.rooman; *Myndert*, Aug. 24, 1691, in Albany; Engeltie, Oct. 29, 1693, in Albany; Engeltie, Oct. 9, 1695, m. Nicolaas Hansen; Grietje, Nov. 10, 1697, m. Simon Volkertse Veeder; *Hendrick*, Jan. 5, 1701; Susanna, April 15, 1703; *Barnhardus*, Oct. 29, 1704.

JOHANNES, son of Myndert, m. first, Catalina, dau. of Reyer Schermerhorn, June 15, 1700, and secondly, Ariaantje, dau. of Isaac Swits, Oct. 6, 1709. In 1711 he was "of the Mohawks country on the Mohawk river;" owned land on the south side of the river, in the present town of Rotterdam, extending from the "*Zandig kil*" to the burying ground of the church; was one of the trustees of the Schenectady patent; made his will March 5, 174$\frac{7}{8}$, d. October 14, 1749. Ch. bp: *Myndert*, Nov. 9, 1701, d. in 1748; *Reyer*, Oct. 17, 1703; Johannes, Oct. 28, 1705; Ariaantje, Nov. 9, 1707, m. Capt. Andries Bratt, d. in 1748; Debora, October, 1710, m. Barent Wemple; Barent (Susanna?), Nov. 13, 1712; *Isaac*, Aug. 28, 1715; Maritie, Dec. 5, 1718, m. Lieut. Walter Butler jr.; Rebecca, September 29, 1721, m. Pieter Conyn; *Ephraim*, Feb. 16, 1724; Cornelis, b. April 19, 1726; *Johannes*, Apr. 18, 1731.

JAN, son of Barent, m. first, Sara, dau. of Esaias Swart; secondly, Helen, dau. of Abraham Van Tright of Albany, Nov. 30, 1718. Ch. bp: Maria, Feb. 13, 171$\frac{4}{5}$,

m. Myndert Myndertse; Barent, Feb. 28, 1711; Johannes, Sept. 22, 1716; Elisabeth, Sept. 24, 1719, m. Andries Arentse Bratt; Volkje, April 28, 1722, m. first, Barent H. Vrooman; secondly, Jacob Sanderse Glen; thirdly, Johannes Simonse Vrooman; Margarita, b. Oct. 24, 1724, m. Jacob S. Vrooman; Barent, b. Dec. 29, 1726; *Abraham.*

MYNDERT, son of Barent, m. Alida, dau. of Johannes De Wandelaar of Albany, June 29, 1718. He was sent by Sir William Johnson to the Senecas, to stay till their corn was a foot high and keep their arms and working utensils in repair; returning with his sons, he made report. The Indians, in 1726, request that he "being good and charitable to the poor," or some of his sons, may reside among them, as they are smiths, and acquainted with them, and know their language. Ch. bp: Volkie, April 18, 1719; Johannes, March 25, 1721; Anna, Dec. 22, 1722; Barent and Myndert, July 26, 1724; *Abraham,* b. June 10, 1726; *Hendrick, ——,* 1730; *Barent,* April 2, 1732; Maria, Sept. 2, 1735; *Myndert,* Nov. 20, 1738.

MYNDERT, son of Johannes, m. Sarah Mills. Ch: Maria, b. Dec 12, 1731, d. April 21, 1731; *Myndert; Andries.*

HENRICUS, son of Barent Janse, m. Catharina, dau. of Arent Andriese Bratt; banns Jan. 23, 1731. In 1728 he and Joseph Van Sice were appointed as smith and armourer for the Indians. Ch. bp: Catlyntje, March 26, 1732, m. Johannes

Empie; Barent, Aug. 19, 1733; Folkje, Oct. 17, 1736; Barent, Sept. 3, 1738; Arent, July 12, 1740; Volkje, Sept. 26, 1742; Johannes, April 8, 1744; Jannetje, March 2, 1746; Johannes, Nov. 13, 1748.

REYER, son of Johannes, m. Debora, dau. of Johannes Veeder; she afterwards m. Douwe Fonda. Through his grandfather, Reyer Schermerhorn, he obtained land in the *Woestine* on both sides of the Mohawk river at Hoffman's Ferry; he lived on the south side, opposite the "Seventh flat." Ch: *Johannes,* b. April 18, 1732, d. in the *Woestine* Sept. 14, 1814, in his 83d year; Meindert, bp. April 23, 1736; Volkje, m. Johannes Bratt; *Meindert,* bp. Oct. 24, 1742.

BARENT, son of Barent Janse, m. Debora, dau. of Johannes Wemple, Sept. 2, 1732. Ch. bp: *Barent,* June 3, 1733; Johannes, Feb. 16, 1735; Susanna, Oct. 9, 1737, m. Harmanus Mebie; Volkje, Jan. 4, 1741; Johannes, Dec. 1, 1745.

ISAAC, son of Johannes, m. Elisabet Nieuwkerk. Ch. bp: Annatje, March 27, 1747; *Johannes?;* Gerrit.

ABRAHAM, son of Myndert, m. Rachel, dau. of Wouter Vrooman, Jan. 16, 1744. He d. July 13, 1758, a. 32ys., 1m., 3d.; Nov. 22, 1774, "widow Wimp" m. Abraham Fonda, and d. Aug. 5, 1791. Ch. bp: Alida, April 30, 1749, m. Myndert R. Wemple; Wouter Vrooman, March 10, 1751; *Meyndert,* Feb. 9, 1753, d. Nov. 10, 1804, a. 51ys.; Nicolaas, Mar. 16, 1755; Maria, Nov. 27, 1757.

ABRAHAM, son of Jan Barentse, m. Antje Van den Bergh of Albany, Aug. 19, 1758. [Abraham Wemple and Antje *Vredenburgh* were living at the *Boght* in Watervliet in 1797.] Ch. bp: Helena, Oct. 28, 1759, m. Willem Van Arnhem; Rachel, Mar. 15, 1761; Johannes, April 24, 1763; Folkje, Aug. 19, 1764; Johannes, Oct. 5, 1766; Volkje, Oct. 1, 1769; Johannes, April 4, 1773.

JOHANNES, perhaps same as the last, m. Annatje Smitt. Ch: Annatje, bp. March 4, 1755.

JOHANNES, son of Reyer, m. first, Margarita, dau. of Abraham Mebie, Nov. 22, 1757. She d. Feb. 11, 1767, a. 27ys.; he m. secondly, Maritie, dau. of Nicolaas Visscher "*Van Knastagujoone*," April 18, 1768 (?). She was b. 1741, and d. Sept. 23, 1804, a. 63ys., 8m.; and he m. thirdly, Hester Van Arnhem, who was b. 1734, and d. Jan. 2, 1822, in her 88th year. Ch. bp: Debora, Feb. 12, 1769, m. Christoffel Peek; Annatje, June 9, 1771; Catalyntje, Feb. 16, 1777; Nicolaas Visscher, May 28, 1780, m. Nancy Veeder; Susanna, April 14, 1782; Johannes R. Wemple made his will July 13, 1812, proved Oct. 10, 1814, spoke of wife Esther, son Nicholas, grandsons John W. Peek, John Haverly, John Heuston and John Wemple, also of his three wives above mentioned. He died Sept. 19, 1814, and was buried in the *Woestine*.

HENDRICK, son of Myndert, m. Aefje, dau. of Johannes Van Eps, Jan. 11, 1755. Ch: Alida, bp. March 7, 1756.

JOHANNES, son of Johannes and Maria Veeder, both of Kachnawage, m. Nov. 1, 1767. His house was burnt there May 22, 1780, by John Johnson's Indians.

EPHRAIM, son of Johannes, m. Anganieta Brouwer, May 18, 1750. In 1799 he lived in Florida, Montgomery county. Ch: Johannes, bp. May 23, 1756.

MYNDERT, son of Abraham, m. Dorothea Brown, Sept. 12, 1787. Dorothea, wid. of Myndert A. W., d. May 29, 1831.

BARENT, son of Myndert, m. Margarita, dau. of Douwe Fonda. His widow Margaret kept a public house at Caughnawaga; her house was burned May 22, 1780, by Johnson's Indians, and her son Mina (Myndert) was made prisoner, but released at Johnstown. [*Simms's History*.] Ch. bp: Meyndert, November 16, 1755; Douwe, Dec. 11, 1757.

BARENT, son of Barent and Sarah Smitt, *getrouwt* in het Maquaasland, Jan. 6, 1759. During the Revolution he lived at Caughnawaga, where his house was burned May 22, 1780, by Johnson's Indians.

MYNDERT, son of Myndert and Sarah, m. Sarah, dau. of Simon Vedder, Nov. 10, 1764 He d. in West Glenville Dec. 18, 1821, a. 83ys., 11m., 23d.; she d. Nov. 7, 1828, in her 85th year. Ch. bp: Sarah, July 21, 1765; *Simon*, March 20, 1768; Myndert, Nov. 18, 1770, d. in West Glenville Jan. 15, 1843, a. 72ys., 1m., 27d.; his wife Elisabeth, d. April 14, 1860, a. 82ys., 11m., 22d.; Maria, May 30, 1773; John, Oct. 15, 1775;

Neeltje, Nov. 3, 1776, m. Jacob Swart; Rhoda, March 5, 1780; John, April 14, 1782; Rebecca, March 20, 1785.

ANDREW, son of Myndert (?), m. Helena, dau. of Andries Bratt, Nov. 4, 1765. [Andries Wemple of Montgomery county, being an adherent of the king in the Revolutionary war, his property was confiscated.] Ch. bp: *Myndert*, Aug. 24, 1766; Andries, Nov. 6, 1768; Pieter Conyn, March 17, 1771; Pieter Conyn, June 20, 1773.

MYNDERT, son of Myndert and Alida, m. Geertruy, dau. of Jacobus Myndertse, March 25, 1765. In 1790 she m. Doctor Dirk Van Ingen. Ch. bp: *Jacobus*, July 2, 1769; Alida, b. Aug. 13, bp. August 18, 1771; Alida, bp. Sept. 17, 1775, m. James McKinney; Maria, June 3, 1781.

SYMON, son of Myndert and Sarah Vedder, m. Wyntje Lewis (Servis). Ch. b: Myndert, Nov. 4, 1789; Simon Vedder, Dec. 17, 1793; William, June 9, 1796; Arent, Aug. 31, 1798; Jacob, June 26, 1800; Harmanus, June 16, 1802.

MYNDERT, son of Andries, m. Elisabeth, dau. of Jellis Yates, July 4, 1790. Ch. b: Andries, June 19, 1793; Jellis Yates, Oct. 3, 1795; Lena, Sept. 4, 1798; Ariaantje, Sept. 19, 1801.

MYNDERT, son of Reyer, m. Alida, dau. of Abraham Wemple. Ch. bp: Catalina, Sept. 23, 1770; *Reyer*, July 5, 1772; Abraham, July 9, 1775; Johannes, Oct. 26, 1778; Walterus Vrooman, Jan. 19,

1783; *Myndert*, b. July 22, 1785, d. July 1, 1844; Deborah, b. Aug. 26, 1788.

JOHANNES, son of Isaac, m. Maria, dau. of Isaac Swits. In 1783 he lived in the *Suider hoek*, east end of State street, 62 feet west of the Schermerhorn property, now in possession of Dr. Harmen Swits. Ch. bp: Elisabeth, March 15, 1772; Isaac, Sept. 12, 1773; Folkje, Sept. 10, 1775; Volkje, July 6, 1777, m. Johannes Winnè, was buried perhaps Sept. 25, 1804; Gerrit, Sept. 26, 1779; Engeltje, June 9, 1782, m. Aaron Bratt of Rotterdam, d. in Gorham Jan. 19, 1854, a. 71ys.; Maria, Aug. 29, 1784, m. Peter Ward; Jacobus Swits, b. April 12, 1788; Abram, May 17, 1791.

JOHN A.; Nancy relict of John A. Wemple, d. in Glenville Jan. 13, 1870, in her 90th year.

REYER, son of Myndert, and Willempie, dau. of Arent Peek, both of the *Woestine*, m. Nov. 11, 1795. Ch. b: Myndert, Aug. 10, 1796; Myndert, Jan. 4, 1798.

JACOBUS, son of Myndert M., m. Catharina Becker. Ch. b: Myndert, Oct. 30, 1796; Gerrit, Oct. 15, 1798; Jacobus Mynderse, Dec. 14, 1800; Peter, Oct. 23, 1802, d. in Albany April 24, 1873.

Maj. MYNDERT M. R., son of Myndert Reyerse, m. March 28, 1808, Elisabeth Van Schaick. He d. July 1, 1844; she was b. Oct. 6, 1789, d. Sept. 6, 1854. Ch. b: Walter V., May 12, 1809, d.

May 6, 1868; Alida Ann, Jan. 1, 1812, d. Nov. 3, 1813; Eleanor, Aug. 9, 1815, m. Norman Frost, d. Oct., 1871; Mary Ann, Sept. 26, 1817, m. Martin C. Myers; John V. S., Dec. 18, 1820, d. Aug. 15, 1822; William H., Sept. 18, 1823, d. June 30, 1848; Elisabeth, May 4, 1827, m. Charles R. Derrick, d. Feb. 16, 1855.

WENDEL (WENDELL).

AHASUERUS, son of Evert jr., of Albany, and Elisabeth Sanders, m. Anna, dau. of Jan Baptist Van Eps, Sept. 4, 1720. He was buried in Albany July 11, 1752. Ch. bp: Elisabeth, Feb. 12, 1721, in Albany; Susanna and Lena, June 29, 1723, the latter m Johannes A. Van Antwerpen; *Jan Baptist*, March 6, 1732.

JOHANNES, attorney-at-law, son of Evert Wendel of Albany, m. Maria Catharina, dau. of Cornelis Van Santvord, July 16, 1741. He was buried in Albany Sept. 22, 1751. Ch. bp: Engeltje, Aug. 8, 1742; Anna, April 22, 1744; Engeltie, Jan. 19, 1746, m. Jacobus Van Eps; Evert, Feb. 28, 1748; Jacoba, Nov. 26, 1749; Geertruy, Sept. 22, 1751, in Albany.

JAN BAPTIST, son of Ahasuerus, m. Jacomyntje, dau. of Cornelis Van Dyck, Aug 31, 1754. She was b. Sept. 12, 1733, d. Nov. 17, 1760. Ch. bp: *Ahasuerus*, Dec. 25, 1755; Maria, Nov. 5, 1758; Maria, Dec. 2, 1759, m. Simon Van Petten; —— Jan Baptist Wendel, m. secondly, Elisabeth, dau. of Nicolaas Groot, and wid. of Arent Van Antwerpen, Jan. 15, 1762. In 1786 he lived at the west end of State street beyond Water street alley. Ch. bp: Annatje, Aug. 1, 1762; Annatje, Sept. 30, 1764, m. Arent S. Vrooman; Maria, Oct. 4, 1767; Nicolaas and Jacomyntje, April 22, 1770.

HARMANUS, merchant, son of Harmanus jr., of Albany, m. Catrina Van Rensselaer. He d. before the baptism of his last child. Ch. bp: Harmanus, Jan. 22, 1768; Harmanus, Sept. 30, 1770, d. Dec. 3, 1841, at the residence of his son-in-law, Henry Vine; Elisabeth, April 4, 1774; Catarina, March 2, 1777.

AHASUERUS, son of Jan Baptist, m. Eva, dau. of Johannes Peek. He d. Feb. 22, 1848, a. 92ys.; she d. April 8, 1852, a. 86ys. Ch: Johannes, bp. Mar. 2, 1783. Ch. b: Margarieta, July 3, 1786; Johannes, Oct. 19, 1788; Jacomyntje Van Dyck, March 30, 1794; Cornelius Van Dyck, July 8, 1797; Joseph Harmen, Nov. 18, 1805.

GERRIT, m. Machtelt, dau. of Hannes Heemstraat of Niskayuna. Ch: Elisabeth, bp. July 13, 1783; Abram, b. Feb. 2, 1786; Johannes, Nov. 16, 1788.

ROBERT H., son of Hendrick jr., of Albany, m. Agnietje, dau. of Pieter Fonda. He was an attorney-at-law, and at the age of 24ys. removed from Albany to Schenectady; was b. in Albany Feb. 7, 1760, d. in Schenectady July 7, 1848, a. 88ys., 5m. His wife d. April 1, 1828. Ch: Hendrick, bp. Sept. 29, 1784, d. March 13, 1868; his wife d. Dec. 1,

1870; Peter Fonda, b. July 3, 1786;
Maria, b. Feb. 9, 1789, d. Oct. 26, 1809;
Jacob, b. April 16, 1791, d. at Shelby's
Basin, Orleans county, Oct. 12, 1843;
Giles F. was buried Feb. 9, 1824; Alida,
bp. Jan. 10, 1796; Robert Henry Lan-
sing, b. Feb. 19, 1799; Mattheus Trotter,
b. Dec. 14, 1801.

WERTS.

JOHN, m. Catharina Hoogeboom. Ch:
Peter, b. Feb. 20, 1791.

WESSELLS.

WESSELL, m. Maria, dau. of Arent
Van Antwerpen. He was b. March 28,
1715, d. June 14, 1789. Ch. bp: An-
natje, Oct. 12, 1740, m. Johannes Clute;
Sara, June 26, 1743, m. Daniel Cornu;
Lucas, April 14, 1745; Anna, June 7,
1747; Lucas, Nov. 26, 1749; *Arent*,
June 17, 1752; *Harmanus*.

ARENT, son of Wessell, m. Maria T.
Truax. [A Maria Wessels d. 1800.]
Ch: Wessell, bp. July 27, 1783.

HARMANUS, son of Wessell, m. Sophia,
dau. of Pieter Truex. He d. March 10,
1813, in his 59th year; she d. Oct. 8,
1838. Ch: Wessell, bp. Nov. 9, 1783,
d. in Glenville Sept. 9, 1858, a. 75ys.;
Margaret, his wife, d. Nov. 25, 1853, a.
72 ys.; Jacobatje, b. Dec. 31, 1790.

WESTLY.

JOHN, m. Elisabeth McFarland. Ch:
Nancy, bp. Sept. 24, 1786.

CHARLES, m. Mary Thornton. Ch. b:
Mary Thornton, March 1, 1785; Ann
Hunt, Dec. 24, 1787.

WESTVAAL.

JACOB, and Annatje Wever. Ch: Annatje, Oct. 15, 1775.

PETRUS, and Sophia Van Aken. Ch:
Johannes, bp. June 19, 1779.

PETRUS, and Barbara Aghenpagh,
both of Hellenbergh, m. Nov. 12, 1788.
Ch: Annatje, b. Nov. 24, 1799.

WEVER.

JOHANNES NICOLAAS, and wife Anna
Elisabeth, were members of the church
in 1737.

DANIEL, from Paderborn, and Claartje, dau. of Willem Marinus, m. Feb. 13,
174¾. Ch: Catharina, bp. Jan. 27, 1745.

JOHANNES, and Christina Bellenger.
Ch. bp: Gerrit, Dec. 3, 1758; Margarita, May 25, 1760.

JOHN, and Elisabeth Achenbagh. Ch:
Peter, b. Dec. 26, 1786.

JERONIMUS, and Elisabeth ...... Ch:
Catarina, bp. Oct. 6, 1762.

FREDERIC, and Geertruy Bellinger.
Ch: Elisabeth, bp. Jan. 25, 1781.

JACOB, and Geertje Van Vliet. Ch. bp:
Benjamin, May 16, 1779; Lydia, March
4, 1781; Zacharias, Dec. 24, 1786;
Blandina, b. March 23, 1789.

FRANS, and Elisabeth Achenbagh,
both of the Hellenbergh, m. Aug. 17,
1785. Ch: Baltus, b. Sept. 7, 1790.

JOHN, and Catharine McNeal. Ch:
Henry, b. Oct. 31, 1790.

HENRY, and Geertje Simonds. Ch. b: Henry, Oct. 8, 1796; Sarah, Oct. 11, 1798, both bp. July 15 (*sic*), 1798.

JOHANNES, and Anna Gates. Ch. b: Jacob, July 30, 1801; Stephen, May 7, 1805.

WHEATON.

WILLIAM, and Hannah King. Ch: Thomas Ladd, b. Aug. 11, 1797.

JOSEPH, of New Jersey, m. Margaret, dau. of Jacob Mebie, May 14, 1758. Ch. bp: Catarina, Nov. 22, 1761; *Reuben*, Oct. 2, 1763; Annatie, Aug. 18, 1765; Elisabeth, Oct. 16, 1768; William, March 10, 1771; Maria, Feb. 26, 1775.

THOMAS, and Annatje Moll. Ch. b: Margrietje, May 17, 1785; John, June 4, 1791; Rebecca, Dec. 13, 1793.

REUBEN, son of Joseph m. Maria McGee. Ch. b: Joseph, June 17, 1787; John, Jan. 13, 1790; Willem, Sept. 12, 1791; Thomas, April 19, 1793; Margarieta, Dec. 17, 1794; Jacob, Oct. 4, 1796; Reuben, May 1, 1798; Dennis, April 20, 1800; Elisabeth, April 10, 1802; Catharine, Aug. 6, 1804.

WHEELER.

JACOB, and Sophia Starkweather. Ch: John Johnson, b. April 8, 1789.

WHITAKER.

THOMAS, and Sarah Dokstader. Ch: Sarah, bp. July 20, 1780.

WHITE.

NICHOLAS, *geboren in* Ireland, and Clara Van Slyck, m. Aug. 3, 1761.

PETER, m. Elisabeth Barheyt, Oct. 26, 1788. Ch. b: Philip, Jan. 13, 1789; Teunis, Dec. 28, 1792; Mary, June 14, 1794; Eber, Oct. 18, 1798.

WICKS.

JEREMIAH, and Jannetje Lansing. Ch. b: John, April 24, 1795; Zopha April 5, 1798; Maria, May 10, 1803.

WIEST.

COENRAT, and Maria Van Aken. Ch. bp: Petrus, Jan. 10, 1777; Benjamin, June 24, 1781; Margarita, June 11, 1784.

WIGHTMAN.

JACOB, and Maria Margarita Temmers (Tyms?). Ch: Jacob, bp. Feb. 23, 1783.

WILEY.

JOHN, from Pennsylvania, and Susanna Peek, m. April 10, 1768. Ch. bp: James, Dec. 10, 1769; Margarita, July 8, 1771.

JOHN, widower, and Ann Needham (Ann Lydel, widow), m. Feb. 1, 1785. Ch. b: Lytle, Oct. 28, 1785; Reuben, Aug. 23, 1787; Susanna, Feb. 2, 1792.

JAMES, and Willempie, dau. of John Peek, m. Dec. 24, 1791. Ch: John, April 1, 1793.

JURRIE, and Catharina Merkle. Ch: Maria, b. Nov., 1797.

WILKIE.

THOMAS, m. Maria, dau. of Christoffel Velthuysen, Dec. 11, 1785. Ch: Annatie, bp. Nov. 5, 1786.

CHRISTIAAN, and Ann Dodd, (Dodge), both of Remsenbos, m. Sept. 2, 1790. Ch. b: Maria, May 21, 1791; Christiaan, Sept. 15, 1792; Catharina, Nov. 7, 1794; Anna, Aug. 18, 1796; Frederic, Sept. 24, 1798.

WILLARD.

LEVI, and Sophia Smith, m. Oct. 29, 1794.

WILLIAMS.

SAMUEL, son of Thomas, of Albany (?), m. Francyntje Akermans. Ch. bp: Thomas, Aug. 23, 1719; Jannetie, b. July 13, bp. July 16, 1727; Jan, bp. 1730; Dorothea, Oct. 21, 1733.

LODOWYCK, and Rebecca Delamater. Ch: Anna, bp. Dec. 3, 1749.

HENDRICK, and Francyntje Clute. Ch. bp: Maria, March 7, 1756; Jacob, Feb. 12, 1758; David, Feb. 10, 1760; *Pieter*, June 10, 1764.

FREDERIC, and Cornelia, dau. of Johannes Barheyt, m. Aug. 14, 1785. Ch. b: Hendrik, April 5, 1786; Annatje, July 5, 1788; Johannes, July 20, 1790; Johannes, Dec. 27, 1792.

CORNELIUS, m. Tanneke Clute. Ch: Henderick, Oct. 27, 1782; Elisabeth, b. Jan. 24, 1787; Francyntje, Dec. 12, 1788.

JACOB, and Maria Markell. Ch: Henderick, bp. July 15, 1783.

PETRUS, son of Henderick, m. Engeltje, dau. of Johannes Barheit. Ch. b: Francyntje, Sept. 23, 1788; Annatje, Sept. 20, 1790; Hendrik, Aug. 25, 1792; Cornelia, Nov. 26, 1794; Johannes, Dec. 9, 1796; Jacobus, Feb. 18, 1799.

WILLIAM, and Polly Philips. Ch: Zilpha, b. Dec. 14, 1789.

DAVID, and Johanna Hoogteling of Lysjes kil, m. March 15, 1789. Ch. b: Sarah, Oct. 27, 1789; Francyna, Sept. 13, 1791; Charity, July 1, 1793; Maria, Sept. 14, 1795; Rebecca, May 1, 1798; Hendrik, Jan. 1, 1801; Catharine, May 20, 1802.

WILLIAMSON.

JOHN, and Mary Passage. Ch. bp: George, Dec. 26, 1781; Elisabeth, May 8, 1784; John, b. March 23, 1786; Peggy, b. May 10, 1800.

WILSON.

ROBERT, of Cherry Valley, and Anna Gardiner of Schenectady, m. Dec. 26, 1791.

JAMES, and Magdalena Schermerhorn, m. Aug. 26, 1757.

WILT.

FREDERIC, and Hanna Cipler. Ch: Dorothea Sophia, bp. Aug. 21, 1760.

FRANS, and Jacomyntje Setel. Ch: Maria, bp. June 15, 1768.

WINCHELLS.

JOHN, of Albany, and Mary Dunlap of Schenectady, m. May 6, 1787.

WINNÈ

LEVINUS, son of Pieter, of Albany, m. Susanna, dau. of Johannes Wendell of the same place. Ch : Johannes, bp. July 30, 1735. [*See Albany Families.*]

DANIEL R., of Albany, and Jannetie Bancker of Schenectady, m. May 21, 1763.

ANTONY, and Rebecca Van Loon. Ch : Christina, bp. Sept. 30, 1799.

HUGHO, son of Frans jr., of Albany, m. Annatie Clute. Ch : Frans, b. July 30, 1794. [*See Albany Families.*]

JACOB, m. Nelly Van Petten, Feb. 15, 1797.

JOHN, son of Pieter of Albany (?), m. Folkie, dau. of Johannes Wemple. Ch : Susanna Maria, b. Aug. 21, 1798. [*See Albany Families.*]

WIRTS.

MOURITS, and Jannetje Noortman. Ch. b : Eva, Aug. 19, 1794; Margaret, Oct. 26, 1796.

WISE.

JOHANN DANIEL, and Anna Maria ...... Ch : Carel Wilhelm, bp. Sept. 25, 1779.

WITBECK.

SAMUEL, son of Lucas of Albany (?), and Rebecca Buys Ch : Jacobus, bp. Jan. 17, 1776. [*See Albany Families.*]

38

WITTICK.

ABRAHAM, and Lea Bovie. Ch : John, bp. Jan. 22, 1788.

WOMBELLS.

JOHN, and Maria ...... Ch : Catrien, bp. May 1, 1764.

WOOD.

JAMES, and Maria Nesbit. Ch. b : William, Sept. 17, 1785; Joseph, Dec. 18, 1787; Catharina, bp. Sept. 14, 1789 : Alida, b. Nov. 15, 1791; Jochim Van der Heyden, Sept. 18, 1794; Joseph Nesbit, Nov. 8, 1797; Johannes, Sept. 15, 1799; Elisabeth Smith, Aug. 18, 1802; Catlina Ryley, Aug. 19, 1804; Maria, March 25, 1806. [James Wood, a Revolutionary soldier, d. Feb. 11, 1827, a. 67ys.]

JOHN, goldsmith, m. Machtelt, dau. of Abraham Quackenbosch. He resided in a house next west of No. 108 State street. Ch. b : Abraham, June 13, 1784; Johannes, Jan. 7, 1792; Peter Ouderkerk, April 5, 1795.

WILLIAM, and Sarah Grant. He d. before the baptism of his dau. Rachel. Ch : Rachel, b. May 19, bp. June 20, 1786.

WOODCOCK.

BENJAMIN, and Mary ...... Ch : Benjamin, bp. March 10, 1758.

WOOLEY.

DANIEL, and Anna Halstead. Ch : Richard, bp. May 27, 1782.

WRIGHT.

SAMUEL, of Duanesburgh, and Catharina Thornton of Corrysbos, m. Jan. 15, 1794. Ch. b: David, Dec. 15, 1794; Anna, April 15, 1797; Ann, June 3, 1799.

EDMUND, and Dorcas Thornton. Ch. b: James Thornton, Aug. 14, 1794; Antje, Aug. 24, 1796; Fisher, July 12, 1799.

HUGH, and Ann Dunlap, m. August 28, 1792.

WYKOFF.

CORNELIUS, printer, and Elisabeth Richmond. Ch. b: Mary Shippy, Dec. 4, 1795; Peter Richmond, June 6, 1797.

WYL.

FRANK, and Jomyna Wyl. Ch: Catrien, bp. Oct. 6, 1765.

WYLDY.

WILLIAM, and Mary Stanley. Ch. bp: Mary, July 1, 1750; *Thomas*, Dec. 20, 1752; John, Dec. 13, 1754; Samuel, Sept. 4, 1757.

EDWARD, m. Maria Magdalena Moor, Nov. 28, 1773 (*sic*). Ch. bp: Annatie, June 27, 1773; Nathaniel, Aug. 13, 1775.

THOMAS, son of William, m. Maria Drake (Dake). Ch. bp: Jacomyntje, Jan. 27, 1775; Maria, Dec. 15, 1777; William, Jan. 17, 1781; Edward, March 20, 1783. Ch. b: Annatie, April 1, 1785; Cornelius, Oct. 21, 1787; Eva, Nov. 10, 1790; Margarieta, April 15, 1793; Hendrick, July 19, 1795; Cornelia, Sept. 8, 1799.

EDWARD DANIEL, m. Mary Mac Culloch, Jan. 24, 1769.

WILLIAM, and Sophia Sheits (Schell). Ch. bp: Mary, April 4, 1779; William, Aug. 23, 1781; Sophia, May 31, 1784.

WYSER.

JOHANNES, and Ruth Wiley (Wilsey). Ch. bp: Cornelius, June 22, 1777; Catarina, Sept. 5, 1779; Martinus, Dec. 30, 1780; Catrina, July 13, 1783; John, b. Nov. 23, 1785; Sarah, Aug. 10, 1789.

YATES.

JOSEPH, came to Albany soon after the surrender of the province to the English in 1664. He probably learned his trade or practiced it with Marcelis Janse Van Bommel, whose daughter, Hubertje Marselis, he m. In 1693 he had 7 children living; in 1713 lived on the east corner of Green and Beaver streets; was buried May 22, 1730. His wife was buried July 13, 1730. Ch. bp. in Albany: *Christoffel*, April 16, 1684; *Robert*, b. Nov. 4, bp. Nov. 11, 1688; Selia, bp. May 7, 1693; *Joseph*, March 17, 1695; Sara, March 6, 1698; *Abraham*, March 1, 1704. [*See Albany Families.*]

CHRISTOFFEL, son of Joseph, of Albany, m. Cateleyntje, dau. of Adam (?) Winne, July 12, 1706. He was buried Feb. 26, 1754. Ch. bp. in Albany: *Joseph*, April 20, 1707; *Adam*, Aug. 15, 1708; Catalina, Oct. 7, 1711; Catalyna Oct. 19, 1712; Hubertje, Nov. 7, 1714; *Johannes*, Oct. 14, 1716; Anneke, Oct. 5, 1718; Maria, April 29, 1722; *Abra-*

ham, August 23, 1724; *Pieter*, Jan. 8, 1727. [*See Albany Families.*]

ROBERT, son of Joseph, "merchant," settled in Schenectady, where he m. Margriet, dau. of Claas De Graaf, Feb. 13, 1712. He made his will Nov. 12, 1747, proved April 2, 1748, spoke of sons Joseph and Abraham, to whom he left his real estate, also his tan-yard on Mill lane, buildings, leather, working tools, hides, &c., "belonging to my cordwainer's trade." He d. March 4, 1748, in his 60th year. Ch. bp: *Joseph*, July 12, 1714, in Albany; Elisabeth, January 7, 1716, m. Ephraim Smith; Maria, Jan. 25, 1718, m. Gerrit Van Antwerpen; Claes, Oct. 25, 1719; Sara, Aug. 19, 1721, m. Jacobus Mynderse; *Abraham*, April 3, 1724; Christoffel, b. Dec. 17, 1726.

JOSEPH, son of Joseph, of Albany, m. Hendrikje Hooghkerk, May 28, 1719. She was buried Jan. 19, 1750. Ch. bp. in Albany; Joseph, March 9, 1720; Luycas, April 22, 1722; Albertus, Oct. 4, 1724; Judic, Feb. 12, 1727, d. Feb. 5, 1805, a. 77ys., 11m., 28d.; Johannes, Sept. 7, 1729; Abraham, Dec. 20, 1730; Abraham, Dec. 24, 1732; Huybertje, June 16, 1736. [*See Albany Families.*]

ABRAHAM, son of Joseph, m. Hester Drinkwater in New York, Sept. 10, 1726.

JOSEPH, son of Christoffel of Albany, m. Eva, dau. of Jellis Fonda, Jan. 17, 1730. About 1734 he settled in Schenectady. Ch. bp: Catalyna, Jan. 17, 1731, in Albany, m. Cornelis Peek; Rachel, May 7, 1732, in Albany, m. Cornelis Barheit (?); Huybertje, June 15, 1735, m. Samuel S.

Bratt; *Christoffel*, July 8, 1737; Thanna (Tanneke), April 29, 1739, m. Col. Cornelis Van Dyck; Eva, Oct. 4, 1741, m. Johannes H. Peek jr.; *Gillis*, April 22, 1744; Annatje, Oct. 5, 1746.

ADAM, son of Christoffel, of Albany, m. Anna Gerritse, June 2, 1733; she was buried Sept. 15, 1751. Ch. bp. in Albany: *Jan Gerritsen*, Mar. 23, 1735; Christoffel, April 22, 1739, d. Nov. 8, 1809, a. 71ys.; Joseph, Jan. 13, 1742; Maria, Oct. 19, 1744; Annatje, Feb. 19, 1749. [*See Albany Families.*]

JOHANNES, son of Christoffel, of Albany, m. Rebecca Waldron, Nov. 28, 1737. He made a will Dec. 27, 1775, proved June 4, 1776. The following ch. were then living, except Cathalina and Cornelia. Ch. bp. in Albany: Christoffel, Aug. 27, 1738; Tryntje, Dec. 28, 1740, m. Antony Bries; Cathalina, Feb. 12, 1744; Cornelia, January 12, 1746; *Pieter Waldron*, Aug. 23, 1747; Annatie, Dec. 25, 1749, m. Willem Staats; Engeltie, July 6, 1752; Cornelis Van Schaick jr.; Rebecca, Nov. 14, 1756.

ABRAHAM, son of Christoffel, of Albany, m. Antje De Ridder. He was mayor of Albany; d. June 30, 1796, a. 73ys. Ch. bp. in Albany: Christoffel, June 7, 1747; Christoffel, July 10, 1748; Tanneke, Nov. 4, 1750; Cornelis, March 11, 1753.

PIETER, son of Christoffel, of Albany, m. Sarah Van Alsteyn. Ch. bp. in Albany: Christoffel, March 18, 1750; Pietertje, May 29, 1752; Jacob, March 28, 1755, d. at Schaghticoke Nov. 21, 1831,

a. 76ys.; Abraham, Dec. 25, 1757; Cathalina, June 7, 1761; Maria, b. April 18, 1764; Annatje, March 2, 1767.

JOSEPH, son of Robert, of Schenectady, m. Maria, dau. of John Dunbar, Sept. 5, 1737, in Albany. Ch. b. in Schenectady: *Robert*, March 17, 1738; Jannetje, July, 1739; Maria, Dec. 14, 1740, m. Jacobus Teller; Catharina, March 20, 1743, m. Johannes Mynderse; Elisabet, March 17, 1745, m. Cornelis A. Van Slyck; Jannetje, June 7, 1747, m. Cornelis Cuyler; Johannes, July 2, 1749; Sara, July 21, 1751; *Nicolaas*, Dec. 20, 1752; Abraham, Mar. 23, 1755; *Abraham*, Feb. 27, 1757; *Johannes*, b. June 12, 1760.

ABRAHAM, son of Robert, of Schenectady, m. Sara, dau. of Abraham Mebie, April 8, 1749. In 1749 he was called carpenter, in 1753, merchant; 1767 he owned the lot opposite the Court House in Union street. Ch. bp. in Schenectady: Robert, Dec. 10, 1749; Petrus, April 5, 1752; Abraham, Sept. 3, 1754; Maria, July 11, 1756; Maria, July 24, 1757; Abraham, June 3, 1762; Maria, Dec. 27, 1765.

CHRISTOFFEL, son of Joseph and Eva, m. Jannetje, dau. of Andries Bratt, Oct. 16, 1761. He was a surveyor; colonel of a regiment of fatigue men in the Revolution, and " one of the best informed and most efficient patriots in the Mohawk valley."—[*Sims's History.*] He made his will 1785, proved Nov. 14, 1785; spoke of his wife and the following ch., save Catarina. Ch. bp: Eva, Feb. 14, 1762;

Elisabeth, May 7, 1763, m. Jillis Fonda; Eva, Jan. 13, 1764, m. William Johnson Butler of Niagara; Helena, Nov. 16, 1766; *Joseph*, b. Nov. 9, bp. Nov. 20, 1768; *Hendericus*, Oct. 7, 1770; *Andreas*, Jan. 17, 1773; Annatje, March 12, 1775, d. April 17, 1851, a. 76ys.; Catarina, Oct 12, 1777; Jillis, April 1, 1781; Johannes, Feb. 1, 1784.

JELLIS, son of Joseph and Eva, m. Ariaantje, dau. of Andries Bratt, March 16, 1768. He d. in Glenville Nov. 13, 1812, a. 68ys., 7m., 17d. Ch. bp: *Joseph*, Aug. 7, 1768; Elisabeth, July 29, 1770, m. Myndert A. Wemple; Eva, Mar. 14, 1773; Catarina, Nov. 17, 1776, m. Robert Gally; Hubertje, b. Aug. 2, bp. Aug. 22, d. Aug. 29, 1779; Andreas, July 14, 1782, d. in Glenville Aug. 25, 1846, a. 64ys., 2m., 6d.; Harriet his wife, d. Sept. 4, 1850, a. 69ys., 1m., 9d.; Lena, b. Oct. 3, bp. Sept. 29 (*sic*), 1784; Catlyntje, b. March 8, 1786; Annatje, b. Aug. 4, 1788; Rachel, b. Aug. 13, 1792.

NICOLAAS, son of Joseph and Maria, m. Rebecca, dau. of Abraham Fonda. He lived at No. 5 Church street; after his death his wid. m. ...... Van Vranken. He was not living, Jan. 2, 1802, when his father made his will. The following ch. were then living, except Susanna. Ch. b: Susanna, bp. Dec. 12, 1784; Abram, b. Feb. 7, 1788, perhaps of Onondaga in 1817; Robert, Nov. 11, 1789; Isaac Glen, Aug. 21, 1793; Joseph.

JOHANNES, son of Joseph and Maria, m. Margarita, dau. of Gillis Fonda. He was b. June 12, 1760, d. 1826; his wid.

d. Dec. 26, 1839, a. 75ys. Ch. b: Joseph, Oct. 4, 1786, d. June 12, 1837; Jannetje, Oct. 5, 1789; Jane, 1794, m. Giles Yates, d. July 20, 1848; Mary, Nov. 5, 1795; Jellis Fonda, Nov. 8, 1798; Robert Henry, July 9, 1801; Maria Matilda, June 27, 1805; Catharine Louisa, April 22, 1810.

ABRAHAM, son of Joseph and Maria, made his will March 7, 1809, proved July 10, 1809, gave Joseph Mynderse two morgens of land, to Joseph, Robert, Abraham and Isaac, ch. of his deceased brother Nicholas, "the share that I hold in the tan-yard near the Church mill," &c.

JOHANNES, son of Christoffel of Albany, m. Margarietje, dau. of Jacobus Myndertse, March 6, 1788. Ch. b. (and bp. in Schenectady): Sarah, Jan. 24, 1789, m. Samuel Gray; Christopher, March 7, 1791; Jacobus, Jan. 11, 1793; Catharina, July 7, 1794, m. Sidney Potter; Maria, May 22, 1796, m. A. Giles; Catlyntje, Nov. 10, 1798.

JOSEPH, son of Jellis, m. Annatie, dau. of Isaac Roosa, Dec. 14, 1788. He d. in Glenville Sept. 13, 1838, a. 70ys., 1m., 8d.; she d. Dec 26, 1823, a. 57ys·, 4m., 10d. Ch. b: Ariaantje, Oct. 3, 1789; Marytje, Dec. 23, 1792; Elisabeth, April 18, 1795; Isaac, Feb. 22, 1797; Gen. Isaac J. Yates d. in Greenfield Sept. 13, 1848, a. 51ys.; Eva, March 8, 1799; Jellis, May 6, 1801, d. April 11, 1853, a. 51ys., 11m., 6d.; John, March 5, 1803, d. Dec. 3, 1851, a. 48ys.; Andrew, Nov. 25, 1806, of class 1834, Union College.

HENRICUS, son of Col. Christoffel, m. Catharina, dau. of Johannes Mynderse, Oct. 24, 1791. He was an attorney-at-law; for a number of years state senator and member of the council of appointment, d. in Albany March 20, 1854, a. 83ys.; Mrs. Yates d. in New York Sept. 28, 1841, a. 69ys. Ch. b: Christoffel, Oct. 6, 1793; Mary, August 17, 1795; Henry Christopher, June 13, 1799, graduated in Union College 1818, d. May 12, 1847; Edward, Oct. 21, 1801, graduated in Union College 1819, d. 1833; Stephen, July 12, 1805, graduated in Union College in 1825; Charles, March 1, 1808, graduated in Union College 1829, d. Sept. 26, 1870; Jane Anne, Feb. 29, 1816.

JOSEPH, son of Col. Christopher, m. first, Ann, wid. of James Ellice, Sept. 31 (*sic*), 1791; secondly, Maria, dau. of John and Sybil Kane of Albany, who d. Oct. 26, 1797, a. 26ys., and thirdly, Ann Elisabeth De Lancey, who d. Jan. 4, 1864. He was an attorney-at-law; first mayor of Schenectady; state senator in 1807; judge of the Supreme Court 1808; governor of the state 1823–4, d. March 19, 1837. Ch. b: Helen Maria, Sept. 28, 1797, m. John Keyes Paige, d. Jan. 25, 1829; Jane Josepha, Oct. 25, 1801; Anna Alida, Sept. 14, 1806; Jane Josepha, Nov. 6, 1811.

ANDREAS (Andrew), son of Col. Christoffel, m. first, Mary Austin; secondly, Hannah A. Hooper, who d. Oct. 22, 1859, a. 76ys. He was a minister of the Reformed Dutch church; 1797–1801, professor of Latin and Greek languages; 1814–1822, professor of Moral Philosophy and Logic in Union College, d. at Schenectady Oct. 14, 1844, in his 73d year. Ch. of the first wife: Christopher, b. Aug. 3, 1798; John Austin, b. May 31, 1801, graduated at Union College 1821, professor of Oriental Literature 1823–1849, d. Aug. 27, 1849; Andrew J., graduated at Union College, d. Aug. 8, 1856. Ch. of second wife: James Hooper, b. Oct. 9, 1815, graduated at Union College, d. 1861; Christopher, b. Feb. 12, 1818; Helena, b. Sept. 1, 1819; Joseph, b. May 20, 1821; Ann Elisabeth, bp. Aug. 18, 1822.

ABRAHAM, son of Joseph and Hubertje (?), of Albany, m. Jannetie Bratt in Albany, Aug. 22, 1761. She d. Nov. 22, 1804, a. 70ys., 9m., 25d. Ch. b. (bp. in Albany): *Hendrik*, Sept. 28, 1763; Jannetje, July 17, 1766; Hubertje, June 12, 1769; Annatie, April 20, 1722; Daniel, Sept. 9, 1774, d. June 29, 1802.

CHRISTOPHER, son of Johannes and Rebecca, of Albany, m. Catharina Lansing, July 17, 1761, in Albany. Ch. b. (bp. in Albany): Abraham, Oct. 14, 1763; Evert, Oct. 24, 1764, d. at Fultonville Sept. 10, 1846, a. 82ys.; Johannes, May 13, 1766; Gerrit, April 13, 1768; Pieter, Jan. 28, 1778; Cathalyntje, Oct. 28, 1771; Alexander, Nov. 22, 1773; Annatie, July 6, 1776; Christopher, May 10, 1779; Doct. Christopher C. Yates d. at Parishborough, Nova Scotia, Sept. 23, 1848.

ROBERT, son of Joseph of Schenectady, m. Jannetie Van Ness, in 1765, in Albany, where he settled as attorney-at-law; member of the committee of safety, and of the convention that adopted the state constitution in 1777; one of the first judges of the Supreme Court of this state, and subsequently chief justice; member of the Federal convention of 1787, and of the state convention called to ratify the Federal constitution; d. Sept. 9, 1801. Ch. b. (bp. in Albany): Maria, Feb. 12, 1767; Maria, Oct. 19, 1768; William, Sept. 2, 1771; Joseph, Nov. 3, 1773; John Van Ness, 1779, d. Jan. 10, 1839; Pieter, Aug. 30, 1783.

CHRISTOPHER, son of Adam, of Albany, m. Catharina Waters, July 19, 1766. He d. Nov. 8, 1809, a. 71ys. Ch. bp. in Albany: Annatie, Feb. 10, *in d' avond Kerk gedoopt*, Feb. 11, 1767; Annatje, March 27, 1768; John Waters, Oct. 25, 1769, cashier of New York State bank, d. March 29, 1828, a. 58ys.; Sara, Dec. 14, 1771, d. Feb. 6, 1794; Marytje, Feb. 12, 1775; Christoffel and Adam, Feb. 9, 1776.

PIETER WALDRON, son of Johannes, of Albany, m. Ann Margarita Helms (Hellems, Kellens). Mrs. Mary Yates, wife of Peter W. Yates, d. Nov. 23, 1794, a. 45ys.; Peter W. Y., counsellor-at-law of Albany, d. at Caughnawaga March 9, 1826, a. 79ys. Ch. b. (bp. at Albany): Cornelius Erasmus, July 21, 1768; Margarita, Jan. 28, 1770; Cornelia, Sept. 27, 1771; Cornelia, May 14, 1773; Maria, Dec. 23, 1775; Rebecca, Aug. 20, 1780, m. John King, and d. in New Lebanon Sept. 28, 1829; Magdalena,

December, 15, 1782; Engeltie, July 12, 1786.

PETER W. (same as the last ?), m. Mary Terbush (Ter Boss), Dec. 19, 1798. Ch. b. (bp. in Albany): Elisabeth, May 28, 1800, "it was intended to call this child, and she is called Catharine by her parents," (*Albany Church Records*); Catharine, June 28, 1801.

CHRISTOPHER, son of Pieter of Albany, m. Rebecca Winnè. She d. July 11, 1763, a. 68ys. Ch: Pieter, b. July 15, 1784.

HENDRICK, son of Abraham, of Albany, m. Rachel Van Santen (Van Zandt), Jan. 19, 1786. She d. April 5, 1846, a. 80ys., 7m., 27d. Ch. b. (bp. in Albany): Abraham, February 14, 1787; Rebecca, Sept. 19, 1788; Gysbert, Nov. 20, 1790; Henry, Dec. 1, 1792; Jan, March 22, 1797; Sara, May 9, 1799; Sara, March 7, 1801; Judith, Aug. 14 (20), 1803.

ADAM, son of Johannes and Catalyntje Goewey, of Albany, m. Margaret Cardenright. Ch: Eleanor, b. Dec. 21, 1791.

JOHN, m. Geertruy Van Vranken. Ch: John, b. Jan. 4, 1793.

YELL.

JOHN, and Mary Long. Ch. bp: Susanna, Jan. 21, 1778; Margariet, Aug. 17, 1779.

YOUNG.

PETER, and wife Anna, members of the church in 1737.

BENJAMIN, m. Maria, dau. of John Fairley. Ch: Hanna, bp. Aug. 29, 1772.

GUY, m. Dirkje Winnè. Ch: Rebecca, bp. April 12, 1778. [*See Albany Families.*]

JOHANNES, m. Dorothea Kossilman. Ch: Margarita, bp. Oct. 8, 1779.

ANDREAS, m. Catarina Cogden (Ogden ?). Ch: Mary, bp. April 17, 1782.

SETH, m. Martha Fairley. Ch: Henry, b. Jan. 1, 1788.

CALVIN, owned a lot on west side of Ferry street, between Front street and the river, in 1789.

YSSELSTEYN (ESSELSTEYN, VAN ESSELSTEYN).

MARTEN CORNELISE, was one of the early settlers and proprietors of Schenectady. On Oct. 23, 1668, he sold his bouwery to Claas Frederickse Van Petten and Cornelis Viele, and removed to Claverak;—Jan. 12, 167⅔—Marten Cornelise, b. in the city of Ysselsteyn, and Mayke Cornelise, his wife, b. in Barnevelt, both living in Claverak, made their joint will. He was not living in 1705. They had one son, Cornelis Martense, from whom have descended the Esselsteins of Columbia county.

ZELLENNAN.

AMBROSIUS, and Margariet ......, both from *Duytsland*, now living in Schenectady, m. Jan. 21, 1759.

APPENDIX.

THE GLENNS OF BALTIMORE.

This branch of the family sprang from Jacob Sanderse, son of Capt. Johannes Glen of Schenectady, b. Feb. 27, 1686. He left Schenectady when a young man and went to Boston where, in company with Oliver Wendell, he engaged in business. Subsequently he removed to Maryland and settled, it is said, near Elkton, Cecil county. It is not known whom or when he married, nor whether he had more than one child, *Samuel*.

SAMUEL, son of Jacob Sanderse, was b. in 1737, probably in Cecil county; in him the name first appears spelt with two ns, and it has ever since continued to be so spelt in Maryland. He m. June 7, 1762, Jane, wid. of William Beedle, and d. in the city of Baltimore, on the 24th of June, 1802, a. 65ys.; his wife d. on Aug. 15, 1808. Of this marriage there were b. Jacob, May 4, 1765, m. Charlotte Bauldwin, Nov. 5, 1789; his ch. moved from time to time to the western part of Virginia and to New York; *Elias*, Aug. 26, 1769; John Washington, Dec. 12, 1776, m. and left one dau., who m. ...... White.

ELIAS, son of Samuel, m. Ann Carson, at St. Georges, New Castle county, Del., Aug. 21, 1794. He settled in Baltimore about 1811; in 1812 was appointed by Mr. Madison, United States district attorney, and his commission was renewed by Mr. Monroe. In 1824 he was appointed United States district judge by Mr. Monroe. After being on the bench for twelve years, he resigned in 1836 on account of failing health and retired to his country seat, Glenburnie, now a part of Baltimore, where he d. on the 6th of Jan., 1846, a. 76ys. Ch. b: *John*, Oct. 9, 1795; *Mary*, March 30, 1797, m. David M. Perine of Baltimore;

Elisabeth Renshaw, July 7, 1798, m. Robert W. Armstrong of Baltimore; Elias Barnaby, Feb. 11, 1800, d. April 19, 1801; Jefferson, Feb. 19, 1802, d. unm. May 15, 1831; Jane, Nov. 14, 1803; Ann, Aug. 17, 1805, d. July 5, 1806; *William Carson*, May 25, 1810.

JOHN, son of Elias, m. Nov. 12, 1822, Henrietta B., dau. of William Wilkins, merchant of Baltimore. As a lawyer he early developed such marked capacity in his profession that he soon rose to the head of the bar, and when he retired to take a seat upon the bench, relinquished the largest practice in the city. In 1852 Mr. Filmore appointed him United States district judge for Maryland, and he then took his seat upon the same bench that his father had occupied. He d. in 1853, a. 57ys. His ch. were *William Wilkins*, b. July 20, 1824; *John*, b. Feb. 20, 1829; Ann; Mary; Ella, m. James Kemp Harwood of Baltimore; Lucy.

MARY, dau. of Judge Elias Glenn, m. David M. Perine of Baltimore. Ch: *Elias Glenn*; Anne; Susan; Mary; Rebecca.

ELIAS GLENN, son of David M. Perine, m. Eliza, dau. of Lewis Washington of Virginia, and had issue.

WILLIAM CARSON, son of Judge Elias Glenn, m. May 19, 1835, Martha E., dau. of Gen. James Serrall of Cecil Co., Maryland. He d. July 7, 1860. Ch: James Serrall, d. unm.; Elias, d. unm,; Rosa, m. William G. Hollingsworth; Anna.

WILLIAM WILKINS, son of Judge John Glenn, m. Oct. 29, 1857, Ellen Wykoff Smith of Philadelphia. Ch: John, b. 1858; William Lindsay, b. 1863.

JOHN, son of Judge John Glenn, m. Oct. 13, 1859, Anna Carrie Smith of Philadelphia, sister of his brother's wife. Ch: John, b. 1863; Letitia, b. 1864.

INDEX.

312 *Index.*

CPSIA information can be obtained
at www.ICGtesting.com
Printed in the USA
LVOW13s0928281217
561013LV00024B/150/P